# The Professional's Guide to Surveillance Training

By

Peter Jenkins

Published by Intel Publishing

Surveillance Tradecraft
The Professional's Guide to Surveillance Training

Published by:

Intel Publishing
Riverside Cottages
Nidd Walk
Pateley Bridge
Harrogate
HG3 5NA
United Kingdom
info@surveillance-tradecraft.co.uk

Further copies are available via www.surveillance-tradecraft.co.uk
Telephone: 01423 712265



ISBN: 978 09535378 22

**5th Edition**

A CIP catalogue is available from the British Library

Typesetting and Design: Eye Spy Publishing Ltd

Cover Design: Peter Jenkins/Intel Publishing
Front Cover Illustration: Jon Moss - www.jonmoss.org.uk

Printed and Bound in Great Britain
by Bell & Bain Ltd, Glasgow

---



DISCLAIMER: The Author and publishers cannot accept any responsibility for any proceedings or prosecutions brought or instigated against any person or body as a result of the use or misuse of any information described in this book, or any loss, injury or damage caused thereby.

# DEDICATION

To those valiant servicemen and women
who return to their homeland
listening to the toll of the church bell in
Wooton Bassett, England

*I will not cease from mental fight*
*Nor shall my sword sleep in my hand*
*Till we have built Jerusalem*
*In England's green and pleasant land.*

*William Blake 1804*

# CONTENTS

# CHAPTER SUBJECTS

## CHAPTER 1 COVERT SURVEILLANCE

- Definitions, types and objectives
- Methods of surveillance
- The surveillance operator
- Personal appearance and dress
- Types of surveillance target
- Third party awareness
- Loss versus gain
- Principle phases of surveillance

## PLANNING & PREPARATION CHAPTER 2

- Planning and objectives
- The target person
- Sources of information
- The surveillance start point
- Target reconnaissance
- Recce reports
- Surveillance triggers

## CHAPTER 3 COMMUNICATIONS

- Types of communication equipment
- Mobile and handheld radios
- Antennas & frequencies
- Covert systems
- Radio security
- Brevity code systems
- Radio call signs and networks
- Voice procedure
- Spot codes
- Encryption
- The click system

## SURVEILLANCE EQUIPMENT CHAPTER 4

- The car bag
- Basic equipment
- Night vision optics
- Vehicle tracking
- Technical triggers
- Surveillance vans

## CHAPTER 5 FOOT SURVEILLANCE

- Foot tactics: stake out, pick-up, follow, housing
- ABC system: follows, handovers, cornering, losses
- Foot surveillance compromises
- Shadow cars
- Covert communications
- Cafes & public houses
- Buildings with multiple exits
- Buses & trains
- Underground rail networks
- Deploying from a vehicle

## MOBILE SURVEILLANCE (ONE) CHAPTER 6

- Tactics: handovers, losses, changing direction, stops
- Mobile tactics: stake out, pick-up, follow, housing

- Stakeouts: primary, secondary, tertiary
- The surveillance team
- Types of vehicles
- Mobile equipment
- Mobile communications
- Action on a standby
- Mobile voice procedure
- Car parks and dead ends

## CHAPTER 7 MOBILE SURVEILLANCE (TWO)

- Progressive tactics
- Parallels
- Losses
- Motorway tactics
- Night mobile surveillance
- Motorbike surveillance
- Rolling stakeouts
- Single handed surveillance
- Surveillance compromises
- Road traffic accidents

## STATIC SURVEILLANCE CHAPTER 8

- Observation posts
- Vehicle OP's
- Surveillance vans
- Van compromises
- Covert cars (boot fits)
- Urban OP's
- Planning an OP

## CHAPTER 9 RURAL SURVEILLANCE

- OP team insertion: routes, countdown markers, drop off points
- OP team extraction: routes, countdown markers, pick up point
- Rural OP planning & reconnaissance
- Types of rural OP
- Camouflage & concealment
- Alternative plans
- Animals & wildlife
- Establishing the OP
- Construction of rural hides
- OP equipment
- OP compromises
- Field craft
- Close Target Recce (CTR)

## TECHNICAL SURVEILLANCE CHAPTER 10

- Technical surveillance counter measures
- CCTV: cameras, recorders, monitors
- Rural rapid deployment systems
- Hard wired audio monitoring
- Radio transmitting devices
- Cellular network transmitters
- Telephone monitoring
- Computer & data monitoring
- Counter surveillance equipment
- Legal issues

## CHAPTER 11 SURVEILLANCE DETECTION

- Definitions: anti surveillance & counter surveillance
- When anti surveillance drills will be used
- Planned and unplanned detection routes
- Counter surveillance detection routes
- Anti surveillance on foot
- Anti surveillance whilst mobile
- Anti surveillance detection routes
- Single handed and team SDR's
- Continuous SD routes
- SD routes with stops
- Automatic number plate recognition

## STILL & VIDEO PHOTOGRAPHY CHAPTER 12

- Correct exposure: aperture, shutter speed, focal length
- Digital SLR cameras
- Image size, resolution & compression
- How a digital SLR camera works
- Exposure modes
- Depth of field
- Lenses: types, speeds
- Film speed and ISO, up rating
- Metering & exposure compensation
- Focusing
- Video photography
- Covert video cameras
- Bag fits & body worn systems

## CHAPTER 13 EVIDENCE AND LAW

- Human Rights Act
- Regulation of Investigatory Powers Act
- Criminal Procedure and investigations Act
- Protection from Harassment Act
- Key definitions
- Trespass
- Use of trackers
- Data Protection Act and CCTV
- Evidence gathering
- Describing people
- Night vision
- Memory & perception
- Surveillance logs & reports
- Witness statements
- Eye witness testimony
- Preservation of evidence
- Surveillance briefings and debriefings

# TRAINING & FINDING WORK CHAPTER 14

- Applying for work
- Training companies
- Surveillance qualifications
- Training courses
- Foot & Mobile surveillance
- Technical training
- Surveillance detection
- Rural surveillance
- Digital photography
- Professional witness
- Top 10 mistakes

# ACKNOWLEDGMENTS

This book is the last one, unless I decide to do an 'Andy McGrisham' and write a novel in retirement. Surveillance Tradecraft has been very, very hard work indeed and I would like to acknowledge and thank the following for their support.

First and foremost to my wife and children who have had to put up with me throughout this project, which often meant long periods away and a great deal of time spent at the keyboard.

Eye Spy Publishing Ltd, Mark Birdsall, the editor for his extremely hard work and effort during the typesetting and production stage. A professional with an eye for detail and artistic flair who has made this book appear how it is. Debbie Plisko for her support especially through the winter. Both good friends who have helped make this book possible.

The members of the surveillance training team that have been behind the success of ISS Training Ltd. Their attitude, professionalism and diligence over the past few years, has been exceptional wherever we have worked be it in the UK or around the world. Brian Gregory QGM & Bar, in particular, who has been part of the ISS family and worked so hard.

Thanks also to those many individuals who we have trained, who have passed on their ideas, comments and assistance and have become good friends along the way.

Those 'Quiet Professionals' and 'Team Guys' we have worked with over the past few years, they know who they are - keep safe.

Quentin Sands for his thoroughness correcting my grammar and spelling at the proofreading stage.

Thank you for supplying equipment and images from:

Jon Moss Illustration
Eye Spy Intelligence Magazine
Google Earth
Globe Police Solutions UK
Hidden Technology Ltd UK
Audiotel International
Photographicmoives.com
Shai Gear LLC
Flir Systems Ltd

And our sponsors who are listed at the back of the book:

## *The Next One!*

# introduction to SURVEILLANCE TRADECRAFT

Peter Jenkins

In 2000, I wrote 'Covert Surveillance' as a basic manual and an introduction to surveillance training. The book was immensely popular within the security industry and so a revised version entitled 'Advanced Surveillance' was released in 2003, this book has sold worldwide but has slowly become out dated in some respects. Although the basic and fundamental techniques are much the same, this third book covers more topics in more depth. It also keeps up with advancing technology, which now plays more of a role than ever in surveillance.

This book is not only aimed at the person who is new to surveillance but also to those experienced operators who require a reference book and training manual. Surveillance cannot be learnt by reading a book alone; it is a skill that requires the correct teaching and plenty of practice and experience.

All the methods and techniques mentioned in this book are already 'out there' in the public domain, either in written material on websites or Internet forums. They have also been featured in television documentaries or in films, therefore I am not letting any secrets out of the bag because they are already out.

Covert surveillance is a means of gathering information and subsequently this information becomes evidence or intelligence. It is a skill that can provide the investigator with vital information when other avenues have failed.

Surveillance can be from a static point, on foot, from a vehicle or by using technical devices. In most cases a combination of all four is used, with targets often taking public transport and even attempting to detect or avoid surveillance.

Surveillance is a team effort. Everyone in the team has an important role to play, none less than the person who is actually watching the activity and reporting on it to the rest. He or she is the eyes and ears of the surveillance and is in effect painting a picture over a radio so the team can understand what is happening. The more accurate the description, the better response from the team as a whole. The most important factor for any surveillance team is communication. Without any form of communication between the team members (such as radios) you will have no teamwork. As far as surveillance equipment is concerned, your radio sets are probably the most important asset that you will have - in addition to your camera.

Throughout the book I have referred to the Surveillance Team and the Surveillance Operator. It is appreciated that in some enforcement organisations and especially the commercial investigation environment there are restrictions in both cost and manpower and it may not be possible to use such a large surveillance team. It is not uncommon for surveillances to be conducted two or three handed. However, I consider a team of three operators to be sufficient for most practical tasks and it is on a three man team that I have based the techniques and methods described in this book.

I do not advise undertaking surveillance single-handed and strongly recommend that this is not carried out, especially by the novice. I have carried out many single-handed surveillances and had good results, in fact excellent results but I have also lost many targets in traffic and also suffered compromises. However, even as part of a team, you will often find yourself on your own with no back up and so having to operate on your own for a period of time is inevitable. Acting as a team, surveillance is 'imposed' on a target but when you are on your own a target is 'followed' and there is a vast difference between the two, as this book will explain.

I have heard many investigators state, 'My client will not pay for two investigators on the same job, I do not have that luxury'. To me that indicates that the investigator has not done his job correctly in convincing the client of the NEED for two or more operators to conduct surveillance. A short while ago, I was asked to carry out personal injury surveillances in the UK for a large American company. The company expected me to do it all single-handed which I was not prepared to do and so I did not take on the work. I understand that in some countries outside the UK, single-handed surveillance can be reasonably straight forward depending on circumstances but this is discussed in more detail in the book.

On the surveillance Circuit, especially when carrying out 'personal injury' type investigations, two operators are probably the norm, one with a van the other with a car. This is what I would expect to be the minimum manpower to conduct surveillance professionally.

Surveillance work is 80% boring, and 20% excitement. Very often the amount of time spent waiting for something to happen far outweighs the amount of time that the target is active. Long periods of boredom and frustration have to be overcome and this can only be achieved by personal discipline and experience. A mobile surveillance is not a 'pursuit' or a 'chase' with the need to drive at excessive, aggressive speeds but is carried out in a calm, relaxed, professional manner and most importantly, with self control.

The surveillance operator is often tasked to obtain evidence. This evidence may be used in legal proceedings and the operator may have to give evidence in court. The defence or prosecution, may attempt to discredit you, your evidence and how it was obtained in order to assist their case. As a professional, you must be a credible witness and be able to justify your actions, which means keeping within the law at all times.

There are no rules in surveillance, but there are certainly guidelines. We cannot say that when a target comes to a halt then 'this operator does this and another does that', every situation is different. However, there are procedures which help us and there are certainly things that we should do and there are others that we should not.

If you are involved in surveillance or are just reading this out of pure curiosity, I am sure you should find the content both informative and educational. If you would like to know more, come and visit us on a training course, the details of which are at the rear of the book.

Good luck and best wishes

**Peter Jenkins, ISS Training Ltd**

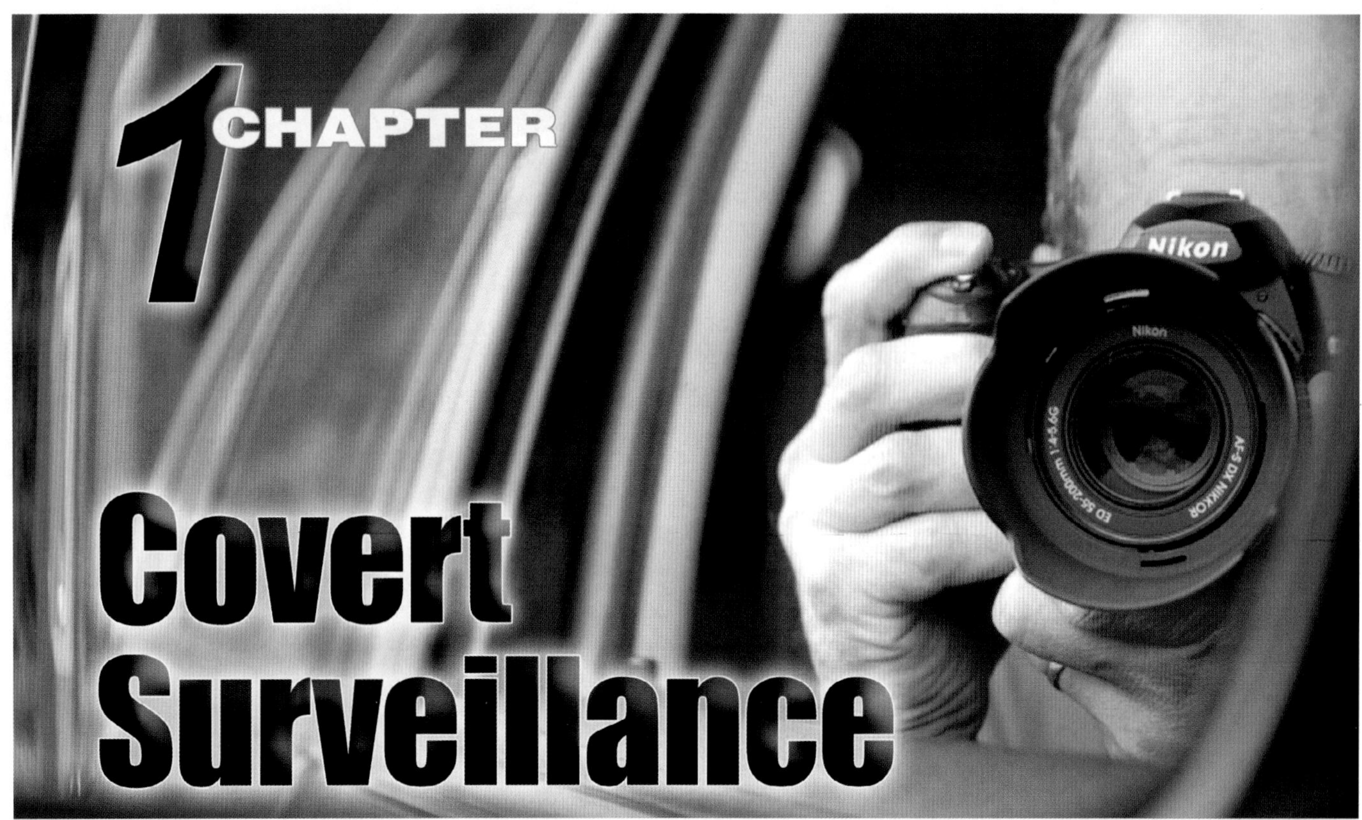


# Chapter 1 Covert Surveillance

In this first chapter, we define the types and methods of surveillance, detail the qualities of a good surveillance operator and describe the areas that provide grounding for the chapters to follow. First of all, let us find a generic definition of surveillance:

*Surveillance is the continuous watching or listening (overtly or covertly) of people, vehicles, places or objects to obtain information concerning the activities and identities of individuals.*

## COVERT SURVEILLANCE DEFINED

**CONTINUOUS** If we break this definition down, we say that surveillance is 'continuous' watching. By this we mean that the period of observation(s) has to go unbroken (unless this fact is recorded). An example, if we commence surveillance at 7.30am, follow the target for a number of hours, then at 10.00am we accidentally lose contact in heavy traffic and then half an hour later we manage to relocate again and continue with the surveillance. This in effect has not been a continuous surveillance as the target has been out of your control for a period of time.

**WATCHING OR LISTENING** Surveillance can be watching or listening (or both). The majority of our surveillance relies on what we see, therefore your eyesight (aided or unaided) has to be perfect. If we are obtaining information by using our ears, this can be carried out technically using audio listening devices or by being close to the target so that we can overhear conversation and obtain good intelligence.

**PEOPLE** Invariably we are concerned with individuals. There are many reasons why we put people under surveillance but essentially we need to monitor and record:

- *Where they go*
- *What they do*
- *Who they meet*
- *When they do it*
- *How do they do it*
- *Why they do it*

**VEHICLES** Surveillance is often carried out in motor vehicles. This could be to monitor deliveries made by the vehicle or because this is the normal mode of transport used by our target.

Although many people drive today, do not assume that you will be following a target in a car. If a target leaves a house, a number of options are open to them, they can walk, cycle, get picked up, take a taxi or use public transport. Quite often in major cities, targets may take public transport rather than drive.

**PLACES** Sometimes the surveillance of a place or premises could be the primary source of information and the activities of individuals may be secondary.

This could be a target's house or even a business premises. We have often put surveillance on commercial premises in order to record what deliveries are made and by which company. In this case, we have not been concerned with the actions of individuals.

**• OBJECTS** We may carry out observations on an object. In the past we put a derelict house under surveillance that was being targeted by thieves. They had removed the expensive stone roof tiles and had stacked them up to one side for collection later. It took four nights of observations until the thieves arrived and the Police were notified. The gang were caught removing the tiles in a truck.

## TYPES OF SURVEILLANCE

**Overt Surveillance:** Overt surveillance is an open observation where we deliberately let the target know that a surveillance is being conducted. This type of surveillance is not carried out often and normally acts as a deterrent to an illegal or illicit activity.

An open police presence can be described as "overt surveillance"

Closed circuit television cameras (CCTV) found in town centres and car parks could be considered as overt because we can see that they are there and therefore they act as a deterrent.

**Covert Surveillance:** Covert Surveillance is a secretive watch where the target is not aware of our presence or activities. We are trying to be totally covert, not only should we be hidden from the target but also from anyone else not connected with the surveillance team. This 'anyone else' we call the 'Third Party' and we have to be very 'Third Party' aware whilst carrying out observations. Many surveillances are compromised not because a team member has been seen by the actual target but by other third parties such as local residents and passers-by - more about third party awareness is covered later.

## OBJECTIVES OF A SURVEILLANCE

Surveillance can be carried out in order to:

**• Obtain evidence of a crime or unauthorised activity**

You may be obtaining evidence of a theft, fraud or other criminal act. Your evidence may be used in legal proceedings and so you have to preserve the integrity of that evidence which has to be obtained fairly and justifiably.

**• Obtain detailed information about the targets activities**

In order to build up 'the big picture', surveillance may have to be carried out in order to identify habits and routines, the places they visit and other people they associate with.

**• Develop leads for investigation**

Surveillance should provide the investigator with other sources or leads that can be followed up to provide further intelligence.

ISS CASE

## OVERT SURVEILLANCE

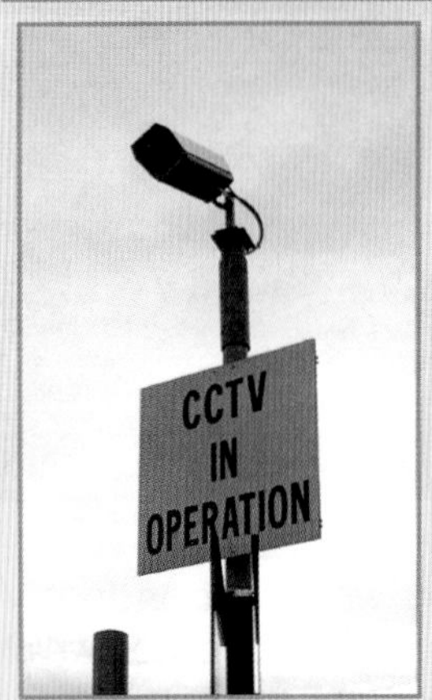

In the past we carried out an overt surveillance on a milkman who would purchase his milk more cheaply from a certain dairy farmer rather than from the dairy franchise that he was tied to. He had been served an injunction forbidding him from buying his milk from anywhere but his franchise company and as we could not maintain surveillance on him covertly (he drove an electric milk cart at five mph in the dark at 4.00am) we went 'overt'. He was aware he was being observed and adhered to the injunction. He is probably still looking over his shoulder to this day!

In another instance, we had to make it obvious to a particular individual that he was being watched. This can be very risky but the job was carried out with caution. I sat directly outside the target's gates (where you are not supposed to be) and waited for him to emerge. When he did, he took a good look at me sitting in the front of my car. I then pulled out behind him without any cover and followed him for a while at a reasonable distance. I made a few changes of direction with him and when I was certain that he had noticed me, I pulled away and let him run.

The last thing I wanted was to be led into a trap where his colleagues would be waiting with iron bars. One of the major disadvantages to this type of surveillance is confrontation with the target and should really be avoided.

- **To know at all times the whereabouts of an individual**

Surveillance operations may be carried out on a target's premises the night prior to, and the same morning that a search or arrest warrant may be executed. It has happened to some agencies in the past where they have gone along to an address to execute a warrant, only to find no one at home after they have burst through the door.

- **To confirm the reliability of informant information**

At times we are trying to establish the truth and to prove or disprove allegations or suspicions. If an allegation is received from an informant, we cannot take it for granted that it is the truth. Therefore we will embark on an investigation to prove whether the allegation is true or simply malicious.

Realistically, any information provided by a client should be treated with caution.

- **Obtain information for later use in an interview**

Enforcement agencies interview suspects or targets in accordance with the Police And Criminal Evidence Act (PACE). A good interviewer should be confident and there is nothing better to boost that confidence than to have a surveillance report and photographs or video of the suspect carrying out the 'illicit act'. If there is denial from the suspect or a not guilty plea, the interviewer will be at a definate advantage.

- **Locate people (by watching their haunts and associates)**

Quite often people provide false addresses if they suspect that they may be under investigation or have a reason to suspect that they may be under surveillance. Keeping observations on a known place that they frequent, a pub for example, will provide us with a 'starting point' for a surveillance. From this surveillance we may establish where the target is residing. In a similar fashion, if we know that an associate frequently meets with the target, it may be easier to put surveillance on the associate.

ISS CASE

A number of years ago, we were instructed by a female to put her husband under surveillance as she suspected him of having an affair with one of her friends and had a strong suspicion that he was meeting her female friend in their lunch hour.

Unfortunately, a heated argument, the client had told her husband that she was going to have him followed. Because of this, it was decided to leave him alone and follow the female friend instead - it takes two to tango as they say.

The female friend left work at lunchtime and drove to her home which was close by. Very shortly afterwards, the clients husband arrived, parked at the rear and entered the house directly in front of our surveillance van. Video tape was obtained of them both entering and then leaving the house at the same time with happy grins on their faces. A good result for us but a poor one for the client.

# EVIDENCE COLLECTION

- **Secure information for search warrants**

Enforcement Agencies cannot simply apply to a Magistrate for a search warrant. Good evidence needs to be obtained to substantiate the need for such a warrant. Surveillance logs, covert video or photographs can provide the evidence required to obtain a warrant.

- **Obtain evidence for use in Court**

Much of the information obtained by investigators and surveillance operators is for legal purposes and is sought by a solicitor or a commercial company. This evidence will often be used in criminal and civil proceedings. Because of this, our evidence has to be accurate, truthful and beyond reproach.

- **Identify people**

Quite often we may carry out a surveillance in order to know what a person looks like, so that further investigations or surveillance can be carried out at a later date. We may have to identify people to eliminate or discount them from enquiries.

## METHODS OF SURVEILLANCE

Surveillance can be conducted in various ways but the methods are divided into five types. They can be conducted separately but more often different types of surveillance are combined.

Regardless of which method of surveillance is used, all rely heavily on teamwork. Surveillance is a team effort and to have effective teamwork you require good communications using radios.

Single-handed surveillance is not recommended but even in a team we often find ourselves the only person in the follow, as the other members have been held up or are detached. There is a section later in this book that deals with single-handed surveillance for that reason.

- *Foot Surveillance*
- *Mobile Surveillance*
- *Static Surveillance*
- *Public Transport*
- *Technical Surveillance*
- *Combined Surveillance*

**FOOT SURVEILLANCE** If we have planned our surveillance correctly we should have an idea whether our target will be going about his business on foot and so we have to prepare for this. The majority of our information and intelligence may be obtained whilst out on foot. A mobile surveillance by car is only a mode of transport which takes the target from A to B. It is when he gets out of the car at the other end and is on foot that we need to get in close and obtain detailed information.

## MOBILE SURVEILLANCE

We do not advocate carrying out a mobile surveillance single handed. Mobile Surveillance is carried out to follow moving targets by car or other motorised vehicle and this should always be carried out in a team or with at least two operators in separate vehicles.

An essential ingredient in mobile surveillance is communication. Communication and radio voice procedure is vital to the success of a mobile surveillance. The mobile operators must be able to observe the target, provide radio commentary, navigate, and record information simultaneously and drive safely at the same time.

ISS CASE

## CAUGHT IN THE ACT

A client who ran a trout farm received information that one of his staff was stealing fish food and selling it to an unknown person at a particular motorway service station on Saturday mornings. The first thing the client did was carry out a stock take but this proved that everything was in order. Still not satisfied, he asked us to put the individual under surveillance to see if he went to the service station as alleged. Rather than put him under surveillance with a two man team, it was decided to carry out the operation with one man (for cost reasons and to minimise the risk of losing him). Rather than follow the target, we waited at the service station for the target to arrive.

We arrived at the service station and parked up in a small observation van. After an hour and a half, our target was identified as he entered the main car park and parked up. Our observation van was then driven into a suitable position to take video footage. After a short period, another van arrived and parked alongside the target van and sacks of fish food were transferred from one vehicle to another. A wad of cash was handed over for payment.

The video was shown to the client and he was satisfied that a theft had taken place. The culprit was interviewed, admitted the theft and resigned. It became apparent that he was able to cover his tracks on the stock take quite easily - he wasn't feeding the fish!

The operator must be flexible, and be prepared for ever changing situations such as the target leaving his car and proceeding on foot, using public transport or meeting with others.

**STATIC SURVEILLANCE** Static Surveillance is where the surveillance operator(s) are in a static position from where they can keep observations such as: a car, a building, hedgerow, surveillance vehicle, or even whilst on foot. Static Observation Posts (OPs) can be long term or short term and may be divided into a further two groups Urban and Rural depending on the local topography.

You may be asked to conduct surveillance on a factory gate to monitor the vehicles that leave or arrive. Initially we may consider sitting in the front of our car from where we can observe. If this is too risky, we may then consider using a surveillance van as an OP. If we cannot park in the street, there may be some form of building or structure from where we can watch. If not there maybe a hedgerow or a ditch that we may be able to observe from, although this takes skill and experience. On a short term basis, an operator on foot could also keep observation providing he has a reason for being there, such as using a phone box or waiting at a bus shelter.

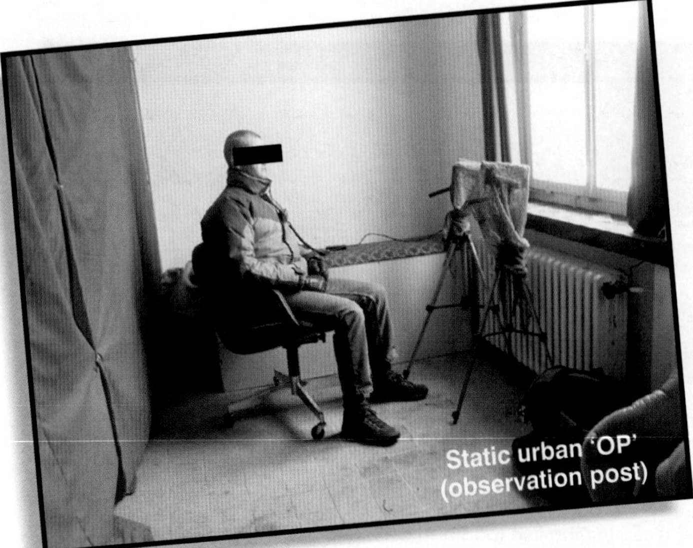

Static urban 'OP' (observation post)

Static OPs are used when the target comes to your area of observation and you await their arrival with a camera. The Static OP is also used as a 'trigger platform' to inform mobile operators that the target is departing from or arriving at a particular area, such as the home or office.

**PUBLIC TRANSPORT** Surveillance on public transport is often carried out by foot persons who are backed and supported by a mobile team. Targets can travel by:

- *Private Hire Cab*
- *Taxi*
- *Bus*
- *Underground Rail*
- *Overground Rail*
- *Rickshaws*
- *Ferry*
- *Trams & Light Railways*

**TECHNICAL SURVEILLANCE** Technical or electronic surveillance is a means of gathering information with the use of technical devices such as:

- *Vehicle Trackers*
- *Radio Microphones (bugs)*
- *Tape Recorders & Microphones*
- *Telephone Monitoring Devices*
- *Covert Video Recorders*
- *Computer Intercepts*

Each item will have its limitations, but used purposefully can be a very effective tool in gathering information and providing technical support to the other types of surveillance.

**COMBINED SURVEILLANCE** The make up and formation of a surveillance team will be decided at the planning stage. The team leader should be able to make an appraisal and may decide what resources are required. For example, on a large task with a budget to suit, the team leader may decide to use a van for the 'trigger' and two cars and a motorbike for the follow. It may be expected that the target will go out on foot in a busy city centre, therefore an extra foot person may be carried in one of the cars.

On one occasion we surveilled a speeding driver often surpassing 120mph on the motorway. Not because he thought he was under surveillance, he just drove that way, and so it was decided to use two cars and a vehicle tracker. He was left to run when necessary and when he stopped we knew exactly where in order to move in close and monitor his activity.

So, effectively we are using various types of surveillance and resources in order to make up a combined surveillance team.

## THE 'IDEAL' SURVEILLANCE OPERATOR

A good standard of surveillance by an individual or team can only be acquired by training, practice and most of all, experience. It is important not to stand out in a crowd and the operator should fit in with his surroundings at all times. His dress code should suit the area in which he is operating and his vehicle should be given the same consideration.

Your target should not be able to remember you, recognise you at a later stage or be able to describe you to another person.

**Your target should not be able to remember you, recognise you at a later stage or be able to describe you to another person....**

- **Personal qualities**

Not everyone is born as the 'ideal' surveillance operator. The making of a good operator will depend upon that persons aptitude, his training, and, most of all experience. The ideal surveillance operator should ideally have the following qualities:

- **Confidence**

Confidence comes with training and experience. A person on a surveillance that lacks in either will be a liability to himself and to the team. Regardless of what skills we have in life, if we are proficient in what we do we will have confidence in doing it and will operate that much better.

- **Be quick thinking and quick to react**

The target can be very unpredictable in his movements and actions, therefore we have to adapt very quickly to ever changing situations. We also have to react very quickly when using a radio in order to direct the team and let the team know of the targets movements and intentions.

- **Multi tasking**

In the commercial world, surveillance is normally carried out 'one up' in the car. That means that you have to drive safely, anticipate the actions of the target whilst giving a commentary over the radio. You have to navigate using a map or Satnav, keep an eye out for the third party and obtain video evidence, all at the same time - it takes practise and aptitude to do so many things at once.

- **Have patience**

Many people consider surveillance as being an exciting occupation. From the operator's point of view, many hours are spent doing absolutely nothing, waiting for things to happen and this waiting requires great discipline. When the action starts, you have to put yourself into gear and be where you are supposed to be, doing what you are supposed to be doing. If you are new to surveillance be prepared for spending most of your time waiting for something to happen with little bursts of activity.

Be capable of acting naturally at all times and move unobtrusively

**• Be capable of acting naturally at all times and move unobtrusively**

What will get you noticed in surveillance more than anything else is unnatural behaviour especially whilst on foot. You should be seen but not noticed. On surveillance courses we often see students standing in doorways whilst trying to keep observations on the doorway across the other side of the street. After 30 seconds or so, the inexperienced operator starts to get itchy feet and shuffles about, craning his neck, peeping and generally moving about acting unnaturally, when all he had to do was stand still and do absolutely nothing.

The way that we carry ourselves and move about is also important. In surveillance, we never run. If we run, we start to attract attention, not only by the target but also by third parties. The only time you should run is when you have a reason for doing so, such as running across a road.

**• Be able to fit and merge into a variety of backgrounds**

The way you dress and act (including the type of vehicle you use) must suit the area in which you are operating. Carrying out a surveillance wearing a suit and driving a new vehicle will soon show out in a rough housing estate. Conversely, wearing scruffy jeans and T shirt and driving a wreck of a car would soon be noticed in a more up-market setting.

**• Have good eyesight and good hearing**

The majority of our evidence comes from what we actually see, therefore our eyesight has to be good. It does not matter whether we wear glasses or contact lenses but as long as we can see clearly. In addition to being able to see well at a distance, your close up vision also has to be perfect for writing notes, reading a map, or to programme a Satnav or a camera. At times we may be very close to the target so we can overhear conversation and so our hearing has to be very good too.

**• Have a good memory**

Combined with good eyesight and hearing, we must be able to remember facts and sequences of events. We may not always be in a position to write down events as they happen or commit them to recorder and so memory and the information we remember has to be accurate.

**• Be a good talker and actor**

For a number of reasons we have to converse with the general public. It may be to satisfy the curiosity of a concerned member of the public (third party) who has seen you parked in a particular place. It may be to quiz a member of the public for information during your enquiries. You may even have to speak to the target to obtain information, although this is not often done. However, he may approach you if his suspicions are aroused and so you need to be able to act and talk your way out of a situation with confidence.

**• Be physically fit and healthy**

We do not necessarily have to be at peak fitness but at least reasonably fit so as not to be out of breath on a long foot surveillance. If you are taking part in an OP you also need to be reasonably healthy, fit in body, fit in mind. Coughs and sneezes not only get you noticed but will also impair your effectiveness as a team member.

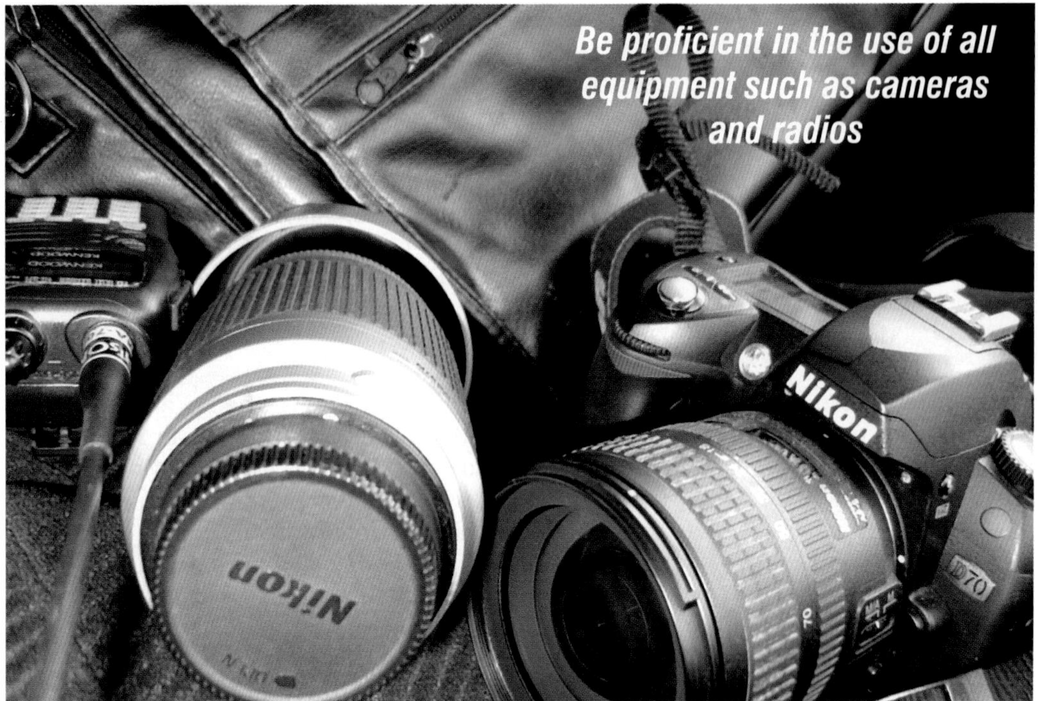

Be proficient in the use of all equipment such as cameras and radios

**• Be astute to the local situation where you are working**

A mobile surveillance can move at a fast pace and cover a large geographical area. When entering an unfamiliar area, take stock of the situation and consider any 'third party'. You may have entered a rough inner city housing estate where crime could be rife with drugs being dealt and high unemployment. Many people may be on the look out for anything or anyone that does not fit in or looks suspicious. If you do not notice this quickly or feel the atmosphere, you will soon find yourself being chased out of the neighbourhood or, at worse, attacked.

**• Be able to work on your own initiative as well as a team**

Surveillance is all about teamwork and communication. The longer that you work together with the same team, the better you will perform which will reflect in your results. However, as an individual, you must draw on your knowledge, skill and experience to act on your own initiative in order to make a contribution to that team.

**• Be a confident and proficient driver with good navigational skills**

Surveillance operators within the police and military must pass an advanced driving course prior to carrying out any mobile surveillance. In the commercial world, your driving skills have to be good in order to operate safely and effectively. After all, you would not expect a person who has just passed a driving test to be able to operate effectively as part of a mobile team.

Within some Police Forces and Enforcement Agencies, mobile surveillance is often carried out with two operators per car (two up). One operator will drive and control the vehicle whilst the other operates the radio and deploys on foot when required. In this way the responsibilities are shared between the crew and in some respects, this makes life easier for each individual, although going 'two up' does have its drawbacks. Within military surveillance organisations and especially on the private surveillance circuit, surveillance is often carried out single-handed or 'one up'.

**• Be proficient in the use of all equipment such as cameras and radios**

This is an important factor and the surveillance operator has to be an expert in all the equipment that he uses.

Being able to follow a target and take him to a destination is only a means to an end; in most cases, it is what actually happens at the 'other end' that provides the evidence and the results. If you missed that vital piece of evidence because you were unfamiliar with your camera or you did not know how to change batteries at the critical time, the job may have been a complete waste of time. Do not let your team or your client down by providing poor excuses because you were unable to operate your equipment properly.

**• Have a 'sixth sense'**

After training, the most important quality a surveillance operator can possess is experience. An experienced operator will get a 'feel' for the job and the way it is progressing. He will be able to predict possible outcomes, purely because he has 'been there' and seen it before. What we try not do in surveillance is assume what the target will do. An inexperienced operator will regularly guess and assume what may happen. This is dangerous, if you expect a target to do one thing, he will probably do something totally different.

## PERSONAL APPEARANCE AND DRESS SENSE

**What Gets A Surveillance Operator Noticed?**

There are three main reasons why you may be compromised and you constantly have to be aware of:

- *Multiple Sightings*
- *Unusual Behaviour*
- *Cross Contamination*

Many people carrying out surveillance related investigations fail to appreciate this. Compromises occur because the operator goes in too close and too hard at the wrong times, so when he really needs to go in hard and close he is already burned.

**• Multiple Sightings**

As previously mentioned, you should be seen but not noticed and be the ultimate 'grey' person. After the target has seen you on several separate occasions he will remember you, especially if you give him a reason to by the way you dress or act. Therefore, if you are working as a team, each member should have their share of taking the 'Eyeball', thus sharing the amount of exposure. Always ensure that you are behind or to the side of the target (out of his 10 to 2 o'clock arc of vision) and never in front and avoid eye contact at all costs. If you stay out of the 10-2, you should never be seen or noticed.

**• Unusual Behaviour**

The way that we act and carry ourselves is very important and if not checked will soon have us noticed. During the early stage of surveillance training courses we find that the hardest thing for a student to do whilst on foot is to stand still and do absolutely nothing. The target may have entered a shop, and so the team are plotted up waiting for him to emerge. We see them hiding behind shop doorways 'peeping' out, suspiciously leaning against lamp posts, pretending to look in a shop window which has not been used for years or standing against a park bench rather than sitting on it, pretending to be on the phone.

Their actions are unnatural and therefore come to the attention of others. Admittedly, it is not easy trying to act naturally whilst having a hidden agenda (the surveillance) and this only comes with practice and experience - you have to learn to relax.

Be aware of 'fiddling' underneath your jacket when adjusting your radio, a passer-by may notice the radio set. In addition, try to avoid constantly touching your earpiece, as it is unnatural and an aware target will pick up on it.

**• Cross Contamination**

Should a target suspect you as being a surveillance operator, he will most likely keep an eye on you. Therefore, although acting in a team, we should never make physical contact with any other member, even using hand signals. This will only 'cross contaminate' the other operator and the target will now be aware of two people following him. Cross contamination is discussed fully in the chapter on foot surveillance.

## THE WAY WE DRESS

The way that we appear and dress is very important, especially when operating on foot. The area in which you are working should govern your dress sense. The team should all be dressed differently, if we were all to wear a black fleece, black T shirt, blue jeans and brown boots we may as well carry out the surveillance on our own or at worst wear a uniform.

Remember, one reason for being spotted is multiple sightings. The target will always see you but to notice you is a different matter. You need to minimise being noticed as much as possible and this begins with the way we dress.

**• Contrasting Colours**

Try to avoid clothing with contrasting colours or bright colours. A dark top over a white shirt or stripes that run down your jacket sleeves can be very noticeable. If you need to wear a suit, consider wearing a darker shirt rather than a white one.

Contrast does not just relate to black and white, the same considerations have to be given to red

**This surveillance student has failed to follow a strict rule - 'conceal equipment at all times'**

and white or green and yellow. If you are working at night consider wearing darker clothing and avoid white trainers.

• **Distinct Clothing**

You should be seen but not noticed, therefore you have to be the grey person that does not stand out in the crowd.

Many that work in the surveillance sector are former military or police. By nature they are practical outdoor people and tend to wear very similar styled clothing, which in essence could be considered a uniform and should be avoided if you dress in this fashion. Let us take a look at some similarities:

**Students arrive at ISS on day one of a surveillance course. Note the uniformity of their dress wear - this will change with experience, training and knowledge**

**SUBTLE CHANGE OF APPEARANCE: This operator's appearance has been changed by simply using a baseball cap and tying back her hair in a pony tail**

# CLOTHING AND ACCESSORIES
## *WHAT NOT TO WEAR AND USE*

*It is best to stay away from designer labels and certain outdoor brands*

*'511' cargo pants*

*Sunglasses should only be worn in appropriate conditions or environment*

Freelance security operators tend to use PDA-style mobile phones

*Military-style watch and compass will be noticed*

*Avoid bright trainers*

# IMPORTANT CHECK LIST

**Jackets, often weather proof**

- Gore-Tex
- Fleece material
- Duvet/Puffa

**Branded Names on jackets, trousers and footwear**

- North Face
- Nike
- Berghaus
- Regatta
- Rohan
- HI-Tec
- 511

**Trousers**

- Blue jeans
- Cargo pants

**Footwear**

- Trainers
- Walking/trail boots
- Military black boots

**Wristwatch**

- Divers or Aviators watches
- Chronographs
- Branded Names

**Mobile Phone**

- PDA style cell phones
- Blackberry, iPhone

**Accessories that are worn or carried**

- Sunglasses
- Belt-worn tools
- Rucksacks
- Baseball Cap

**Bearing**

- Fit
- Upright posture
- Confident gait
- Well groomed
- Short tidy hair
- Tattoos

***This operator has committed two dress errors - the contrasting pale jacket with black shoulder bag strap, and the white training shoes***

Ensure that you also dress for the weather. The last thing you want to do is leave your car to carry out a foot surveillance on a wet and windy day when you have forgotten to take a jacket or coat with you. You will be the only one in the street getting wet and consequently stand out in the crowd.

In a similar manner, you should dress for the occasion if at special events. On a recent surveillance at a trade fair, the surveillance team all wore business suits because that was the dress of the day in order to blend in. Jeans and trainers or casual dress would not have been acceptable in this instance.

Female team members should dress like females! There are many women that carry out surveillance but not very many compared to the men. Therefore having a woman on the team can be very advantageous but do not lose the initiative by the way you dress. We see many girls on surveillance courses who dress just like the men (blue jeans, trainers and a dark fleece) rather than use their wardrobe to make them look different from the rest of the team.

**DRESS ACCORDING TO YOUR VEHICLE** This sounds odd but ensure that the way that you dress suits your vehicle. If you are driving a top of the range car, you do not really want to be dressed scruffily, conversely, you may look out of place wearing a suit whilst driving a wreck of a car.

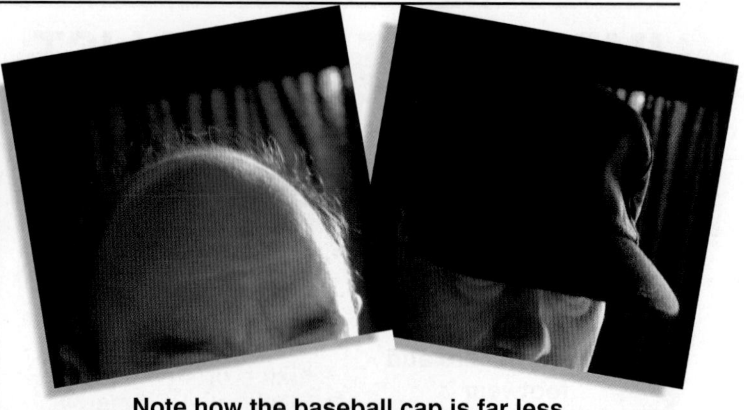

Note how the baseball cap is far less prominent in this case

**DISGUISES?** It may be wise to carry a change of clothing with you, such as a lightweight or reversible jacket or a hat. A plastic carrier bag in your pocket can be used to put your jacket in, thus changing your overall appearance. If you have long hair, you could wear it down and then tie it back with a bobble or tuck it under a baseball cap.

You may wish to change your appearance slightly by wearing a baseball cap, this is okay but do not continually put it on and off. The target may notice these frequent changes in appearance and so confirm suspicions. Be aware of wearing black 'bobble' hats or rolled up balaclavas, this will make you look dubious and be the focus of attention.

A change of outline is recommended by the removal of a hat or scarf. Putting on or taking off a jacket, plain glass spectacles, or even putting your hands in pockets to change your overall appearance can help. Do not use disguises, especially wigs because even the best can look obvious. An alert target will notice a change of appearance and again, will only help to confirm any suspicions. Do not wear sunglasses unless everyone else about you is also wearing them. Surveillance is not about looking good, its about avoiding being noticed.

A heavy padded coat can quickly change the body's outline

## ISS CASE

A number of years ago we were on a surveillance task involving personal injury fraud, when one of the team (Dave) had driven the observation (Obs) van into position and then walked back to his car, which was parked a distance away.

Not long after he returned to his car, he received a phone call from the police asking if he was the owner of a dark blue BMW, registration 1234 etc.. and was he aware of the cars' whereabouts. Dave stated to the police that he was sitting in it and asked why they had called. The police informed him that a local resident had reported seeing a scruffy and unkempt looking person suspiciously getting into an expensive BMW.

Always carry an amount of change and money with you. If the target gets onto public transport or takes a taxi he will have to be followed. If he enters a pub or café you may have to go in with him. Do not forget money for car parking, tolls and trolleys at supermarkets.

**STANDING DOWN** If you feel that you may lose contact with the target, you would consider keeping much closer but by keeping close you risk showing out. It is therefore better to let the target continue and experience a loss. If you are compromised, you may not be able to return to that target for a number of weeks, it is far better to let the target run and remember... *there is always another day.*

**TEAMWORK** Any experienced person trained in surveillance, will tell you that to carry out a surveillance single-handed is not only difficult but down right foolish. Not only do you run the risk of losing contact with the target in traffic but also and more importantly, you run the high risk of compromise and possible confrontation. As a rule, we do not carry out single handed surveillance, if we did, we would feel that we would not be doing our clients any favours. We would not be acting professionally and feel that we would be deceiving the client into handing over their money when the odds are against us achieving a successful outcome.

If a client says, 'I can't afford for more than one person' I turn the job down and let some other person in the phone book take it on and bid them good luck.

Teamwork is essential in surveillance and in order to have effective teamwork you require effective communication. The team have to be fully conversant with radio voice procedure and radio discipline, you have to trust the other members of the surveillance team and act on your own initiative without being told where to go and what to do.

A team leader has enough to think about and should not have to continually direct the surveillance. If the target stops, the team should carry out a set drill in order to control him. The team leader should not have to direct individuals with particular tasks.

In the early stages of training, all three members of a foot surveillance team tend to get 'eyes on' to the target all at once. This is expected, as they are keen and it is only natural that they all want to be in control of the target and have a piece of the action. Remember, only one person has to see the target at any one time, the 'Eyeball', who is giving a radio commentary and painting a picture of events for the benefit of the others who are out of sight.

During this time, if you are not the Eyeball, you have to listen to the commentary and trust what is said totally.

## TYPES OF TARGET WHO COME UNDER SURVEILLANCE

Many people can be the target of a surveillance for many different reasons and can come from all walks of life. Listed below are the various categories of awareness levels that the target may fall into. When obtaining a brief from a client, it is very important to know whether the target has been put under surveillance in the past, so do not forget to ask at the briefing stage. If they have, you should be told of the outcome, especially if there was a compromise as you will then have to be on your guard and adapt your tactics.

- **Aware**

The aware target disciplines and trains himself to look for 'watchers' and 'followers' and he may carry out anti-surveillance tactics as a matter of course every time he appears in the open. He will certainly do it prior to an activity. This type of target is usually from the criminal element that has knowledge of surveillance procedures or is a subject who expects to be followed.

They can be tricky to put under surveillance but a larger team and more covert tactics will enable you to control them.

• **Semi-Aware**

The target categorised as being semi-aware would expect to be followed or watched as they have a reason for doing so. For example, someone with a large insurance claim for injury may be on the lookout as they are aware that false claims are being investigated. This target will be alerted by noticing things that are out of the ordinary and unusual without having to look too hard. You must not spook them or they will become very aware.

They may adopt some overt anti-surveillance tactics to identify whether they are being followed but they may not really know what to look out for. Their anti surveillance drills are soon noticed by an experienced team.

Never make an 'unaware' target become 'aware' by encounters such as this on a narrow bridge with few persons around

• **Unaware**

This target does not consider or think about being watched or followed and can be very complacent about his activities and is easily caught out. This does not mean that they are guiltless. We have put people under surveillance in the past who were carrying out serious criminal acts but because they have been carrying out these activities for so long without being caught out, they become complacent.

• **Hidden**

The target we consider 'hidden' is more likely to be the hardened criminal. Rather than appear out in the open to carry out their activities, they remain out of sight and have their 'foot soldiers' to carry out their work for them. If they do appear out in the open, (as everyone has to do at sometime) they will probably carry out anti and counter surveillance measures. This type of target is difficult to put under surveillance and can only be infiltrated by undercover operators or informants.

On a recent investigation we were asked to follow a sales manager, we were told that he had not been under surveillance before.

The target carried out some unusual manoeuvres as he left work in his lunch hour, but had no reason for doing so and we had no reason to believe that we had been compromised. After talking to the client again, asking if he had been followed before, stated: 'Well, one of our staff did try to follow him in his lunch hour a couple of weeks ago but he was noticed, which is why we have called you in!'

The target is more likely to be aware at various times or places.

- *When he is leaving his home or his base*
- *When he is about to commit a crime or act*
- *After committing a crime or act*
- *When he returns to his home or base*
- *When he has been 'spooked'*

Be alert and aware at these times and proceed with caution. These awareness levels are described more fully in the chapter on Anti Surveillance.

• **A 'Lost' Target**

Losing contact with the target of surveillance is inevitable from time to time even when working with large teams. Losses occur for many reasons, for example, traffic congestion, busy roundabouts, traffic lights and lack of concentration. When this occurs the surveillance team must adopt a search pattern. It assists greatly if the operators draw on knowledge and background of the target in an effort to pick him up and continue the surveillance. The type of target who expects to be followed will undoubtedly attempt to lose the tail. Never let over-enthusiasm in pursuit of the target result in 'showing out' and a compromised surveillance.

If you find yourself following a lost driver he may carry out manoeuvres that you may consider to be 'anti-surveillance'. This could include; changing speed, suddenly stopping, making 'U' turns or going around a roundabout a few times. These are classic anti-surveillance manoeuvres but are also the signs of a lost driver, so you should decide at an early stage, is the target lost or is he trying to catch you out.

***Losses happen, they are a fact of life and an occupational hazard in surveillance***

## THIRD PARTY AWARENESS

Most surveillance work is considered 'covert'; we are being secretive about what we are doing and we do not want the target to know that they are under surveillance. More importantly, we need to remain unobtrusive from the general public and anyone else who is not connected with the surveillance. We call them the 'Third Party' and we have to be third party 'aware' at all times. It is the third party who causes at least 80% of all compromises and if not careful, the surveillance can be blown well before the target has appeared out in the open.

These compromises are not unique to Neighbourhood Watch type areas. Whether we are working on the roughest estates, the remotest rural areas or the sleepiest suburbs, we have to be astute.

You may be quite a distance from the target's house or premises (possibly acting as back-up to the trigger) but you still have to take precautions when deciding where to 'plot up'. During a mobile or foot surveillance act accordingly, never run or drive erratically and try not to be the focus of attention.

**WHEN STATIC** Your vehicle has to fit in with the area in which you are working in order not to attract unwanted attention.

If you are not using a surveillance van or an OP to 'trigger' the surveillance it may be that you have to remain sitting in your vehicle. In this event you have to be far away enough from the target for them not to notice you but close enough for you to identify them. There are a number of precautions that we can take to minimise the attention we bring on ourselves. Some of them are common sense but they are easily forgotten.

**This vehicle without its wheel trim immediately attracts attention through its contrasting trims**

• Do not carry out multiple 'drive pasts' of the targets address. If you have to take another look at the property get out of the car and walk, or ask another team member to do it. Ask yourself, can I get a 'long look' from a distance and use binoculars.

• When parked turn your engine off, don't forget your lights, square off your wheels and take your foot off the foot brake, you do not want to appear as if you are on a mission! Park pretty, a vehicle parked 'unnaturally' will stand out and if you are the only vehicle in the street, you will not last long and remember to take your seat belt off and lock your doors.

• Park the vehicle where houses or offices do not overlook you. Use cover such as hedges, walls and other vehicles. If working on industrial estates be aware of CCTV cameras that may be present.

• Consider sitting in the passenger seat, any passer-by or local would naturally presume that you are waiting for the driver to return. Maybe sit in the rear seat with a jacket on a hanger over a window to provide some temporary cover, especially when taking photographs if there are people about.

• Always have your 'working tools' close to hand so that they can be used at short notice. Your camera, phone, wallet, binoculars, dictaphone, notebook and pen should always be within easy reach but remember not to have them in view so that passing third parties can see them. This does not mean that the car is clean and sterile but it needs to look natural and used.

• In warm weather, when windows are open, keep your radio volume turned down, passers-by may hear transmissions.

After having been sitting in the same place for a while you may feel that you have to move your position or bring in a replacement because you've been there too long. If so, your replacement should not position himself in the same spot, this will only confirm the locals' suspicions and will possibly compromise another vehicle. If you are attracting some third party, make the team aware so that they do not sit in the same place.

You may be part of a surveillance team and not even be the person that has 'eyes on' whilst waiting for the 'Standby'. The position where you park up and how you act is equally important: take a good look around you and try to see yourself from the 'third parties' perspective.

Be prepared to be approached and have a cover story ready. Remember, that in everything we do we must

Frequent drive-pasts along urban streets such as this will soon attract local attention

always act naturally, adopt an identity and have a reason for being there. Cover stories are many and may be left to the imagination but ensure that your reason for being there is realistic and probable. I have got away without being approached for hours just by wearing a fluorescent Hi-Vis vest or having the vest thrown over the dashboard. Also in the past I have told enquirers that I intend serving a Divorce Petition on someone who is trying to avoid me and am awaiting for them to return.

Have the right attitude with enquirers, being off hand with people will only irritate them and attract further attention. Be confident and try not to act 'shifty'. Whatever you do, do not pretend to be the Police, not only is it illegal, it will attract more attention than you wished for.

## THE REST OF THE STREET

Remember that your target may not be the only person in the street who has a reason to be under surveillance. I am sure that in an average street there is at least one fraudulent social security claim, a personal injury insurance claim, a drug dealer, a criminal, a matrimonial affair, someone that was recently burgled and the local 'paranoid' expecting men from Mars. All of whom have reason to be on their guard. Just because you are watching one property, it does not mean that all the other properties are considered safe. So be careful.

## DURING MOBILE SURVEILLANCE

Whilst taking part in a mobile surveillance we have to drive in a manner that will not attract attention. Aggressive, high speed driving is not only dangerous but you will be noticed and reported. If you are in a situation where you are directly behind the target and held at a junction, act naturally and avoid eye contact in his mirrors. Do not slowly

Make sure your actions in a vehicle such as photographing your target are not seen by anyone

## ISS CASE

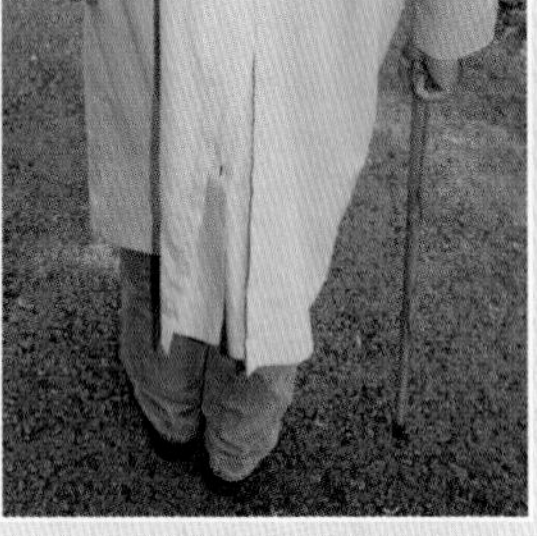

On a surveillance case involving theft, one operator had the trigger from the van. I myself was sat in a quiet nearby street away from the target. At about 8.30am, I noticed a large man come out of a house some 30 metres to my front. Before he got into his car he looked up and down the street and gave me a 'double take'. He was then followed by his daughter and both got into their car and departed.

About 15 minutes later, the same man returned, parked and entered the house giving me another look on the way in. I was not really put off by this so stayed where I was. Some 45 minutes later, the same man came out of the house now walking with a slight limp and using a walking stick!

I had to laugh and guessed that he must have a disability or injury insurance claim on the go and he obviously thought that I was interested in him. I thought to myself, 'I'll be back here again soon!'

creep up behind the target vehicle hoping that he will not notice you, he will. You are a member of the public on a public road and have every right to be there so act normally.

### WHEN STOPPING

If your target comes to a halt, do not stop directly behind without any cover and definitely do not screech to a halt. You may need to get your camera up and running so have a quick look about you before you start filming including above you. Most passers-by may not even notice you or even care, but it only takes one person to see that you are up to something. Consider jumping into the back seat for cover.

### DEPLOYING ON FOOT

If you have to get out on foot, don't ever run (unless you're crossing a road). Anyone seen running in a public place attracts attention, people are naturally curious and they will want to know why. Again, act naturally and give yourself a reason for being there.

To summarise, in order to minimise 'showing out' to third parties, adopt the following procedures:

- Be aware of the area and situation in which you are operating.

- Be extremely observant of your surroundings when close to, and away from your target. Do not forget to look 360 degrees around you and above you at windows and buildings.

**Always carry some form of identification**

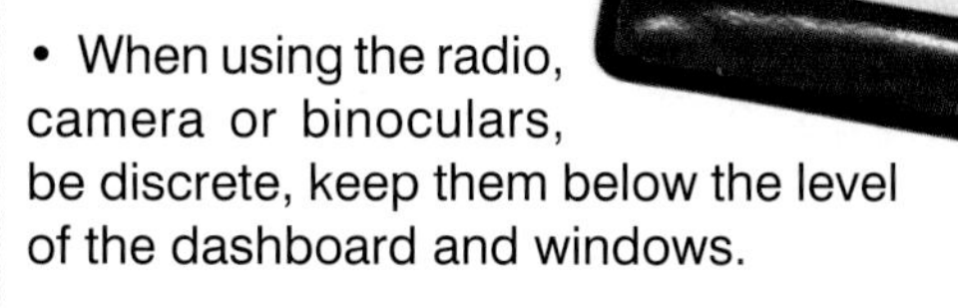


- Be aware of Neighbourhood Watch Schemes or criminal elements.

- Keep all equipment such as radios and cameras out of view and covered up, This also applies to any paper-work, files or photographs. Do not let radio transmissions be heard through an open window.

- When using the radio, camera or binoculars, be discrete, keep them below the level of the dashboard and windows.

- Use the other team members to keep a look out and back you up if you have to do something you consider risky; for example, photographing items in the rear of the target vehicle.

- Adopt an identity and always give yourself a purpose, a visual cover story and reason for being there.

- Have a convincing cover story ready if a member of the public challenges you, make it realistic. Curious neighbours will not tolerate excuses such as 'mind your own business'. This will arouse their suspicions further and they are likely to inform the Police.

### DO YOU INFORM THE POLICE OF YOUR PRESENCE AND OF THE INVESTIGATION?

There are many different trains of thought on this matter, both have their advantages and disadvantages but as a rule we do not usually inform the Police of our activities, unless it is to our advantage.

## ISS CASE

A few years ago we carried out a surveillance on a sales manager who was suspected of carrying out other work and so he was put under surveillance in order to see what he did during the day.

We carried out the job by triggering the surveillance with a van, which I was in. Covering the left option some half a mile away was Mick in a car, he was parked up in a country walk car park where members of the public would arrive in order to walk their dogs. Half a mile away covering the right option, was Keith on a motorbike who used a lay-by to lie up in. The target did not leave home until 12.30pm and drove for about six miles to his place of work, when he arrived, the team re-plotted. As we were doing so, Mick and I were separately 'hemmed' in by the Police using plain cars and were questioned as to who we were and what we were doing, they were obviously upset about something.

It transpired that the Police were from the regional Drugs Squad and they had placed Mick under surveillance through no fault of his own. Unbeknown to us, the Police had an OP in a public house that overlooked the country car park and were waiting for their targets to arrive. From their OP they would have seen this person arrive early morning (Mick) who would just sit in his car and do nothing, now and again he would take a drink from his flask or be seen to talk on his mobile phone.

After a while another person (Keith) would arrive at the car park dressed in black and riding a motorbike, he would exchange words with the driver of the car for a few minutes and then disappear. Half an hour later or so the rider would return for another chat and a share of a flask of coffee. To the Drug Squad, this was 'it', this was their target, Standby Standby!

When our target went mobile, so did we and so did the Police! During the journey, the Police obviously switched on to the fact that Mick was not alone as he was backed by me in the van and Keith was on the bike. It was revealed afterwards that the Police suspected that Mick was driving with his own 'counter surveillance' team behind him and so they decided to 'strike' and stop us when they did.

As team leader, I was quizzed by the plain clothed Police sergeant and was asked if I ever tell the Police when we operate in certain areas. I said 'No' and told him my reasons, 'We always get the nosey patrol car who comes looking for us and compromises the job'. The sergeant was sympathetic but we were asked to stay away from the country car park for the remainder of the week.

When working in 'rough areas' where there is a high risk of criminal element and the operators could be under threat, we would inform the local Police of our presence providing them with our vehicle details. In the past we have provided the Police with our details when working in particular areas. Not long after being on the ground, a Police patrol car would arrive in the area searching and trying to spot us. This has happened on many occasions and does nothing to assist our cause.

You will undoubtedly be stopped and questioned by the Police on occasions, therefore always carry some form of identity card to prove to them that you are an investigator. You are not obliged to give specific target details, but politeness and common sense should prevail.

### LOSS VERSUS GAIN (EXPOSURE LEVELS)

During any covert operation there is always a risk of 'showing out' and being compromised, experience and training will help to minimise this risk. You will either show out personally, your vehicle will be noticed or it will be your actions that draw the targets or a third parties attention. As an operator you will only have so many 'lives' and having too much exposure will lose them one by one.

Every time you go out on a surveillance give yourself 10 'lives' (or heat states as they are often referred to) just like a cat. Now every time that you have any exposure to the target, knock off a life or two. For instance, if the target goes into a hotel and you decide to go close in order to

An operator must decide whether to go in 'hard and close' if the target enters a building, meets another 'player' etc.

overhear what is being said at the reception, you may want to knock off one or two lives, as you have been in close and had some exposure to the target. You may now be down to a score of 9 or 8. These 'exposure levels' as we call them have to be monitored and considered wisely and are explained in more detail in the chapter on Evidence.

As we have already discussed, it is imperative that you are aware of the targets surveillance awareness level before embarking on the job. Consider what your aims and objectives are, as these will dictate how you operate on the ground and will not put you at unnecessary risk. For example, if we are on foot surveillance in a city centre, investigating a target who is suspected of fraudulently copying music CD's, we do not want to go in too hard and too close when it is not necessary.

The target may go into a newsagent, a clothes shop, and a chemists. When he does stop, although you have to keep control over him by covering the door to the shop - you have to decide whether it will be of an advantage to go in with him. Unless you are going to achieve anything, I would recommend that you stay out. If he was to visit HMV or Virgin Megastore then (remembering the aims and objectives) I would most certainly get an operator in close if it was of evidential value. What you have to decide is: *What am I going to 'gain' against what am I going to 'lose'?*

By going in close you may gain some good intelligence but in doing so, you will lose a number of lives. Guard your exposure levels if you have had a 'close encounter' with the target. If it is necessary that you get in close again, let the team know that you are 'warm' and so a different operator can go in close, remember, it is all about teamwork.

An experienced team member will know if he has been seen or noticed. Often we are very sensitive when the target looks in our direction and we are over cautious to the extent that we think we may have shown out. If this be the case, you should make a quick decision as to whether the operator or team should pull out of the surveillance.

## PRINCIPLES OF SURVEILLANCE

### Principle Stages or Phases

The surveillance operation can be broken down into the following four stages which is a continuous cycle of events or phases.

- *Stakeout*
- *Pick Up*
- *Follow*
- *Housing*

For example, we deploy on a surveillance, arrive at the target location and plot up in the area (the Stakeout). It maybe that one person can get in close, get eyes onto the house (the Trigger). The target comes out of his house and gets into his car (the Pick Up). He then drives for two minutes (the Follow) and stops at a newsagent shop and enters (the Housing). The cycle then starts again, we obtain a trigger on the newsagents door, the target comes out and gets into his car (the Pick Up) and drives away (the Follow), after a short while he arrives at his place of work (the Housing). So you see this sequence of phases can happen many, many times during the days surveillance. Let us look at each phase in more detail.

**THE STAKEOUT** What this means is that the team plot up in the area and box the target in so that he cannot move through the box without it being noticed. There are various types of stakeout and these are described in more detail later. More often than not, one person will be able to see the target or his premises and will be able to give warning of possible activity, we call this 'The trigger'. Sometimes, no one will be able to see the target and so the exits to the target street or particular roads have to be covered until the target is seen to be moving.

**THE TRIGGER** The start of the surveillance can be the most difficult and critical part. The whole operation can go wrong at the outset if the target cannot be 'triggered' and

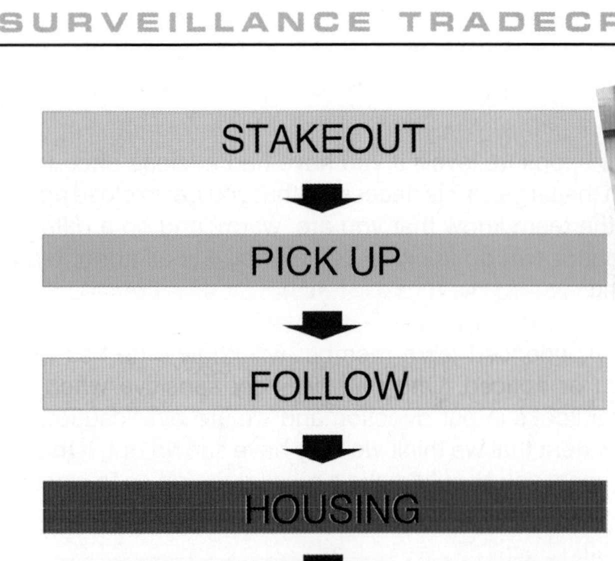

initiated away from his house or premises. It is the task of the trigger person to keep the target house or premises under observation in order to alert the remainder of the team when the target departs. It goes without saying that if we don't have a trigger and a pick up, then we will not have a follow.

**THE PICK UP** As soon as the target appears, the trigger should alert the team of possible movement. The call 'Possible Standby Standby' should be given over the radio net. This alerts the team putting them on standby for activity. Initially call a 'possible' standby until the target is actually committed to move. Otherwise, if a target comes out of the house, retrieves something from his car and the re-enters the house, you do not want the team to react. They will be pulling away from their safe positions, throwing coffee out of their windows when it is not necessary. If this is the case, come up on the radio net with the call 'Cancel Standby', to which all call signs should acknowledge.

When you are positive of movement, you can then confirm, and call a standby and a direction of travel.

**THE FOLLOW** The Follow is the term used when the target is on the move. He is considered 'mobile' if he is in a vehicle and 'foxtrot' if he is on foot, this is very important. At this stage you know where the target is and he should be under control at all times so the team can be deployed to the best advantage.

During this phase we do not always follow like ducks in a line but surveillance is 'imposed' upon the target and there is a vast difference, especially when on foot. The various techniques and methods used during the follow are discussed in the respective chapters. Do not always assume that the target will drive a car, he could travel by taxi, bus, train, bicycle or any other mode of transport.

**THE HOUSING** Housing the target after a follow can often be a tricky part of any surveillance and could be the most important. The housing could be a very short stop or could be a long wait. Therefore, the team have to act with a sense of urgency, re-trigger the target as soon as possible and re-plot at the location straight away. If you happen to get the trigger on a stop, come up on the radio net straight away and tell everyone. Once a trigger is established only then can the team settle down and relax a little knowing the target is under control.

By identifying the address or premises that the target enters may provide that final, vital piece of information you have been waiting for throughout your surveillance. You may have observed the target for many days but he now suddenly arrives and parks his vehicle in an unknown street. It is imperative that an operator is close enough to identify the property that he enters and this may possibly mean deploying an operator on foot as quickly as possible. Whilst doing so the team have to hold their positions in the event he goes mobile again.

In the next chapter we discuss the various methods of planning and preparation that are required before deploying on the ground.

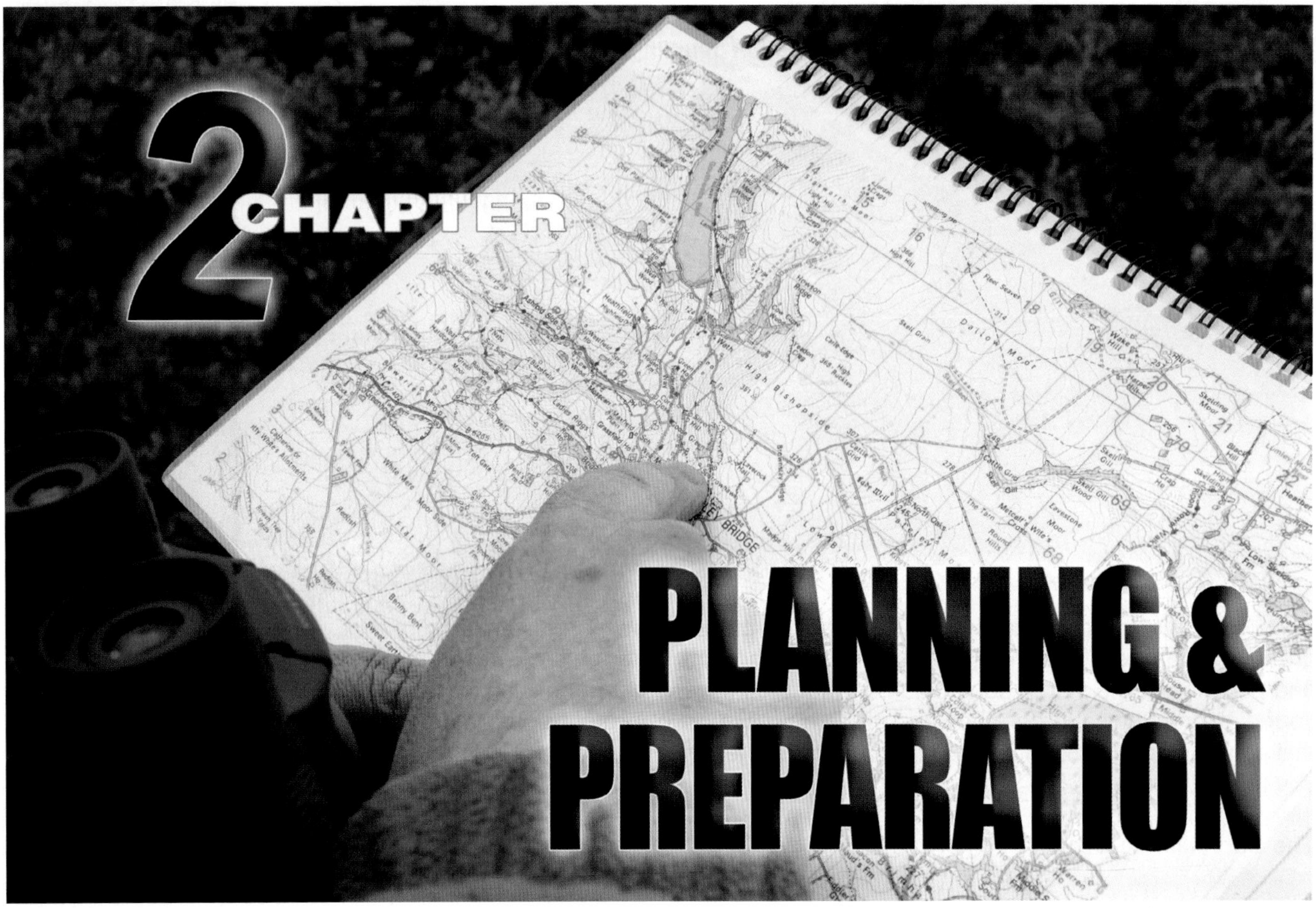

# CHAPTER 2

# PLANNING & PREPARATION

It is essential that detailed planning and preparation is carried out prior to any surveillance taking place. It would be foolish to just turn up at the target address on the morning of surveillance and hope that it goes well, because it probably won't.

## IS SURVEILLANCE THE SOLUTION?

When obtaining your brief, decide whether surveillance would provide the answer to your clients' problem. There are many reasons why a surveillance should be carried out but could the answers to your investigation be found out by other means?

Pretext telephone calls, visits to neighbours, or even speaking to the target of inquiry on a pretext can often lead to the results that you require. In addition, covert video cameras or trackers may provide you with information that you can act upon, without having to resort to lengthy and costly surveillance.

## WHAT ARE YOUR OBJECTIVES?

Look at the whole picture. You may have to break the investigation down into phases or objectives so that each one can be realistically achieved, do not expect to achieve the result that you want all at once.

Students prepare for a surveillance

For example, you may be tasked to investigate possible copyright infringement of your clients' product, you may be asked to establish:

*Where the target premises are?*
*Who is involved? How many staff?*
*How are they manufacturing the product?*
*What materials are used to make the product?*
*Who is supplying the materials?*
*What is the level of sales and distribution?*
*How are they marketing the product?*

Target under observation

Each objective could be tackled individually or put into groups or phases of the investigation. With forethought and planning at the start, you should be able to achieve your aims in a logical order and very often you may find that achieving one aim, will provide information that leads you to another.

### The Surveillance Option

If surveillance is the option that you have decided to take, you will require as much information as possible from the client concerning the target of enquiry and the circumstances in order to formulate a plan.

***It is essential that you establish whether the target has been under surveillance in the past and that you establish his 'awareness level'. It will affect how you plan and conduct your own surveillance.***

Having decided on your aims and objectives, you should then work in a methodical manner to arrive at a viable plan. Whether the task is a simple short single handed affair, or a complex team task requiring the use of static and mobile operators. All require some form of detailed planning and essentially there are two main areas that we need to look at prior to going out on the ground: the **Target** himself and the **Start Point** - often a home address or place of work.

If you can gather as much information about the target at the clients briefing or before we leave the office, the better prepared you will be.

## THE TARGET

Attempt to obtain as much information about the target as possible, this can be provided by the client or by your own enquiries. Ensure that you get as much as possible from the client; with a bit of thought you may be able to gain more information from them - they have a habit of forgetting important facts as they do not always understand our methodology. Points to consider are:

- **Target's name, nick-name or aliases**

Ensure that you know what the target is known by. Your target may be called Paul but all his life he may have been known by his middle name or nickname. If you have to make pretext enquiries and you have his name wrong you might arouse suspicion.

- **His address and associated addresses**

Ensure that the address that the client provides is correct; you do not want to be watching the wrong property. Double check with the Electors Register if possible, and the phone book. Invariably, if you telephone directory enquiries and ask for the person by name, they should tie it up with the address you have. You will be told either; the telephone number, whether it is ex-directory or that the number is not listed. If the latter is the case you will know that the target is not responsible for the bill and/or may no longer be resident. If you have to ring directory enquiries do so on a landline or payphone rather than from a mobile phone. Mobile directory enquiries are often a couple of months behind in their information.

- **Telephone number**

It is always handy to have the target's telephone number. If you arrive at the address for the surveillance and there has been no movement after four or five hours, the curtains have not opened or the milk is still on the doorstep, you would be thinking, 'Is anyone at home?' A realistic

## ISS CASE

In one case we could not identify whether it was our target or his son that had left an address but we decided to follow him just in case. The trigger person was left in situ in the event that we were wrong, but whilst there, he telephoned the target's address and asked for him by name. We were lucky as the reply from a female was, *'I'm sorry but you have just missed him, he left two minutes ago'.*

In another enquiry we could not identify the target who was with two other similar-looking men. By having his mobile phone number we were able to video all three of them at once whilst another member of the team rang him on his mobile (above). The one that pulled out his mobile to answer - was our target.

pretext call to the house would tell if there is anyone about. If there is no answer you may hear an answering machine providing a mobile number that you did not have.

If you do talk to someone on pretext, make the call realistic and never hang up on anyone, they only get suspicious. What would you think if someone did it to you?

**• Description**

A full up to date description of the target should be obtained. In the next chapter we deal with how a description is given so use this as your checklist.

**• Is a photograph or video available of target?**

If you can get a photograph or a piece of video tape then use it. Ensure that the photograph is up to date and there have been no changes - hair styles, facial hair and so on. Make sure that you study the picture, take it with you and do not pay 'lip service' to it. I have often seen investigators with photographs but they have not really looked at them or compared it with the subject.

A few years ago, we carried out a surveillance on the Isle of Man and we were armed with a photograph that was some 15 years old, taken when the target was 18. It was difficult to identify the target at first but certain characteristics could be seen in the picture and so it proved useful.

***Old telephone directories can be useful in finding current ex-directory numbers***

**• Mode of Transport**

Not everyone drives a vehicle; therefore you need to know the target's mode of transport as you will have to prepare for travelling by the same means. He could use public transport, get a lift, walk, or ride a motorbike.

If he uses a vehicle you need to know the vehicle, make, model, shape, colour, registration and any other identifying features.

• **Family details or other occupants of the household**

The *Electors Register* should identify all the adults in the household, although it is accepted that the records are not always accurate. It would help to know how many male adults lived in the house (if your target is male), you do not want to follow the first one that leaves which may be the wrong person.

In addition, if there are children living at the house, you can expect them to leave for school on their own or have them taken on the 'school run'. This is a time when the team need to be on the alert for possible movement.

Families often live in areas we call 'tribal'. By this we mean that other members of the family live in the same area or estate. You may find that the target's sister lives three doors down and the parents live two streets away. This is handy to know, especially if you have a loss as it is somewhere to search. In addition, if the target stops at one of the addresses, you know whether to go in close or not, as it may not be that important to the investigation.

• **Employment**

The details of the target's work or trade are required. The type of job, his workplace or area, his position, the shifts and hours he works including overtime. If he is unemployed, the day, time and place he signs on for unemployment benefits may be of use, especially if you have to pick him up there.

• **Habits or Routines**

Be aware of any habits or routines that the target may have. For example, a target would leave his house and religiously stop at a nearby newsagent in the morning to buy his paper and cigarettes. On the third and fourth day of surveillance, we didn't plot up at his home address, which was difficult to cover but chose to plot up at the newsagents where we had no problems picking him up each day.

You should also know the targets regular haunts such as pubs and clubs. You should also have information relating to his friends or associates.

• **Awareness level**

Ensure that you establish whether the target has been under surveillance in the past and what their awareness level is likely to be. It would also be useful to know whether they are likely to be potentially violent should a compromise occur.

## SOURCES OF INFORMATION

There are various sources of information that can assist us at the planning stage:

• **The Client's Brief**

Obtain as much information from the client that you can. Beware of the client that is over zealous with information, it can often be misleading or inaccurate. You should decide what is important and what is not, obtain a full description.

• **A pretext visit to the target's address to identify him**

If you have to call at the target's address, do so only as a last resort and preferably use someone that will not be involved in the surveillance. If you do, do so with caution

We were tasked to obtain a photograph of an individual who was suspected of stalking and harassing our client by post and e-mail. No one knew what he looked like and so a photograph was needed for the client's security team in the event that the stalker showed himself. He lived in a run down area on the 5th floor of a block of flats to which access was controlled by security guards. There were 14 floors in total.

Using the on-line *Electors Register* (www.192.com) we established the name of the target's neighbour and made up a parcel to be delivered to her. Using a fake ID card and wearing a jacket very similar to an international parcel courier, we attended at the address and waited for someone to enter. Rather than approach the guard who may scrutinise our identity, we waited for a resident to enter and 'tailgated' them in. In fact, as we were carrying the package, the resident actually held open the first two doors for us.

Once on the 5th floor we were able to call at the target's address and told him there was no answer from his neighbour and would he accept delivery for her? This he did and we obtained excellent covert video of the target at his front door whilst we made conversation with him for several minutes.

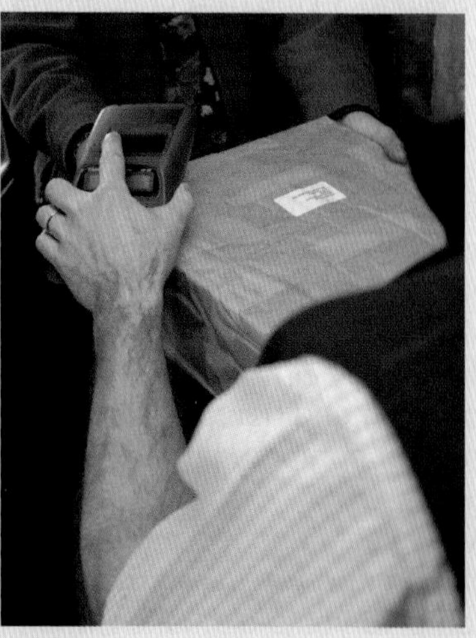

and have a realistic reason for being there. Enquiries to locate the previous occupant (whose details you have obtained from the Electors Register) are a reasonable excuse for a visit. Do not make up an elaborate story or deliver a free prize or a bunch of flowers, people only get suspicious.

- **Telephone Directories**

There are many directories available which contain information: BT Directories, Thompson's Directory, Yellow Pages, Business Pages and so forth. Sources on the internet such as www.192.com are very useful and it lists phone numbers, electors information and neighbours.

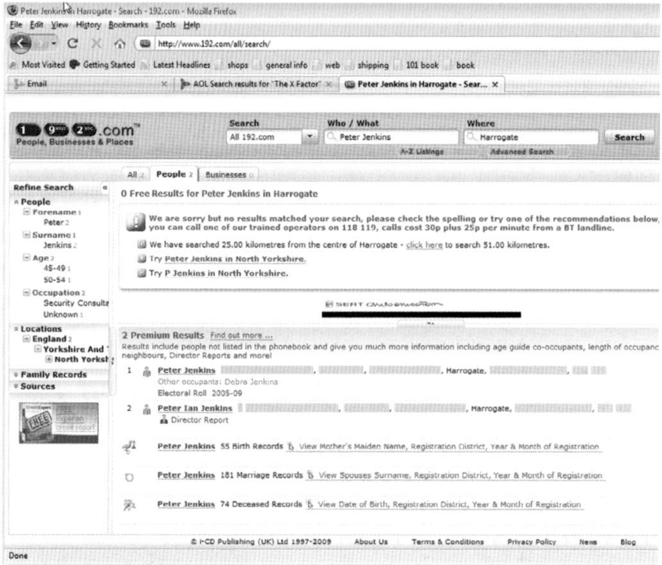


- **Trade Directories**

Trade Directories (such as *Kelly's* and *Dunn & Bradstreet*) list specific professions and are available in most reference libraries.

- **Electors Register**

As mentioned above, this is a good source of information but soon may no longer be available to the general public. Treat the register with caution as the information contained can be inaccurate.

- **On-Line Computer Searches (Equifax & Experian)**

Organisations such as Equifax and Experian collect financial data such as credit history and credit ratings that may be of use to you, and this information can be obtained 'on-line' to those who subscribe or via the Internet. They also have a 'locate' facility, which can be used to trace a person if they have moved. Quite often, a person will move house and then obtain a credit card or other form of credit and when they apply they have to provide their previous address. When the data is entered into a computer, the new address gets tied in with the old address.

## THE INTERNET

A wealth of information can be obtained from the Internet, from individual websites to search engines.

Below are some useful websites to use for researching and these have been found to be very effective in the past. In a recent investigation, we had a name, an address and a brief description. The name was dropped into the search engine of 'Facebook' and it revealed a picture of the target, it also listed two others who were associated with the investigation. Online searches were then carried out on these two 'associates', one of which had a business website which revealed much of what we were after. The information was also dropped into 'Friends Reunited' to reveal what family one of the targets had, his daughters 'Bebo' site also provided us with information.

- **People Information**

Drop the name of a person you know (or yourself) into any of these websites and see what you come up with, you may be surprised. '123people' is a search engine that searches all of the social networking sites and lots more.

**www.123people.com or www.123people.co.uk**
**www.friendsreunited.co.uk**
**www.facebook.com**
**www.bebo.com**
**www.myspace.com**
**www.lookupanyone.com (USA)**
**www.linkedin.com**
**www.192.com**

- **Mobile Phone Numbers**

In the UK the website **www.mobile118.co.uk** lets you type in a name and a town and provides you with the details of a mobile phone number for that person if they

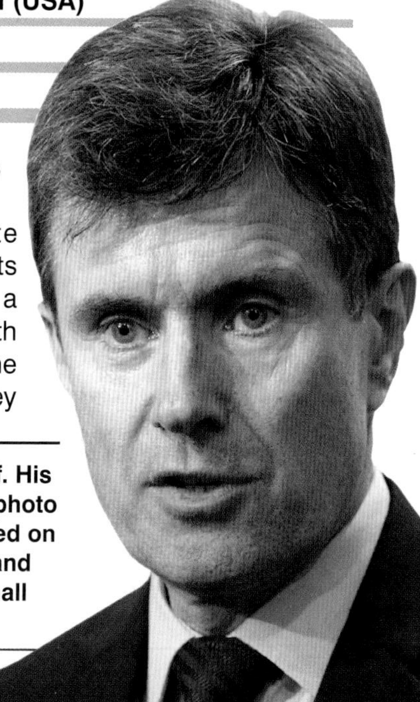

**Sir John Sawers - MI6 Chief. His details, address and family photo album were innocently placed on Facebook by his spouse and caused a furore in Whitehall**

Facebook is a convenient tool for establishing friends and acquaintances

are under contract or have registered a 'pay as you go phone'.

On a few occasions, we have the need to identify the owner of a mobile phone when we only having the number. One ruse that has worked for us on a few occasions (prior to the Data Protection Act) is to call the number in the middle of the night when there is a chance the phone will be switched off or go unanswered. Leave a message on the answer phone stating words to the effect of, 'Hi its Pete, can you give me a call as soon as you pick up, its really urgent, thanks'.

Hopefully, our target will call you the next morning, when he does you ask who's calling and from what company and you will have all or part of your answer. You then will need to close the call by apologising and saying you think the message was left on the wrong persons answer phone.

- **Website Information**

Sometimes it is useful to know the owner of a particular website or URL. Quite often, you find websites advertising their business or company but do not have an address on the contacts page, which is often disconcerting. If you visit **http://whois.domaintools.com/** or **http://who.is** and enter the name of a website into the search bar, it may reveal the registrant's name and address. This is not always successful if the registrant has decided to 'opt out' at the time of registering.

## GOOGLE IT!

For all other information, 'Google' it or drop it into a search engine, you'll be surprised at what shows up. Google everything but be wary of just putting in a name on its own or you will have thousands of useless hits. Try to link it with something, for example, rather than just Google 'peter jenkins', input 'peter Jenkins surveillance' or a house number together with the postcode. Try some of these:

- *Names*
- *Mobile Phone numbers*
- *Land line phone numbers*
- *Fax numbers*
- *Post code and house number*
- *A company name*

The post code search is effective and can list estate agents details, planning applications, offices, other websites and a host of other information.

- **Local Press**

The local press can often help you with information, especially if you have a particular date or point of reference. Many local newspapers also have a website, have a look at these in the event that they also have their own search engine. If you search for your target's name

## KEEP INFORMATION PRIVATE

The real names detailed here have been changed but recently I was on a train journey to London, taking advantage of the wireless internet to do some work. Sitting opposite was one of those annoying people who like to talk loudly on their mobile phone and generally annoy everyone in the vicinity.

The person made a call and said, 'Oh hello, this is Claire Randall from York Social Services can I speak to Darren Hart'. Wanting to have some fun I immediately 'Googled' York Social Services and found their web address was www.york.gov.uk.

I then Googled, 'claire.randall@york.gov.uk' and it came up with five hits. Three of which were downloadable PDF documents, which involved some of the social services meetings that she had been involved with. I then Googled Darren Hart Social services on the off - chance and this again revealed that he worked for the Social Services in Leeds.

Then, just for my self amusement, I switched on the Bluetooth facility on my laptop and scanned the area for other Bluetooth signals. Six were identified in the area, one of the phones was named 'Bombshell'. Claire Randal was the only one in the vicinity with blonde hair so I guessed it was her. I nearly said something to her but thought otherwise...

The rule here is keep your conversations private

and if he has been written about in the paper, it should come up with the story, and if you are lucky, a photograph.

- **Companies House**

Via the internet at **www.companieshouse.gov.uk/** you can, for a small fee, obtain information about limited companies, their accounts and their directors.

- **Land Registry**

By visiting **www.landregistry.gov.uk/** you can for a small fee, obtain copies of the sale deeds to a property which will indicate the owners who bought it, the cost and also the extent of the land that they own.

- **Local Enquiries & Local Knowledge**

It may be necessary to make some enquiries from local shops or neighbours but do so with caution and remember to have a realistic cover story ready.

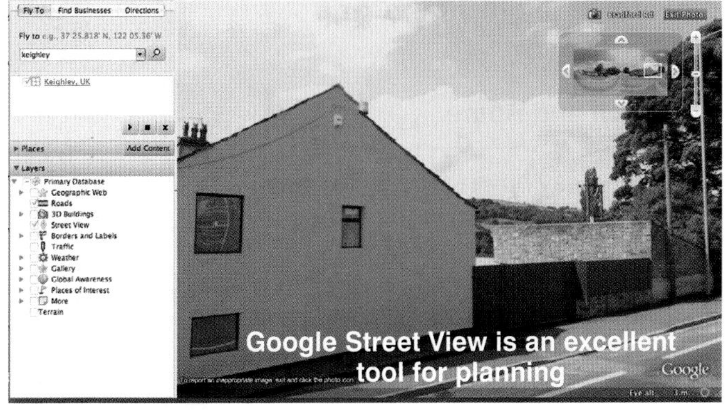

Google Street View is an excellent tool for planning

### THE SURVEILLANCE START POINT

Prior to any surveillance being carried out a reconnaissance visit should be made of the target location. This visit is made to enable you to plan and organise the task. This could be residential, business premises or an area in which the target is going to be or likely to visit.

You will carry out a pre-surveillance (or Recce) in order to help you decide:

- *The size of the team*
- *Make up of the team and which type of vehicles to use*
- *Equipment you may need such as cameras and radios*
- *Dress code to suit the areas and target*
- *Time spent on the surveillance, which affects the budget*
- *Length of time spent on the ground*
- *Likely trigger points*
- *Any possible hazards*

There are certain things that we can do before actually going out on the ground. By looking at a map, be it an A-Z or an Ordnance Survey, we can establish what type of area we will be operating in such as urban town or rural village. If we use the internet site 'Google Earth' and 'Google Maps' not only do you obtain street maps but also very detailed aerial photographs and even photographs at street level of the roads and buildings.

Once we have arrived in the area, there are certain things that we should look out for and a sample of a recce report is found below detailing the factors that should be known or considered.

On a walk past approach from the other side of the street and cross over in front of the target to give you maximum observation time

### Aerial Photographs

Aerial photographs can be a very useful aid to planning if they can be obtained. As part of our pre-surveillance routine, Google is checked for aerial photographs on every job.

Use the photographs with caution as shadow will make features look different and check the age of the photograph as buildings and roads can change very quickly. Consider the seasonal change also, a photograph taken in the summer will not show a true likeness during the winter.

### The Recce (Drive Past and Walk Past)

Your recce will possibly be conducted by an initial drive past in order to establish the exact address and to obtain any valuable information, this may be conducted with a covert video camera filming the area.

Do not just do a drive past for the sake of it, think, 'what am I going to achieve?' You should be obtaining information such as:

- *Gates, paths, driveways, doorways and cut through access routes*
- *Vehicles (make, model, registration, colour)*
- *Parked vehicles (which way do they intend to go)*
- *Signs of life: windows open, curtains closed or open cooking smells, lights on, steam from windows*
- *Street lighting, security lighting or cameras*

After a drive past, you may wish to carry out a walk past in order to observe from a closer point of view and in a much slower time. Do not carry out a walk past as soon as you have driven past, stay away from the area for a short period of time. Dependent on how aware the target is likely to be (or the locals), it may be that only one walk past or drive past can be carried out before you present yourself as multiple sightings.

A memo recorder is a valuable tool as there is a lot to remember

Ensure that you have a cover story ready if approached and ensure that your dress and demeanour fit in with the area and walk a natural route. It is often suggested to walk a dog on a walk past but you cannot hang around for too long. Be aware of other dog owners wanting to stop and chat, or worse still the dogs start fighting and draw attention to you.

## RECCE AND PRE-SURVEILLANCE REPORT

This should comprise of a report together with a sketch map or diagram of the area.

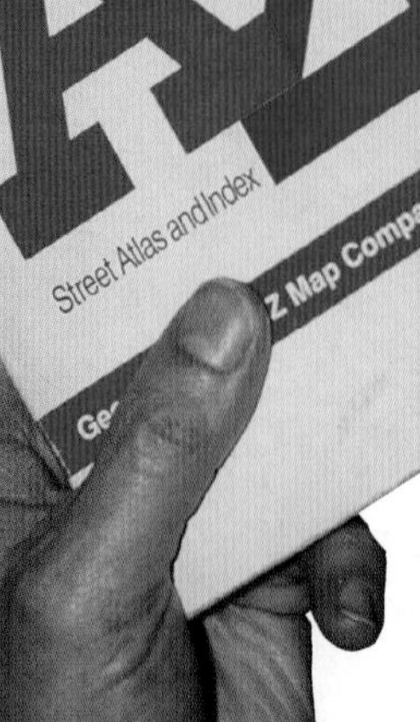


### A-Z Map

Provide details of the A-Z map book including page and grid reference. If an ordnance survey map is used, provide an eight figure grid reference.

### Approach and Route

Operators may have to make their own way to the target's location rather than be led there by the team leader. Directions should be taken from a main local landmark to the target or to a central RV (rendezvous point) and include the distance.

**Rendezvous (RV)**

The team do not want to meet up in the target's street for obvious reasons, therefore an area within a short distance should be selected where you can RV on the morning prior to the job starting such as in a car park or lay-by. Ensure that the RV is safe so that the team does not look suspicious by meeting at this location early in the morning.

This RV or another may be selected as an emergency rendezvous (ERV), in the event of the team having to split up and meet at a later time after a loss or a compromise.

**Area in General**

Ensure the address is correct and provide a description of it, especially if it is difficult to locate. If there isn't a number on the door double check. Carry out a recce 360 degrees surrounding the target premises - do not consider the front of the premises alone, there may be hidden access to the rear.

Draw a sketch plan of the immediate area indicating all routes in and out by vehicle or on foot and consider how many observation (trigger) positions are available and their locations.

**Target Address**

Provide a detailed description of the address; it may be that you can only carry out one 'drive past' and so the more information you have, saves valuable 'lives'. Point out any identifying features that can easily be recognised from a distance such as prominent satellite dishes, window frames or painted porches.

**Escape Routes**

The possible routes that the target can take must be identified. Do not just carry out your recce from your car, get out and have a look around. You must identify all mobile (road) routes and any foxtrot (footpath) routes that he can possibly take. Do not forget to look 360 degrees surrounding the target address and check for exits at the rear as these may also have to be covered.

**Always check the front and rear of the target house**

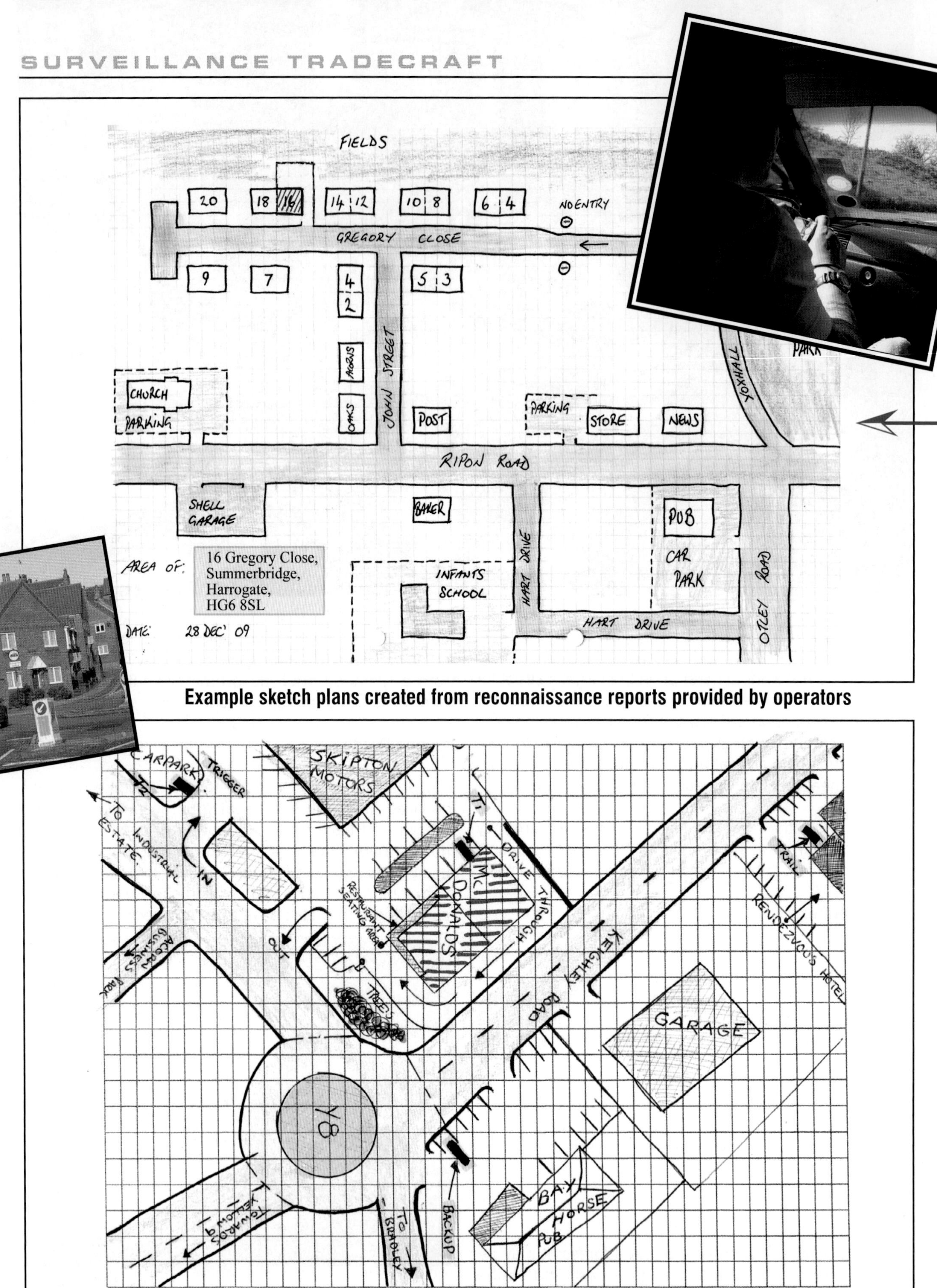


**Example sketch plans created from reconnaissance reports provided by operators**

RECCE REPORT

**Name: Debbie McDonald**
**Date & Time: 28 Dec 2009, 08.50hrs**

**Name: Roger Taylor**

**Address: 16 Gregory Close, Summerbridge, Harrogate, HG6 8SL**

**Vehicles: Pale Blue Audi A3 (YL09 CMF)**

**Map Reference AZ: Page 45, E/5**

**Route:** From the roundabout that intersects the A61 and the B6141 in Ripley, 4 miles north of Harrogate: take the second exit on the B6141 sign posted Pateley Bridge. Continue for 7 miles and you arrive at Summerbridge village. On entering, you pass a playground on the right. The next option on the right is John Street, immediately after the village post office. Gregory Close is at the top and runs east to west.

**Team R.V:** Village cricket ground car park is located 500m south of the village on Otley Road. This is fairly safe but be aware there is also a 'recycling' area in the car park.

**General Area**: Summerbridge village is located in a rural area surrounded by farms. The B6141 main road running through the village supports the other villages and towns to the west in Nidderdale Valley. This quiet but busy village is supported by a number of local shops and amenities including a post office and a petrol station.

**Immediate Area:** Gregory Close is accessed by either turning off Yoxhall Crescent (which is into one way traffic) or via John Street. It is a long cul de sac and number 18 is some 60m from the end on the right. The house is easily identifiable as it is the only property on that row with a gate (brown wooden) and all of the window frames are brown whereas all the other properties in the street are white PVC.

- 2 -

There is a car-port to the right side as you look at it and there is a small garden to the rear. There is no pedestrian or vehicle access to the rear.

**Escape Routes:** From the house by car, escape is via John Street only and down to Ripon Road where they can turn left or right. From the house you can only travel so far along Gregory Close towards Yoxhall Crescent by car until you hit the no entry signs. However, access can be obtained past the 'no entry' on foot to the park area.

**Vehicle Sightings:** At the time of the recce a pale blue Audi A3 (YL09 CMF) was reversed parked on the driveway. It had a yellow 'tree' air freshener hanging from the rear view mirror.

**Trigger Positions:** The area of No. 16 is quite tight, but a van positioned in the Close opposite No. 6 would get a good 'long look'. It would not be able to call a direction on Ripon Road though. The target is known to have a dog and so the approaches would be covered if he departs on foot towards the nearby park.

An alternative would be to put the van half way up John Street which will be able to call a direction as he turns on Ripon Road but will be a quick standby.

**Back Up Locations:** A call sign will need to cover the junction of John Street and Ripon Road in order to call a direction. There are a few parking places such as the church car park and the local SPAR store. The fastest escape routes are west towards Pateley Bridge, east towards Ripley and south towards Otley.

**Sightings:** There were no sightings at the time of the recce except for the car.

**Additional Information:** This is a neighbourhood watch area and there is an infants school nearby on Hart Drive. This area was very congested with school traffic at the time of the recce.

### Vehicles

List the details on any vehicles sighted at the time of carrying out the recce. You may have to pay a visit early morning or late evening to establish further vehicles. Note how they are parked as this will not only tell you which direction they may go in, but also tell you from which direction they have arrived.

### Trigger Locations

Every surveillance needs a trigger. Therefore you need to decide how you are going to get an 'eyeball' on the house and how you will trigger the surveillance. Consider all the options - discussed later in this chapter - but keep it simple, there is no need to have a complex plan in order to get a trigger.

### Position for Back Up & Support

Locations could be identified where the mobile units could 'lie up' in a safe area (Lie Up Position or LUP) whilst waiting for a 'standby'. This is often personal preference and left to individual operators once they are on the ground. The position has to be within radio range and should not attract attention from 'third parties'.

### Sightings

Sometimes you will see the target and other persons during the recce. Make a note with descriptions and timings.

### Miscellaneous

Note anything else of interest that may be of value to the team. Note any particular hazards that may present them-

Be aware of 'third parties' when you are 'laid-up' and do not have the trigger

selves such as: parking restrictions, schools, traffic conditions, security patrols and neighbourhood watch. Carry out a radio check from where you intend to put your trigger or OP.

Take a camera with you! Always take a camera with you to obtain photographs of the area and if the target shows, you may be able to get an ID picture.

If you are carrying out a recce, look at the whole picture. Check 360 degrees around the target property and think, 'How can we trigger this?'

**The Plan**

On completion of the recce, you will have to formulate a plan of action in order to carry out the task, within the bounds or restrictions placed on you by the client. Points to consider are:

- *The size of the surveillance team as this will effect costs*
- *Gender make up of the team, male or females or both*
- *Team vehicles, such as cars, a van or a motorbike*
- *Communications and radios*
- *Specialist equipment such as night vision optics*
- *How you will record your findings and evidence (surveillance logs, memo recorders)*
- *Calculate the man-hours into actual costs to provide an estimate of costs including mileage, accommodation and incidentals*

***In order to plan and carry out a successful surveillance, it is essential that a recce is carried out at the target's address and that as much information is obtained about him... remember - keep it simple***

**SURVEILLANCE TRIGGERS**

How we actually trigger a target away needs to be kept as simple as possible. If you can do it from your car without arousing suspicion, then you do not to have to deploy someone to hide in a ditch. Always consider the easiest and most practical way first.

During the stakeout the trigger man plays the most important role in the team, he has to be alert at all times and have total concentration on the target premises. The operator has to be covert and should not be in a position that is obvious. An aware target is more likely to be alert at the pick up phase and anything unusual will be noticed, remember this will be his territory and his domain and he will know it better than you do.

Once in position, the trigger should be asking himself: What is my reason for being here? Do I look natural and how long can I get away with being here?

At the first sign of possible movement by the target, the trigger person puts the team on 'Standby'. He should provide the team with a radio commentary of the targets actions such as getting into a vehicle. He should also state the targets intended route, the route being taken and a description of the target.

This is probably the most crucial part of the surveillance, especially if you have no knowledge of the target or his intended movements. A target is likely to know short cuts and back street routes in the local vicinity to his house and may well take them to avoid heavy traffic. Therefore the target is more at risk of being 'lost' in the first few minutes of the surveillance than at any other time.

**There are various ways of triggering a target:**

- *Car*
- *Van*
- *Covert Car*
- *Foot Person*
- *Static O.P*
- *Tracker*
- *Informant*
- *Audio Transmissions*
- *Video Transmissions*

**CAR** The simplest way to trigger is from your car although you risk of being noticed quite easily. Consider sitting in the passenger seat or the rear of the car. Ensure you are

A typical surveillance van

Trigger from foot operator in telephone booth

parked properly and in a place that does not draw attention. Whatever you do, don't simulate a breakdown! This is what they do on the TV and it only attracts unwanted attention.

**VAN** Most surveillance teams on the commercial circuit use surveillance vans which can be parked up in a street with someone in the rear. They can then remain for long periods of time in a close position to the target. Vans are discussed more in the chapters on equipment and observation posts.

**COVERT CAR** A car parked up on a street does not attract any attention, especially if it blends in with the area. A covert method we use to trigger away aware targets who may be suspicious of vans is by means of a 'Boot Fit'. By this we mean that an operator is concealed in the boot (trunk) of the car and is able to observe a particular area. The person is likely to have to remain there, in uncomfortable conditions, for many hours.

**FOOT PERSON** A trigger may have to be obtained by a foot person, either at the start of a planned operation or they may have to quickly deploy from their car if the target stops. Foot triggers are more likely to be short term and you have to have a reason for being where you are, such as a bus stop, a phone booth, a seating area, cafe etc.

**STATIC O.P.** The various types of static OP's are described in some detail later on but they can be located in a building, hedgerow, caravan or any other static point from where the target's premises can be covertly observed.

**TRACKERS** Technical devices such as car trackers are ideal triggers when you have a target who is extremely aware or located in rural areas that are difficult to observe.

This provides you with the opportunity of keeping your distance, especially if the target is looking for watchers when they first go mobile. Trackers are very accurate and can send a signal to your mobile phone when the target moves.

**INFORMANT** If the team can be informed of an imminent move by the target, this could greatly assist their effectiveness at the pick up stage. The informant is someone who is known to the surveillance team.

To have a client or person to inform you of a standby is a luxury that is rare but very welcome when the chance arises.

## ISS CASE

On one occasion we had to follow a company vehicle suspected of making unscheduled stops. It was difficult to 'trigger' without risking compromise but the client was able to telephone us and give prior warning of his departure. He would telephone saying that the vehicle was loaded and would be departing within the next five minutes. This allowed the team to relax in safe areas until we were put on standby, the team would then close in and take up their positions for the follow.

**AUDIO TRANSMISSIONS**

A simple audio transmitter or radio microphone can be covertly placed in the target area such as a garden hedgerow in order for you to listen to what is happening, such as doors opening and closing and vehicle engines starting. Audio triggers have been useful when triggering away targets who live in flats or apartment blocks where there is a risk of missing them coming out.

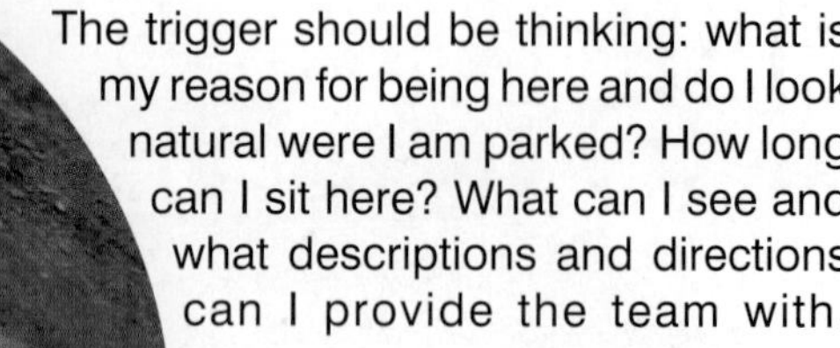

An audio transmitter concealed in a flower pot

**VIDEO TRANSMISSIONS** A video camera located in a hedgerow or concealed in a car and directed towards the target can transmit video pictures by UHF/VHF or Microwave signals. An operator, located nearby in a safe area can trigger the surveillance by watching the target area on a small television monitor. When activity is viewed on the screen, the team can be put on standby. The camera will be able to tell you in what direction the target is travelling and possibly what he is wearing and other relevant details.

These devices are not too expensive and can be used to good effect when other conventional means fail or are considered too risky. We are now using sophisticated cameras which observe an area and then by means of an SMS text, informs you of activity over the 3G network. You can then dial into the camera from the same mobile phone and observe the activity taking place.

## TRIGGER POSITIONS

Having already mentioned recce reports we will spend some time discussing the various trigger options that are available to us. Every mobile or foot surveillance will need an operator to trigger the surveillance and call the 'standby' in order to put the team into action.

Only one person needs to trigger the target away and the remainder of the team have to rely on this person to call a standby. They have to trust him to be alert, not to fall asleep or be distracted.

The trigger should be thinking: what is my reason for being here and do I look natural were I am parked? How long can I sit here? What can I see and what descriptions and directions can I provide the team with.

Triggers are in some way the same as Observation Posts (or OPs), but they are primarily used to trigger away a mobile or foot target rather than keep a continuous static observation.

There will be aspects of this that will also be found in the chapter on Observation Posts as much of the principles are very similar.

Regardless of which type of trigger you choose you must consider the following from your position:

- **Can you see the Target?**

From your position you must have a clear and unobstructed view of the target, be it the front door of the house, the gate, vehicle or a road junction. Be aware if the view is likely to become obstructed by passing or parked vehicles or pedestrians.

**ISS CASE**

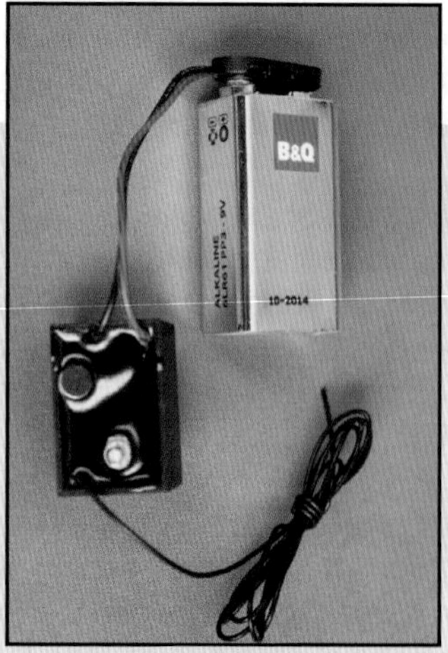

During one surveillance we had to trigger a target out of a block of flats where we could not observe the front doors or the car park. A cheap VHF transmitter was concealed in the foyer of the flats which transmitted the sounds of people walking down the stairs and using the main doors. We were able to listen in and put the team on 'standby' every time we heard the main door slam shut. This provided us with the extra time we needed to put a footman in position to cover the exit, in order to check and confirm the target leaving.

In another instance, the target lived in an upper floor flat. Access was via an alley at the side of the property, which led to a rear door. Video had to be obtained of her leaving the property and it was difficult to get any advanced warning. By the time you saw her and brought the camera up she was gone. A device was concealed in the alleyway which gave us the edge, as we were able to hear her locking the door on departure.

You need to be close enough to identify the target but far away enough for him not to see you.

**• Can you observe the approaches?**

The approaches to the target should also be able to be observed. This will help when waiting for a target to arrive and give you that extra time you may need to have your camera up and running. When the target departs you will need to inform the team of his direction of travel. Additionally, you may need to observe if any third party approaches your location.

**• Are you overlooked?**

Be aware of people above you in buildings or offices. If they are constantly looking down on you, you do not want to attract any attention. Be aware of CCTV cameras, especially on industrial estates.

**• Can the target see you?**

In surveillance we say: 'If you can see the target, the target can see you'. You do not want to make your trigger position obvious or attract attention. The trigger's position should not be right outside the target's front door but out of his '10 to 2' arc of vision. This area may be the target's home, his domain and territory, therefore he may notice anything that is unusual or out of place.

**• Can you move in and out safely?**

You will need to move in and out of this position without attracting attention or curiosity. Remember, for everything that we do in surveillance we have to act naturally and have a reason for being there.

## TRIGGERS FOR A MOBILE SURVEILLANCE

Together with the street plan opposite, we can look at the various trigger positions open to us. The scenario is that we would expect the target to leave the house by the front door, depart on foot or get into his vehicle and go mobile.

### TRIGGER POSITIONS

**A** From a car in this position we are behind the target and so he does not have to pass you when he goes mobile. You can see the front of the house, the car and

Can you see the target? Make sure you are out the '10-2'

also the next junction so that you can call a change in direction. When on plot, ensure:

- *You are out of the '10 to 2' arc*
- *You are not overlooked*
- *Not parked right outside someone's window*
- *Do not appear as if you are on a mission (turn off lights, engine, square wheels and remove your seatbelt)*
- *Sit in the passenger seat*
- *Have a reason for being there*
- *Have a cover story ready*

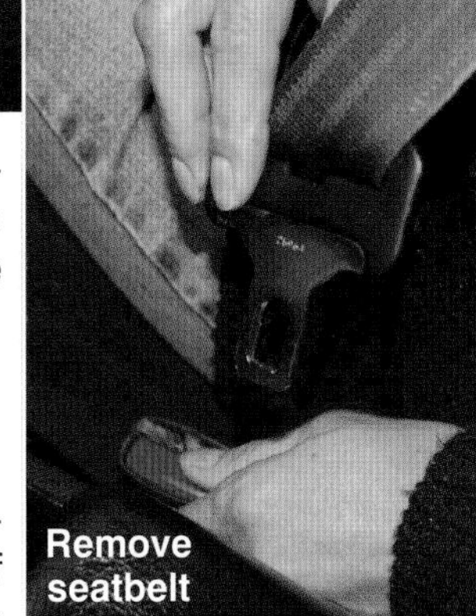
Remove seatbelt

We could also insert a surveillance van where we can afford to get a little closer to the target. Ensure:

• All of the above points

• You are driven in and extracted, do not drive in yourself then jump in the back of the van

**B** From your car you are well away from the target. You could position yourself to look directly at the target or use your mirrors. If using your mirrors, rehearse to yourself what you will say on the radio if the target goes mobile. Even experienced operators often give the wrong commentary because with the mirrors everything is back to front. Consider:

• When the target goes mobile he will be towards you and will get a 'free look' at you

**C** Still using our car or van, we do not necessarily have to be in the same street, from this 'long look' position we can see from across the park or waste ground. Consider:

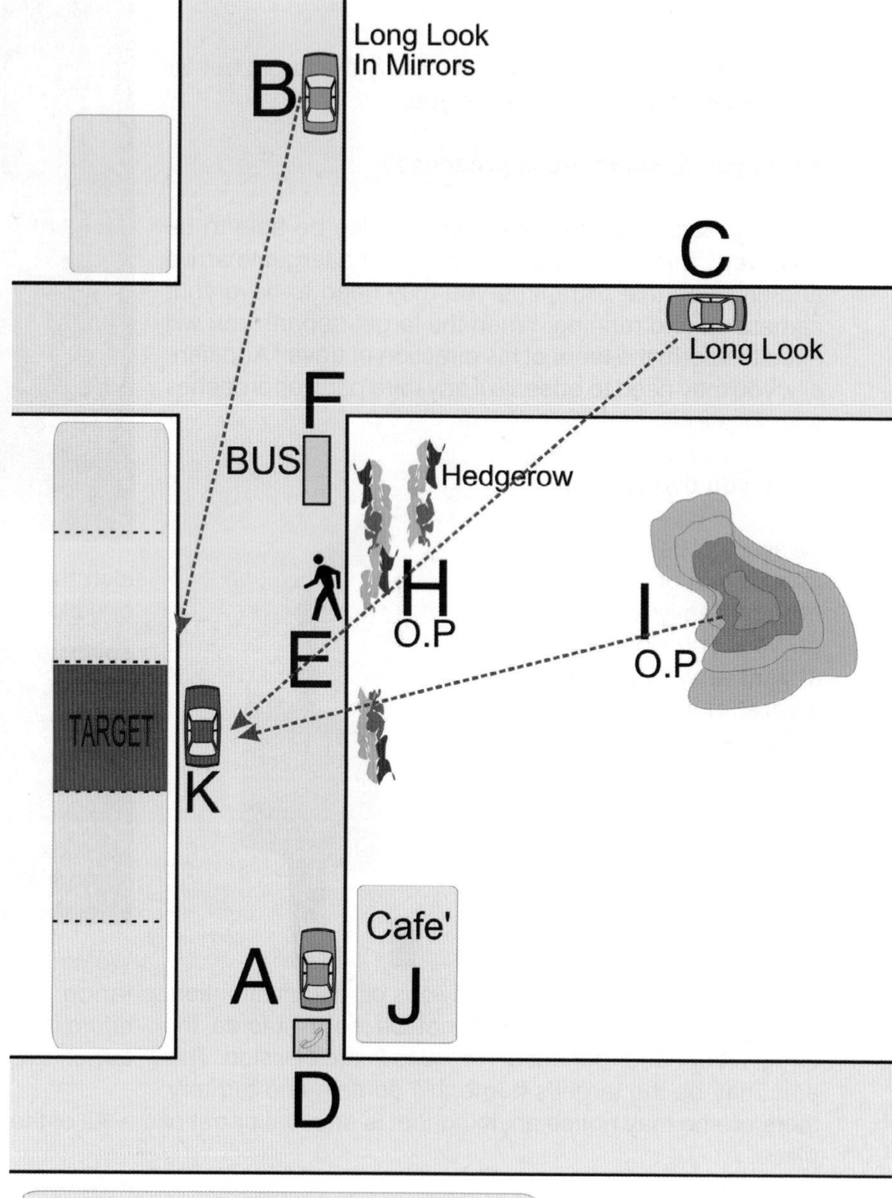


• This 'long look' is good if the target is aware

• If you have been on the surveillance previously and it is not necessary to go in close in order to identify

• Be aware of obstructions to your view

**D** A foot person could be deployed to provide the trigger although this is usually a short term measure. Many phone boxes have advertising graphics over the windows which allows you to see out but prevent others from seeing. This provides good cover. If using a phone box consider:

• You will have a good all-round view

• If someone is in it, then wait. It will provide you with additional time to hang about on the street

• Once in the box, *pick up the phone!* You have to act naturally and someone in a phone box not using the phone looks suspicious

• If you cannot hold the position for too long, get another team member to take over from another location

• After the Standby, you should be able to be picked up by a mobile unit or return to your own vehicle

**E** If there is no cover but you still have to deploy a footman, do so with caution. You will get away with it so long as you have a reason for being there.

**F** In a manner similar to the telephone box, the bus shelter gives you a reason for being there. Again this is only short term as you can only let one or two buses go past without getting on. If there is a queue then get into it, what better cover. If a queue starts to build up behind you then let it. If a bus arrives, all you have to do is step back and let everyone else get on. Do not feel out of place doing this, everyone else will be in their own little world and minding their own business as they get on the bus and probably will not notice you.

**G** If there is a building opposite (used or unused) then this could make an ideal trigger location. Caution should be used when entering and leaving the location and you have to decide whether to extract the trigger when the target goes mobile.

**H** Surveillances become tricky or difficult when you cannot get a decent trigger. In the past 19 years in the private sector, I have carried out many surveillances where we have had to use a 'rural' trigger from a hedgerow, ditch or thick foliage, even in built up areas.

It works, but it takes skill, planning and discipline and for obvious reasons is specially suited to former military personnel with training in covert movement, camouflage and concealment. Once the trigger is in position, he has to consider what to do after the target goes mobile. Does he:

• Stay where he is until the end of the day, he may have to trigger the target in and out numerous times during the day

## ISS CASE

We had to identify the driver of a car as he left a cul de sac. The only way to get close enough was to actually stand on the curb side; so, one of the team, dressed in overalls, clutching a sandwich box and a rolled up newspaper giving the appearance of waiting for his early morning lift, was able to identify the driver and call a 'standby'.

• Should he self extract, return to his vehicle and attempt to re-join the team

• Should he be extracted by another team member and go with his vehicle

A distant rural trigger could also suit your purpose, why get in close if you do not have to?

### TRIGGERS FOR A FOOT SURVEILLANCE

Together with the street plan of a precinct shopping area, (below) we can look at the various trigger options open to our foot team. The scenario is that we would expect the target to leave the burger bar where he works by the front door in order to establish where he goes during his lunch hour. There are no rear exits to the premises, he normally leaves for lunch at 12.30pm.

### TRIGGER POSITIONS

A Having a person trigger from inside the burger bar has its advantages and disadvantages. On the plus side:

• You can obtain a good identification, the staff may wear uniforms and look similar, so identification is important

• You should not miss the target out, as you are fairly close

• You should be able to give a direction, when he leaves

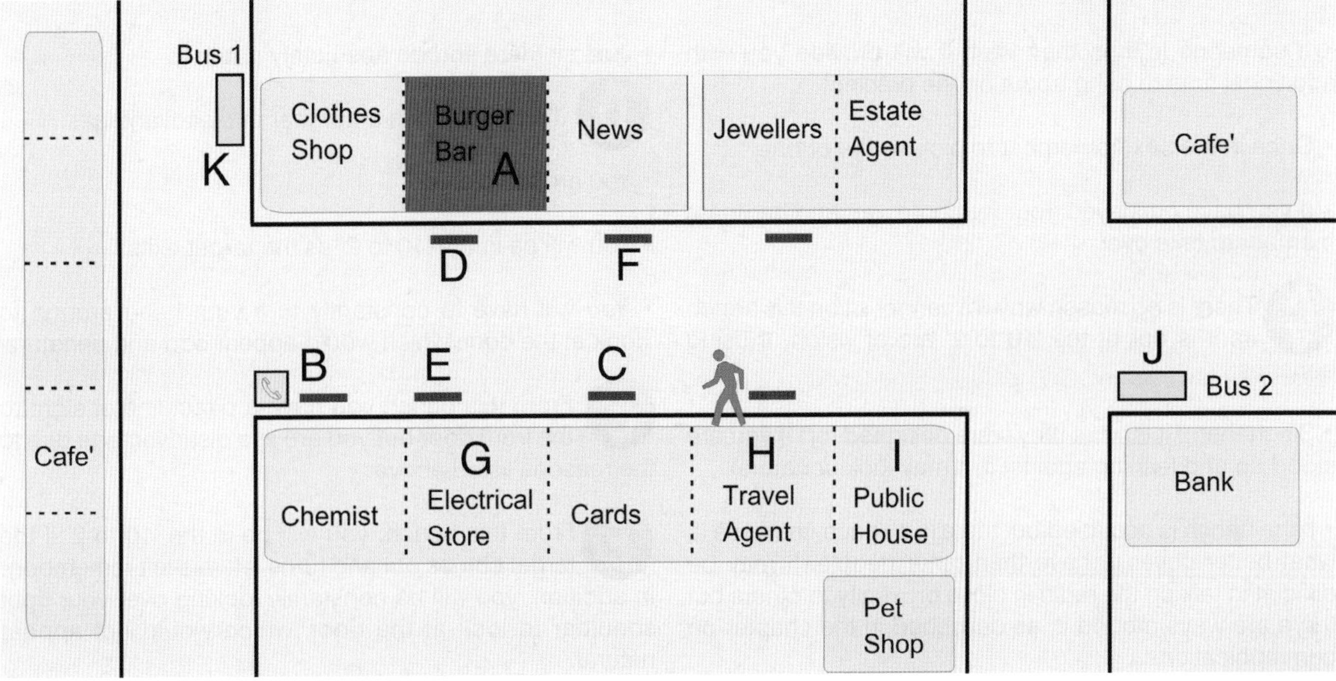

## ISS CASE

During a three-man job in Ireland; the target lived in a very remote area, which was criss-crossed with single track roads. The only place to trigger the target was from on top a small hill some 600m from the house. The team had nowhere to lie up as there were no lay-bys and no real reason to be in the area and so they had to keep on the move. With the aid of a spotting scope, I was able to trigger away the target who was picked up by the rest of the team. Once they "housed" him, I was extracted and picked up.

• You may be able to cover any other exits if there are any

On the minus side:

• You may be in close and so a sighting may cause you to lose a 'life'

• If the shop is very busy, you may miss him out

**B** The phone box would be an ideal option as the wait is short term, because we know roughly when we can expect the target to leave. From the telephone box:

• You will have a good all-round view

• If someone is in it, then wait. It will provide you with additional time to hang about on the precinct

• Once in the box, remember to pick up the phone

• If you have outstayed your welcome, get another team member to take over

**C** There is no reason why we cannot sit on this bench as it is out of the '10 to 2' arc of vision. If using benches:

• Sit on them; it is what they were designed for! If you are stood up and leaning against it, it may look unnatural

• If the bench is occupied but there is a space, then use it, what better cover to have than other people. It may be difficult to talk on the radio in close proximity to others but there are ways around it, as described in the chapter on communications

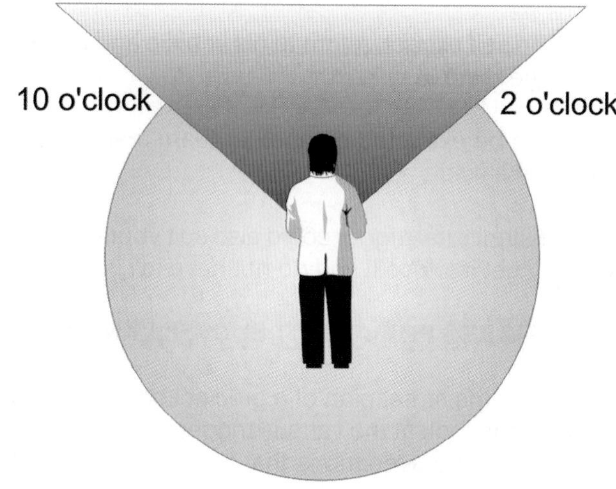


• Just sit there and do absolutely nothing.

**D** This bench has a number of disadvantages:

• You are too close

• You will be in the '10 to 2' as the target exits

• You will have to constantly turn your head around to look at the door, which would appear odd and unnatural

**E** From this bench you have a direct line of sight to the front door but you are at a disadvantage due to the reasons listed above.

**F** From this bench, you will be in the '10 to 2' if the target comes out and turns left (his left remember). In addition, you will be constantly looking over your right shoulder to look at the door, which would not appear natural.

***Using a vehicle mirror to trigger a target. It's important, however, to call the target's correct direction as the image is back-to-front. In this instance, he has exited the bakery and turned right***

Have a reason for being somewhere and avoid lurking

**G** You could place the trigger in the Electrical Store but:

- You are in the '10 to 2', although you may have cover from within the shop

- It may be difficult to pretend to browse and keep your eye on the target. Remember, as soon as you look away, the target will be out and gone

- If you are not acting naturally, you will become the focus of attention for store assistants and store detectives

**H** From outside the travel agents or any other shop doorway, there is no reason why you can't just stand and wait. STAND STILL, do not bob and weave about or you will attract attention.

- You are out of the '10 to 2'

- You have a clear view across the street

- You have a reason for being there (you are waiting)

- Do not 'peep' around corners

- A travel agents window is designed to be looked into (similar to an estate agents)

- If you use a shop doorway, make a cursory check of what the shop is selling. Loitering outside jewellers is not recommended

**I** If you have a clear and unobstructed view of the doorway from the pub, then there should be no reason why you should not consider this trigger position.

- You do not really want to consume alcohol, so keep to soft drinks

- Obtain a position where you would look naturally in the targets direction

**Other Team Members Positions**

Once you have established a trigger, that person will have control over the target. You may have another two members on the team. They have to be positioned away from the target, remember, only one person has to see the doorway. These team members should be off the street but for now we will place them in the following locations, as we will cover this aspect in more detail in the chapter on foot surveillance.

**J** At the bus shelter you are far enough away from the target and you give yourself a reason for being there. If the target walks away from you, you can take up the follow. If he walks towards you, you can take control from where you are as you do not have to move anywhere.

**K** From this bus shelter you are 'off the plot', which is good. You will be listening in to your radio for a standby and a direction of travel. If the target comes out and goes left (his left remember), you can take up the follow. If he walks towards your corner, you can take control at the corner without you having to move.

We now have the beginnings of teamwork and are now 'imposing' surveillance on the target rather than just following him.

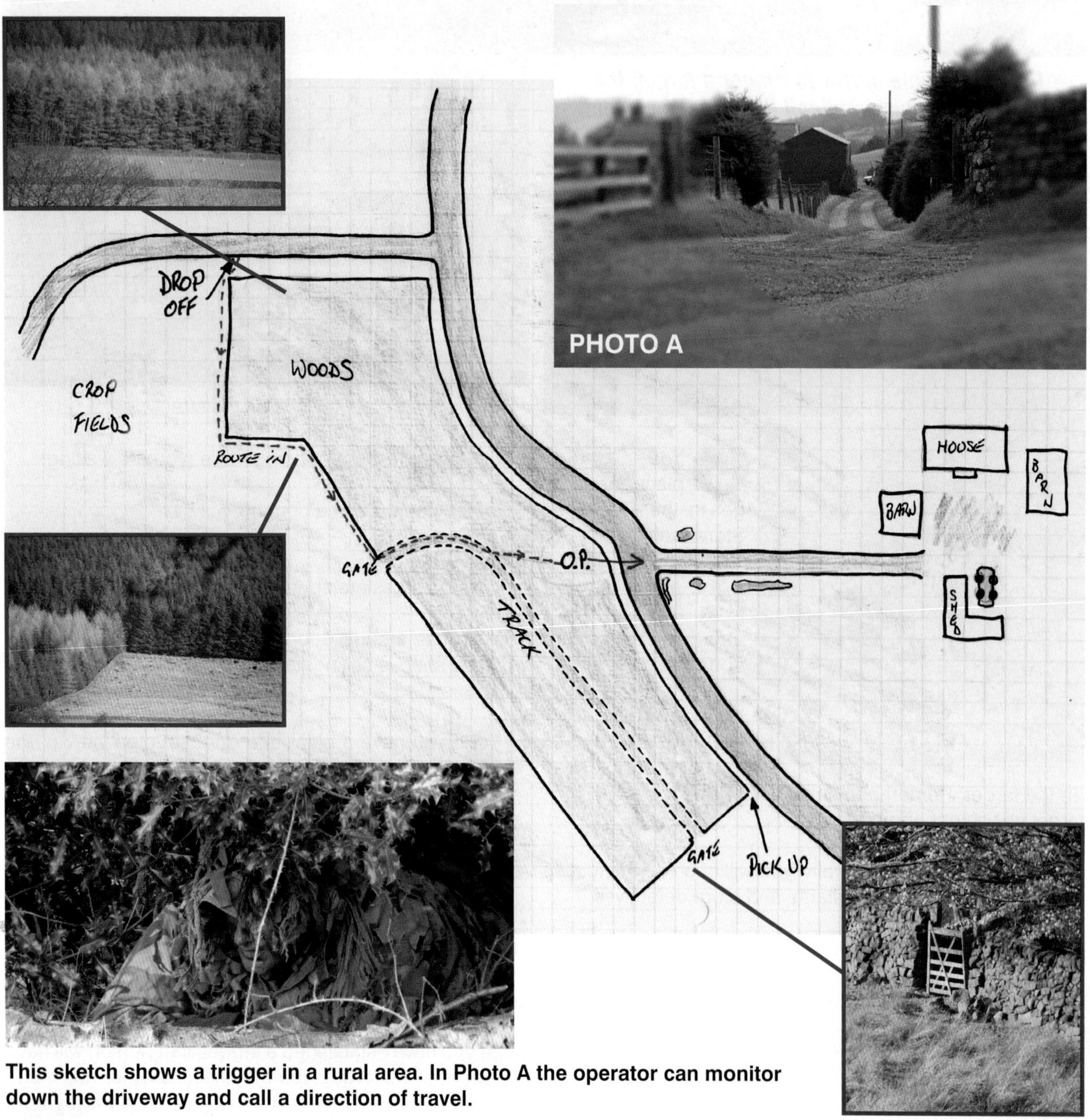


**This sketch shows a trigger in a rural area. In Photo A the operator can monitor down the driveway and call a direction of travel.**

Communication is probably the most important factor when there is more than one operator working on the same task. Team tasks can succeed or fail depending on whether good communication is maintained between team members. All team members should be well exercised in voice procedure and the giving of a radio commentary.

***Surveillance is all about teamwork, without communications you will have no team to work with***

Communication is about being able to speak or indicate to another, in a manner that is precise, detailed and clear to the receiving party regarding what the target is doing. In this instance, the sender will be passing information about a target's actions and intentions, or will be issuing instructions to the remainder of the surveillance team.

Communication (or comms) can be passed in any of the following ways:

- *Mobile phones*
- *Radio transmissions*
- *Hand signals*

**MOBILE PHONE**

Mobile telephones are not recommended as a substitute for radios but they are essential as your secondary comms. The cost of operating a mobile phone is probably one of the first disadvantages that springs to mind, but mobile networks can be very temperamental and calls have a habit of suddenly ending due to loss of signal.

With radios, you will be able to call and speak to an unlimited number of people at the same time, with a mobile, you can only speak to one person unless you are using 'conference' calling but this is not ideal.

The main advantage with mobiles is that they have an unlimited range of transmission where you can get in touch with anyone throughout the country. Each member of the surveillance team must be in possession of a mobile phone. Operators often find themselves out of radio range, especially after a loss and the only means of communication is by mobile phone.

Your mobile phone is your secondary means of communication, it should always be handy and set to silent but vibrate mode if you are on foot. Always ensure that your 'Bluetooth' is also switched off and set to 'undiscoverable'.

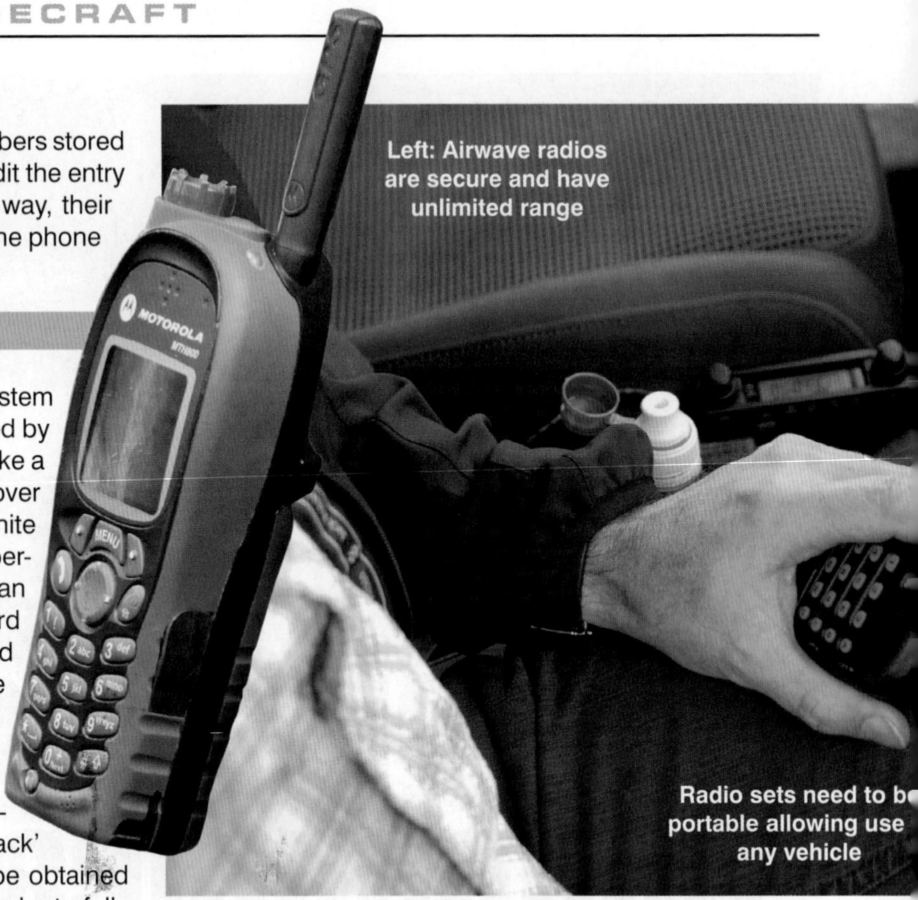

Be sure to have all of the teams telephone numbers stored on speed dial for easy access. Alternatively, edit the entry adding 'AA' to their name i.e. 'AA Pete', this way, their names will automatically appear at the top of the phone book.

Left: Airwave radios are secure and have unlimited range

Radio sets need to be portable allowing use any vehicle

## AIRWAVE (TETRA) RADIO

A recent communications advancement is a system called TETRA or AIRWAVE currently being used by the 'blue light' and public services. Used just like a standard hand held radio, it actually operates over the mobile phone network and so range is infinite and audio quality superb. Should they be operated in an area with a bad phone signal, they can also be used 'back to back' just like a standard radio. The small handsets can be used hand held on foot or in a vehicle and do not require any external antennas. They can be fitted with covert ancillaries.

At the present time in the UK, TETRA is available to anyone if only used in the 'back to back' mode. However, a special licence needs to be obtained from the Home Office to civilian agencies in order to fully use them.

## RADIOS

Communications are a very important factor in surveillance work where investigators have to work as a team. Therefore radio equipment is paramount and has to be:

- *Reliable and robust*
- *Have sufficient transmit/receiving range*
- *Portable*
- *Secure*
- *Simple to operate*
- *Good battery life*

### Radio Frequencies

Two different wave lengths are available to the commercial investigator in the UK and the correct one should be selected to obtain maximum performance for the type of area that you are normally working in.

• Ultra High Frequency or UHF should be used in very built up towns and cities or if you are constantly working in buildings or shopping malls. In the UHF range this is normally between 430 - 472MHz.

• Very High Frequency or VHF is the most commonly used and is ideal for most situations, it is adequate for both built up areas and out in the open. In the VHF range, the frequency is normally between 162 - 175 MHz.

It is preferable to have a power output of at least five watts to provide you with sufficient power and transmitting range, the majority of hand held radios can be set to five watts. Any less and you may not have a sufficient range. Car to car sets ideally need to be transmitting on at least 20 watts output.

If you purchase your own VHF/UHF sets, a 'Business' operator's licence has to be obtained from the Radio Communications Agency OFCOM: **(www.ofcom.org.uk).** This is usually organised by your radio dealer or you can apply online, and the licence costs approximately £75.00 for five years and can cover up to ten radio sets. When the licence is issued you will receive a selection of operating frequencies onto which the radios can be set.

Due to over-crowding of the airwaves within these frequency ranges, it is possible that you will hear other people on the air (breakthrough) who are using the same frequency and likewise, they would be able to hear you. This 'sharing' of frequencies could create a problem during surveillance as your commentary could be interrupted and third parties will be able to hear your commentary.

Many modern radio systems utilise a system called CTCSS coding. This system enables the radio set to automatically transmit a coded signal to your other sets and 'opens them

Motorola's digital radios are the future in secure comms.
ISS use these models for operations and training

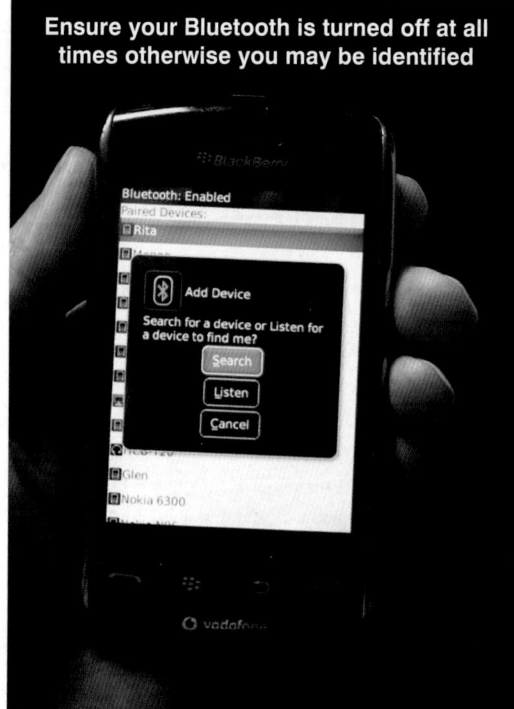


up' to receive your messages only. Radios using the same frequency without the compatible CTCSS coding will not be able to be listen in to your commentary nor will you be able to receive the others transmissions.

## DIGITAL RADIO

Companies such as Motorola now supply radios that communicate to each other digitally. This offers clearer reception but more importantly, more security as the signals cannot easily be intercepted. The transmission range is equal to that of their analogue counterparts. The latest digital sets such as Motorola's MOTOTRBO series are only slightly more expensive than analogue sets.

### Types of Radio Sets

Radios come in various forms, the main two types being hand-held transceivers (the walkie-talkie) or vehicle mounted sets. Both sets have their advantages and disadvantages:

### Vehicle Mounted Sets

Vehicle mounted sets (as their name suggests) are normally mounted and concealed in a surveillance vehicle and will give you a high transmitting range, drawing its power from the vehicles battery. An output of twenty watts or more with an external mounted antenna will provide a range over many miles depending on terrain.

### ISS CASE

Acting as target during a training exercise, I was sitting on a train whilst under surveillance from the team. I switched on my phones Bluetooth and scanned the local area for other Bluetooth signals and made a note of the five phones or 'names' that it picked up. A short while afterwards, I went into an art gallery and again scanned the area for Bluetooth devices. One of the same names cropped up again. An hour later, and back on a train again, a third scan revealed the same person and therefore a possible compromise for that person (multiple sightings).

In a similar exercise, we were teaching rural surveillance to a government agency and the class were practising camouflage and concealment on the edge of a forest. Their personal camouflage and hide camouflage was excellent and they were very difficult to see even from about 5 metres away. However, a scan for Bluetooth devices identified an individual who was made to show himself.

It will not be practical to have a mag mount antenna located in the centre of your car roof like a taxi, as it would look too conspicuous. Therefore, it should be located on the rear bumper area or put inside the car itself. If it is put inside, ensure that the antenna is upright and that the base is on something solid such a metal plate or even a biscuit tin lid in order to provide what is termed a 'ground plane' and to reflect the radio radiation. Alternatively, a 'boot clamp' fitting is preferable and more covert. A purpose built antenna fitted into the roof or wing of the car, made to look like an ordinary radio aerial is the most preferred and is even more covert.

A typical radio communications car-to-car set

A vehicle mounted set requires approximately 12 volts DC to operate it and this can be obtained from the vehicle's own power supply via the cigarette lighter socket for a temporary measure or alternatively and preferably, have it connected to the cars power system. If you use the cars power sockets, check that they are still operable when the engine is switched off as some makes don't. In addition, some vehicle mounted sets will only work when the ignition keys have been turned to the first click.

These large sets can also be used as a base station or used in a static O.P. when greater transmission distances are required. The radio set can draw its power from the mains supply transformed down to 12 volts or run from a stand alone car battery.

### Hand Held Radio Sets

Radio handsets offer more flexibility, as they can be carried about your person during foot surveillance, be located in your car or used in an OP as they have their own power supply. They can be fitted with accessories that will enable you to use the radio covertly such as an ear piece and a concealed microphone, they also utilise their own short antenna.

When used in a vehicle, the transmission range may only be up to one kilometre but this can be greatly increased by connecting the hand set to an external antenna or a purpose fitted antenna as described above. This is a preferred method by many surveillance operators and in the past I have had some 20 kilometres range (across open ground) with a hand held set from a car.

When using a hand held set in a vehicle, ensure that you keep it below the level of the dashboard, you do not want the target to see you using it in his mirrors. In the same vein, when using the radio, do not keep bobbing your head up and down as you speak each time into the microphone, act naturally. Try not to let your fingers or thumb curl over the microphone, as you will muffle your commentary.

### Different Types of Radio Sets

The Motorola GP340 is a popular radio, it is robust and will take a knock or two. However, the ancillaries can be expensive and any changes to the radio settings such as adding new frequencies have to be carried out by an authorised dealer, which incurs more costs.

### PMR 446

There are some radio sets easily obtainable in high street stores and electrical shops that are classed as PMR 446. This is Public Mobile Radio operating on 446Mhz for which you do not need a licence. They have a very limited range and are not really ideal for surveillance, not just because of the limited range but also they are very easily intercepted because they all operate on the same frequency.

## ANTENNAS

Whether you are using a hand held radio or a vehicle set, it is very important that you have

Simple controls make radios easier to use

Kenwood TH-22e radio

the correct antenna (aerial) fitted otherwise you will have problems when transmitting and receiving. The antenna is probably one of the most important parts of your radio. It has to be the correct type and length and it cannot be any 'old piece of wire' plugged into the set.

The antenna should ideally be vertical and has to be the correct length to correspond with the frequency used and this can be done by a simple calculation. For example, a radio using a frequency of 174Mhz requires an antenna that is .43 of a metre long (or 43cms, or 17 inches). When you buy a mag mount antenna or those for vehicle mounting, they are slightly longer than necessary so that they can be cut down to size for this reason. A pair of pliers or a hacksaw normally does the job.

The length of antenna is calculated by dividing the number 300 (a constant) by the frequency. We then divide the answer by 4 to give the length in metres, what is known as a quarter wavelength.

So if we take 300 and divide it by our frequency of 174Mhz, this equals 1.724 (our wavelength). Divide this by 4, which equals 0.43 (our quarter wavelength) or 43 centimetres.

E.g. $\frac{300.00}{174.00} = 1.724$ then $\frac{1.724}{4} = 43\text{cm}$

I would agree with you if you said that it would look a bit odd to have a hand held radio with nearly half a metre of black wire sticking out of the top and you have probably already noticed that the antennae on these sets are fairly short. These are called 'helical' antennae and are in fact cut to the correct length; it is just that the wire is coiled up like a spring inside the covering. Some of our covert antennae are extended to a quarter wave length but are worn in a harness where the antennas length runs across the shoulders for better reception.

If the radio has 'line of sight' to another set, you should achieve maximum transmitting range. When objects such as buildings, trees or hills come between them, the range will be drastically reduced. Radio waves find it difficult to pass through water which essentially is what your body is made up of. Therefore if your covert set is stuffed tigh under your armpit, you may experience problems w range. Clipped to the belt in the small of your back o your hip is preferable to maximise range.

If you are in an OP where you are lying down, be aware of the transmission range reducing as you are close to the ground. The higher up you are the better the range therefore it would be advisable to use an elevated antenna by attaching it to a fence post or up a tree.

## DIPOLE ANTENNAS

This is a very simple and effective way of increasing your transmission range with an external antenna, especially when in an OP.

It is fairly simple to make your own 'dipole' antenna, which is very effective for use in vehicles, or OPs when it is not practical to use a mag mount antenna. A dipole can be made by taking an old mag mount antenna and cutting off the magnetic base. Looking into the cut end of the cable (or coax) you will note that the section is made up of four elements; the outer protective sheath, a fine wire mesh sleeve (called shielding), a strong plastic core with a copper wire running through it.

Firstly you need to calculate the length of your antenna, let's say it is 43cms. Now you need to cut away about 44cms of the outer sheath and throw it away so that you now have exposed the bare shielding surrounding the inner core. Next, very carefully make a small hole in the shielding where it emerges from the outer sheath and pull the inner plastic core back through it being careful not to sever the shielding. You should end up with a hollow shield branching off in one direction and the inner core branching off in another, so that when laid flat out your cable should be in the shape of a 'T'.

All you have to do now is to wrap electrical tape around the 'T' in order to stop the wires from fraying and breaking loose. Measure and cut the length of the antenna (the inner core) and the shielding (ground plane) so that each is 43cms long.

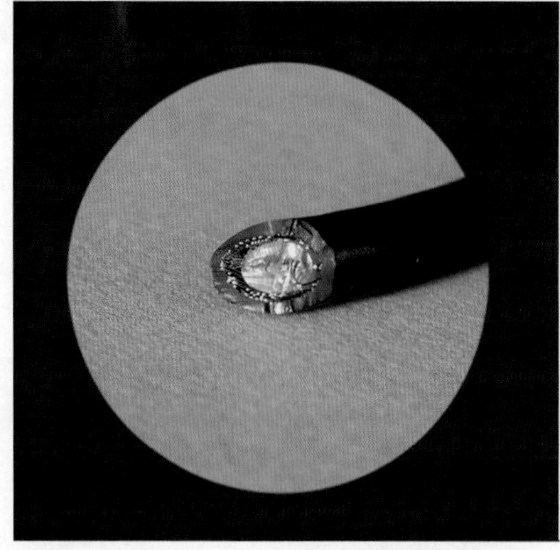

With a BNC connector at the other end, plug it in to your radio and you are ready to transmit. Ideally the two elements (wires) should be set in the shape of a 'V'. In the photograph, you will see one that is concealed in a protective tube that can be laid flat or hung from a tree or post for use in rural OPs.

## COVERT RADIO SYSTEMS

A semi-covert set of wires can be purchased for about £40.00. This comprises of a 'Walkman' style earpiece and a lapel microphone. The earpiece is not 100% covert as it can be seen but it is very effective if you are operating on a budget and let's face it, how many people walk around these days with something in their ear? Mobile phones, hands free kits, MP3 players and iPods so you will get away with this type of equipment to a certain extent. The microphone is worn just under the collar and operated with a PTT switch to transmit. Just be aware if all members of the team have wired earpieces, otherwise it would look like the iPod fan club having a day out together!

Another style of earpiece is the 'Curly Wurly'. This is a robust earpiece which is more suited to overt security work

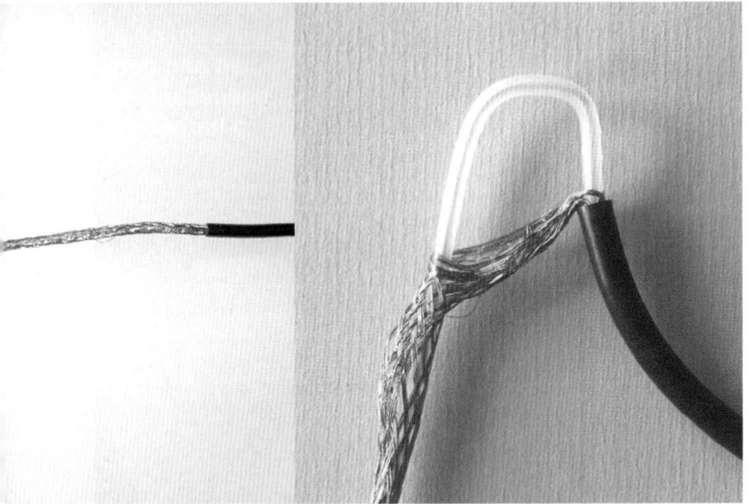

***A dipole antenna can easily be constructed from old coax cables. They can be attached to simple objects such as a coat-hanger or protected within a tube for outdoor use***

such as close protection or door work than covert surveillance as it is so noticeable. The 'Curly Wurly' is ideal for rural work as it can be easily removed and put back in again, where wireless earpieces can easily fall out and get lost.

The more professional accessories comprise of a carry harness similar to that of a pistol shoulder holster, which carries the radio. Built into the harness is the antenna, microphone and an induction device which 'transmits' voice to a small ear piece placed in the ear. There are no tell - tale wires to the ear piece which appears very similar to a hearing aid. This equipment is very effective and was once described as being 'the closest you would ever get to being telepathic'.

A dipole suspended from a tree needs to be camouflaged

For women operators, the set can either be body worn or concealed in a handbag. In this instance the microphone, inductor and PTT switch are all contained within the shoulder strap. These handbags are in common use by store detectives. They are not always ideal for surveillance, if the wearer happens to enter a café or restaurant, it would be odd to keep the bag over the shoulder

There are two types of covert rig, the 'inductor' and the 'induction loop'. The inductor is a small plastic tab about 5cms long which is pinned to clothing in the area of your collar bone. This inductor transmits signals to your earpiece (which has to be fitted in the ear on the same side as the inductor) and also has a built-in microphone.

The induction loop is what it says it is, a loop of flesh coloured wire that is worn over the head like a necklace and is also fitted with a microphone. With the loop, it does not matter in which ear you wear your earpiece.

**Walk and Talk**

Students on courses often find it very difficult to use covert radios in a natural manner until they have gained confidence after a few hours of practice. Remember that we have to act naturally in everything we do and it is not always easy when you have a lump of equipment strapped to your body and you are required to walk down the street whilst talking to yourself.

Have confidence in the equipment, this will come with constant practice.

• Relax, speak at a normal level and do not talk directly into the collar or microphone. It looks odd to see a person walking down the street with his chin glued to his chest.

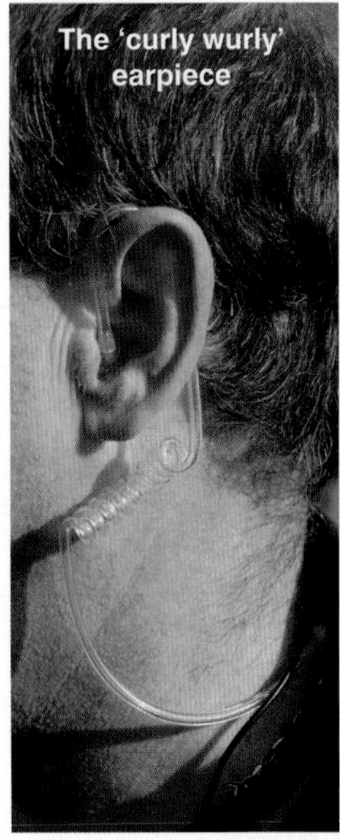
The 'curly wurly' earpiece

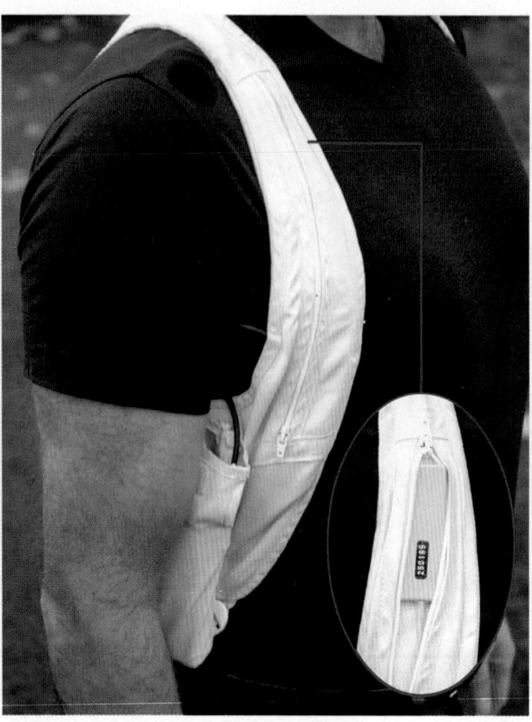

Radios can be worn on a belt and not necessarily in a harness

• Do not worry about talking to yourself there are many people that do it! Obviously if you are in close proximity to someone (especially children) be extra cautious. If you have to talk and the situation is difficult (you may be next to someone on a bench), then pretend to be using your mobile phone but remember to switch off the ringer or you would look silly if it suddenly goes off.

• You may have your PTT switch running down the inside of your sleeve, so keep your arm relaxed. Do not walk with your arm outstretched and appear as if you are carrying a bag with a bomb in it, relax the fingers and keep it out of view. If you are close to the target, keep your hand in your pocket.

• If you prefer to wear your pressel in your trouser pocket, check how the rest of the team are wearing theirs. If all are wearing it the same the team could give off a 'signature' as each one will have at least one hand in their pocket. Be conscious of having one hand in your pocket all of the time. If you do, keep your elbow tucked in and not stuck out like a tea pot handle and do not let the other arm swing about as if you are marching.

• Refrain from constantly touching the earpiece, an aware target may notice this - counter

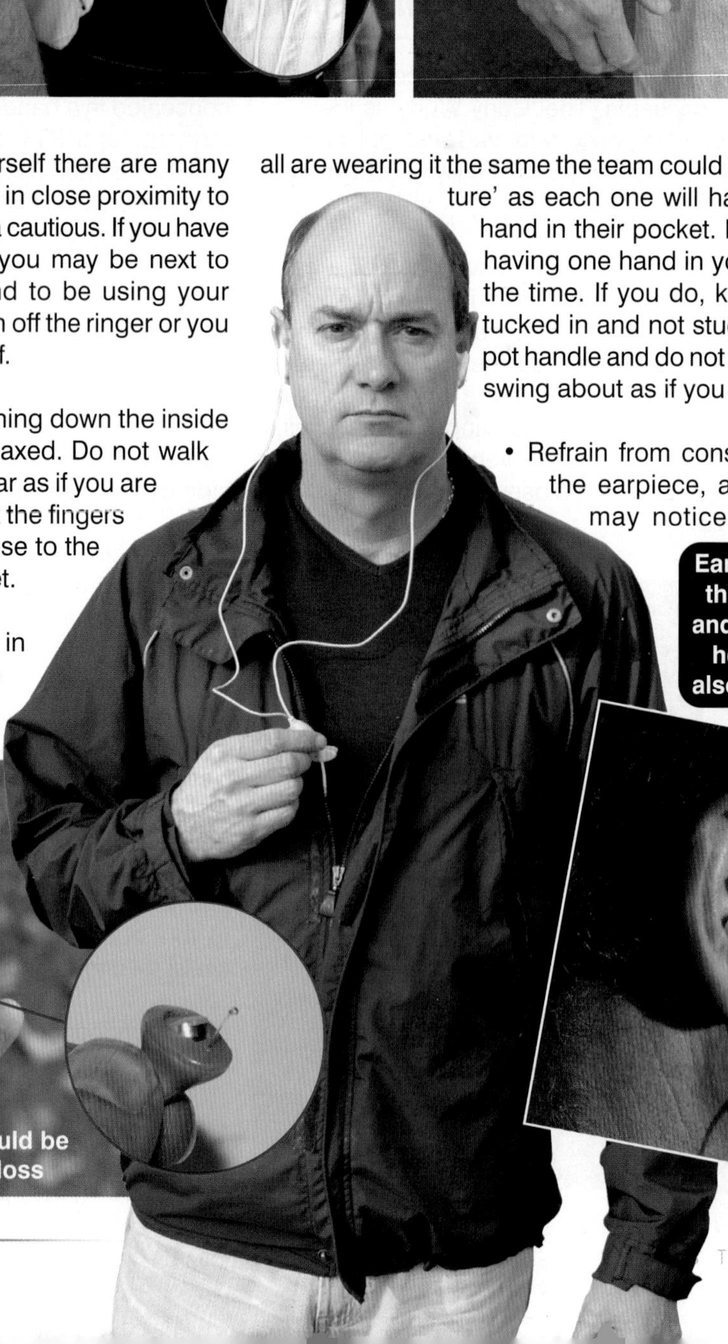

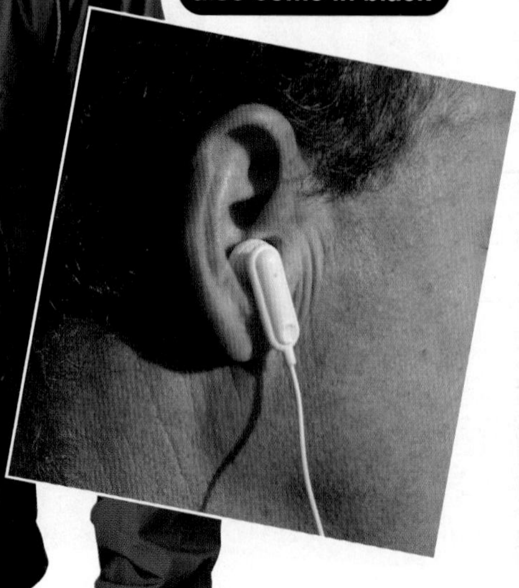

Earpieces such as this, are popular and resemble iPod headsets. They also come in black

When not in use - earpieces should be housed in a pouch to prevent loss

# Keep your covert equipment covert...

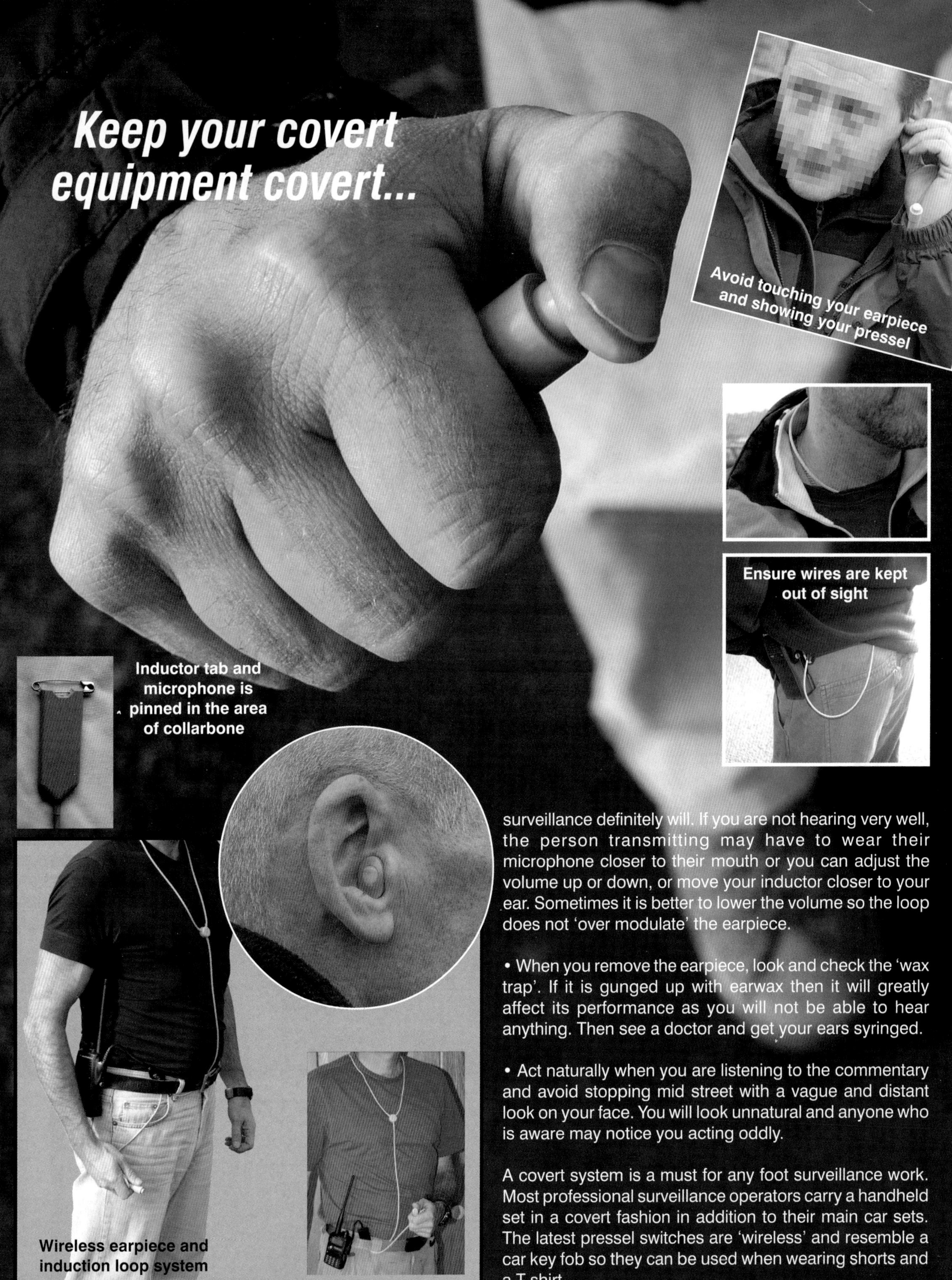

Avoid touching your earpiece and showing your pressel

Ensure wires are kept out of sight

Inductor tab and microphone is pinned in the area of collarbone

Wireless earpiece and induction loop system

surveillance definitely will. If you are not hearing very well, the person transmitting may have to wear their microphone closer to their mouth or you can adjust the volume up or down, or move your inductor closer to your ear. Sometimes it is better to lower the volume so the loop does not 'over modulate' the earpiece.

• When you remove the earpiece, look and check the 'wax trap'. If it is gunged up with earwax then it will greatly affect its performance as you will not be able to hear anything. Then see a doctor and get your ears syringed.

• Act naturally when you are listening to the commentary and avoid stopping mid street with a vague and distant look on your face. You will look unnatural and anyone who is aware may notice you acting oddly.

A covert system is a must for any foot surveillance work. Most professional surveillance operators carry a handheld set in a covert fashion in addition to their main car sets. The latest pressel switches are 'wireless' and resemble a car key fob so they can be used when wearing shorts and a T shirt.

## RADIO SECURITY

Radio transmissions are open to interception and so security is an important factor when transmitting messages. There is little you can do to avoid interception, except from use 'secure' digital radios which encrypt all messages or use veiled speech and brevity codes.

There are a number of people that may wish to listen in to your radio transmissions:

- *The radio enthusiast or radio ham*
- *The person that unintentionally listens in to you by chance*
- *The person who intentionally listens in*
- *The Radio Ham*

These people may spend thousands of pounds on radio receiving and scanning equipment in order to enjoy their hobby. They are able to pick up radio transmissions and talk to other enthusiasts from all over the world. If they pick up your transmissions, they may be listening for a short while in order to satisfy their curiosity but they may make a note of your operating frequency and return to it at a later date to see what you are up to. Radio hams are 'proud' of what they do and are likely to report to the authorities any misuse of radios, voice procedure or bad language

- **The Unintentional Intercept**

This could be anyone scanning the airwaves just by listening out for anything of interest. They may not be purposefully looking for surveillance operators but if they hear transmissions relating to 'target' or places that sound familiar to them, their interest will be aroused even more.

- **The Intentional Intercept**

Operators are more likely to be overheard by amateur radio hams than government agencies

Some of the criminal fraternity make use of 'scanners' that are freely obtained from electrical stores and radio shops for as little as £75.00. They will tend to listen into Police broadcasts but they will also lock onto your frequency if you are nearby. These scanners usually lock onto the most powerful and nearest radio signal; they are small and can be carried about the person, used in a house or even in the car. These people may react to transmissions, if you are overheard stating that you are 'plotted up on the junction of Haworth Road and Gate Lane do not be surprised if you are paid a visit!

There is not much you can do to minimise the risk of interception by eavesdroppers except to use secure radios, therefore the following should be considered:

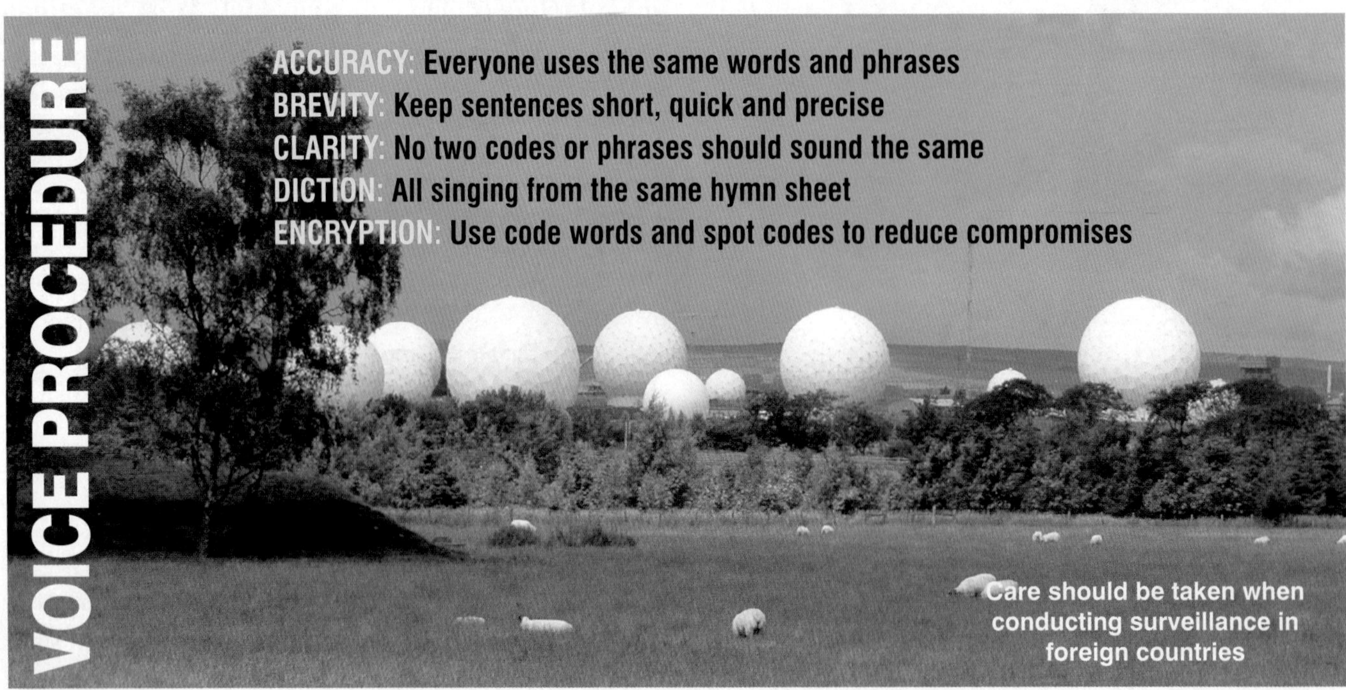

Care should be taken when conducting surveillance in foreign countries

- *Use mobile telephones to send sensitive information*
- *Keep transmissions to a bare minimum*
- *Change frequency regularly*
- *Refrain from sending 'identifiers' such as street names and place names*
- *Use pre-arranged brevity code words and phrases*
- *Use spot codes*

**Encrypted Radio Sets**

Radios that transmit encrypted (or scrambled) signals are available to the investigator and are essential if you are sending very sensitive information; they are not much more expensive to purchase but can have a limited transmission range

**Brevity Codes and Identity Systems**

As mentioned, the security of information given out over a radio is very important. Without encrypted radios it would not be practical to give sensitive information such as names, addresses, telephone numbers and vehicle details over the air. Anyone who is able to monitor your frequency or channel will soon know about the subject of your enquiry and your operation.

In addition, unidentified people or premises should be given an identity if they cannot be named and are unknown to you. It is possible that the subject of a surveillance will meet up with others and they will have to be identified or given a name/nickname.

There is a simple system, generally used on the security circuit, which lets us assign identifier codes to our target, and anyone that he/she has contact with and there are several variants to it. **For example:**

## BREVITY CODES

| | |
|---|---|
| A male is referred to as an | *ALPHA* |
| A vehicle is referred to as a | *BRAVO* |
| Property, such as a house or building is a | *CHARLIE* |
| A female is referred to as an | *ECHO* |
| Unknown person/vehicle referred to as a | *UK* |

- **Individuals**

When used in context, the primary target (if it is a male) would be known as 'Alpha 1'. Should he meet up with another male, that male would then become 'Alpha 2' and so on.

**This wireless 'PTT' is more covert than using a system which requires a wire running down your sleeve. Especially useful in close environments**

If an unknown male arrives at the target's address, he would initially be referred to as a 'UK Alpha'.

In a similar fashion, the primary female target would be known as 'Echo 1'. Or if 'Alpha 1' is your Target, his wife or partner may be referred to as 'Echo 1'.

By assigning individuals I.D. codes it creates less confusion when giving a radio commentary. During a surveillance, the Target may meet up with an unknown male (who could be described as: male, white, thick black hair wearing a blue jumper with a white stripe across). Rather than use this awkward description every time you want to mention him, it is easier to refer to him as 'Alpha 2'.

- **Vehicles**

The primary vehicle used by 'Alpha 1' would be 'Bravo 1'. Should you arrive at 'Alpha 1s' home address to commence a surveillance and find two vehicles in the driveway they could be designated 'Bravo 1' and 'Bravo 2'. Any subsequent vehicle related to the task would be further assigned 'Bravo 3, 4 and 5'.

- **Premises**

In a similar fashion any property or building is referred to as a 'Charlie'. The primary building such as 'Alpha 1's' home address would be referred to as 'Charlie 1', his place of work as 'Charlie 2' and so on.

This system or variants of it, is generally used on the security circuit.

## PROCEDURE

Radio commentary has to be clear, precise and quick. The terms listed above assist in the speed of transmissions, making them understandable by all. For example, the following message given by a 'trigger' would be long winded and insecure:

***'STANDBY STANDBY, That's Mr. Jones and his wife leaving the house, walking past the blue Escort and getting into the red Peugeot'***

and could be given as:

***'STANDBY STANDBY, Alpha 1, Echo 1, exit Charlie 1 going complete Bravo 2'***

or another example:

***'That's Jones and the male with the long grey coat and beard walking from the blue Escort back into the office building'***

could be given as:

***'That's Alpha 1, Alpha 2, foxtrot from Bravo 1 to Charlie 2'***

You will note that the messages are shorter, to the point and to some extent, encrypted. The system is simple and effective when used properly and eliminates the need to mention any names that should otherwise be given in 'clear'. It does not take long to master with practise.

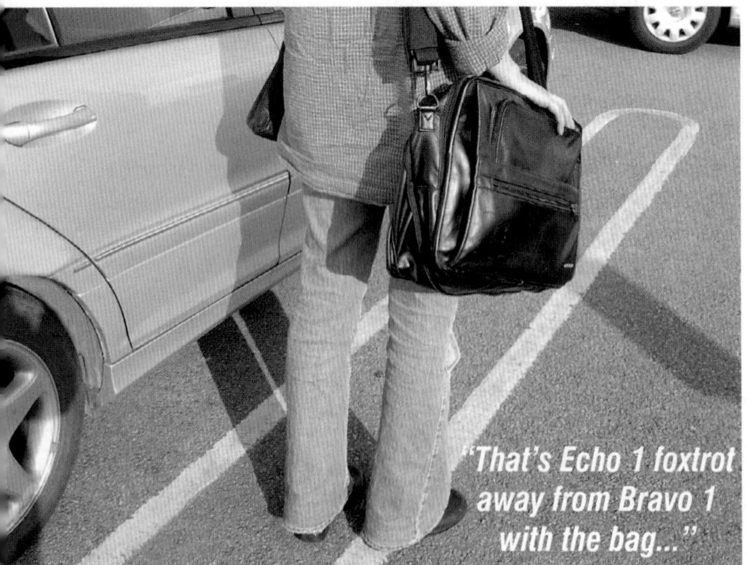
"That's Echo 1 foxtrot away from Bravo 1 with the bag..."

It is the task of the team leader to designate all initial identity codes on a briefing sheet prior to any surveillance task. The team leader will also nominate new codes during the surveillance as new targets, vehicle or places come into play.

When the Target is walking we refer to him as being **'foxtrot'** and when in a vehicle he is **'mobile'.** It is very important that you do not get it this mixed up. If a target is on foot and an operator mistakenly calls, ***'That's Alpha 1 mobile towards the college..'.*** All of the footmen are going to be panicking and start heading back to their cars under the impression the target is driving away.

### NUMERICAL BREVITY CODES

Some companies and agencies use numerical codes as part of the voice procedure. For a well rehearsed and practised team this system works. For someone who is not used to it, does not use it frequently or is new to surveillance it can easily become a hindrance to the team. The list is long but a few examples are:

| | |
|---|---|
| '777' | STANDBY |
| '999' | STOP STOP |
| '55' | I HAVE |
| '66' | PAST ME |
| '68' | BACKING |
| '69' | TRIGGER |
| '74' | HANDOVER/TAKEOVER |
| '83' | HELD |
| '91' | TOWARDS |

And used in conjunction with some of the following brevity codes:

| | |
|---|---|
| HANDLE | ENTRANCE/EXIT TO A BULIDING |
| ON CARPET | ON PLOT |
| FOGGY | UNSIGHTED |
| NEST | ROUNDABOUT |
| HAWK | JUNCTION |

## ISS CASE

A few years ago, I was working with a foreign Special Forces unit, one of the Team stated that they used a 'secret code' which they had borrowed from one of their own Federal Agencies. It turns out that their secret code was the one described here, which has its origins born out of the British Intelligence Corps working in Germany against the Eastern Bloc during the Cold War.

| | |
|---|---|
| STARLING | TOWN CENTRE |
| SWALLOW | BRIDGE |
| SPARKLERS | TRAFFIC LIGHTS |
| FLOOD | PETROL STATION |
| SHAKER | TAXI |
| RATTLER | TRAIN |
| LEEK | CAR PARK |
| HEAVY SAND | HEAVY TRAFFIC |
| X-RAY | TARGET PERSON |
| YANKEE | TARGET VEHICLE |

So as part of a commentary you may hear: ***'Kilo: 777, 55, X-Ray 1, foxtrot, 66, 91 the swallow'***

Which means:

Call sign Kilo: ***'Standby Standby, I have the target walking past me towards the bridge'***

Not only can getting a single number wrong cause a lot of confusion but not being 'fluent' can also lead to compromising the codes as well. I have seen a situation where an operator giving the commentary comes out with a sentence of numbers and codes, and then realises his mistakes and ends up coming out with the same message but in 'clear' which has really defeated the object.

Whilst this is good for teams using comms that are not encrypted, the nature of the codes can sometimes lead to compromise if you are overheard using them. Imagine being sat in the lobby of a hotel and you are overheard by a third party saying: ***'Kilo: 777, 55, X-Ray 1, foxtrot, 66, 91 the shaker'.*** Mr Third Party is going to be thinking, ***'What the **** is that all about?'*** and will continue to keep his eye on you, as you have now got his full attention.

### RADIO CALL-SIGNS AND NETWORKS

The Police, Military and other Enforcement agencies use specialist call signs as a matter of course. Call-signs not only identify the individual operator but also give an indication to what unit, sub-unit or team he belongs to. Complex call-signs and networks are only necessary when there are many operators on the ground with varying tasks.

As a simple network the following diagram shows how the team are labelled, remember, all call-signs can transmit and receive each other. You will note that the team comprises of four cars; Car 1, Car 2, Car 3 and Car 4 (see diagrams overleaf). These are the call-signs that they will use throughout the surveillance irrespective of where they are in the surveillance convoy. Car 2 and Car 3 may have a passenger who would be expected to deploy on foot when the need arises. These operators respective call-signs become Foot 1 and Foot 2 in relation to their own vehicle. Should Car 3 pick up Foot 2 for some reason, that person still retains the call-sign of Foot 2.

The disadvantage of this network is that it can tell an eavesdropper how many cars are on the team. Should someone be scanning and hear, ***'Car 4, roger that...'*** it tells them that there are at least 4 cars on the team.

Should the team be on the ground and a base is used as a control point, such as an operations room they could use call-sign 'Zero' or 'Control'.

**Pretending to talk on your cell phone while in radio communication is fine - but over use of the ruse should be avoided - especially if all team members are doing the same.**

# RADIO NETWORKS

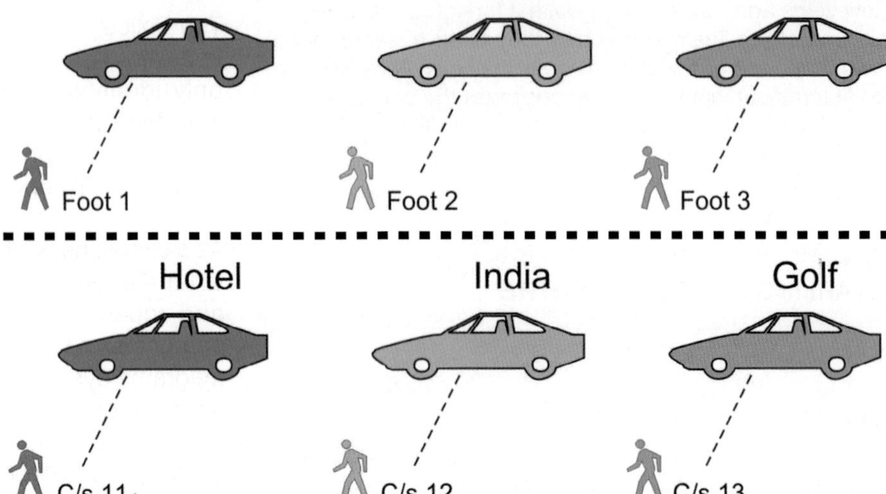


On the commercial surveillance circuit it is rare that we go out with two operators in one vehicle (two up) mainly due to the cost implications. When operating 'one up', we tend to keep to a personal call-sign, for example, Peter (PAPA) and Greg (GOLF).

Another effective call-sign system especially when you are using large teams that are operating on foot as well as mobile is shown in the picture. Each car has its own individual call-sign such as Golf, Papa or Kilo. When you are 'complete' your vehicle you use this call sign. However, if you deploy on foot, you then use your foot call-sign such as 11 (one one). This enables other operators to identify whether you are in your car or out on foot.

**Establishing Communications**

Prior to starting the task, make sure that all radios are working properly and carry out a radio check to ensure that everyone can transmit to and receive each other. If there is a problem, sort it out there and then before getting out on the ground. Ensure that the batteries are charged and that antennas are fitted correctly and tightly. Fresh batteries should be placed in covert earpieces, ready for use.

Radio procedures differ from organisation to organisation such as military or police. The military way of calling a station always states the other persons call sign first and then state your own. So that PAPA wanting to speak to ROMEO would be:

| VOICE PROCEDURE | MEANING |
|---|---|
| 'ROMEO, PAPA?' | (Romeo this is Papa) |
| 'ROMEO, send' | (This is Romeo, send your message) |

The police way of doing it is the opposite way round:

| VOICE PROCEDURE | MEANING |
|---|---|
| 'PAPA to ROMEO receiving?' | (Papa is calling Romeo) |
| 'ROMEO, go ahead' | (This is Romeo, send your message) |

Both differ and neither way is any better than the other, so use the procedure that you are used to.

**Radio Check!**

As mentioned, you must establish comms and carry out a radio check before going out on the ground and also when in position on the ground. If comms is poor due to distance for example, and you cannot receive the trigger person, it is 'you' that will have to move to a better position (higher up, move closer or transmit over flat ground) because the trigger is the person who is static and cannot move anywhere.

Try to avoid calling all stations at once asking for a radio check. A disciplined and well rehearsed team will answer in alpha numerical order. An unrehearsed team will all answer at the same time causing confusion on the radio net.

The sequence of a radio check between call-signs PAPA and ROMEO (with PAPA sending) would be:

**'ROMEO, PAPA, radio check'**
**'PAPA, okay over'** ('difficult' if barely audible, or 'unworkable' if message is not understandable).
**'ROMEO, okay out'**

Some responses to a radio check differ from team to team or organisation to organisation. Some say, **'Loud and Clear'** (or Lima Charlie), some say, **'five R five'** which means strength 5 out of 5.

If you do not get a reply, send another radio check, if you still do not get a reply then check:

- *Is your set switched on!*
- *Is your volume turned up*
- *Are you on the correct channel or frequency*
- *Is the battery secure and charged*
- *Is the antenna securely in place*
- *Make sure any ancillary equipment is plugged in properly*

If this still does not get a reply transmit over the air 'Nothing Heard'. If the other station is able to hear you, they will know that you are unable to receive them by your call. In addition, any other team members will know that there is a communication problem and they would then be able to offer to relay any messages. As a last resort, use your mobile phone to call the other team member in order to establish what the problem is. More often than not, if a radio fails to operate or work it is due to operator error, so check and check again.

If you are wearing covert body worn sets and you have a comms problem, then check and carry out the following:-

• Your earpiece is in your ear and switched on. Some wireless earpieces give off a faint hiss, this tells you the battery is okay.

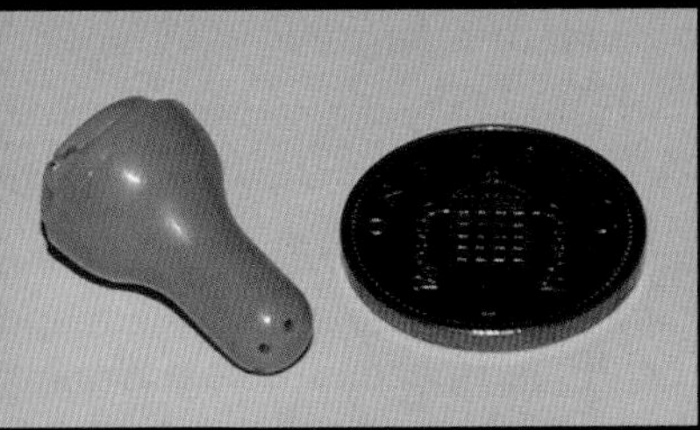

• Turn your radio off, wait for a few seconds and turn it on again. You should hear a confirmatory beep from the radio in your ear.

• Listen for commentary, if you do not hear anything, ask for a radio check or a 'five count' (1, 2, 3, 4, 5) so that you can adjust your volume to a comfortable level.

• Be careful of turning the volume up too high as this will 'over modulate' the earpiece and you will have difficulty listening.

If we have a four car team using the call-signs as illustrated on page 56 (Car 1, Car 2, Car 3, Car 4), the response should always be in numerical order. For example:

'All call-signs this is Car 1, radio check...'

The response:

*'Car 2, Okay'*
*'Car 3, Okay'*
*'Car 4, Okay'*

Followed by:

'Car 1, Roger that, all cars received'

If Car 2 responds and then there is a pause (possibly because Car 3 has a problem). Car 4 should normally wait for about five seconds before he acknowledges, allowing Car 3 time to respond.

Many people from various organisations use the voice procedure that is best suited to them. In surveillance, the radio commentary has to be fast, accurate and to the point, to this end it is greatly abbreviated and pro-words such as OVER or OUT are normally dropped altogether. Many people incorrectly use the word OVER to finish a transmission, this word actually demands a response. There is also no need for pleasantries such as: please, thank you or obliged.

## VOICE PROCEDURE

There are various common phrases or words used when transmitting over a network called 'pro-words'. At the rear of the book there is a Glossary of Terms, which details a number of pro-words and phrases commonly used in surveillance voice procedure.

When Kilo cannot receive Golf, Hotel must relay

**Relay To...**

Quite often, one operator may not be able to receive another due to the fact that he is out of range or there is an obstruction such as a hill blocking transmissions. If this is the case, then another operator (who may be located in between the two operators having difficulty) can pass on a message or 'relay' it between them by saying, 'Relay' and then pass the message on.

A relay car is better located on high ground as it will receive and transmit signals over a wider range. In town centres, the top floor of a multi-storey car park is an ideal location so long as you can get out quickly, otherwise you just float about and back or shadow the team.

If your team is strung out along a valley for example (whether in cars or OPs) and the Eyeball transmits, 'That's Alpha 1 still digging in the garden'. Rather than the next operator along just acknowledging with 'Roger that', actually pass the message down the line, such as, 'Roger that, relay, Alpha 1 still digging in garden'. This way, everyone on the team is kept informed.

**Eyeball Permission?**

Some enforcement agencies, especially the Police, use a strict method of control over the radio network. When the Eyeball is giving a radio commentary, he is in total control of the radio net and no one should interrupt the commentary for any reason.

Within these particular teams, if another member of the team wishes to speak, they firstly have to ask permission from the eyeball, for example:

***'Car 1 has the Eyeball, that's the target still inside the premises, no change.'***
***'Car 2 to Car 1, Permission?'***
***'Car 1, go ahead...'***
***'Car 2, can you tell me what the target is wearing?'***
***'Car 1, yes, blue jeans and black T-shirt.'***
***'Car 2 received, back over to you.'***

This system has its advantages and disadvantages, for the people that use it regularly, it is a disciplined system and works for them. It could be argued that this system is rather long-winded and unnecessary. If you need to say something, why not wait for a suitable break in the commentary and quickly say it. Experience will tell you when you should not interrupt at an important time and when you can. The following commentary would be much shorter and quicker:

***'Car 2 to Car 1, what's he wearing?'***
***'Blue jeans and black T-shirt.'***
***'Car 2 Roger.'***

## RADIO DISCIPLINE

When words or car registrations have to be spelt out over the air the 'Phonetic Alphabet' is often used and is internationally recognised as a means of doing so. This is so that the letters of the words cannot be mistaken for any other and thus avoids confusion.

## PHONETIC ALPHABET

| | |
|---|---|
| A ALPHA | N NOVEMBER |
| B BRAVO | O OSCAR |
| C CHARLIE | P PAPA |
| D DELTA | Q QUEBEC |
| E ECHO | R ROMEO |
| F FOXTROT | S SIERRA |
| G GOLF | T TANGO |
| H HOTEL | U UNIFORM |
| I INDIA | V VICTOR |
| J JULIET | W WHISKY |
| K KILO | X X RAY |
| L LIMA | Y YANKEE |
| M MIKE | Z ZULU |

***All surveillance operators should know the phonetic alphabet***

**Target Identity Codes (I.C. Codes)**

A number of Enforcement Agencies for many years have used a system of codes in order to describe a person's ethnic origin. This code in recent times has been the subject of debate as it has been suggested that it is not politically correct to use it. However, the code has been in place for many years and is still used today in some circles.

**Commentary During a Surveillance**

During a mobile or foot surveillance, a running commentary should be given by the lead vehicle (Eyeball) to the remainder of the team to inform them of the targets movements and intentions. It is possible that the 'Trail' car is some 600 metres behind and 'driving blind' and so he will be relying on the commentary in order to put him in the right direction. Commentary during a mobile surveillance is described fully in the chapter on mobile surveillance but should be clear, precise, timely and most importantly, relaxed. I always teach that it should not be so relaxed that everyone becomes complacent but rather like an airline pilot giving a firm and clear brief to his passengers. There is nothing worse than having someone on the team who is over excited and hyper active in their voice procedure. All this does is have a negative effect, it rubs off onto the rest of the team and control is soon lost.

During a surveillance the targets direction of travel (whether on foot or mobile) must always be given as 'Left', 'Right', 'Straight' or 'Reciprocal' (recip). These directions are always in relation to the Target's 'Left' or 'Right' and not yours as you look at him. They are very important calls

If you are no longer 'backing' say so!

and so must be repeated just like a 'Stop Stop' or 'Standby Standby' not only to emphasise a change in direction but also in the event of a part of the transmission being lost or unheard.

**Clipping or... "lippin"?**

Sometimes (and it differs from radio to radio) transmissions get 'clipped' by pressing the pressel after we have started talking or we let go of the pressel before we finish speaking. When transmitting you should press the pressel, wait a second and then speak to ensure that the whole message gets transmitted (press, pause, speak). If you find an operator who keeps clipping his calls, you have to tell them straight away, otherwise they will not realise it and you will miss an important call.

## SPOT CODES

Spot codes are used to designate road names and junctions by means of allocating them a colour and a number. This provides two things; security on the net (by not having to give specific road names over the air) and also to quickly communicate to the rest of the team, the targets location and intentions.

On the commercial circuit, they are normally used if you are operating in an area long term or when security is very important. If working abroad they are a must if you find it difficult to read, and pronounce the local street signs (if there are any). It is far easier to say, **'..that's at Blue 4 towards Blue 5..'** rather than try to say, **'that's gone Left Left on Hugenshlaftendunst Strasse towards the Hauptbahnhoff.'** Not only is it difficult to say but the team also has to try and understand what you said.

Just by stating, **'That's at Blue One to Red One'** tells a picture of what direction the target is travelling and also his approximate location which is described more in the chapter on mobile surveillance.

It is also easy to compromise spots if you are not careful. A transmission such as, **'..that's into Silsden Village towards Red 2...'** tells an eavesdropper where Red 2 roughly is, so treat the system with caution.

Depending on the locality, a small number of streets in the vicinity can be spotted; alternately a small village could have all its major junctions spotted as shown in the diagrams.

**It is easier to say 'that's gone Right Right towards Red 4' rather than Llanfair Pwllgwyngyll!**

**'Spotting' maps whilst operating abroad - in this case Switzerland**

## Hand Signals

Hand signals are to be used when there is no other means of communication or when silence has to be maintained in a situation such as an O.P. Should you be out on foot and communications is lost, you may have to resort to subtle hand signals and 'nods' of the head in order to communicate. However, hand signals are to be avoided if at all possible as they create 'cross contamination'. If the Target suspects that you are surveillance he will keep an eye on you. If he sees you make a gesture to someone else, you have now compromised them by association.

## Encryption of Numerical Information

When other sensitive information such as telephone numbers, house numbers or vehicle registrations have to be transmitted by radio they should be encrypted in the event that they are intercepted by an unauthorised listener.

A simple system we call 'LUDO' can be used to transmit numerical figures. The pro-word 'LUDO' should always be given prior to the numbers being sent, so that the recipient knows that they are encrypted.

Should you want to transmit the telephone number: 750259, add a 1 to each figure, so that it becomes: 861360. Note that a 0 becomes a 1 and that a 9 becomes a 0.

When you transmit your message, it would be in the form of: **'Telephone number, LUDO 861360'.**

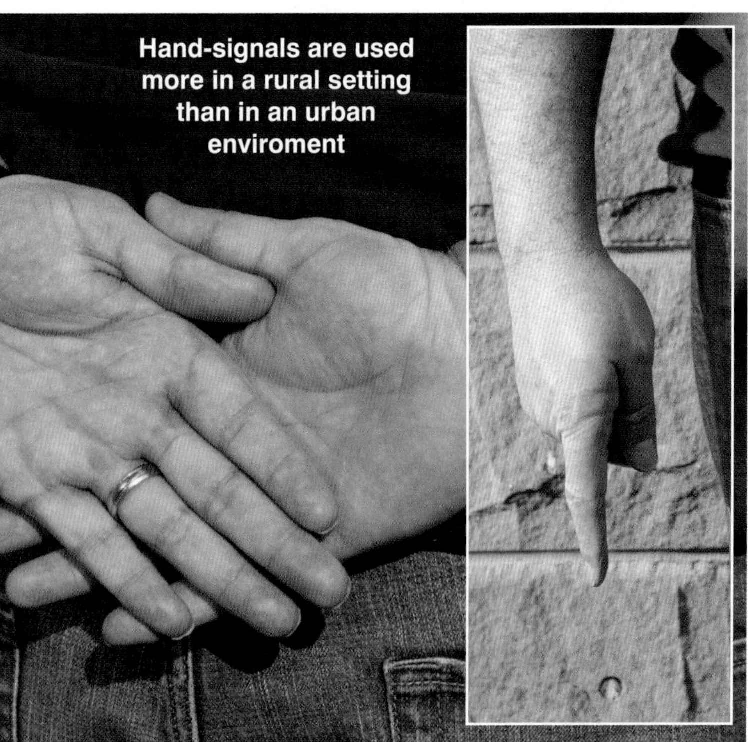

Hand-signals are used more in a rural setting than in an urban enviroment

This registration number will be encrypted as "LUDO, Papa, 910, Bravo, Mike Sierra"

The recipient having heard the pro-word LUDO, then subtracts 1 from each figure to obtain the original number.

In the same manner, house numbers or vehicle registrations can be given so that A123 ABC becomes LUDO A234 ABC, or house number 169 becomes LUDO 270.

The LUDO 'factor' used here has a value of 1 (the numbers alter by 1). This can be altered to 2, 3 or even 4 on a daily basis if your security demands it.

There are many systems of encoding numerical information, one other simple method is to double the original number before it is transmitted or another is to reverse the whole number. It does not matter which system you use, so long as the recipient knows what to do with the information in order to make sense of it.

***If in doubt, transmit sensitive information by mobile phone or text.***

## Breakthrough

From time to time you will get 'breakthrough' on the radio net as someone nearby will also be operating and transmitting on the same frequency and CTCSS codes. It happens as there are only so many frequencies to go around. Not all will be surveillance teams but other radio users such as: construction sites, security guards, delivery drivers and taxis.

If you hear breakthrough, do not respond. Ignore it and switch channels. If you respond, the other will only listen into your transmissions and may even mess you about by holding down their pressels or playing music over the net. It is possible that you may be able to hear the others but they are not able to hear you, especially if they are high up and using more powerful transmitters than you are.

## ISS CASE

A few years ago, I was working on a quiet surveillance in Castleford, West Yorkshire, the target never moved. Over the radio net we had 'break through' from another surveillance team who were arriving in the area of a retail park. I overheard, 'that's a stop stop at the B&Q Store, I'm going static in McDonald's car park, covering the roundabout..'. I thought to myself, 'that's only 300 metres down the road, I haven't got the trigger so I'll go and take a look out of curiosity'.

Another call sign, came up over the air and said that he had the Eyeball on the Target and from the style of commentary I guessed that they were former police, it sounded good, they appeared to have the target under control. After a few minutes, I heard something like, 'Brian, are you still in Micky Dees, I'll come and join you..'. 'Yes Yes' was the reply.

Right, I thought, right lets see what happens now! As I was sat in the McDonald's car park, I thought that I had identified Brian and his car and it was soon confirmed when his partner pulled up alongside, both windows were wound down and they began to converse.

Having being bored for the past few hours I decided to have a laugh at their expense. I pulled up along side 'Brian' and wound my window down, he was aware of my presence and I indicated for him to do the same. When he said, 'Yes, can I help you?' I handed him my business card and said that I am in the area all week and if they needed a hand then to call me. I then wound my window up and drove away!

He must have sat there and thought, 'Where did this guy come from and how did he know?' I have never found out who it was to this day, so if you are reading this and recognise the event please get in touch!

### THE CLICK SYSTEM

When it is not practical to speak, for instance you may be inside a shop or café or when it is difficult to use the radio, a procedure known as the 'Click System' can be used.

This system enables you to communicate by pressing the pressel switch (PTT) a given number of times, in answer to direct questions received. The receiving radio receives and hears these presses as 'clicks'.

There are a number of variations to this system depending on the organisation using it. The military tend to use two clicks as YES (double click) and no clicks for NO. Whereas Enforcement Agencies would interpret two clicks as NO.

The Police and various Enforcement Agencies use this system:

| | |
|---|---|
| **4 clicks on PTT** | **= Ask Me A Question (AMAQ)** |
| **3 clicks on PTT** | **= Yes** |
| **2 clicks on PTT** | **= No** |
| **5+ rapid clicks** | **= Standby, Standby** |

In practical terms, the target may get onto a bus and hopefully a foot person will get onto the bus also. Prior to getting on, you have told the remainder of the team what you are doing. The team realise that you are getting on the bus and therefore they would not expect you to give a verbal commentary as you may be in close proximity of others.

Hopefully you will have another member of the team following the bus in a car to act as your back up. From the bus you want to communicate with your back up so you will instigate the conversation by giving four clicks (ask me a question). Your back up should hear the clicks and respond.

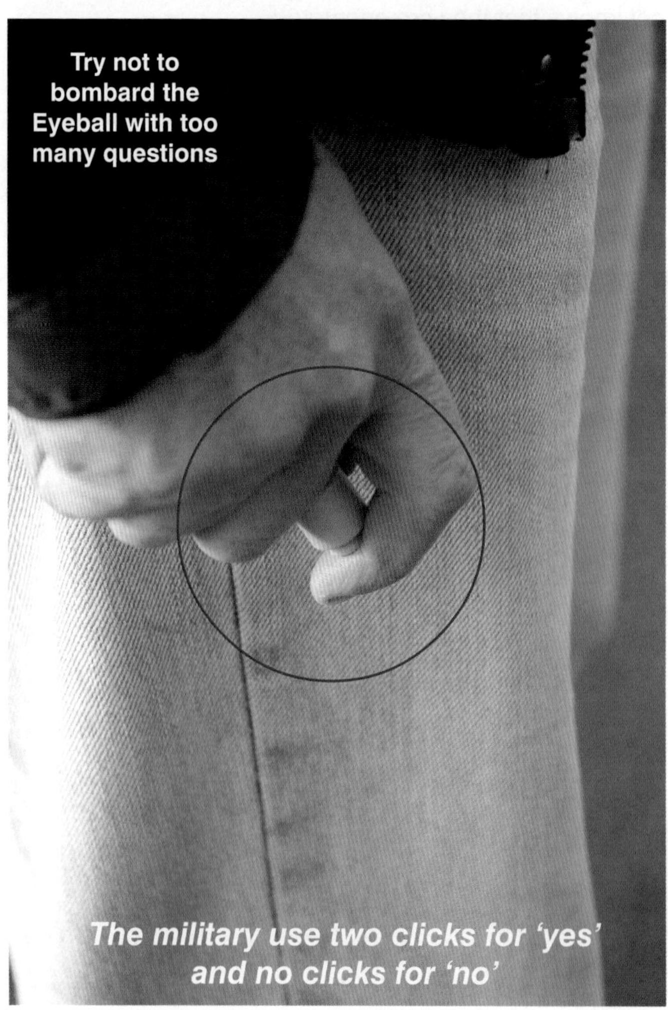

**Try not to bombard the Eyeball with too many questions**

***The military use two clicks for 'yes' and no clicks for 'no'***

Antennas can be custom built to blend-in with the vehicle

**'Four clicks received, are you okay?'**

To which you respond with three clicks (Yes)

**'Three clicks received, do you have control of the Alpha 1?'**

Click, Click, Click (Yes)

**'Is the target with anyone?'**

Click, Click (No)

**'Roger that, two clicks received. Can you give a standby when the target gets off the bus?'**

Click, Click, Click (Yes)

**'Three clicks received, roger that, do you want anymore questions?'.**

Click, Click (No)

A few minutes later you may want an up date on the situation.

**'Is there any change?'.**

Click, Click (No)

**'Roger that, two clicks - no change'.**

When the target makes a move to get off the bus, you need to give a standby and this is done by a series of rapid clicks to which your back up should acknowledge with,

**'Roger that, rapid clicks, Standby Standby.'**

Be careful not to bombard the eyeball with unnecessary questions. The eyeball may be in a position where he is trying to overhear conversation or remember certain facts. The last thing he wants is someone gibbering over the net into his earpiece at the wrong time.

Remember, you can only ask direct questions which require a Yes or No answer.

**Care of Your Radios**

Your radios are the backbone to your surveillance and so you have to take care of them to ensure that you get the most out of them and that you can rely on them at all times.

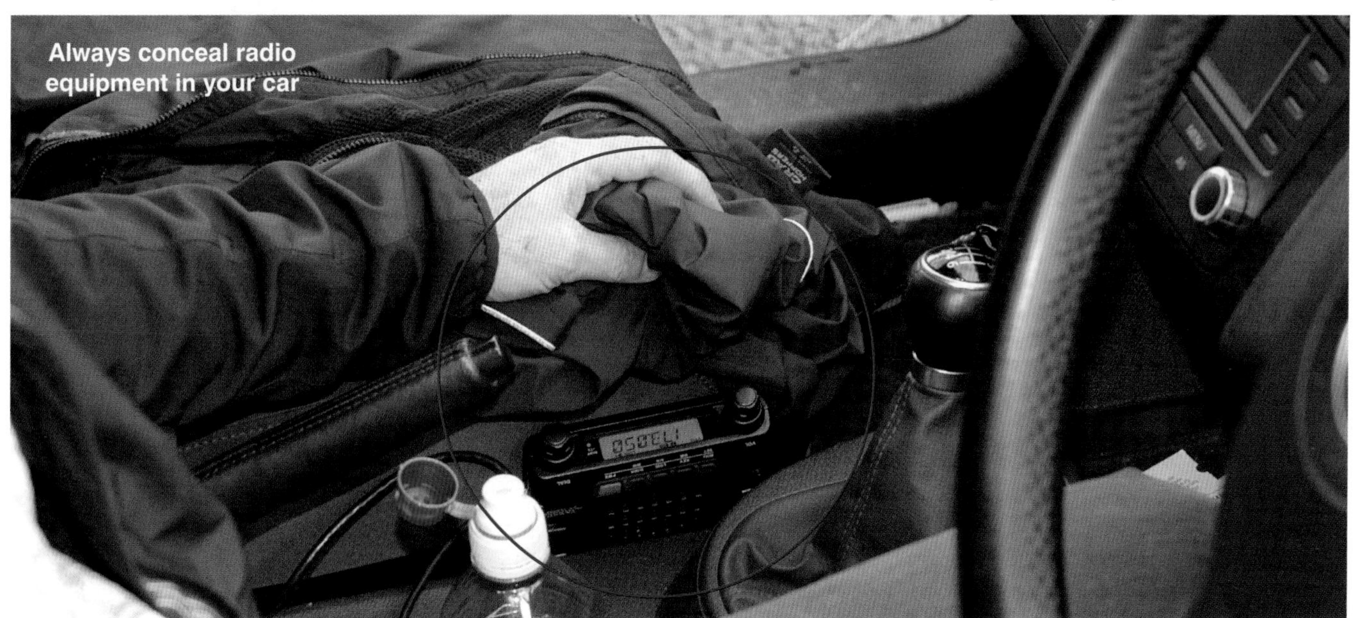
Always conceal radio equipment in your car

- Always keep them clean and dry
- Do not let them get wet
- Never switch the set on unless there is an antenna fitted, you will damage it
- Fully discharge the battery before recharging
- Switch the set off when changing batteries or any other ancillaries
- Be careful when removing ancillaries, you may damage connections and sockets
- Try not to bend or crease the wires in your covert loops and inductors
- Regularly check loose antenna screws and cables that may have become 'pinched' after being trapped in car doors
- Clean and check earpiece wax traps

*Say exactly what you see, say it calmly, clearly with precision and at the correct time...*

**Best Practice**

The best practice in surveillance commentary is to say exactly what you see, say it calmly, clearly with precision and at the correct time. Always listen to the radio net before transmitting as there is nothing worse than being in the middle of a transmission when someone else steps right on top of you when they should have waited.

It is not always essential to use codes and brevity but they do help speed up what you are trying to put across. There is no such thing as right or wrong in 'surveillance speak'. Each agency, organisation or company has its own way so if it works for you, it works. The style of commentary used throughout this book is the one generally used by most surveillance operators working the security circuit in the UK.

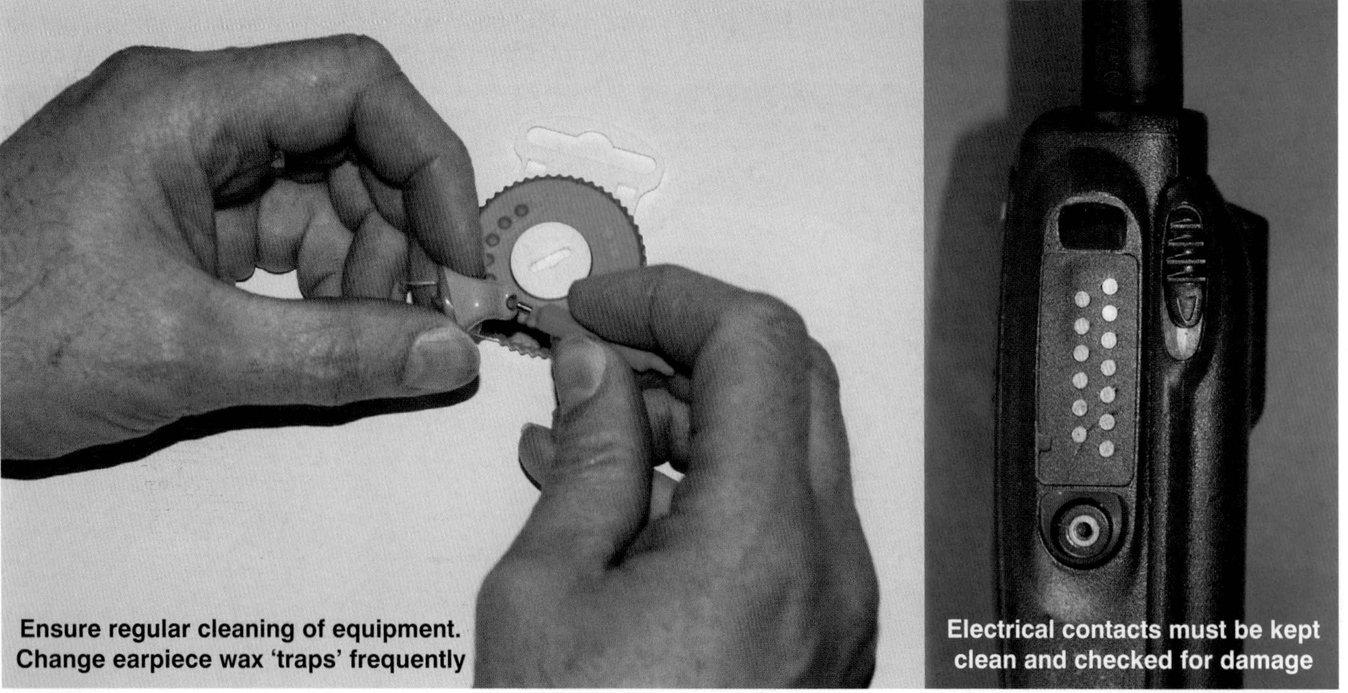

**Ensure regular cleaning of equipment. Change earpiece wax 'traps' frequently**

**Electrical contacts must be kept clean and checked for damage**

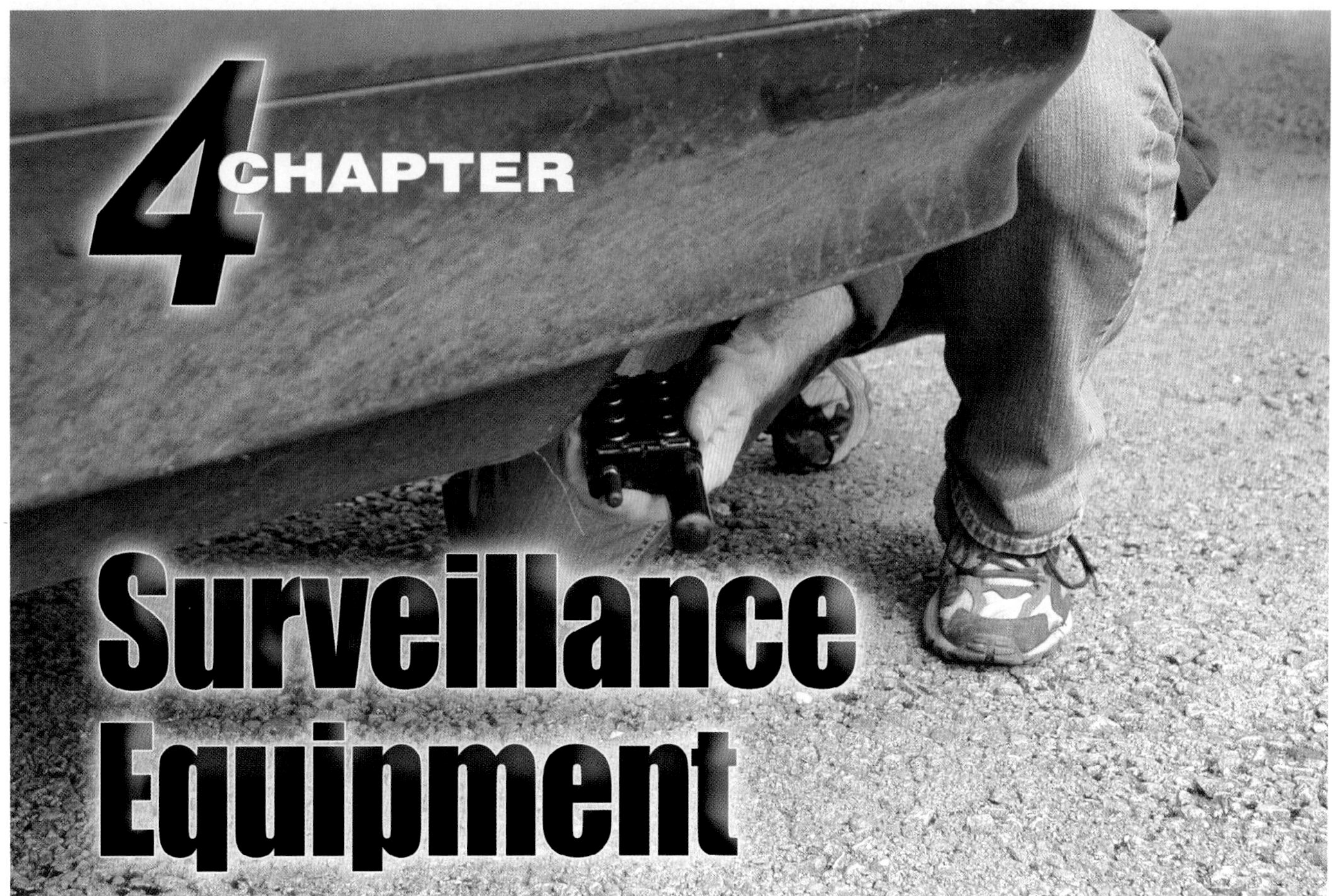


The essential equipment that you need to operate effectively can be obtained for around £1,500. Equipment has to be cost effective, long lasting, efficient and most importantly, reliable. It is not always the best policy to buy a cheap alternative if the success of the surveillance relies upon it. Rightly or wrongly, in the commercial world, you are only as good as your last job so you need to get it right every time. Most surveillance operators make use of a small 'car bag' which is easily portable and carried to and from vehicles, hotels and the office.

The minimum equipment an operator should carry on his person or in his vehicle should be:

- *Radio*
- *Memo Recorder*
- *Log Sheets or Note Book*
- *Camera (Video, Stills or both)*
- *Binoculars*
- *Mobile Phone*
- *Money*
- *Penlight Torch*
- *Maps & Satnav*
- *Identification or Driving Licence*
- *First Aid Kit*

**Radio Equipment**

Communications are a very important factor in surveillance work where investigators have to work as a team. Therefore it is essential that the correct equipment is fitted into the vehicle and on your person in the event you have to deploy on foot.

**Memo Recorders**

Digital memo recorders are a must and are ideal for recording events as they happen, especially when you do not have time to write down notes during a mobile surveillance. I do not recommend recording the whole days events, only record when activity occurs. The digital memo recorders can have a date and time stamp on them so that you can refer to the time a recording was made.

You should transfer your recorded notes as soon as possible to a hand written log.

**Log Sheets or Note Book**

Dedicated log sheets or a notebook should be kept as described in the chapter on Evidence. It is handy to have your logs attached to a small clipboard.

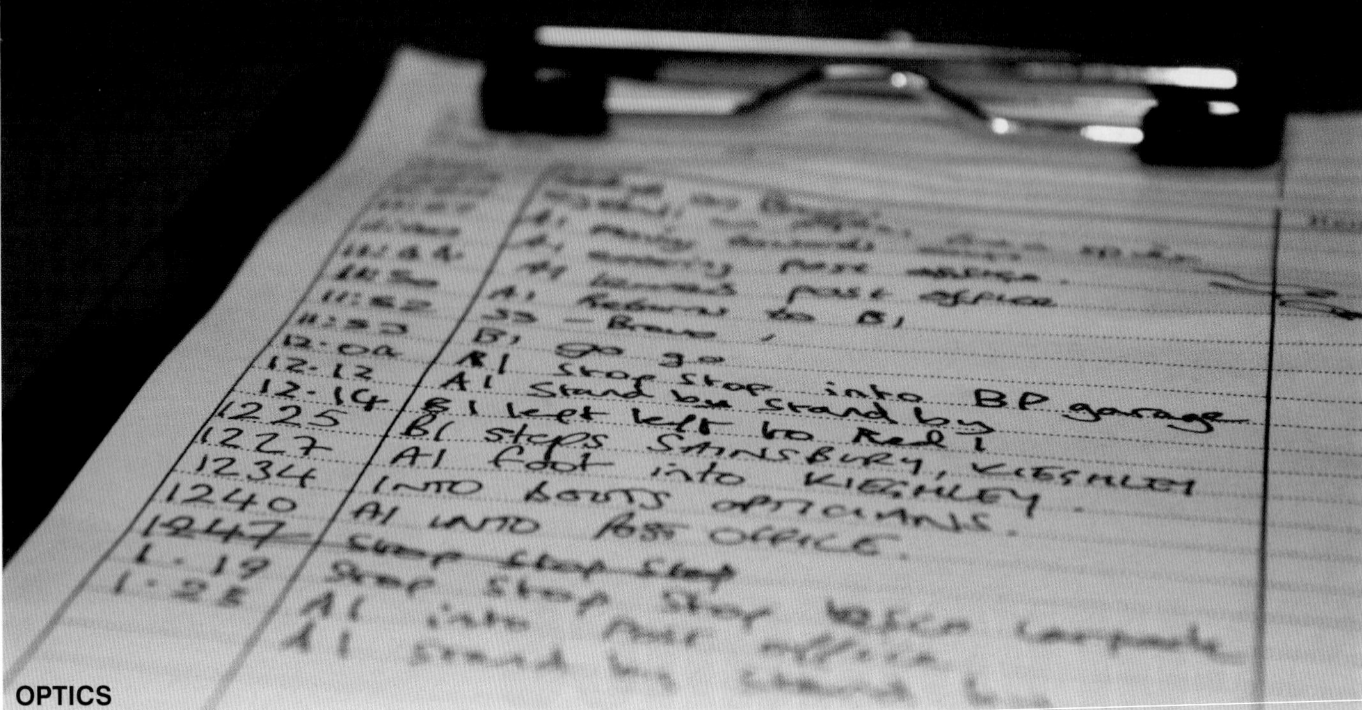

## OPTICS

As an aid to your vision and to bring your subject closer, various optical instruments are available, they should be handled with care and the lenses should be protected at all times.

### Binoculars

There are many different types of binoculars available and a pair should be selected for their cost, robustness, size and magnification. It is not always the best thing to opt for the most powerful pair you can lay your hands on, nor the smallest pair. Many people think that the smaller they are, the more covert they will be but at the end of the day, you still have to lift your hands up to your face in order to use them - whatever size they are.

These are stabilised binoculars - but very expensive

### • Magnification

The power of a pair of binoculars refers to the number of times the subject in view is magnified. Lenses with a power of 'times 8' (8x) magnify the subject by bringing it 8 times closer. This has the effect of making an object which is 400 metres away appear to be only 50 metres away.

Binoculars are commonly quoted with a magnification number such as 8 x 25. As mentioned, the 8x refers to the lens magnification, the 25 relates to the diameter in millimetres of the objective lens (the larger lens at the front). This is important as the larger the objective lens is, the more effective they will be in low light. If you intend to use your binoculars mostly in the dark hours such as dusk and dawn, then the larger the objective lens the better.

A magnification of about 10 times is suitable for most purposes. Any higher could result in sore eyes and headaches if used for long periods of time and holding them steady may be a problem without a tripod or mount.

### • Field of View

The field of view may be referred to in an instruction booklet. This is the extent of the view to the left and right as you look straight ahead. It is expressed in either degrees or in metres at a range of 1000 metres. That is to say that a field of view of 70 degrees will show you 70 metres of landscape at 1000 metres distant. Or, in other words, 35m

using a zoom lens always initially focus close in, and then pull out of the zoom to the required setting.

**Lens Hoods**

When viewing a subject always be aware of the position of the sun. If the sun is to your front, remember that any direct sunlight entering the optics will also be magnified and may cause eye damage and blindness. The light may also be reflected off the lens and be seen to glint by your target. To remedy this, use a piece of fine dark netting (or stocking) held over the lens with an elastic band. A good piece of kit originally designed for snipers and hunters is SunGuards 'KillFlash', a specially made guard that fits onto the lens to cut down reflections.

to the left of the axis and 35m to the right. The greater the magnification the less is the field of view.

**Telescopes or Spotting Scopes**

Telescopes are ideal when in a static location and you require more viewing power than binoculars. The magnification/lens size guides are the same as for binoculars. However, with a more powerful scope the field of view may be quite narrow and thus 'shake' is more pronounced. In this case it will need to be tripod mounted especially in an OP for a long period of time.

Many telescopes utilise a zoom facility which enables you to range the power from 8x through to 25x and upwards. If

**Money**

Cash should always be carried and a handful of change should always be left in the car for car parks, tolls and public transport.

**Torch**

A small penlight torch is useful for map reading or note taking at night and will save your night vision more than if you put on the interior light. If the torch beam is too bright, cover it with a piece of sticky tape to diffuse it.

## SAFETY KIT

***If you have a small compartment in the floor of your car or in the boot, they are good for storing safety equipment that you do not use often. Items such as: tow rope, jump leads, high-visibility vest, space blanket, first aid kit, chemical lightsticks, screenwash, torch, water, safety light, voltage inverter, de-icer, ice-scraper, multi-tool kit, hand-wipes, spade and tyre weld.***

## ISS CASE

A four-man surveillance team were following skip trucks belonging to a waste company. Whenever one of the trucks made a drop, one of the team had to remain behind and get a photograph of it in situ. This meant that one operator would always be left behind for a short while. Having a Satnav was a life saver, especially when the team were now quite a distance away after the target made many left and right turns.

To hear on the radio net, '..that's gone right right into Gibraltar Crescent..'. really helped. I just typed the street name into the Satnav and followed the directions, as I got closer the radio signal got stronger and I was soon back with the team.

A large 'Maglite' type torch is strong and durable and handy for emergencies at night. It can also double up as a means of protection if the need arises.

**Maps and Satellite Navigation**

Maps are a must in surveillance, whether they are A-Z street maps or larger scale 1:50,000 Ordnance Survey maps. Satnavs such as a Tom Tom or Garmin are worth their weight in gold these days especially if you are at the back of a mobile team and trying to play catch up. Satnavs also give you important information such as traffic cameras, car parks and one way systems.

Try and use your Satnav in 2D mode or 'birds eye' view rather than 3D or 'oblique' (as pictured below). This way you will be able to identify the street layout, cut-throughs and parallels in the vicinity. Try and keep the devices off the windscreen and put them covertly somewhere on the dashboard (a lump of 'Blu-Tack' always helps). At night, remember to adjust the brightness of the screen so not to illuminate your face.

A Satnav is a must if working abroad as well as at home

**Identification Cards**

Most people carry some form of identification and it may be wise to carry your driving licence with you during surveillance. Inevitably, you will be stopped by the Police from time to time who will ask for some form of identification. If you have your licence with you, not only are you able to show who you are but you also minimise the risk of being asked to produce your licence and any other documents at a later time at a Police station. If you belong to a trade association such as the 'Association of British Investigators' or have a business card, then carry these with you also.

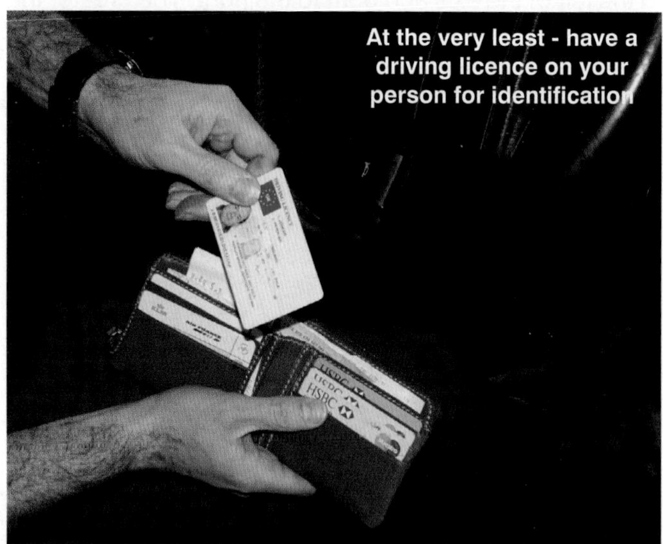

At the very least - have a driving licence on your person for identification

### NIGHT VISION OPTICS

Night vision equipment or image intensifiers as they are known, are easily obtained these days and can be bought quite cheaply. They come in various forms but the main types are single mono scopes or goggles that fit over the face.

The image intensifying optics rely on the available light in the sky (which the eye cannot see in darkness) which comes from stars, moonlight, clouds and glow. The intensifier magnifies the available light by millions of times to produce an image. When viewed, the image is seen in shades of contrasting green, white and black.

Image intensifiers can also 'see' infra red light and can be used in conjunction with an 'invisible' infra red light source.

Courtesy: www.flir.com

**Thermal imaging has its advantages over image intensifiers**

**During daylight thermal imagers will also identify people who are concealed and camouflaged in undergrowth. They can also identify people in buildings**

**The H-Series portable thermal imaging camera from Flir Systems Ltd**

## THERMAL IMAGING

This enables viewing in shadows and areas of low light. Never switch on or use these devices in daylight - unless they are fitted with the correct filters as the internal components will be damaged.

Ensure that you take care of the eyepiece, quite often this comprises of a little rubber flap that closes when you remove it from your eye. This prevents loss of light so does not give your position away in the event that your target is also using night scopes. Night scopes will also ruin your night vision in the eye that you are using to view through, so be aware of not being able to see clearly through that eye for a while.

Many light intensifying scopes can be attached to SLR cameras and Camcorders using specially designed fittings. These provide very good quality low light imagery and are described more in the chapter on digital photography.

Also available are infrared imagers, these do not intensify the available light but require an infrared light source for them to operate. Yukon's 'Ranger' night vision scope is reasonably cheap, offers a 5x magnification and can be used up to 500 metres in the dark. The unit appears to have two lenses like a pair of binoculars but in fact only one is the lens, the other is the IR illuminator. These optics also have a video output so that you can connect them to a digital DVR for recording events.

**Pyser's PNP Night vision scope is excellent for attaching to a still or video camera**

A high-end military and enforcement grade image intensifier - around £5,000

Night vision images showing surveillance targets - in this case a barge and house

A very low-cost image intensifier - around £200

Infrared beacon used to illuminate shadowed areas

### Infra Red Lighting

As already mentioned, infra red light from a torch fitted with a special IR filter enhances the performance of image intensifiers. Other devices are available which can be used for covert applications. Infra red light waves are normally transmitted at either 850nm or 950nm wavelengths. A floodlight transmitting on 850nm will give off a slightly red glow signature which is not 100% covert as opposed to 950nm which is invisible to the naked eye and totally covert.

- **IR Floodlight**

This floodlight requires 12volts to operate but effectively floods an area of approximately 20 metres away with invisible IR light. It is fitted with a light sensor which enables it to shut down during daylight which is useful if operating it from a 12v battery.

The Yukon Ranger is an infrared scope rather than an image intensifier. A DVR can be attached for video recording

An infrared filter has been attached to this torch allowing it to emit invisible IR light

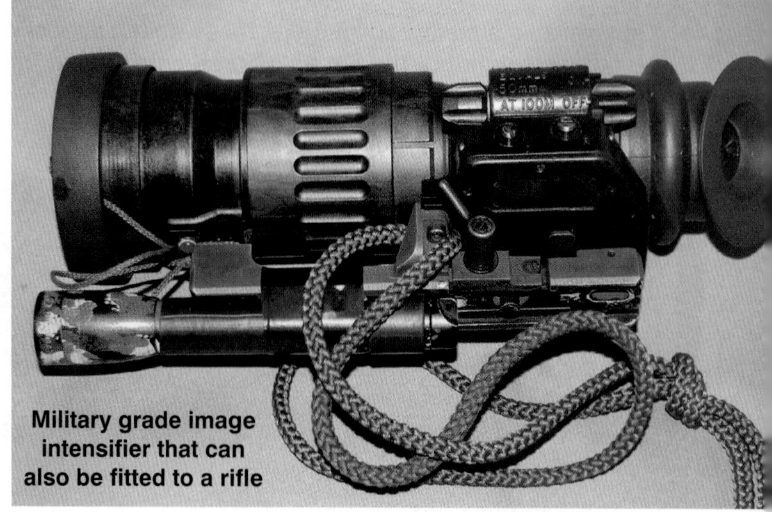

Military grade image intensifier that can also be fitted to a rifle

IR - light sticks help you see in shadows and dark areas

• **IR Beacon**

This small device, the size of a match box emits infra red light from a series of diodes. This beacon is battery powered and can last for four days, providing enough IR light to illuminate a small sized area such as a doorway or a small room. This beacon can be concealed in a target area to be viewed and then observed from a distance.

• **Chemical Lightsticks**

Chemical Lightsticks (manufactured by Cyalume) provide a disposable invisible light source. These lightsticks are in the form of a sealed plastic tube containing chemicals. When activated they produce an intense light source and last for about eight hours.

An infra red version is available and when activated nothing can be seen by the naked eye. When viewed through an image intensifier it will illuminate a small area with invisible light. Again, these are particularly useful illuminating dark doorways or marking access routes when retrieval of the light source is not paramount.

## VEHICLE TRACKING EQUIPMENT

Vehicle tracking devices are playing more of a role in support of conventional surveillance these days. Not only are they freely available, they are reasonably cheap to purchase and a cost effective way of carrying out surveillance. They are extremely accurate but it must be remembered that technical equipment has limitations, it is prone to failure and the information that the device provides only tells you where the vehicle is. It does not provide any other information about the Target's activities.

Essentially, there are two types of trackers: **Passive** and **Active.**

**Passive trackers** are attached to a vehicle (or products) and store data such as locations, speeds and directions of where they are. These trackers cannot be interrogated nor do they send data to you for live tracking. They have to be removed from the vehicle at a later date and the data is then downloaded into a computer for analysis.

**Active trackers** can be fitted to a vehicle and report its location and status to you live as it happens or when you request it. These devices normally contain a SIM card as they use the mobile phone network to communicate to your mapping software on a computer, a server or to your mobile phone.

**Why Use Trackers?**

There is nothing better than having actual 'eyes on' the target. A good surveillance team will be able to keep control of the target by always having him in view but this is not always possible. We tend to use trackers for the following reasons:

- *To monitor routine activity*
- *To monitor activity of an aware target*
- *To recover after a total loss*
- *To provide a trigger and keep control when 'Un-sighted'*
- *To track the movements of products*

Spy-Craft supplies a very small tracker called the Enduro which can operate for up to 90 days

• **To monitor routine activity**

Surveillance can be costly in terms of manpower, resources and expense, therefore if you can achieve a result by deploying a tracker you will save a lot of time, a lot of effort and your clients money. Trackers may be used at the start of an investigation to establish patterns of movement and areas visited by the target, which may then warrant further and more detailed investigation or conventional surveillance on a particular day or time.

Some Enforcement Agencies who have to comply with RIPA, may argue that they would deploy a tracker in order to display that the surveillance is 'proportionate'. By this, it would be less proportionate to deploy a tracker on a target for a week than to have 4 cars and 8 people with cameras following him around for the same period.

• **To monitor activity of an aware target**

An aware target is likely to carry out anti surveillance drills in order to detect surveillance and those that may be following him. He is also likely to drive at excessive speeds in order to detach himself from surveillance. Therefore a target can carry out as many drills as he wants to, check his rear view mirrors all day and even deploy counter surveillance but a tracker placed on the car will always have him under control.

Trackers fitted to a vehicle can also minimise risks to surveillance teams from harm. Many Enforcement Agencies, even the Police, have to conduct risk assessments in order to minimise dangers in what is a hazardous occupation. If an aware target identifies surveillance, the team may be attacked; led into a trap, or forced to drive dangerously in urban areas.

• **To recover after a total loss**

If you have a target that is in and out of very busy traffic in city centres where there is high risk of losing him, a tracker may be installed to act as a back up to conventional surveillance. If you lose sight of him, it is no problem to request a position and control is regained within a short space of time.

Students being taught how to deploy and recover trackers at ISS Training

I know of some commercial investigators that carry out single handed surveillance together with the deployment of a tracker. This way, they can keep their distance to avoid being spotted and if they have a loss, they can quickly pick up the target again via the tracker.

- **To provide a trigger and keep control when 'Un-sighted'**

It may be that the target resides in a rural area or even an urban area which is very difficult to trigger. A tracker can be installed so that as soon as the vehicle moves, it sends a report to the operator so the team can be put on standby. The vehicle can then be tracked technically until one of the team picks it up conventionally and the surveillance commences.

More time spent under the vehicle gives you more time to find an optimum place for deployment

In addition, if the target were to enter an area which is out of bounds to a surveillance or it is deemed too dangerous or risky to the team, the tracker can come into its own and the task can be carried out technically. Let's say that you are on a team following a vehicle which turns off the main road and enters a forestry block or continues up a long narrow track. To send one car behind it to keep control is risking compromise so this would be an ideal time to interrogate the tracker live.

Live monitoring can now take place and an accurate radio commentary be given by the person with the controlling laptop. He will be able to give the speed, changes in direction and any stops or starts as they happen, whilst the surveillance team position themselves to 'box' in the target. When the target moves and breaks the box, the team can then pick him up and continue conventionally. If the target stops in the forest, you will be able to identify where the stop took place by obtaining a latitude/longitude co-ordinate. Later, you can revisit the exact location by programming a Satnav to get you there.

- **To track the movements of products**

Trackers are not only used to track vehicles. Due to their small size, they can also be used to track products being shipped anywhere in the world. Trackers will operate if they have sufficient power and they can receive a signal from the navigational satellites.

## HOW DO PASSIVE TRACKERS WORK?

These trackers are very small and can operate for up to three weeks or more on one set of batteries. One model, the Trackingkey, is fairly inexpensive and easy to operate. After installing a good set of batteries. The device will need to see the sky for approximately 15 minutes to get a good fix from the satellites.

It can then be placed in or under a vehicle and left for a number of weeks. After retrieval, it is plugged into the USB port on a computer and the data can be transferred using the supplied software. It can be read in two ways, one by bringing up internet based mapping such as 'Google Earth' over which it lays a trail of the route the vehicle has taken, indicating the stops it made. The other way is to view the file (.HTML file) that opens up in a browser, such as Firefox or Explorer which details all of the journey information. You are also able to click on the reports co-ordinates and if online, you are taken to Google Maps displaying an aerial image of exactly where the vehicle stopped. This HTML file can be printed, emailed or saved.

***Thursday, November 08, 2007***
*Departed From :* [illegible]
*Arrived At :* [illegible]
*Total Driving Time : 16 minutes, 24 seconds*
*Total Mileage Driven : 9.9 miles*
*Maximum Speed : 53.4 mph*

| Departed | Driving Time | Arrived | Location Arrived | Distance (Miles) | Stopped Time |
|---|---|---|---|---|---|
| 07:41:10pm | 09m:52s | 07:51:02pm | [illegible] | 5.0 | 1h:39m:47s |
| 09:30:49pm | 06m:32s | 09:37:21pm | [illegible] | 4.9 | 1days 16h: 12m:28s |

***Saturday, November 10, 2007***
*Departed From :* [illegible]
*Arrived At :* [illegible]
*Total Driving Time : 1 hours, 42 minutes, 6 seconds*
*Total Mileage Driven : 36.9 miles*
*Maximum Speed : 68.4 mph*

| Departed | Driving Time | Arrived | Location Arrived | Distance (Miles) | Stopped Time |
|---|---|---|---|---|---|
| 01:49:47pm | 39m:48s | 02:28:35pm | [illegible] | 12.3 | 1h:20m:39s |
| 03:59:14pm | 29m:15s | 04:28:29pm | [illegible] | 4.5 | 14m:05s |
| 04:42:34pm | 03m:43s | 04:46:17pm | [illegible] | 2.5 | 24m:37s |
| 05:10:54pm | 06m:43s | 05:17:37pm | [illegible] | 3.3 | 47m:51s |
| 06:05:28pm | 22m:37s | 06:28:05pm | [illegible] | 14.4 | 20h:26m:46s |

**A sample tracking report from a passive tracker**

***Whatever you do, do not insert the batteries or switch on the device at your office or home and then drive to your target. Should the device be found and compromised, the target will be able to track back where the journey started!***

**How do Active trackers work?**

There are a few different types of active trackers, which use different ways of communicating to the operator.

The device takes readings from the satellites every few seconds and stores the location data in its memory. Depending on how the device is configured, it will either continue storing the data until you send a request signal to it, or it will constantly feed you the data so that you have 'live' tracking.

The device will have a SIM card built into it, which is how it reports back to the operator over the mobile phone network. The operator will have a computer with a SIM card modem and dedicated mapping software in order to track the vehicles movements. Alternatively, the device will report to the manufacturer's computer server. If this is the case, the operator has to be online so that he can log onto the server and view the journey.

The device needs to 'see the sky' in order to get a signal from the satellites and it will receive the signals through plastic, wood and fabric but not metal, therefore, care has to be taken when placing the device. In addition, it needs a phone signal in order for it to operate and send the co-ordinates back to you. Should the device go into an area with a poor phone signal it will continue to store the location data but only push them to you when a good signal is regained.

Some of the cheaper devices are less sophisticated. You send the device a text message from your mobile phone and within a few seconds you get a reply containing the location co-ordinates and speed. You then have to drop these co-ordinates into Google's mapping browser (on a computer or mobile phone) and the map displays the location of the tracker.

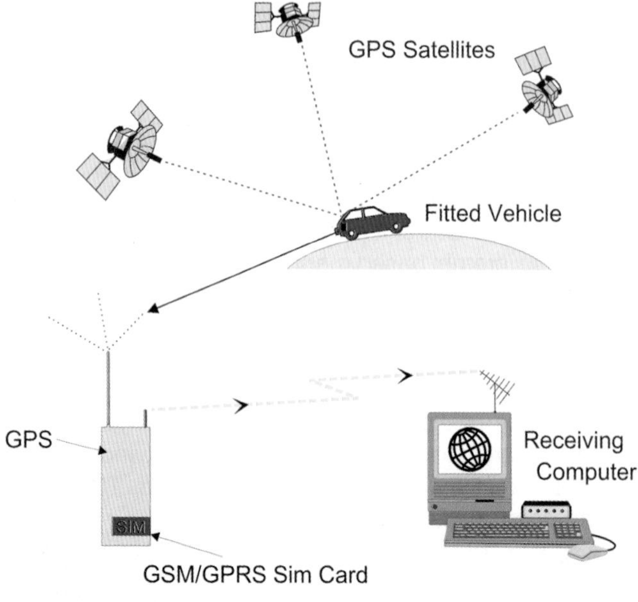


**The results from an active tracker can be monitored live on either a map or aerial image**

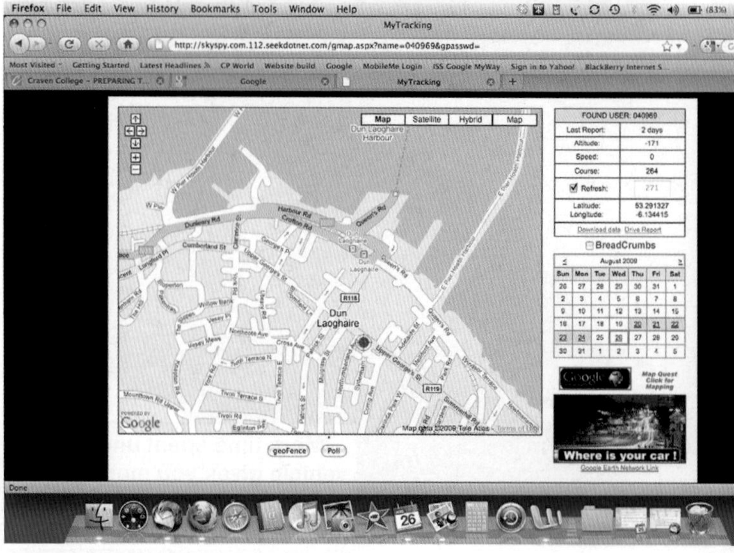

## TRACKER DEPLOYMENT

Prior to deploying a tracker, there are certain checks to be made to prevent compromise or losing the device.

If possible, examine a car the same make and model of your targets to identify where the device can be placed. The time 'on target' has to be minimal and quick when it is deployed

Check that the targets car is roadworthy and not likely to be in a garage having its exhaust repaired, the tracker might be seen by a mechanic

Do not touch the car, you may activate an alarm or leave a sign on dirty bodywork

Ensure the magnets have got a good hold. Use a cable tie if you are not confident it will hold in position

Ensure the batteries are fully charged

Ensure that it is switched on and operating correctly immediately prior to deployment. Erase any prior or historical data from the device

Deploy the device in a public space rather than on private property (trespass)

Check that you can still communicate to it after deployment, if not it may have to be recovered straight away

Keep an eye on the battery state. If it gets to 30%, consider taking steps to retrieve it or replace the batteries

Do not place it near the exhaust pipe or it will be damaged and do not place it under wheel arches

Make a written note of where it is placed, someone else may have to retrieve it

### Alternative Ways of Tracking

#### • Personal Tracker

Another device on the market in the UK is the TR-101 'Personal Tracker' manufactured by 'GlobalSat Technology' and costs in the region of £130.00. This is actually a mobile phone with a GPS built into it but you can only store 3 telephone numbers into it, which are assigned to a speed dial number. Quite simply, you send the device a text, it automatically sends you one back with the co-ordinating data which you drop into Google Earth or similar. If you are carrying the device and you get into trouble, you can press and hold the alert button down; the alert button assigns a recipients mobile telephone number and an alert is automatically sent with your location on it. The recipient can then dial the trackers number and you can have a voice conversation. If weatherproofed and concealed covertly on a vehicle, it is a very cheap way of carrying out live tracking.

**TR-101 'Personal Tracker'**

#### • Mobile Phone

A cheaper and improvised way of tracking is to use a mobile phone. Take an old mobile phone and install a 'prepay' or 'pay as you go' SIM card into it with some credit

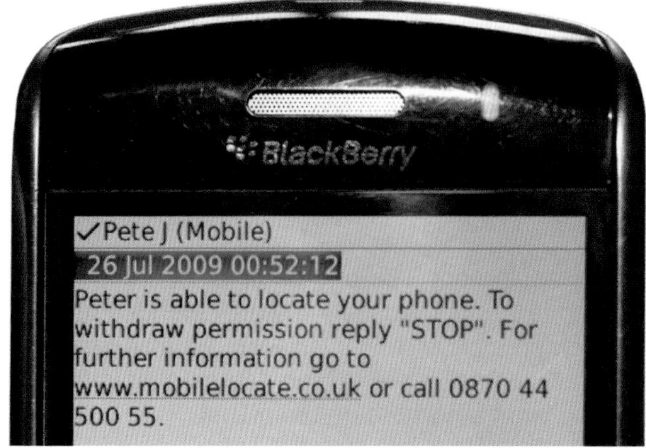

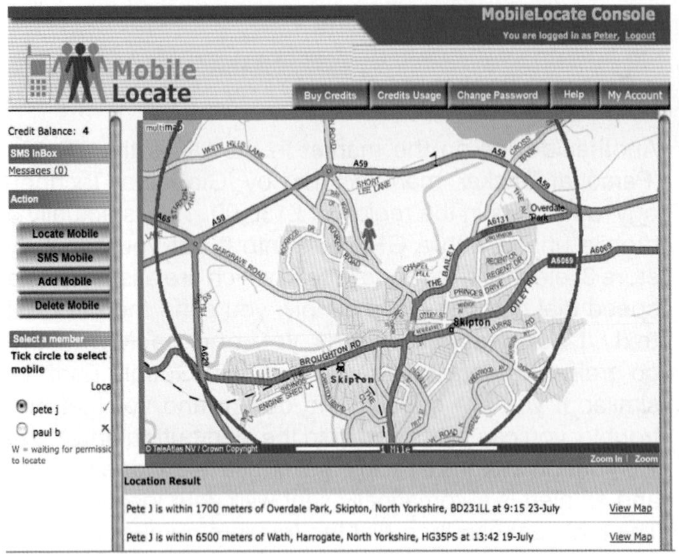


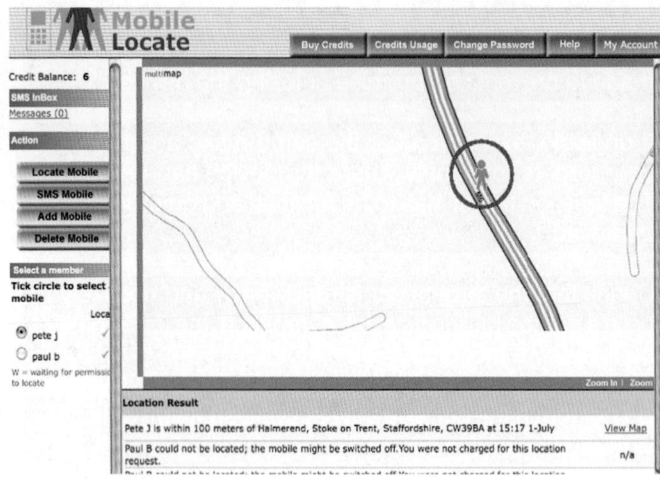


**Screen shots from mobile phone tracking - the picture on the right is of an accurate 'fix' due to the close proximity of a mast**

on it (to avoid contracts). Then register online with a tracking provider such as **www.mobilelocate.co.uk** or **www.verilocation.com.** For a small registration fee and a small fee every time you want to locate the phone, it provides a useful alternative option.

When registering the phone, an initial security password is sent to it by text in order to marry up the phone with the account holder. As an additional security precaution, the phone being tracked is randomly sent a text notifying the user that the phone is being tracked. This is to prevent abuse and the unauthorised tracking of a persons phone without them knowing.

However, to use this as a vehicle tracker, you register it and conceal it in a car. It does not have to see the sky as it does not use GPS to obtain a location. Its life will depend on the battery and how much it is used but you should get at least four days tracking unless you use a modified car charger to connect it to the vehicle power supply.

If you want to know where your children are and they have mobile phones, this is the way to do it but remember they will be sent random texts reminding them that the phone is being tracked.

The accuracy is varied as in some urban areas (where there are more masts) you may get a fix radius down to about 100m. In more rural areas the radius could be as wide as 3km.

Tracking equipment, like any other electronic device is subject to failure and so it should only be used as an aid or to back up a physical surveillance. What is frightening about satellite tracking is its high degree of accuracy and that it can work anywhere on the planet.

**Technical Triggers**

When it is not possible to observe and trigger a target (for one of many reasons) it would be advantageous to have a system that gives prior warning of the vehicle going mobile. The surveillance team may then be put on 'Standby' and be covering their 'areas' in order to pick up the vehicle for a follow.

A device marketed as the 'Go Tag' can be covertly attached to the underside of a vehicle by magnets or can be wired into the vehicle itself. Approximately two inches square, the device remains dormant until the vibration of the starting engine activates a transmitter, which can be received from some 500 metres away.

The transmitted signal is received on a unit such as a scanner (held by an operator) which gives a bleeping tone when activated. The operator can then put the surveillance team on 'standby' and await the target going 'mobile'.

**The 'Go-Tag' device**

## ISS CASE

The 'Meerkat' was used when we had a rural OP watching a quarry where illegal dumping of waste was taking place. The access gate was some 350m away and could not be seen, so the Meerkat was deployed to cover the gate. When a vehicle arrived and entered, the OP team were alerted of its arrival and were able to crawl forward from their lie up position to a closer observation point and obtain video of the vehicle in the quarry.

### The Meerkat

The 'Meerkat' is a piece of equipment that can give you early warning of movement for a trigger or it can be used as an early warning of intruders, especially if you are in an OP and you need to cover the area to the rear of your position.

The device is weatherproofed and can be buried or concealed in undergrowth. It comprises of a PIR detector which senses movement and is connected to a 5 watt radio transmitter. When movement is detected, a series of clicks are transmitted over the radio net to alert you. It is also fitted with a microphone so that you can listen in to the activity, if required.

### Vehicle Locking Immobiliser

A very ingenious device which is custom made, is a small transmitting unit that immobilises a cars remote locking/unlocking system. When switched on and placed in the vicinity of a car, it will disable any radio remote controlled locking system within 15 metres of it.

Why is this useful to surveillance? It can provide a surveillance team with an additional few seconds on a standby in order to take a good quality identification shot. If you are using video, by the time you have switched on your camera, pressed record and have actually started filming, the target is often already into the car and the photo opportunity is lost.

With this device, the target approaches the car pressing the remote key fob but the doors do not unlock. Trials have shown that men take at least 30 - 35 seconds attempting to open the car with a remote as they walk around it. Women take about 15 seconds before they give up and put the key in the door!

Vehicle locking immobiliser

Although, the faulty locking system could alert an aware target, it is more likely that he will presume that the batteries are flat in the remote. This device placed under the target car with magnets, will ensure that you get a delay every time. If an Enforcement Agency needs to effect an arrest, this device can give them a head start to move into position.

Please note that these devices are not licensed for use in the United Kingdom.

## SURVEILLANCE VANS

An important piece of equipment is the surveillance van, the majority of surveillances that I take part in, will have a van on the team. Primarily the van can be used to provide the 'trigger' for a mobile surveillance. As a static observation post the operator can observe, record and report events taking place outside for many hours.

The type of van is very much up to personal preference but it should not be too big. It should not be a high vehicle as it will stand out above the rest in a car park or a line of traffic. From the front and rear it should look like a car and therefore may also be used for mobile surveillance.

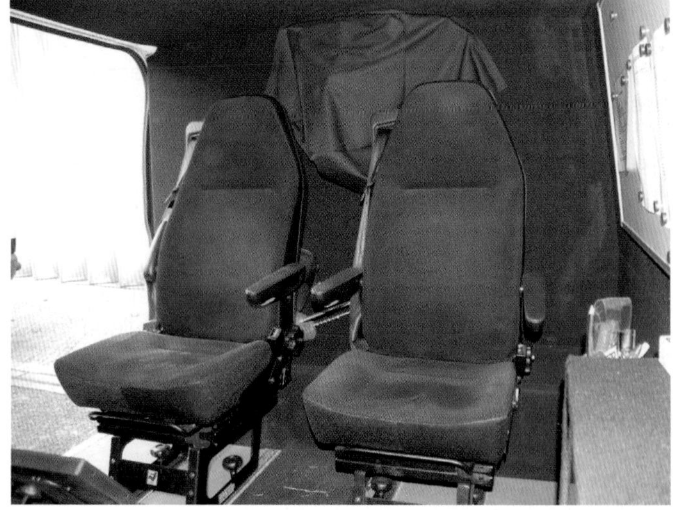

**Colour**

Which colour should your van be? If it is white will it stand out, or should it be a dark colour? The choice is yours, where dark vans will not stand out as much, a white van can be used just as well as there are many of them about. The van can be left plain or magnetic removable signs can be used to change its appearance.

***These micro drones supplied by MW Power Systems can fly for up to an hour with a range of 5km. They are virtually silent and can carry an array of still cameras, live video or thermal imagers***

If you decide to use magnetic advertising signs ('Jim's Electrical' for example) consider adding a mobile telephone number to it. If any curious third party decides to ring the number to enquire about the suspicious van in the street, you will be called and alerted to their curiosity and be able to provide them with a suitable response.

**Observation**

Obviously you will need to be able to observe your target without them being able to see you. The rear windows of the van should be covered with a film that gives you the ability to look out without anyone being able to see in. Many different types are available and come in roll form from car accessory dealers.

This 'Mirror Tint', comes in colours of silver, gold and blue. When applied, visibility out is near perfect whilst from the outside it is almost impossible to see in, unless noses are pressed against the glass or in certain light conditions. Many tradesmen's vans have this film fitted and so it does not always stand out or appear odd.

Another film similar to mirror tint is the Smoke Tint. This is black in colour and is just as effective when the inside of the van is made light proof from the front. The smoke tint is preferable as it does not tend to stand out as much as the reflective mirror.

Another alternative is to have a false wall built at the rear doors through which you will be able to observe.

If viewing through an aperture ensure your camera is not shiny. Black tape is useful in concealing the unit

A surveillance van provides an excellent trigger platform

Ideally, if any suspicious persons can see right through the van it will satisfy their curiosity that no one is in there.

The rear of the van also has to be made light proof from the front for the reflective windows to be effective. Plywood, or a curtain suspended from a rail behind the drivers seat, is sufficient. This also gives you the ability to view through the front and side windows when necessary.

**Windows and Vision**

Your surveillance van needs to be operational in all weathers. A rear windscreen wiper is essential in the event of rain. You should be able to operate it from within and without the ignition being switched on. The exterior glass can also be treated with 'Rain X Rain Repellent' or 'Jewel Ultra Rain Screen' which prevents rain from sticking to the glass so that you can see out clearly.

Likewise in cold or damp weather the inside of the window is likely to mist up, therefore the screen de-mister should be rewired to enable it to be operated in the same way. If your vehicle is going to be adapted it would be recommended to use a secondary battery rather than the vehicles primary battery so you do not run the vehicle battery flat.

Some van operators use a 12 volt hairdryer obtained from camping shops, attached to a spare battery. This gets rid of condensation after a minutes blast of warm air. Alternately, you can use a special fluid from motorcycle shops or motor valet suppliers called 'Rain-X Anti Fog'. This prevents helmet visors from misting up and when applied to the insides of the windows is quite effective.

If you have to improvise, put a small amount of washing up liquid on a cloth and wipe over the window; it will give the same result.

**Interior**

The inside of the van should be panelled with plywood and painted black. This provides you with insulation from the cold, makes the vehicle more sound proof and

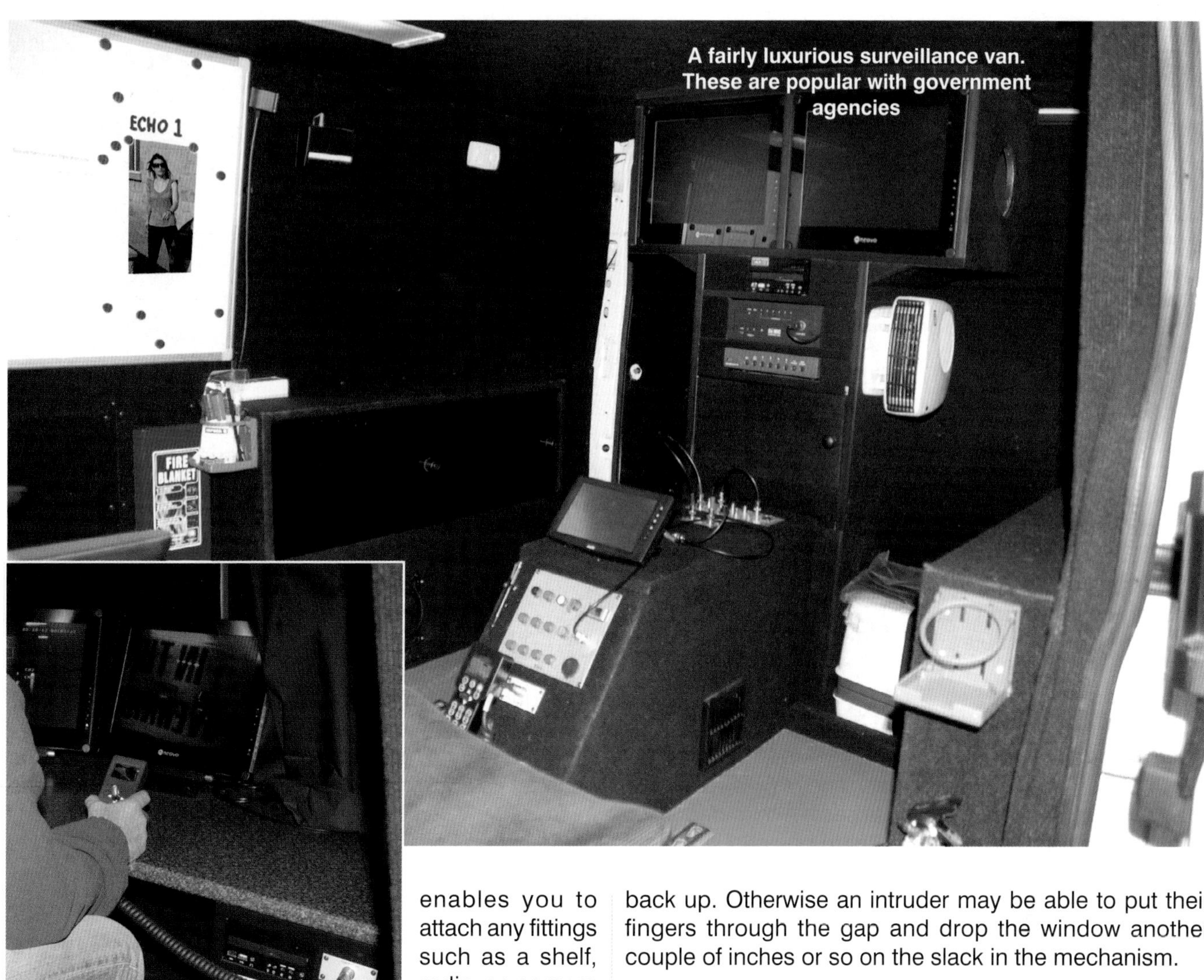

A fairly luxurious surveillance van. These are popular with government agencies

enables you to attach any fittings such as a shelf, radio or camera mount.

Something comfortable to sit on should be provided such as a bean bag. There is nothing worse than being uncomfortable and cramped for long periods of time, always try to sit facing the target rather than having to crane one's neck, it becomes uncomfortable after a short period.

Some form of ventilation should be provided by means of a proper ventilator or by just opening the front windows half an inch or so. In hot weather fresh air is required, in colder weather a flow of air is required to prevent windows misting. When you wind your window down, actually wind it down a few inches further than required and then wind it back up. Otherwise an intruder may be able to put their fingers through the gap and drop the window another couple of inches or so on the slack in the mechanism.

It may not always be viable to observe through the rear window and so the vehicle should be parked in such a manner that viewing is carried out through the front windscreen or through the side windows whilst sitting in the back. If the weather is extremely cold it may be wise to put some form of hot water bottle on the dashboard under a cloth to prevent the glass from misting and freezing. The rear view mirror should be detachable in order to provide a clear view and to remove a potential obstruction for your photographs.

**Alarms**

In addition to a standard vehicle alarm a second alarm horn could also be installed to be operated from within by means of a switch. On occasions, third party curiosity may invite them to take a closer look at the unfamiliar vehicle nearby, a quick burst of high decibel alarm as they touch the vehicle should keep them at bay! In addition, it will deter car thieves from stealing the vehicle whilst you are still in the back.

**Food & Drink**

Take adequate food and drinks for the duration of your stay. Avoid messy foods and a flask is indispensable. Ensure that you take plenty of water in hot weather to avoid dehydration, some vans can soon become like baking ovens. Be aware of hot drinks from a flask in cold weather, they will mist up your windows.

**Hygiene Provisions**

You may be in situ for many hours where it may not be possible to leave to use the toilet. Therefore adequate provision has to be made for urinating or defecating such as a bottle or disposable tub.

**Keys**

Once in position the keys should be removed from the ignition and placed in a handy spot by the dashboard for easy access. A member of the team should also carry a spare set to be used when the van is being inserted and extracted.

The van is mentioned again in more detail in the chapter on static surveillance.

A 12volt hair dryer is an excellent device for combating condensation

The equipment list for an operator is virtually endless, as there is so much that can be used to assist an investigation. You should remember that the equipment is only to be used as an aid and will not carry out the investigation for you. To this end, the equipment is only as good as the person operating it. You should be familiar with the equipment, know how to use it proficiently in the daylight as well as in darkness and know its full capability and all its limitations.

The surveillance industry and equipment is constantly changing - therefore training is required to keep current

As a surveillance operator you will probably obtain more information whilst out on foot. The exposure risk is high and confidence is a very important factor. A foot surveillance carried out single handed can be risky and so a minimum of two operators is recommended. A good standard of foot surveillance by an operator or team can only be acquired by constant practice and experience.

Difficulties will most certainly occur when carrying out foot surveillance if there is a lack of communication between the team, either by poor commentary or poor equipment. Without radios, confusion arises and the likelihood of a loss of contact or actually 'showing out' is very high. Covert radio equipment is necessary and communication with each other is essential as described in the chapter on communications.

## THE SURVEILLANCE OPERATOR

As previously mentioned, the ideal operator could be described as being the 'Grey Person' or Mr 'Nobody' but a Mr 'Everybody' who looks like Mr 'Average'

During surveillance, there are three things that will always get you noticed, especially whilst on foot:

- *Multiple Sightings*
- *Unusual Behaviour*
- *Cross Contamination*

## MULTIPLE SIGHTINGS

It is obvious that the more times a target sees you, the more chance of him remembering you. You will always be seen but being noticed is something different and being noticed is what we are trying to avoid. He will remember you if he is 'surveillance aware' or by the way that you dress and act whilst out on the street.

Wherever you are, you should attempt to stay out of the '10 to 2' arc of vision. You should remain to the side or behind the target at all times. If you find yourself in a situation where you do get in front of the target, get out of

## ISS CASE

On training courses we often use targets that are unknown to the team and who have never seen the course before. This provides good feed back to the class in order to establish their 'exposure levels' and whether the target has identified them. The class are always briefed, 'If you stay out of the targets 10 to 2 you will never be seen or noticed by him'. When it comes to the de-brief, those noticed by the target are ALWAYS those who were in the 10 to 2.

the way as soon as possible; get into shop, a doorway or side street but do not linger in his '10 to 2'. If you find yourself in front, listen to the eyeballs commentary and do not look back. Don't forget, the arc of view extends above you and below you, not just to the sides.

***Remember: If you can see him, he can see you***

### UNUSUAL BEHAVIOUR

In everything that we do, we have to act naturally and have a reason for being there, but this is easier said than done. On training courses we find that students realise that this is one of the hardest things to do in surveillance. Anyone can walk down a street or stand in a shop doorway but give them a radio and a mission (e.g. watch that shop front) and they turn into a different person. They talk noticeably into their collars, constantly touch their earpiece, shift about, peep and 'balloon' around the high street as if trying to dodge a swarm of bees. This is expected in a beginner but as training progresses and most importantly, confidence builds up, they eventually become effective covert operators.

The following few paragraphs are an excerpt from an article written by the author in response to a question on an internet security forum where the question was asked, 'How do we become and remain the grey man?'

It depends what you are trying to be 'grey' for and I presume that it is for surveillance?

## GOING GREY

*A good friend of mine explains that the way you want to dress for surveillance is in clothing similar to a young bachelor: remember when you first left home and didn't have your mum to wash your clothes? Well, you shove everything into a washing machine, (blues, reds, whites and blacks all mixed in together), throw in a ton of washing powder and crank it up on boil. What colour does everything come out? Yes, you guessed it (greyish) and that is the way you want to be dressed for surveillance..... or maybe not...*

*If you are on your own, maybe, then there is no problem, If you are working within a team, you should all be dressed differently (not all dressed in the grey boiled clothes!). If all the team were to wear dark fleeces, blue jeans and black trainers we may as well put on a uniform - get different.*

By 'grey' we say that you have to fit in with everyone else in the same environment, it is as simple as that but there are a few things to keep in mind.

The first thing to understand is why we get noticed to a target and the main two reasons are multiple sightings and unusual behaviour. We will forget about the unnatural behaviour part for now and concentrate on multiple sightings. If you are seen once you are probably forgotten about, seen twice - it's a coincidence; seen a third time - more than a coincidence. Remember, being seen is not the same as being noticed. Being seen 3 times will get you noticed and so it is our appearance, manner and clothes that you have to be aware of to minimise these multiple sightings.

You can carry out a surveillance in a bright yellow jacket and a red hat but you can only let yourself be seen wearing them once. The hooks in our subconscious memory will hook straight into it again the next time you are seen and you will become noticed after only two sightings - not good. It is these sightings that you want to minimise by blending in with everyone else around you which is why we say avoid bright colours and more importantly contrasting colours. Don't wear a black jacket over a white shirt - it screams out, especially if you are driving a car behind a target.

Don't forget to dress according to the car you drive - dressed in 'rag' order, driving a new BMW will also get you noticed. Get neutral or even fashionable as well! Remember if you are ex' police or ex' military leave your 'liberty rig' civvies in the store and throw away the key. If I thought I was being followed, I would force the team out on foot and then have a good look at what people are wearing even before carrying out any anti surveillance drills. I would look for: trainers, outdoor chukka boots, divers style watch, gore-tex jacket (probably with a North Face or Berghaus logo on it), cargo pants or Chinos and observe their gait - the way they walk. And for heavens sake don't wear sunglasses unless everyone else about you is also wearing them. It puts a contrasting band across your face and if the whole team are wearing them, standby, cos' the Men in Black are in town! Surveillance isn't about looking good which is a good excuse for being so ugly!

Keep it simple: take a look around you - fit in with everyone else in the same environment as every situation and place, is different.

Regarding vehicles, treat them with the same caution. Avoid black cars, especially with blacked out windows - they look too sinister or too diplomatic. Definitely avoid white ones (although you would get away with a small white van). You see a white car in your rear view mirror and what do you do? You automatically slow down and take another 2 or 3 looks at it in order to identify whether it is a police car. Don't give a target a free look.

## CROSS CONTAMINATION

Now and again, you may have a problem with your radios or there may be a need for you to meet up and talk to another team member. Strictly speaking this should never be done because if the target suspects that you are surveillance, he will keep a subtle watch on you to see what you do. If you then go and speak to another team member, you will then compromise him by what we call 'cross contamination'. The target's interest will now switch to the other team member.

You should also be aware that a more sophisticated target may employ counter surveillance and it is these people that will be looking for you. You do not want to make their job easier by compromising the team.

When on foot, the back up should always acknowledge the eyeballs transmissions. This gives confidence to the eyeball knowing that his back up is present and in place. If the Eyeball were not to hear any other radio transmissions or acknowledgements, he is likely to start looking around and behind him to see if his team are there. In doing so he might cause cross contamination with them.

## ISS CASE

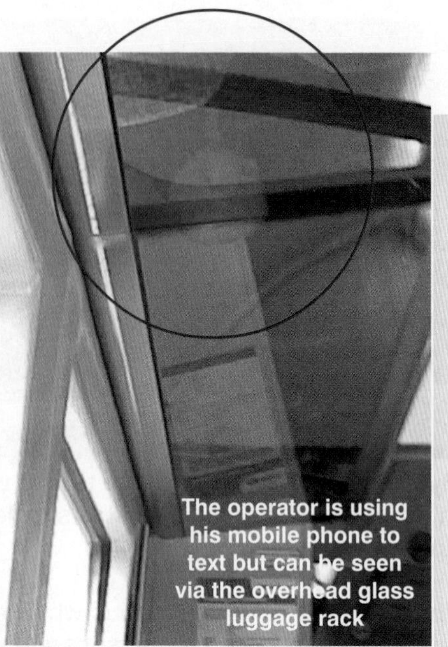


You can also cross contaminate inadvertently by the use of mobile phones; in a couple of instances on training exercises we have identified the surveillance team using phones. I was a target of surveillance on an exercise in Virginia and met up with another target who was also under surveillance by a separate team. We met up in the food court of a very large shopping mall and I was able to identify the guy that had a trigger on me. After I had met up with Alpha 2, he was able to identify or suspect who had the trigger on him also.

After a while, my trigger took out his mobile phone and started to make a call. On the other side of the food court I saw Alpha 2's trigger watching out of the corner of his eye, answering his mobile phone. I told Alpha 2 that one of my surveillance appeared to be on the phone to his surveillance team. I was not one hundred percent sure but this was confirmed when they looked at each other and one of them hung up and finished the call as did the other at exactly the same time. So, by using the cell phones in view of the target can cause problems.

In another instance, I was a target on a train and was under control by the surveillance team. The person with the trigger was sat opposite but behind a row of seats and too close to talk on his covert comms. He took out his mobile and sent a text. Shortly afterwards, another team member sat at the end of the carriageway (who I could see down the aisle) took out his phone and answered a text message and replied to it. I could see the two team members texting each other and thus they were cross contaminating.

### FOOT SURVEILLANCE TACTICS

If we look at the diagram, this provides us with a basic street layout as you would expect to find in a town centre. In our scenario we wish to put a member of the Burger Bar staff under surveillance in his lunch hour, in order to see where he goes during that time. We need to 'plot up' or stakeout the area using a three-man team.

Remember our phases of a surveillance; the **Stakeout**, the **Pick Up,** the **Follow** and the **Housing,** so we will commence with the Stakeout and Pick Up phase.

**The Stake Out Phase**

We have already discussed various trigger positions, so we have decided to put our trigger person in the telephone box outside the chemist.

The trigger should be in a position close enough to identify the target but far enough away not to be seen and out of the '10 to 2'. He needs to carry out a radio check with the other team members and ensure that they are in position, ready to take the follow. If nothing is happening you may be in for a long wait, the trigger should come up on the radio and report, 'No change, No change' on a regular basis. This is for several of reasons; it lets the team know that nothing has happened, it acts as a radio check giving confidence to the other members.

On a surveillance radio network, there is nothing worse than long periods of silence. If nothing is heard, operators start to lose confidence and think that something has gone wrong. They start to fiddle with the radio to see if it is working okay and possibly move position to see what is happening, so keep the team informed at regular intervals.

During surveillance training we have found that one of the hardest things for the students to do was to stand still and do absolutely nothing. If the target had entered a store, one of the team has gone in with him, leaving the other two outside to cover the exits. The two acting as back up find it hard to keep still without feeling obvious. If there is a shop doorway, stand to one side of it as if you are waiting for someone and stay there rather than shifting about and appearing anxious.

If there is a seating area or bench then sit on it, they are natural places for you to remain static. In addition, if there is an empty phone box nearby then get into it.

In the diagram shown on page 87, we have call sign Foot 1 giving the trigger, located in the phone box. From here he can cover the exit door, give a 'standby' when the target appears out in the open and also give a direction of travel.

Foot 2 and Foot 3 need to be located either side of the target and out of sight. Foot 2 has taken a position up in the bus shelter, left of the target outside the bank, and Foot 3 has taken up a position in another bus shelter which is right of the target and around the corner on West Street.

Remember, only one person has to see the target (the

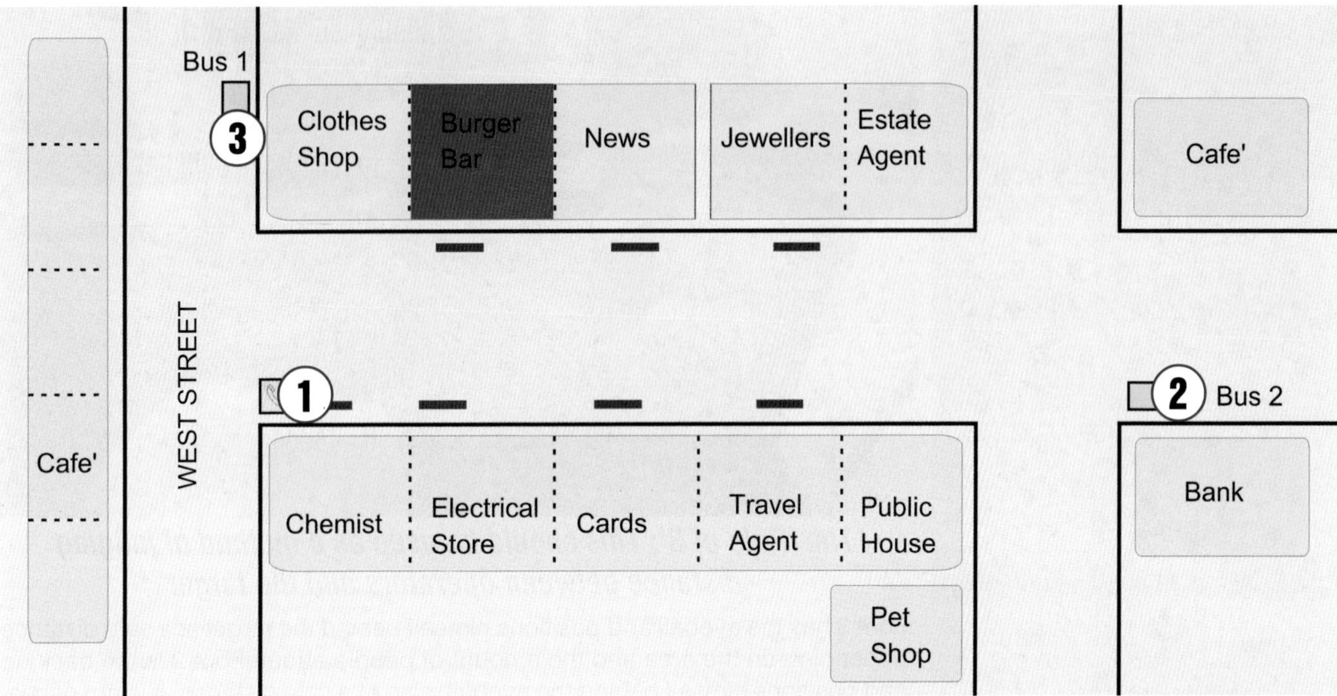


eyeball), the other two team members have to be 'off the plot' and out of the way. You do not want the target to come out of the premises, turn left or right and have a head on collision with the others.

## STANDBY STANDBY!

When the target appears, the eyeball should immediately call, **'Standby, Standby'.** This is a wake up call to the team to say, 'let's go' and listen in to the commentary. The eyeball should give a direction of travel and a brief description, for example:

***'Standby, Standby, that's Alpha 1 Out Out and gone Left, Left, wearing black (top) on Blue (bottoms) and foxtrot up the high street towards the fountain'.***

As the target has come out and gone left, Foot 2 should not move anywhere, he can stay where he is for the time being. Foot 3, having heard on the radio that the target has gone left will realise that he is walking away from his position. That should be his cue to leave the bus shelter, come around the corner onto the high street and take the 'first follow'. He would come up on air and state, **'Foot 3 has'** (the eyeball), and then takes up the commentary. The backing call sign should then acknowledge, **'Foot 2 backing',** straight away.

We say that there are no rules in surveillance but a very important guideline is the fact that the trigger person never moves on a standby (unless as a last resort) to take the first follow.

**A trigger is obtained from this phone booth**

Remember it is a team effort, so the trigger person 'triggers' the target out and another member takes up the first follow. If the target were to be aware at anytime, it would be when he leaves the premises and notes the reactions of people outside. Therefore, the trigger person who can see the target, so the target can see him, should remain where he is until out of the targets view, before moving.

## THE FOLLOW PHASE

As soon as practically possible the surveillance team will filter themselves in a position as illustrated in the diagram below.

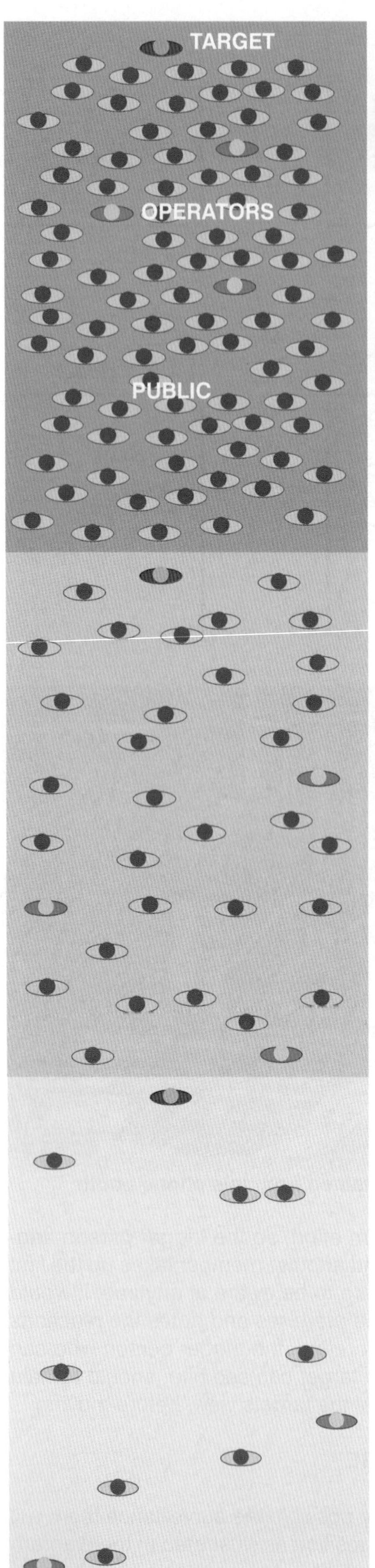

**_The 'Rule of 3': This should be used as a method of judging distance between operators and the target_**

Foot 3 has the eyeball and positions himself behind the target at a safe distance depending on the area and the amount of people about. Foot 2 is the back-up and positions himself behind the eyeball, also at a safe distance. It is not necessary for the back-up to see the target. Trail takes up a position on the other side of the street. The team is now positioned in what is called the classic A, B, C formation. This formation is not set in stone and dependant on the area, the size of the team and awareness level of the target.

## DISTANCING - RULE OF THREE

In order to judge how close or how far away you should be from the target and each other, you also have to consider the targets pace, your own pace, the cover that is available and the distance he is away from you and whether there are any changing situations such as transferring from a busy crowded shopping mall to a quiet street.

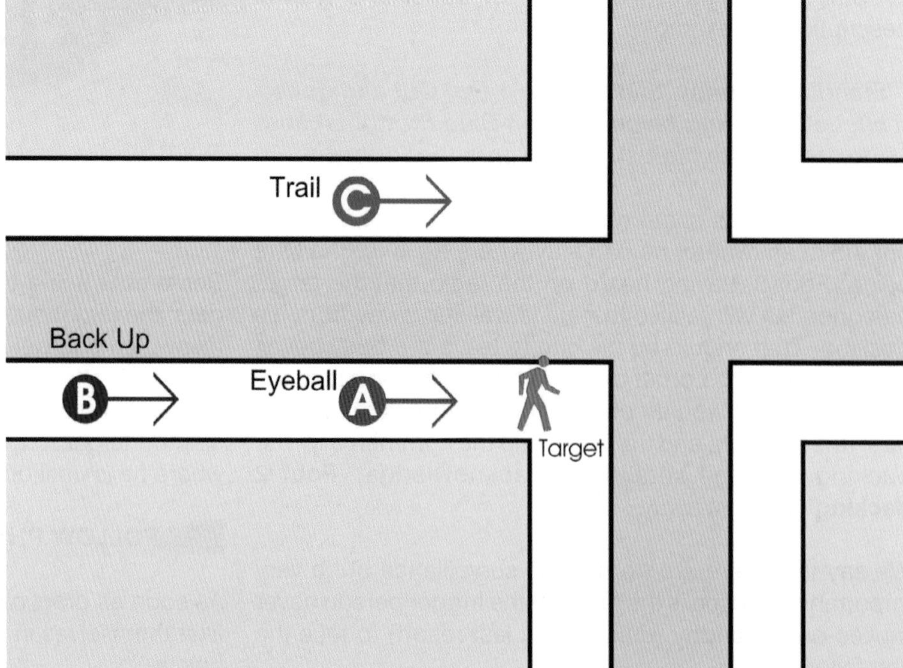

As a rule, you should look at the area and try to be '3 people' distance apart. So in a very crowded place where everyone is bunched up, you would be close together. Whereas, in a more open area you would be further apart as shown in the diagram.

A. **OPERATOR 'A' (Foot 3)** is behind the target with a reasonable distance between them depending on cover, crowds and the area.

B. **OPERATOR 'B' (Foot 2)** is on the same side of the street and is 'backing' Operator 'A'. There is no need for him to see the target and he should be able to see Operator 'C' listening to the commentary.

C. **OPERATOR 'C' (Foot 1)** operator is positioned on the opposite side of the street from the target and is slightly behind him.

## THREE MAN TEAM (A, B, C METHOD)

A foot surveillance team requires mobility and frequent changing of its operators in order to prevent compromise.

In diagrammatic form, the formations appear regimented and give the impression that the positions have to be strictly adhered to. This is not so, as once on the ground, the experienced operator will take up his position without thinking. The use of three men in a team permits greater variation in the position of operators and also allows for a member who may be getting 'warm' to be replaced by another operator from the team. It reduces the risk of losing the target and affords greater security against showing out.

**Impose Surveillance**

Should the target cross from the nearside of the precinct to the offside (left to right), the eyeball and back-up should not follow him, this is why we 'impose' surveillance on a target, rather than 'follow' him.

To recover from this situation, operator 'C' can take the eyeball, as he is already in a position on the other side of the street, and operator 'B' can then move to the other side of the precinct in order to 'back' the eyeball. Operator 'A' can stay where he is and cover the other side of the street. Remember, this would only be used only when the topography needs it. You would not do this in a quiet housing estate.

Foot surveillance is about team work and communication. If you lose sight of the target, we use the term 'temporary unsighted' so that another team member can take control if need be. During the surveillance, remain out of the targets '10 to 2' at all times and use whatever is around you to act as temporary cover. You should not be diving in and out of cover, but you need momentarily, to have something between you and the target so that if he turns around, you will not be in direct view. You might use pedestrians and street furniture.

If you are operating in a pedestrian precinct type area, keep to the sides so that you can easily enter a shop if the target turns around or looks behind him, do not walk down the centre.

*I am not entirely convinced of this but a student on a training course once stated that it may be useful to know whether the target is left or right handed. He claimed that a person who is left handed, when looking back over his shoulder is likely to turn his head to the left and look back. Therefore always keep to his rear and on the right side and vice versa. Try it, see what you think.*

Be aware of other body language traits made by the target. If they walk to the outside of the pavement, expect them to cross the road or if they walk into the pavement,

# STREET

they may be about to enter a building. Someone constantly looking at a wrist watch may have an appointment or meeting and searching and patting pockets may indicate that they are looking for car keys. An increase of speed after a phone call could indicate activity.

***Remember: If you can see him, he can see you***

Use 'street furniture' to provide temporary cover from view, it could be:

- *Other pedestrians*
- *Telephone boxes*
- *Advertising boards*
- *Parked cars*
- *Bus shelters*
- *Trees*
- *Lamp posts*
- *Shop doorways*

On the street you have to make constant appraisals regarding the target's intentions and always think to yourself, What if he....

***Stops...?***
***Crosses the road...?***
***Enters a building...?***
***Turns around and walks towards me...?***

The A, B, C method in very crowded streets can be difficult to adhere to, and at times it may be necessary for all three operators to be on the same side of the street or, conversely, on the other side. If you are close to the target, do not let him hear your radio commentary.

Use street furniture to give yourself a reason for being there

The A, B, C method on a street with little or no traffic such as a housing estate can create difficulties, it may be that only one operator is on the same side of the street as the target, with the other two operators on the opposite side. It may be that only one operator is deployed if the area is quiet. If a vehicle is used as back up, a footman can be picked up and re-deployed ahead of the target, if needs be.

**The Shadow Car**

It is not often that you would be deployed on foot without a vehicle to back you up. If the target's vehicle is under control by a team member, another may go mobile in order to support and 'shadow' the foot team.

This car can move and park-up for short periods whilst shadowing the team. The car can act as a relay in order to re-broadcast the eyeballs radio commentary to the other footmen and also to the cars which may be out of foot comms range, in order to keep them updated and for one of them to maintain a log. The shadow car can carry out various other tasks such as replacing or recovering footmen when necessary.

When acting as a relay, you do not necessarily have to re-transmit the whole message coming from the Eyeball, only the relevant parts.

Eyeball Footman: **'Standby Standby, that's Alpha 1 out out and gone left left towards the church'.**

Shadow Car: **'Golf Relay, Standby Standby, Alpha 1 out and gone Left'**

If you are out on foot and you hear a callsign start to relay, manage your calls on the radio net to account for this. Say your message, then pause a second so that the relay can do his bit before you carry on.

RNITURE

• If the target approaches you, never act surprised but act naturally. Have a good cover story ready in the event you are questioned. It is more realistic to dismiss the target as a 'nutter' rather than go into an elaborate and unrealistic excuse.

• Always remember that you may be seen but not necessarily noticed, therefore act naturally at all times and be aware of your dress sense.

• Do not dodge behind corners or into shop doorways if the target turns round, this only attracts attention to you. Do not forget that shop windows can reflect the activity of persons on the opposite side of the street. They can be of use to you but they can also be of use to the target.

• Always act naturally if the target turns round and retraces his steps, walk on and avoid eye contact. Remember, another team member should automatically take control. Whatever you do, do not look behind you. If you look back over your shoulder, the target will be doing the same.

• When in a confined area always endeavour to be doing 'something' but act naturally doing it. Give yourself a reason for being there.

## TACTICS IN FOOT SURVEILLANCE

A surveillance operator is a member of a team and he must at all times be in communication with the others. In the event of radio failure, you should carry out a quick check of your equipment to rectify the problem. Failing that, you will have to resort to using your mobile phone. The use of these signals and tactics must be automatic and apply to every team member.

When on the ground consider the following:

• Always ask yourself, am I in the right position? How can I benefit the team? If you are not in the right position, get into it.

• Avoid eye to eye contact with the target. If you do have eye to eye contact, you know and he knows that something is amiss which might lead to a compromise.

The 'shadow car' should relay messages accurately and quickly

**When giving an initial quick description start by providing details from the top and work downwards. For example, 'that's Alpha 1 wearing black on blue carrying a grey sweatshirt'.**

• In crowded areas, walk on the outside of the pavement. This gives better vision and less obstruction. The nearside of the pavement is good cover when the streets are less crowded.

• Do not take unnecessary risks, always consider 'loss v gain'.

• Ensure your mobile phone is in silent mode.

• Stay out of the '10 to 2' - you will not be seen.

• Be third party aware at all times.

**Change of Eyeball (Handover)**

It must be realised that the closer the operator is to the target, the more likely he is to be seen and noticed, therefore he must be changed at regular intervals in order to prevent a compromise. In some ways you could follow him all day on your own and not be noticed, so long as the target does not turn around. However, surveillance is not like that and so we have to act accordingly.

After having the eyeball for a period, you may feel that you have had a bit of 'exposure' or you feel 'warm' and therefore could do with a change to let someone else take over.

There are five occasions when we would normally carry out a handover:

- *When you are 'warm', or you have had the eyeball for sometime*
- *When the target changes direction*
- *When the target stops*
- *If you are compromised*
- *If the target goes out of your view*

The larger the team, the more changes can be made, but do not make changes for changes sake and it is normally the eyeball that will decide when to handover.

**Simple Handover**

When walking down a street and you require a handover, you should ask your back up if he is in a position to take the eyeball; this is what we call a 'planned handover'. If he replies **'Yes, Yes',** then you can handover to him by turning in to a shop, a side street or moving to the other side of the street and letting the back-up come through to take the eyeball.

Trail should then move in a position to act as back-up and tell you that he's backing.

**The Target Performs a U Turn**

You should always be observing the targets body language to help you anticipate his actions. If he suddenly does a U turn, be aware of being startled and caught out like a rabbit in a cars headlights and avoid having eye contact with him. It may be difficult to call over the radio, '..That's a reciprocal, reciprocal, towards..' because the target may be too close and will either see you, or hear you talking over the radio. Continue to walk naturally, avoid eye contact and put your hands in your pockets so the target cannot see your radio's pressel switch.

Two things you can do: either give rapid clicks on the radio to alert the team, (hopefully your back up will call the reciprocal turn as you carry on past the target). Also taught is the phrase 'Snake Snake Snake', to indicate a U turn whilst on foot. This is a phrase that you can say without

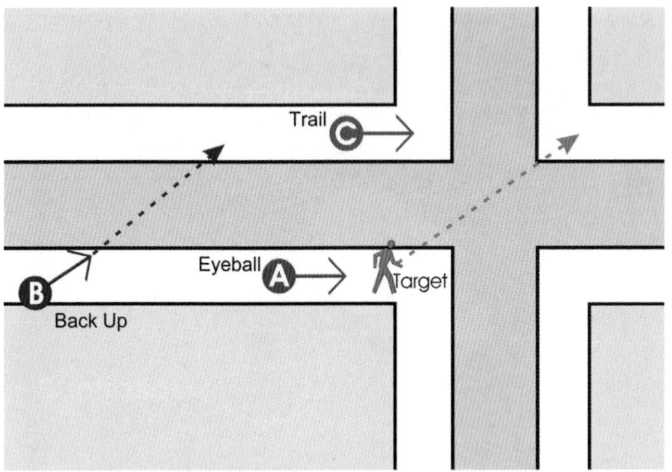


**If the target crosses the street there is no need to follow him across as there should be an operator on that side of the street to take control**

moving your lips, try it! So if you are behind the target and he turns around, call 'Snake Snake Snake' and the remainder of the team should understand what is happening.

### Cornering Drills

Should the target change direction by turning a corner, we need to maintain control over him. What we should never do is turn the corner and go around with him in the event that he suddenly stops. He may stop because he is suspicious of you, he may be browsing in a shop window or he may be waiting to cross a road. For this reason, we do not want to go around a 'blind' corner or this 'zone of invisibility' as it's called.

As soon as the target turns and goes out of your view, you should call, **'..that's gone left left and unisighted to me..'.** This indicates that the eyeball is now up for grabs to anyone that can take control.

As the eyeball does not want to go into this zone, one of the team members should 'clear the corner' and let the eyeball know if it is clear to come round or through.

You will note in the diagram below that the eyeball (operator 'A') gives advanced warning of a junction or a corner. This should be the cue for operator 'C' to move up to the corner on his side of the street to enable him to see and clear the corner. If the target has stopped, operator 'C' will state, **'It's a Stop Stop, hang back'.** If the target has turned the corner and continues up the street, Operator 'C' can say, **'Corner clear, come through'.**

As we are changing direction, it may be a good time to carry out a handover, in case the target is changing direction in order to identify followers; you do this, once operator 'C' has cleared the corner, rather than turn the corner and continue the follow and commentary. The eyeball should cross directly over the road to take up a 'C' position. The back-up can then come around the corner and take over as eyeball and the operator (C), who has cleared the corner then acts as back up.

We have now carried out a basic cornering drill where we clear the corner and carry out a handover at the same time. This can also be carried out if there are just two of you on the ground.

If you are on your own, there is no way that you would want to go around a blind corner. Therefore to recover this, you should consider moving to the other side of the street and effectively clear the corner for yourself as you look left and right and then move into a safe position to follow.

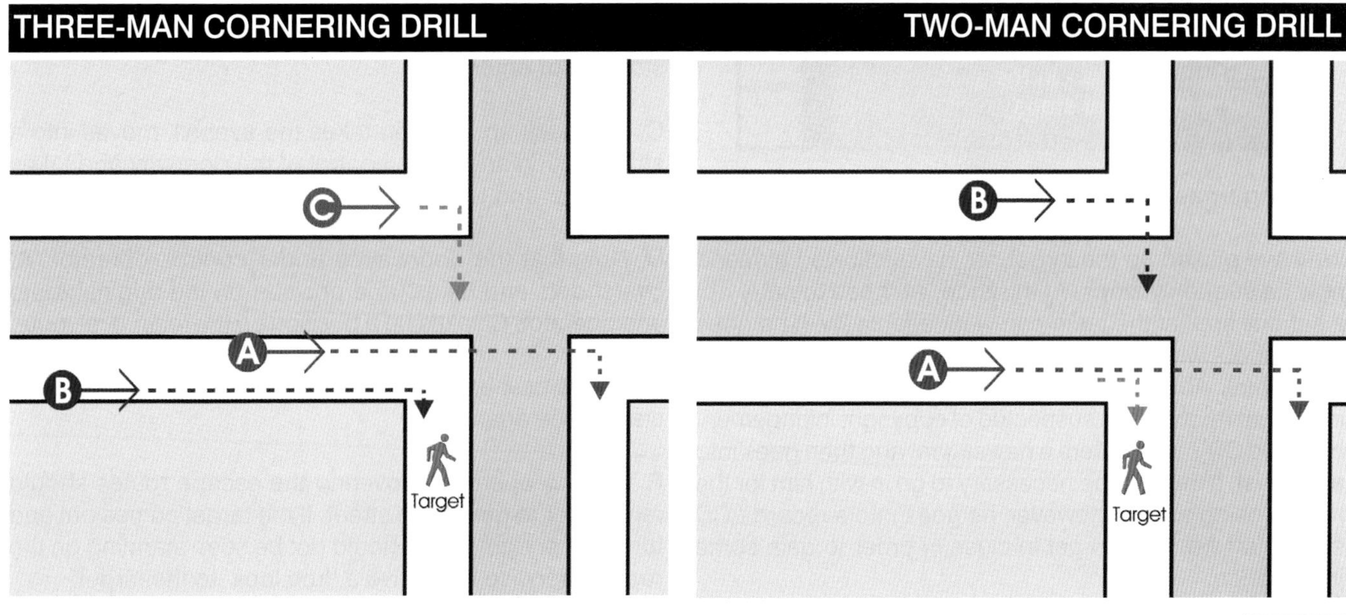

If the target turns into a street or alleyway it must be 'cleared' before a colleague follows - in the event the target stops

**The target turns right and goes 'unsighted' to operator 1; Operator 2 takes control and 'clears' the corner**

**Housing Phase**

We have picked up the target, we have followed him and now he suddenly stops. At this stop, we need to carry out a set drill so that the team can work effectively. If he goes into a shop, we must decide if it is necessary to go in with him. Think about your aims and objectives. If you are investigating a person suspected of copyright infringement of music CD's who enters a newsagent and then goes into a chemist, it may not be necessary to go in with him for the risk of losing a life. If however, he goes into a record / CD store then we need to get in close in order to gain some intelligence.

**Action on a Stop**

If we have the target under control walking down a street and he then enters a shop (newsagent) we have now entered our 'housing' phase of the surveillance and so we now have to re-plot and stake it out to prepare for the 'pick-up' phase.

We have decided that we are not going to enter and so a set drill is put into action as in the diagram.

**A.** The eyeball **(A)** should call, **'It's a Stop Stop at the newsagents'.**

**B.** He should then carry on straight and overshoot, stating, **'I'm going to overshoot, back-up, can you?'** (take the eyeball). Hopefully the reply would be, **'Yes Yes'.** Whilst overshooting, he confirms exactly where the target has stopped or entered.

**C.** The back-up **(B)** then takes the eyeball, moves into a safe position and takes control of the doorway and takes the trigger and tells everyone that he has control.

**D.** Now that the doorway is under control, operator **'A'** overshoots and takes up a position on the original route and operator **'C'** takes up a position on the reciprocal route.

**E.** We are now back to our pick-up phase and the process starts once again.

**F.** The two operators covering the escape routes should remember to get off the street. If the target comes out and turns left or right, they should not be seen standing on the road, otherwise it will give a 'free look' to the target.

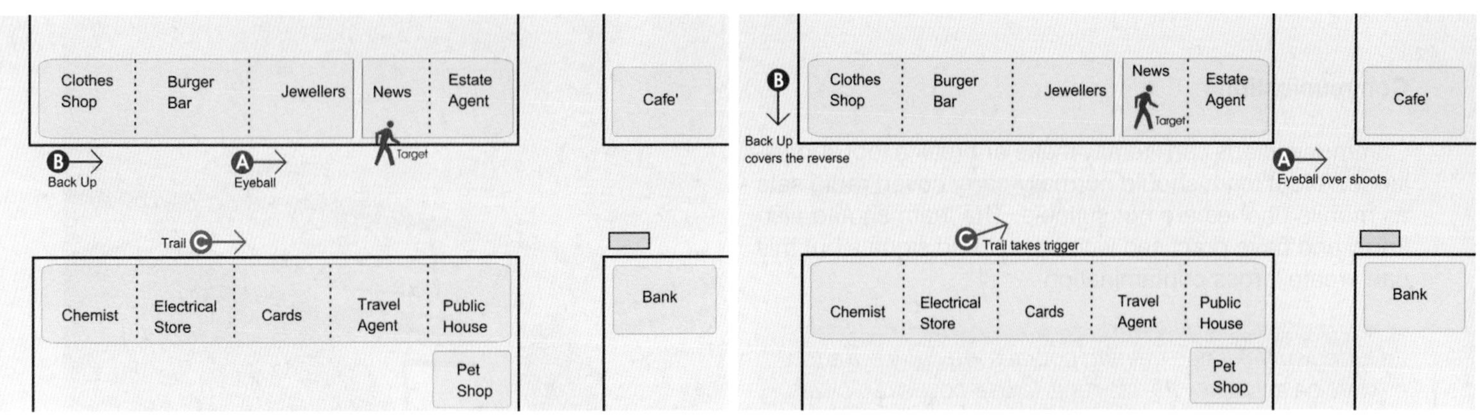


**When the target makes a stop the 'eyeball' continues past to cover the original direction; trail gets a 'trigger' on the door and the back-up covers the reciprocal**

Should it occur that one of the team can see the newsagents from his car, there is no reason why he can not take a trigger on behalf of the footmen. This prevents the footman from getting unnecessary exposure and allows them to move clear.

### Get In Close

If you decide that an operator needs to enter the premises with him, try to let the back-up go in rather than the eyeball. Tell the team that you are going 'complete' (or in with him) so that the team can expect you to 'minimise' on the radio. If you need to communicate to the team, you can resort to the click system. However, we normally use this procedure if an aware target enters somewhere, to see if he is being followed in by the person behind.

On occasions, it would be impractical to hand over when the target enters a premises and you have to get in straight behind him. For example, we often carry out a training exercise where the team have to establish the names and addresses on envelopes being posted by the target. When the target enters a post office, we have to get someone in right behind him to get close in order to read the envelopes. If someone else is allowed to get in-between in the queue, we lose the initiative.

For the team members on the outside, consider that the eyeball may be trying to obtain information by listening into the targets conversation. Therefore, do not start talking unnecessarily, it can be distracting.

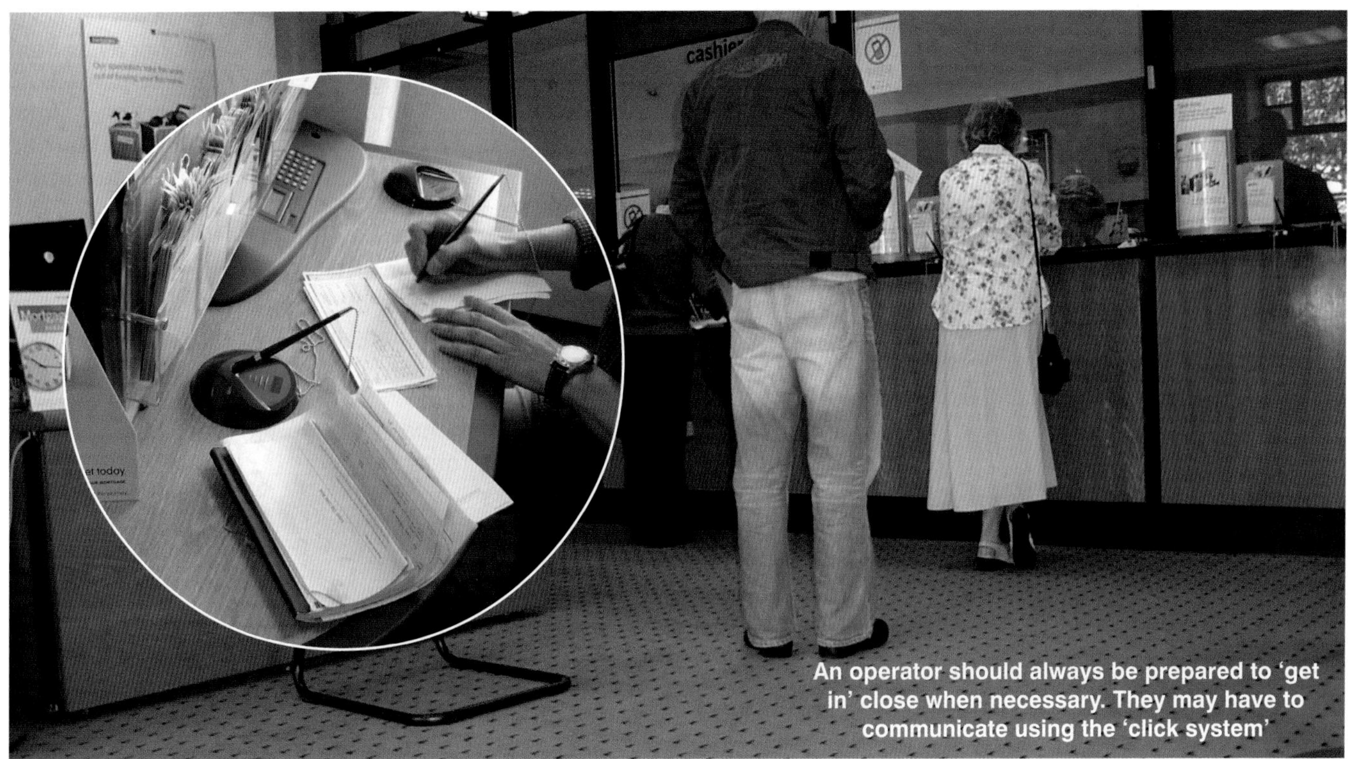

An operator should always be prepared to 'get in' close when necessary. They may have to communicate using the 'click system'

## Communications

Communications can literally make or break a foot surveillance. A foot team should normally carry covert radio sets as mobile phones are not suitable. The team should also know and have practised with basic hand signals but this can create 'cross contamination'.

*During surveillance training courses we carry out a foot exercise and allow the students to use covert radio sets. They appear to do reasonably well, except for dropping their heads into their chests in order to speak into the concealed microphone. This is not necessary as the sets allow you to talk quite openly whilst acting normally.*

As the eyeball, you should now be giving a commentary on the target's movements. Many surveillance operators prefer the back-up to acknowledge his transmissions every time or just now and again, after every three or four transmissions or on a change of direction. After the eyeballs transmission, all the back-up has to say, very briefly is, **'Foot 1 Roger'** or **'Foot 1 Backing'.** This tells the eyeball that his messages are coming across and also gives him confidence because he knows that his back-up is in position.

## Action on a Loss

Should the target go out of your view you must alert the team with the call, **'Temporary Unsighted'** and give a reason such as, **'Temporary unsighted due to traffic'.** If you regain sight, you can inform the team by calling, **'Eyeball Regained'.**

Operators must avoid becoming or looking anxious when searching for a lost target

Now and again the team will suffer a loss where the target has disappeared. This has to be acted upon very quickly as the longer the target is 'unsighted' the further away from the team he will be getting. A set drill should be carried out in the event of a loss and the eyeball should call, **'Total loss, total loss at...'** as soon as possible, stating the location. After a loss, a search procedure has to be carried out:

- The eyeball should decide which is the most logical route or quickest escape route that the target must have taken and head for this, searching to his left and right as he goes along.
- The back-up should take the second most logical or quickest escape route.
- Trail should hold the 'point of loss' in the event that the target returns through it.

***If the target enters Stead & Simpson, for example, the 'eyeball' must overshoot to confirm that they are in the shop and have not turned into the alleyway or door (circled)***

• By holding the point of loss, that operator is also in a good position to act as back-up if contact is regained in any direction. He is also in a position to relay radio messages to the team who may be getting further apart.

• If contact is regained, the eyeball should call, **'Standby Standby, that's Alpha 1 gone Left Left at the point of loss and is continuing along East Street'.**

When a loss occurs, be extremely careful how you search for the target in respect of your actions and body language. Try and be subtle and casual as you check left and right in nearby buildings or shops. The target may be watching you as you carry out the search so do not give yourself away by appearing anxious and alert.

**If an operator is required to enter a cafe/pub etc. they must endeavour to find a good vantage point**

**Cafés & Public Houses**

If the target goes into a café you must decide whether to follow him in or not, remember, he could be meeting some-one. If you do decide to go in, consider your heat states and the fact that you may have to 'lift off' after the target leaves if you have been exposed.

If you go into a café  but it is not necessary that you get in close to the target, you may need to position yourself where you can 'dominate' the room. By this we mean that from where you sit you should be able to see the target and the exits, including toilet doors.

**This glass-fronted cafe allows the operator to view inside without entering**

If necessary, get as close as possible to the target without being obvious in your intent. Consider sending two people into the café (preferably a man and woman) to make their presence appear more natural and sit opposite your partner but out of the '10 to 2'. You can then talk on a radio giving the appearance that you are in conversation.

• Do not feel awkward in public places, you have a right to be there, you are a member of the public.

• Always have cold drinks. If the target suddenly leaves, it may appear odd for you to leave a hot drink or meal on the table and walk out.

• Pay for your beverages as you receive them. If the target departs, you do not want to be left in a queue waiting to pay.

• Sit close if a meeting is in place, you do not necessarily have to face the target to overhear conversations.

• Use the crossword page of a newspaper to write and make notes if necessary.

• Fast food restaurants such as McDonalds are rather impersonal places where the staff do not interact with customers except to take their money. Smaller cafes are likely to be more friendly and so expect to engage in conversation with staff or the owner.

• Use the click system to communicate to the rest of the team. It is the trigger person outside who should respond to you or the relay car.

• Switch your mobile phone onto 'silent' mode.

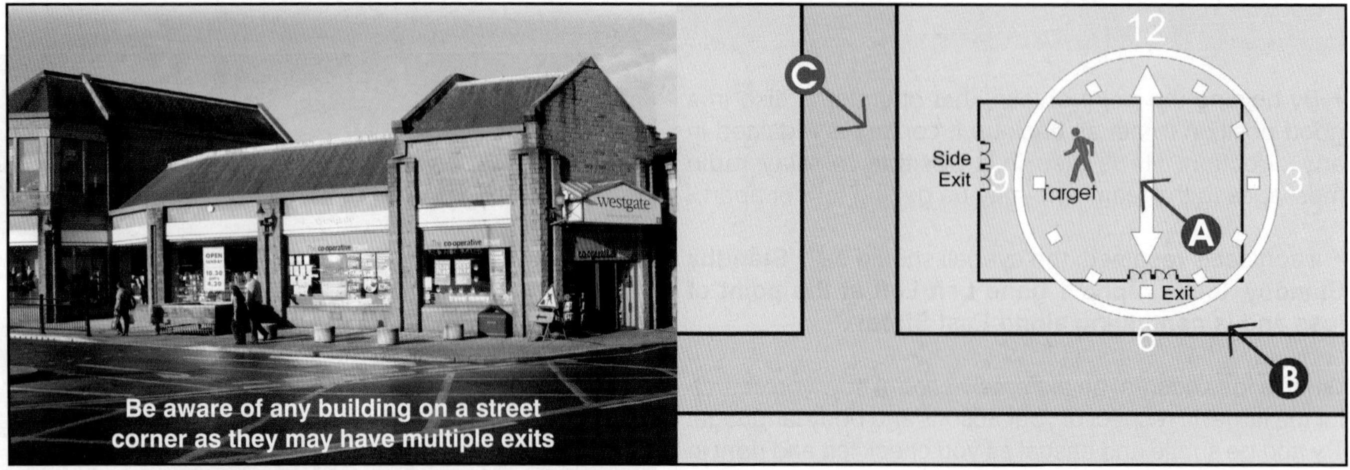

Be aware of any building on a street corner as they may have multiple exits

**Buildings with Multiple Exits**

If you suspect that the premises the target has gone into has another exit or is located on a corner, operator 'A' should not only overshoot, but also check the rear and side for possible exits. If there are any, he should notify the team and get a trigger on those exits too.

We say that if a target enters a large building or mall he always goes in at 6 o'clock by imagining a clock face over the area. Therefore, if an operator checks the side of the building and notices an exit on the right side he can call, '..there's an exit at 3 o'clock and I've got it covered..'

Should the target exit from the side of the building, operator A can call, 'Standby, Standby, that's Alpha 1 out out at 3 o'clock and gone left left..'

Be aware of both uniformed security guards and store detectives. They are trained to recognise anything out of the ordinary and they will soon notice you if you do not act naturally. Many store detectives make use of covert radios and you will soon become the target under surveillance; in addition, it is likely that you will be tracked by closed circuit TV.

Also be extremely careful if you enter a store with a bag containing a covert camera such as a sports bag. Store detectives will naturally 'lock' onto anyone entering a shop carrying a bag, for obvious reasons.

Many large stores are also used as a 'cut through' for shoppers and so the target should be kept under control visually until all the exits are covered. It may be necessary for the whole team to enter the store depending on its size.

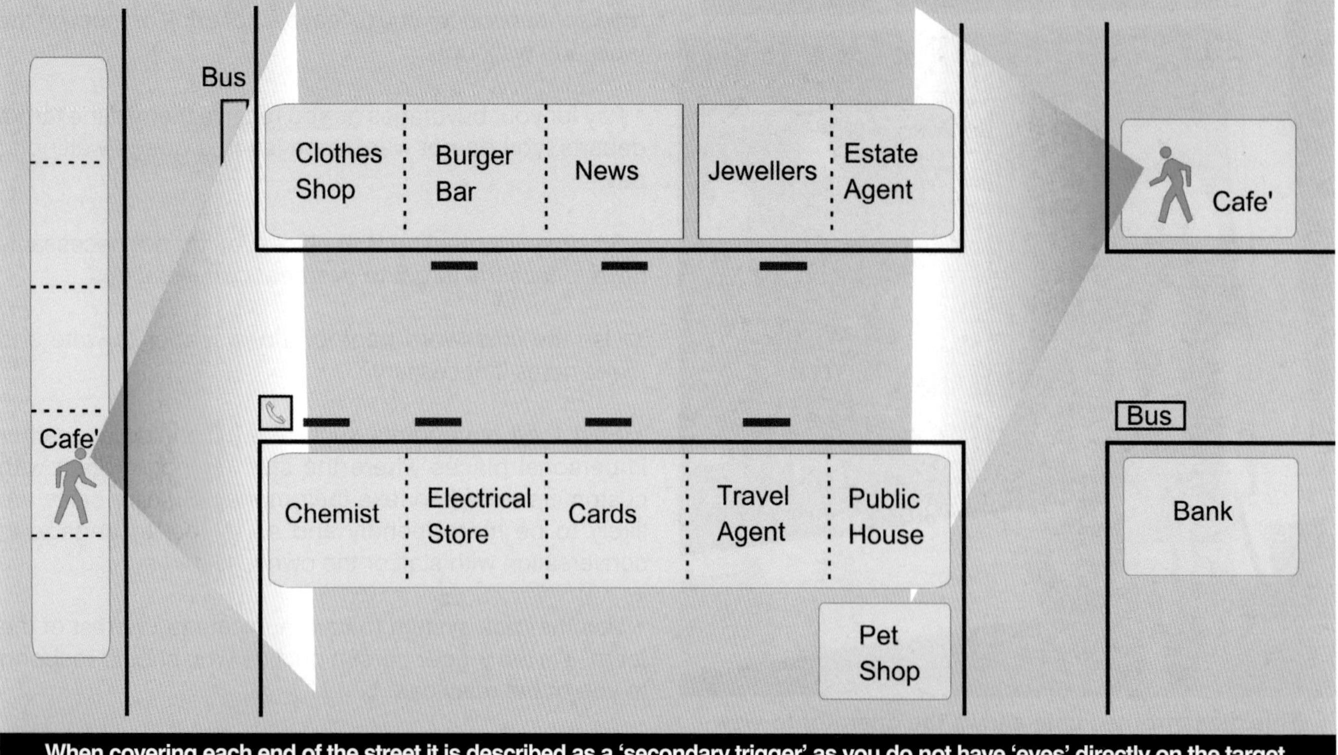

When covering each end of the street it is described as a 'secondary trigger' as you do not have 'eyes' directly on the target

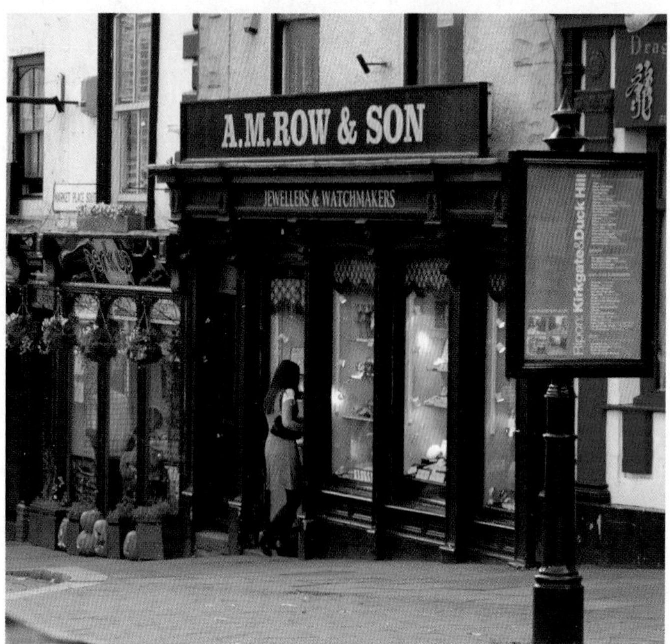

**Operators should be wary of loitering in sensitive areas such as banks, jewellers etc.**

## Indoor Shopping Malls

Treat indoor shopping malls as you would streets and position yourself appropriately and you should be aware of security guards and CCTV cameras in operation. If you act unnaturally you will be tracked.

Some areas have multiple levels and so be prepared to use stairways inside shops, elevators and escalators. If your target enters a shopping mall with multiple levels, it would be wise to deploy an operator on the floor above in anticipation of the target going up.

In surveillance we normally term the ground floor as 'Ground Floor', the next level up is 'White 1', then 'White 2' and so on. Should there be a basement or level below ground level, it is termed as 'Black 1', 'Black 2' etc.

So if the target enters the mall on the Ground floor and continues shopping, an operator should be deployed above on White 1 for a couple of reasons. He can possibly get a trigger from above whilst looking down (but remember the arc or '10 to 2' also looks up and down). Also, if the target heads for an escalator up, you do not have to follow him as someone else has the top of the escalator covered.

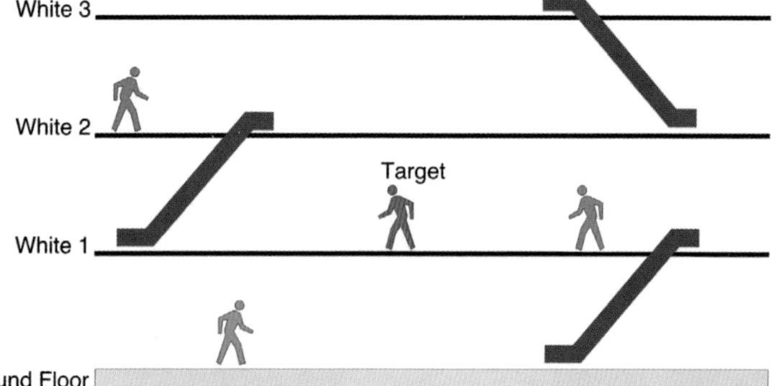


Foot 1, **'That's Alpha 1, foxtrot towards the escalator, that's Alpha 1 onto the escalator and up up towards White 1, I no longer have'**

Foot 2, **'Foot 2, roger that, I have Alpha 1 on White 1, at the top and gone left left towards...'**

Foot 1 can then either back Foot 2 or leapfrog ahead and position himself above on White 3. If you have a third operator deployed, they may want to remain on the ground floor ready for when the target comes back down again.

## Window Shoppers

Quite often it is difficult for a target who just seems to window shop to be kept under control (or in other words, does not actually stop and go into a store) where we would carry out our normal stop procedure.

If a target stops to look in a window, rather than call a 'Stop Stop' over the radio (which actually signifies the housing phase, instructing the team to plot up) the call **'Check Check'** is made. This signifies that the target has temporarily stopped and that the team should hang back slightly. Should you be operating in shopping precincts you may find it easier just to hold and control the end of the streets and 'bounce' the target along.

## Escalators

Many indoor shopping centres, large stores and underground train stations have escalators which should not cause too much of a problem. When using an escalator:

- Try avoiding the same escalator as the target, especially if he is aware. If the target turns around, he may see all of the team. Put only one member of the team on the escalator at any time.

• Keep to the right side and use other pedestrians as cover. Drop your upper body by slightly lowering your right shoulder in order to lower your profile

• There may be a short period when the target is 'unsighted' as he disappears over of the apex at the top, so quickly take control or he will be lost

• Should the target get to the top and then suddenly turn and take the escalator back down; avoid eye contact, do not take the same escalator down but carry out a hand over. Make your way down by using another escalator, the stairs or the lift.

**Lifts & Elevators**

Should the target enter a large building with many floors, the team should expect the eyeball to minimise on his radio and possibly resort to 'clicks' to communicate. If the target makes for an elevator, you could follow him in but consider:

• Is it necessary and will we achieve anything? (Loss v Gain). An operator having been in close. may have to lift off from the surveillance afterwards as he has been over exposed.

• Is it safe or wise to enter with him? The target might be a threat and have a go at you.

• Remove your covert earpiece, it may be seen or heard in close proximity. Do not put it in your shirt pocket otherwise it will still pick up the transmissions from your induction loop and will be heard

• Avoid eye contact at all times.

• Take control of the button panel. If you do, you can ask the target which floor he wants (as any person would do), you then get off at the same floor or the one above or below.

• Be prepared for casual conversation with others or the target himself.

• Switch your mobile phone onto 'silent' mode.

• Relay the floor to other team members as soon as possible.

Intelligence agencies often use an ATM immediately after a target has done so in order to 'mark' the transaction

If the target's intended floor is unknown (as he had taken control of the button panel or someone else has) your best option is to take the second to top floor if he is going up. This way you will be able to identify which floor he gets off at, and you get off at the floor above. If he gets off at the same floor as you, good, if he remains in the lift he only has one other option open to him, the top floor.

After being in close proximity to the target, you have to consider that you have had much exposure without necessarily being compromised.

**Telephone Kiosks**

Telephone booths can be used by the target or yourself at any time for various reasons:

• By the Target

• To make or receive a phone call - the obvious

• To perform anti-surveillance

• To get out of poor weather whilst waiting for someone

• By yourself

• Use the box as natural cover from where to observe; keep in mind that it should only be a short term wait

• Act naturally, remember to pick up the phone and pretend to speak

• If there are two boxes adjoining can you get into the second box and listen into the target's conversation? If you do, place your back towards him, don't let him see your face or earpiece

• Be aware at night time as the phone booth may be illuminated

If absolutely essential, you may have to get in a lift with your target

If a person stands on the right and drops their right shoulder whilst lifting the leg - the profile is lowered

Some enforcement agencies teach operators to 'clear' a phone box after a target has used it. This should be treated with caution as you will discover in a later chapter

You should always be wary of any stop at a telephone kiosk. The target, even if making a call, has a clear view to three sides and it is a natural tendency for him to look around outside whilst talking on the phone. Some public call boxes have advertising pictures stuck to the glass windows in them, these adverts enable you to see out of the box but observers cannot see into them. They are a good form of cover if you need to take photographs or video film.

**Clearing a Phone Box**

Some enforcement agencies are taught to 'clear' a phone box. This means that after a target has used a phone box an operator should quickly check it for anything that may have been left behind, but only when the target is away from it. In addition, a quick call is made to the office from the pay phone. At a later time and through official channels they can obtain a list of all calls made from the phone box. If you identify the time of your call, the targets number will be listed as the one prior and you have now identified the number called by the target.

In similar fashion, if the target uses an ATM machine, an operator should put his card into the machine to record and mark. Then later, again through correct channels, you can identify the account used by the target.

I would treat clearing phone boxes with extreme caution. A very aware target is likely to use a phone box (or pretend to) and then leave. Knowing that the phone might be checked, he will keep an eye on it to see what happens in order to identify surveillance. A sophisticated target may even have counter surveillance deployed, so that they can identify if the phone box is cleared by surveillance.

**Parks and Open Spaces**

These areas can be tricky and you have to use the open ground as cover by keeping your distance especially if there are not many people around. Use the pathways on a parallel with the target and be careful that you do not follow him like a lost duck. If the target stops, use benches to sit on, lay on the grass and sunbathe if necessary. Just look around you, see what everyone else is doing and do the same.

Be conscious of other pedestrians: dog walkers, joggers, mothers with children and children's play areas. When the target leaves the park area make sure that all the

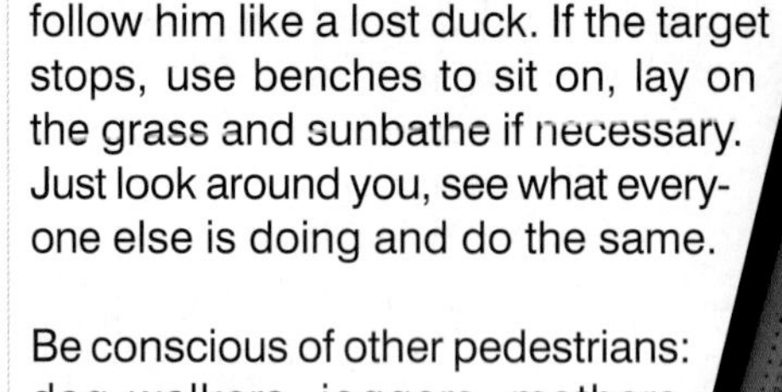

Common sense dictates that single male operators should avoid youngsters play areas

When the 'taxi light' on the roof is illuminated - the cab is available for hire

team do not converge on the same exit point as you attempt to close up. It is possible you will be leaving a wide open park space and be straight into a confined urban area.

## PUBLIC TRANSPORT

### TAXIS AND PRIVATE HIRE

At times your target may take a taxi or private hire cab. Taxis can be flagged down and stopped in the street. In major cities, the TAXI sign is usually illuminated if it is free. Private Hire cabs are pre booked by telephone or email. Treat this as you would a mobile surveillance but be aware of certain dangers:

• The driver will probably know all the short cuts and 'cut throughs' and so he will make many short left and right turns, therefore handovers should be carried out more frequently if you are in a following vehicle.

• Expect him to stop at short notice and stop anywhere. Taxis can also use special lanes in traffic which are prohibited by other road users.

• If you are also following in a taxi, be careful of what you say to the driver as you do not want your driver to alert the target's driver. Some taxi drivers can be very protective over their colleagues.

• Make a note of the taxi firm if it is a private hire company. If you have a loss, you may be able to phone the taxi company and 'blag' the destination from the controller.

On a surveillance job this happened to us so we telephoned the cab company and said that the person who had been picked up from 'Smiths Offices' had forgotten their mobile phone. They told us where he was dropped off so that we could send someone round with it. The ruse worked!

Target uses a taxi: If the operator is forced to follow a target in a taxi be aware that the driver does not communicate your intention to the target's driver

An operator must get in close to overhear any destination information imparted

## BUSES

If the target heads for a bus stop, inform the team as soon as possible as you will probably have to get on with him. Do not get unnecessarily close whilst waiting for the bus to arrive and consider keeping away from the bus stop altogether especially if there is no one else around.

As the bus draws near, attempt to obtain the fleet number, registration number or other identifying feature and relay this to the team. You may have an operator in a car backing you and he does not want to end up following the wrong bus, they can all look alike!

Inform the team that you are getting on the bus so that they will know that you will be unable to communicate. If you can overhear the targets destination, you can ask for the same. Keep a hold of your pressel switch whilst asking for the ticket, as this will be transmitted to your team.

An operator should endeavor to sit behind the target

You do not want to be in the targets '10 to 2', so attempt to sit behind him so that he does not have you in his view. If he goes upstairs on a double decker, remain downstairs at the rear and cover the stairs. Obviously, if there is a strong possibility that he may meet someone on the bus, then you need to get close.

If you have your back-up following in a car you will need to communicate with him and so instigate comms by giving four clicks when you can. If the target shows intention of getting off (anxiously looking out of window, doing up jacket, picking up bags), then give the team a 'standby' as they can then prepare themselves for deploying someone on foot.

If you are quick enough, consider putting a team member on the bus at the stop prior to the targets. If he is an aware target and possibly carrying out anti surveillance, this should put you one step ahead. Similarly, put an operator on the bus at the next stop after the target has got on.

*'One One: Standby Standby... that's Alpha 1 on the red bus'... One Three 'errr hello?'*

## RAILWAYS

Should your target arrive at a train station, the team leader will decide whether to put an operator or two on the train with him. The size of the surveillance team will obviously dictate what course of action to take. If it is envisaged that the target is likely to use a train or that it is part of his routine to do so, you can be better prepared and deploy a larger surveillance team. A train journey can be broken down into three parts, the beginning, middle and the end; it is at the end phase or destination when you are most vulnerable.

On entering the station and ticket office, the following should be adopted:

**It is difficult to obtain the target's destination if they have purchased a pre-paid ticket or bought one on the Internet**

• If the destination is unknown, the eyeball gets right behind the target at the ticket counter. He is to establish the targets destination by overhearing the target or by 'blagging' it out of the counter assistant.

• If the ticket is obtained from a machine, you will need to get in very close in order to see over the targets shoulder and obtain the details of the journey.

• The eyeball purchases return tickets and informs the team of the details by radio. A car call sign should relay the details because radio communications will be difficult due to the station noise and electrical cables.

• Keep control of the target on the platform; if there are not many people about, keep away and out of his sight until the last minute that the train arrives. Do not stand on the side of the target from which the train will be approaching, otherwise the target will be constantly looking in your direction as he waits.

• Keep an eye on any information displays or monitors. Many modern platforms have an information board stating the next train's destination, arrival time, and stops. If you have a while to wait, you can keep your distance or consider getting a trigger from another platform.

**Doors in some carriages are manually operated**

Operators should keep an eye on the train arrival/departure board for information. This should be passed on to the team

**Operators must 'get in' close to identify the target's destination**

• Remember to put your mobile phone onto 'silent' mode. You do not want the whole train looking at you if it rings and make sure that the 'Bluetooth' system is switched off.

• If you find yourself in a bad position and feel the need to move, do not just stand up and move for no apparent reason. Wait until the train pulls into a station and get off - then get back on the train further down the carriage.

• If the journey is a few hours duration, switch off your radio in order to preserve battery power but switch it back on whenever you approach a station.

• The team leader should decide whether to put two or three operators on the train and deploy a mobile unit to the trains destination, if is practical.

• When the train arrives, remember that on some carriages you have to press a button in order to open the doors.

• The eyeball should keep control at all times and remain alert, the target may get off the train at an earlier halt than expected, especially if he is surveillance conscious.

• The remaining team should locate themselves in the carriages either side of the targets carriage and preferably facing the adjoining carriage door. If the eyeball is unable to tell you that the target is moving carriages, you should at least be able to see it happen.

**If the carriage is full when you depart - it could become empty as your journey continues**

**Be aware of overhead electricity cables which will affect wireless earpieces causing them to squeal and can be problematic**

**Be careful of losing sight of the target because the platform can be very congested. Similarly, be aware of unpredictable behaviour - in the event he is seeking another platform or train**

If you are the eyeball, you may find it difficult to communicate to the rest of the team, especially when the train arrives at a station. The click system should be used as we have already described. If the target starts to get off the train, then rapid clicks can be given (standby). If the target stays where he is 'two clicks' should be given to let the team know that he is still on the train. This procedure can also be used on a bus.

As the train approaches the station, attempt to identify which side of the train you will be getting off and also the

***Do not stand on the side of the target from which the train will be approaching, otherwise the target will be constantly looking in your direction as he waits.***

The target's options are many when they exit a station

direction of the exit as you step off, left or right. To avoid getting off and finding yourself in front of the target, use the same door as him so that you are naturally behind.

When the target moves to get off the train, as much notice should be given to the rest of the team. It is likely that at least one operator may end up ahead and in front of the target as everyone gets off the train. If this is the case, the eyeball should inform the team member how far the target is behind him so that he can quickly move out of the way. If you do end up in front, do not look back behind you to see where the target is.

Keep close control of the target and keep the commentary going as communications will be difficult. Hopefully, one of the car call signs will be in the area of the station ready to act as a relay.

It may be planned that any foot call signs on the train have to be picked up by their cars. It may be that fresh footmen have to be deployed to take over as the target leaves the train station. If this is the case, the radio traffic should be minimised and only be used to commentate where the target is. Any administration such as finding out where your car is located, who is taking over from you etc, should be carried out on the phone to avoid interrupting important commentary.

Following a target on a train is fairly simple, as he has nowhere else to go. The difficult part of the surveillance is when he arrives at his destination, as so many options are open to him. He could:

- *Get on another train*
- *Take the Underground*
- *Continue on foot*
- *Get into a taxi*
- *Take a bus*
- *Be met by a car*
- *Have his own car parked nearby*
- *Cycle*

**OVERSEAS WORK:** **If operating in foreign countries, ensure you are familiar with transportation systems**

If a surveillance team has to get ahead of the train, the driver's skills have to be first class and the use of a Satnav is essential

## LONDON UNDERGROUND RAILWAY AND METRO SYSTEMS

The London underground is a vast network used by thousands of people each day and is probably the easiest and quickest mode of transport within London. Because targets can frequently and easily use the underground system, we have to adopt certain procedures when dealing with this situation.

We have to be very guarded in these areas of the third party, pickpockets and security staff. Any un-natural behaviour displayed will certainly attract someone's attention.

The main problem as far as surveillance is concerned is the fact that the surveillance team whilst under ground have limited or no communications with the world on top.

Conventional radios do not work to those above the surface but do work very well to others underground at the same time. The latest secure 'Airwave' radios (used by Police and other agencies) rely on the mobile phone system (for encryption and unlimited range) and so are unreliable underground. They do have a facility to switch to operate as a conventional radio but this means having to fiddle about with the set (concealed under clothing) and so risk compromise.

Our target is on the street heads for a tube station, the person in control reports, **'that's 'Alpha 1' towards Manor House tube station'.** Everyone on the team should now switch on and expect to really close up on the target otherwise he will go down into the Tube system and be lost in the crowds.

Clearing corners can be difficult in tight areas - in this case, however, the mirror can be used as an aid

With the advent of Oyster Travel Cards, the days of a surveillance operator getting very close to the target as he obtains a ticket from a machine are more or less gone. Pre-Oyster, the drill was to get in close to the target, attempt to identify the destination and pass this information 'up top' so that they can dispatch a surveillance car, taxi or a motorbike to cover the destination and provide support. If the target has an Oyster Card, he is straight through the barriers and into the system with no indication of his destination - this can really hinder a surveillance operation.

Each member of the team should also be in possession of one of these 'magic' cards to enable them to freely move about the underground system.

Operators must get in 'hard and close' to the target as you access the train barriers. If you do not have a fare you may have to 'tailgate' someone to enter

Use other rail users as cover but you must be quick when the target reaches the top or bottom of an escalator

Their best cover to remain covert is the hundreds of other people going about their daily business. The team will get in very close to the target on the escalators down and within the tunnelled walkways. On a packed platform, at least one operator will have 'eyes on' the target with the others in close proximity but using other commuters as cover or waiting on a nearby opposite platform.

If, for some reason you have not managed to obtain a ticket or have no Oyster Card, consider 'tailgating' a member of the public. By this, you have to get very close to someone as the control barriers open and go though at the same time before they close again. At the destination, you will have to do the same or you will be challenged by a member of staff. Remember to call back later to pay for your fare!

The eyeball, has to keep the commentary flowing: **'That's towards the Piccadilly Line South, Piccadilly Line South'** and the back up acknowledging the calls all of the time by repeating it back **('Roger that, Piccadilly Line South').** This also acts as a relay by passing the message to those operators behind and further up the escalators. Be aware of your voice booming down tunnels and walkways so try to keep it low.

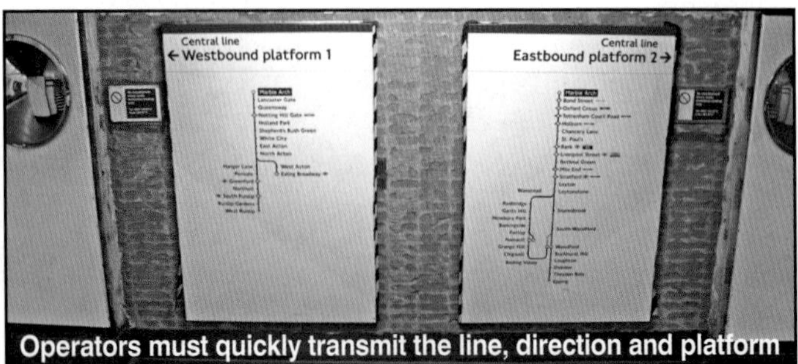


Operators must quickly transmit the line, direction and platform

Be prepared for the target running as he gets to the bottom of the escalator or stairs adjoining the platforms. It may be that a train has just arrived and he rushes to catch it. It would not be unusual to run at this time as everyone else does it. Expect a certain amount of unusual behaviour on the underground system as the target changes direction frequently and appears lost, the reason being - he may be lost! It is easy to get confused when you are in an unfamiliar place, especially when one of the train lines is out of service and detour routes are in place. Take a look around you and observe the signage.

On the platform, keep an eye on the travel display, this should tell you how long you have to wait for the next train. The eyeball should be close and on the blind side of the target (not the side the train approaches from, which is

Use mirrors to help keep control of the target and give warning of approaching trains

On the Tube in London the majority of trains enter stations from the left; therefore do not stand on the left side of the target because he will be looking towards you

normally from the left). The other members should be spread out or be waiting just off the platform for the train to arrive. On arrival, everyone should close up and get on the train with at least two operators in the same carriage.

When on the train, an operator could be within reach of the target and one or two other team members may be in the same carriage. Ideally they should be spread about the train on different carriages all within visual contact with each other. Trouble can start when the target makes to get off the train. It may be difficult for an operator to talk on the radio when he is surrounded at close quarters by commuters and so the 'click' system may have to be used.

When boarding a Tube train in the centre of London, the carriages can be very crowded. As the train moves towards the suburbs, passengers exit leaving the carriage sparse - and with less cover for the operator. It can be advantageous to leave the train and reboard further down the platform if you are 'too close' to the target

If a seat is available use it

Whilst on the train, the team will have to be conscious of their covert equipment remaining covert. Whilst a wireless earpiece can look much like a hearing aid or a Walkman headset, a radio pressel switch could be mistaken for a trigger to a suicide bomb and someone bumping into you with a radio on your hip might give you a questioning look. If you are wearing your radio on your hip or belt, be aware when you sit down because the arm rests either side of the seats are fairly close together. If you are not careful, one will catch the base of your radio as you sit down, unclipping it and causing it to fall away when you stand up again.

Most commuters get on the train and quickly find a seat, so do this as well. If you are standing at the end of the carriage by the doors when there are plenty of free seats, it will look odd, so sit down.

Be aware that if you get on a train on the outskirts of London heading towards the City, the carriage may be very sparse with commuters. The closer you get to the City the busier it gets, therefore you have to be conscious that it is possible you will lose sight of the target. If this is the case, you have to move closer (possibly by getting off the train and getting back on again through a closer door). Also consider the opposite; getting on the train in the centre where it is extremely busy and you are very close to the target but then travelling away from the City where the carriage becomes empty.

When the target gets off the train, the team have to keep close control amongst the heavy crowds. Some of the team may end up in front of the target at this stage, which is not always ideal but they will 'peel off' when they can to get out of the target's view. Hopefully, all of the team will have heard the rapid series of clicks indicating that the target is getting off the train. Keep a keen eye out for the yellow 'Exit' direction signs as you pull into the platform, this will give you an indication of the target's direction as he gets off. If you feel that by getting off you will end up in front of the

target, move within the train to get behind him and get off by the same door.

On the escalators, an operator will need to decide, whether to be right behind him or to give him some distance. Much of the decision is down to how aware the target is and whether he is likely to be looking for surveillance. An operator will be close as the crowds will allow for and will stand behind others for cover. Just leaning slightly to the right and holding onto the handrail helps as this drops the right shoulder and lowers your profile slightly without appearing to be hiding.

The top of the escalator can be a dangerous place because the target can turn sharply to get onto another line or can go through the exit barriers. One of the worst targets to follow on the underground is one who does not really know where he is going or how to get there. Rather than keep moving at a steady pace which is good for the followers, he frequently stops and starts whilst looking at the maps or signage, which creates a real challenge to any surveillance team.

Pay particular attention of the target's body language. If he reaches for his Oyster Card, this may indicate he about to leave the station. If you get close to him at the exit barrier, you may be able to see how much credit he has remaining on the card from the display.

Exiting the station can also be testing. The team is up close and personal and suddenly you are out onto a quiet open street. Conversely, and equally testing, is coming out of the tube at Tottenham Court Road or Oxford Circus which is packed solid with pedestrians - keeping control is difficult. Surveillance on the London Underground is certainly a challenge but not impossible. It takes a practised and well rehearsed team to keep control.

As the train arrives you have to close in to keep control of the targ

When in close proximity of others, ensure your pressel switch is out of view

## DEPLOYING ON FOOT FROM A CAR (MOBILE TO FOOT)

When the target departs on foot or leaves his vehicle, the surveillance team has to act with urgency in order not to lose contact at this critical stage. Prior to surveillance commencing, the team leader should have planned and briefed his team what to do in the event that the target goes on foot (foxtrot).

If the team is involved in a three car follow and the target parks up and walks into a town centre, a foot operator should deploy straight away to take control of the target. The remainder of the team can then position their cars for the departure and then join and 'back' the eyeball on foot. Think ahead, if the target enters a car park, it is likely that he is going to park his car and go on foot, so you should be thinking of deploying the second he enters the car park.

Do not be too eager to deploy - if the target has to obtain a parking ticket and return to the car to place it in the window, wait. There's no point you getting out of the car otherwise you will have nothing to do but lurk around the car park looking like a car thief.

Ideally, one operator should remain and cover the target's vehicle in case the foot team have a loss and the target returns to his car. At times a footman will have to 'dump' his car and risk parking fines and wheel clampers. If practical, another operator can move the footman's car to a safer location for him.

The car covering Bravo 1 should now manoeuvre to get a good trigger on the car and also try to cover the exit to the car park so he can call a direction of travel when exiting. When the target is under control of the footmen, you may consider taking a quick look inside his vehicle; note how long the car parking ticket is for and anything else of interest.

If you are 'two up' in the same car and the passenger gets out on foot, remember where you were dropped off, as this should

If the target enters a pay and display car park - don't be too eager to get out of the car as the target has to buy a ticket

# DEPLOYING ON FOOT

**WHEN DEPLOYING ON FOOT REMEMBER:**

- Before you deploy, ask yourself: 'Is it necessary, do I have to get out yet?'
- Never screech to a halt, act naturally and never run or appear to rush
- Always reverse park your vehicle to enable you to manoeuvre away quickly
- Cover up any equipment, paperwork or maps
- Inform the Team Leader of your intention to go on foot, this is normally done by carrying out a radio check with your body set to your car or a team member as you deploy
- Don't forget your mobile phone and wallet
- Ensure your car is locked and remember where you parked it or where you were dropped off.
- Do not run
- Take control of the target

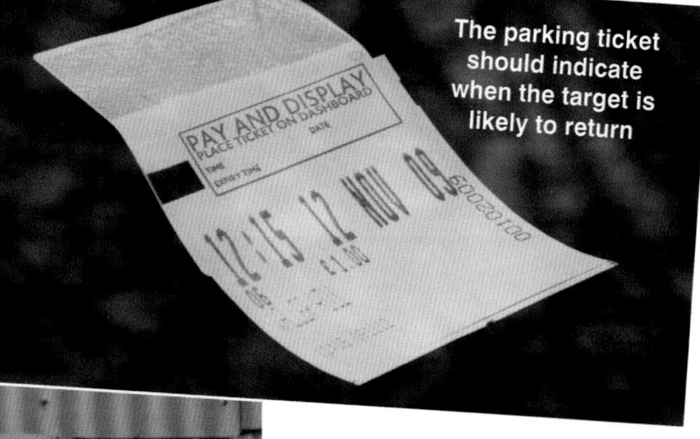

The parking ticket should indicate when the target is likely to return

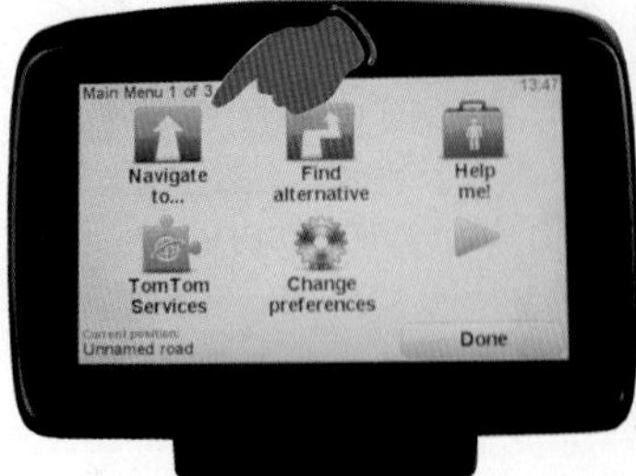

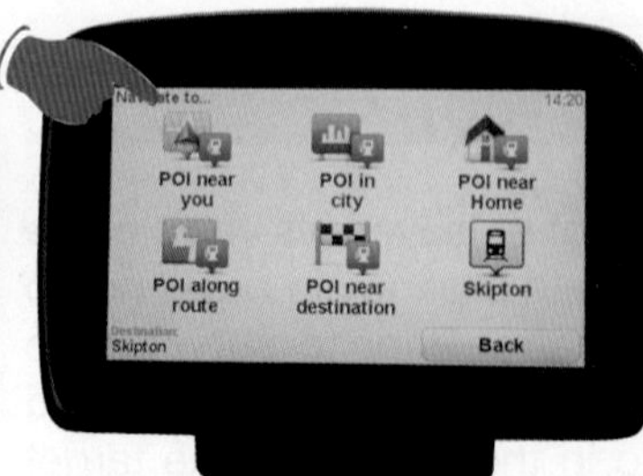


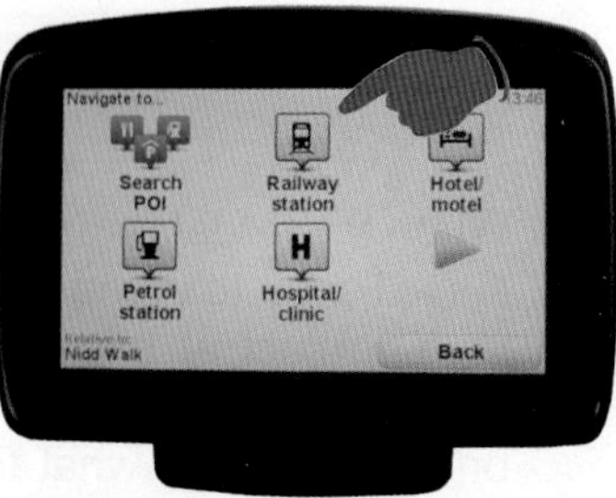


**If the target is expected to take a train ensure you know how to use your Satnav to bring up 'points of interest' such as train stations in order to help get ahead of the train**

be the same place where you get picked up again afterwards. If it is not practical to do so, ensure that you designate a place to get picked up from.

### Vehicle Back Up (Shadow Car)

When the team is deployed on foot and has control of the target, one of the operators should remain with his vehicle in order to act as back-up and 'shadow' the team. Not only can he pick up and re-deploy any footmen but if the target gets into another vehicle or onto public transport you will still have a mobile option.

The 'shadow car' can also act as a radio relay as the cars radio set will be pushing out much more power. This gives confidence to the foot team and also relays the messages back to the cars where the loggist may be located.

### Returning to your Vehicle

As soon as the target heads back towards their car, the eyeball should call 'That's Echo 1 generally back towards Bravo 1'. This gives the team warning, especially the operator covering Bravo 1. When returning to your vehicle, consider:-

- Footman to handover the eyeball to a mobile operator who is covering Bravo 1 as soon as possible. The footmen will want to get back to their vehicles as soon as possible

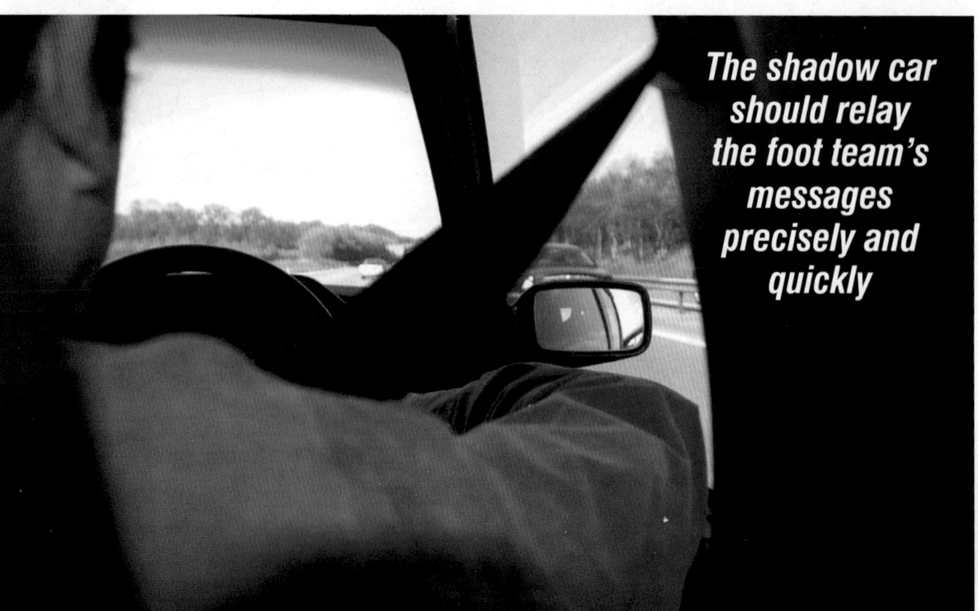

***The shadow car should relay the foot team's messages precisely and quickly***

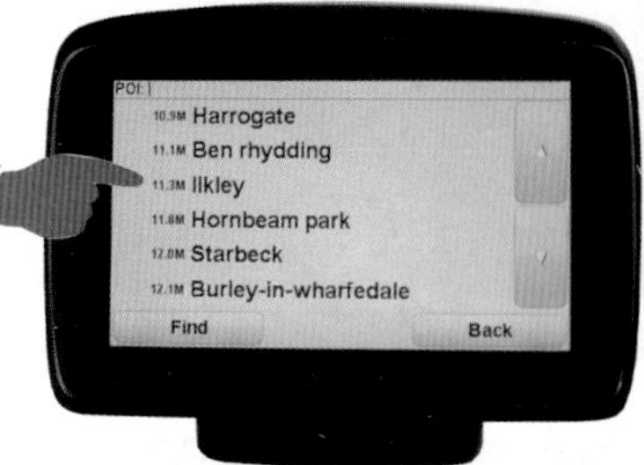


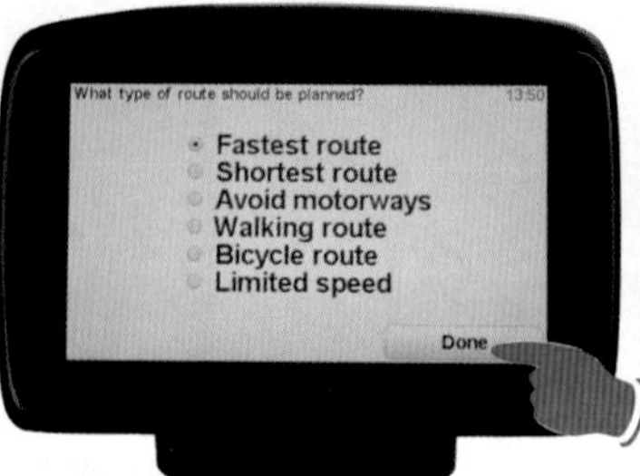


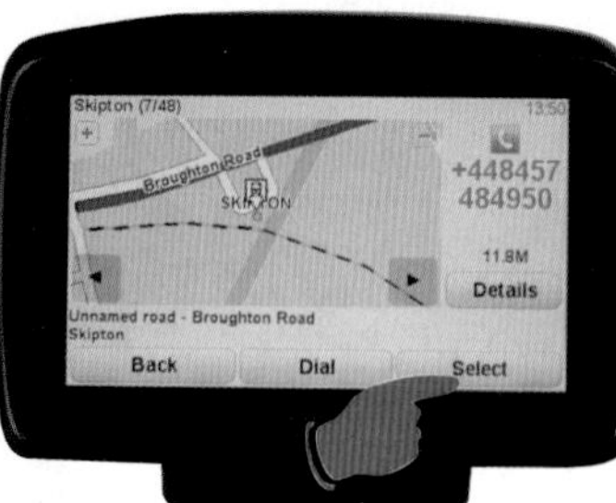


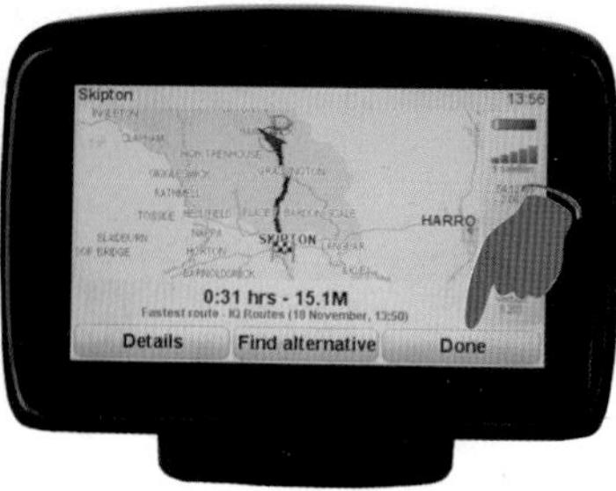

• Turn your covert radio off (it will interfere with your car set). Take out your earpiece, put it in its pouch and put it away. Do not put it somewhere on the cars dashboard, you will lose it

• Take a look around you, think third party and lock your doors

• Tell the team that you are 'complete' (back in the car) and move to your tactical position ready for going mobile

**Working 'two up'**

If you are two up in the car and one of you has been dropped off on foot, head back to the same place or the place that was designated to be picked up from. DO NOT come over the radio net asking for your cars location, 'Car 3 where are you? I need picking up...'. This will interrupt very important commentary regarding what the target is doing on a standby. If you have to obtain directions, use your mobile phone and don't clog up the radio net. Better still, your partner in the car should send you a text message with the pick up point to save you from asking.

Also at this stage, you may want to consider changing over roles such as the driver taking over the radio in the passenger seat and the returning footman getting into the drivers seat. This enables a quick transition if the target stops again and gets out on foot. You would not want to deploy the same foot person in another town later in the day, especially if the target is very aware. If you do change over roles, the driver should move into the passenger seat when his partner is on his way back to the car (not when he gets to it) otherwise you may attract unwanted third party attention as you rush around changing places.

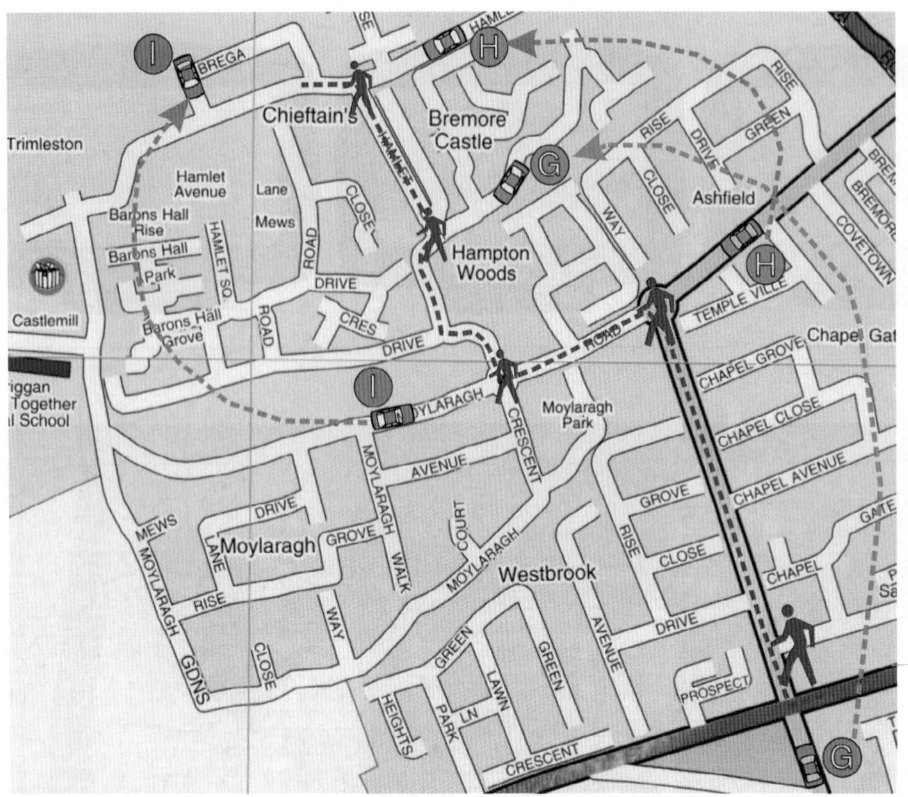

## Rolling Stakeout

Perfect foot surveillance is when it is combined with a vehicle in support. It is possible to conduct surveillance of a target that is on foot without getting out of your car. This is very tricky to carry out and a good local knowledge of the ground and area is important and aids such as a Satnav helps a great deal.

The target who may be walking down a street is controlled by a car call sign. A second call sign will be ahead of the target or covering a junction where the target could change direction and there may even be a third call sign ahead or to the side of the target. The car that 'has' gives the commentary and calls any change of direction, the car should be ahead and in position to pick him up when he goes unsighted. When this second car takes control, the first now moves ahead and takes up another tactical position (he should try to use parallel routes rather than drive past the target). He takes up a new position and the target is passed from one car to another or 'bounced' along without actually being followed.

Mobile surveillance is probably one of the most difficult types of surveillance to carry out, as there are so many factors that are against you. The target has to be followed without detection and without you losing contact with him. At the same time you have to keep a log of events, communicate with the other members of the team, navigate, photograph and consider the target's future intentions, all at the same time.

A mobile surveillance should not be a 'mad car chase', carried out at excessive speed with aggressive manoeuvring, screeching brakes and handbrake turns, but should be in a calm, relaxed manner and most importantly, being in control. As previously mentioned, a surveillance should be 'imposed' upon a target rather than a target being 'followed' - there is a vast difference.

## THE SURVEILLANCE TEAM

We refer to a mobile surveillance being carried out by a team rather than an individual. Carrying out a surveillance on your own is asking for trouble as the risk of compromise is very high from the outset and loss of contact in traffic is inevitable.

An operator on his own will soon be spotted and will therefore jeopardise any further surveillance, he may also lose the target at the first road junction he approaches. The success of a surveillance is dependant upon how many operators are used. An effective surveillance team should include a combination of cars and motorbikes.

It is appreciated that in the commercial sector, clients are very cost conscious and that a surveillance can be expensive to carry out. If you have to supply a potential client with an estimate of charges it is essential that you inform them of the importance of using a **minimum** of two operators in **separate** vehicles to carry out a mobile surveillance, which will be reflected in the costs. I would also explain to a client the pitfalls of using only one operator to conduct surveillance.

### The Team

Many surveillance teams that work on the commercial circuit work in pairs, one in a van the other a car but larger teams are also common. Pre-planning will decide on the size of the team.

Police and enforcement agencies often work 'two-up', whereas in the military and commercial sector we operate on our own 'one-up'

Factors to consider are:

• Is surveillance the answer? Can you achieve your aims by any other means such as good old fashion detective work or deploying a tracker?

• The costs per surveillance operator

• The target's awareness level - this is very important

• Area that the target is likely to be in, i.e, busy town centres, cities, rural or motorway and the likely areas he may visit - you may need a motorbike or a taxi

• Whether a static OP is required to act as 'trigger'

You are most likely to lose a target when they initially go mobile

• Is an extra foot person required to double up with a mobile operator?

A well trained and experienced surveillance team will enable a mobile surveillance to be carried out with the minimum of effort. Members can act on their own initiative without having to be instructed by the team leader, especially when the target comes to a halt and the team splits to surround him or 'boxes' him in. The team leader should be there to make important decisions only, whereas it is the eyeball that dictates and controls the target and establish where the remainder of the team is located.

Whenever possible make use of a static operator in a van or an OP to give you the 'trigger'. The most likely time to lose a target is within minutes of his departure, especially if his departure time is unpredictable and he knows his own area well. Surveillance is normally considered easy or difficult from the way that it is triggered.

## SURVEILLANCE VEHICLES

Ideally, all of the team's vehicles should be different in all respects, it would be a waste of time having two grey Ford Focus' on the same task. Ideally the colour of the car should be a dark shade, obviously a bright orange car will stand out.

**What would you want in an 'ideal' surveillance car?**

On training courses, we ask the class what would they consider to be the ideal surveillance car. They are told that they are each given £10,000 each and to go out over the next hour or so and come back with what they consider the best surveillance car to operate in. These are the common characteristics chosen:

### Common Make & Model

A common production line make and model of car such as a Ford, Vauxhall or Volkswagen of which there are plenty about. The vehicle should not have any identifiable features such as spoilers, low profile tyres or excessively tinted windows. If it is a high performance car, consider removing the 'SRi' or 'Turbo Injection' decals from the rear otherwise it could attract unwanted attention.

### Dark and Popular Colour

The colour of the vehicle is important and a neutral and nondescript colour is better than something bright like canary yellow or white. You will always be seen but being noticed is something different, especially after numerous sightings. Greys, dark greens or dark blue should help you blend in that much better. Avoid black cars (especially with tinted windows) as they can look rather diplomatic or sinister and draw attention. A white car is easily mistaken for a Police car. Imagine you are driving along a road and you see a white car in your rear view mirror - what happens next? You suddenly take your foot off the accelerator and scrutinise your mirrors until you decide whether that car behind you is or is not a Police car! It draws the eye.

**CAR SELECTION** White car... police car? Yellow car? Neutral colour (centre) is prefered choice for surveillance

### Minimum 1.6+ Litre Engine Size

We are not embarking on a mad car chase but if you become detached from the team or held up by a slow motorist, you need some power in the vehicle for you to overtake quite quickly, especially large slow moving vehicles. A 1.8 or 2 litre engine should suffice.

### Safe and Roadworthy

The car should be safe to drive at high speed and be able to cope with numerous 3 point turns and tight manoeuvring. The car should be absolutely roadworthy in all respects and strongly built with airbags.

### No Noticeable Markings

The vehicle should be fairly plain with no visible or distinguishing marks. Extra fog lamps, low profile tyres or fancy alloy wheels should be avoided. Likewise, excessive scratches, dents, damage and malfunctioning lights will help to identify and make the vehicle more noticeable. Ensure that all the wheel trims are present and are of the same style.

Manual or automatic?

Damage on the wheel arch is noticeable

***Camouflaging your vehicle will not help you 'blend-in'!***

It is not recommended to use vehicles with personalised registration plates, or those that will easily be remembered such as having the letters ROD, BAT or SAM.

**Automatic Transmission**

This is down to personal preference but some operators prefer to drive an automatic car. When you are holding a radio fist mic', giving a radio commentary, programming a Satnav, navigating, using your Dictaphone and grabbing your camera all at the same time, it helps not to have to change gear.

**Air Conditioning**

Air conditioning is a good feature to have especially in hot weather. The only draw back is that you have to sit there with your engine constantly running, which could attract unwanted attention. On balance, I would rather have air conditioning than not.

**5 Door**

Again, this is personal preference and if you are involved in a surveillance where you are likely to be picking up or dropping off foot people on a regular basis (or OP teams) this is a must and avoids the passenger having to get out to put the front seats forward to let people get into the back. If you are operating in hostile areas, rear doors will be an advantage if you have to evacuate a casualty fairly quickly.

**Avoid Uniformity**

All of the above are good features to look for in a surveillance vehicle but what you have to be mindful of is that if we all go out and buy a car to suit, you may end up with six tidy Ford Focus', all grey, 1.8 litre, automatic, air conditioning, with 4 doors! Beware of uniformity.

## WEEKLY MAINTENANCE

Obviously, your vehicle has to be roadworthy at all times and you should make a habit of checking your car on a regular basis; points to look out for are remembered by the mnemonic **POWER:**

**P** **PETROL.** Ensure that you fill up with fuel every morning of surveillance and have a spare can in the boot.

**O** **OIL.** Check the oil level at regular intervals.

**W** **WATER.** The coolant water needs to be topped up to prevent overheating and the screen washer needs to be kept full, especially in the winter months.

**E** **ELECTRICS.** Ensure that the lights work correctly, especially if driving at night. The target may notice if you have a light out and you also run the risk of being stopped by the police if you have a light out.

**R** **RUBBER.** Ensure that your tyres have enough tread and the air pressure is correct. Do not forget to check your spare tyre as this is often overlooked.

**Beware of uniformity in vehicle selection**

## ISS CASE

I once had a white Vauxhall Nova van which was used on just about every job that we did. At one stage we took on an apprentice who had undergone training and he became quite proficient. However, not long after my protege, he came to see me, proud as punch exclaiming, 'I've bought my own surveillance van.' I was quite impressed until I saw it. Yes, you guessed it, a white Vauxhall Nova van. *I'm not sure what he's doing now...*

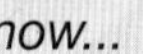

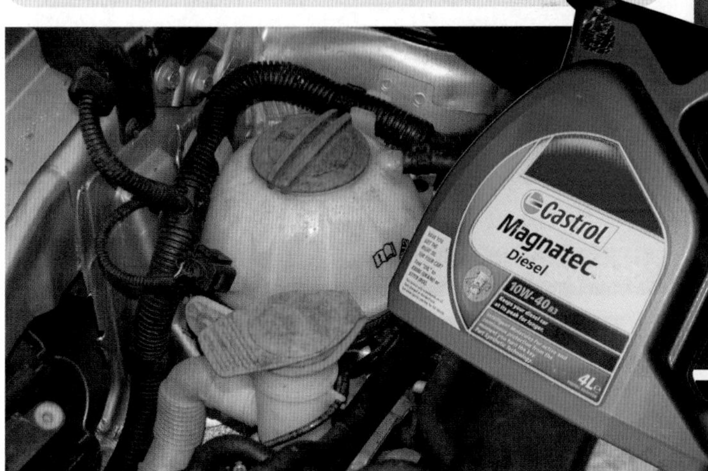


Keeping your windows clean is essential

Voltage inverter is useful for keeping your radio, camera and phone on charge whilst on the go

Also consider the cleanliness of your car, inside and out. The interior should be kept clean and tidy but not too immaculate, you do not want the car to look sterile but lived in and used. If it is too untidy, (I have seen many cars full of old newspapers, magazines and a week's worth of fast food wrappings), it will attract the attention of someone who is aware. If I were searching for a surveillance operator's car, this would be the one that I would look out for and take notice of. Any items of importance should also be kept out of view such as maps, brief sheets and radio parts.

The cleanliness of the exterior should also be considered. If you are working in an area that is more 'up-market' then you would not want to be driving around in a vehicle covered in dirt and grime as you may appear suspicious and be reported. Conversely, if you are operating in a rougher area, driving about in a shiny-waxed vehicle, you will also stick out and thus be noticed. Small points but worthy of consideration.

### SAFETY EQUIPMENT

In addition to your car bag containing your surveillance equipment, there are certain items that you may want to keep in your vehicle for safety.

Tyre sealant is essential for getting you back on the move quickly following a puncture

Clean glass reflects light better than dirty glass

Keep your windows up or people can see in - especially at night

- **Hi Visibility Jacket.**

By wearing this you can sit and wait for hours in some places without being bothered, it can afford you some cover. If you are not using it, then get it out of the way as it will show out; don't leave it on the dashboard.

In addition, if you encounter a road traffic accident it is something quick to throw on if you assist. A lot of people in this industry have first aid or paramedic experience and it will help establish authority if you are trying to take control of a situation where people are looking for guidance before the emergency services arrive.

- **Torch**

This is obviously useful at night. A torch such as a 'Sure Fire' is quite small but extremely powerful. A large heavy torch such as a 'Maglite' can take up more room but may come in handy for your own protection.

SAFETY FIRST: Always carry a minimum amount of safety gear

- **Windscreen Wash**

A bottle of screen wash and a cloth should be handy in order to keep the inside and outsides of the windows clean. Dirt and dead flies will play havoc with your camera if you are using auto focus modes.

During the day clean windows reflect ambient light from the sun and clouds. At night, street lighting, moonlight and other car headlights also have the same effect. These reflections make it difficult to see inside the car as the reflected light is bouncing all over. A car with dirty windows makes it easier to see through because you don't have all of the reflections, so clean them to your advantage.

If they tend to mist up quickly, especially in cold weather, the interior glass can be wiped with some cleansers that also de-mist without having to turn the 'blowers' on.

SAFETY FIRST:
Always lock your doors

• **De-Icer Spray**

Not only does it clear your windows quickly in cold weather, but as a last resort it could be used for self protection as the aerosols have quite a powerful spray and will keep an attacker at bay from a distance.

• **Protection**

There is a product on the UK market called 'Stoppa Red'. This is a small aerosol that sprays coloured dye into the face of an attacker and could be quite handy if you are in the back of a surveillance van and someone breaks in. I would check the legalities of using such products with the suppliers before purchase. An air horn or a shriek alarm might shock an attacker into fleeing.

• **Voltage Inverter**

This is a very useful piece of kit to keep in the car, it transforms the cars 12 volt DC power supply to 220 volts AC. This enables you to run mains operated equipment and chargers for radios, phones and cameras.

• **First Aid Kit**

A first aid kit if needed for yourself, the surveillance team and any other emergencies that you may come across. Trauma dressings, plasters, splints and basic analgesics should be included. If everyone in the team has a first aid kit, ensure that you all store it in the same place in your vehicle and if someone needs it, use theirs' not yours.

• **Tyre Weld**

A flat tyre is quickly repaired with 'tyre weld' which comes in the form of an aerosol can that can be injected into the flat tyre in order to get you out of a hostile situation quickly. Similar repair kits also help if you have a radiator leak called 'Radweld'.

• **Roadside Assistance**

At a relatively small cost, this is probably the most effective insurance policy that I have ever taken out. Of the times that I have broken down, three out of five happened when I was on my way to somewhere important or I was in a remote area. Unless you are a good mechanic, membership of one of these organisations is a must.

**Lock Your Doors**

This is a personal preference but it is advised that you lock your car doors whenever you are inside, especially in built-up areas. In the past I have seen suspicious third parties actually go up to a car, open the door and confront the driver and it was quite frightening for them. There are some 'hard' people about especially in some rough estates who would not think twice about having a go at you. After all, you are in their area, you may be interrupting their activities and they do not want you there, whoever you are.

Even worse, is having the actual target approach you and pull open your car door, you can consider yourself well and truly compromised if this happens. Do not forget to lock the rear doors as well; it can be even more embarrassing if the target gets into the back seat!

**Mobile Communications**

Many operators and agencies adopt their own style of radio call signs and codes and so there are no hard and fast rules regarding this. Use whatever system you are used to or happy with.

In simple terms, each vehicle could be termed: Car 1, Car 2 and Car 3. However, if someone is eavesdropping on the radio net it will not take long to establish how many

Keep your windows up and your radio below the level of the dashboard - unlike these two!

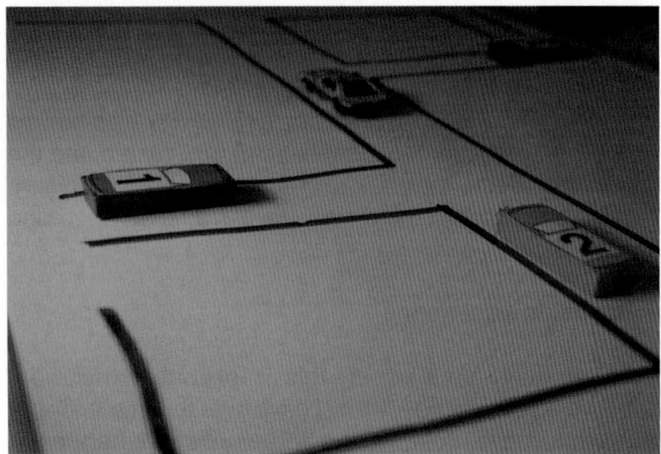

## The Crew

Generally, you may find yourself on your own but a vehicle crew can consist of a number of operators. Remember, that even two operators in a vehicle (two up) can arouse suspicions, especially when waiting for a trigger.

Ensure maps and radios are kept out of view

Four men in a vehicle can look hostile so be aware of how you look to third parties. It is recommended that one operator per vehicle is used at most times, unless an extra operator is required to deploy on foot at short notice (on the commercial circuit that is).

If two persons are used (as is often the case in the Police and other Enforcement Agencies) decide on the tasks of driver and footman/radio operator. Their appearance should fit with the vehicle and area of operations. The second operator could sit in the rear seat behind the driver in order to remain out of view and give the appearance of being 'one up'. In addition the second operator sitting in the rear can easily take covert photographs or video when necessary.

Enforcement Agencies will often use two operators in order to share responsibilities so that one person concentrates on the driving whilst the other operates the radio and provides the commentary. This has its 'pros and cons' and may arouse suspicion from some 'aware' targets. If you have to sit in your car for a period (even if it's a short halt whilst following) try and move over to the passenger seat. If the target (or anyone else) sees you, they will naturally presume that you are waiting for your driver to return without arousing too much suspicion.

Do not wear brightly coloured clothing or have anything noticeable on the dashboard or dangling from the mirror that draws attention. A change of jacket or the wearing of a hat for a short period is advisable.

cars are involved. Hence, we tend to use the phonetic alphabet for car call signs, i.e: Golf, Hotel, India etc..

If you are using a hand held radio (or a fist mic) try to keep the radio set below the level of the dashboard and do not bring it up to your mouth - if your target is checking his mirrors he will see you. Third parties will also notice you if you are not careful. In a similar vein, do not make a habit of bobbing your head down whenever you speak on the radio, this too looks peculiar and may be noticed.

When you are static, ensure that your radio equipment is out of view and that radio transmissions cannot be heard through open windows, especially on hot days.

If you are two up in the car, make it look natural when conversing on the radio, actually appear as if you are having a conversation rather than two heads looking in opposite directions - be natural.

The operator in the back should use the seats as cover and sit to one side

## THE MOBILE SURVEILLANCE

**Identify a good RV where the team can meet up before deploying on the ground**

Considering the phases of our surveillance operation (Stakeout, Pick Up, Follow and Housing) we will now discuss the tactics used in a mobile surveillance.

### The Stakeout or Plotting Up

The stake out is the positioning of the team with a trigger in place, to ensure that the target is boxed in and cannot escape. There are other terms used for the stakeout such as: on plot, on the grid, on the diagram, in the box and on the carpet.

On arrival in the area where the surveillance is to commence, you will probably meet up with the team at a pre-determined rendezvous (RV) nearby. The team members would now carry out a recce of the general area to familiarise themselves with the layout of the location and escape routes. You need to carry out a recce of the target's address by carrying out a drive past and possibly, also a walk past.

If you have a sketch map drawn from the initial recce, use it in order to identify where the target address is before you actually get to it. The last thing you want to do is to drive down the target street, crawling at 5mph whilst trying to identify the target property - you will be noticed by someone. If you consult your sketch plan, you can see which side of the road the targets address is on, how far down it is and you can identify it from a safe distance before you get on top of it.

On a drive past you need to consider the following:

• Any sign of life or activity such as: lights on, windows open, curtains open or milk on the doorstep

• Any vehicles and their details, how they are parked and which way they intend to go

• Any trigger positions where you can plot up or put the van in as described earlier

**In streets like this, the recce should identify the target address, together with a 'marker' such as a hanging basket, along with the colour of the front door as all these properties look the same**

A walk past enables you to obtain more detail at the target's property such as a registration number

Some stakeouts have to be fairly tight especially in busy areas so the target does not escape

• Check and double check that the address you have identified is the correct one - this is important

• Consider dropping off a foot person in order carry out a walk past to take a closer look and obtain more detail

Considering the phases of our surveillance operation (Stakeout, Pick Up, Follow and Housing) we will discuss the tactics used in a mobile surveillance stake out. There are other terms used for the stakeout such as: on 'plot', on the 'grid', on the 'diagram', in the 'box' and on the 'carpet'.

## STAKEOUTS

The stakeout phase can be carried out in different ways, which we will look at separately.

- *Primary Stakeout*
- *Secondary Stakeout*
- *Tertiary Stakeout*

## PRIMARY STAKEOUT

A primary stake out is when we have a close trigger in place to see and initiate the surveillance, he should be able to see the front door of a property, the gate or vehicle. The other call signs are positioned in a loose box around the target, covering the escape routes and ready to react.

This primary stakeout should always be considered first as you have a trigger that can give advanced warning of any activity so that the call signs can then close up and move to their pick up positions.

In the diagram, you will note that there are only two exits out of the estate and these have to be 'covered' by the mobile units. By this we do not mean that call signs Hotel and India actually sit on the junction, they only cover them.

It may not be physically possible to sit there (double yellow lines, busy traffic for example) or practical. What it does

**DRIVE PAST** On a drive past there is a lot to remember - a dictaphone can be a useful surveillance device

ISS US surveillance course. On some stakeouts you may not be able to physically see the target, therefore vehicle trackers can be used.

mean, is that the mobile units can park anywhere they like (if it is safe and away from the target) so long as they can get to their respective 'pick-up' points in time, on a standby.

In **DIAGRAM 1** you will note:

• **Golf** has the trigger. He has to be close enough to be able to identify the target but far enough away not to be noticed. Remember, if you can see the target, he can see you. Golf will trigger, give a description and call a direction at the first T junction.

• **Hotel's** responsibility is to 'cover' the west exit and pick up the Target if he goes right at the T

• **India's** responsibility is to cover the east exit and pick up the target if he goes left at the T

When the target goes mobile, Call sign Golf will not move and so it will be Hotel or India that is responsible for 'taking the first follow'.

## SECONDARY STAKEOUT

Sometimes it is not possible to get an 'eyes on' trigger of the target address and therefore no one can call a standby when the target initially goes mobile.

The only option is to place an operator at each possible exit (or escape route) on the route that the target may take on his departure.

If the options are many, the team leader should decide on which exits are the most likely to be taken. All the team members should know the whereabouts of their colleagues and the escape routes that they are covering. It may be that frequent drive pasts have to be made of the target in the event he has slipped the net or to check for any activity.

In this stakeout, the operators have to be alert and observant at all times whilst they cover their options. It is not

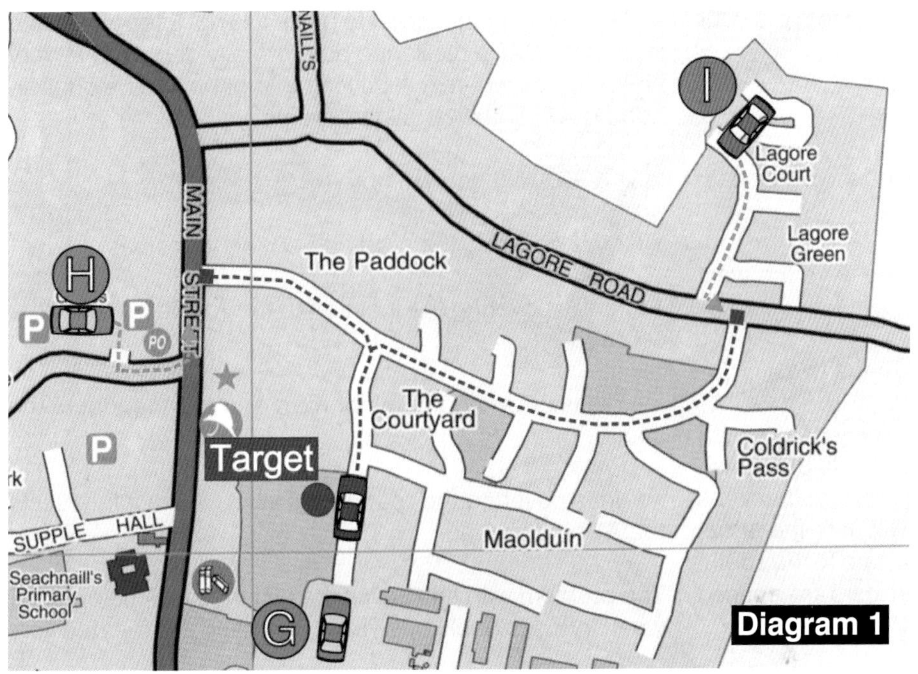


Diagram 1

If covering a junction you must be focused so the target does not slip past

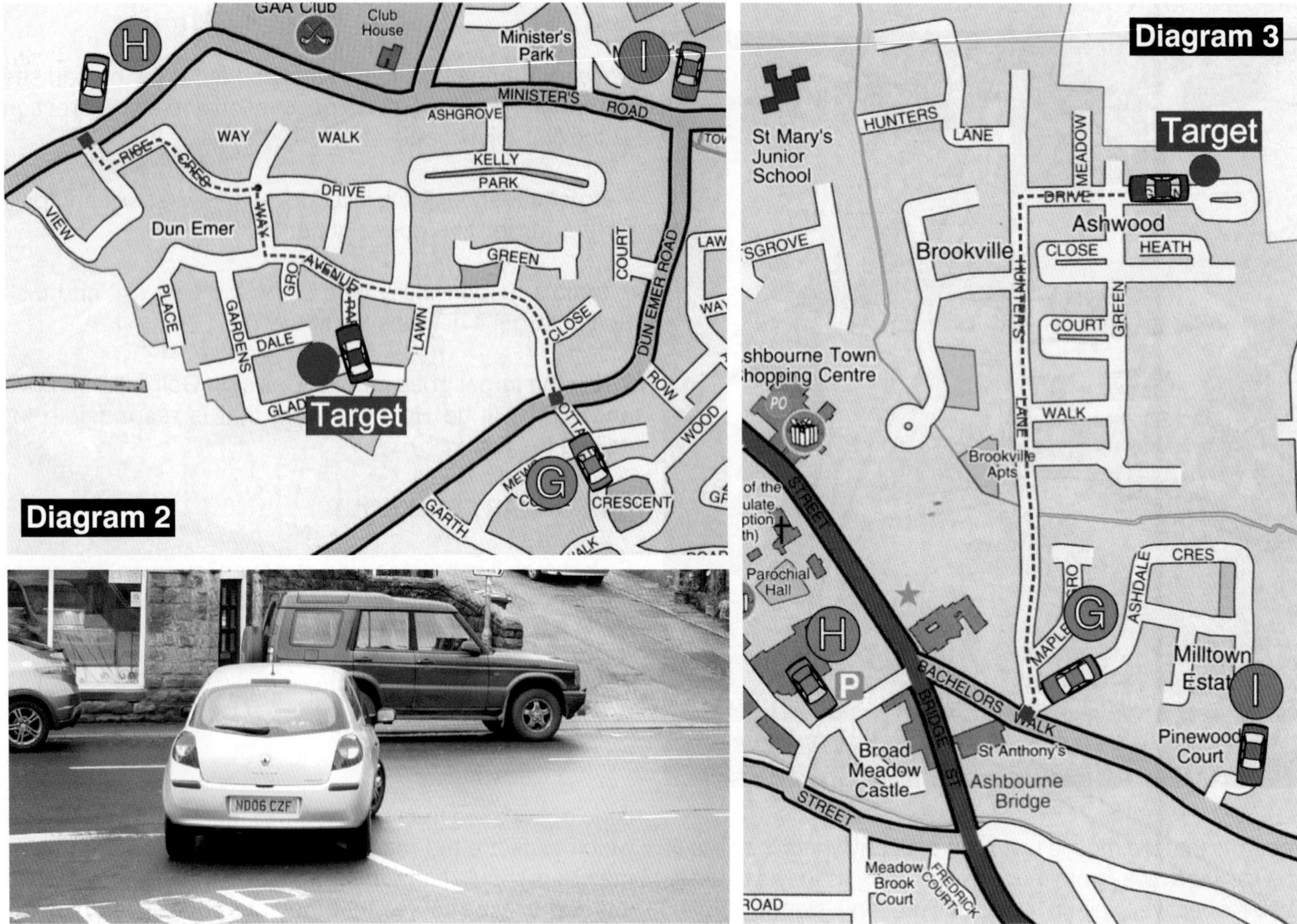


always ideal as the standby is a very quick one and does not give much time for the team to react. In addition, it may be that a similar vehicle has quickly driven past the option you are covering and so you will now have to move and get close to it in order to confirm or deny that it is your target.

In **DIAGRAM 2** you will note:

• Golf's responsibility is to cover and observe the east option

• Hotel's responsibility is to cover and observe the west option

• India's responsibility is to float between the two

Each call sign should identify how to quickly get to each others options on a standby, as they will have to play catch up. India is positioned in the middle in order to 'back' as soon as possible. In **DIAGRAM 3** you will note the target is forced to take the only exit out of the estate to the south. And in **DIAGRAM 4** you will note, the team cars are 'spaced out' even further.

**Tertiary Stake Out**

This type of stake out is similar to the above but on a wider scale, where each escape route is covered by a call sign and you wait for the target to pass. It is not used very often in commercial surveillance but normally deployed in very hostile areas where it is difficult to plot up in a neighbourhood or when the target is extremely aware.

In **DIAGRAM 5** you will note:

• Golf is covering the road and option to the east

• Hotel is covering the junction to the A1 motorway to the south

• India is covering the minor road and roundabout to the south

• Kilo is covering the road to the west where it intersects the A1 southbound

The problem with this is that the distance is a major factor when trying to back the eyeball. We used this method very

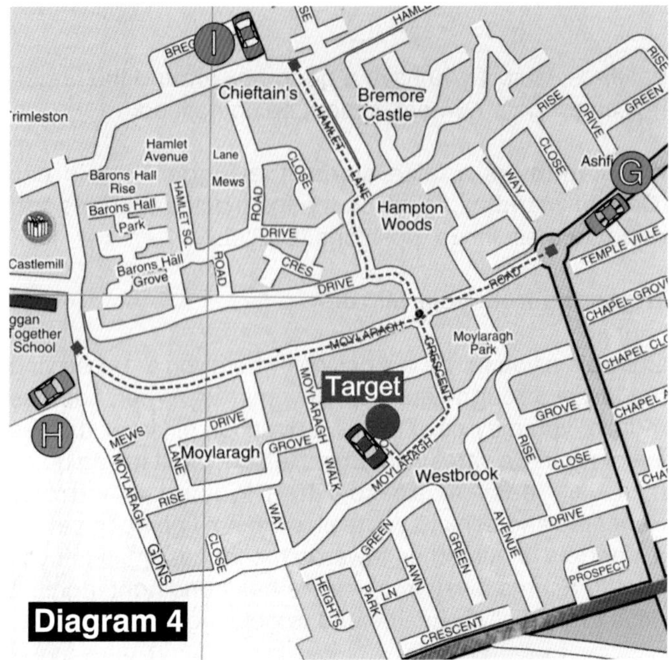


recently when working in a rural area where it would have been ideal to insert a rural OP to act as a trigger but it was not possible at the time. By the time the backing call sign caught up with the eyeball, the target had travelled some 20 miles.

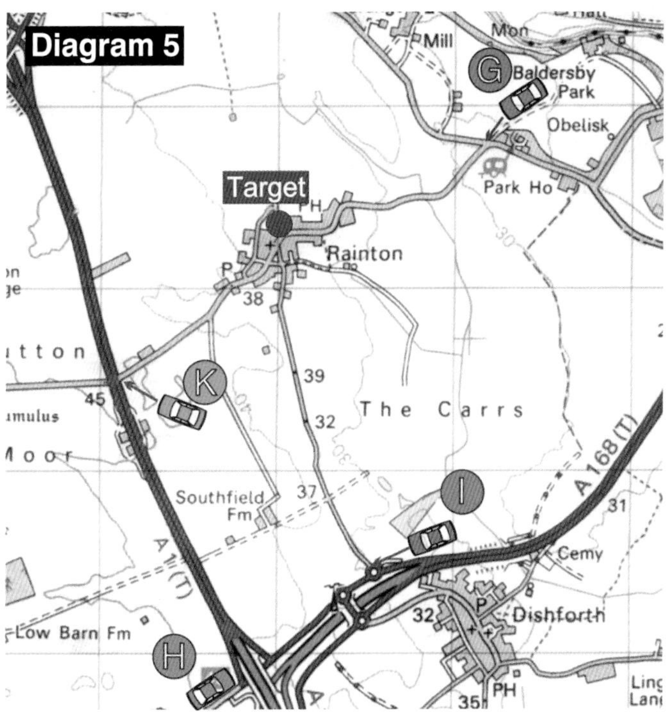


## THE TRIGGER

Once you have the trigger in position, it is his job to maintain the eyeball on the property and report any events to the remainder of the team. Nothing may happen for a number of hours and so the task requires great concentration. If nothing happens, then report to the team, 'No Change, No Change' on a regular basis and at least every 15 minutes. This not only informs the team that you are still in control but also keeps them up to date and doubles up as a radio check.

If there is a problem with communications such as being out of range, it is the mobile units that have to move to a better position to get better reception, as the trigger person cannot move.

The mobile units have to 'plot up' in a position that is safe, where they will not arouse any suspicion from third parties. These units do not have to see the target address but have to get off the plot completely and cover the targets options to escape. They need to be in a position to take up the follow when the target moves. These positions can be anywhere, so long as they can get to the point where they can intercept the target when he goes mobile.

When static, ask yourself the following: What is my reason for being here? How long can I stay here and do I look out of place? If nothing is happening, trust the trigger person and try to avoid carrying out 'drive pasts' unless requested. This often happens out of boredom rather than having a deliberate effect. The time you decide to drive past to take a look, the target will be coming out or looking out of his window onto the street.

Using a van enables you to obtain a close trigger, call a direction of travel and prevents having to carry out drive pasts

### Cross Contamination

The stake out phase can be extremely boring but you have to remain alert to your surroundings at all times. When boredom cuts in, I have seen operators (not the trigger) drive to each others location for a chat for a short period and then move back to their position. Just about everyone I know in the surveillance industry including myself, has been guilty of it at one time or another. Just be aware of cross contaminating another operator or drawing attention to yourself when drawing up alongside a colleague's car.

Don't 'pair up' and cross-contaminate each other

**Action on a 'STANDBY STANDBY!'**

As soon as the target appears out in the open or there are signs of movement, the trigger person should call, **'Possible Standby, Standby'** and commence a running commentary on the target's activities and description. This 'standby' is a wake up call to put the rest of the team on alert.

As soon as the trigger gives a 'standby', the mobile units should carry out the following:

- Instantly acknowledge with your call sign in alpha numerical order. When the team moves, no one should be left behind

- Be ready to turn your engine on and put your seat belt on

- Listen very carefully to the 'trigger's' radio commentary, he will be giving descriptions, vehicle details and directions, remember them.

- Move from your 'plot up' (or Lie Up) position and draw near to the spot where you intend to pick up, or intercept the target

- Be prepared to pick up the target and take the first follow or act as back-up

- Do not come up on the radio to ask 'What's happening?' If there is a period of silence from the trigger it may be because he is filming or taking photographs, be patient.

- If you hear **'Standby standby, that's Bravo 1 mobile towards Red 1 and unsighted to me'.** Expect a period of silence on the radio net as the target manoeuvres within the box until he is picked up by a team member. There is nothing worse than hearing over the radio net, 'Who has the Eyeball?' by a panic stricken team member. Have patience, wait, if you have a good box around the target, he cannot go anywhere without being noticed.

If a standby is a false alarm, the trigger should call **'Cancel Standby',** to which the team acknowledges and return to their 'lie up' positions (LUP's).

**Triggering from your Mirrors**

Quite often you will be in a position where you are observing the target through your rear view mirrors. When he goes mobile, you may have to call a direction of travel such as left or right. Be careful not to get left and right mixed up as it is very easy to do so when looking in mirrors. Rehearse and think to yourself, what am I going to say on a standby. 'If he comes towards me he has gone left, left and if he turns away from me he has gone right, right'. It pays to mentally rehearse and to get it right first time.

**Trigger Person Do Not Move!**

Remember that surveillance is all about team work; when the target moves, inform the team of the direction. If he goes out of your view, let them know that you are 'unsighted', this is their cue to take the eyeball. If a team member hears the phrase, 'unsighted to me', he will realise that the target is out of view and control and therefore the eyeball is 'up for grabs'. Whoever sees the target first can take over the commentary and direct the team.

When the target moves off, keep still, do not move or react with the target. Most compromises by inexperienced operators occur when the target initially moves off and is quickly followed. Imagine, the first thing the target does when he pulls out is to check his rear view mirror, especially if he is aware. So don't be there, wait until he is out of your sight before moving.

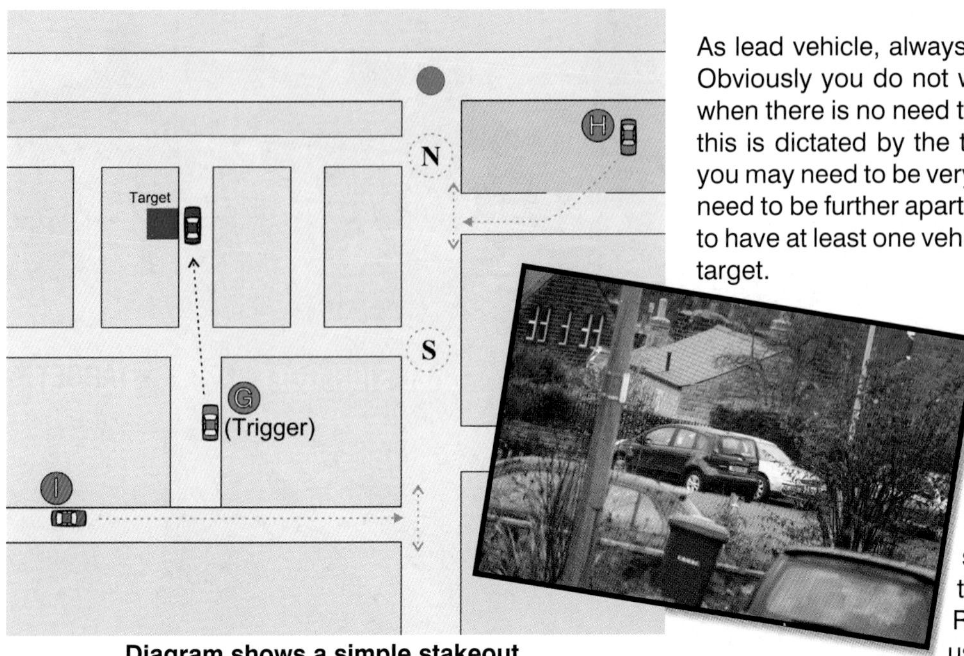


**Diagram shows a simple stakeout**

**As Trigger, never move off until you are out of the target's mirrors**

Referring to the diagram above, if the target moves towards the north exit on the estate, it would be Hotel's responsibility to pick him up and call a direction on the main road. If he goes left towards the mini roundabout, Hotel can call this and India can come round and take the first follow. If the target takes a right on the main road, Hotel can call it on the radio and so India can stay where he is until the target passes and then takes up the follow. This is operating as a team should do, passing the target from one person to another. Up to this stage, no one has actually 'followed' the target but surveillance has been 'imposed'. At your briefing, it would have been decided whether the trigger vehicle is to stay where it is, or whether it joins in the follow.

If the trigger vehicle is a van, we will often leave it where it is until the target has cleared the area in case the target returns. It is useful to bring the van with the team as it can take part in the follow (with caution) and it can also be used to re-trigger the target when he has been 'housed'.

**Team Positions - The Surveillance Convoy**

Once on the move, the lead vehicle or 'eyeball' should be in control of the surveillance and at that moment in time is in charge of the radio net. He should let everyone know by calling **'India Has'** (the Eyeball), the response straight away should be **'Golf Backing'** from the back up. India will now be giving a running commentary to the remainder of the team, to which no one should interrupt except for the backing call sign when acknowledging.

As lead vehicle, always drive normally and be confident. Obviously you do not want to be right behind the target when there is no need to but common sense prevails and this is dictated by the terrain and area. In built-up areas you may need to be very close, whereas in rural areas you need to be further apart. As a general rule, always attempt to have at least one vehicle for cover between you and the target.

When approaching an obstacle such as traffic lights, a junction or a roundabout, you may need to be as close as possible to avoid being held back. On approach, never crawl up behind the target, if you do this you will soon be spotted or have the target's suspicions aroused. Remember, you are a public road user going about your normal daily routine and therefore you have to act normally.

As soon as the team has settled down, the team should automatically acknowledge the eyeball.

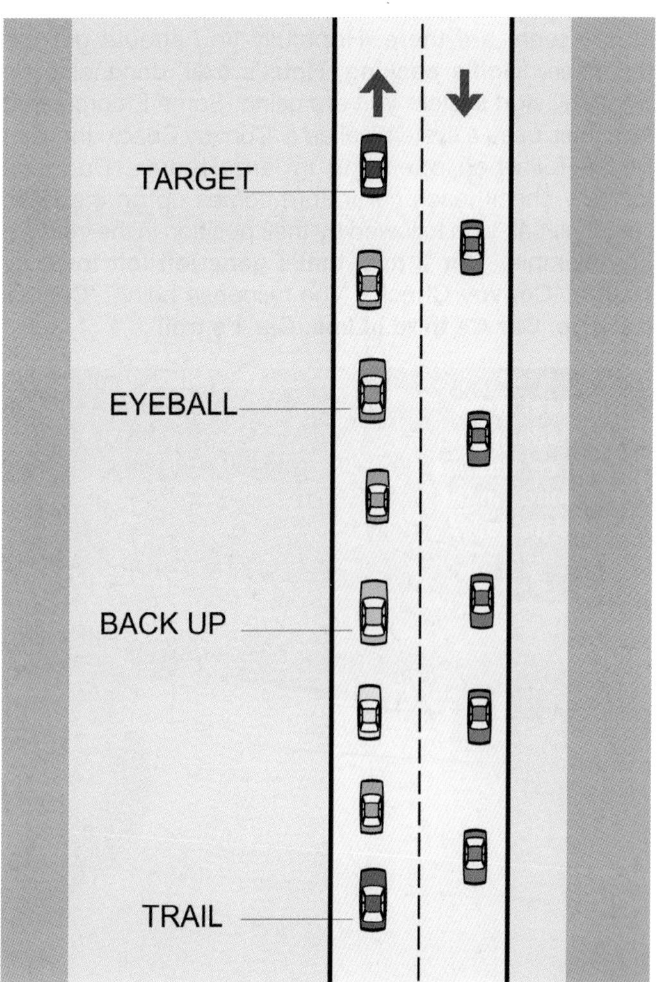

CALL SIGN GOLF

TARGET

CALL SIGN INDIA

***The team needs to close up at road junctions controlled by traffic lights***

If your team members have not acknowledged that they are with you, carry out a quick radio check to ensure that all the team are there. Hopefully you should get the response, **'Golf's backing, Hotel's trail'** depending on what call sign system you are using. Some Enforcement Agencies used a system called a 'Convoy Check' that can be useful when operating in large teams. During a 'convoy check' each car in turn comes up on the radio with their call-sign followed by their position in the convoy. For example, **'Car 3 has, that's gone left left towards Halifax. Convoy Check?'** The response being, **'Car 2's back up, Car 4's third in line, Car 1's trail'**.

In rural areas consider your distance and use the bends in the road as cover

Generally, the backing call sign acknowledges every transmission from the eyeball with his call sign (Golf etc.). This ensures that the team are receiving the commentary, gives confidence to the eyeball and clarifies that there is actually a call sign backing. Each other member of the team normally comes up on the radio net with their call sign atfrequent intervals, especially after changes of direction.

If you are the eyeball and you do not hear an acknowledgement from a call sign after a period of time, it is your job to carry out a radio check to clarify that they are still with the team. If you cannot establish comms, then you have to get the backing car to relay messages to them or get onto the mobile phone as soon as possible.

**Distance and Positioning**

Very often you will come to a halt whilst waiting in a queue of traffic, you may be directly behind the target or have a vehicle for cover. Either way, do not get too close to the car in front for safety reasons. If you are too close, you will not have enough manoeuvring room to be able to pull out in an emergency. As a general rule, make sure that you can see the tyres of the car in front or a section of the road surface.

As a general rule, but this also depends on the ground and terrain that you are in. The eyeball car should impose surveillance on the target. The backing car should be at a distance as if it was putting the eyeball under surveillance. The third or trail car should also have the same considerations as if imposing surveillance on the back up car. We

A convoy may be forced to 'bunch up' together when the target is held by a slow mover

Make sure that you can see the tyres of the car in front, this way you will not be too close

find on courses that everyone wants to see the target at the same time and this is quite understandable until an element of trust in the eyeball is obtained. Remember, if you can see the target, he can see you, so don't be afraid of using distance and cover at the right time.

If you are in the back up position and you have become slightly detached or held up, tell the eyeball that you are no longer backing. This is important and prevents the eyeball from carrying out a quick handover or asking for one. As soon as you are in position to support again, tell the eyeball that you are backing.

If you are driving in rural areas, try not to be constantly in the mirrors of the target if you have no vehicles for cover.

If you get detached you have to make ground as quickly as possible

Use dips in the road as cover

Use the road, hills and bends in order to catch glimpses of the target as he encounters them thus 'clipping' the sight of his rear bumper. For the remainder of the team, do exactly the same to the team member in front but not be too evenly spaced apart as this could look unnatural and make the convoy appear to be in formation, especially on a long straight road.

In heavy traffic, try to look through the car in front of you rather than weaving in an out trying to see around the car in front, it is un-natural.

**Be Kind To No One But The Team**

If you are in a long queue of slow moving traffic, sometimes it helps if you have one vehicle in between for cover. If you do not, consider letting a car come in between you and the target from an adjoining side road, only do this if it is to your advantage. Do not flash your headlights but give a discreet finger wave to let them out.

However, be very careful if you do this as the driver that you have just let in will now be in a good mood because

Do not let anyone in from a side road unless it is to your advantage

In heavy traffic you need to 'close up' and be directly behind the target

they have just been let in. If they also decide to let someone else in further up the road, and then they let someone else in, before you know it you are four or five cars behind the target; so, be very careful if you decide to let someone in as cover.

If you do want a car to pull out in front of you, make a determined effort to avoid eye contact with the driver, otherwise they will catch your eye and take it as an invitation to pull out. We say that we should be courteous to no one but the surveillance team, with out being obviously aggressive. If you are in a long queue of traffic (waiting for lights or approaching a roundabout) and your team members are being held back, do not be afraid to call them forward on the radio when the traffic conditions are safe.

Provide a gap to your front and let them slot into it. Obviously, you do not want to carry out this procedure in the target's mirrors, you will be noticed.

Quite often, a car may be detached and trying hard to catch up but is held up by a slow mover. If the eyeball or backing car can see that it is clear up ahead and that there is no risk of adjoining traffic turning onto the road, you could call the road 'clear' in order for the rearmost car to blindly overtake the slow mover. This technique should be treated with extreme caution and should not be attempted by the faint hearted as you are putting your total trust in the car that is calling it 'clear'.

## MOBILE COMMENTARY

Whilst carrying out a mobile surveillance, the commentary given by the lead car to the other members of the team should be precise, straight to the point and immediate. Whilst you as eyeball are in front, the remainder of the team may not be able to see the target and be some distance

Using dot maps are essential when operating in foreign areas especially when you cannot read or pronounce road signs

behind. Remember, the commentary is for their benefit not yours.

Certain phrases and descriptions are used to simplify messages and to assist the operators because they will not have any visual contact with the target. Although these phrases may appear obvious or unnecessary, they are to assist you and the team to prevent any confusion and subsequent loss of contact.

All messages are to be kept short and accurate. A message lasting half a minute could mean that the target has travelled half a mile in that time and changed direction, so do not waffle on and repeat yourself unnecessarily. The only things that should be repeated are important statements such as **'Stop stop', 'left left', 'right right'** etc to emphasise important changes. Commentary such as, 'that's approaching a T junction, approaching a T junction...' is not considered that important to say twice as it takes away the importance of a message when it really matters.

You should keep the team up to date with an accurate running commentary giving details of the targets:

- *Direction of travel*
- *Speed*
- *Intentions to turn (which indicators are used or the position of the wheels)*
- *Any deviations made*
- *Its current position in relation to local landmarks (his position, not yours)*
- *Any unusual driving tactics*
- *Loss of contact, temporary or otherwise*

**Direction of Travel**

When giving the direction of travel, use large visible local landmarks as an aid as street names can lead to confusion if you are not familiar with the area and they can also be difficult to spot at speed. The direction of travel may be given in one the following ways:

**'That's following the signs marked A629 Halifax...'**

**OR**

**'No deviation, passing windmill on the nearside...'**

**OR**

**'Continuing straight towards Halifax...'**

**OR**

**'Still straight towards Red 4...'**

Ensure the target has actually made the turn before you call, 'that's gone right, right towards Skipton'

**Left and Right, Nearside and Offside**

When giving any indication regarding the target's movements, messages should be repeated to make sure that everyone is informed at once. This eliminates other team members using 'air' time by asking for repeated messages. For instance, if the target turns Right, he's turned **'Right Right'.** If he stops he's come to a **'Stop Stop'.** We repeat the call two or three times in the event that the operator is 'clipping' their calls and the call is missed by the team.

The terms Left or Right should only be used when describing a change in direction and should not be used when pointing out a landmark. For example, **'Target passing church on the Left'** is wrong and should be, **'That's passing church on the Nearside'** (or Offside as applicable).

The reason for this difference is so that any team member who may be held back in traffic and may be getting out of radio range can still attempt to catch up with the surveillance by listening to the commentary. Should the radio message be 'broken' and all that is heard are the words **'Church.//.Left',** he would presume the target has turned left at the church. Whereas if he only heard the words **'Church.//.Nearside'** he would decide to continue straight (with no deviation) knowing that a landmark (the church) had been indicated on the nearside.

A change in direction should always be followed by a **'towards'** or an **'at'** or an **'into',** in order to emphasise the direction. For example, **'that's gone right right towards**

'That's passing the Black Swan of the near side'

When vehicles drive on the right-side of the road, the nearside is considered as being right, for example 'that's passing the 7-11 on the nearside

**the football ground'** or **'that's gone left left at the phone box'.** Changes in direction are very important information and the guy at the back wants to know exactly where to make his turn or make a run on a parallel road.

Should the target use his indicators at any time, the eyeball should inform the team of his intentions; for instance, **'that's held at a 'T' junction with a nearside indicator'.** This enables other operatives to prepare for the turn by getting into the correct lane or taking other action. If he is not indicating but his wheels are aligned and turned to the left then on a balance of probability, he is also intending to turn left.

If you are behind the target vehicle which is at a junction or crossroads and indicating to turn, do not indicate the same yourself. Should the target decide to drive straight across at the last second, you will be committed to making that turn because you indicated. Indicating might be an anti surveillance move by the target.

Satnavs can be a useful aid when trying to identify street names

### Reference Points

As the target vehicle passes identifiable landmarks (reference points) the eyeball should pass this on to the remainder of the team. For example, **'that's passing church on the nearside'.**

These reference points should be large and prominent so that the operators can see them easily from a distance and can establish how far the target is ahead of them. In this way, they can decide whether to close up or hang back as necessary.

Do not use moveable objects as reference points such as 'passing a yellow car on the nearside' as it will have probably moved by the time the last man gets to it. Phone boxes, petrol stations, advertising boards, buildings, shops, bridges and churches are ideal reference points.

Try to avoid calling the street name as they may be difficult to see

Be careful of using street names as reference points (unless you are familiar with the area or they are really prominent) such as, **'that's passing Strutton Ground on the nearside'.** If you are back-up, the last thing that you want to do is have to slow down to find and locate a small street sign in order to read it, so use large prominent features if you can. Many operators use Satnavs and so calling out street names might be helpful as they can read the streets on the device as they approach. Just be careful when calling out street names on an insecure radio network as you may risk compromise from eavesdroppers.

### Advance Warnings of Obstacles

Should there be some form of obstacle or hazard to your front such as a set of traffic lights or a roundabout, inform the other team members; for example **'that's approaching a roundabout/crossroads/set of lights'.** This will

As soon as you are aware of a roundabout ahead - inform the team as it is a 'hazardous' area

Traffic lights can be a hazard anywhere in the world

allow the team to close up, as there is a possibility that a loss could occur here.

Also warn of obstructions such as road works, tractors, learner drivers, cyclists and pedestrians that may be a danger to the team. If there is a speed camera or a Police car travelling towards the team, then let them know as you would not want them to risk getting a speeding ticket or to be overtaking at speed with a Police car coming towards them.

**Traffic Lights**

On approaching traffic lights pass all relevant information back to the team regarding their state. The other members may be required to accelerate to catch up. Let the team know the sequence of the lights as they change, and the target's position in the queue of traffic. The trail car should inform you of his position and when he is through the junction.

Let the team know the state of the lights in plenty of time. If you are approaching the lights and they have just turned to green, call, **'that's approaching lights on a 'fresh green..'.** This indicates that the lights have just turned to green, which should give time for the whole team to get through. Alternatively, **'that's approaching lights on a 'stale green'.** Which indicates that the lights have been on green for quite a while and there is a likelihood that they may change to red at any time.

**Speed and Lanes**

Relay the speed of the target frequently, but especially when their speed changes. We tend to 'bracket' the speed such as, 'three zero to three five' (30-35mph) and remember it's the target's speed and not yours. Inform the team in which lane he is travelling (such as motorway or dual carriageway) or on approach to a junction or roundabout with more than one lane. On a road with multiple lanes such as a motorway, we can nominate the three lanes; the nearside, the centre lane and the offside lane but this can get confusing when there are four or more lanes. For this reason we tend to number the lanes from the nearside so that if the target is in the centre lane of a three lane carriageway he would be in lane '2 of 3'.

A: That's approaching the roundabout in lane 2 of 2
B: That's onto the roundabout, not one not one
C: That's taken the second the second towards 'Midlands'

**Roundabout Procedure**

When the target approaches a roundabout, the team must be given plenty of warning in order for them to close up, especially if the roundabout is busy. The position of the target must be given as he approaches the roundabout, when he is on it, when he passes exits and most importantly when he exits the roundabout.

In a similar fashion mentioned earlier, when referring to using the terms nearside as opposed to left left, we adopt similar procedure to identify which exit the target has taken off a roundabout. This procedure avoids confusion especially if a team member is having difficulty receiving comms.

If the target vehicle is onto a roundabout and he takes the third exit (Right) the mobile commentary would be as follows:

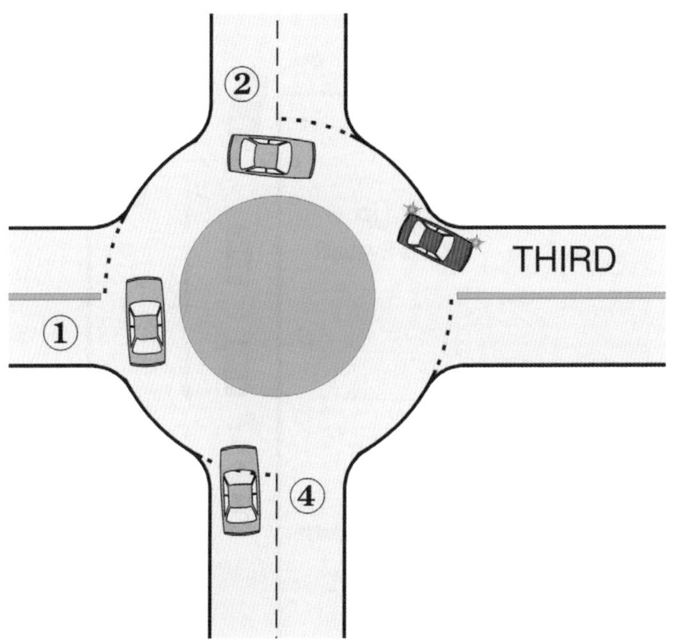


## VOICE PROCEDURE

**'That's up to the roundabout in lane 2 of 2'**

**'That's at the roundabout and held, wait'**

**'That's onto the roundabout'**

**'Not One, Not One', as he passes the first exit**

**'Not Two, Not Two', as he passes the second exit**

**'Taken Third, Third on the A629 towards Halifax', as he takes the third exit**

You will notice the change of phrase between using the terms One, Two or Three and First, Second, Third. Each exit is numbered in a sequence of One, Two, Three as the target passes it, but if he takes a particular exit the phrase changes to First, Second, Third and so on.

This system was devised in the event of poor communications. If a team member was having difficulty receiving the commentary but heard **'Second, Second',** he would automatically know that the target has taken the second exit whereas if he heard **'Two, Two'** he would know that the target had passed option two and was continuing round. In order to add credibility to your commentary, it may be worth adding that extra bit of information such as the road name or direction, so we may hear:

**'Not One, not One,'**
**'It's the Second, the Second, A610 towards Nottingham'**

If there is a 'No Entry' from the roundabout (traffic can join but not leave) then this is not counted as it is not an option that the target can realistically take.

**If the target stops at a petrol station like this, overshoot and do not park up as illustrated**

If you are using the spot (or dot) codes, this will eliminate the use of calling options and directions and thus keep the commentary more secure. E.g. **'That's approaching Yellow 9, that's at Yellow 9 and held, that's from Yellow 9 towards Red 1...'**

## HANDOVERS

Occasionally, (in order to avoid being noticed) you will need to change lead vehicles in what is called a 'handover'. These handovers should be carried out at natural places such as roundabouts and road junctions.

As back up, (who should be behind the eyeball with one or two vehicles in between), you should be ready to take over as eyeball at short notice in the event that the target suddenly turns or stops (an unplanned handover). Your concentration must be on the target's actions and the eyeball's commentary and therefore you have to think ahead at all times.

After a handover the backing call sign should immediately tell the Eyeball that he is backing after a handover. If for some reason, the back up car becomes held or slightly detached, he should tell the eyeball that he is 'no longer backing', this prevents the eyeball from asking for a handover as he then knows he has no back up. Common sense.

As eyeball, you should decide when to hand over and this should be carried out frequently, depending on a number of factors. Essentially you would carry out a handover at the following times:

• As soon as practically possible after the initial pick up. An aware target will notice the first vehicle that pulls out behind him and possibly keep his eye on it. However, if it soon turns off, the target will relax somewhat and ignore it.

• When you have had the eyeball for a while and there is risk of compromise if you stay with it any longer, especially if you have been directly behind the target with no cover.

• Whenever there are two or three changes in direction. As eyeball, you do not want to take the target around one corner, then another and then another, you will alert him. If he is carrying out anti-surveillance drills, you will only confirm that you are following him, so hand over after changes in direction. Frequent changes are better than none at all.

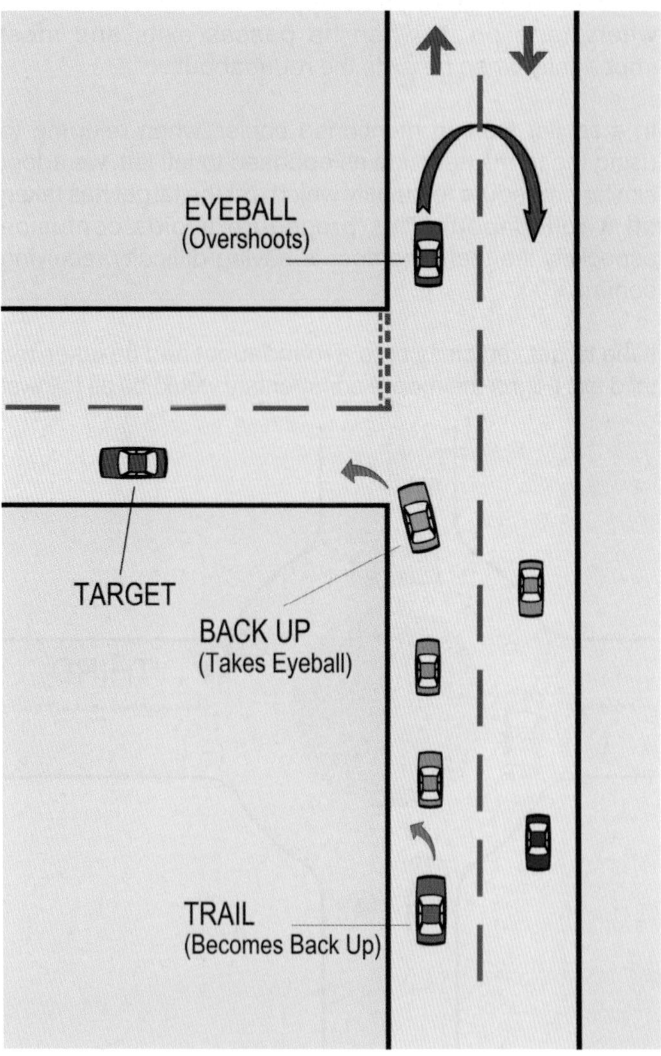

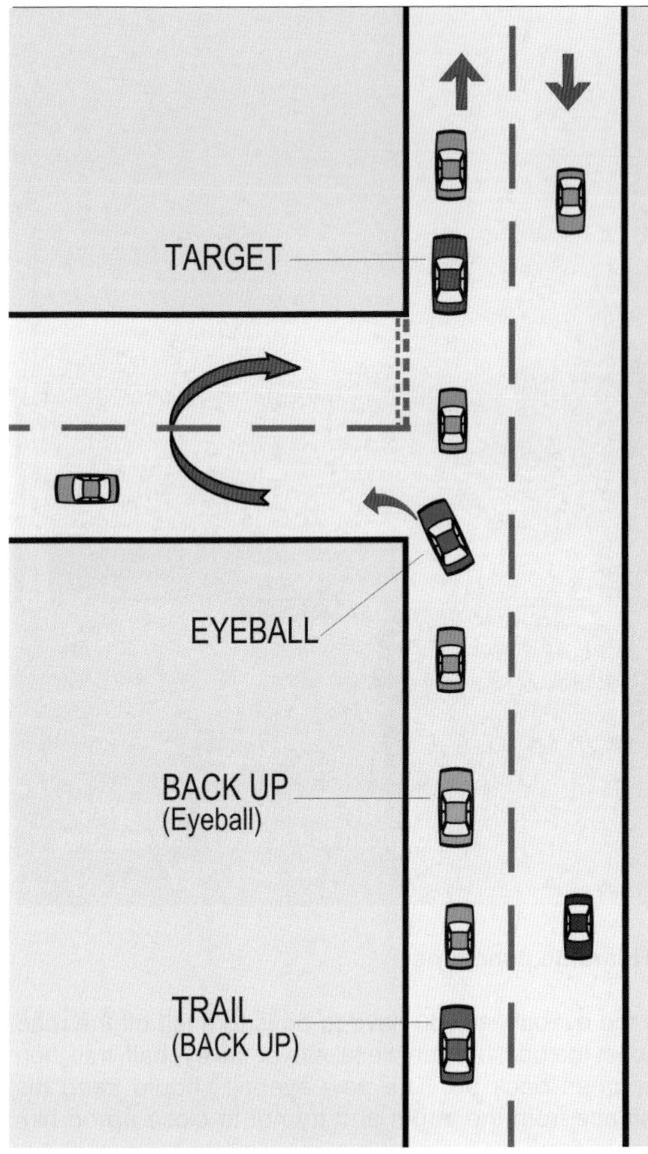


• If the target stops at the side of the road, it will look a bit obvious for the eyeball to stop directly behind him. So in order to act naturally, the eyeball should overshoot, keep going and hand over the eyeball to the back up. If the vehicle moves off again, you then have a different car taking the eyeball and triggering it away.

• On entering a car park. If a target is suspicious, he may pull into a car park to see if you follow him in. Therefore we normally hand over as the target enters a car park.

• When you are compromised. If this situation occurs, you will have to clear the area and so your back up may keep an eye on the target, it may be a case that the whole team disperses.

**Setting Up a Handover**

There are certain places where a handover can be carried out without being obvious to the target. What we would not expect to happen, is for you to ask for a handover, move over to the nearside and let your back up come screaming through by overtaking you. If this were to happen and the target were to see it in his rear view mirror, he would probably expect the 'boy racer' to overtake him also, but when he doesn't and hangs onto his tail, he soon becomes suspicious.

There are two types of handovers, 'planned' and 'unplanned'. Unplanned would be when the target suddenly turns into a car park and a quick handover is carried out, i.e **'That's gone left left into the Shell garage, back up can you now?'**

A planned handover is when it is set up with plenty of time beforehand. It is normally carried out at a designated place and normally at a 'natural' point where the eyeball can naturally peel off the road. In order to instigate a handover, the Eyeball should come up on air and ask, **'Back up are you in a position?** (to take the eyeball)' or **'Back up, can you?'.** If they are, you should hear the response, **'Yes Yes'.** Or, it can be set up at a designated place or a spot e.g. **'Back up can you at the Shell garage?'** or **'Back up can you at Red 6?'**

At this time, the backing call sign should now close up on the eyeball car. This is so that when the eyeball peels off, the back up is already in a good position - otherwise the eyeball would peel off and the back up will be forced to accelerate to close up and then hang back from the target, which may appear unusual.

Locations for handovers can be anywhere where you can easily leave the road and rejoin it again quickly:

Don't handover on a right turn you may hold up the team if there is oncoming traffic

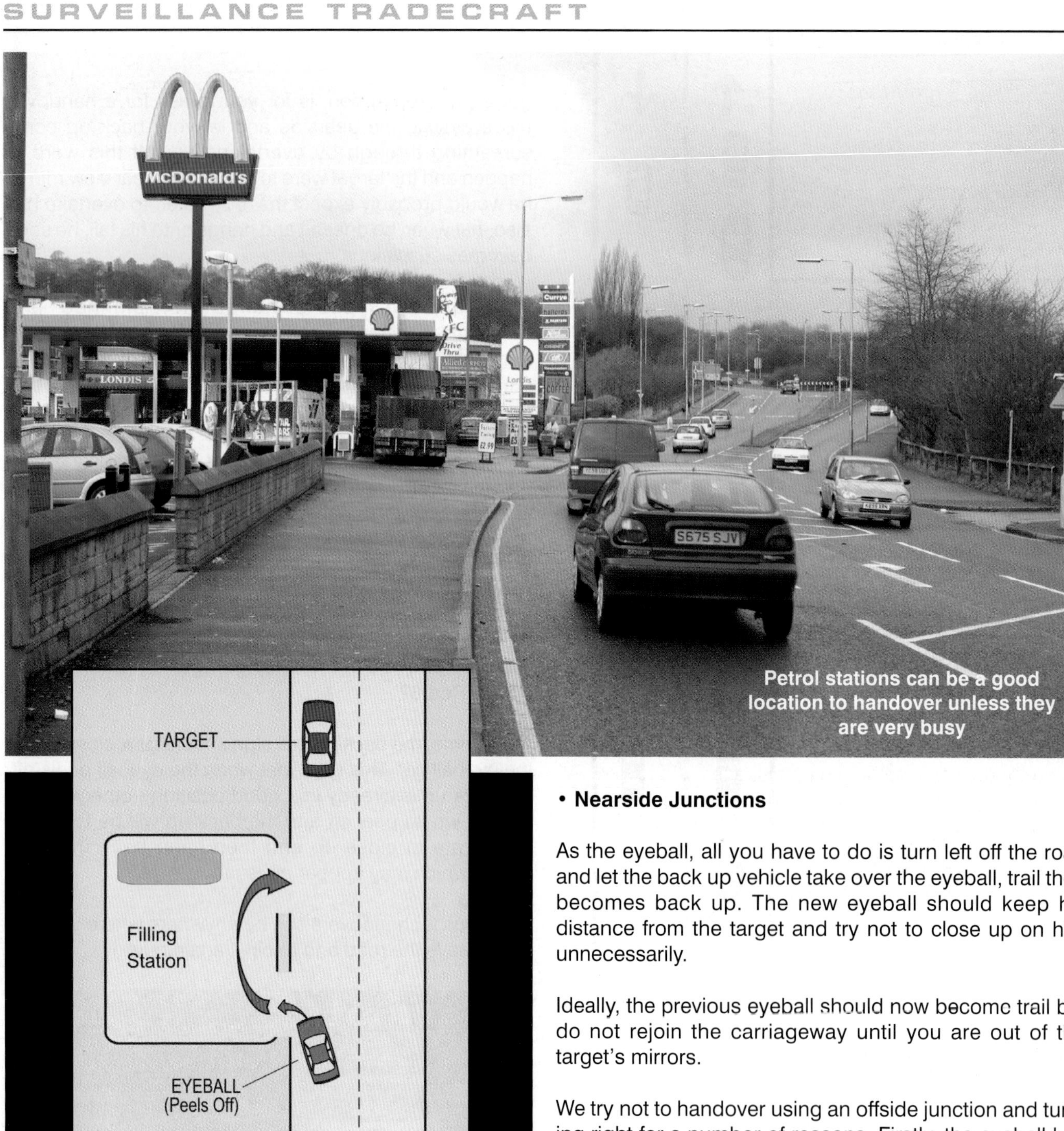


Petrol stations can be a good location to handover unless they are very busy

• **Nearside Junctions**

As the eyeball, all you have to do is turn left off the road and let the back up vehicle take over the eyeball, trail then becomes back up. The new eyeball should keep his distance from the target and try not to close up on him unnecessarily.

Ideally, the previous eyeball should now become trail but do not rejoin the carriageway until you are out of the target's mirrors.

We try not to handover using an offside junction and turning right for a number of reasons. Firstly, the eyeball has to cross over oncoming traffic in order to turn off, in doing so he may hold up the team behind him. If he manages to cross the road, he may encounter traffic when getting back again as he now has to cross the traffic again.

• **Petrol Stations**

In a manner similar to the above, all the eyeball has to do is pull into a petrol station and let the back up come through. Again, do not pull out onto the main road until you are out of the target's mirror.

Protocol dictates that you should now become trail. However, if the back up car has been detached and is not

If you intend handing over at a roundabout, set the handover up in plenty of time

in a position to actually 'back' the eyeball, then you must get out and act as back up straight away. You can always change over positions at a later time.

**• Roundabouts**

Roundabouts can also be a natural place to handover. As soon as you see the sign prior to the roundabout, you should offer up the handover and check that your back up is in a position to take over.

Do not handover at a roundabout controlled by lights

There are essentially two ways of handing over at a roundabout. Firstly, the eyeball can take the target onto the roundabout, call the exit and then continue going around the roundabout letting the back up take over. Secondly, the eyeball can peel off at the first exit (if the target hasn't taken this one) and hand over this way. If you do this, ensure that you can turn around and get back in the team quickly. You do not want to find yourself joining a dual carriageway and not being able to turn around for miles on end.

If following a sophisticated target who may have counter surveillance deployed. Think twice about handing over at roundabouts, as these are ideal 'choke points' that a CS team may cover to observe a surveillance team coming through and carrying out a handover.

Handovers at roundabouts can be dangerous when following a sophisticated target as you will discover in the chapter on surveillance detection

Do not handover in congested traffic as it will be difficult to get back in with the team

• **Laybys**

Caution should be used if handing over at a lay-by. If there are cars already parked there, they will afford you some cover but empty ones may not. As eyeball you can pull into a lay-by and let your team come through, whatever you do, do not pull out again if you are still in the target's mirrors.

**When Not to Handover**

There are no hard and fast rules to this but you should remember:

• That turning into offside junctions, you may hold the team up behind you as you wait to cross oncoming traffic

• Do not bring cars through. The backing car should not overtake you and then slow down behind the target

• Do not handover at traffic lights. As you turn off and handover, you may get held by the same lights and so become detached

• Do not handover at large roundabouts, especially if they are controlled by traffic lights

• Do not handover where traffic is very heavy and prevents you from rejoining the team. Prior to a handover, check your mirrors. If there is a very long line of traffic behind you ask yourself, 'will I get back into the traffic if I peel off?'

• If you handover on a motorway by coming off at a junction, check the map or Satnav first to ensure that you can rejoin the carriageway, otherwise you will be gone for a long time.

Remember the targets awareness level and the amount of exposure you have had will dictate the frequency of handovers.

## WHAT HAPPENS WHEN THE TARGET STOPS

Whenever the target stops, the eyeball must immediately transmit **'..that's a STOP, STOP on the Nearside'** (or whatever is applicable). Although the eyeball vehicle may have to keep moving and pass the target, it is important that the other vehicles stop quickly or take appropriate action. If the eyeball has had to overtake the target, the back up vehicle naturally then becomes 'eyeball' to get a trigger and the trail car should hold back and take up a position ready for the next follow phase.

This should be practised and carried out as a drill whenever there is a stop. In addition to stating that there has been a stop, the eyeball should indicate the target's whereabouts in brief detail, '..that's a STOP STOP on the nearside at a post office'.

**Housing Phase**

We are now into the 'Housing' phase of our surveillance and so we now have to re-plot (or stake it out) ready for the 'pick-up' phase.

If he gets out of his vehicle, the eyeball should be giving a commentary on the target's actions and the team leader can then decide on what course of action to take, such as

**You can handover by coming off a motorway and rejoining it, however, ensure that this possible before doing so**

Park 'pretty' - make sure your vehicle and wheels are parallel to the kerb

Close all windows

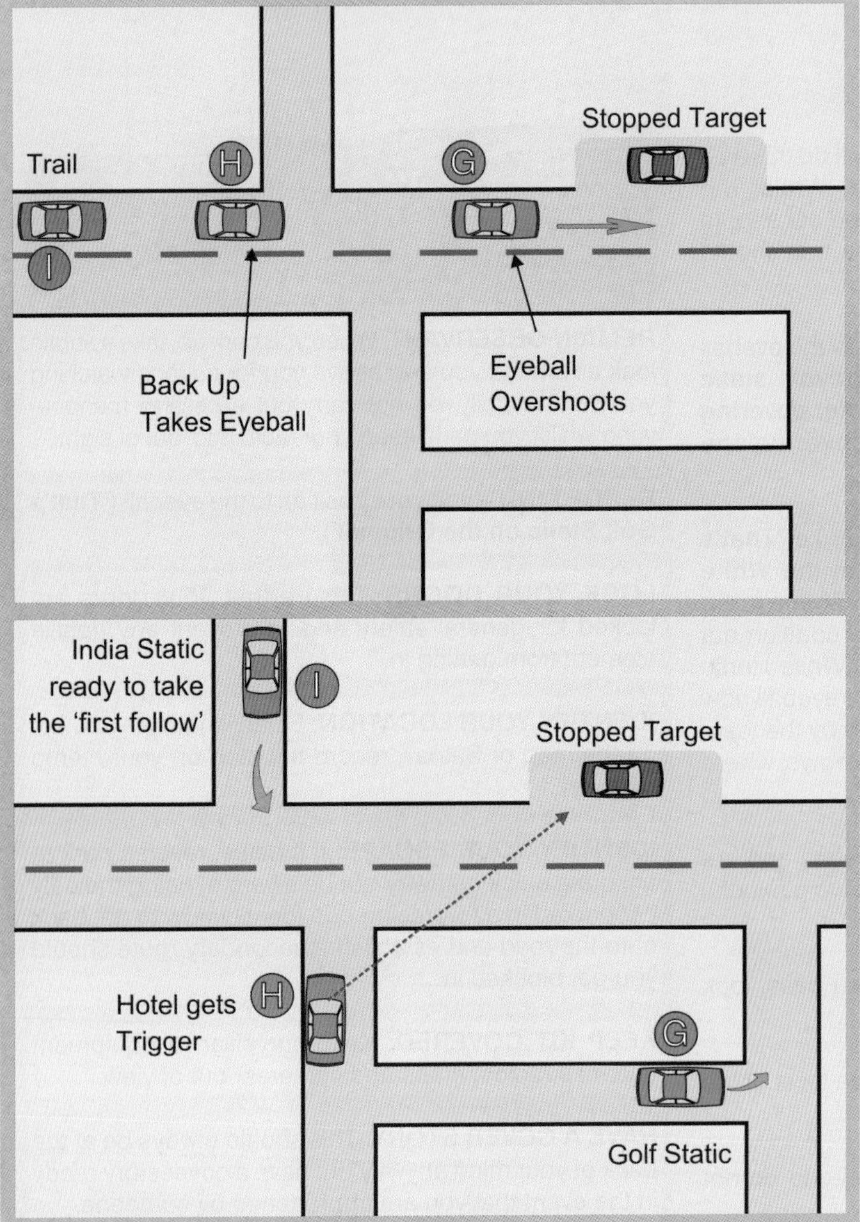

'Square' your wheels

Never park like this...

putting footmen out. An experienced team will do this as a matter of course on their own initiative. Whilst the commentary is being given, the previous lead car should take a position ahead of the target and the trail should hold back and take up a position behind him.

On doing so, the cars should quickly call in to the eyeball and report their positions. E.g. **'Golf has Bravo 1 static outside the post office'. 'Roger, that's Hotel covering the original'. India, roger, that's me covering the reciprocal'.**

The cars do not want to report too much detail, i.e. **'That's Hotel covering the original, parked up in the White Horse car park 500 metres ahead..'**. Think radio security, don't name your exact position. In addition not everyone on the team will know where the White Horse Pub is, so keep it simple. By reporting in, the eyeball now knows that all the escape routes are covered by the team and if a call sign gets into trouble, he knows where assistance is needed.

Be aware of your actions if you are the eyeball and are having to pass the target on a stop. Be aware and mindful of the following

• Don't stare and gawp at the target as you pass, look straight ahead

• Keep your radio out of sight and below the level of the dashboard

• Relax, do not have your head on a swivel and do not appear anxious

• Do not suddenly brake as you pass, as you look in your mirrors or check for somewhere to pull in

• Do not suddenly or aggressively turn off in front of the target. If he thinks he is being followed and you suddenly turn off right in front of him, you will attract his attention - keep going then turn off naturally.

**When Plotting Up**

When manoeuvring into a position, you should remain alert. Just because another car has the trigger, it does not mean that you can switch off. You should:

## PLOTTING UP DRILL

**REMAIN OBSERVANT:** When you park up, take a subtle look all around you and above you for anyone watching you. Act naturally, do not carry out excessive manoeuvring whilst you park, keep your radio mic' out of sight.

**REPORT IN:** Report your position to the eyeball **('That's Golf Static on the Original').**

**LOCK YOUR DOORS:** Ensure that your doors are locked for general safety and to prevent any hostile element from getting in.

**IDENTIFY YOUR LOCATION:** Establish where you are on the map or Satnav, record the stop on your memo recorder.

**IDENTIFY YOUR ESCAPE:** If it helps, reverse park to ensure a quick getaway but be aware of being the only car parked in a row facing out. Identify how to get back onto the road and establish a secondary route should you get blocked in.

**KEEP KIT COVERED:** Keep surveillance equipment (such as radios, maps and cameras) out of view.

**HAVE A COVER STORY:** This should always be at the back of your mind anyway but have a cover story ready in the event that you are approached by someone.

The eyeball to keep the team updated with '..no change..' on a regular basis.

When you get a standby and the target goes mobile again on the original direction, (remembering that the trigger shouldn't move) it should ideally, be trail that comes round and takes the first follow. Remember, that when the target stopped, the call sign that overshot does not necessarily want to take the first follow as it was behind the target when he stopped.

Every situation is different but the main aim is for an operator to re-trigger the surveillance and the other team members to cover the possible routes the target may take when going mobile. On a standby or when the target moves off, it should ideally be a fresh vehicle that takes the first follow rather than the one that had the previous eyeball.

When the target moves off again, call the direction of travel and let the team know when the target is 'unsighted' to you so that another team member can cut in and take the commentary.

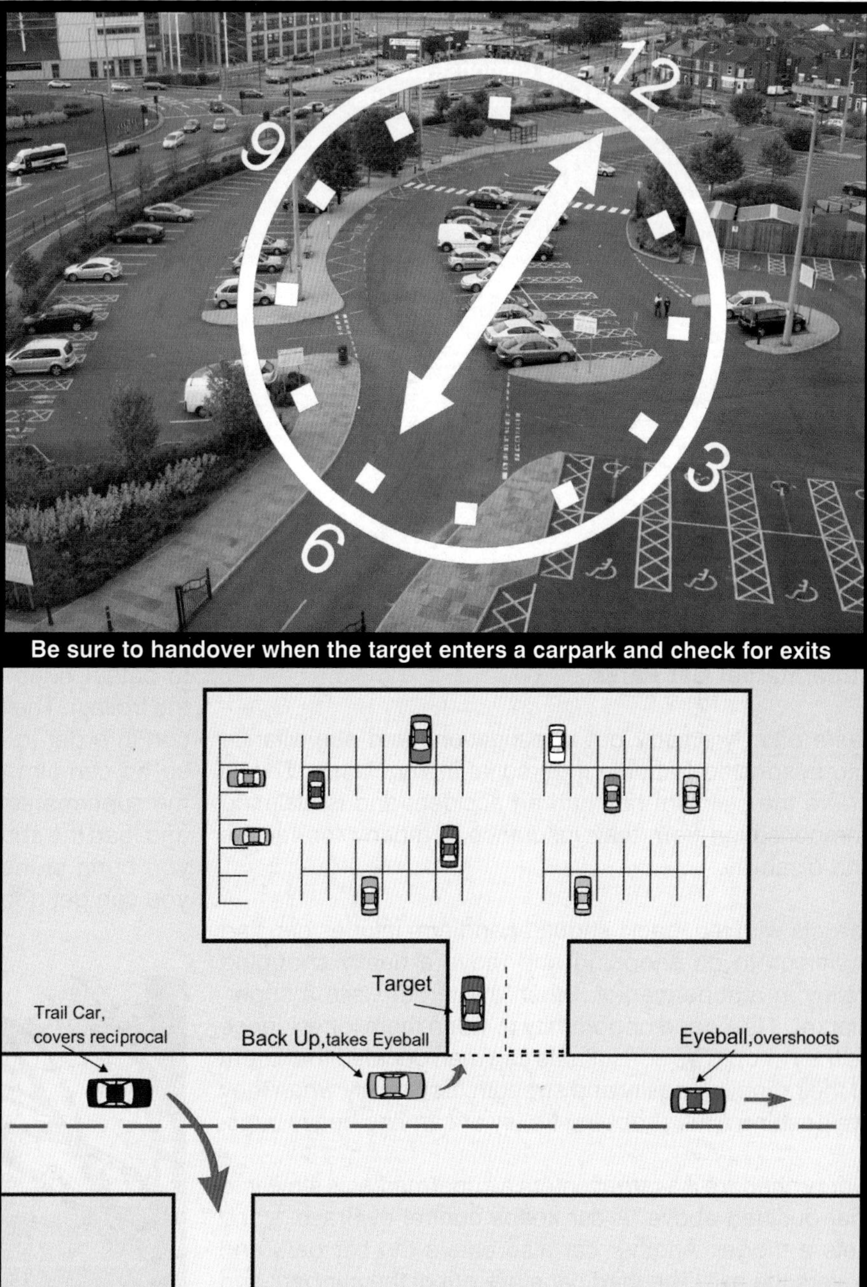


### Stopping in a Car Park

We normally carry out a hand over when the target enters a car park. This is a stop and so the eyeball should not follow him in but hand over to the back up. An aware target may be checking to see who follows him in.

• The eyeball should overshoot, try to identify any other exits and find a plot up location.

• The back up now up takes the eyeball and controls the target in the car park. Do not follow him down the same lanes but use the parallels as cover. If the target enters a car park, it is fairly likely that he will get out on foot. When the target comes to a halt, inform the team of his whereabouts in the car park using the 'clock ray' method.

• The eyeball (trigger) vehicle should now position himself so that he can clearly see the target and also the exit to the car park. This way, not only can he give a standby but also a direction of travel as the car exits the car park.

• If the car park has multiple exits, these should be identified as soon as possible and relayed to the team who must then get in a position to cover them. In large car parks, it may be necessary to have more than one car in there.

• Do not be too hasty to get out on foot, the target may have to obtain a parking ticket to display in his windscreen before he departs on foot. In which case, he will be returning to his car before departure.

• Do not park between the target and the exit or between the target and the pay and display machine, he will have to walk past you.

If carrying out personal injury surveillance it is essential to cover the car - as demonstrated in these photographs - the target lifts heavy bags into the boot

## Supermarket Car Parks

Quite often we carry out investigations and surveillance into suspected fraudulent personal injury claims. This is where the claimant has had an accident and is claiming compensation from their insurance company for injuries and disability.

Targets with leg, back, shoulder and arm injuries can find it difficult to go shopping and move a heavy shopping trolley in a supermarket. When the target visits a supermarket, it is a good opportunity to video them for evidence as they shop. The consultants can then decided the extent of their mobility, agility and strength. Especially when they are pushing a full shopping trolley or carrying heavy bags.

Our procedure if a target enters a supermarket is similar to that outlined above. A car keeps control of Bravo 1 and gets a trigger. Another car also enters the car park and covers the exit. The third car stays out of the car park and covers the escape route. The operator covering the exit deploys on foot into the supermarket with a covert camera to obtain video inside (remember to take a coin for the trolley). The trigger car may then move position in order to get a good 'video' position so he can film the target as they leave the supermarket exit, walk to their car and load the shopping. It may be that you bring in the van to do this, so you can get good close up video.

When the target leaves the supermarket return to your vehicle as soon as possible

When plotting up attempt to get a good video filming position

When the target is at the checkout and enough covert video is obtained, the foot person returns to his car and covers the exit from within or outside of the car park. The operator covering Bravo 1 videos the target exiting the store, walking or pushing the trolley to Bravo 1 and loading the shopping into it. He then triggers it away when it goes mobile.

### The Cul-De-Sac and Dead End Streets

The target may drive into a cul-de-sac to either visit an address or to carry out an anti surveillance manoeuvre. Two scenarios can be envisaged: one, when you know that the road is a dead end, or two, you have been caught unaware and do not realise that it is a dead end until you are into it and it is too late.

The following actions can be taken when the target turns into a cul-de-sac:

• If you know the road is a dead end

• The eyeball is to continue straight, driving past the turning and checks to see if there are any routes out by car or on foot

Triggering a target in a cul-de-sac can be difficult. This is where a 'boot-fit' is ideal

Try not to follow into cul-de-sacs

Park the van with caution and make sure it does not stand out by being the only vehicle on the street

• Back up to carry out a drive past of the turning (or deploy a foot person) to identify where the target has stopped and get a trigger on the entrance/exit

• Trail to enter the cul de sac to positively identify where the target has stopped. This can depend on whether the road is a long one or very short. This can be done either by driving in or by going in on foot

• The team should reorganise to pick up the target when he goes mobile again. It maybe that you can only trigger the exit to the cul de sac

• If the house or premises is unidentified, an operator may have to check it after the target has gone mobile or return to it at a later time

• The cul-de-sac is not recognised until you have turned into it

• Don't panic and act naturally

• Consider if by doing a three point turn and driving out again you will arouse suspicion. If possible do this out of sight of the target

• Park naturally on the roadside and walk away from your vehicle, possibly through a footpath if there is one

• Drive onto a resident's driveway and make a pretext call at the front door. You can then depart, driving out of the cul-de-sac

• Act naturally, do not look at or pay any attention to the target and avoid eye contact. I would consider entering a cul de sac as having lost a life and therefore keep out of the way for a while

• If you are in a long cul-de-sac, try and get a trigger from within or stay down there until the target has departed

In the following chapter, we look at the more progressive aspects of mobile surveillance.

Reverse parking is a good idea to ensure a quick getaway. However, make sure your vehicle is not the only one parked this way

In this, the second chapter on mobile surveillance, we look at the more progressive and advanced techniques used by a mobile team. Also included is an important section on single-handed surveillance and surveillance compromises utilising a number of interesting factual case studies.

**Multi-Storey Car Parks**

Multi-storey car parks can be tricky to cover, especially when there are multiple exits. When the target drives into a multi-storey car park, expect him to find the first available spot and park in it. If you can obtain a spot close by, all well and good but quite often you may have to go up one or two floors to obtain a space.

Every situation is different but the following is suggested:

• When the target enters, the eyeball vehicle hands over to the back up then remains on the outside of the car park, checks and covers the exits

• New eyeball takes the target into the car park, reporting where it stops, deploying a foot person as the target goes on foot

• Trail remains on the outside of the car park, covering the escape route.

• The footman, having picked up the target, will remain with him and follow him into the street, hopefully to be backed up by another. When deploying on foot, remember what floor level you are parked on. When walking through narrow stairways in car parks be aware of how far your voice travels when giving a commentary.

• Be aware of the target returning to his vehicle after collecting a parking ticket

• Remember to examine the target vehicle parking ticket for the amount of time parked and note anything of interest that is possibly left on view inside. You may also want to make a note of the mileage but do this only if it is safe to do so.

***Remember where you have parked your car!***

**Indoor Shopping Centres and Car Parks With Barriers**

Be aware of car parks where you obtain a ticket from a barrier upon entering. Usually, you have to keep your

Good control has to be maintained in a multi-storey car park they can escape via many different routes or exits

parking ticket with you and pay at a machine located in a nearby building or at the stairwell to the car park prior to departure. This means that you have to pay on returning to your vehicle, which may cause difficulties in keeping control of the target.

After paying, you normally have a 15 minute period to actually leave the car park before the barrier refuses to let you through the exit.

**Showing an Empty Car**

At times you may have to let the target pass you whilst you are stationary. This normally occurs when triggering from a position up ahead of the target. If so, you may want to show an 'empty car' to make it look unoccupied by 'ducking down' before the target passes you.

If you do this make sure:

• That no one sees you, have a quick look around you, think third party

• Turn your engine off and your wipers off

• Switch off your lights and indicators

• Make sure that your foot is off the brake pedal or the rear lights will flash brightly

• Do not have your windows wound right down

**Parallels**

If you can use parallel routes to the target, it prevents 'following' the target like ducks in a line and therefore minimises your exposure. Parallels should only be carried out if you

**Ideally exit the car park before the target. However, you should already have team members plotted on the exits**

are familiar with the ground, or if you are confident in your map reading.

Parallels also assist during a handover; rather than peel off, handover and then emerge back into the flow of traffic, you can continue straight on a parallel and then rejoin the main road further down (see diagram - right).

**If giving a radio commentary be careful as your voice will echo down stairwells and parking areas**

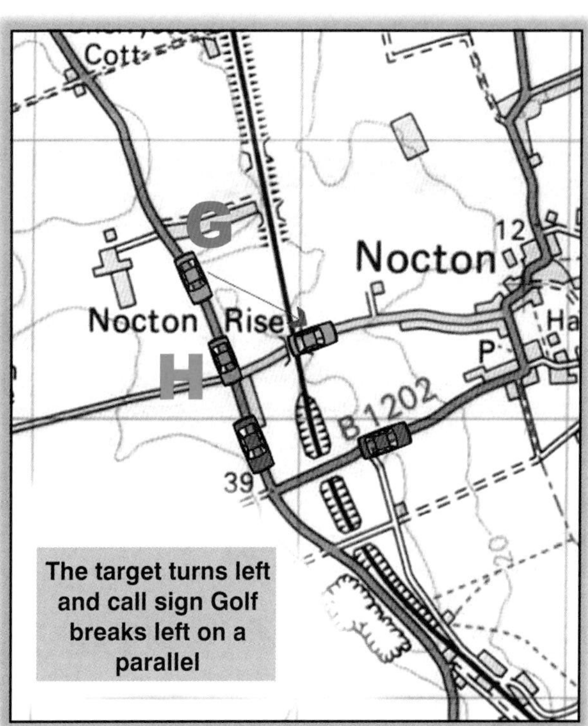


**The target turns left and call sign Golf breaks left on a parallel**

## STOP STOP AT RED 1

Using the diagram, let us look at how this scenario is handled when the target stops for fuel at a petrol station in a small industrial area. There is only one way in, one way out at the other side and there are various hazards nearby such as a busy roundabout leading to a dual carriageway and a railway level crossing which often closes for 15 minutes at a time.

Call sign Golf 'Has', Hotel is backing and India is the trail. The target turns right and enters the petrol station, a handover is carried out. Golf continues straight towards the roundabout and Hotel takes him into the petrol

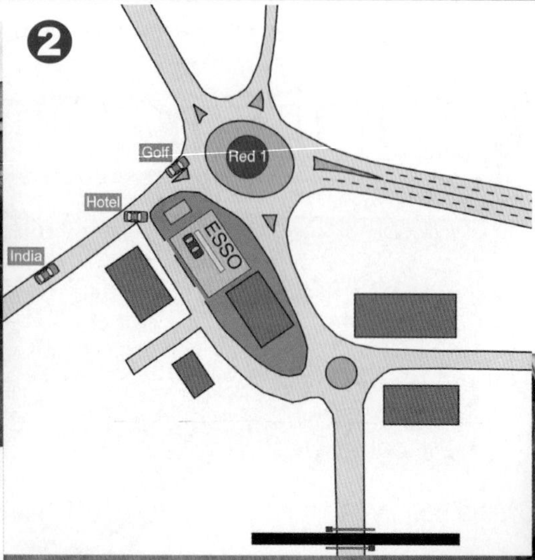

**Golf overshoots as Hotel takes control**

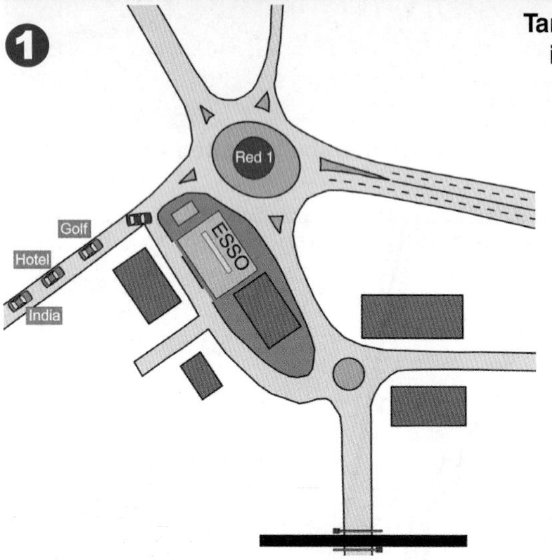

**Target turns left into garage**

**Entrance to the BP garage**

station, India hangs back to cover the entrance. The target stops, Hotel overshoots slightly and gets a trigger on Bravo 1.

Hotel now identifies that there is only one way in (6 o'clock) and only one way out (12 o'clock) from the petrol station and he then directs his team if they have not already plotted up on their own initiative.

**'Hotel has Bravo 1, that's Alpha 1 obtaining fuel'**

**'Call signs be aware, Bravo 1 will be forced out at 12 o'clock, India, can you cover the exit?'**

**'India, Yes, Yes'**

**'Hotel, no change, no change. Golf can you cover the main roundabout at Red 1?'**

**'Golf, Yes, Yes'**

**'Hotel, no change no change, Alpha 1 getting fuel'**

**'Hotel, that's Alpha 1 foxtrot towards the pay kiosk'**

**'India, static covering the exit at 12 o'clock, where there's a mini roundabout. Be aware of a level crossing after the third exit'**

**The roundabout at the 12 o'clock**

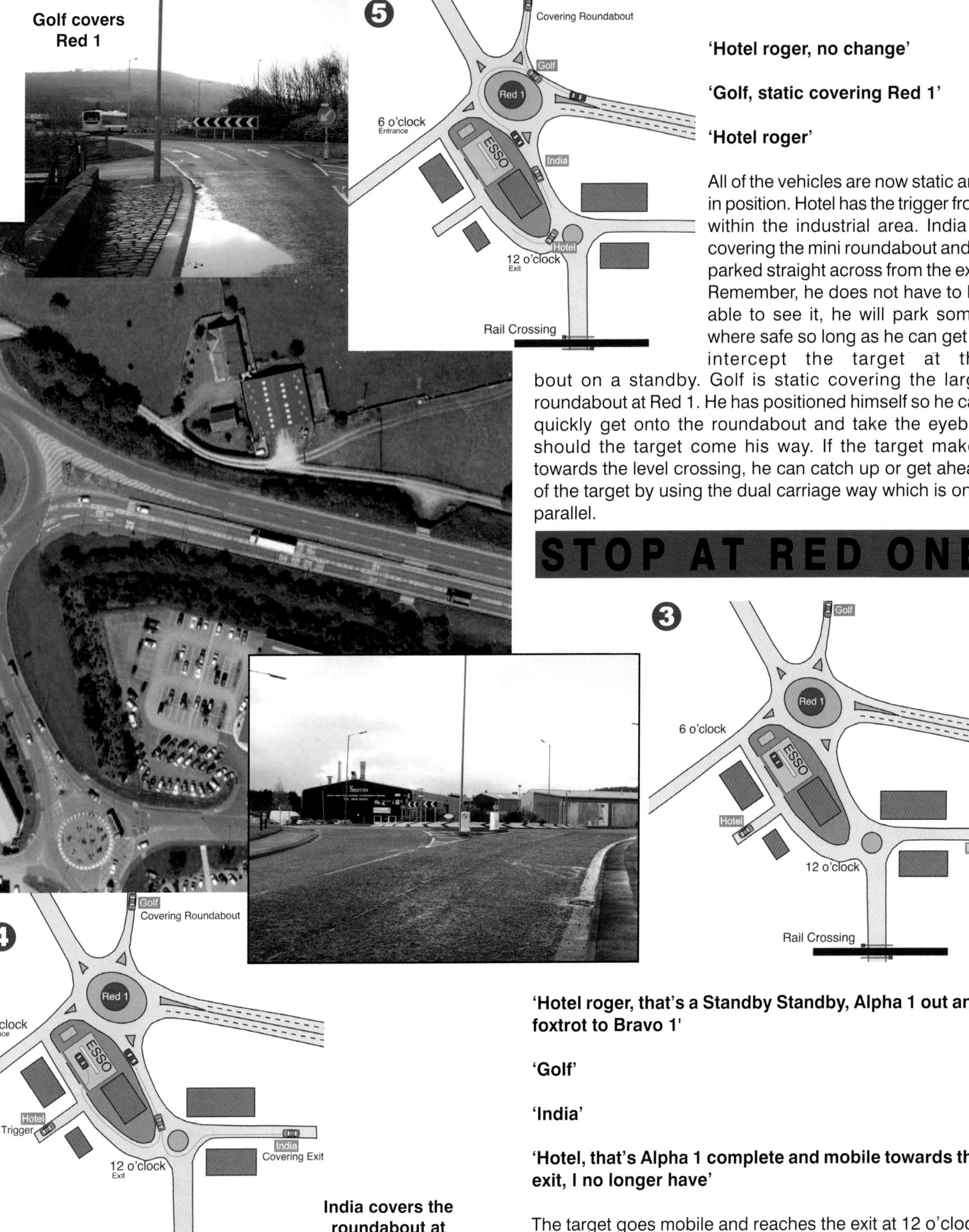


Golf covers Red 1

**'Hotel roger, no change'**

**'Golf, static covering Red 1'**

**'Hotel roger'**

All of the vehicles are now static and in position. Hotel has the trigger from within the industrial area. India is covering the mini roundabout and is parked straight across from the exit. Remember, he does not have to be able to see it, he will park somewhere safe so long as he can get to intercept the target at the bout on a standby. Golf is static covering the large roundabout at Red 1. He has positioned himself so he can quickly get onto the roundabout and take the eyeball should the target come his way. If the target makes towards the level crossing, he can catch up or get ahead of the target by using the dual carriage way which is on a parallel.

# STOP AT RED ONE

**'Hotel roger, that's a Standby Standby, Alpha 1 out and foxtrot to Bravo 1'**

**'Golf'**

**'India'**

**'Hotel, that's Alpha 1 complete and mobile towards the exit, I no longer have'**

India covers the roundabout at 12 o'clock

The target goes mobile and reaches the exit at 12 o'clock where there is a mini roundabout. He takes the first exit towards the main roundabout (Red 1) and then takes the fourth exit at the large roundabout towards Red 3.

Hotel does not move as he is giving the trigger. The first car to pick up Bravo 1 would be India, covering the mini.

Golf is plotted up down the third exit covering the roundabout at Red 1.

**'India, I have. That's Bravo 1 at the exit and taken the first, the first at the mini towards Red 1'**

**'Golf'**

**'Hotel'**

**'India, that's Bravo 1 approaching Red 1 in lane three of three with an offside indication.**

**'Hotel backing'**

**'India, that's at Red 1 and onto the roundabout. Not one, not one, not two not two and unsighted to me, I no longer have..'**

**'Golf has. Not three not three, taken the fourth, the fourth towards Red 3'**

**'India Backing'**

..and away we go.

You see, the target was not followed but surveillance imposed by bouncing him from one call sign to another. The commentary has to be accurate and fast to keep him under control.

**The Fast Driver**

Some targets will drive like maniacs. Not just because they suspect that they will be followed but because they do this as their normal pattern of behaviour. So it may be worth inquiring at your briefing stage on how your target is likely to drive.

| | | |
|---|---|---|
| 05:10:27pm | 30m:59s | 05:41:26pm |
| 06:06:58pm | 36m:55s | 06:43:53pm |

***Thursday, November 27, 2008***
*Departed From :*
*Arrived At :*
*Total Driving Time : 6 hours, 12 minutes, 20 seconds*
*Total Mileage Driven : 328.6 miles*
*Maximum Speed : 141.1 mph*

| Departed | Driving Time | Arrived |
|---|---|---|
| 07:51:12am | 00m:37s | 07:51:49am |
| 08:03:58am | 2h:53m:24s | 10:57:22am |
| 01:28:10pm | 2h:22m:57s | 03:51:07pm |
| 04:17:23pm | 47m:44s | 05:05:07pm |
| 09:42:52pm | 07m:38s | 09:50:30pm |

***Friday, November 28, 2008***

**Report from tracker where the target's speed exceeded 141 mph**

A target driving at high speed is more likely to be concentrating on the road ahead than he is on the road behind him. Though occasional checks of his rear view mirrors will be made in order to look for Police.

Fast speeds on the road can be the cause of fatal accidents and so I would be inclined to think to myself, 'Is the job really worth it? Do we really have to push ourselves, at the risk of an accident to keep up?'

These drivers can be difficult to put under observation and so a pattern of movement may have to be established so the surveillance can be carried out in stages. Tracking devices are an excellent tool against very fast targets, not only can you obtain a pattern of movement over a period of time but also let them run at high speed. When they have stopped, it will be easy to identify where and then re-locate them. The faster a person drives, the narrower their field of vision becomes to the side and behind them.

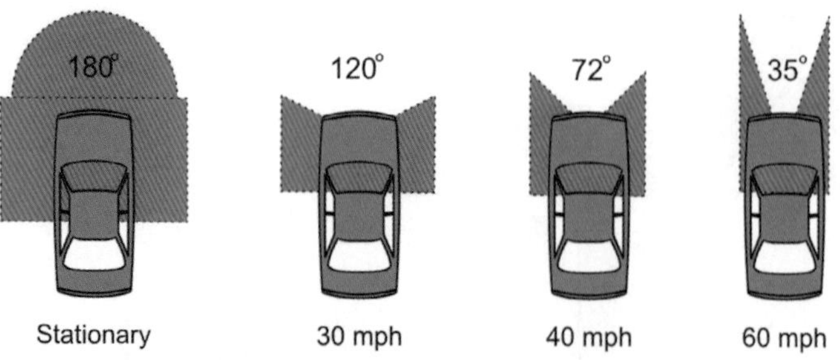


**Your field of vision narrows the faster you drive**

**Loss of Contact**

Losing contact with the target is inevitable from time to time and is an occupational hazard in surveillance. You can have a team of six cars and two motorbikes, to help minimise your chances of losing the target, but it can still happen. We say that in this industry there are only two types of surveillance operators, those that have losses and those that tell lies.

A loss will occur for many reasons, such as traffic congestion, busy roundabouts, traffic lights and most often, lack of concentration. If you hear the call, '**Temporary Unsighted**' you would normally expect to hear, **'Eyeball Regained',** shortly afterwards. If the 'unsighted' calls come one after another, expect to hear a **'Total Loss, Total Loss'** shortly afterwards to indicate the target has disappeared.

The longer the target has been 'unsighted', the further he may be getting away from you and therefore, the more difficult your task becomes in picking him up.

When a **'total loss'** is given by the eyeball, the following procedure should be put into action: The eyeball will state where the total loss occurred, then a search pattern should be adopted. Every situation is different, be it a T junction, a roundabout or a fork in the road, so no hard and fast rules can be applied but consider:

• Eyeball calls the 'total loss' and continues in the original direction or the most logical and fastest escape route

• Back up vehicle to take first nearside turning after point of loss or the second most logical or quickest escape route

• Third vehicle to take first offside turning after point of loss or the most logical escape route. It could also remain at point of loss and check immediate area and then hold this junction/roundabout or area.

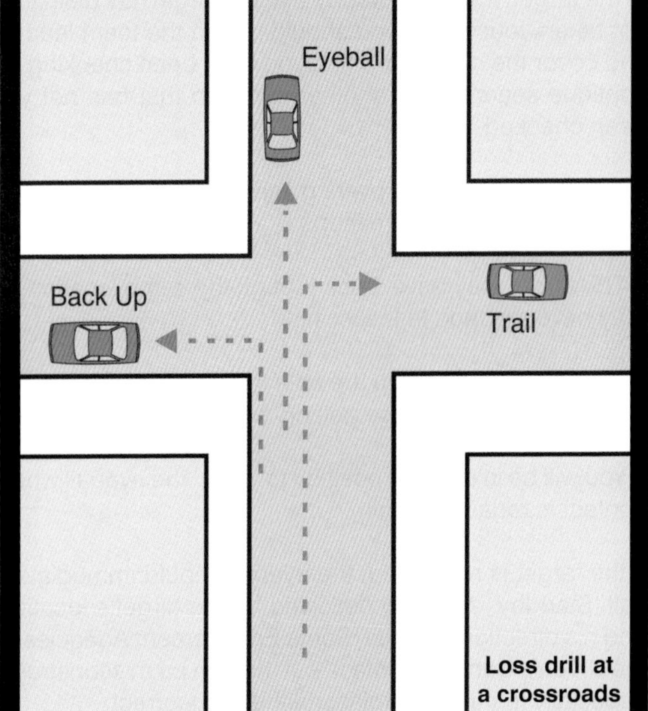

Loss drill at a crossroads

Having a loss in heavy traffic can be a nightmare. A motorbike in this case is a vital asset

Common sense should prevail regarding the time and distance travelled along these routes relative to the speed of the target. If you feel happy that the target has definitely not taken your route, you should inform the team leader, and cover the direction which you have been checking or continue searching in another direction that has not yet been chccked.

The operator who is covering the point of loss remains there, for a number of reasons:

- The target may travel back though the same location or may have stopped in the vicinity

- From this position you are able to relay radio messages as the team may now be getting further and further apart

- You will be in the best position to 'back' the eyeball when contact is regained again

If the target is re-located, the eyeball should immediately call 'Standby, Standby' followed by the target's location and his direction of travel. Some Enforcement Agencies in the UK call 'Contact Contact' but this can be misconstrued especially in military circles; neither is incorrect.

Keep it in mind that some of the team members during their search may now be out of radio range and so the location and direction of the target should be repeated over the air. If necessary, you may have to use your mobile phone.

If the loss occurs at a roundabout you should treat this in the same way as you would at a crossroads or a junction with multiple exits, each one should be checked.

If the target is not located, you will have to consider sending someone back to the target's home address or place of work in the event that they return. The other team members should be checking the places where the target is known to frequent.

## MOTORWAY DRIVING

Surveillance on a motorway can be easier or more difficult depending on your outlook. Although vehicles can travel at much greater speeds, they can only go in one direction and can only leave the highway at certain points and so they are 'contained' to a certain degree. With this in mind, we have to realise and appreciate the problems that motorways and motorway service areas can present.

If your target's base is close to a motorway be prepared for him to use it and ensure that you have a full tank of fuel. Remember, if you have to peel off from a motorway to obtain fuel your target and the team can be miles away by the time you rejoin the carriageway and you will have to drive at breakneck speed in order to close up.

### Speed

The change from rural and urban driving to motorway driving is obvious and it must be appreciated that we can travel a long distance in a matter of minutes at high speed. Therefore, it is important to be able to correctly assess and judge the speed of the target vehicle, so that the convoy does not become too 'strung out'.

**Be aware of 'look-alikes' it is so easy to lock-on and give commentary on the wrong car. The team should be informed of any similar or identical cars on the road. If you are unsure - close up and confirm the registration**

Because motorways stretch for many miles, the eyeball can be retained for longer periods by the same vehicle but only when there is plenty of cover from other vehicles. Each vehicle in the convoy can allow a greater distance between one another and from eyeball to the trail the distance can be as much as a mile or more. So long as radio reception is still good, there are no road hazards imminent and all the vehicles have the power to close up when required, you can keep well spaced.

Speed indication should be given often on the motorway. Should the target increase his speed from 70mph to 90mph you may find that trail is having to do 100mph in order to close up. This is an example only and not intended to entice anyone to speed.

### Mirroring

As with urban driving, it is important for the eyeball on a motorway surveillance to make sure he does not copy or 'mirror' the actions of the target. Should the target pull out and enter another lane the eyeball should maintain the same speed but remain where he is until such time as it appears safe to move out into the same lane as that of the target. If you think ahead and anticipate that the target is just overtaking another vehicle (such as a slow moving truck) you should stay where you are until the target has pulled back into the nearside lane. An inexperienced surveillance operator will often inadvertently mirror the target's movements.

If the target is on a dual carriage way and approaching a roundabout in the nearside lane, he may quickly change lanes to the outside lane as if turning right at the roundabout. If this occurs, do not be too hasty to mirror his movements but call for your back up to come though on the outside and take control, this prevents you from directly mirroring the target.

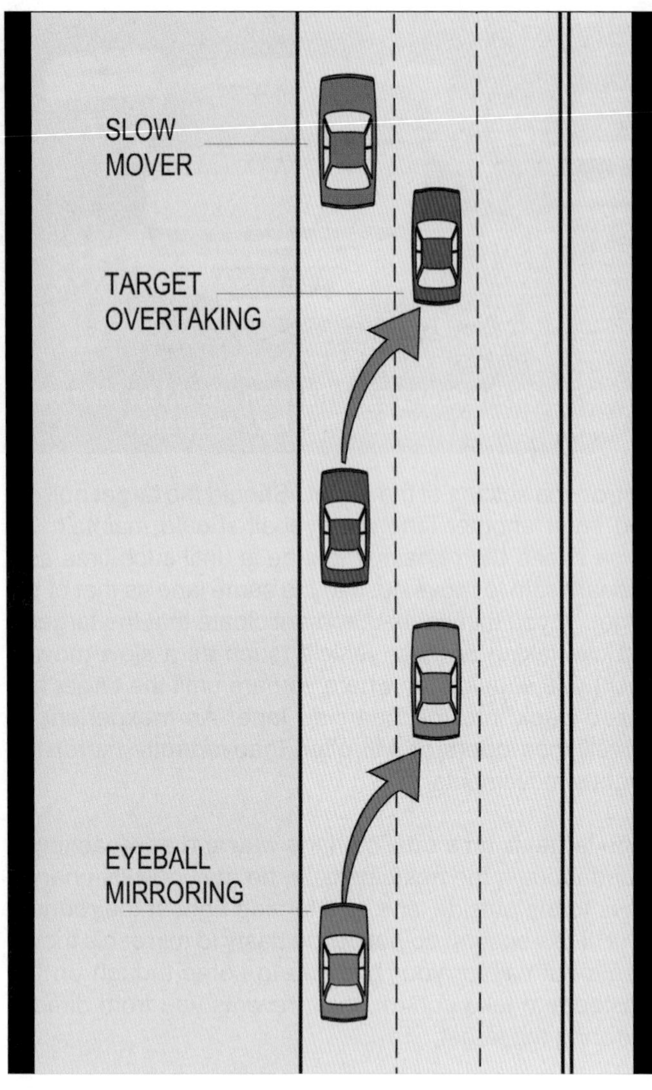


## Motorway Signs and Marker Boards

When travelling on a motorway reference points can sometimes be rather sparse. Bridges and electricity pylons can be used as reference points as they are high up and can be seen from quite a distance.

As we approach the exits from a motorway we are given warning by directional signs which are placed at one mile and half mile intervals (in some cases 2/3 and 1/3 mile) prior to the exits. Each of the exit warning signs details the distance, junction number and road classification numbers coming up.

You must remember that vehicles on motorways can only go one way until such times as they get to exits. If following slow moving targets, much discipline is required in order to prevent 'closing up' on the target and being forced to overtake. If the eyeball on the motorway does become too close they should overtake the target and position themselves at the next exit in order to get behind him as he passes. At this junction the operator must also prepare for the target leaving the motorway as well. Never simulate a breakdown on the hard shoulder in order for the target to overtake you, you will be noticed.

## Approaching Motorway Junctions

On the approach to a junction the eyeball should always give prior warning and the team should close up. On passing the countdown markers the eyeball should be giving a fast commentary as he approaches each, stating the lane that the target is in and his speed. For example:

**'1 mile marker board, junction 16, speed seven zero (70)'**

**'1/2 mile marker board, junction 16, nearside lane, speed seven zero (70)'**

**'Countdown markers, three hundred nearside lane, two hundred, nearside indicator, one hundred, gone left, left, at Junction 16'. Some agencies use the term 'Off Off' rather than 'Gone Left Left'.** Or

**'Countdown markers, three hundred, two hundred, one hundred Committed, Committed M1 south'.** If the target does not deviate and continues on the motorway.

*One mile marker board, junction 'One-Six' in lane 2 of 3*

*Half mile marker board, junction 'One-Six' in lane 1 of 3*

## Handovers

When following on motorways let the handover occur by the eyeball leaving at a junction and then rejoining the carriageway whilst the back up takes over. Ensure that you have read your map and established that you can rejoin at the junction. Sometimes it is safe to handover by bringing the back up through by letting it overtake you, but keep some distance from the target and do so with caution.

Just as you hand over, re-iterate where the target is so that the backing car can lock onto it:

**'Back up, can you at the next junction?'**

**'Yes Yes'**

**Roger that, that's Bravo 1 backing the yellow truck, I no longer have'**

Remember, the back up will have closed up to take control but the target may still be some distance away and it is easy to report on the wrong vehicle.

When the target comes off and leaves at a junction, it is likely that he will encounter a roundabout or a junction at the top of the slip road. This is a good time to carry out a planned handover so you are not seen to take the target off the motorway and then follow him as he changes direction. Be aware of large roundabouts at motorway intersections, some are controlled by traffic lights.

## What if the Target Stops on a Motorway

If the target pulls over onto the hard shoulder, it could be for a number of reasons; he might have broken down or he could be carrying out some form of anti-surveillance. If this happens, act naturally and continue past. Whatever you do, **DO NOT** simulate a break down and pull up on the hard shoulder some distance behind or in front, you will be noticed. If the target has genuinely broken down he may walk towards you for assistance. If he is carrying out anti-surveillance you have now compromised yourself!

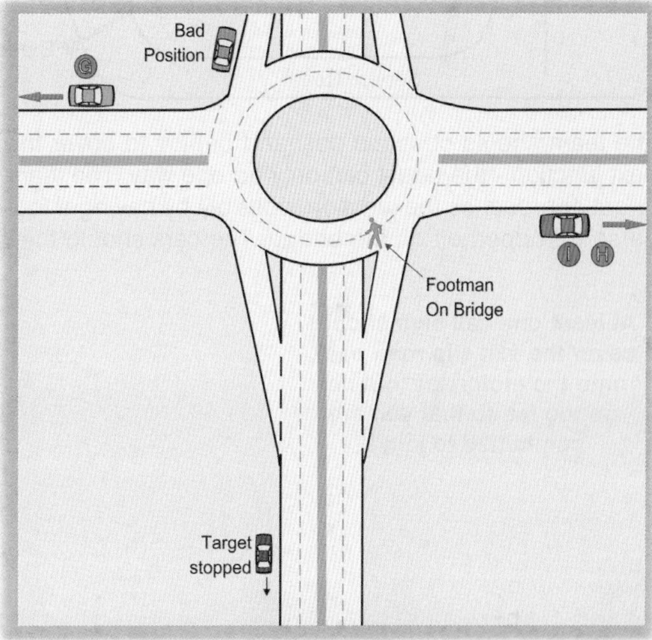

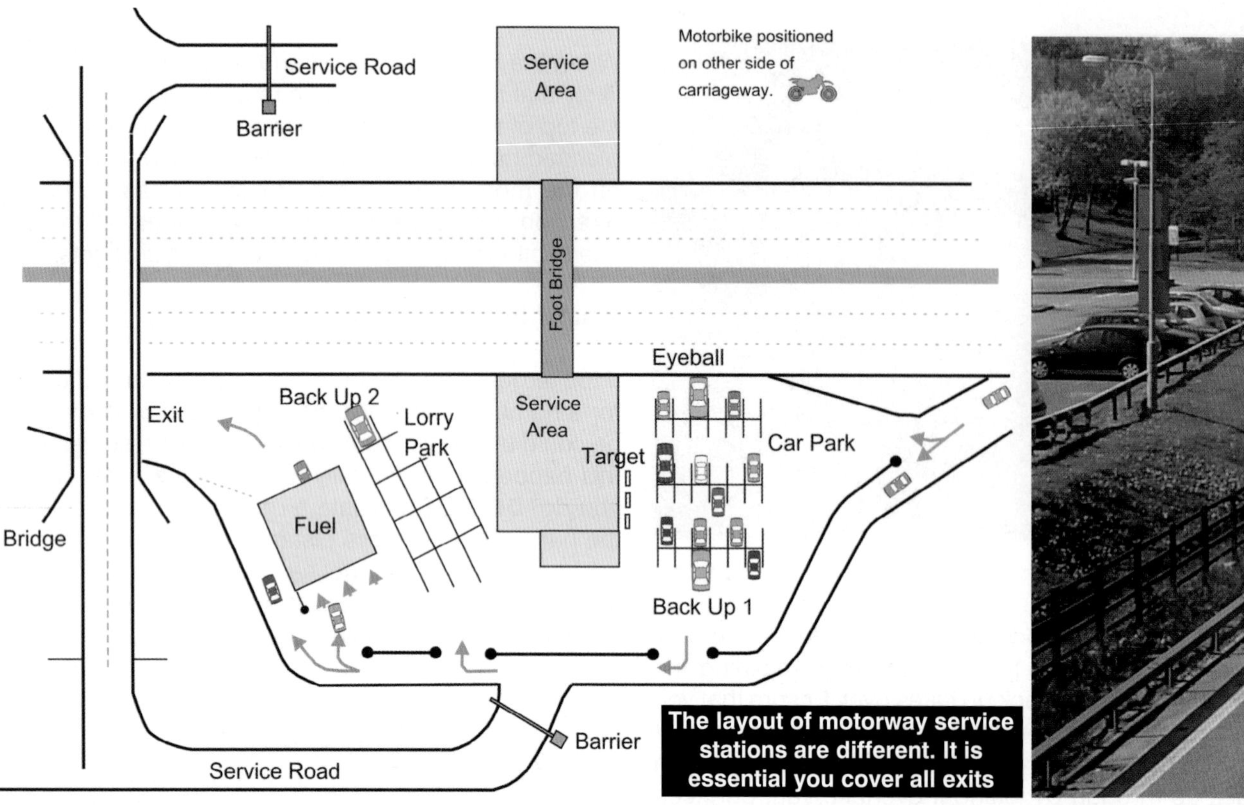


**The layout of motorway service stations are different. It is essential you cover all exits**

The team should continue past and deploy to cover the next junction - the target can only go one way. The team target approaches the junction, possibly by having a foot person dropped off on the bridge. The cars should then position themselves in the best possible place in the event that the target continues on the motorway. They should also be in a position to cover the eventuality that the target leaves the motorway at the same exit that is being covered. If you are on foot, do not stand above the motorway lanes as this makes drivers nervous, observe the motorway from one side.

**At least one call sign should cover the exit slip road back onto the motorway, but not go too far so that you are committed to join it**

Do not just expect the target to drive past after a short period. If he has genuinely broken down you could be in for a long wait. If you are the one observing the motorway do not forget to check any breakdown recovery vehicles that pass you, your target may be on the back of it.

If junctions are not too far apart or you have a motor-cyclist, it may be worth sending an operator on a drive past in the opposite direction in order to establish what the target is doing.

### Motorway Service Areas

These areas usually have a large cafeteria or service areas and give access for the public to park their cars and seek refreshment before continuing their journey.

Because of the proximity of the parking areas to the motorway and the possibility that a target can change the direction he is travelling in by using the service roads, we have to cover the options which are open to him by deploying operators in the following positions.

Upon entering a motorway service area a three car team should carry out the following:

• Eyeball should carry out a handover and take up a position in the area of the filling station or exit to the motorway

• The new eyeball takes the target onto the service area and keeps him under control, possibly deploying a foot person

• Back up covers any other exits away from the service area such as the service roads to hotels and so on

• Consider sending a motorcyclist or any other vehicle to take up position on the other side of the carriageway in the event that the target takes a footbridge across and meets with an associate on the other side. This is not always necessary and depends on the awareness level and the level of sophistication of your target.

• Be aware of one way systems in these areas.

## NIGHT MOBILE SURVEILLANCE

When driving at night, it is very difficult for the target to identify the vehicle or occupants of the car behind, especially when it is close. As the following car's headlamps are so bright, we tend to be blinded to anything but the lights themselves and so in busy times such as 'rush hour' we can afford to get closer to the target's vehicle.

Conversely in rural areas, a surveillance car may soon be spotted at night time and it may not be practical to 'hang back' too much. Ensure that any handovers are carried out frequently and always in the mirror of the target. This should satisfy the target's curiosity if he suspects that he is being followed. Prior to handover, ensure that you confirm which the target vehicle is, especially if it is between two or three other vehicles - you don't want to follow the wrong vehicle.

When handing over, you are trying to convey to the target, 'look at me, I am indicating to turn off, I am turning off, I am not following you'. So, carry out plenty of handovers in the targets mirrors.

Ensure that all your sidelights and headlights are working properly, a faulty light will soon be noticed. If you have to navigate by reading a map, try to refrain from using the 'courtesy' light as this will light you up like a beacon and also ruin your night vision - use a small pocket torch instead. Consider removing the courtesy light bulb altogether, so it does not light up the car when you open the door.

• **Where to Sit at Night**

In urban areas, you will have to decide where is a good place to park up without revealing that you are sitting in a car. There are different ideas on this. Do you sit right underneath a lamp post or away from it?

Being sat directly underneath a lamp post illuminates the car but not its occupants

If you park right under the lamppost the car will be illuminated but the interior will be cast in shadow, therefore use the dark shadow as cover, especially if you lower the seat back to reduce your profile or sit in the back. If you park away from the illumination of the lamp, the light itself will shine into your car to light you up or to make you stand out in silhouette.

Either way, it pays to use other cars as cover rather than you being the only one on the street.

As previously discussed, ensure that your widows are kept clean so that you cannot be seen inside. Try to avoid winding your windows down for the same reason. A wound down window looks just like a black hole, which someone outside the car can see straight into.

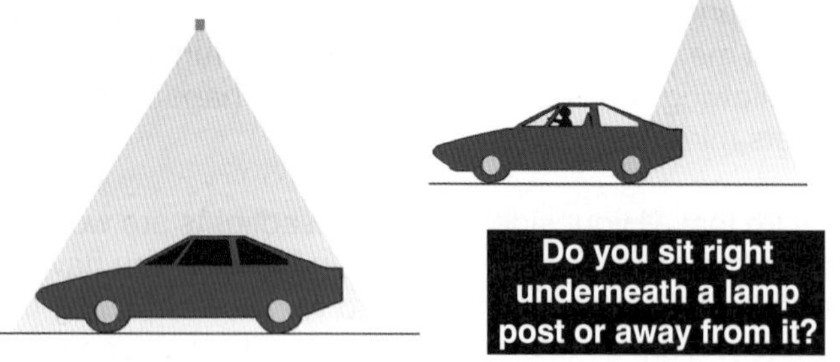
Do you sit right underneath a lamp post or away from it?

• **Touch Red!**

Quite often, the back up or trail will have difficulty seeing where the other team members are in the convoy ahead of them. The call **'Touch Red'** on the radio is often used to request that the eyeball (or person in front) taps their break pedals twice in order for those behind to see the brighter glow of the brake lights and thus indicates where they are. Be careful when you call this and don't ask anyone to 'touch red' on an approach to a junction or a roundabout as everyone in the line of traffic will be using their brakes.

• **Lights Away!**

Let's say that the target has entered a pub car park at night and you can only trigger the entrance from a distance or from a standing O.P. It will be difficult to identify the target as other vehicles may also leave the car park. Due to this, if a vehicle leaves we call **'Possible Standby Standby, Lights Away'.** This means that a vehicle has left but cannot be identified and therefore a team member has to check it and confirm whether it is the target.

Don't ask to 'touch red' when traffic is 'stacking up'

## Motorbikes

A motorbike is an essential aid when carrying out mobile surveillance through heavy traffic in busy towns and cities but they have their limitations. In their favour, they are harder to notice, they are fast with good acceleration and they can access areas that cars cannot. Using a motorbike greatly minimises the risk of a loss.

A surveillance rider's task is fairly specialised and requires a lot of training and experience. The rider has to be very proficient in bike handling as his task is probably one of the most dangerous on the team. A good rider will be able to act on his own initiative without having to be tasked by the eyeball, he will know when to hang back or when to come through and take the eyeball.

Not only can he take part in the surveillance but he can also provide support to the team. For example, if you are the trail, are held back in heavy traffic and need to close up but cannot get around it, the motorcyclist can help. If he cuts through the queue of traffic, pulls in front of someone and applies his brakes he can hold back the traffic and prevent them from moving forwards. As a gap appears, the biker calls forward the straggling team member who then overtakes the held traffic and jumps into the gap created by the biker. In a similar manner, if the convoy is struggling to get out at a road junction, the biker can position himself in the middle of the adjoining road, hold any oncoming traffic back and let the team come through. As I mentioned, a bikers task can be a dangerous one!

During the stakeout phase, the biker has to find an ideal place to lie up whilst waiting for the standby. Sometimes this can be difficult but he can afford to be further away from the target than anyone else, as he has the power to accelerate and get to where he is meant to be quickly.

Some bikers will co-locate with one of the mobile units (in the back of their car). The biker can then relax as he does not have to be 'attached' to his bike in order to receive comms. You will find a biker doing this quite often when the weather is bad! Remember that a motorbike has a limited range, therefore on long surveillances, it is likely that he will have to re-fuel at a petrol station or from a spare can carried by one of the team.

The professional surveillance rider will have his bike and helmet fitted with appropriate radio equipment. His radio will be worn about his person or he will have it fitted and powered from his bike, in some cases the biker will have one of each so that he can deploy on foot.

It is natural for a biker to push ahead on a motorway, but in surveillance he must hang back until required

In situations like this the biker will come through on his own initiative

During the follow, the biker should pay attention to the commentary and should act on his own initiative or when called through by the eyeball. If the target gets held at a set of traffic lights, he should automatically close up in case any of the team becomes held. If the lights change against the team, the biker can quickly clear the lights and take control. The rider will want to hand the eyeball back to the car team as soon as possible afterwards.

The biker can use other vehicles for cover but should also be courteous and safe. If he starts to annoy other motorists they will try to bump him off the road, flash their headlights at him or beep their horns, which will attract attention.

**Take care of your biker and he will take care of you**

### THE BIKER SHOULD BE USED:

- In heavy traffic such as busy towns and city centres, especially when there is a chance of the eyeball losing control
- At major roundabouts and junctions controlled by traffic lights, he should close up
- To provide suitable support to the mobile team
- To take the most direct and logical route when a loss occurs
- When following very fast or very slow targets
- To back up a footman who may be on a bus or train. It may be that your biker has to travel to the target's destination and arrive before him
- To pick up a foot person and re-deploy him
- To provide a trigger when the other vehicles are 'warm' or cannot obtain a good trigger position
- To cover the opposite side of a motorway service station

## Standing Down The Surveillance

At the end of the surveillance, the team leader will order the team to 'Stand Down' and lift off from the surveillance. When doing so, a meeting point or an RV should be nominated where all the team can meet up prior to debriefing and leaving the area. This RV should be an area which is safe and away from where the target or his associates are likely to visit or pass.

## Summary

• When the trigger gives a 'STANDBY', all call-signs should acknowledge. No one should be left behind!

• The vehicle nearest the target and giving the commentary is the 'eyeball' or the vehicle that 'HAS'

A team RV is normally a public place where vehicles can blend in and refreshments are often available

On a loss take the quickest and most logical escape route

• If you are backing, tell the eyeball straight away. If you become detached, also let him know with 'No longer backing'

• During the follow, the second (back up) and third cars will be at the rear, often out of sight

• The eyeball will give radio commentary on the speed and direction of the target and of any road hazards

• Cars will change positions as dictated by the eyeball

• In rural areas and motorways a greater distance can be allowed between target and eyeball. Bends in the road, hedges and other vehicles can be used as cover

• In built-up areas and especially busy towns, surveillance vehicles must close up and the eyeball should be very close, at times being directly behind the target

• Cars should keep to the nearside of target's rear when in close proximity to reduce the chance of attracting attention. People use their nearside mirrors less often

• If you are held immediately behind the target, drive and act naturally. The driver should 'minimise' on the radio and the back up vehicle should take over the commentary temporarily

• At night time, it is more difficult to follow in country areas without showing out

• Drive with normal lights, ensure that they all work properly

• If you are the back up and you become slightly detached, tell the eyeball that you are no longer backing

As soon as practically possible commit your observations to your log from your memo recorder

**Log Keeping**

Obviously a record of events should be made during a mobile surveillance just as they would if you were static. The use of a dictaphone or memo recorder is ideal as you can record the times and the events taking place. It may not be wise to write up your log sheet whilst in the middle of a surveillance at a temporary stop in case you miss something. Save the writing up of logs and reports until you are back at your base or as soon as practically possible. After the surveillance, it may be wise to plot the target's route on a map. This will reveal any patterns or unusual routes that they may have taken.

It is down to personal preference how the log is maintained. Normally, each operator maintains his own log on a dictaphone and then commits it to a written log at the end of the day. These are then handed to the team leader to compile a 'master' log which will ultimately, be sent to the client.

## THE ROLLING STAKE OUT

A rolling stake out is where the target is kept under control whilst the whole team has him surrounded, rather than being strung out in a line behind him. For example, your target is known to arrive by train and you do not know his mode of transport or where he is going, it can be tricky to cover.

The rail station will be plotted up, with the three cars in position, one getting the trigger on the exit, two covering the escape routes. It may be that you have a foot person deployed to take the trigger and follow.

The target arrives by train, he exits the station and continues to walk down the road. You could deploy a foot team of say two persons to take control but as the target moves further and further away from the start point (the rail station) it is not wise to leave all of the cars there - there is no reason, they have to keep up with the target.

In a rolling stake out the target is left to run but 'bounced' from car to car

Therefore, in this instance, one car may 'back' the foot team by remaining behind them and then moving, halting and waiting for a few minutes before moving up again. The other two cars now leapfrog ahead and re-plot to cover the side roads and options that the target might take. In essence, the whole team is constantly moving with the target by leapfrogging ahead. With practice and experience, a target can be kept under control like this using cars alone, without having to deploy a foot person. Use of parallels, good map reading and knowledge of the ground, really help during a rolling stakeout.

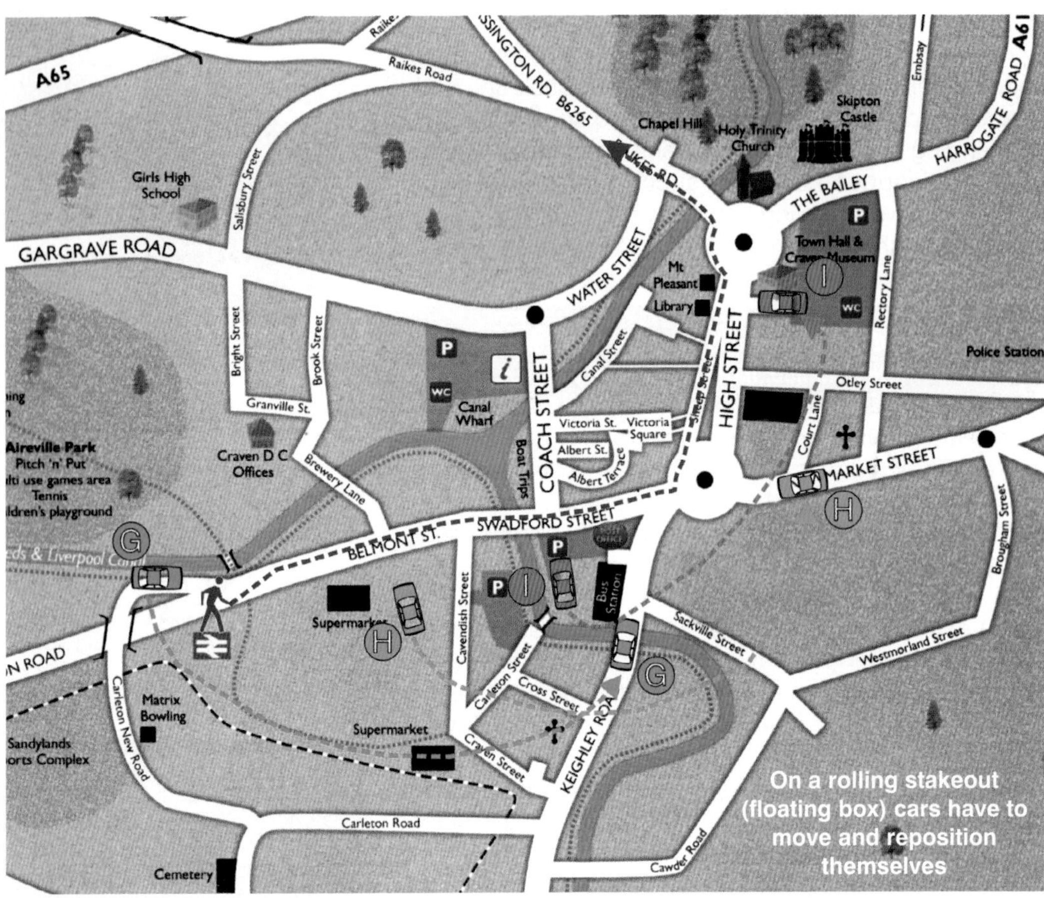

On a rolling stakeout (floating box) cars have to move and reposition themselves

## SINGLE HANDED MOBILE SURVEILLANCE

Many private investigators and surveillance operators carry out surveillance single handed. In the UK this can be very difficult because we live in an environment where we have been educated to be alert. In some countries, single handed investigators have an easier task but will still encounter the same problems.

In my opinion, if you consider yourself to be a professional investigator and surveillance operator, you would not be acting professionally by carrying out a surveillance single handed.

I often receive enquiries asking how much it would cost to carry out surveillance and I always answer the same way, 'You will need two or more surveillance operators in separate vehicles in order to minimise the risk of losing contact and more importantly minimise the risk of a compromise. Anyone who claims that they can do it cheaper by only using one person should be treated with extreme caution because they will risk compromising the job and the client.

If you experience a loss when on your own - making a decision at a junction must be instantaneous

Over the years experience has shown that the serious client understands what I am telling them and agrees to my suggestion. Therefore as a professional operator, it is up to you to educate and convince the client for the need to have two or more operators to do the job properly. Although more expensive, it is cheaper in the long term and your evidence will be much better especially if you are carrying out 'personal injury' type surveillance. You should always highlight the problems that will be encountered if operating on your own.

Sometimes as a member of a surveillance team, you will find yourself having the 'eyeball' with no back up, as the remainder of the team is detached and so, in effect, you are carrying out a single handed surveillance. I, and many of my colleagues have had successes during single-handed follows over long and tricky journeys, but not very many. Often the target has been lost in order to avoid a compromise, which is the better of two evils.

***We do not recommend carrying out single handed surveillance, it but if you have to...***

Before any surveillance, plan for it properly and get know the targets awareness level; has he been followed before? Will he be checking in his mirrors and carrying out anti surveillance, or will he be totally oblivious to a surveillance? Carry out a full recce of the target address or the premises from where he is to be followed. Identify the vehicle or mode of transport he is likely to use. If parked up, which way is he intending to travel? It may be better to 'pick up' the target at another road junction on his route, rather than sit near the property, where he is likely to be more aware.

Remember that we are talking about single handed surveillance. Consider carrying out the surveillance in stages if at all possible, in order to minimise compromise. Let's say that we are trying to establish where a target is working. It may be possible that on one morning's surveillance we make it our objective to: identify the target, establish what vehicle he is using (or other mode of transport), the time that he leaves and the direction that he travels in. On the following day, we make it our objective to plot up in the direction he intends to travel and then carefully follow him to his destination.

When driving alone try to keep your distance. However, when entering a built-up area you are forced closer

**GETTING THE MONEY SHOT** When on your own you

**Plotting Up**

Do not sit close to the target's address, the further away the better; remember, if you can see him, he can see you. Be very third party aware and adopt an identity by giving yourself a reason for being there. Don't make it obvious that you are watching a particular address and use hedges and walls to provide you with some cover to avoid prying eyes. Consider sitting in the passenger seat to give the impression that you are waiting for someone. If you have the equipment, consider using a technical trigger or a tracker to give you warning that the target vehicle is about to move.

Triggering in bad weather can be a problem because when alone you have no one to confirm identification or peform a drive past

When the target goes 'mobile', do not pull out directly behind him as you will be spotted, especially by an aware target. We only get one chance, so if at all possible, wait until the target is out of view before pulling out. Use another road user as cover, or alternatively, cover the first or second junction on his intended route and wait for him to pass.

quickly and find a position to get your camera up and running

## During the Follow

If you are behind the target and have no vehicles providing cover, peel off at regular intervals and put another road user in between you and the target. Whatever you do, do not rejoin the road if you are still in the target's mirror; if he is aware, he will be checking to see if you pull out. Try not to peel off if there is a string of traffic behind you, you may not be able rejoin the carriageway very easily.

Depending on the amount of traffic, you may be able to afford to have two or three cars providing cover, but remember that if you hit a roundabout or a junction you need to keep control of the target as these are high risk areas where a loss is possible. If you lose contact, it may be difficult to locate him when you are on your own. Logically, you should search along the most likely travel route, or make your way to any locations that the target is known to visit.

Always act naturally; if the target is held in traffic, avoid 'creeping up' behind him in the hope that you will not be noticed - you will be. If the target is held at a junction and indicating to turn, do not indicate yourself and try to avoid 'mirroring' the target's movements.

At night time, you can afford to get close to the target in busy traffic, as the target will only see a pair of headlights and not the colour/type of vehicle you are using. Ensure that all your lights work correctly. If the roads are sparse with traffic, you will have to 'hang back' and turn off frequently.

## Action on a Stop

When he comes to a stop, don't pull in directly behind him. Use cover to park behind or peel off to one side, if you are too close, act naturally and drive past before stopping. Avoid eye contact.

When the target stops, you have to consider whether he will get out on foot or if he will drive off again. Keep your eyes on the target and try to anticipate his intentions by reading his body language and actions such as removing a seat belt, turning the engine off or retrieving items from the passenger side.

Always have your 'working tools' close to hand so that they can be used at short notice. Your camera, binoculars, memo recorder, notebook and pen should always be within

Do not 'creep' up behind the target when it is held. Drive naturally.

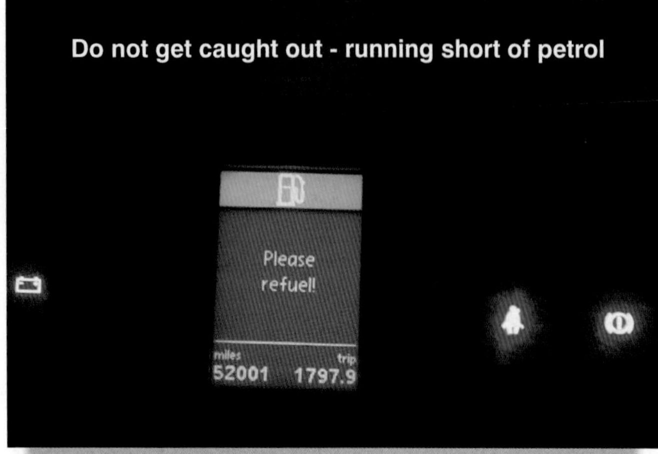


Do not get caught out - running short of petrol

easy reach but remember not to have them in view so that passing third parties can see them.

The target may enter a car park (multi-storey or open) and it is important that you keep him under tight control. If he is entering a car park you can expect him to get out on foot; so, be prepared and adopt a sense of urgency and park up quickly before the target disappears. You must decide whether or not to obtain a ticket from the machine. Whilst you are looking for change and putting a ticket on your windscreen, the target could be away and gone forever. If you get a parking fine, add it to your invoice!

Do not take unnecessary risks and do not over expose yourself. Remember the aims and objectives of the surveillance and stick to them. If the brief is to establish what software the target buys at the computer shop, we don't need to follow him into the newsagents, the chemists and the bookmakers, so, let's stay outside and get in close only when it is necessary.

With technology advancing as fast as it is, some operators on the surveillance circuit are now carrying out single handed surveillance with the assistance of a tracking device. A tracker can give you a trigger that enables you to keep your distance and if you lose the target he can be quickly regained again.

**Be aware if a target enters an industrial estate. They are likely to stop frequently and carry out U-turns if they are lost or seeking an address**

### The ABI Investigators Journal

The above section on 'Single Handed Surveillance' was published in the 'Investigate', the journal of the Association of British Investigators and it received comments from readers.

One response was by an investigator who operates in Australia who stated that most of his surveillances are carried out single handed and that he never has a problem with losing the target or having compromises. He also added that he had thousands of excellent results over a number of years. He also stated that operating on one's own is more challenging and tests the individual skills of the investigator. This was my response:

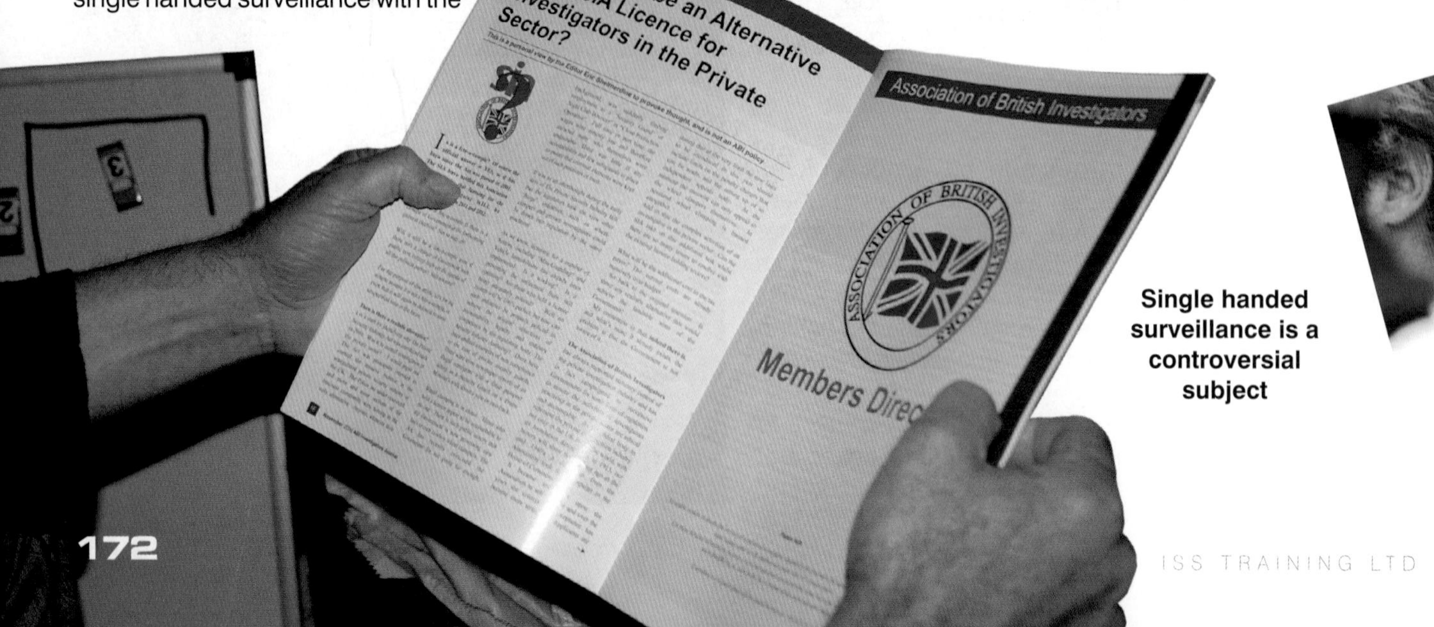


**Single handed surveillance is a controversial subject**

Dear Sir,

I write in response to Mr K of Australia in the last issue of Investigate regarding my article on 'Why Compromises Occur' and specifically the comments he makes about single handed surveillance and I would like to make the following points in return.

The article was written with a view to carrying out surveillance generally in the UK, after all we are the Association of 'British' Investigators. To some extent, I fully concur with Mr K's contradictory comments. I do not contest that his company has carried out thousands of surveillances single handed and has had excellent results. However, it would appear that surveillance is easily carried out in Australia. I have not worked over there and therefore could not comment but I have carried out work in the United States and parts of Europe where it can also be very easy to carry out surveillance on one's own. A single handed operator would get away with a lot more in other parts of the world than he would here in the UK.

In the UK we are all naturally vigilant, the population has had past experiences with terrorism, growing crime and anti-social behaviour, which makes everyone more aware of what is happening around them, which does not help the surveillance operator. I beg for Mr K to come and visit us in the UK and carry out a single handed surveillance in areas such as Gipton in Leeds, Bransholme in Hull or Pennywell in Sunderland (where we have carried out many personal injury investigations). In these areas, the local population will know the colour of your underwear before you can say 'single handed'. What also complicates in the world of personal injury claims (in the UK), is the fact that the claimants solicitor will, as a matter of course, tell the claimant that he will be put under surveillance at some stage... they do not want to lose cases and subsequent revenue.

Our company, and many others is this industry 'enjoy' being able to use 2 or more investigators on a task, as it is what we (and our clients) expect to do the job professionally. Many corporate security managers (our clients) are former policemen who would not expect anything less. I totally agree that working on one's own is far more challenging and tests the investigators skills but it does not help when you have been rammed off the road.

I understand the need for some investigation companies, who can only budget for one investigator but this is down to them, their relationship with their client and the amount of profit that they want to take from each job.

We have also been in this industry for a while and have seen all sorts of irregular practices, especially where single-handed surveillance is concerned. I would like to say that being employed or working on one's own for a large investigation company can often lead to 'incompetence and lies' if that is the correct phrase to use in this instance. I do not wish to tar every employer with the same brush but I make these observations from personal experience as an employer and contractor, from reports of those investigators attending our courses and from many conversations with those also in the industry.

If you currently employ a number of surveillance staff and expect them to carry out single handed surveillance, take a close look for the person who keeps on having 'losses' or reports back that 'nothing happened'. Imagine these scenarios;

Joe works for ABC Investigation Company on a wage of £8.00 an hour. He goes out to work on surveillance, after a couple of hours he needs a call of nature or is hungry and leaves the area for a short period. He returns to the target address with his Big Mac and guess what? Yes, the target's car has gone. Does he tell his boss what has occurred? No, he reports in his log that nothing happened all day.

Joe goes out to work the following day, the target comes out and he looses him in traffic after a few minutes.. oops. The third day, the target comes out again and he loses him in traffic once again.. another oops. Does Joe (who wants to keep his job) report back to the office that he keeps having losses? I don't think so, he writes in his surveillance log that the target never came out all day, or writes down that the target came out, appeared to be 'very aware' and was 'left to run' to avoid compromising the job. Hmm..

Joe's boss is now putting on the pressure because he is having so many losses. Joe wants to keep his job and so sticks to the target like glue. Joe does so, which results in him being compromised all the time and fails to get any video evidence. Does Joe tell his boss that he is now having lots of compromises? No, he says that the target never came out..... Joe then gets a new windscreen fitted to his car after it was smashed by the target.

Joe, due to being under pressure from working on his own, eventually gets caught out when a case is heard in Court. Joe's surveillance log reports that there was no movement to or from the target house all day. The target's barrister cross examines him and asks him how he failed to notice, or log in his report the fact that the fire service attended at the house, to put out a kitchen fire on that particular day.... Big oops.

I would really like to survey all those who carry out single handed surveillance in order to get a true picture of successes, losses and compromises to produce a report but I am sure I will not get a true picture or response. One major problem is the fact that many of these 'Joes' are not members of any trade body and therefore will not know what goes on in the industry; many of them probably wont even read this article.

I note that there were no letters from investigators based in the UK who took exception to my article, was it because they agreed? I am open to constructive criticism but remember the whole point to that article was to understand why we get compromised. It still stands that you will get noticed if you are seen on multiple occasions or you are doing something odd or unnatural. Both of which are greatly increased if you are on your own.

P.S. If an investigator called Joe asks you for a job...............

Peter Jenkins
ISS Training Limited

## SCOTTISH WARNING

This is a story published in the Edinburgh Evening News in October 2009.

A retired policeman, now a private investigator was fined £1,150 for following a prominent businessman's wife in her car. He was charged under Scottish Law for a Breach of the Peace.

The court heard that Mrs Cross left from the address she was staying at in Fife to take her son to school in Edinburgh, after dropping him off she noticed a grey BMW following her. She continued driving into Edinburgh for a meeting, with the BMW still on her tail. She was suspicious of this car and noted the registration number.

She parked at the city's Castle Terrace to go to a meeting and when she came out the car again tailed her. She drove on to Lothian Road and out to the Gorgie area and noticed the BMW still behind her. She stated, 'The passenger in the vehicle appeared to be moving between the front of the vehicle and into the rear'.

The court heard Mrs Cross, now in a state of panic contacted police who said they would meet her at a petrol

If you have been behind the target with no cover, do not be afraid to peel off the road and rejoin after a short while letting cover in. However, do not pull back out again in the target's mirror

station. The police met Mrs Cross at the petrol station and accompanied her to her home in Fife. When they reached her home the police saw the BMW and pulled it over.

The court heard that substantial surveillance gear was found in the car including binoculars, a camcorder, a digital camera, SAT NAV and a laptop. The investigator, Mr. Allen, admitted following Mrs Cross and breaching the peace.

**Comment**

*In Scotland, a breach of the peace is the most common non-motoring offence brought before the courts. Case law states that to be guilty of a breach of the peace, the accused must cause fear and alarm.*

## SURVEILLANCE COMPROMISES

This section deals with surveillance compromises. Compromises are a fact of life in surveillance and an occupational hazard as they will occur with the best of operators.

They can either be caused by the target noticing you or the third party. Although you have to be third party aware at all times, sometimes you just have to 'brass neck' it and get your camera up and running regardless of whoever is about. If you have been on a surveillance for the past four days and nothing has happened and then all of a sudden on day five, activity occurs, you have to go in for the 'money shot'.

In the commercial world, in some respects you are only as good as your last job and you get paid for results not excuses. Can you imagine having to report back to a client after five days surveillance with a three man team and a hefty invoice. You are asked, 'So why didn't you get any video of the target transferring the goods from one van to another?' You answer, 'A man standing in a bus stop was watching me and if he had seen me with a camera he may have reported me to the police..'. That type of excuse is not acceptable and the client is unlikely to pay your bill - you have to get the video.

## ISS CASE

I recall being in the back of a van where it was imperative that we had eyes onto the targets house located in a cul de sac. Within an hour or so, a neighbour had come out of his house and took a good look at the van, he also tried to look into it by peering through the one way glass. He was seen writing down the registration and so we now had to consider either leaving it there or moving it. The latter was decided and as my partner walked up to it he was approached by the neighbour and was asked why it as parked there. He was given an excuse and we covered the target by a different means.

Although not strictly compromised, it is considered as a 'soft' compromise and we were forced to change our approach.

On another occasion, we had a three man team following a target who was delivering fake soft drinks to pubs in some rough areas. I was in a phone box using it as cover to take photographs. I had noticed that someone had walked passed me and entered the pub and thought nothing of it. A few minutes later, the same man appeared with a colleague and stood in the pub doorway pointing in my direction. Again, I considered it as a soft compromise and got out of there, luckily I already had the 'money shot' of the fakes being delivered.

We consider two types of compromises; hard and soft. Over the past 20 years I have had a few of each but mainly soft compromises.

**Hard Compromise**

In the mid-nineties, I was working single handed in the North East on a personal injury surveillance. Working single handed is not normal working practice in our company as it has its flaws but we were constrained by the client at

Stay out of the '10 to 2' at all times but do not be directly behind the target

Always think 'loss versus gain'. Don't go in hard and close if it is not necessary

the time. I had to establish whether an individual was currently working contrary to his insurance claim and to obtain video of such.

The target left his home in the morning and was followed some six miles to another town where he parked and entered a shop that sold baby clothes. He was in there for quite a while and so a walk past was carried out and he

Witnesses at this bus stop provided corroborative evidence when the author was rammed by a van driver

was seen inside working behind the counter. The client was informed of the progress and they now asked for me to go into the shop and buy something to obtain a receipt. Although I have two children, I didn't feel comfortable with this - a 30 year old bloke in a baby clothes shop. However, as instructed, I went into the shop, bought some baby clothes and left with a receipt. I then went back to my van and covered the shop from a distance. A short while afterwards, the target came out and was followed again as he drove home.

Once at home, I plotted up and covered the house once more but after about 15 minutes I noticed the target's wife looking out of the window in my direction. I was in the back of a small van and felt happy with my position but I sensed that something wasn't right and so I decided to leave the area. As I drove out of the end of the street, I noticed the target walking towards me and waving his arm about in an attempt to flag me down. I gave a casual wave in return and continued on without stopping.

It was obvious that he was suspicious of my presence and had gone out of his back door in an attempt to ambush the van so I drove on. After about three miles I stopped to make a phone call as I didn't think the compromise was that serious, on looking in my rear view mirror, I noticed the target driving towards me at speed! I hastily drove off and thought it would be easy to shake him off but after going around a roundabout to get onto a dual carriageway, the target was now coming towards me and decided to crash into me and ram me off the road.

I stopped on the verge 100m from the target who never came over to me and I phoned the police. They then arrested "me" on suspicion of driving without undue care and attention! It became apparent that the target had also telephoned the police just before me and stated that I had rammed into him! No charges were ever brought either way as witnesses standing at a bus stop confirmed what actually happened. I later discovered the target had been under surveillance in the past by another investigator.

A number of things were learned that day:

- *Don't ever carry out single handed surveillance*
- *Ensure whether the target has been under surveillance in the past*
- *Whoever manages to telephone the police first is considered the victim and always favoured..*

## COMPROMISE SURVEY

There are many other compromise stories that have occurred and are worthy of a book in their own right. On our website there has been a survey for the past year inviting investigators to submit stories about compromises that they have had and a few are listed here. I spoke to a few on the phone and this is what they have had to say:

## BOBBY'S STORY

"I used to carry out a lot of personal injury type surveillance in Northern Ireland, most of it was single handed because the client would not authorise two operators but I was getting some good results.

"I had one target who I knew had an association with Loyalist paramilitaries and so had to be very careful. The target left home on the first morning and drove to a building site where he appeared to be working. I had to risk it and so I drove into a compound next to the building site and jumped into the back of my van and started to video the target working on the site.

"After an hour or so the target and two others started talking about my van, it was obvious that they were concerned about it as they kept looking towards me. I was quite concerned but felt that I could not jump into the front and drive off as they would have been after me. I thought that they may have suspected that I was social security, tax investigators or at worse the security forces.

"The target and another bloke then came up to the van and peered in through the front and sides. They also tried to see through the one-way glass in the rear but I had a curtain over it so they couldn't see in. I just froze, I absolutely crapped myself and waited for them to start banging on the roof. After a few minutes they went back into their own compound and one of them started up a dump truck. I thought that they were going to use it to block me in and so I decided to quickly jump into the front and leg it. I drove at high speed and cleared the area feeling extremely relieved but worse emotion was yet to come.

"When I parked up and got out of the van I realised that I had not locked the drivers door! If they had tried the door handle they would have been in and I would be buried in concrete by now." **Lesson Learned:**

- *Ensure that your doors are locked as soon as you get in.*
- *Don't work single handed*
- *As soon as you feel theatened - get out*

FIGHT OR FLIGHT? **Alerted targets will either confront you or flee**

## GEOFF'S STORY

"In my early surveillance career, I was very keen to get results when I worked for a large insurance investigation company that specialises in personal injury claims.

"I was tasked to carry out surveillance on a target who was suspected of submitting a false claim in respect of his injuries. I was briefed that the target was a former soldier with some surveillance experience but was told to carry out the job single handed and was assured by my boss that it would be okay. I intended to do the job with the help of a tracker in the event I had a loss as this job was to last for seven days.

"The target lived on a modern housing estate where no one parks up on the street so the address was difficult to cover, it was also too risky to deploy the tracker, so I gave it a miss.

"During the first two days I managed to obtain some video of the target in and around his house as he didn't go anywhere. On the third day, he took his dog for a walk in the fields and woods in the local area. I managed to get some video of him from a distance but another dog walker spotted me from behind whilst I was filming.

"It turns out that the dog walker knew the target and told him that I had been filming him as he turned and started after me. I began to run back to my car but then changed my mind and ran into the wooded area, I think at this time the target had pinged my car as it was the only one parked in the area. I then hid in the woods, crapping myself because I could hear the target searching for me and shouting that he was going to beat the shit out of me.

I telephoned my boss asking for some back up to come out and assist but he just said that I will be okay and that if I stay hidden, I should be able to come out later.

"The target spent some time looking for me and so I stayed where I was and after three hours decided to head back to my car. As I got close, I saw the target sat in his car which was nosed up to mine at the front, at the back was a huge bloke sat in another car and they had blocked me in. I phoned my boss again and he said that he would get someone to help me out, I was pretty worried and told him that I was going to phone the police. He convinced me not to and said help was on its way - I think he didn't want the police involved as it would be embarrassing if his client found out.

"I stayed hidden in the woods and seven hours later, I was picked up by another employee, we did a drive past of my car and the target had gone. Still crapping myself, I quickly jumped into my car and drove off, the target and his mate had gouged deep scratches in the cars paintwork.

"I never had anymore work from that company afterwards. A few months later the company sent me a witness statement to sign to go with the video that I took. I never signed it and never posted it back so I do not know what happened with my evidence. If I learned anything that day, it was not to go out on your own, the other thing, telephone the police as soon as you get in the shit. As its your neck on the line." **Lessons learned:**

- ***Read the brief - the target was switched on and knew about surveillance.***
- ***Don't go out on your own.***
- ***Telephone the police as soon as you feel threatened.***
- ***Don't work for someone that thinks more about his client than his staff.***

## BANKSEY'S STORY

"I was on a surveillance in Manchester and the target was working as a taxi driver from a small cab company next to a small train station. I was plotted up on my own and had a good view of the taxi company, I was able to film the parking up and going inside etc. Close by and behind me was a pub and I occasionally kept seeing people stick their head out of the pub door and then go back inside. They did not bother me and so I dismissed it.

"When I got home, I noticed that someone had stuck two fluorescent stickers on the rear of my car which read 'DSS Snooper'! Obviously, those from the pub had a laugh at my expense." **Lessons Learned:**

- *Be more third party aware and move as soon as you feel uncomfortable with your surroundings*

## CHARLTON'S STORY

"I was watching a target in Bradford who had claimed that he could not walk without the aid of walking sticks after being in an accident. I filmed him for two days as he delivered leaflets for the local Asian community and I was on my own. The area was a very run down inner city where drugs and crime were rife.

"On the third day, I was in the back of my van when I noticed two dodgy looking characters walking towards my position on the same side of the road. They were very street wise and gave the van a few looks which were more than passing glances. After walking past, they turned around towards the van and started looking into the front cab and the back windows. I could hear them say, 'there's some f****r in there'. One of them noticed the window was down about half an inch and started to pull down at the window with is fingers. At this stage, I decided to jump through into the front and into the drivers seat.

When lowering windows in the van take up the slack by raising them slightly. Otherwise it is possible for someone to force the window down a few inches

"As I appeared, the two started banging on the windows, screaming and yelling at me. One of them was leaning forward and I could see a long screwdriver in the inside pocket of his jacket, they meant business so I just put my foot down and got out of there, not to return." **Lessons Learned:**

- *Remember to wind your windows back up after dropping them an inch to take up the slack*
- *Have a back up nearby to help you out when in trouble*
- *Don't go out on your own*

## MARTIN'S STORY

"This was a stupid mistake that caused a compromise. I was in the back of my van filming through a gap in the curtains whilst shooting through the front windscreen. The target lived in a small estate at the bottom of a long cul de sac.

"The target had been in a road traffic accident and was claiming insurance for injuries to his back and neck. I had filmed him in his garden as he set up a rotary washing line and then hung out the washing. About an hour later, he got into his car and drove out of the street and had to pass me on his way, I filmed him as he went. He just got passed me and then stopped, reversed and came to a

Be aware of your video cameras recording lamp - switch off at all times

halt right in front of my van. I could see him staring at me, he got out of his car and stood directly to my front and stared into the van. He then started yelling, 'I know you're in there, get out!' and he started to push and rock the van as if to shake me out. I knew I was compromised and had nothing to lose, so continued to video him whilst he bounced up and down on the bonnet (cracking video!). After a minute, he got back in his car and drove back to his house, his last words were, 'I'm phoning the police'.

"I drove off rather sharply and realised how I had been seen. The red recording lamp at the front of my camera had not been switched off! I couldn't believe I made such a simple mistake. Not only do I make sure the lamp is switched off through the menu settings but have also painted out the lamps on all my cameras." **Lessons Learned:**

- ***Make sure that the recording lamp on your camera is switched off***
- ***Clear the area completely after a compromise***

## NOBBY'S STORY

"I had been following the same target for two evenings on a matrimonial job. It was quite tricky because I had to follow him by car and then go into anywhere he went in the event he met someone, the job was single handed. On the second evening, he had been to a pub, had one drink and left at about 8pm. I followed him through Stroud and after about 15 minutes he was held at a set of traffic lights.

"To my surprise, the target got out of his car, ran over to me and yanked open my car door shouting, 'You're not very good are you, Inch High private eye?' He then snatched the keys out of my ignition and threw them as hard as he could down the road! He got back into his car and drove off with his wheels squealing.

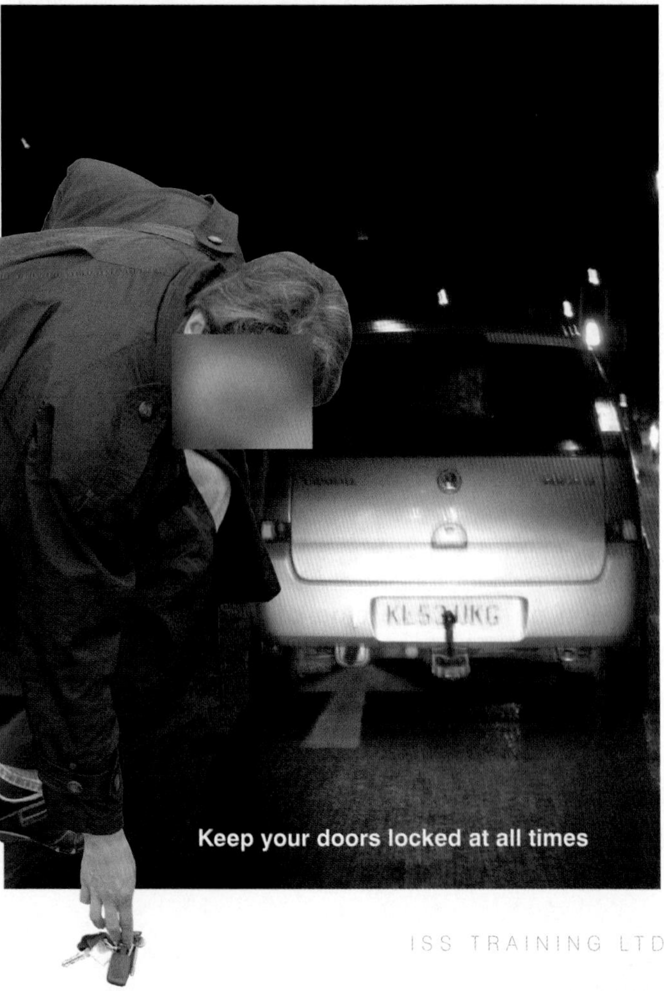

Keep your doors locked at all times

"I was left stranded in the middle of a road junction causing a jam whilst I searched for my keys. I had to report back to the client which wasn't fun and she never paid my bill." **Lessons Learned:**

- ***Don't go out single handed, even if it is only a 'matrimonial'***
- ***Find out if your client has told her husband, 'I'm going to have you followed'***
- ***Lock your doors***

## FRANZ'S STORY

"I work for one of the biggest personal injury investigators in the UK and they ask us to go out single handed, which I think is ludicrous. Anyway, the company don't know it, but I try and put a tracker on the targets car whenever I go out because it's so easy to have a loss when on your own.

"On this particular case I had visual control of the target but was having trouble getting a fix from the tracker, which reports to my Blackberry phone. We were held in a queue approaching a roundabout and I was texting the tracker hoping to get a position. The target was in pole position on the roundabout and pulled away, then I heard a bang and felt a jolt as I crashed into the rear of the target! I was distracted by my phone, the target had stalled his car and I just ran into the back of him. Ooops..

"There wasn't much damage but the target insisted on exchanging details. I had to give them truthfully as he had taken my cars registration. He didn't realise who or what I was and he went on his way. I told my employer that I had a loss early on and didn't see him again that day. I had to sneak up his drive that night to get my tracker back because I couldn't follow him again." **Lessons Learned:**

- ***Don't get distracted when you are immediately behind the target.***
- ***Keep your cameras covered up at all times***
- ***Work in teams of two***

## MACHETE MADMAN!

This case went to Court in 2006 (R v Clark 2006). I have not been able to speak to anyone involved but gleaned the story from the Internet and local papers.

In 2005, an investigator from a UK company was carrying out a personal injury surveillance in the Midlands on a female, the client was an insurance company. The task was carried out single-handed. The investigator spent a few days observing the targets house and even made pretext calls to the neighbours, word soon got around and the target became aware. It appears that the target also worked for an insurance company at one time and so she would know that she may be subjected to surveillance at some point. The agent made a pretext call to the targets address and the door was answered by the husband. The husband, knowing who the caller was, dragged him inside, tied him to a chair and threatened to kill him with a machete.

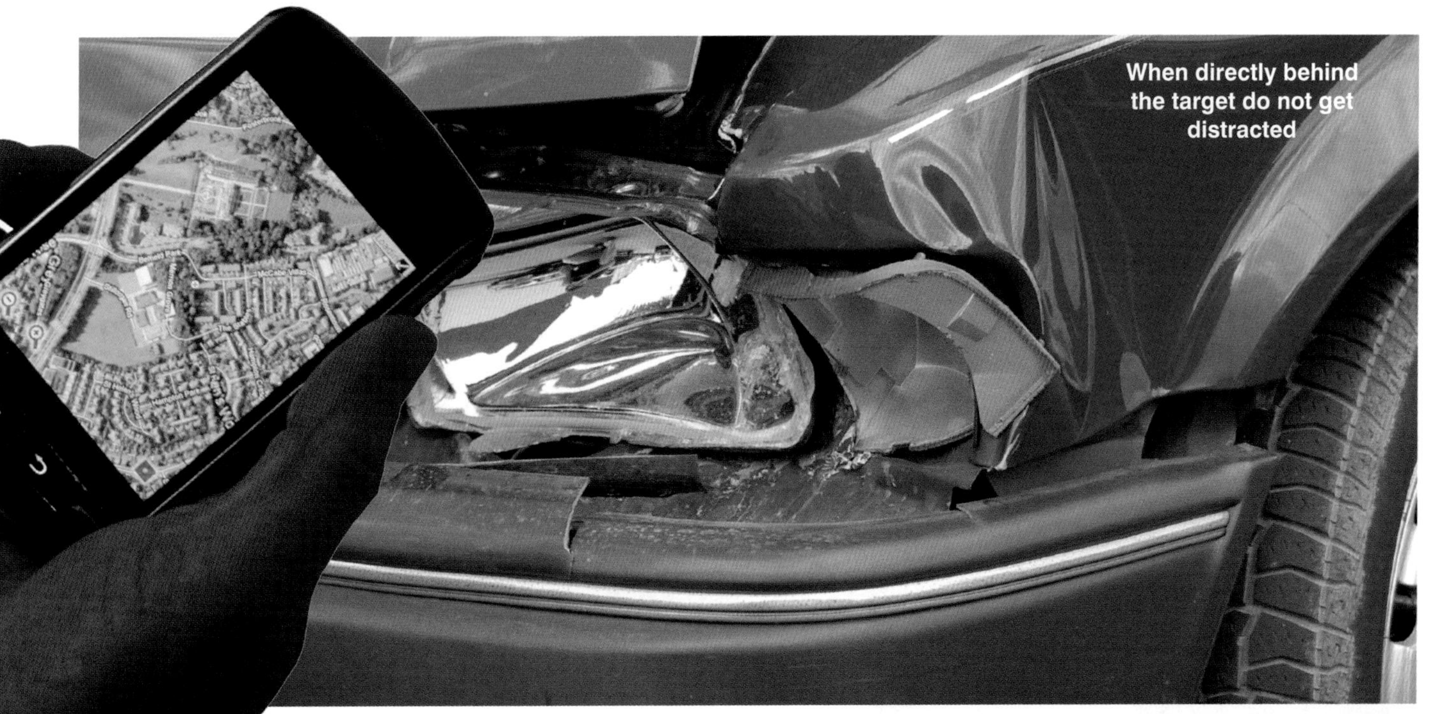

When directly behind the target do not get distracted

Recognise threats early and be prepared to leave the area quickly

The daughter also joined in by holding a knife to his throat. The husband then put a bag over his head, poured a flammable liquid over him and threatened to set him alight. The target intervened and he was allowed to go free and called the police.

As a consequence the family went to Court over the incident and the husband received a custodial sentence, the daughter received a police caution. **Lessons learned:**

- ***Don't work on your own without any back up.***
- ***Don't make any pretext calls to neighbours***
- ***Research your target***

## JACKIE'S STORY

I was following a delivery driver in Blackpool, Lancashire as it was known that he added extra stock onto his van. The company sold and supplied computer printer ink cartridges and the client wanted to know who he was selling them to.

The driver knew his routes well and it was difficult to keep up with him at times. Every time he stopped I had to video the boxes that he took into the premises.

The target stopped at an outdoor market in Preston and delivered four boxes, it was risky getting the video as there were so many people around but this was an unscheduled delivery which had to be videoed. After he left, I continued to follow him for about 20 minutes until I received a phone call from my wife. She said that the Police had telephoned the house asking if we owned the car that I

was driving. My wife told the police that we did and added that I was a private investigator and was using the car on a surveillance. The police told her that someone (it turned out to be the target) had telephoned the police claiming that they were carrying a large amount of cash on them and that they thought that they were being followed to be robbed.

I had been following him for quite a while and he could have seen me. I think that I was spotted in the market by a trader, who told the stall holder who received the delivery. The stall holder obviously telephoned the target driver. **Lessons learned:**

- *Don't go out single handed, convince the client for a team*
- *I could have gone to the market stall and made a test purchase as the delivery was being made or shortly afterwards*
- *Watch out for the third party and don't take risks*

**Conclusions**

The above stories were selected from about thirty that were submitted via our website survey. The reasons for compromise were many but the most re-occurring reason was the fact that investigators or operators were carrying out surveillance on their own. The answer is simple - Don't do it!

Self-protection sprays are a useful device in a hostile situation but check they are legal to use in your country

**ROAD TRAFFIC ACCIDENTS**

This is not a lesson in first aid and I would strongly recommended that anyone carrying out surveillance work undergo first aid training. It is likely that you will encounter an accident at some stage in your career because a great deal of time is spent on the roads. This section should be used to complement your first aid skills and training.

**What to do if you encounter a road traffic accident**

Call the emergency services, 999 or 112 from a mobile. Try and be specific where the accident is; note the road number, any adjoining street names and the nearest village or landmark. If on a motorway, note the number written on a post - this will indicate exactly where you are. They will also want to know what has happened, how many cars and how many casualties.

Stay calm, put on a hi-vis vest if you have one handy, this gives you an authoritative appearance, people are more likely to listen to you and follow instructions.

Secure the scene; get passers by or others to either stop traffic or redirect it past the scene. All cars should switch off engines, put hazard warning lights on, put triangles out and look out for hazards such as fuel spillages that may ignite. Try and redirect traffic, the last thing you want to do is hold up an ambulance by stacking up the traffic.

Make an assessment, check each vehicle or pedestrian for injuries. The injured should be prioritised, if anyone is unconscious deal with them first, check:

**Airway** - ensure nothing is blocking their airway; airbags, dentures, teeth or debris from the accident, this is your first priority. If the patient is unconscious, loosen neck clothing, open their airway by tilting their head back gently and lifting the chin. If they appear unconscious, give them a slight tap for any response

**Breathing** - check that the patient is breathing. This may be shallow and difficult to detect. Put your cheek close to their mouth to feel breath, watch for the chest rising. If not, you should commence mouth to mouth resuscitation.

**Circulation** - ensure that the patient has a pulse, this may be weak and hard to identify. If not, you will have to apply chest compressions to get the heart pumping. Stem any bleeding from injuries immediately or the patient will go into shock. Apply compression dressing for excessive bleeding from arms and legs.

If a neck injury is not suspected, place an unconscious patient who is breathing in the recovery position and cover with a blanket. Give your patient reassurance and comfort - talk to them, tell them your name, ask them theirs, tell them that help is on its way.

**DO NOT** move a patient if you do not have to, treat them in the car if necessary. Wait for the emergency services.

Remember; stay calm, take charge of the situation and reassure the injured until the emergency services arrive.

Lamp posts on a highway should be marked similar to this at regular intervals

Much surveillance work involves observation from a static location in order to carry out a continuous watch on an individual, a premises or even objects. The static Observation Post (OP) is where we are in a fixed position with no requirement to follow the target by the OP team. We could be tasked to observe a warehouse to note all deliveries made, or to watch a private house to photograph the occupants when they leave. The reasons for carrying out a static surveillance are many and the methods used to carry out such a surveillance are described in this chapter.

## STATIC OBSERVATION POSTS

In addition, the static OP may be used to provide a trigger with a mobile or foot team in position. The surveillance van (if used as an OP) can follow on behind a mobile surveillance (or even take part in it, if used carefully) and move into a new static position when the target arrives at his destination or stops.

### What is an OP?

- *A static position from where you can observe, report and photograph activity*
- *It can be covert or overt*
- *Long or short term*
- *Urban or rural*
- *Located in vehicles, buildings or rural Hides*
- *Located on foot for short term purposes (night & day)*

### Vehicle OPs

As described in the chapter on Surveillance Equipment, a fully equipped surveillance van is worth its weight in gold to the surveillance team. Having the ability to move your OP into a position, observe and photograph the target and then depart without arousing any suspicion from the target or locals, is paramount to a covert investigation. It can be difficult to sit in the front of your car on a housing or industrial estate and carry out observations without arousing

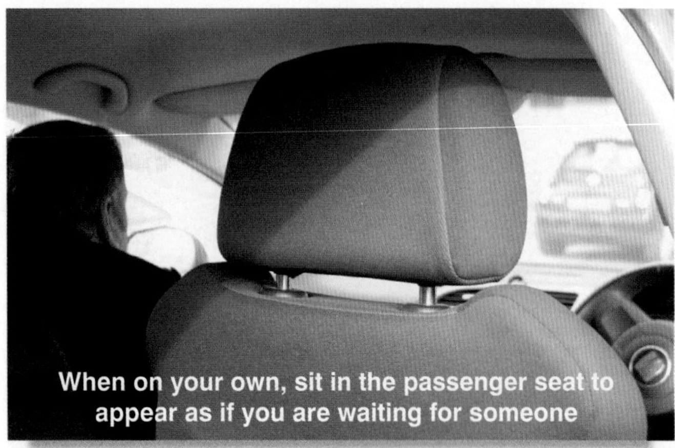
When on your own, sit in the passenger seat to appear as if you are waiting for someone

suspicion. It is extremely difficult to last for any length of time before you are reported to the police. With an increase in crime rates, the general public are normally alert to anything suspicious.

Occasions arise when it is necessary to observe for long periods from a car and the operator can feel exposed and uncomfortable when doing so. If you have to, try and sit as far from the target as possible, preferably having to look obliquely at the target rather than straight at it. Use any cover that may shield part of the car such as other vehicles, walls, hedgerows and trees. If you are sitting in the passenger seat this will give the appearance that you are waiting for the driver to return. If sitting in the rear, use a jacket on a hanger to provide you with some cover. Many motor accessory shops sell small roller blinds that attach to car windows to act as sunshields. These are effective for providing temporary cover, especially when attached to the rear windows of the car.

**What if I am challenged?**

If you are challenged by a member of the public, have a good cover story ready and make it sound realistic and convincing. On occasions, it may be worth telling the curious person that you are waiting to 'serve' divorce papers on a person and you are waiting for them to return home as they are being evasive. Use your imagination but do not let it run away with you.

**A skip similar to this was purpose built to contain a hide from which to observe. Refuse was then added to make it look realistic. It was then moved into position**

## SURVEILLANCE VANS (MOBILE OP)

During your pre-surveillance, you decide that the only way to observe the target premises is by use of a surveillance van; the vans position is important and you must decide whether to observe though the rear window or through the front or the sides.

When positioning the van, consider:

• What is your reason for being there?

• Your OP position in relation to the target; can you see the target clearly, are there likely to be any obstructions? Can you identify who leaves the property and in which vehicle?

• Is your position obvious? If there are no other vehicles on the street, you may show out

• If the target goes 'mobile' are you able to give direction of travel to the remainder of the team?

• Does the target have to pass you on his way out?

• Does the van intend to join the team and follow the target when he leaves? If so, is the van facing in the intended direction

• Are you in a cul-de-sac with only one escape route? If so, park the van facing towards the exit route in case you have to extract quickly

• Is it feasible to 'self extract' or is it too risky?

• An aware target may be suspicious of vans

Be aware of parking restrictions - especially in private residential areas

Large vans with blacked-out windows are more noticeable depending where you are operating

The smaller van has a low profile and can be parked in a row of traffic

## The Insertion

If possible park the vehicle where there is some cover from the view of others, especially in residential areas. If you have to park outside a semi-detached or terraced house, then park between the two properties. One neighbour may think that the van is connected with next door or vice-versa and try to limit suspicion about the van.

If it is difficult obtaining a parking position it may be necessary to park another vehicle the day before the surveillance in order to 'reserve' a space. It can then be driven away to make a space for the van the following morning. If you do this, ensure that you understand and adhere to any parking restrictions to avoid parking fines, clamps or being towed away. In addition, make sure the car you leave behind is 'sterile'; remove briefing sheets, maps or anything else that identifies you, in case it is stolen.

Before moving into position carry out a recce by driving past in another operator's car rather than the van. Carry out a walk past if required, find the most suitable spot to position the van so that you get the best possible view. Note anything about the target premises: Are they occupied? What vehicles may be parked out of view? Is there milk on the doorstep? Are any windows or curtains open?

Moving into position can be achieved in a number of ways depending on the size of the team and how aware the neighbourhood is. You can have a partner drive you into position and then lock the door and walk away from the vehicle. Prior to this, a 'cover' car may have cleared the area for safety and be keeping a look out as the van is inserted. Secondly, you can drive yourself into position

The interior of a van can be simple or sophisticated as you desire

When the street is congested with parked cars you may have to 'reserve' a space by parking a car overnight. This can be driven away in the morning leaving a space for the van

Obtain local parking permits

and then hop into the rear of the van. Obviously, the first choice is recommended and much safer. Should you be seen to hop into the rear of the van, the surveillance would be compromised before it has even begun. Only experience will tell if you can get away with self inserting.

Always leave the ignition key under the dashboard or in the glove compartment where you can easily reach it, if you have to depart quickly. A team member should also carry a spare key that he uses during the insertion and extraction. Remember to obtain a parking ticket if needed.

**The Van Observation Platform (OP)**

When the surveillance is being carried out in what would be termed a risky or hard area, your back-up needs to be close and radio contact is essential. At any sign of compromise or trouble then it would be wise to terminate the surveillance and leave the area. So, regular radio checks should be carried out at least every 20 minutes.

In the past, the following encounters and problems have occurred when using surveillance vans:

- Neighbours standing beside the vehicle discussing its presence
- Police arriving after being called by suspicious neighbours
- Curious people attempt to look into the one-way glass
- Children playing and shaking the vehicle in an attempt to set off the car alarm
- Tyres being deflated by playing children
- The vehicle being accidentally blocked in
- Attempted break-in of the van
- Parking tickets issued whilst an operator is in the back
- A ladder on the roof rack (placed as part of cover) being stolen

Curious neighbours may take a close look into the van. It is best to use some form of curtain to conceal the interior

## ISS CASE

On a surveillance task in the past, a van was used for a period of three weeks to observe the comings and goings from a house in Lancashire. The residents of the street appeared not to notice the van but the target gave it more than the occasional glance a few times. One morning, when it was known that one of the targets would leave the house, the rear doors of the van were left open with a number of cardboard boxes in the back for him to see.

The target had seen us moving the boxes about and this satisfied his curiosity. After he had departed, the cardboard boxes were flattened and the observation of the house continued from the rear of the van.

You may be working on an investigation where you will only get one chance to watch for the information that you need, so remaining in position all day is vital. However, the safety of the operator should be considered paramount and the surveillance terminated, should any problems occur.

Once in position you can set up your OP for your requirements. Start the surveillance log detailing as much information about the target area as possible. Set up the video camera on its tripod, set the camera for correct exposure and focus, adjust any other special equipment that you may need and have it organised so that you know where it is when you need it. Also, inform the team leader or your back up when you are established and report anything of interest. Ensure your radio volume is turned down and your phone ringer is switched off.

If there is no activity, report a 'No Change' to the team at regular intervals.

**Amount of time spent in the van**

Once set up in your observation van you can be totally self contained and remain there for as long as you wish. It is not uncommon to find observations being carried out for periods of ten hours or more and it takes a committed operator who can cope with the demands of the task, confined in a small space with long periods of boredom.

Should the OP be in for long periods you can either change the operator and his vehicle or just change the operator and use the same vehicle. When a change of operator is made it is better accomplished by driving out of the position, making the change and then returning. Whilst the change is being made, another operator should move into the same spot to take a temporary trigger and to reserve the parking space.

**Vehicle Disguises**

In most cases, a plain unmarked van is sufficient to carry out observation. Should you feel the need, it could be disguised in a manner of ways.

Window film comes in various colours choose an appropriate one

Avoid using props to disguise the van such as ladders. They may inadvertently attract attention from would-be thieves

ISS CASE

On an investigation involving personal injury fraud, we had to establish that the target was physically able to use his lower limbs. (He had suffered broken legs and had a neck injury due to a road traffic accident).

Using the surveillance van with an operator in the back, the van was driven in front of the target and he was 'followed' from the front riding a racing bicycle. Video film was obtained of him cycling around eight miles, thus disproving his claim.

Magnetic signs advertising a fictitious company are useful and can be attached and removed within seconds. It would not be wise to have a fictitious address on the sign in case a suspicious person decides to check it. A mobile telephone number would not seem out of place and could be included on the sign. Should anyone be suspicious of the van's presence, they may telephone the number written on it. If they do, an excuse can be given as to why it is in the area and you will also know that certain residents are suspicious of it being there.

**Use of Vans in Mobile Surveillance**

Should the van be used as a trigger and thereafter be used as a mobile unit, caution should be taken not to 'show out' and the vehicle should be used as little as possible during the follow. If the van is required later to act as a trigger or moved into a position to obtain evidence later on in the surveillance, it should remain at the rear of the 'convoy' until required. We try to have a van on every surveillance team for this purpose.

**The Extraction**

When it is time to extract the van, the operator inside may have to de-rig cameras or other equipment. He must do so quietly, without moving hastily and take time - the extraction is just as important as the insertion as far as security is concerned.

Inform your back-up when you are ready to be extracted. They may carry out a drive past first to check that the area is clear. On approaching the van on foot, the back up should let you know of his position by radio. If possible, he should always approach the van in your field of view so that you are aware of his arrival.

**Why Do Van OPs Become Compromised?**

At times the surveillance van will become compromised for a number of reasons and more often than not by third parties rather than the target. If a compromise occurs, the

For long-term surveillance a camera mounted on a tri-pod is useful

vehicle should be extracted as soon as possible to prevent any risk to the operator inside.

The van OP may be providing the trigger to the surveillance and so this is the most important asset to the team. Therefore, care should be taken in its placement, the way the operator inside behaves and the way that it is extracted.

We can minimise the risk of compromise if we look at the reasons why the Van OP is brought to another person's attention.

### Operators Own Fault

- **Position**

Ensure that the van is parked 'naturally' and has a reason for being there. A van that sticks out like a sore thumb will soon attract unwanted attention. If you feel that the van will stick out then do not use it, attempt to get 'eyes on' by a different method or from a different location. Be aware of 'stealing' someone's parking slot. Some people are very possessive of a gap in the roadside and will not like someone else parking in 'their' space, even if it is public road.

- **Insertion**

Try not to 'self insert' the van and then climb over into the back unless you are absolutely sure that you are safe to do so. If it is early morning, remember to switch off your sidelights. If being driven into position, the operator driving you in should not be seen to sit in the front and talk to you. If the driver has to talk, have a reason for doing so, such as pretending to be on a mobile phone.

When the driver gets out, think 'third party' and do not appear to rush away from the van. Have a reason for being there and walk away on a route that looks natural and be prepared if challenged.

- **Movement**

When in the back, keep still! There should be no reason for any sudden movement, any rocking of the van will be noticed by an observer. It has been known for some vans to be fitted with damped shock absorbers to prevent rocking but personal discipline is more important.

- **Noise**

Noise can be a contributing factor to compromise especially if you are on the radio or a mobile phone.

**By being 'two up' in a van one operator can drive to 'bounce' the target while the other obtains video. In this case - the target had an alleged shoulder and back injury**

Remember that there is only a thin piece of tin (unless insulated) between you and anyone standing nearby and your voice will carry. Be aware of the natural tendency to start whispering but the longer the conversation continues, the louder you become without realising it, so be careful.

A van is really useful when deployed in an industrial park, especially when you have to get close to the target

• **Sightings**

Make sure no one can see a camera lens poking through curtains. If you have to shoot through the front try and be a few inches away from the viewing aperture. Do not lean into the front of the van if you have forgotten your mobile phone or map - you will be seen.

• **Smoke and Smells**

Only personal discipline will stop a hardened smoker from lighting up in the back of a van. As a non-smoker, I can smell a cigarette from quite a distance. The sight of cigarette smoke or the smell of it wafting from the van will almost certainly give you away.

• **Silhouette**

In some light conditions you can see in through reflective mirror tinted windows, especially in low light - be careful. In addition, if you are shooting through the front, have the rear windows shielded by a curtain as the shape of your body will be silhouetted.

Some smells and the ultrasonic noise from a camera can attract dogs

• **Re-supply**

When the van is inserted, it is up to the 'van man' to be totally self sufficient for the duration. He should be inserted into position with enough to eat, drink and have facilities for going to the toilet and also have a supply of video tapes and batteries.

In the past, I have seen so-called 'professionals' have plated meals from a nearby supermarket delivered to the van so that the 'van man' can have his breakfast! Not only does this attract attention but whilst the van man is tucking in and pouring on the ketchup, it detracts from what he is supposed to be doing.

**Other Peoples Fault**

• **Children**

Children can often be inquisitive and attempt to see through the reflective window out of curiosity. Therefore, have a curtain or blind to prevent anyone from looking through the glass.

• **Dogs**

In the past we have had an operator sitting quite happily in the back of a van when a passing dog would suddenly go wild and start barking at the van. This does not do anything for the van man's confidence

On most surveillances, toilet facilities are not readily available - be prepared

# SHOOTING THROUGH THE FRONT OF THE VAN

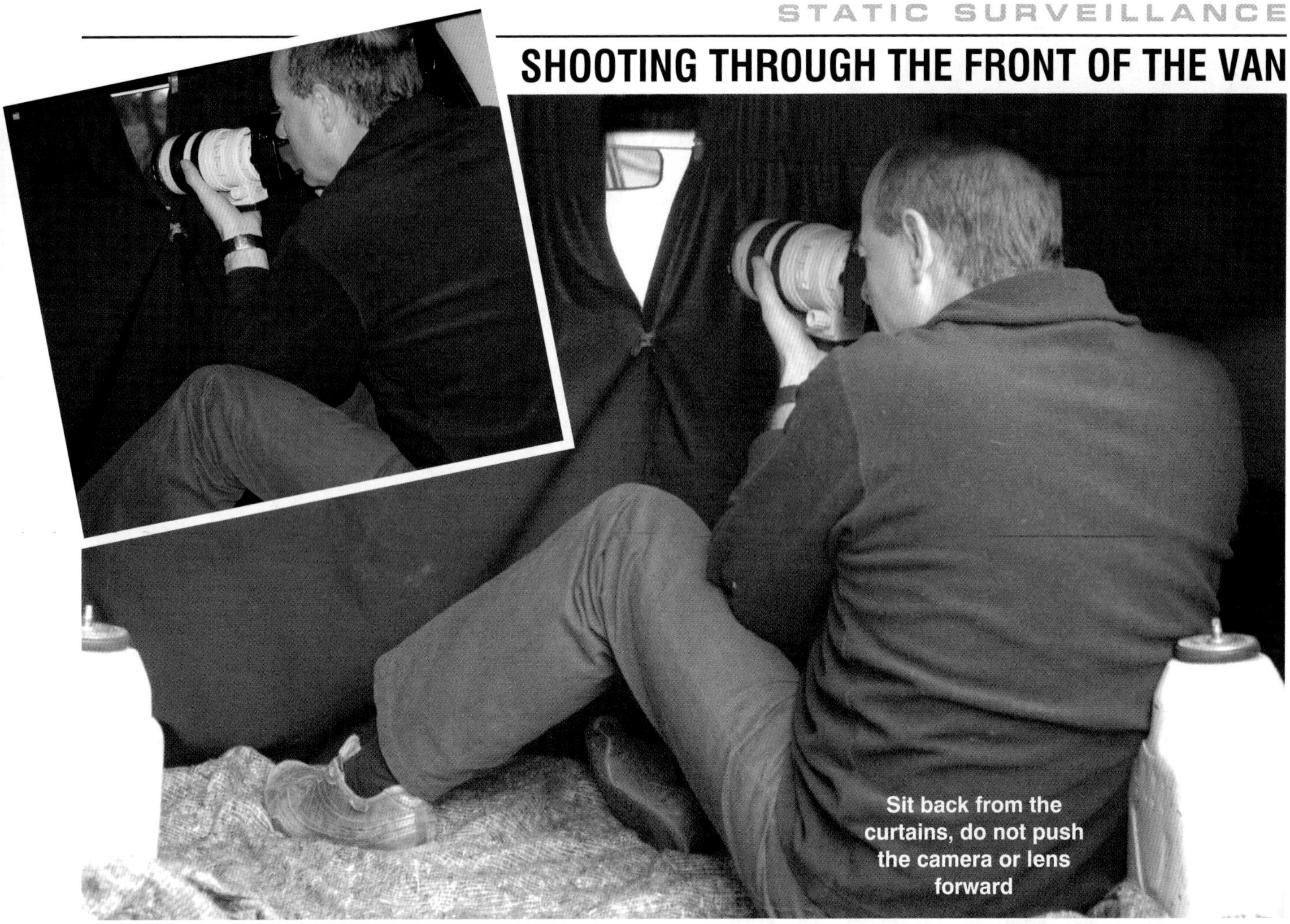

Sit back from the curtains, do not push the camera or lens forward

and will arouse the owner's suspicion. There are various reasons why a dog will react, your smell, a noise, even the inaudible sounds from your video camera and there is very little you can do to counter it.

**What to do in the event of a compromise**

At the first indication of a compromise, inform the team so that they can close in to your location and prepare to extract you. You may have to resort to 'clicks' so that you do not have to speak.

If you can, inform the team what the problem is so that they can be prepared for it and take appropriate action. In the past we have had an attempted break in of the van and managed to prevent it by one of the team driving up behind the van and sitting in his car - which deterred the would-be thieves.

The van should be extracted and driven to a safe area where the operator can exit. During this phase, ensure that you are backed by one of the team in the event that you are followed. If you are the person who has to extract the van, be prepared for confrontation with a resident and have a realistic cover story at the ready.

A van can be extremely comfortable - but most operators use a bean bag to sit on

# BOOT FIT

## THE COVERT CAR OR 'BOOT FIT'

This method has been kept out of the public domain and has not been written about in previous training books but is now known to many due to exposure in the press, books on TV and on various internet forums.

In a similar manner to the surveillance van, an operator is concealed in the boot (trunk) of a car, which is then driven into position. Live monitoring can take place in the most hard and difficult areas as the vehicle appears to be unoccupied. Close up video can be obtained and live reporting can be used to trigger aware targets.

Anti-social behaviour recorded from the boot of a car

To create a boot fit, a suitable vehicle needs to have the space and the spare wheel removed and placed in the back-up car. The boot floor needs to be lined with something comfortable as you could be lying in there for a number of hours. The parcel shelf is then modified so that you can get your head through and then covered over with a strong frame to form a viewing aperture.

You will need to be self-contained with your radio, camera, food, drink and waste bottles. You will also need to modify a boot release catch in case you have to self extract in an emergency or you will need to be able to fold down the rear seats to escape into the front.

**A small hatchback car can be modified and made comfortable for an operator to get in close in tough areas, where risk of compromise is high**

## URBAN OBSERVATION POSTS

When we speak of urban surveillance, we mean any situation where a surveillance has to be carried out that does not involve the techniques described below in the section on rural surveillance.

An urban surveillance can take place in a village, town, city, industrial estate or housing estate, in fact anywhere which is built up. Obviously rural techniques can be deployed in an urban situation but OPs that are used, are different.

### Indoor Static OPs

The indoor or 'room' OP can be any form of building or structure from where you can carry out your observations, in fact anywhere where you are not in a vehicle or a hedgerow such as:

- **Hotel room**
- **Disused or occupied office**
- **Portacabin**
- **House**
- **Factory/mill/warehouse**
- **Shop**
- **Caravan**
- **Flat or apartment**
- **Boat**
- **Garden shed**
- **Loft space**

## HOTEL ROOMS

We have put a few OPs in hotel rooms. This can be very useful as long as you obtain a room that overlooks the target area. Your cover story will have to be very realistic to satisfy the nosiest and most curious of landlords, receptionists and staff. Only a suitable pretext will get you the room that you want.

On one occasion, we required a specific room on one side of an hotel. One of the team members went to book the room and used the pretext that he was an ambulance driver, away for a few days break but still on-call. He stated that he had a poor reception on his mobile phone and asked if he could have a room as high up as possible. He was

## ISS CASE

In the past we had to establish an O.P. to observe an inshore oil tanker which would moor up along a river quayside. There was nowhere to carry out observations apart from an old school house (used for storage) located on a neighbouring company's premises.

Our client was granted permission for us to use the old school house. Once inside, it was found that there was no upper flooring in the building and so we hired a scaffolding tower from a builder's merchants in order to provide us with a viewing platform. The tower was approximately 40 feet high and we were able to view out of a 'crucifix' window and through holes madeby removing roof tiles.

From the top of the platform we were able to covertly observe, photograph and video the events that took place below us.

being shown the hotel rooms for suitability and the first one shown was on the wrong side of the building. He told the receptionist that he could not get a phone signal in that room and so was shown another. He eventually got a 'good signal' on the correct side of the building and the hotel room was booked!

Another ruse to obtain the correct side of the hotel, is to say that you car has a faulty alarm which keeps going off in the night. To ensure your car is safe and not wishing to bother the other guests, you can easily disable it from your room, should it go off.

As with everything we do in surveillance, we have to have a reason for being there and this is equally important in hotels as the owners are often interested in people and what they do. You also have to have a reason for staying in your room for long periods of time. Taking a laptop computer on the pretence that you are 'getting away' for a few days to get on with some work is realistic enough.

If out of the room, be aware of inquisitive cleaners and staff so ensure all your equipment and paperwork is out of sight.

A pinhole lens camera and DVR is used to monitor a hotel corridor through the spy hole

Beware of silhouetting yourself in OPs

An overnight OP was put in this garage in order to catch vandals damaging the allotment

### Individual OP Tasks

The principal tasks of an operator in an OP are to:

- Trigger, to give warning of movement (the Standby)
- Observe, to observe and watch events
- Record and Photograph, to compile logs and take photographs and video record activity
- Operate Radio, to relay incidents to the mobile teams or loggist
- Sentry, to warn of unwanted visitors to the OP

An experienced and well-trained operator will be able to do all of these tasks to enable a minimum of two men to run the OP. It is not unusual to do all these activities single-handed, in the commercial sector.

### Manning Levels

Manning levels will depend on various factors, but an observation lasting over a day should, ideally, be manned by a minimum of two operators. You should consider:

- The time spent in the OP (hours or days)
- The aim of the OP. Is it a short term trigger or long term intelligence gathering?
- The size of the area to be kept under observation and the amount of activity to be recorded. One person may watch and photograph whilst the other records information and reports by radio
- The size of the OP site. Is there enough room for two or three of you?
- The amount of equipment taken in to the OP

In my 'previous life' in the Marines, we would operate in four man teams and it would not be unusual to run an OP for three days at a time. With four men: two would observe, record and report; one would be a sentry watching the rear; the other would be sleeping or eating. We would change roles every few hours.

**Re-Supply**

On most occasions you should go into the OP totally self sufficient taking with you enough food, water, video tapes and batteries for the duration because any comings and goings may get you noticed. This is not always possible and so a re-supply may be necessary to bring items to you or you may need to pass out surveillance logs or video films. The modern operator is likely to have an internet enabled laptop or PDA in order to send back images or video.

There are two ways of taking things in and out of your OP:

- ***Live Letter Box (LLB)***
- ***Dead Letter Box (DLB)***

The Live Letter Box is where a person would come to the OP or brush past and in doing so, pass or collect items to/from the OP team. A Dead Letter Box is a pre-designated place where an operator will leave the OP at night and then leave/collect the items. Another team member can then collect them.

The DLB must be easy to find and recognise at night, preferably with some identifying feature close by such as a telegraph pole or a gate. It must also be hidden from view and at a natural place for a vehicle or person to stop for a short period.

## PLANNING THE OBSERVATION POST

**Pre-Surveillance Report**

A thorough recce should be carried out of the area you will be operating in. The following is a basic pre-surveillance report for siting an OP. It is assumed that you have already carried out a map recce.

**Ensure that you are not overlooked**

**Target Address/Location**

Ensure that the address is correct and provide a description of it, especially if it is difficult to locate. If there is no number on the front door or gate, double check. Draw a sketch plan of the immediate area indicating all routes in and out by vehicle or on foot. Identify possible OP locations to trigger the surveillance and suggested 'lie up' positions for the back up units.

**Approach and Route**

Operators may have to make their own way to the target's location rather than be led there by the team leader. Directions should be taken from a local landmark to the premises or to a central RV point. Obtain local street and Ordnance Survey maps and consider the use of aerial photographs.

**Recce 360 Degrees**

Carry out a 360 degree recce surrounding the target premises (do not only consider the front of the premises, there may be hidden access to the rear) and consider how

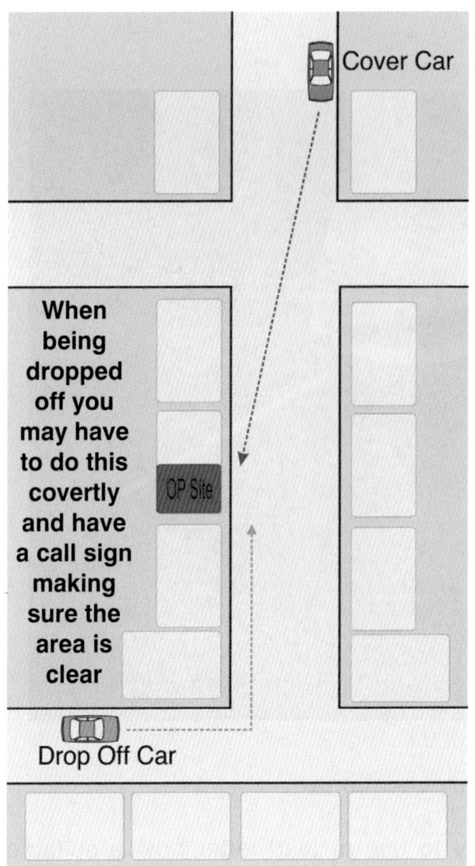

**Which room would you put your OP in? The window on the left may look odd with the curtains closed during the day and the gap looks suspicious. Therefore the window on the right may be preferable as long as you are set back from the window**

many observation positions are available and their locations. Remember, the OP position could be in a van, car, hedgerow or building.

The following factors should be considered when choosing your OP location:

- **Drop Off & Pick Up Points**

You may be dropped off in the daytime, at night time and in urban or rural areas and so easy accessible locations have to be identified. Your drop off point and pick up point has to have cover and security from third party attention. Alternatives have to be identified in the event of one of them being compromised.

- **Route In and Out**

The route in and out of the OP should provide you with easy access and be covered from the target's view if possible. The route in does not always have to be the same as the route out and always consider third parties.

- **Can You See the Target?**

Once in the OP you should be able to see the target clearly. If the target's premises cover a large area, you should have a good field of view or even consider using two or more OPs to observe it. Check if your field of view will become obstructed by passing or parked vehicles or any other obstructions.

- **Can You Observe the Approaches?**

The approaches to the target should be observable. This will assist when waiting for a target to arrive and give you that extra time you may need to have cameras up and running. On the target's departure you may need to inform the team, giving his direction of travel. In addition, you need to see the approaches to your OP in the event of a 'third party' approaching.

- **Are You Overlooked?**

If the OP is in a built-up area, be aware of anyone above you, in buildings or offices, looking down. Likewise should you be in a rural situation be aware of anyone on high ground who may be able to look down onto your position.

- **Can the Target See You?**

Is your OP in an obvious position? You do not want the OP to be in a position that will attract and draw attention.

## ISS CASE

On one occasion we carried out a recce for a task where the main gate and security lodge of a large company had to be kept under surveillance. This company was situated in a very large, modern industrial estate where mounds of earth had been created to provide 'natural' divisions between the boundaries and these were covered in bushes and small trees. It was our intention to put a rural OP in the foliage from where we could observe the main gate and security lodge.

Two of us went on the recce quite overtly, suitably attired as 'Highway Maintenance' workers, armed with petrol strimmers and the intention of clearing away over grown grass at the side of the road. Whilst one was able to get a close look at the target area and create a diversion with the strimmer, the other was able to identify an OP position and create a hide in the foliage. A string line was then laid to enable us to follow it in the dark which led us into the OP position.

Over the following three nights we were able to move into the position and carry out the surveillance without any difficulties.

- **Position for Back Up and Support**

A suitable position should be found where your back-up and mobile units can be located. The position should be close to the OP so the back-up can assist you quickly if compromise occurs. The position has to be within radio range.

- **Emergency Rendezvous**

An emergency rendezvous (ERV) should be located and known by all the surveillance team. If the OP is compromised or the surveillance team is split up, they can make their own way to the ERV to reorganise themselves and plan what action to take next. It may be that you decide the ERV to be the OP itself, as this is where you are. It would be easily defendable and secure (if in a hostile area) and everyone already knows where it is.

- **How Long to Establish**

Estimate how long it will take to move into position and establish the OP to commence observations. This will effect your timings when planning the insertion. It might be a simple matter of driving a surveillance van into position or it might take an hour or so setting up.

- **Likely Hazards**

Note any particular hazards such as: parking problems, traffic conditions, security patrols, neighbourhood watch, animals and floodlighting at night and CCTV cameras.

- **Dead Letter Box Locations**

If it is necessary to use a dead letter box, a suitable location should be found.

- **Rest Area, Meals, Toilet Facilities**

Depending on how long your surveillance is going to be, you may require an area where you can rest, eat and go to the toilet within the confines of the OP. In addition, the back up and mobile units will also require these facilities.

Keep well back from windows - avoid silhouetting

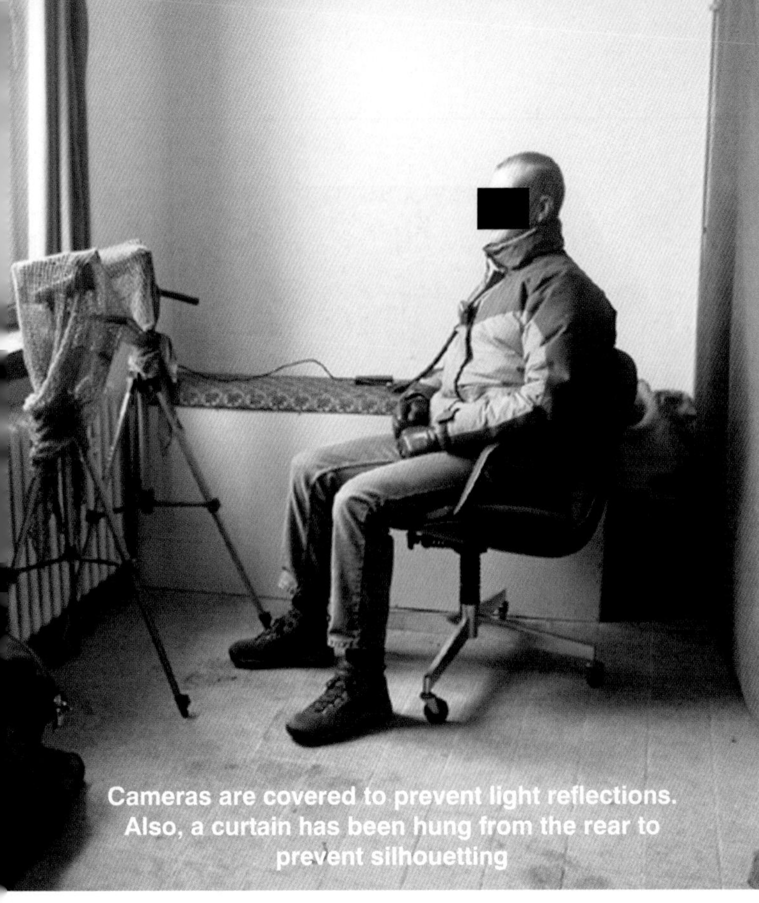
Cameras are covered to prevent light reflections. Also, a curtain has been hung from the rear to prevent silhouetting

- **Special Equipment**

Decide what special equipment you need for the surveillance. Items such as tripods, powerful lenses, night vision scopes, electronic devices, screens or camouflage nets need to be considered.

- **Team Base Accommodation**

Should the team be staying in the vicinity of the target area for a number of days, then suitable accommodation should

An elevated radio antenna should be used to boost comms

be found. When choosing a hotel consider that you may be getting up fairly early in the mornings and that your comings and goings may appear suspicious to the staff. Travel Lodge type hotels are convenient and offer some privacy.

- **Additional Information**

Add any relevant information that you think is necessary such as any sightings of suspects, any vehicles noted at the time and whether a pretext visit was made.

**Selection of an OP**

The indoor room OP is used less often than the surveillance van as it is not always possible to obtain a good position from where the target can be observed. However, when carrying out your pre-surveillance, always consider the static OP.

- Ensure that your routes in and out of the OP are protected from view. Insertion and extraction are the most vulnerable times. Have your back-up positioned nearby after clearing the drop off location. It may be that the insertion is quite overt, perhaps appearing to be dropped off by taxi.

- Make sure you can see the target and the target's approaches to the target area. Many room OPs are situated on upper floors and overlook the target area.

- Ensure that you are not seen whilst observing. Site your observation position as far back from the window or viewing aperture as possible.

- Do not silhouette yourself by having a light background behind you or a bright window. If the room is darkened wear dark clothing and make a dark background by hanging a length of dark material to a screen behind you.

Use hessian or cloth to act as a screen. This should be set back a few feet from the window

A staple gun is handy for attaching screens and cord, though they can be noisy

• If possible, fix net curtains over the windows. If not, a cloth screen hung between you and the window (a few feet back and not covering the window itself) will provide you with cover so that slits can be cut, through which you can observe. House plants or ornaments on a window sill do not look out of place and will provide you with 'natural' cover.

• Have an escape route planned in the event that you need to leave the OP quickly.

In a private house you can use window ornaments and pot plants as camouflage

• Check if there is a power supply to recharge batteries. What toilet facilities are available and is there is a water supply?

If there is a risk of compromise or someone stumbling across your position, use a wedge to secure doors

This device can be used to help suppress the sounds of coughing

If using a van in cold weather be aware of the condition of your windscreen - the glass on your vehicle may be the only one free from frost

Your eye is drawn to the red netting rather than the broken glass/viewing aperture

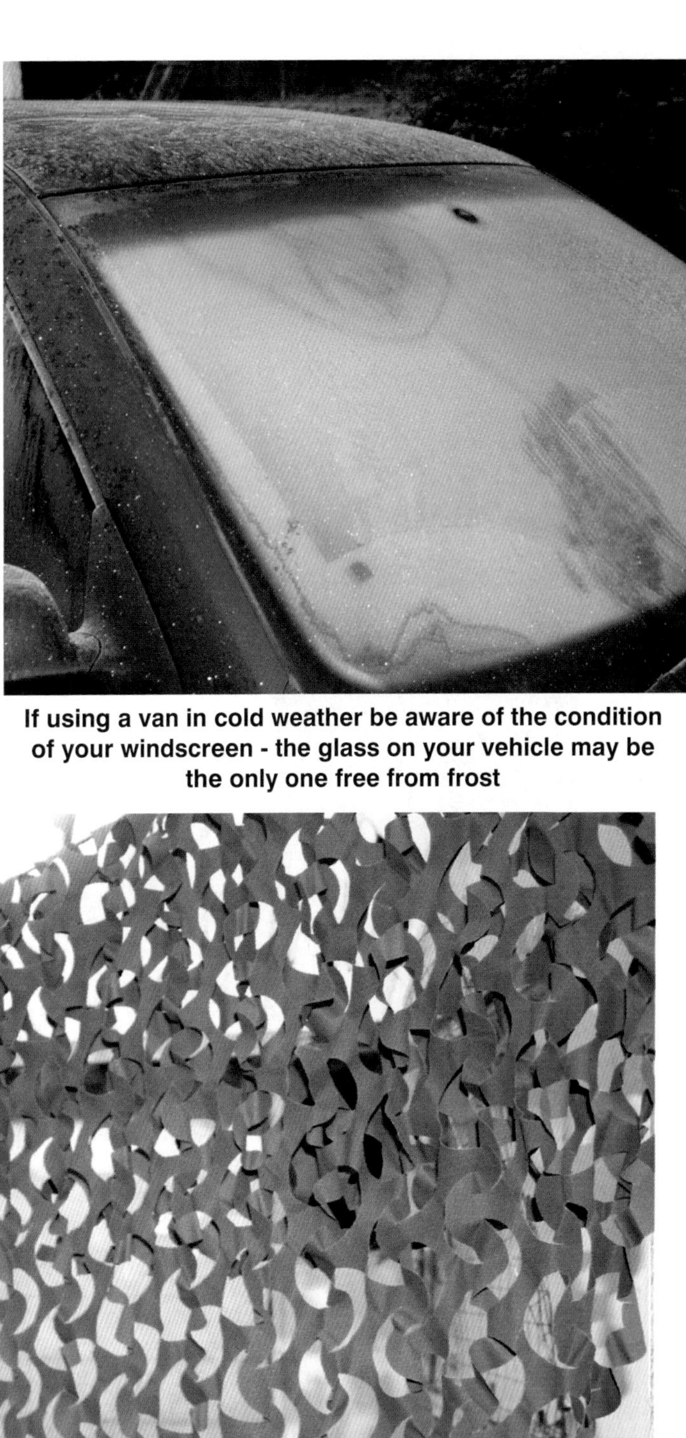

Camouflage netting can also be hung up to use as a screen

ISS CASE

Inside the OP

# EYES ON PLATFORM 2

A number of years ago we kept a business premises under surveillance for nine days. The targets (our client's former employees) were suspected of infringing copyright by manufacturing the same products and attempting to sell them to customers at cheaper prices.

We discovered that their business premises were located in an industrial unit adjacent to an unmanned railway station near Leeds. It comprised of a large yard area and a warehouse with large roller shutter doors which we needed to see into.

At first, it appeared to be very difficult to put under long term observation. However, an ideal OP position was found on the railway station platform in a disused toilet that had been boarded up except for a small square window. Inside, it was dark, cold and smelly (it was February) and it was evident that a tramp had used it as a refuge at some time.

A view from the OP into the roller shutter doors

Over a nine day period, we would walk along the railway platform in our fluorescent jackets, enter the OP early morning, carry out our surveillance and extract after all the staff had gone home. The two of us would remain in there all day, totally self sufficient, as we could not leave because the small window faced on to the target.

Through two observation holes in the wooden walls my partner, Steve, would use the video camera whilst I took still photographs and made notes on a dictaphone. We were approximately 70 metres from the warehouse and had a good view of the yard and inside the unit. At times the staff would be only 3 or 4 metres away.

From our cold OP we were able to identify what materials and machinery were being taken into the unit. As the target's new business started to unfold, we were also able to identify what products they were producing and where they were being despatched to.

From the OP we had gathered a lot of information for our clients needs and over a period of months we would regularly go back to the OP to check on activity. At one stage, a large white board appeared on the rear wall detailing the customer's orders that could be read with binoculars and photographed with a 600mm lens.

Our evidence was used in the High Court as it clearly showed that some of the machinery being used had been built to order and infringed our client's copyright. The small building has since been demolished and replaced with a new one.

Our OP was sited in the white hut on the left

***In the next chapter, we look at carrying out surveillance in a rural area.***

# 9 CHAPTER

# Rural Surveillance

On occasions, a surveillance operation may be required in a rural setting to watch a farm or any other premises located in the countryside. If the use of an observation vehicle is not practical then the task still has to be accomplished. To establish a watch on the target the operator may have to be totally camouflaged and concealed in his local surroundings for sometime, to achieve his aim.

You do not necessarily have to be in the countryside to mount a rural OP. The techniques and methods described below are equally useful in cities or towns when the only position to carry out observations may be from a hedgerow, ditch, undergrowth or a small wood. Your OP may be required for the sole purpose of providing a trigger for a mobile team.

In the recent past we have carried out many surveillance tasks which required complete camouflage. Some of these were in urban areas. It may appear that it is verging on the extreme to be adopting these military style methods, but at the end of the day it is a means to an end. If you can achieve a result by photographing a target and the only way of doing so is by lying on your belly in a hedgerow then that is what has to be done.

**Personal Qualities**

For obvious reasons, this type of task is suited to someone with experience and more likely to be someone with a military background or someone who has had the relevant training. Some of the information in this chapter is taught to infantrymen during their basic military training and many of the techniques are also used by more specialist troops, where it is essential that these methods are adopted to ensure their survival. For the investigator (who is possibly less experienced) the techniques are crucial, in order that they remain undetected.

**Types of Rural Observation Post**

As mentioned, the OP can be in a variety of places, a hedgerow, on an industrial estate, a railway embankment, a ditch at the side of the road or in the edge of a wood. It

You don't necessarily have to be buried in the ground to be concealed

may be a short or a long term position. In most instances it is possible to construct a simple OP using camouflage netting and then covering this with natural foliage.

There are various types of OP and the choice is normally dictated by the amount of cover available and, more importantly, the amount of time that the OP is to be manned.

**Types of OP**

- *Standing OP*
- *Surface OP*
- *Sub surface hide*

**• Standing OP**

The standing OP would be a very short term measure rather than a full-blown long-term OP. It is more likely to be used to trigger a surveillance where an operator has little equipment, such as a combat jacket, face veil, radio and a pair of binoculars. Imagine that you are on a mobile surveillance and the target drives from the main road into a premises located in a rural area. It may not be possible to trigger and observe from your car; so, you will have to deploy on foot to get 'eyes on' from what we call a standing OP. The standing OP can also be used at night to get close in order to trigger a target away.

**• Surface OP**

As its name suggests, this OP is carried out by lying on the surface without having to dig down in order to create some cover. Ideally the position will be in thick undergrowth or in a dip providing you with cover. The use of natural cover (foliage) must be used together with camouflage nets to reduce the risk of compromise. The surface OP is used for short term measures or when the threat of compromise is considered to be minimal as this sort of OP will leave you fairly exposed.

**Standing in an OP is often necessary but strenuous**

Sometimes your observation post may be set back in the undergrowth, but you will have to crawl foward to observe when activity occurs

A hide of this type is quick to deploy but requires practice and experience to build and you also need to have confidence in your camouflage and concealment techniques.

• **Sub Surface Hide**

Sub surface OPs require detailed planning and an experienced OP team in order to operate effectively. The team will have to take the necessary materials with them in order to construct the OP such as shovels, sand bags and camouflage netting. The OP may be in a ditch and so suitable camouflage netting should be placed over the top, followed by natural foliage.

If this is not possible, then a shallow 'scrape' may have to be dug out (in the dark) in order for you to remain concealed below the skyline. An area of turf is removed from the OP site, the ground is dug out to form a hollow and the soil removed from the area, a low roof is then built over the top. The turf and camouflage is replaced on top of the roof and a small entrance made. The operators can then live in the 'hide' for a number of days perhaps without replenishment. Plenty of back-up in the surrounding area will be needed to protect the OP team during construction which is normally carried out at night.

This type of OP can be very hard work to set up and it is likely to be used for two or three days or even longer. In the commercial world, this type of OP is rarely used. It is more likely to be used by military close observation teams or Police CROP (Covert Rural Observation Post) teams.

**The operator is not inside the foliage but still difficult to see**

# SUB SURFACE HIDES

Area cleared and dug down

A strong overhead frame erected

Natural foliage applied for concealment

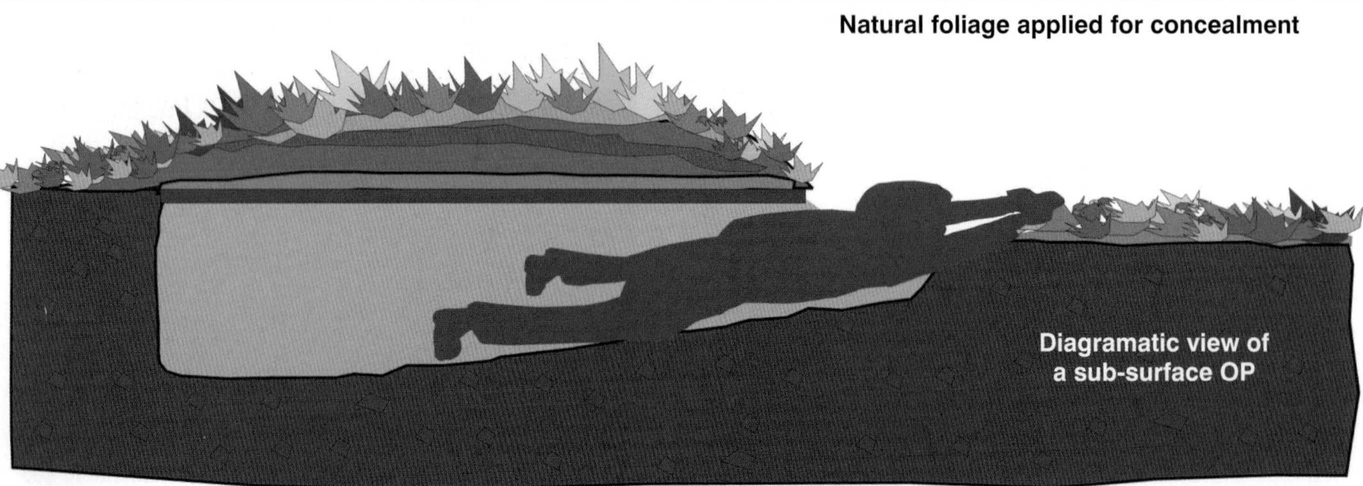

Chicken-wire added for support

Sheeting for waterproofing

## CAMOUFLAGE AND CONCEALMENT

Camouflage and concealment is probably the most important factor in this type of covert role. You may be positioned within 10 metres or less of your target and be required to maintain observations. Your target or any other third party should not have any indication of your presence and this should be achieved by blending in with your surroundings. Camouflage and concealment is breaking up the appearance of people or objects to make them appear natural and part of the terrain. It is an art which requires much practice and experience.

If we look at the reasons why we see things and what brings them to our attention, hopefully we will be able to counter them and thus make ourselves become less visible. Things are seen because they are different from their natural surroundings. The main reasons things stand out are:

- *Shape*
- *Shadow*
- *Silhouette*
- *Surface*
- *Spacing*
- *Sudden Movement*

Use face veils in place of cam cream when deploying quick OPs, but try and eliminate your silhouette

• **Shape**

Objects and people can be recognised instantly by their shape. Your body shape or outline is distinct and therefore has to be 'broken down' to look more like a 'blob' than that of human form.

The head, neck and shoulders are the most important. This blurring can be achieved using some form of camouflage netting attached to a camouflaged bush hat which hangs and drapes over the shoulders to break up the outline, to which natural foliage can be added. Should you be using camouflage netting to make a hide, the outline should also be broken down with natural foliage to break down any straight lines that occur.

• **Surface**

Many objects have a smooth surface but bushes, grass and rocks are irregular, therefore a camouflage jacket on its own may not be enough cover in order for you to blend in. By attaching irregular pieces of camouflage material to it, gives its surface an uneven 3D texture. Local foliage attached to the person also assists in the breakdown of the surface and helps you blend in with your surroundings.

Smooth surfaces are often reflective which means they shine, obviously anything that shines will be instantly seen.

Shiny objects to be aware of are: camera lenses, binoculars, watches and jewellery. The forehead, face, hands and wrists also shine so make use of camouflage cream and paints (camcream).

Camera lenses and optics should be fitted with lens hoods or you should attach a fine, cloth mesh over the lens to reduce reflections.

• **Silhouette**

When moving to and from the OP position and, just as importantly, when in the position itself, attempt to keep below the horizon to avoid being silhouetted. Any object silhouetted against a contrasting background is clearly noticeable - such as light coloured clothing in front of a dark background. When moving, make use of cover such as hedgerows and ditches, or crawl if necessary. When using cover, attempt to look through the cover or around it, rather than over the top.

• **Shadow**

In bright sunlight and on moonlit nights, your body shape will give a shadow if you are walking or standing up, which may betray you. Make use of shadow for cover whenever possible as it is difficult for an observer to see into shaded areas. Remember, that when the sun moves so does the shadow.

• **Spacing**

Natural objects are never regularly spaced on the ground, regular spacing means man-made objects. If there are a number of you having to move across country, vary the distance between you so that the line appears irregular. Avoid any areas that provide isolated cover, a single bush in a field may seem an appropriate spot to observe from but it will stick out like a sore thumb. Areas such as this are also more difficult to move in and out of.

Keep spacing irregular unlike above

• **Sudden Movement**

Humans are predators and therefore the human eye is attracted to movement, especially if it is sudden. Movement is one of the most important give-aways. You may be totally camouflaged in your surroundings and made to be invisible but a slight movement from the hand or a turn of the head will catch someone's eye and you will be compromised. If you have to move, move slowly, deliberately, with stealth and make use of cover. Do not be afraid to crawl on your front or on your hands and knees and do not rush.

*Camouflaged scrim nets can be plain green or disruptive patterned but they also need depth to 'break up' the surface and shape*

In nature everything is irregular, therefore straight lines especially in camouflaged nets must be disrupted.

## Concealment

Camouflage and concealment are two very important skills, which will enable you to see without being seen. Once camouflaged, you will need to conceal yourself by making the best use of cover without giving up a good field of view. The following principles should be observed:

*Avoid creating silhouettes by 'sky-lining' against the horizon*

*A base layer of camcream should be applied first as a foundation and then other colours used. Ensure you cover jewellery such as wedding rings with dark tape*

- *Look around cover or through it, not over it*
- *Avoid skylines to avoid silhouetting yourself*
- *Make use of available shadow*
- *Choose clothing and equipment to match the background*
- *Avoid isolated cover such as lone bushes or trees*
- *Move carefully, especially when moving into or out of cover*

**Camouflage Paint and Face Creams**

In order to camouflage the face and hands 'cam cream' will have to be applied. This cream is easily available from army surplus stores. Cover the whole face, forehead, neck, ears, hands and wrists with a thin base layer of brown cream. Then sparingly apply more cream in random dark patches to break up the shape of the face; possibly add a touch of dark green paint.

Remember to do the 'V' of your neck and the back of your wrists, otherwise clothing will ride up and expose your skin. People with black or dark skin should also apply cam cream as the skin reflects light and becomes shiny, cam cream should be non-reflective.

**Spray Paints**

Camouflage spray paints are available in various shades of green and brown which are very effective for camouflaging equipment such as tripod, equipment boxes and binoculars.

**Camcream should be applied liberally and don't forget the hands and ears**

*Camouflage spray paints come in an assortment of colours and shades. They are excellent for painting tri-pods, cameras, weapons and other equipment*

### Communications and Hand Signals

When working in an OP during daylight, silence is essential and so communication may be achieved by using hand signals. When using radios, it is essential that you have comms with your back-up. At times you will be lying very low on the ground or in ditches below ground level, therefore radio signals will be reduced. A 'mag mount' antenna attached to a hand set should be used to maximise comms and should be elevated as high as possible by putting it up a tree or attaching it to a fence post. The dipole mentioned in the communications chapter is ideal for this situation.

Consider using 'Curly Wurly' earpieces as they can be removed easily if necessary. Wireless earpieces are more likely to fall out and get lost.

Hand signals are for conveying silent messages

Try and elevate a remote antenna to extend radio transmission range

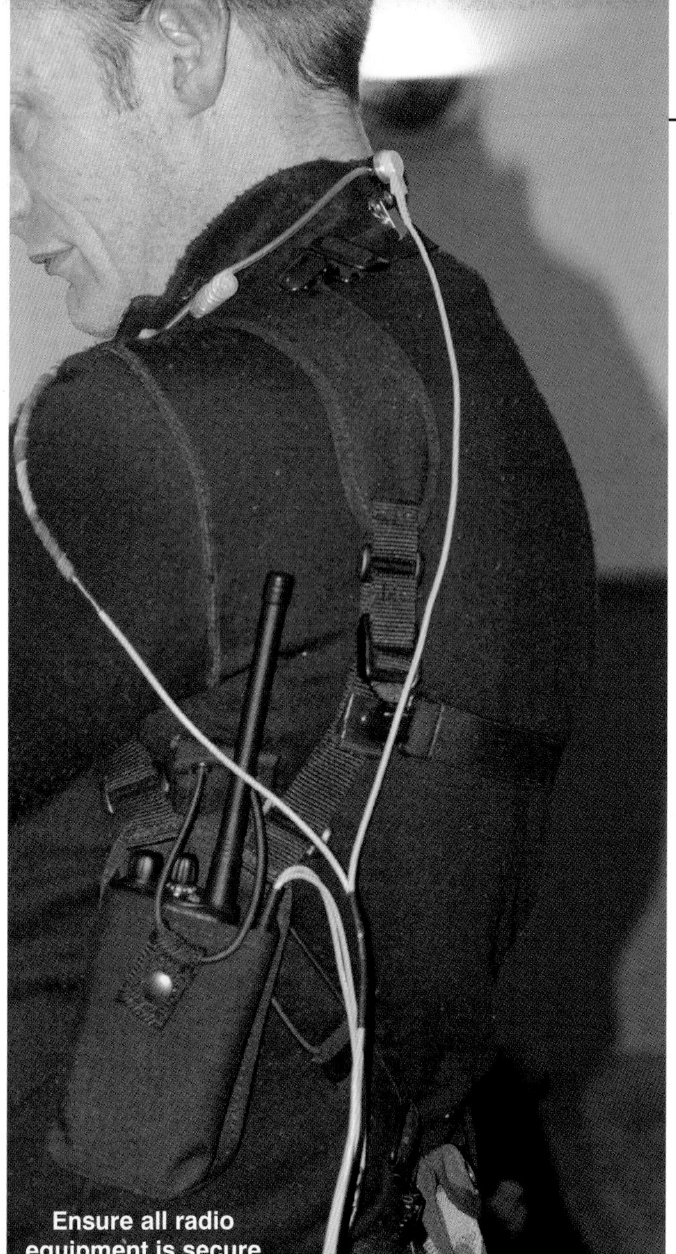
Ensure all radio equipment is secure

The 'curly wurly' earpiece is useful in a rural theatre

## THE RURAL OBSERVATION POST (OP)

When conducting a pre-surveillance, and you decide that the only way to conduct static observations would be from a rural point of view, then there are many factors to consider.

Remember, that these types of OP require great personal discipline. The operator has to work for long periods, often lying down, motionless, in poor weather and in uncomfortable conditions. Your personal camouflage and the concealment of the hide has to remain paramount to avoid detection. You may not always have the advantage of having natural cover immediately available and therefore you may have to create your own in the form of a hide.

We teach that two vehicles should be used for the deployment of an OP or CTR (close target recce) team. The first vehicle (the cover car) drives ahead, checking that the drop off point is clear, shortly followed by the drop off car which stops and deploys the team. In high risk areas, it may be that a third rear cover car is also used to protect the rear during a drop off.

**Planning and Logistics**

The length of stay in your OP will dictate what comforts or necessities to take with you.

Considerations are:

• Food and water; you will need enough for the duration and do you eat hot or cold? Is it tactically safe to use a camping stove, or self heating foods such as 'Hotcan'. You should take enough to drink and a flask is essential

• Toilet paper and something to defecate in should be taken. Ziplock type polythene bags are ideal. If the OP position is to be used over a period of time, it is unwise to relieve yourself in the position. Take all waste with you when you leave

• Should you be in the OP for a considerable amount of time, you may require a re-supply of food and batteries. In addition, you may have to pass on surveillance logs, video tapes and waste. A system should be planned for re-supply by either DLB or LLB

• Take enough batteries to supply radios and cameras. When used in the cold they have a shorter lifespan

• Use a sleeping bag, one between two

• Do you have to walk far carrying heavy rucksacks, batteries and equipment?

ISS CASE

## THE DIESEL THIEF

In this surveillance task, we were tasked to observe a fuel depot with special regard to the fuel pumps. It was suspected that some of the staff that worked on a Saturday, were helping themselves to diesel fuel (they all had diesel cars funnily enough) when none of the management were present on the site.

It was not possible to install a time-lapse video recorder and so an manned static OP had to be used.

There were various locations surrounding the site, which at first view would have been ideal for static surveillance: two car parks to put a van, a building to put an OP in and also watching from the main road. All of which were found unsuitable when carrying out a recce.

The best position to observe from was from a hedgerow, which ran along the rear perimeter fence. Access was gained by walking along a country footpath, crossing over a railway line and into the OP site.

A hide was constructed which included providing cover at the rear from third parties who would walk their dogs on the other side of the train tracks. Concealment was not a problem and we were able to remain their undetected for the duration.

Two members of staff were videoed helping themselves to fuel. One of which would reverse his car up to the pumps and unscrew the filling cap. He would then fill up the tanks of a tanker and then 'crawl' along the floor (thinking he would not be seen) to his car, which he filled up with diesel.

The two members of staff were interviewed by the company security manager. At first they pleaded not guilty but when shown the video, admitted theft, they were both dismissed.

## CARE OF EQUIPMENT

You may be using sensitive equipment such as video cameras and radios in the OP, therefore it is important that they are taken care of and are not damaged by the elements. Rain, sand and dust can get into the smallest of places so do not put equipment down on the ground and keep it covered. If you are operating in a dry environment, consider wrapping your radio in 'cling film' to keep the dust out but be aware of morning dew that will penetrate and remain trapped inside.

### Camouflage your Equipment

Any piece of equipment, especially binoculars, scopes and cameras may possibly require some form of camouflage as they will be forefront in the OP.

Lenses should be covered with some form of fine netting. A green 'cam scarf' obtained from ex-army stores is ideal. Cut a piece to size and attach over the front lens with an elastic band. Also use this material to wrap around equipment or drape over a tripod. A piece of black stocking stretched over the lens reduces lens flare and reflections when shooting into the sun without any considerable loss of light.

A company in the USA called 'LensCoat' manufactures covers for cameras and lenses ideal for rural surveillance. The covers, made from neoprene are especially designed for telephoto lenses. They are supplied in various camouflage colours and help protect lenses from knocks, dirt and the weather as they are waterproof. In addition, the neoprene protects the lens from extremes of temperature. They absorb the heat from the sun and also act as a thermal barrier in the cold.

Vehicle camouflage nets, cut down into small sizes (6ft square) are ideal for quick camouflage when covered with some natural foliage. Items to assist putting up cam' nets are: cord and string, clothes pegs, elastic bungees and extendable fishing rod rests to act as supports.

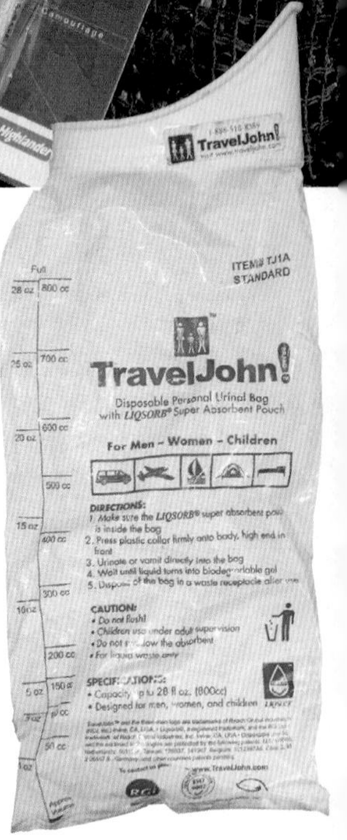

On completion of a task, give all equipment a thorough clean. If it has been damp, air the equipment to dry it out, then test it to make sure that it still works. Replace batteries or recharge them if necessary.

### Suggested OP Equipment

If there are two of you manning the OP, take in two rucksacks. One is to be used

Make-up face wipes are useful for quick removal of camcream

Use camouflage tape and netting to help conceal equipment which is at the forefront of the OP

Ensure all lenses are covered to reduce reflections

This lens is covered with 'LensCoat' neoprene

for the operational equipment such as: cameras, scopes, radios etc, the other for camouflage material, food and drink. This way, if you have a compromise and have to 'bug out' you can grab the rucksack with the expensive and sensitive equipment in it, as a priority.

A company called Artkis, based in the UK, supply a 'Grab Mat' which is a small green mat which unfolds in the front of an OP. It has a couple of elbow pads for comfort and a draw string through its edges. The idea is that all of your OP equipment that is being used is placed on the mat keeping it off the ground. If you have to move out quickly, you just pull on the draw string, gather up the equipment in the mat and run.

Various items of equipment can be suggested: green waterproof sheet, cameras, radios, trowel, small saw, chicken wire, dipole antenna, insect repellent, camouflage netting, secateurs, green string, food, water, sleeping bag (one between two), spare batteries, refuse bags.

For note taking, the company 'Rite in the Rain' manufacture waterproof notebooks with green paper that can be written on with pencil and pen and are ideal for rural OP's.

In a rural situation you are going to encounter insects and mosquitoes and so a good non-scented insect repellent is necessary. Try to avoid those containing 'Deet' as many people have adverse reactions to it and it can also melt the plastic on cameras and binoculars. The best insect repellent I have come across is in fact 'Avon Skin So Soft'. It is actually a moisturiser not a repellent but it keeps most insects away better than any other product.

### Cats Eyes Pick Up Marker

When you are getting picked up at night, you may have to deploy a marker at the side of the road to indicate to the pick up car exactly where to stop.

A cat's eye marker is made up from the glass elements that you would find in a 'cat's eye' found in the centre of the road. These 'eyes' can be screwed into a wooden holder to give the appearance of an animal, or just kept in their original rubber mounting. The reflective material that you find wrapped around a traffic cone is also ideal if cut into a small strip. It can be seen at night, in the headlights, from some distance away to indicate your PUP.

Waterproof writing note pad

Hot drinks flask

Door wedges are handy for draping camouflage nets, especially at night-time and against walls

Clothes pegs are handy for draping netting

Prepare and check your kit before deploying

Elastic bungees are useful for putting up shelters

Leafy wear - off the shelf ghillie suits come in various designs and materials

**Recce the OP Position**

Carry out a day and night time recce if necessary. If you have to walk about during the daytime in unusual surroundings then adopt an identity to suit. Walking dogs is an ideal cover or wear running clothes as if you are orienteering or jogging. Wear a fluorescent jacket as if carrying out a road survey. All circumstances differ so use your imagination but make it realistic.

Prior to going out on the ground, obtain any relevant information from maps, aerial photographs or any previous reports. You have to pick your point of observation carefully, taking the following into consideration:

• What is the awareness level of your target and are others in the locality likely to be aware or notice anything out of the ordinary.

• You will have to identify where you will need to be dropped off and picked up by vehicle. Is there a suitable spot to do this and what are the alternatives?

• Is your walk route in and out covered from view? This avoids casual observers wondering where you are going to and from. Choose your route tactically, keep to hedgerows, walls, tree lines, banks, ditches and railway tracks and avoid crossing open spaces.

• From the OP do you have a good view of the target area. There is no point in having an excellent OP position if you cannot see your target. You do not necessarily have to be right on top of the target - the further away the better, in some circumstances.

• Do you have a good view of the target's approaches. This is important if the target goes mobile, as it gives you those extra seconds you may need to have your camera up and running or to radio your team.

Your route to the target should be walked in 'bounds' using natural cover

• Is the position obvious or are you overlooked? Do not choose a position where you stick out, always be aware of being overlooked by buildings or from hillsides. In addition, you should have a clear view of the approach to the OP in case passers-by come too close.

• Consider your concealment as you may have to construct a hide. Is there any natural cover about, will you have to dig down? What construction materials will be needed: camouflage nets, shovels, sandbags, wire netting?

ROYAL MARINES RURAL ARCTIC OP

• Where is your ERV in case of compromise and where can your back up be positioned?

• Your back up needs to be positioned where he can get to you quickly; his position also needs to be safe.

• Is there provision for a rest area in the location? If you are in a two man OP it may be practical to have a rest area to the rear where one man can sleep and eat whilst the other is observing.

• Allow for any special equipment that may be required such as a spotting telescope or night vision aid. However, you may find yourself in a confined space so take only the equipment that is necessary for the task.

• How long will it take to move into position and to establish the OP? If you are moving at night add plenty of time to move in and establish the OP before your task starts. Establish what time the sun rises and sets and also the state of the moon.

• Note any particular hazards. Are there dog walkers, horse riders or farmers in the vicinity? Familiarise yourself with landmarks and features on the route such as pylons, masts, walls or tree lines to aid navigation at night.

• Carry out a radio check to your back up location. You must have comms.

Equipment should be split into operational and camouflage rucksacks

These cats eyes are set into a camouflaged piece of wood

## RECCE THE DROP OFF POINT (DOP) AND PICK UP POINT (PUP)

- **Identify a Start Point**

Once you have established where your OP is likely to be sited, you will need to establish where you want to be dropped off by car and then picked up again after the task is complete. If at all possible the drop off vehicle should stop on the nearside of the road so that the operators can move quickly into cover and not have to cross the road. An anti clockwise road loop around the target area helps with this and makes the pick-up and drop-off, run very smoothly.

Try to identify a start point from where you begin the run in. This start point may be a road junction where you can set your cars trip (odometer) to zero so that you can measure the distance to your DOP or PUP as it may be difficult to see and identify in the dark. On the start of the daylight recce and drive past, set a video camera running in order to record the route; this can be used for planning and briefing.

A camcorder set into the passenger seat headrest is the easiest way, with the zoom and focus set to obtain the best view. Adjust the seat to obtain the ideal view out of the windscreen.

Gates are a good marker for drop-offs and pick-ups

- **Identify a Drop Off Point (DOP)**

Try and find a natural place that a car can stop or slow down at night without arousing suspicion. A lay-by, a T junction, a dip in a road, a wide gate or under a bridge is ideal. The DOP should be able to afford cover for the team to move quickly into cover for a short period, before moving off.

If you intend to hop over a wall or fence, check that there is not a 3 metre drop on the other side, or any other hazards. On a recent deployment we had someone jump over a low wall only to have a 3 inch nail go through his foot.

Students on an ISS rural course discuss OP rest areas

Video the route during a daylight recce

Road signs can be used as countdown markers

• **Drive the Route**

Carry out a drive past recce of the drop off point and pick up point but only make one pass, driving up and down will soon attract attention. This should be done the day before or a number of hours prior to the actual drop off. Do not drive too slowly or too fast at speeds that would draw attention to yourself. Keep your road sense and do not forget to check your mirrors for third parties.

• **Alternative DOP & PUP**

Normally, an alternative DOP has to be identified in the event that the first choice is compromised. Imagine running in to drop off and a courting couple is parked up where you intended to stop; or, if you are the team waiting to be picked up and the PUP is compromised. You can either wait for a few hours until it is clear or go into an established plan. We normally teach that the PUP is your alternative DOP, and the DOP is the alternative PUP. This makes sense because with good planning and briefing everyone should know where the DOP & PUP is and all that has to be done is to switch each location.

• **Identify a Pick Up Point (PUP)**

The same considerations have to be made for the PUP, which should be at a different place to where you are dropped off. Should you be seen or be compromised when getting dropped off, the location may be watched if you return. Therefore the PUP should be in a different location.

The PUP should also provide the team with cover as they may have to lie up and wait for a period before they are actually picked up.

• **Identify Countdown Markers**

As you set off from your start point, note anything en route that you can use as countdown markers. Countdown markers are used to give warnings to the team of your location on approach to the DOP & PUP. Suitable countdown markers could be: gates, road signs, road markings, buildings, telegraph poles and prominent trees. You should note their distance on the trip counter from the start point mentioned earlier.

On the run in, you will have countdown marker 3 (CDM 3) which should be about 2 minutes away from the DOP. CDM 2, about 1 minute from the DOP and CDM 1 about 30 seconds away from the DOP. All will become apparent shortly...

Cattle grids can also be used as countdown markers

# DROP-OFF - PICK-UP

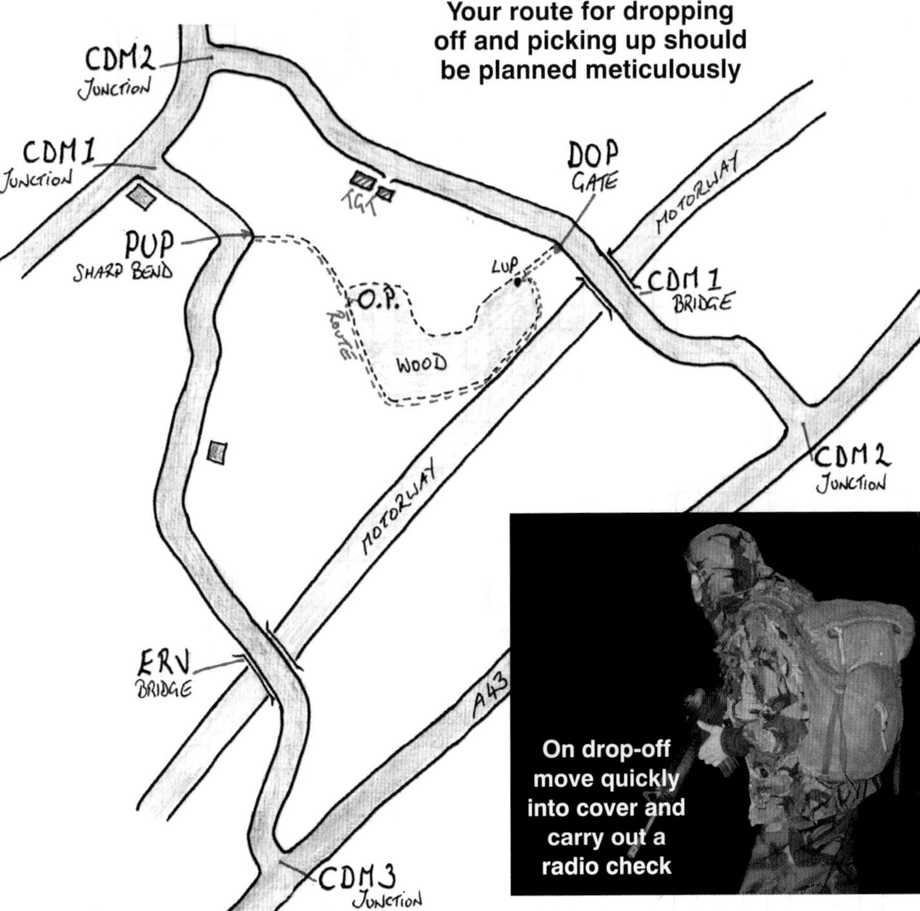


**Your route for dropping off and picking up should be planned meticulously**

**On drop-off move quickly into cover and carry out a radio check**

- **Identify a Lie Up Position (LUP)**

Once the team has been dropped off, a vehicle call sign may remain in the area to act as a radio relay or act as a back up. Therefore, a place has to be identified where he can safely park up without attracting attention to himself.

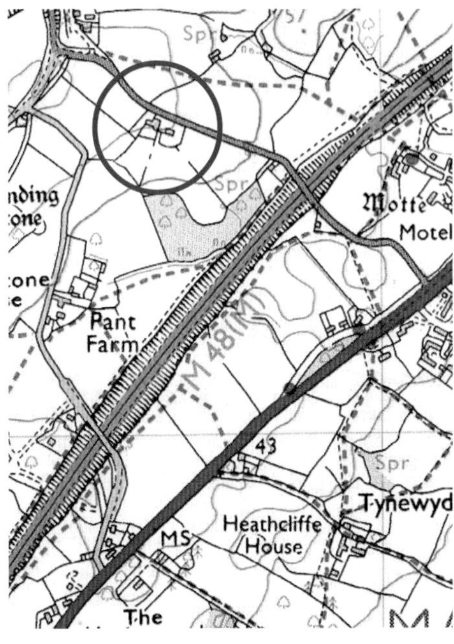


- **Identify an Emergency RV**

If the team is compromised on the way in, in the OP itself, or on the extraction phase, they may have to bolt and run. Therefore, a location has to be identified where it can head for and wait for the back-up to pick them up. It may also be worth noting where the nearest payphone is located in case of lost comms.

**If you have to climb over a gate, do so on the hinge side which is stronger**

**Use of Satnav**

On the recce, it would be useful for you to enter and store each location (Start Point, PUP, DOP, ERV etc.) into your Satnav as a 'waypoint' to give you accurate grid references or co-ordinates. It is also valuable at night for identifying the locations; but, do not totally rely on it, you should still be aware of features on the ground.

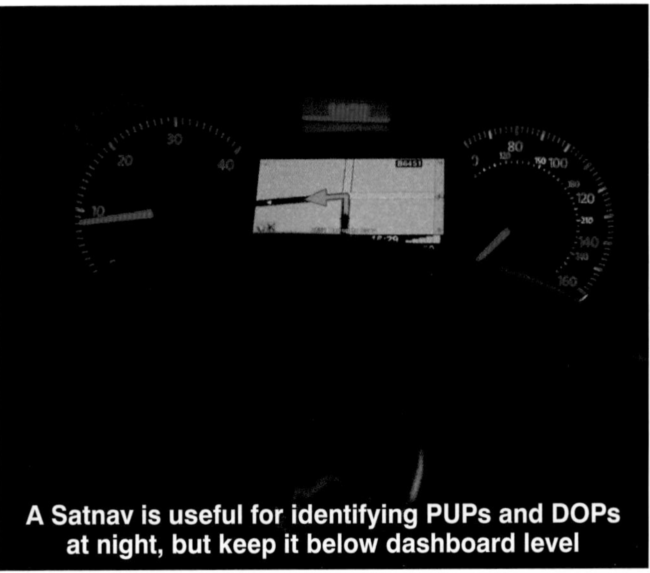

**A Satnav is useful for identifying PUPs and DOPs at night, but keep it below dashboard level**

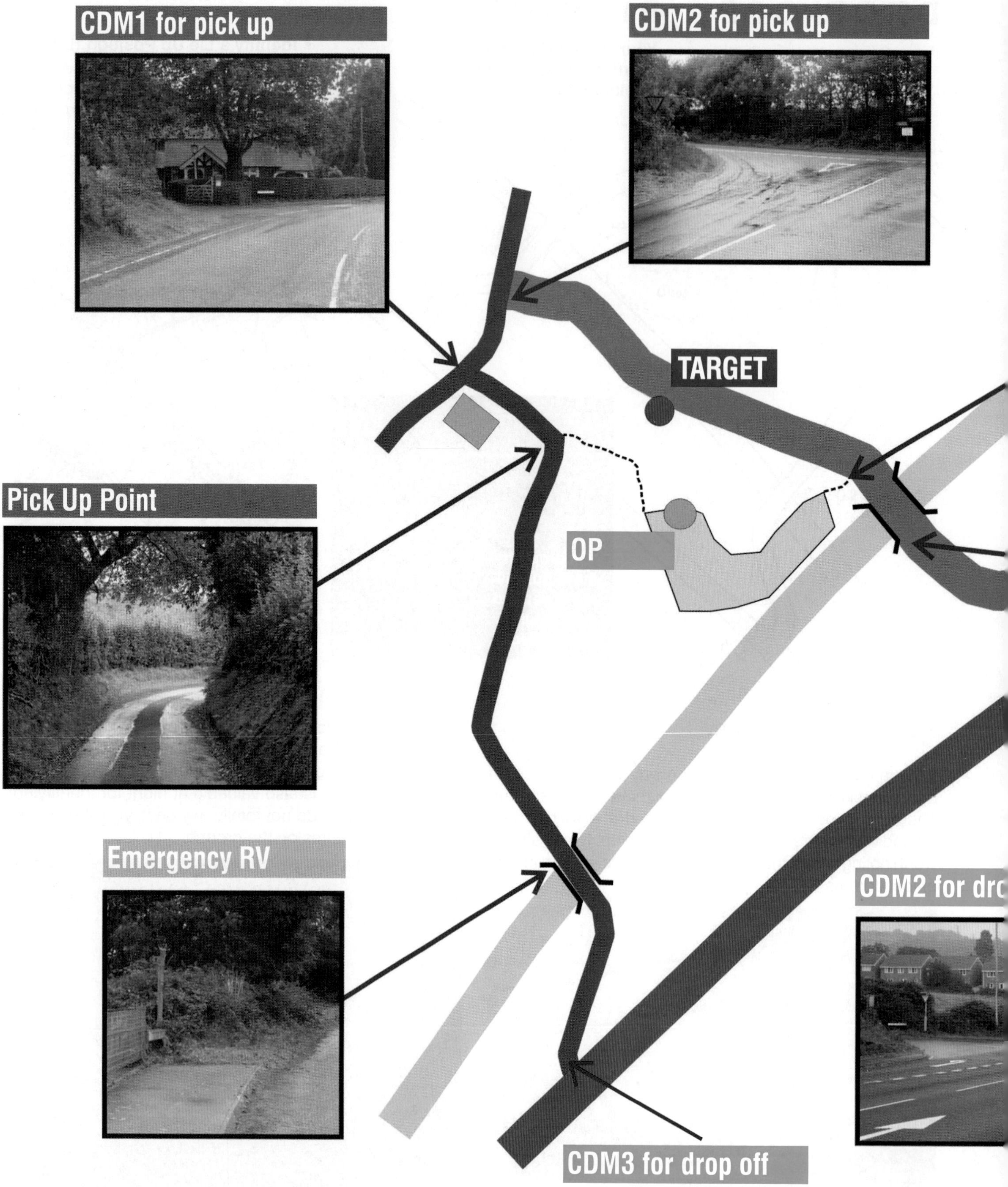

CDM1 for pick up

CDM2 for pick up

TARGET

Pick Up Point

OP

Emergency RV

CDM2 for dro

CDM3 for drop off

** Author's note: Simulated target/graphic*

CDM3 for pick up

Drop Off Point

# THE CIRCUIT

## FOR DROPPING OFF AND THE PICKING UP OF AN OP TEAM

CDM1 for drop off

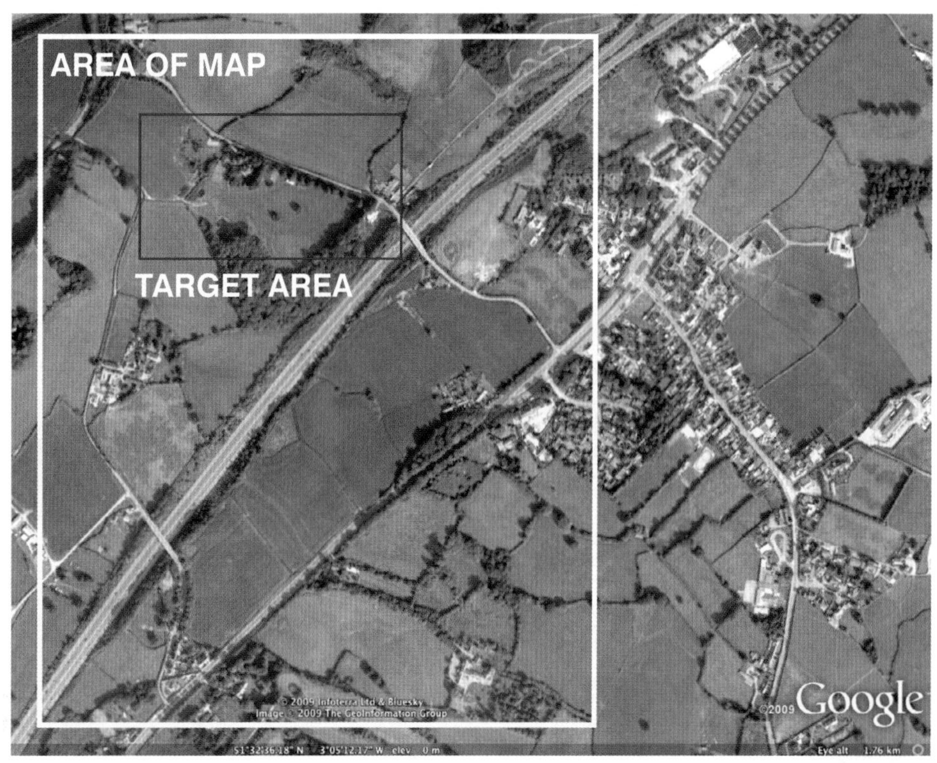

## Rehearsal prior to a night-time deployment

### THE OP TEAM INSERTION

In some ways, once you are settled in your OP all you have to do is lie there. You should be able to carry out your task and you should not be compromised unless you are literally walked on top of. Therefore the most risky part of using OPs is the insertion and extraction when there is a high risk of compromise.

To minimise this risk, consider the following:

• Move in and out in the dark hours

• If there during the day, have a reason if challenged

• Move in bounds, keeping to public paths as much as possible, it looks more natural than walking blatantly across fields

• Be dropped off close-by using a vehicle

**Pre-Deployment Checks and Rehearsals**

The driver of the vehicle is responsible for the condition of the vehicle and for getting you there at the right place at the right time. He should consider the following:

• The car should be reliable and checked for serviceability, there should be no rattles or unnecessary noises such as squeaky fan belts; all lights should be working properly.

• Disable the interior lights, lights inside the doors and the boot. Disable the child locks on all doors

• The vehicle should suit the area in which you are operating. A four door car is best or use a van if necessary

On pick-up you should move quickly out of cover and into the vehicle

• The driver should carry out a map study and be fully briefed on his routes in and out, the start point, the countdown markers and what to do in the event of a compromise. He should also have a cover story ready

• It may be practical to have a cut off switch fitted to the brake lights to avoid glowing lights as you apply the brakes.

If a van is used to drop off multiple teams, they should be seated in reverse order; first in, last out. They should also carry out a rehearsal to practise getting in and out of the vehicle without any snags.

If a car is used to drop off a two-man team, they should be sitting in the front passenger seat and the rear nearside seat. They can both get out of the car on the same side as the cover they intend to move into, without having to move across the headlights or rear tail lights.

**Ensure that you disable all interior lights. Do not forget warning lights located on doors**

## ISS CASE

On one occasion we put a two man OP team into a very rural area in order to observe an industrial waste site. We could drive to within 1.5 miles of the target and then we had to walk the remainder. The insertion route took us about a mile along a canal tow path and we walked quite openly as any other hikers would. Once at the spot where we would leave the path, we would check for any observers and then quickly disappear into the adjacent wood. We would then lie in wait for 15 minutes just in case we had been seen. After it was clear, we changed into our camouflage clothing and moved off to our lie up position (LUP) just short of the OP.

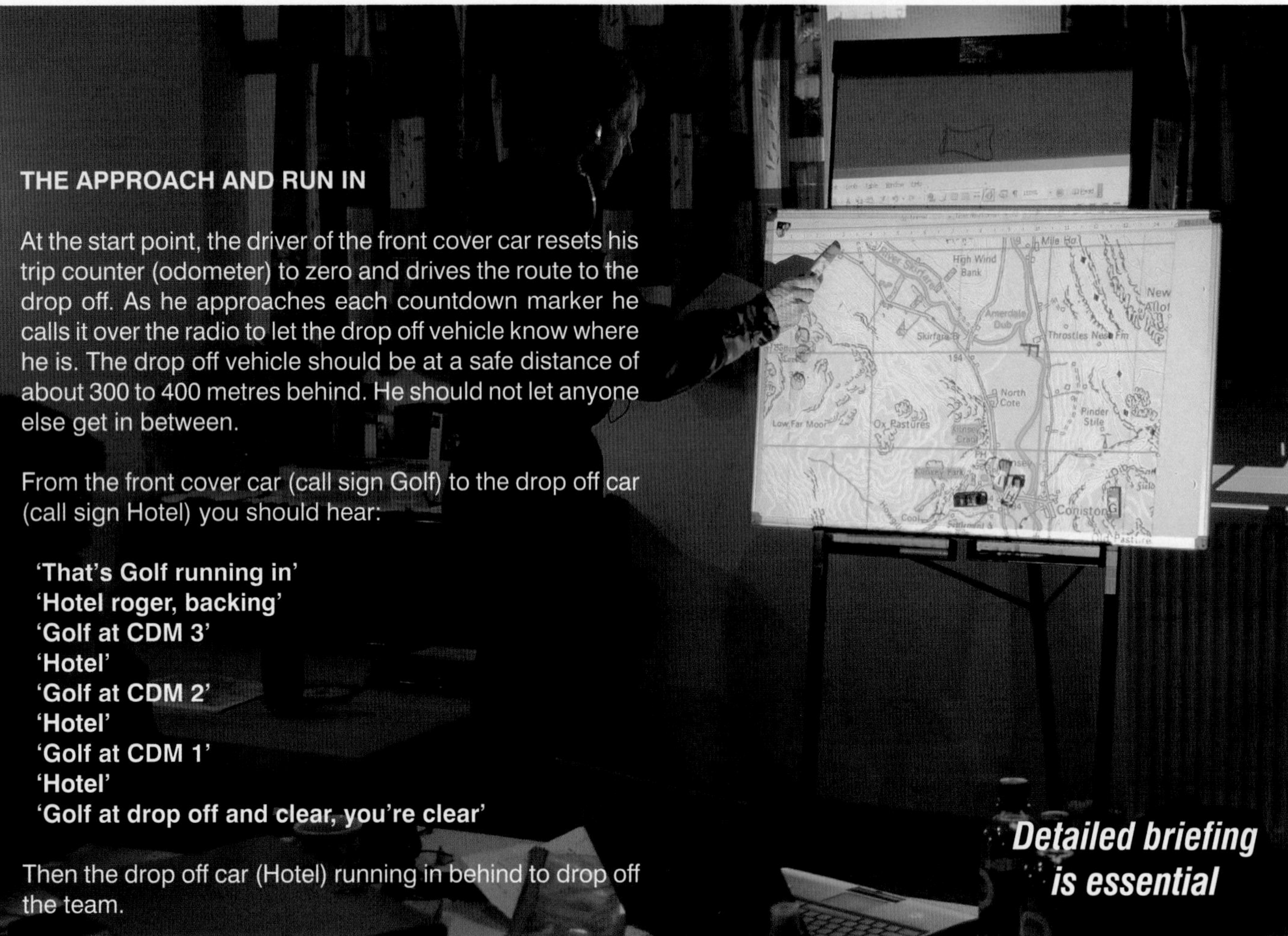


## THE APPROACH AND RUN IN

At the start point, the driver of the front cover car resets his trip counter (odometer) to zero and drives the route to the drop off. As he approaches each countdown marker he calls it over the radio to let the drop off vehicle know where he is. The drop off vehicle should be at a safe distance of about 300 to 400 metres behind. He should not let anyone else get in between.

From the front cover car (call sign Golf) to the drop off car (call sign Hotel) you should hear:

**'That's Golf running in'**
**'Hotel roger, backing'**
**'Golf at CDM 3'**
**'Hotel'**
**'Golf at CDM 2'**
**'Hotel'**
**'Golf at CDM 1'**
**'Hotel'**
**'Golf at drop off and clear, you're clear'**

Then the drop off car (Hotel) running in behind to drop off the team.

Detailed briefing is essential

**'Hotel roger that, running in at CDM 2'**
**'Golf'**
**'Hotel at CDM 1'**
**'Golf'**
**'Hotel at DOP, wait out'**
**'Hotel, drop off complete and mobile'**
**'Golf, roger that'**

When the front cover car calls the drop off clear, the drop off car should be at the 2nd or 1st CDM. The OP team should be listening in to the radio commentary and should act accordingly.

**'Hotel at CDM 3'** - Seatbelts off, civilian jackets off to reveal camouflage jackets underneath

**'Hotel at CDM 2'** - Camouflage paint onto faces or headovers (or balaclavas) on

**'Hotel at CDM 1'** - Rucksacks on knees, hands on door handles and doors open slightly on the first click ready to de-bus

On approach, the vehicle begins to slow down, the driver gives a warning and the operators prepare to de-bus by ensuring they have all equipment necessary.

## THE DROP OFF

The team should de-bus and whist doing so the driver remains in his seat and keeps the engine running; he should also act as a look out to his front and behind him. They should de-bus in silence on the nearside, ensure that there is no talking or unnecessary noise from equipment. Do not slam doors or drop tail gates but slowly push the doors closed; if need be, use your body weight such as your backside for the final push to snap it closed. The drop off should be silent. When you are ready, give a 'thumbs up' signal to the driver so he can move off. Do not double tap the cars body work as a signal, if a piece of equipment gets accidentally knocked whilst you are half way out he will mistakenly pull away. Ensure that mobile phones are on silent mode with the illumination switched off.

The OP team should move into cover a short distance away and carry out a radio check to the car as soon as possible. Then wait for about 15 minutes in order for your senses to

Prepare your camouflage on the run-in to drop-off

get used to the dark and the new surroundings before moving off. Carry out regular radio checks to your back-up and keep them up-dated with your progress as you move forward.

**The Route In**

Allow plenty of time to move into your OP position. If you have to be in position before first light, allow enough time to set up and establish the OP and to check its concealment.

Select your route with care and consider that an ideal route is one that provides:

- Places to observe without being seen
- There is cover from view
- There are no or very few, obstacles en-route
- There is good going underfoot, not rocky or boggy
- Avoids farms and wildlife

Move in with caution; at all times you must:

- Remain alert, stop frequently to look and listen. Do not cross open spaces but keep to hedgerows and wood perimeters to give cover. Move slowly, thus creating less noise. When you stop, open your mouth - it helps you hear more.
- One person must lookout and listen if the other is occupied, perhaps checking a map. Both should never be occupied at the same time
- Move in 'bounds' from one location to another. After each bound, confirm your direction from distant landmarks such as hills, pylons, urban lights, the position of the moon and stars, or use a compass or a GPS.

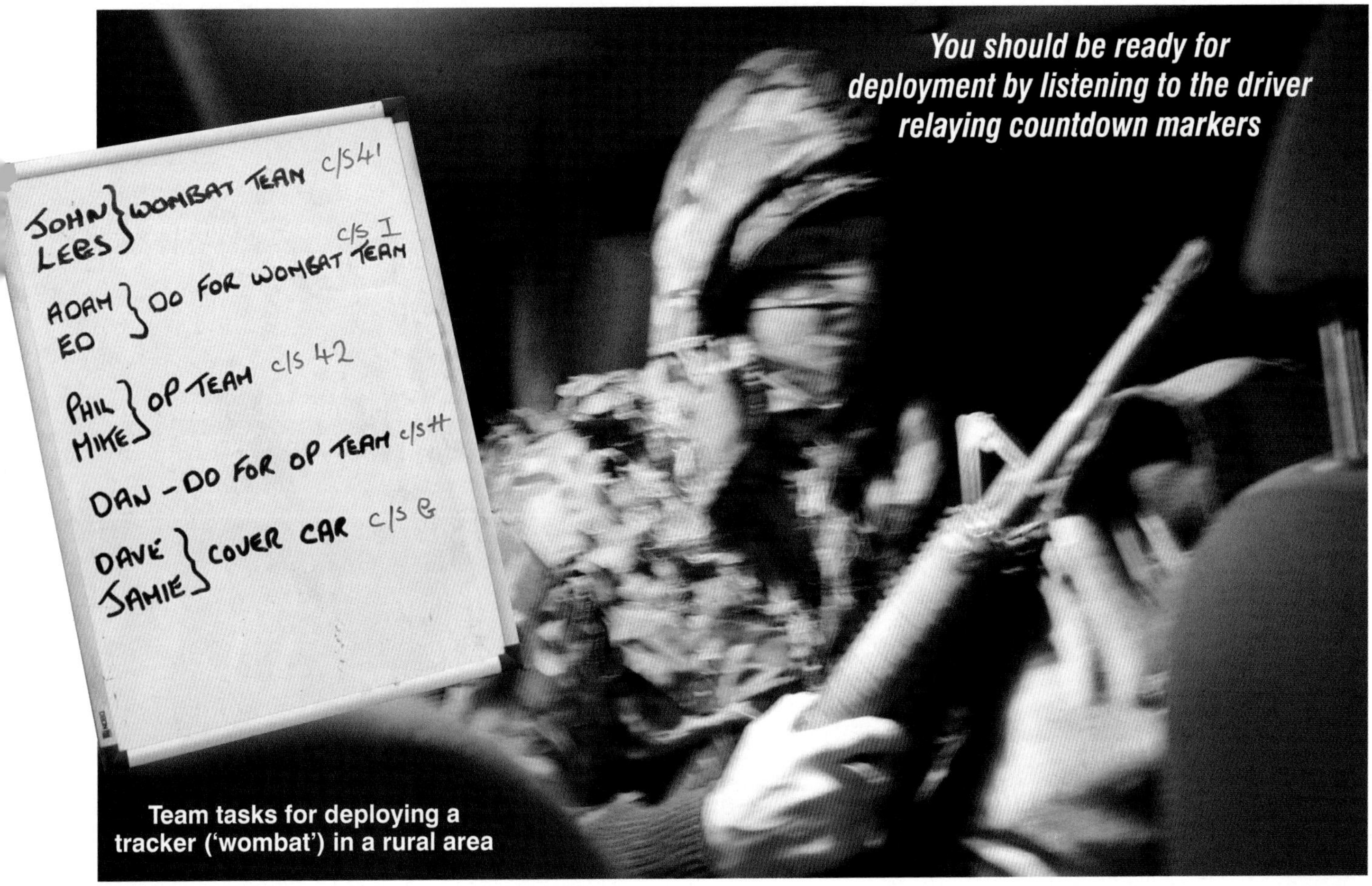

*You should be ready for deployment by listening to the driver relaying countdown markers*

Team tasks for deploying a tracker ('wombat') in a rural area

• Make use of surrounding noise (such as cars passing) which will give you cover when moving.

• Do not take risks. Have a plan ready if compromised and keep your back up informed of your progress. Take note of where you can take cover and hide along your route.

• Avoid open ground or walking directly across fields, always endeavour to use the perimeter. If you have to, keep low and move as quickly as possible.

• Only one of you should have an earpiece in, otherwise the teams hearing will be reduced by half. Only one of you use night vision gear as it will ruin your night vision.

• Enter the OP from the side or behind keeping the position between you and the target and be aware of creating tracks that lead to it.

*Deployment from a vehicle should be 'clean' and silent... do not let any equipment snag*

En route, use different types of cover such as:

• Dead Ground

Dead ground is the ground which cannot be seen into from the target's location such as low ground, hollows, small valleys and re-entrants.

• Ditches

These provide cover from the target's view but they can be obvious approaches and are hazardous if filled with water.

• Trees and Bushes

These provide cover from view but remember that isolated bushes and trees are obvious places to hide and should be avoided if possible.

Give a 'thumbs-up' rather than tap the vehicle

• Plantations, Woods and Tree Lines

These provide cover from observation but man-made plantations can be very difficult to move and navigate through, so keep to the perimeter.

• Country Lanes

Sometimes you have no alternative but to cross or move along narrow lanes but treat them with extreme caution in case of approaching vehicles. Always remember what you pass (such as low walls, fences and gates) that you can quickly move into for cover.

• Habitation and Farms

If possible avoid going near farmland and habitation as animals can be inquisitive and give away your presence.

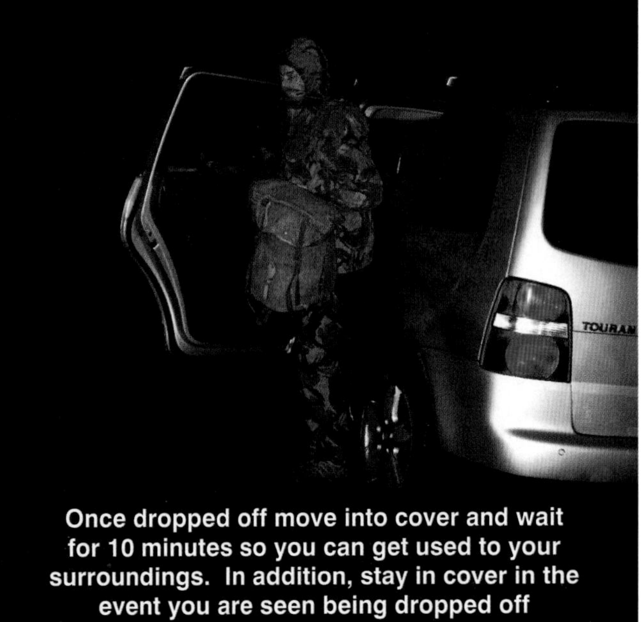


Once dropped off move into cover and wait for 10 minutes so you can get used to your surroundings. In addition, stay in cover in the event you are seen being dropped off

**Use walls, re-entrants, tree lines and fences to guide your route in. Be aware of leaving trials and do not cross open ground**

**Beware of leaving ground signs in the dew or frost**

## Obstacle Crossing

You are likely to encounter obstacles on the route in and out which can pose a hazard as you cross them such as: roads & tracks, gates, walls, stiles, fences, rivers, streams, large ditches and foot bridges. Prior to crossing them, follow the procedure:

• Stop, wait and listen. Check in front and behind you to see that it is clear before you cross

• Cross the obstacle one at a time, one moves whilst the other keeps a look out

• If it is a gate, open it and go through it. It is amazing how many people climb over them when they just had to open it! If you have to go over it, do so at the side of the hinges as it will be much stronger and keep a low profile whilst doing

**Do not cross in front of headlights or you will be illuminated**

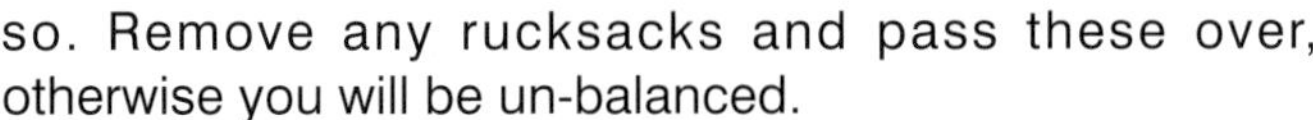

Do not cross the tail lights as this will display movement

Sheep scatter and bleat when alarmed

so. Remove any rucksacks and pass these over, otherwise you will be un-balanced.

• Remove any ground sign, such as mud from your boots, left on fence and gate railings

• Make sure that you have not dropped anything or left anything behind. Check your bearings and move off again

**Animals and Wildlife**

Be very aware of various types of animal that could cause alarm; they should be avoided at all costs.

**Dogs:** Normally confined to farms and outbuildings. They can make a lot of noise by barking to alert the owners.

**Geese:** The Romans used geese as an early warning system and they make a lot of noise when disturbed, especially at night.

**Pheasants:** Pheasants are normally patient and will stay still in order to conceal themselves. However, if startled or nearly trodden on, they will suddenly take flight, making a lot of noise as they go.

**Cows:** Cows are very curious as their eyesight is poor. An OP along the edge of a cow field may bring undue attention from the whole herd as they will be able to smell you before they see you. A whack from a catapult can often disperse them.

At night pheasants make a great deal of noise when 'spooked'

Animals can give away your presence. Move with stealth and make sure you do not alarm them and their owners...

Horses can be friendly expecting to be fed

**Sheep:** When frightened, sheep tend to scatter and bleat loudly and once one starts, they all start. A nearby farmer will soon check on sheep that are continually bleating due to stress, especially in the lambing season.

**Horses:** Horses are expensive and with them comes expensive tack equipment and so horse owners will be alarmed if they hear disturbed and stressed horses. As they are domesticated, horses expect to be fed and so the sight of a human often means food - which may also bring unwanted attention.

## MOVING AT NIGHT

At night we hear more than we see and so silence is vital. Moving silently at night requires very slow and deliberate movement so your route has to be selected carefully.

When moving, consider:

• Stop at frequent intervals, scan the area and listen. If you have night vision scopes, use them

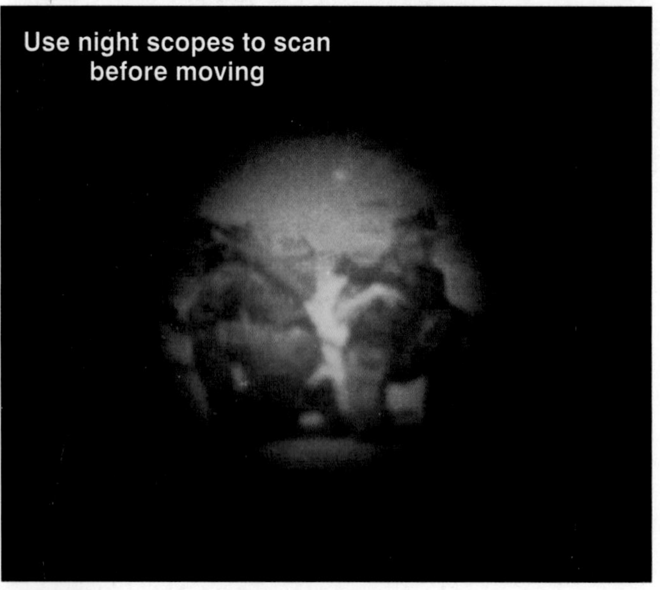
Use night scopes to scan before moving

• When stopping, keep as low to the ground as possible and turn your ears towards the direction of sound. An open mouth will help pick up the direction of the sound

• If you hear any suspicious noises en route, stop, scan and listen until you are happy to move on

• Keep checking your direction regularly by using the stars, distant landmarks or a compass/GPS. If you have to stop to look at a map, get into some cover and keep as low to the ground as possible. Do not let torchlight give away your presence

At one time in the military, it was taught and practised to have a red filter over the end of your torch in order to preserve your 'night vision'. This can be good practice but if the torchlight is seen by a casual onlooker, all they will see is a red light in the distance and may become suspicious of it. There are more 'white' lights seen at night than red lights, so it could be argued that a small amount of white light is preferable.

## ESTABLISHING THE OP

Move into the OP position keeping low to the ground. Once there, remain silent and motionless for a 5 to 10 minute period. Listen and observe in case you have been seen or followed into the OP and get accustomed to the local noises and area.

Attempt to hollow out the foliage by pushing back brambles and foliage. If necessary use secateurs to snip at the foliage to make a comfortable observation position. Remember, one person should be keeping a lookout whilst the other constructs the OP.

A viewing position may have to be constructed using 'chicken wire' and then camouflaged. If necessary, add extra foliage to the outside of your cover. Remember, if you intend using the same position over a period of time, you will have to replace the foliage as it dies off.

Do not forget to cover the rear of the OP. A camouflage net draped inside the OP at the rear will prevent you from being silhouetted by light shining in from the rear.

At first light, if you are able, crawl forward of your position and look back to identify any gaps in your camouflage. If you are unable to do this, radio your back-up and ask him to make a pass and check it for you. If you need protection from the rear, you will need to keep a constant lookout or deploy a 'Meerkat' early warning device.

Establish radio check with your back up as soon as possible. If comms are difficult, remember that there will be little

Your observation position may be a short distance from your rest position

that you can do about it and so it is your back up that will have to move to a better position. If necessary, erect a 'dipole' antenna. It may not be necessary to report by radio every time you see something and so battery power can be preserved by going on air at pre-set times of the day such as on the hour, every two hours.

Some OPs provide enough room for you to sleep in when you are not observing. If this is not possible, then an area to the side or rear of the OP will have to be used as a lie up position (LUP). From here you can sleep or rest away from the 'business end' of the OP. The LUP has to be camouflaged and the route in and out of the OP has to be safe and secure.

**Bramble Hide**

The Bramble Hide is an effective way of constructing an OP in very thick brambles with a portable camouflaged roof for cover.

To construct the roof, take a piece of chicken wire about 1 metre square and spray it with dark paint. Then attach a camouflage net to it using string or cable ties. It then needs to be folded four times from each side towards the centre so that it is compact when held against your chest and easy to open lying on your back. The idea is that when you are in the centre of the thicket, you push the brambles to the side and upwards forming a little cave. The wire mesh (held to your chest) is then unfolded, pushed up and secured to form a concave roof and so offer you protection from view and makes room for you to operate in. If you also sandwich some waterproof material between the chicken wire and the camouflage net, you will be fairly weatherproof from rain.

You should enter the OP by lying on your back, feet first, pushing apart the brambles with your feet to form a tunnel into the centre. Once in, make a turn towards the front of the OP and continue tunnelling a short way. We put a 'dog leg' in the tunnel so that no one can see directly into the OP area if stumbled upon from behind. Once you have made your turn, the actual OP can be hollowed out as described. It may be that you will have to obtain some foliage from nearby to act as a plug to block the entrance.

# THE BRAMBLE HIDE

Peg out the camouflage net

Attach chicken wire and a layer of waterpoofing

The finished camouflaged roof

When finished - fold correctly for easy opening

*Students on an ISS rural surveillance course learn to construct a bramble hide*

The completed hide should be comfortable to work and rest in.

It should be able to accommodate at least two operatives

Use you feet and legs to burrow into the brambles

Snip away foliage with secateurs deep into the hide

A colleague should act as lookout during construction

The entrance way should be concealed with a 'bung'

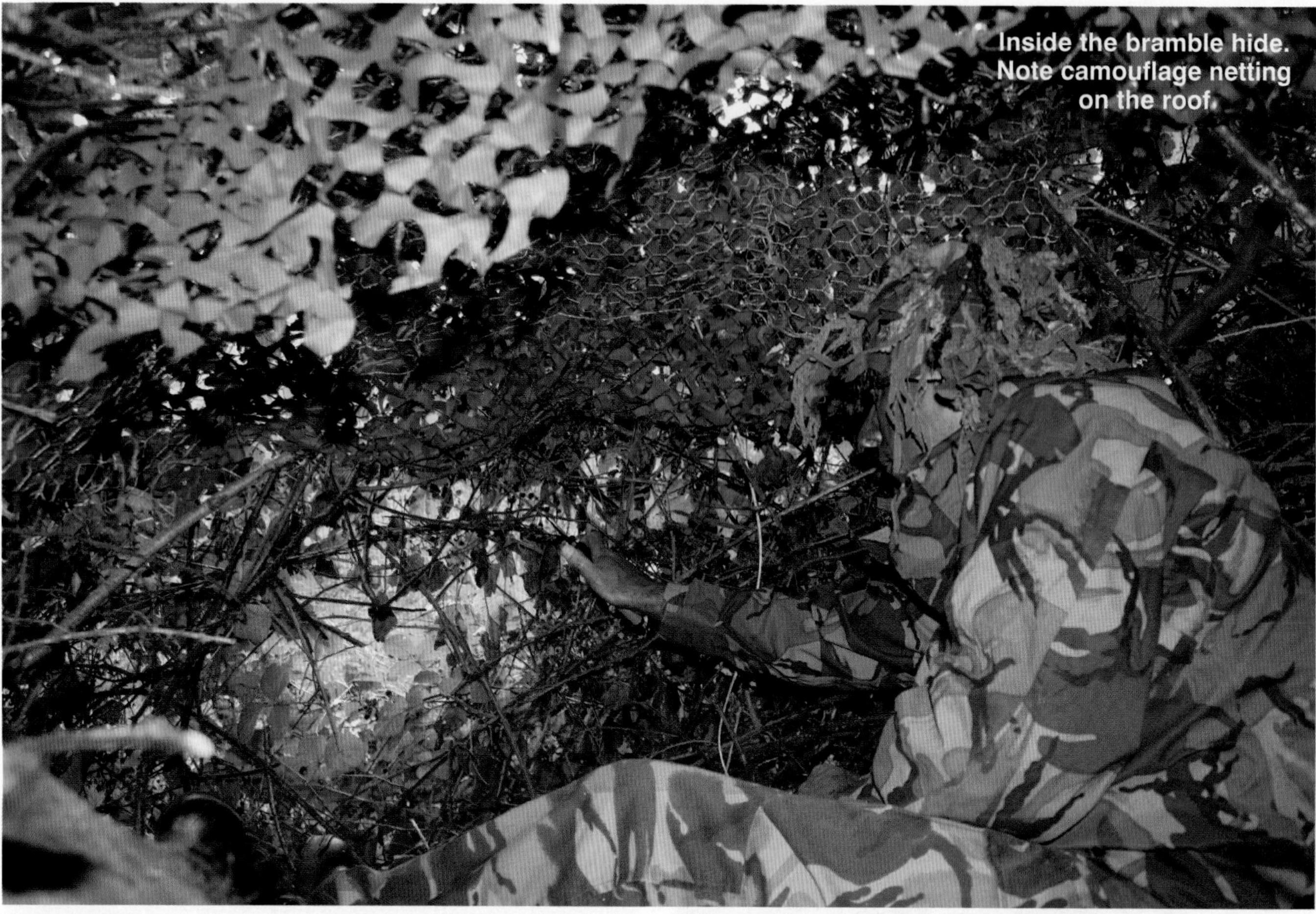
Inside the bramble hide. Note camouflage netting on the roof.

**OP Routine**

Once settled in the OP you should adjust your camouflage and make a comfortable viewing area where you are able to see your target without having to move position.

You should unpack the items that you require to use such as radio, camera, small tripod and a note book & pen or dictaphone. All other equipment should be stored away in your rucksack at all times in case that you have a compromise.

Any food and drink should be pre-prepared, you do not want a mountain of rubbish and wrappings, nor do you want to use a camping stove - for obvious reasons. If you have to go to the toilet, you may have to do this within the confines of the OP.

Carry out regular radio checks with your back up.

## THE EXTRACTION

At the end of the surveillance, you will need to leave the OP which we call the extraction phase. You will need to extract for a variety of reasons:

- *The task is complete*
- *You have been compromised*
- *You cannot see the target*
- *The OP lacks cover or has collapsed*
- *The weather is vory poor*

In preparation you will have to:

• Pack away all equipment that will not be needed

• Inform your back-up when you intend to leave, he can then assist by observing the area to give you warnings of third parties. At this time you can confirm the estimated time to be at your pick up point

• Dismantle all camouflage and bring natural foliage inside the OP to die. Leave the position as you found it, taking with you all refuse, including all human waste

• Move out one at a time and never in haste, be as cautious during the extraction as you were during the insertion

• Inform your back up of your progress along the way out and head for the PUP

## ISS CASE

During a surveillance in a very rural area, the final approach was via a lake as one of the OPs was conducted from the water's edge within banking undergrowth. Dressed in a diver's dry suit and camouflage clothing, a short distance was swum in order to get into position. This OP was maintained all day during the daylight hours and I had to keep the dry suit on for my extraction as it was not practical or possible to take it off. At first, having a pee was a joy of warmth but after a few minutes the novelty wore off with the cold. 14 hours were spent there...

### The Pick Up

Once you have arrived at your pick up point, you may have to wait a short period before your vehicle arrives. Do not become complacent at this time, remain concealed and out of view.

The drill for getting picked up is very similar to how you got dropped off but now takes place in a different spot. The cover car will come through to clear the PUP and warn of any oncoming traffic from the front, whilst the pick up car collects the OP team. By virtue of the fact that the OP team will be first at the PUP and waiting, they will be responsible for checking that it is clear and safe.

### The Run In and Approach for Pick Up

At the start point, the driver of the front cover car resets his trip (odometer) to zero and drives the route to the PUP. As he approaches each countdown marker he calls it over

An OP from the top of a quarry covering a weighbridge where theft was suspected

Use natural walls and foliage whenever possible but ensure you have an escape route

the radio to let the pick up vehicle know where he is. The pick up vehicle should be at a safe distance of about 300 to 400 metres 'running in' behind. The OP team will either put out a stop marker at the side of the road to indicate where to stop, or they will 'vector' the car in by radio and tell it where to stop.

From the front cover car (call sign Golf) to the pick up car (call sign Hotel) you should hear:

| |
|---|
| 'That's Golf running in' |
| 'Hotel roger, backing' |
| 'Golf at CDM 3' |
| 'Hotel' |
| 'Golf at CDM 2' |
| 'Hotel' |
| 'Golf at CDM 1' |
| 'Hotel' |
| 'Golf at pick up and clear, clear' |

Then the pick up car (Hotel) running in behind to pick up the team.

| |
|---|
| 'Hotel roger that, running in at CDM 2' |
| 'Golf' |
| 'Hotel to 41 (OP team) running in at CDM 2' |
| '41 roger' |
| 'Hotel at CDM 1' |
| '41 roger, I have you visual' |
| 'Golf, clear to the front' |
| 'Hotel' |
| '41 to Hotel, you're 50m short' |
| '20m, 10m, Stop Stop Stop |
| 'Hotel at PUP, wait out' |
| 'Golf' |
| 'Hotel, pick up complete and mobile' |
| 'Golf roger that' |

When the front cover car calls the PUP clear, the pick up car should be at the 2nd or 1st CDM. The OP team should be listening in to the radio commentary and should act accordingly:

| |
|---|
| 'Golf at CDM 2' - Prepare to move out of cover. |
| 'Golf at CDM 1' - One of the team puts out the cat's eye marker or commences commentary to 'vector' the car in. |

On approach, the vehicle begins to slow down and stops at the correct place, the driver keeps an eye on the rear. The OP team collect the stop marker, ensures they have left nothing behind and get into the pick up vehicle as quickly and as quietly as possible. Do not slam the doors but close them gently on the first 'click'. When the car moves off and changes gear, use this noise as cover to open the doors and close them properly. Body worn radio sets are then switched off.

The OP team then put on their civilian jackets and remove any cam cream with baby wipes.

Look through cover rather than over it

**DOP and PUP Compromises**

Should you be on the insertion run in and find that the DOP is compromised (by a parked car for example), there are a few things that you can do. One is to continue the circuit and drop off at the PUP (the alternative DOP), the other is to abort for an hour or so and then try again; it all depends on the importance of the task and the time constraints.

When picking up or dropping off, use natural places to halt such as T-junctions

## ISS CASE

On a training exercise, a foreign special forces team were being picked up who had been deployed on a Close Target Recce (CTR). Their stop marker was a plastic Pepsi bottle, which was placed at the side of the road.

All were in position and running in, the front cover car had cleared the PUP. Due to bad planning and the fact that the pick up car was too far behind, an unidentified car had managed to get sandwiched in the middle of the team. The OP team did not realise this. The unidentified car stopped exactly where the OP team were

COURTESY: DOD

concealed, the passenger door was opened and the passenger picked up the Pepsi bottle and drove off, just as the OP team were emerging from their position.

The car's occupants were obviously concerned about litter but they did not realise how close they were to having two armed men dressed in black, climbing into their backseat in the middle of the night. It was a very close call and a good lesson.

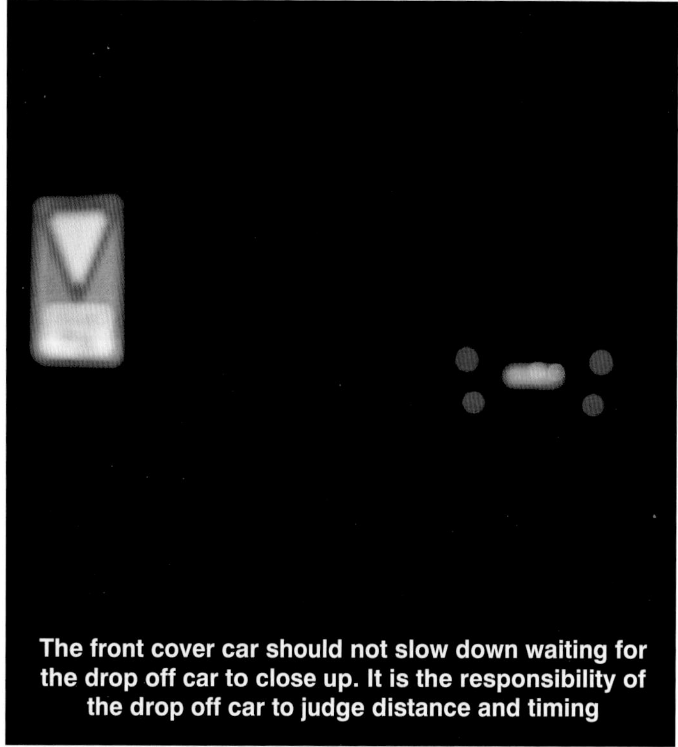

**The front cover car should not slow down waiting for the drop off car to close up. It is the responsibility of the drop off car to judge distance and timing**

# SENSES

Cooking in an OP is not advisable or the wearing of fragrances

Take all rubbish with you - do not leave anything behind

## SURVEILLANCE COMPROMISES

### Why Are Rural OPs Sometimes Compromised?

As we have mentioned earlier, there are many reasons why OPs will become compromised by either the target or by third parties. The reasons for compromise are many but we can minimise the risk of compromise if we look at the reasons why the OP is brought to another person's attention.

Keep all equipment packed away when not in use

### Operators Own Fault

- **Location**

Sometimes the only option for positioning your OP is in an obvious one as it is the only place to give cover. Stay out of the '10 - 2' arc and avoid lone cover such as a clump of bushes in the centre of a field. Avoid being near routes that the public will take and ensure that you are not overlooked.

- **Insertion**

Ensure that you are not seen entering or leaving the location. Use available cover, enter the OP at night or have a reason for being in the area before you slip into your OP. Be aware that on dewy mornings you may leave tracks to the OP site.

Move with stealth

- **Movement**

As we discussed earlier, sudden movement is the biggest giveaway when trying to conceal yourself. You may have the best camouflage but you will be noticed the second

SMOKING PROHIBITED AT ALL TIMES

Ensure cell phones are on silent mode

Camouflage any pruned or broken branches

ISS Training Course. Circa 1915!

you move. Only personal discipline and training will help you to lie perfectly still for many hours.

• **Noise**

It is essential that you keep quiet in the OP. There should be no reason for idle conversation as whispers soon grow into loud dialogue. Be aware of your radio volume and your mobile phone should be in silent/vibrate mode. If using a radio or phone, keep check of your voice level. Quite often you can start off a conversation in a low whisper but very soon you will find yourself shouting the longer the call goes on, almost without realising it.

• **Smoke and Smells**

Smoking is not advisable in an OP for obvious reasons, so if you are a heavy smoker, be prepared for a long wait. Not only will the smell give you away but at night, a cigarette tip will illuminate your face, especially when viewed through night vision optics.

Make sure your Ghillie suit matches your surroundings

• **Silhouette**

Your position should look through cover and not over the top of it or you will be 'sky-lined' by your silhouette. In addition, ensure that you blend in with your background and not be in contrast with it.

• **Re-supply**

If you are in the OP for a long period, it may be necessary to be re-supplied with fresh batteries, films and food and to have your waste taken away. This can be a high risk time and carried out by either dead letter box (DLB) or live letter box (LLB) and therefore a re-supply should be carried out with caution.

• **Lights**

Keep torchlight to an absolute minimum at night, you do not need a lighthouse beacon to read a phone number from a pad. Keep the torch lens as small as possible and get under cover when you have to use it.

Remember to disable the red recording light at the front of your video camera and be careful that the light from the viewfinder does not illuminate your face. In addition, remember to switch off the illuminator on your mobile phone.

• **Lack of Camouflage**

You will need sufficient camouflage on all sides and it has to be of the correct type. Camouflage nets covered in local foliage are very effective but remember that natural foliage may die after a day or so and will have to be replaced.

• **Clues of Presence**

When extracting from the OP ensure that you take everything with you when you leave. This includes all rubbish,

## ISS CASE

A colleague was once in a Standing OP in a ditch on some bare moorland in North Yorkshire. He had to observe a gateway in order to identify the driver of a vehicle, when he stopped to open the gate. He had been in the position for little over two hours when he came on the radio to say that he had been compromised by two horse riders. They had seen him and asked him what he was doing. This was a total fluke and bad luck as the operator had kept well away from paths or tracks and the moor covered such a large expanse. The riders just happened to pass the same spot by coincidence.

string, camouflage nets, human waste and so on. You should endeavour to hide the fact that you were ever there, as you may want to use the same location again in the future and so you have to protect its security.

**Bluetooth!**

Don't forget to switch off the Bluetooth signal on your mobile phone! On a recent training course, the class were superbly camouflaged and concealed in a hide and it was extremely difficult to see them; however a quick scan with my mobile phone revealed that 'Dick Dastardly' was nearby as he had his mobile Bluetooth switched on.

**Others At Fault**

- **Accidental Finding**

On occasions, an OP may be walked upon purely by accident which is why camouflage and concealment is such an important factor.

- **Purpose Finding**

A very aware target may be on the lookout for observation positions and make an effort to 'patrol' his local area and look for signs of your presence.

- **Children**

Playing children can stumble across your position but usually you will have plenty of warning by the noise that they make. You can either burrow yourself in deeper or have a reason for being there if discovered. After a compromise by children it is always best to extract as it will not be long before they tell someone who also comes for a look.

- **Dogs and Farm Animals**

A dog will react and bark at something it is unsure about and there are various reasons why it will react to you: your smell, noise from the OP and even inaudible sounds from your video camera or night vision equipment.

What to do in the event of a compromise

- Be absolutely certain that you have been compromised, you do not want to leave the position unnecessarily
- Wake those who are sleeping
- Inform your back up straight away. They may need to extract you, cause a diversion or intercept those who have spotted you
- Pack items of equipment (only the essentials should be out anyway)
- Move out, decide if it should be covert or overt (silently or at the 'crash')
- Move to the emergency RV for pick up
- Move clear of the area
- Consider sending an operator on a drive past to monitor any activity at the OP site

Nothing can be really done to prevent dogs from sniffing your position

# SPECIAL CASE FILE

## MOUNT WALL - FALKLAND ISLANDS WAR 1982

We had been patrolling for a number of days, we had just spent 2 days in an OP covering Fitzroy and Bluff Cove ensuring it was clear of enemy so that the Gurkhas and Guards could come ashore - but that's another story.

We moved off and later that day we bumped into a recce patrol from the Mountain & Arctic Warfare Cadre and spoke to 'Monty' the team leader and one of his team 'Ray'. They told us how they had been in a contact a few days before at a place called Top Malo House. The Cadre team had had a fierce fire fight with an Argentine special forces unit where Chris Stone and Terry Doyle had both been shot and injured. The Argentines had come off worse in the assault.

Talking to Monty, he gave the advice: '..if you get into a contact, '66 them' - they don't f***ing like it'. A '66' is an American light anti tank rocket, which fires a 66mm diameter missile which penetrates 10 inches of steel and designed to be used against tanks and bunkers. Monty could see that I had two of them strapped to my rucksack.

A few days later, our recce team were located on Mount Wall, a small mountain a few miles from Port Stanley and the most forward of the British forces, it was a large OP as it was very high risk as we were very close to the Argentine positions, some 500 metres. We set up an OP to observe an enemy position and we were also escorting two Air Force specialists who guide in jet aircraft for aerial attacks, there was also a team of artillery specialists who were bringing in artillery and naval gunfire.

My Recce Troop partner and surveillance mentor Yogi Leak (Ken), seen here a few days before the 'contact' on Mount Wall. He joined 14 Intelligence Company and later established his own commercial surveillance business. Sadly, Ken died in December 2011, after a long illness

On day two and after being shelled all night, I was covering the north side of the position with my partner 'Ken'. We were located in a small rocky outcrop. I had just finished my watch and handed over to him to look out but after a few minutes I heard him whisper, 'Tsst Tsst'. I looked at him questioningly and he gave me a thumbs down (Enemy) and he pointed to his front. He indicated that there were three of them, they were very close and appeared to be having a rest. Great!... only 10 metres to our front.

I later searched the internet about this incident and it is reported that a patrol of special forces from 602 Commando Squadron were tasked to clear the high ground on Mt Wall in the event that there British were there.

I called for the Boss - Chris who came to our position with Scotty and Jim to make an assessment. Under whispers, it was decided to call a contact report and bring down some artillery fire to land just to our front, this would make a lot of noise whilst we whacked the enemy patrol before we were discovered. That was the plan....

Ken then turned and said, 'they've seen us..'. Chris decided to go 'noisy' and said, 'Okay Go for it.' All hell broke loose with everyone firing towards the patrol through the rocks.

Remembering Monty's words, I took one of my 66's and prepared it for firing. Ken gave a long burst of covering fire from his GPMP whilst I bobbed up, fired the rocket at a huge boulder the patrol were using as cover. The rocket hit the boulder and went, 'dink'. If Victor Meldrew was there he would have muttered those immortal words.... 'I don't believe it..'

The guys were in hysterics, it was surreal, we were getting shot at and any everyone was having giddy fits. The boulder was so close that the rocket did not have chance to arm itself.

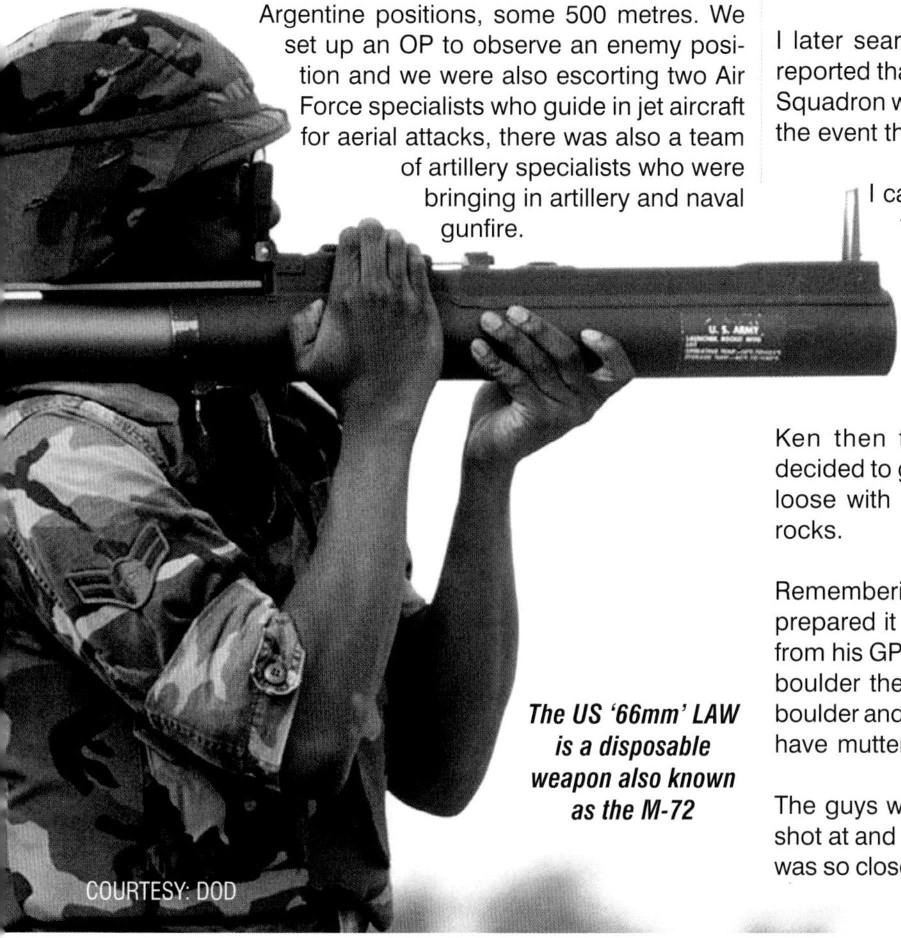

*The US '66mm' LAW is a disposable weapon also known as the M-72*

COURTESY: DOD

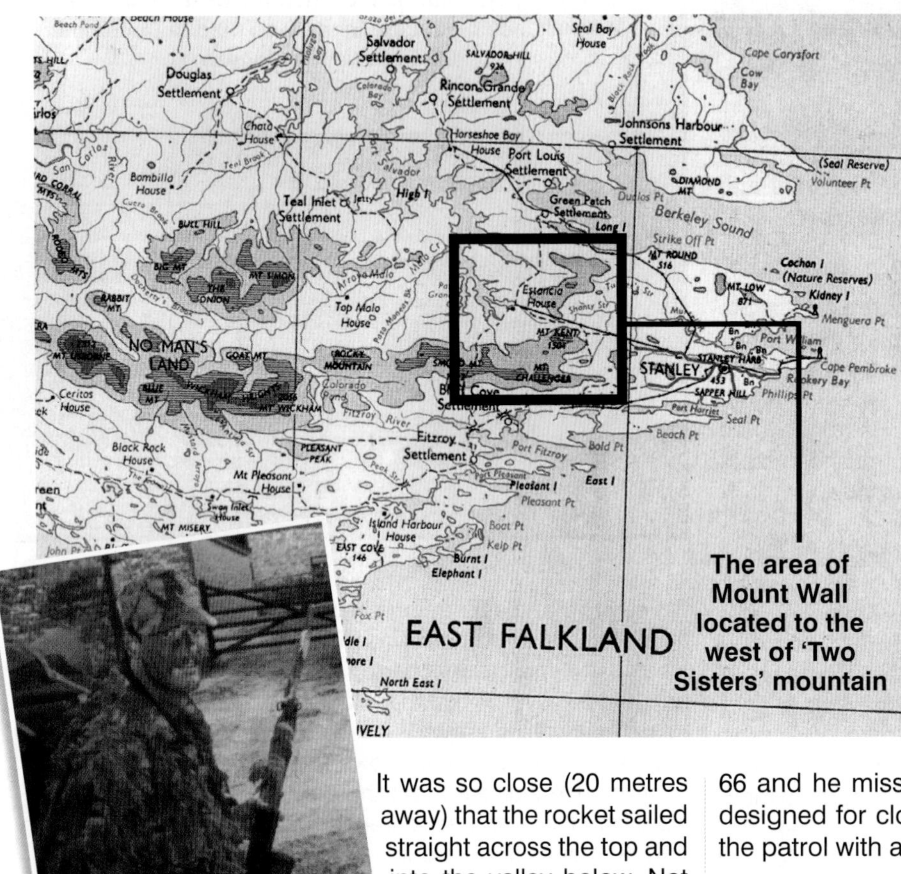


The area of Mount Wall located to the west of 'Two Sisters' mountain

Ken at 'Moody Brook' on the outskirts of Port Stanley shortly after the Argentine surrender

Author returns from a patrol

It was so close (20 metres away) that the rocket sailed straight across the top and into the valley below. Not being disheartened I followed up with a phosphorous grenade (instant smoke) whilst the others put down heavy fire. Chris the Boss was shaking his head, dazed by the loud bang and back blast as the 66 went off.

Steve, one of the snipers on the team managed to catch the tail end of the patrol as they withdrew, he also fired a 66 and he missed as well - I don't think that they were designed for close quarters! He then took out the tail of the patrol with an L42 sniper rifle.

The position was absolutely compromised, we could see mortar rounds landing in the valley to our north which were being directed to our position. It was decided to 'bug out' and we made a tactical withdrawal, some of our rucksacks had to be left behind as they weighed a ton and the forward observers had to destroy their equipment in the event it was captured. Lima Company (to our West) had reported that Argentine re-enforcements were deploying from a couple of trucks towards us and so they moved forward to give us cover as we moved back towards their lines. Luckily, none of our team were hit during the contact.

It was the first contact for 42 Commando RM and the Commanding Officer - Lt Col. Nick Vaux told us the following day that he had watched the contact taking place from his position on Mount Kent. He said, "we were watching the firefight through binos and we also noticed that the Argies were watching as well from Two Sisters' so we DF'd (shelled) them." He continued: "Well done up there" and gave us all an extra ration pack for our efforts.

The compromise was pure fluke, we wanted to dominate the high ground and so did the enemy - but we were there first and had the advantage.

**Royal Marine Commandos learning camouflage and concealment during basic training**

## THE STATIC FOLLOW

It may be that you have to keep a target under control in a rural area where it is too risky to carry out conventional surveillance by 'following'. It may be because you are unable to work in the area as this in itself will attract attention or the target may be very wary of any vehicles at all that are behind him.

If you have a start point and a finish point, a number of OP's strung out over the distance, covering any options should be able to keep him under control.

On the rural courses that we run, we have to control a target suspected of poaching. He leaves home early evening and goes drinking in his local pub some three miles away, he has to drive along two valleys to get there.

After he finishes his drinking, he leaves the pub and drives home. En route he stops somewhere and sets out illegal fishing nets on one of the two rivers on the valley floor. He is very aware and if he notices any vehicles behind him, he will not lay out the nets but continue home. The aim of the exercise is to identify where along the route he stops and set his nets. The following day the team have to deploy rural video cameras in the same spot in order to gather evidence.

The team plan and execute a deployment where four OP teams are strung out over the route. One covers the house, the others deploy along the route and a car covers the pub. All eight personnel (four pairs) are dropped off from a van at certain points where they can move into position.

When the target moves, he is 'bounced' from one OP to the other and passed on down the line. When he goes 'unsighted' to one OP, the next one along should pick him up and so on.

The team bounce him down to the pub and on his way back they bounce him back and identify exactly where he stops. After the task is complete, the OP teams move to their pick up points and are sequentially picked up by the van and clear the area.

# PLAN FOR A STATIC FOLLOW

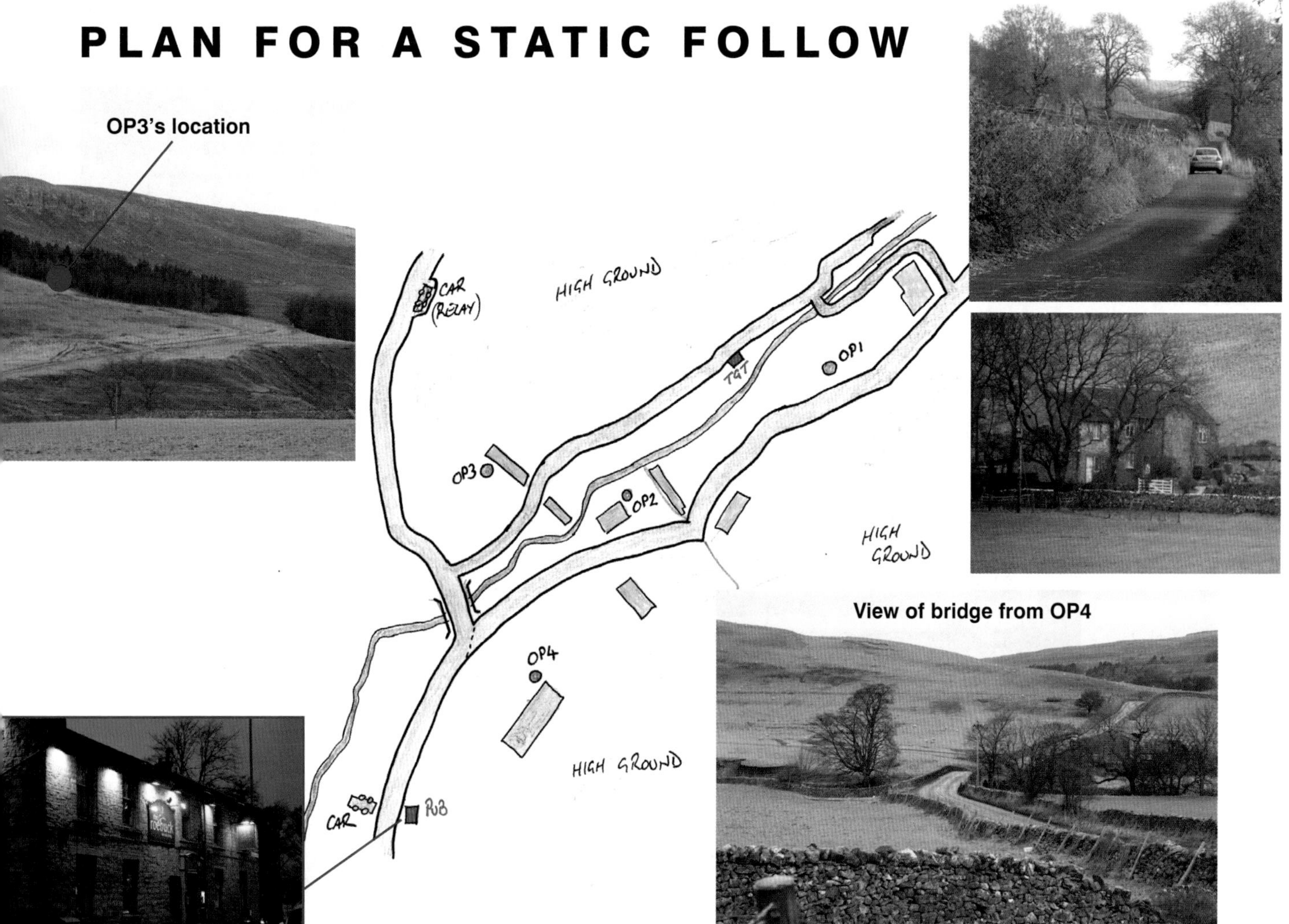

## FIELD CRAFT

Soldiers are taught field craft during their basic training in order to help them observe, and identify friendly or enemy positions. They are also taught how to judge distances in the event that they have to report where targets are and more importantly set their weapon's sights. Below are a few disciplines that are of use to the surveillance operator whilst operating in OPs.

### Observation Skills

If we recall the reasons why things are seen: Shape, Shine, Surface, Sudden Movement, Spacing, Silhouette; we should be able to use this to our advantage when we are observing an area, a target or a piece of ground from our OP.

We can observe in a number of different ways, primarily by scanning and searching.

- **Scanning**

Scanning is a general and systematic search of an area of ground to detect any unusual or significant object or movement. You may scan an area by dividing the ground into the foreground, middle distance and far distance. By looking at the far distance sweep your eyes from side to side and slowly move closer to cover the middle and then the near distance. Scan each area horizontally and move the eyes in short overlapping movements so you do not to leave any gaps; in this way you should not miss anything.

- **Searching**

Whilst scanning, your eyes may 'lock' onto a building or something that has attracted your attention. You should now give this a thorough examination and search paying as much attention to it as possible, using binoculars if necessary.

If your position is overlooked by any high ground, buildings or risky areas where third parties may see you, these should be scanned first.

Objects look closer when they are higher up, when you are looking across a valley, or if the sun is behind you

### Judging Distance

If we recall in the chapter on evidence we discussed the mnemonic ADVOKATE and the fact that we may have to judge the distance that we are from the target. Therefore we have to be able to judge distance accurately and with practice you can become quite proficient.

There are several methods used to judge distance and there are certain aids that can also be used.

**When scanning at night look to the side of your target due to blind spots in the eye**

### Methods of Judging Distance

- Appearance Method
- Unit of Measure

Provided that all the ground between you and the target is visible, you can use any unit of measure that is familiar to you such as the length of a football pitch or the length of your garden.

By estimating how many units of the familiar length (eg. a football pitch) can be fitted - in between your position and the object, a quick calculation should give a reasonable measure of the total distance.

- **Appearance Method**

The appearance method of judging distance is based on what an object looks like compared to its local surroundings. The amount of visible detail of a person at various distances, gives a good indication of how far he is away.

| |
|---|
| At 100 metres, all details are clear |
| At 200 metres, clear in all detail, colour of skin and clothes are identifiable |
| At 300 metres, clear body outline, see colour of skin, remaining detail is blurred |
| At 400 metres, body outline clear, remaining detail is blurred |
| At 500 metres, body begins to taper, head becomes indistinct |
| At 600 metres. body now appears wedge shaped |
| Conditions that Effect Judgement of Distance |

The length of a soccer pitch is approximately 100 metres - you can use this as a guide for judging distance

Certain circumstances and environmental conditions can make your target appear closer or further away than you actually realise.

**Objects seem closer than they are when:**

- The light is bright or the sun is shining from behind you.
- They are bigger than the other objects around them.
- There is dead ground (valley or re-entrant) between you and the observer.
- They are higher up than you.

**Objects seem further away when:**

- The light is bad or the sun is in your eyes.
- They are smaller than the other objects around them.
- Looking down a street.
- You are lying down.

300 metres

200 metres

100 metres

Objects seem further away when looking down the street

Accurate map reading will allow you to estimate distances

**Aids to Judging Distance**

There are various aids that we can use to assist us in judging distance in order to become more accurate.

- **Bracketing**

The bracketing technique is a useful aid. Quite simply, estimate the maximum possible distance to the target and then the minimum possible distance. An accurate estimate of the actual distance can be set midway between the two distances.

- **Halving**

For long distances, estimate what the midway distance is and then double it.

- **Team Average**

When in a group, get each person to judge the distance, add them together and then divide the figure by the number of people, in order to get an average distance.

## THE CLOSE TARGET RECCE (CTR)

A Close Target Reconnaissance or Recce (CTR) is effectively a stealth patrol conducted to collect information about a specific location and detailed information for intelligence. The operators may have to enter a yard, farm, business premises or garden to conduct their search and so stealth and slow movement is vital. The CTR has to be carefully planned and executed using all your field craft skills.

A CTR is carried out for the following reasons:

- *A general close recce of a target premises*
- *To locate a close OP site*
- *To carry out a close search of a premises*
- *To install technical surveillance equipment within, or close to, the target*

**CTR Basic Procedures**

A daylight recce of the area should always be carried out to establish your routes in and out and establish the layout of the target area and to identify any difficulties.

The CTR team should always cover each others movements by moving one at a time and by using as much cover as possible. You should always have a back up ready to cause a diversion or to have them extract you should you become compromised.

A CTR may be carried out to bury cameras in the ground

## ISS CASE

A couple of years ago we had to enter a commercial property that was located on an industrial estate in the bottom of a large disused and converted quarry. The aim was to identify and photograph the chemicals that were stored in the yard contained in 40 gallon chemical drums.

Two of us had set up an OP during the day and kept watch of the premises and yard area. From our vantage point at the top of the quarry we are able to observe all deliveries made during the day and were also able to plan our route in for the night time CTR.

After the premises were locked up and all the day shift had left, we were able to establish that there were still approximately five members of staff left during the night. After dusk fell we moved from our OP to a closer vantage point which overlooked the drum storage area. It was intended that my partner, Ray, would enter the premises and I would keep an eye out for any staff members. Ray carried his personal radio with a covert ear piece and a video camera with an infra red (night shot) capability.

After an hour's waiting in our LUP, all appeared quiet and Ray moved silently forward, balaclava pulled over his face

A view of the site from the OP

and entered the premises. From above, I could monitor his progress through a night vision scope and also warn of anyone entering the storage area.

Every now and then I would give him a radio check and receive 'three clicks' in response to say that he was okay. After a while I received 'four clicks' (ask me a question). I asked him if he had located the 'obvious' and then received three clicks in response - he had located the chemicals.

We had to get in close to identify the writing on the drum

Through the intensified night scope, I could just see Ray in the shadows, his video camera up to his eye and I could see the infra red beam from the camera illuminating the labels on the barrels. After twenty minutes or so, Ray started to move back to my location, slowly and deliberately just as he had done when entering. Once back, we moved slowly back to our OP, then waited for a while in case we had been seen. When satisfied, we checked the video tape (we did not want to leave if the shots had not come out okay) then gathered our rucksacks and left the area and returned to where we had parked the car.

Make the most of covert equipment such as night vision devices. If you have to obtain photographs or images use 'Zero Light' or 'Night Shot' video cameras.

The CTR in some ways is an extension of your observation post and so the same meticulous planning should be considered, especially when dropping off and being picked up. The risk of compromise may be high and so you cannot neglect to make a plan of action for such an eventuality.

### Cache Equipment

It may be necessary to leave a rucksack in a safe area, hidden. If you do this, ensure that it is properly camouflaged and easily located on your return. Use a gate post, telegraph post or another fixed object nearby to use as a reference point to help you find it again later, in the dark. A GPS (global positioning system) is ideal for locating a cache as they can be accurate to within 2 metres.

### Probing

You will be moving at night, carrying very little equipment. If you are suspicious of a noise or movement, go to ground; look and listen until you are satisfied that it is safe to move on. Do not push yourself and go any closer to the target than is necessary, you do not want to risk a compromise.

You may not want to go directly into the target area but you want to examine it by 'probing' and there are two ways that you can do this:

**Use of night vision aids are essential when carrying out close reconnaissance**

**Passive night goggles**

- *Satellite Method*
- *Probe Method*

**You may need to probe your target in stages from different directions**

- **Satellite Method**

This is achieved by selecting a route around your target which allows you to walk 360 degrees, giving you a view from all sides. How close you get (the radial range) depends on the ground and also the target's awareness level and how much intelligence you need.

- **Probe Method**

This method is similar to the Satellite Method but at a number of points along the route, for example, North, East, South and West, you close in on the centre of the target for a closer look. You then withdraw back onto the satellite route and move round to the next probe point. This is a very effective method but can be very tiring and time consuming.

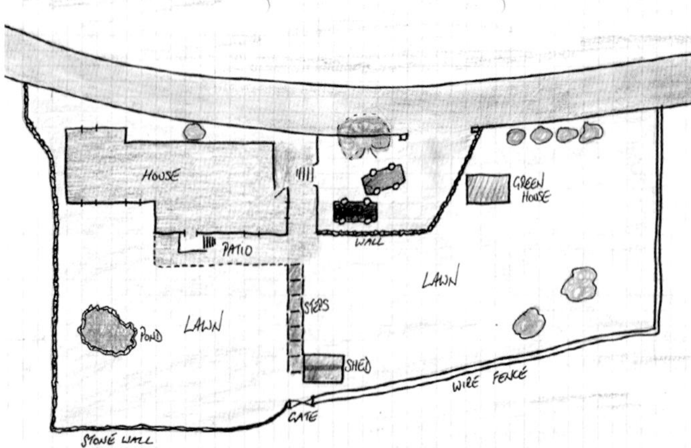


**In addition to photography, you may have to make detailed sketches of the target**

**Conclusion**

Rural surveillance is a very specialised skill that requires proper training and experience in order to carry it out successfully.

We have carried out many static rural OPs over the years, not just in rural areas but also in urban areas where at first view an unskilled investigator would comment that the job was impossible to do. There is a time and place for everything in surveillance work; and so keep an open mind and think about all the possibilities.

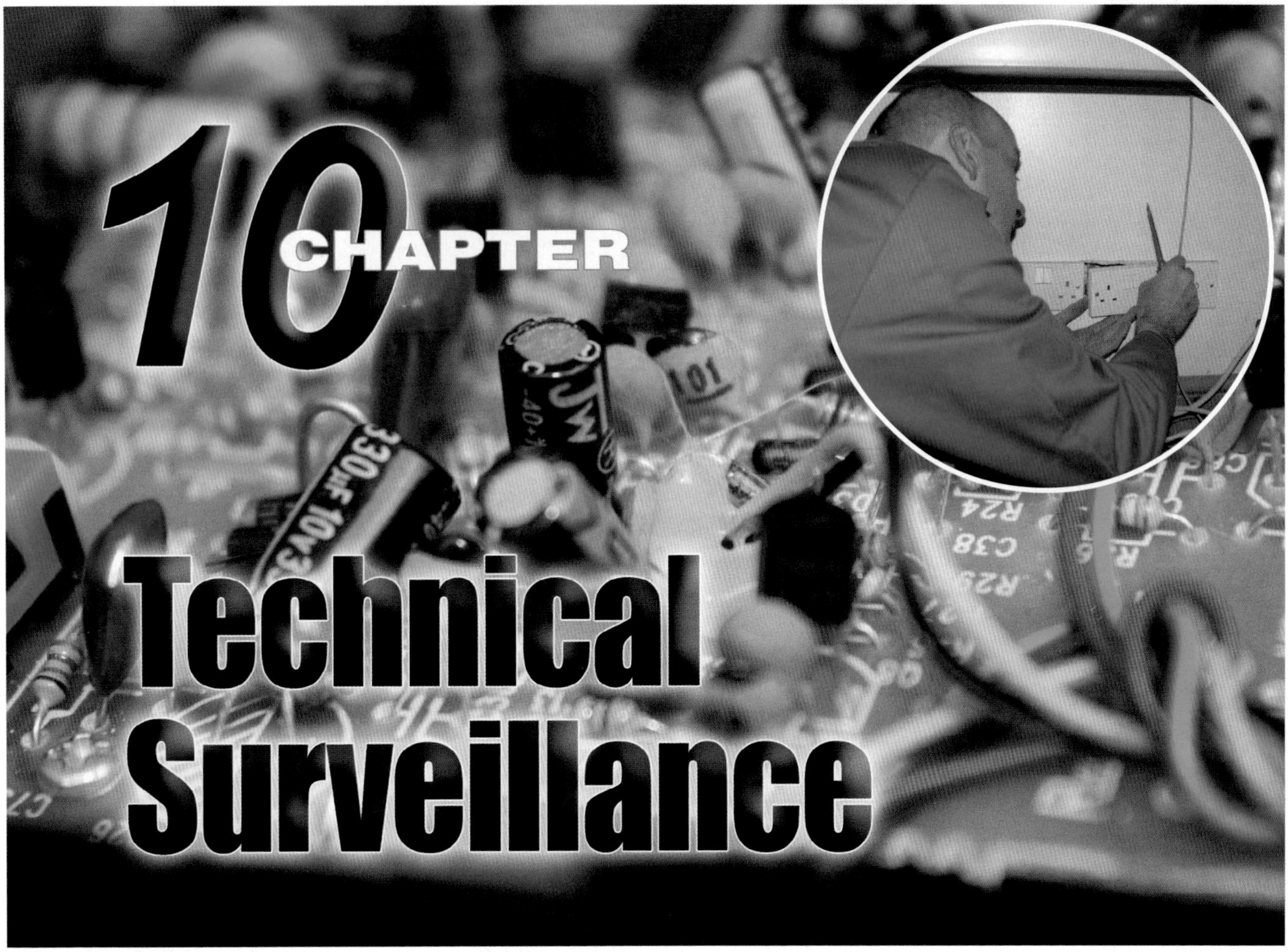

# 10 CHAPTER Technical Surveillance

Technical surveillance methods are constantly changing with advancing technology, so the surveillance operator has to keep abreast of what equipment is out there. This equipment will not carry out the investigation for you but can be used to great effect to support conventional investigations and surveillance.

Technical kit, being technical, has its drawbacks and limitations: much of it relies on electricity to make it work and so power supply is always an issue; also, at some stage in its life, a piece of technical equipment will almost certainly fail and Murphy's Law predicts that this will be when you need it most.

Technical Surveillance can fall into many categories but we will concentrate on:

- *Covert Video (Internal & External)*
- *Room Audio*
- *Telephone Audio*
- *Tracking, Locating or Triggering*
- *Computer Monitoring*

**Covert Closed Circuit TV Cameras**

Covert Closed Circuit TV (CCTV) has an important role in covert evidence gathering. By means of a video camera linked to a recorder and monitor, you will be able to unobtrusively watch events taking place 'live' or, alternatively they can be recorded and viewed at a later date.

We have installed many covert video cameras and achieved excellent results, especially where theft and unauthorised access to premises have been suspected. If covert cameras can resolve a problem it saves the manpower, time and expense of having to provide a manned observation team. In addition, a covert camera may in any case be the only option available to you if the target area is difficult to watch.

**Cameras**

Video cameras are available on the security market that are smaller than a matchbox and are as thin as a wafer. A camera such as this can be concealed in almost any object and placed in a position to view the target area.

Miniature cameras can be fitted with a variety of lenses to work in low light and long range

This camera is concealed within a smoke detector and is very effective for covert use

The camera can be fitted with various lenses that will give you a choice of wide angle or telephoto views. Many cameras come ready built, into objects such as smoke detectors, PIR detectors and wall clocks but it is for you to use your imagination in choosing where to conceal them.

Cameras produce either colour or black and white (monochrome) images. Colour cameras are more expensive but monochrome cameras can produce a better quality picture, especially in low light. The quality of the image is made up of TV Lines (TVL) rather like the pixel quality of a digital image on a computer screen; the more TV Lines

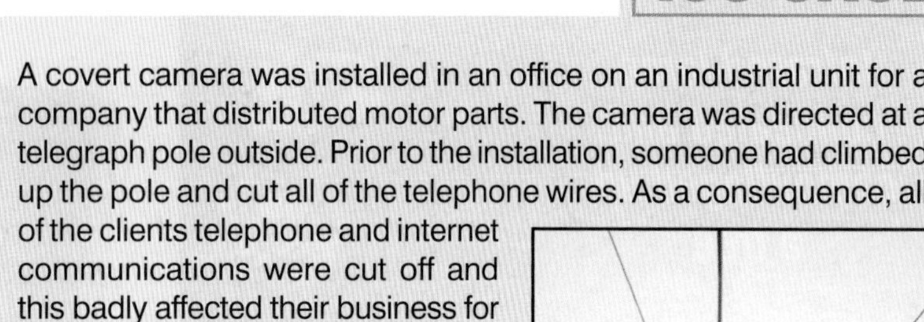

## ISS CASE

A covert camera was installed in an office on an industrial unit for a company that distributed motor parts. The camera was directed at a telegraph pole outside. Prior to the installation, someone had climbed up the pole and cut all of the telephone wires. As a consequence, all of the clients telephone and internet communications were cut off and this badly affected their business for a whole day until it was repaired.

The client's suspected the culprits were from a competitive firm operating on the same industrial estate who also traded in motor parts. The video tape was left to run and three weeks later the same happened again. The video tape identified the culprits who were from the 'competition' who used a forklift truck to lift someone up who took a swing at the wires with a hand axe. The Police were informed straight away and the individuals concerned admitted to committing criminal damage.

Infrared is useful at night-time and low-light situations, but ensure the illuminators are totally covert

This Envirocam is used in remote locations where video can be obtained over a week-long period with a sufficient power supply

the camera supports, the better the resolution. A camera of 380 to 520 TVL should be sufficient for professional use. Cameras also have a different threshold to the amount of light they will operate in, and this is measured in 'Lux'. Zero lux is total darkness. A 0.3 lux camera will operate quite well in low light situations whilst a camera with a 1 lux will not be so good as it needs a lot of light.

At the time of writing, we have a 'NiteDevil'' pinhole camera deployed which has a specification of 520 TVL and a Lux down to 0.0014. It is currently concealed in a wooden gate post and produces excellent quality in very low light. The area is also flooded with infra-red light.

*Infrared lamp concealed and camouflaged up a tree*

**Infra Red**

Monochrome cameras also have the ability to see infra red (invisible) light. Therefore, if you have a situation where you need to record in total darkness, a monochrome camera together with an IR light source should suffice.

Infra red light waves are normally transmitted at either 850nm or 950nm wavelengths. A floodlight transmitting on 850nm will give off a slightly red glow signature which is not 100% covert as opposed to 950nm which is invisible to the naked eye and totally covert. The floodlight in the picture requires 12volts to operate and an area of approximately 20 metres distant will be covered with invisible IR light. The lamp is fitted with a light sensor which enables it to shut down during daylight, which is useful if operating it from a 12v battery.

Many colour and mono cameras also come with an array of infra red LED emitters built around the lens for low light and night time. However, the LED's also tend to emit a red glow which is not 100% covert.

In the wiring diagram you will note that the camera requires power to make it work (12v positive and negative) which takes up two wires. We also have to get

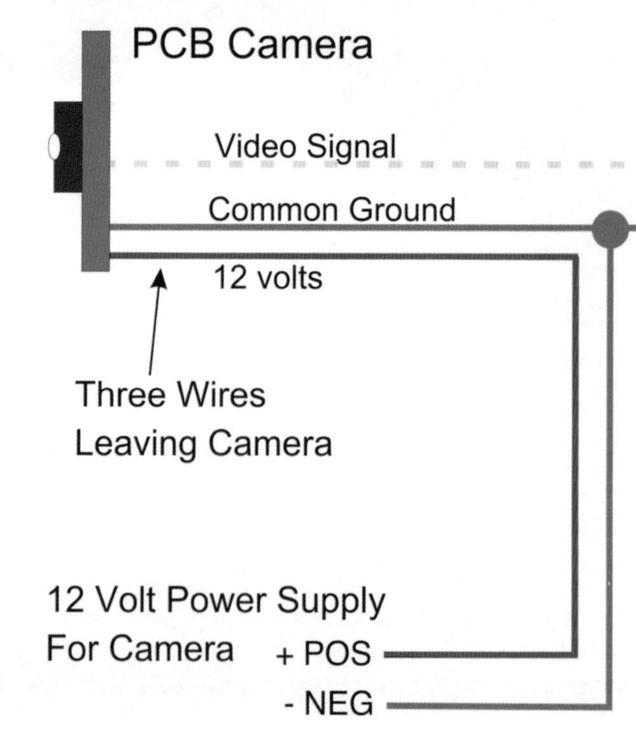

the video signal back to the recorder (positive video and ground/or negative) which takes up another two wires; therefore, four wires in total. Quite often, 4 core telephone cable is used to link a camera to the recorder, which is ideal for short runs up to 100 metres. Most cameras these days come supplied with connectors, cables and power supply which makes installation a very simple process. The hardest task and the most time consuming when installing cameras is actually laying and concealing the cable.

This DVR records four cameras simultaneously. The recordings can be transferred from the hard drive to a DVD

**Time Lapse Video Recorders (VCR)**

Time lapse video recorders are still being manufactured and used even though we are now in the digital age. These recorders can record up to 960+ hours onto a single VHS tape and will stamp the time and date onto the recording.

When recording, always set the minimum amount of recording time on your VCR to ensure the best quality in playback. A 24 hour time lapse VCR will also record at speeds of 3, 6, 12 and 24 hours. The longer you record, the poorer the quality and any movement will appear to be staccato. Most VCR's only accept one camera so if you need two or more cameras you will have to make use of a 'quad' or 'multiplexer' which has inputs for a number of cameras that streams the images onto one tape.

**Digital Video Recorders (DVR)**

4-core telephone cable is useful for long cable runs

The latest digital recorders do not use tapes but store the data (images) on a hard drive and so many weeks or months of data can be recorded. The storage capacity is measured in Gigabytes (Gb) and a 250 Gb recorder is an average capacity machine. One Gigabyte will give you approximately one hour of recording with one camera. Most DVR's will have a minimum of four camera inputs, make use of Video Motion Detection (VMD) and can transfer and burn the recordings to a DVD drive. They may also have the facility to transfer video or images onto an SD card.

The resolution settings can be altered to extend your recording capacity and the lower the resolution, the longer the recording time. I would suggest that you always set the highest resolution because it is likely that the recorders batteries will have to be changed well before the memory is full to capacity and so you will be recovering the data at the same time.

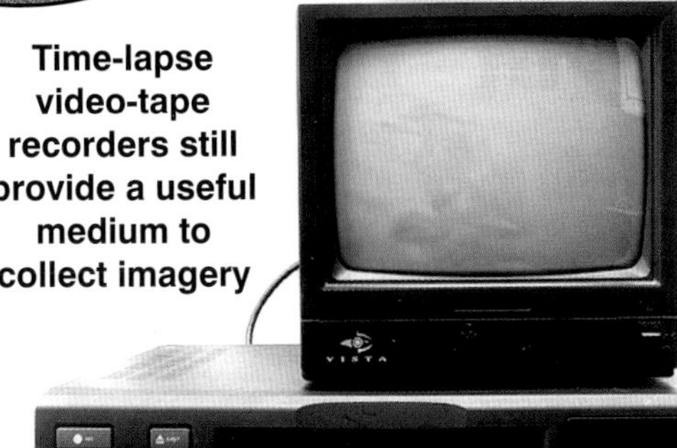

Time-lapse video-tape recorders still provide a useful medium to collect imagery

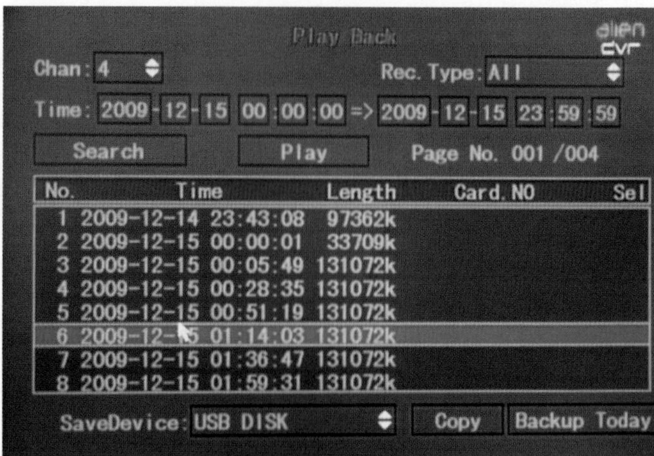


**The DVR has a simple playback facility as the recordings' time-length and size can be customised**

### TV Monitors

You will require a monitor connected to the recorder in order to set up the system and ensure the camera has a good view. These can be colour or monochrome and once the system is set up and recording, the monitor can be removed as it will not effect the recorder. The majority of monitors are now flat screen LCD.

### Radio Transmitting Cameras

If you are unable to physically link the camera to your video recorder by cable it is possible to transmit the video signal by radio waves to a receiver, which in turn is connected to your DVR. The camera and video transmitter will still require a power supply (mains or battery) but no other cables are necessary.

There are many video transmitters on the market and you really get what you pay for. Radio frequencies used for these transmitters in the UK are normally either 1.394GHz or 2.4GHz which do not require a licence. Some transmitters can provide a range of 1000 metres line of sight with a decent 'Yagi' antenna but some ranges are very limited.

### Cameras using the Cellular Network

A very good and effective system utilises the 3G cellular network (the mobile phone network) to transmit images. Some of these units are 'stand alone' and operate from an internal power supply and can transmit video footage over an infinite distance. Bibcom Ltd is a company that supply these type of devices and they are available in many disguises if required. The operator 'dials' into the device from a mobile phone using the 'make video call' facility and the camera's images are viewed live via the mobile phone. This unit also has the additional ability to send an image by text to your phone when movement is detected. You can then dial the device to view the activity.

**CAMERA CONCEALMENTS**

**GSM cameras manufactured by Bibcom Ltd**

**Why are the 'Crime Watch' videos always poor quality?**

Courtesy: BBC

Video tapes shown on TV of thefts taking place in shops often show that the picture quality is rather poor. This is due to a variety of reasons:

- Camera is sited in the wrong position
- Poor resolution camera
- The wrong lens such as too wide angle
- The lens is out of focus
- The lens not cleaned regularly
- Old tapes used in the recorder, they stretch and become magnetised after a short period
- Poor and old wiring
- A tape recording speed that is too slow
- Poor lighting
- Cheap, inexpensive equipment

**Old style VHS tapes tend to get stretched and magnetised if used too often resulting in poor quality recordings**

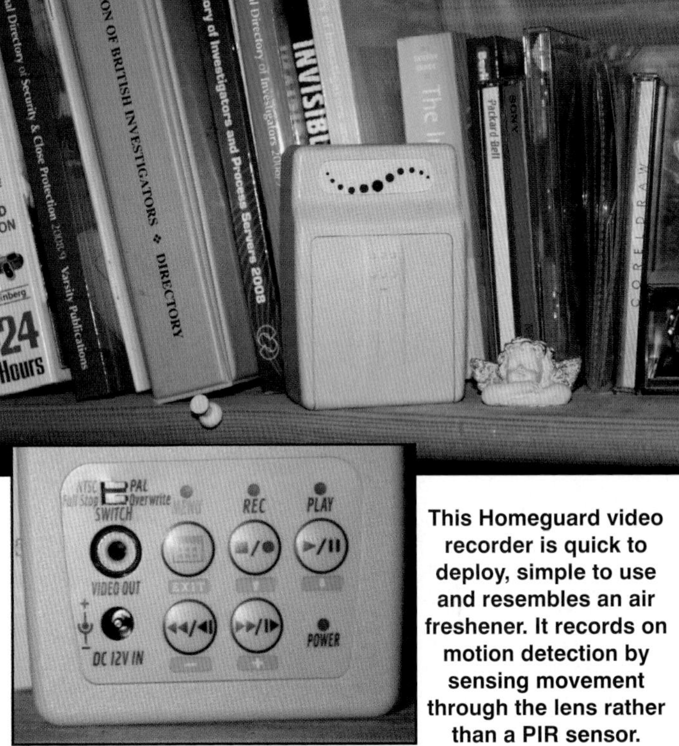


**This Homeguard video recorder is quick to deploy, simple to use and resembles an air freshener. It records on motion detection by sensing movement through the lens rather than a PIR sensor.**

More often that not, it is the tape that produces a bad picture because the user has used the same tape over and over again. Tapes should be changed for new ones on a weekly basis, which is another reason why digital recorders are preferable.

**These miniature Watec cameras are excellent quality and can easily be used with a variety of lenses**

Globe Police Solutions manufacture rapid-deployment camera systems

## RURAL RAPID DEPLOYMENT CAMERA SYSTEMS

Video photography in remote and rural areas is quite often needed to capture activity. A camera needs to be left in situ to record for a defined period and then retrieved at a later date in order to view the footage. Some systems use the mobile phone network in order to 'dial in' to the camera in order to view activity remotely on a laptop or mobile phone.

The cameras need to be weatherproof as they may be buried in the ground for concealment; they also need to be covert, especially the lens as this is the exposed part. The power system has to be very effective as it may have to run for up to a week and the batteries can be very bulky and heavy.

**Digital Video Recording Systems**

Most of these systems are excellent for rapid deployment. The units normally comprise of several low light cameras,

A laser pen is attached to the camera for sighting onto the target when deploying at night

An IR camera located up a tree. For additional concealment, a stocking net needs to be placed over the front lens

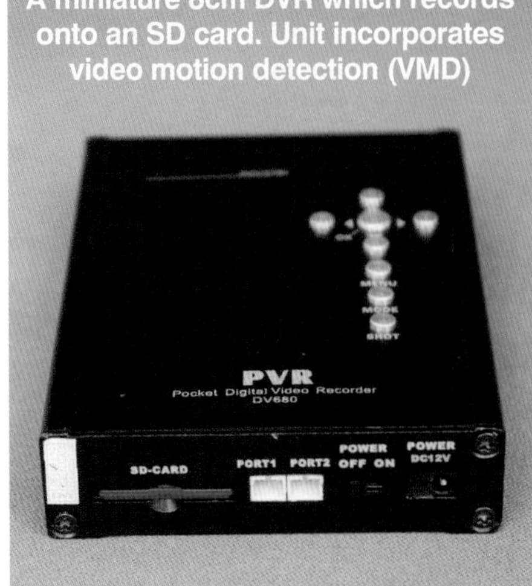


A miniature 8cm DVR which records onto an SD card. Unit incorporates video motion detection (VMD)

a digital video recorder and monitor (for setting up and playback) and the power supply. The type of video recorders differ and can store data onto a hard drive or SD type memory card. They can operate from mains supply or 12 volt car or leisure batteries. The very latest lithium batteries can run a camera system for five days without recharging, however, they are expensive.

Most have very similar recording features in order to preserve battery life and hard drive space. An internal timer can be set to record at chosen times of the day. Video motion detection (VMD) is very useful to enable the system to lay dormant until movement is detected and the recorder comes into life. Once movement is detected, the recorder will continue to record according to how the system is programmed i.e. 10 secs, 30 secs, 1 minute, 5 minutes or longer; if there is continuous motion, the system will keep recording.

Most motion detection systems have the ability to 'zone off' areas where there is movement which may accidentally start recording. This is good because if there is an area where branches on trees are moving about in the wind, or there is a road in the distance with traffic moving along it, they can be zoned off.

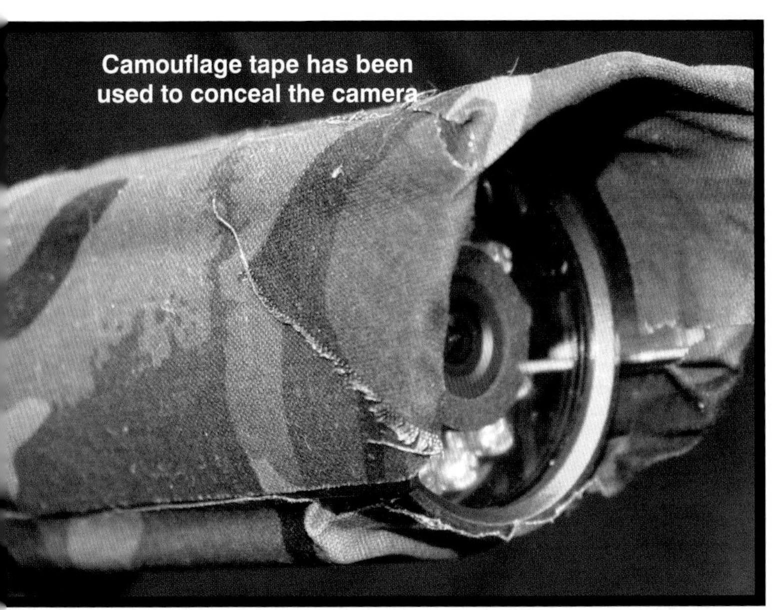

Camouflage tape has been used to conceal the camera

This pipe conceals a DVR and a power supply which is buried and left in the ground to record. The camera unit can be remoted by cable up to 3 metres

If you are using the motion detection facility, ensure that the camera is fixed to something that it is rock solid, not a branch or pole that may vibrate or move otherwise the camera will move about and set the camera recording. If necessary, use the motion sensitivity control to 'tweak' the system. You may find that the recorder has a high, medium and low setting; I would suggest setting it to low initially to avoid any false recordings.

Images taken with a NiteDevil pinhole camera. (See page 266-267 showing camera set-up)

Some lenses have built in infra red LED's (light emitting diodes) for use at night. They are effective to a range of 5 to 10 metres and are excellent for reading a car's number plate. They do have their disadvantages as they use up more power from the batteries and they are not 100% covert as they give off a slight pink glow in the dark. In addition, if you are using motion detection, expect many false recordings as moths fly into the IR beam and set off the motion detection. Quite often you can review a recording and find there is nothing on it because a moth has flown past and disappeared by the time the recorder has activated. In addition, infra red light can also reflect off heavy rain drops and cause the VMD to activate.

Any movement captured in the area zoned off in red triggers the recording system

## EnviroCam Rapid Deployment Systems

This small and neat video recording system is supplied by Globe Police Solutions and is excellent for quick camera deployments. It comes supplied with various focal length lenses, from close up and wide angle to telephoto and it has IR lighting. The recordings are stored on an internal 150Gb hard drive or an SD card and are date and time stamped. The internal batteries last for about 18 hours but an external lithium power pack can run it for approximately 5 days.

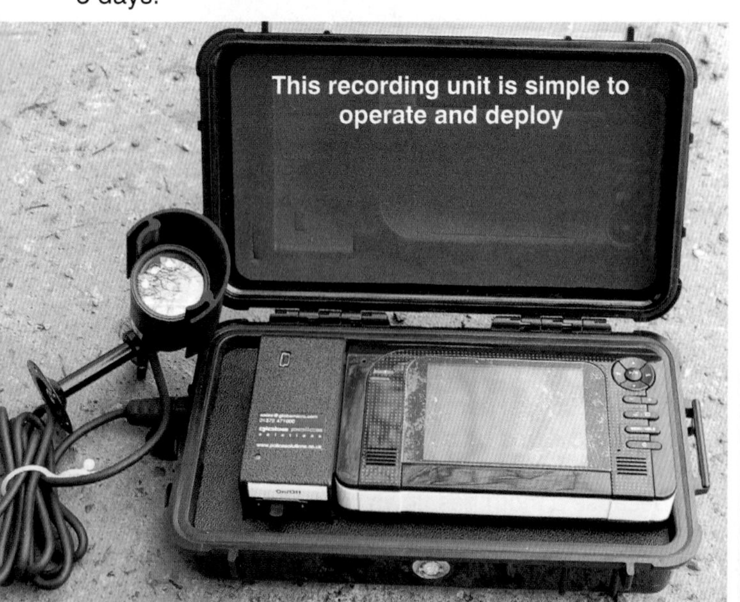
This recording unit is simple to operate and deploy

The latest version, transmits any motion detection to a server via the 3g mobile phone network. You are then able to monitor any activity that is taking place, live.

## The Envirocam 3

This system built by Scanguard, is also very effective and has all of the features of the above system. With a built in modem it can be remotely controlled and monitored from a distance. Recordings are stored on a removable hard drive so that you do not have to disturb the unit for long when servicing it.

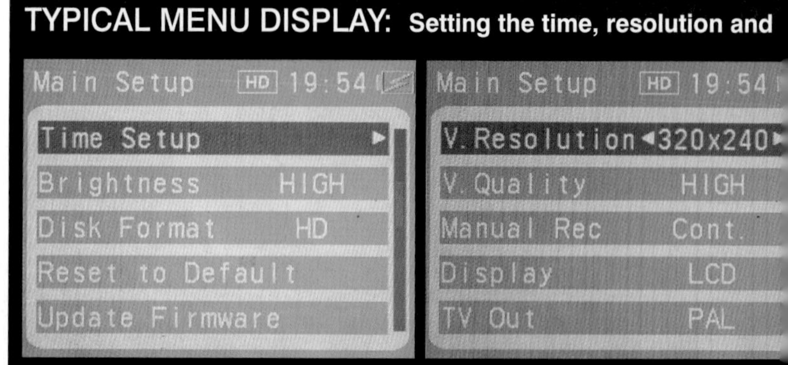

Camera concealed in a simulated pile of cement

The cameras can be camouflaged with paint, tape or material and mounted with brackets onto tree trunks or other solid surfaces. Sometimes the lens has to be mounted into a roadside object such as a sign post, bollard or a fake boulder.

### Camera Deployment

If you are using these camera systems, there are various checks to be made before, during and after deployment. It may be that you have to deploy in the same manner as an OP team would, described in the relevant chapter. You should check:-

- *Batteries are charged and connected correctly*
- *The SD card is reformatted and has enough memory*
- *Camera lens is clean and concealed in a 'Trojan'*
- *The date & time is set correctly*
- *Other settings such as motion detection are set correctly*
- *All connections are firm and weatherproofed*
- *The unit is weatherproof and covered with soil proof bags*

It is recommended that the resolution and recording quality is set to the highest possible setting, as it is likely that the batteries will fail long before the hard drive is actually full. Various focal length lenses should be available to enable you to site the cameras as various distances from the target area. You should be familiar with their limitations and what they are actually able to see. For example, a 3.5mm lens will cover a very wide angle of view but will only be able to read a number plate of a vehicle 3 metres away. A camera fitted with a 12mm lens will be able to read a number plate at 20 metres but will have a narrower viewing arc.

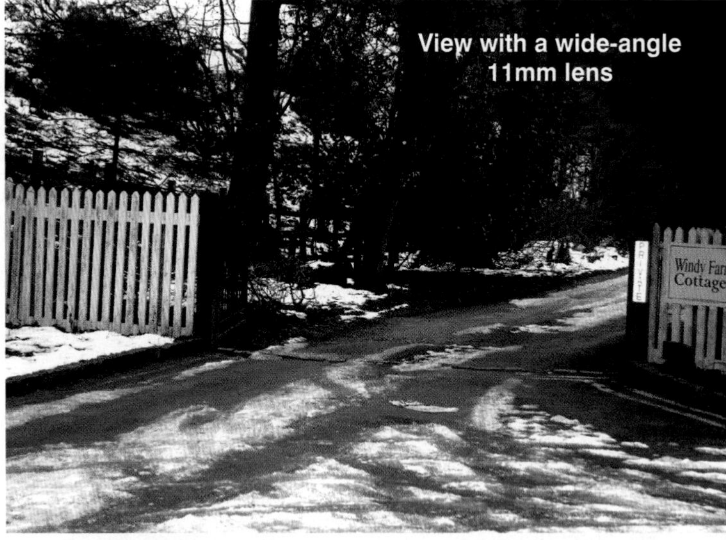

View with a wide-angle 11mm lens

View with a wide-angle 4.5mm lens

The camera deployment can be carried out covertly or overtly, either by going in early morning or late at night, using the darkness as cover with a back up close by keeping watch. Sometimes it is better to deploy the system overtly wearing Hi-Vis jackets and hard hats as you will appear to be carrying out roadside ground works.

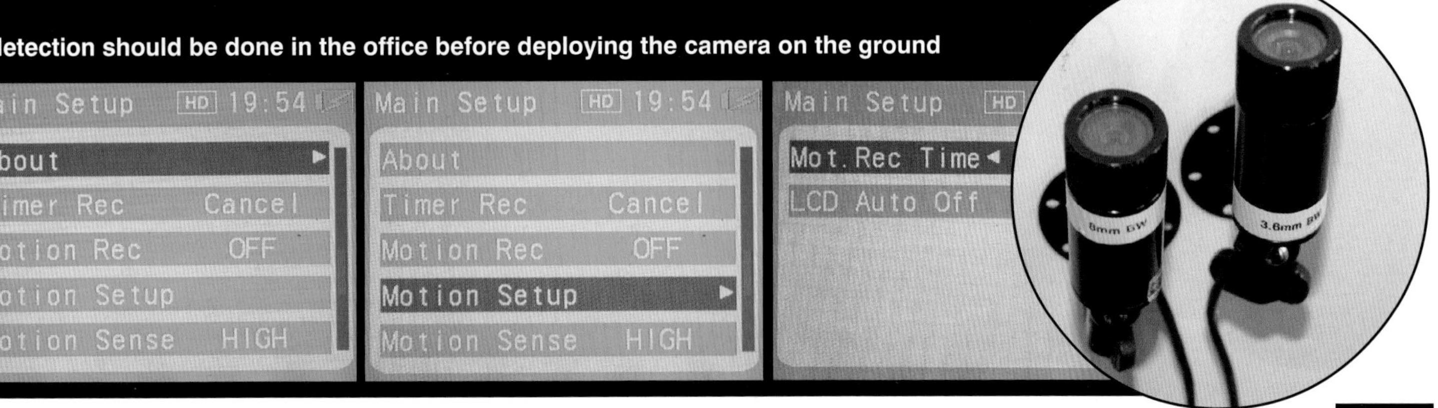

detection should be done in the office before deploying the camera on the ground

Concealment of cables and recording unit is paramount

**Action at the site**

On arrival at the site, carry out a radio check to your back up who should be acting as a lookout. Have a quick look around the area to ensure it is clear of third parties.

If you are sighting the camera at night, you may find it useful to attach a laser pen to the top of the lens pointing in the target direction. This will enable to you correctly aim the camera in the dark.

It is possible that the equipment will have to be covered in camouflage material and pushed into a hedge for concealment or it may have to be buried in the ground but be sure not to leave any ground sign that will give it away. Find a secure place for the camera and ensure it is concealed well and covers the correct arc of view; remove any twigs that may affect the video motion detection. Run the camera's cable back to the recorder and bury it if you can, to prevent rats and other animals nibbling through it. Ideally, the recorder should be as far away from the camera as possible as you may have to return to it frequently to recover data or replace batteries. You should

A camera is concealed inside a fence to view through a 2mm aperture

High-speed camera lens which is as effective as a night vision camera

avoid disturbing the camera which is at the 'business end' as much as possible. It may also be necessary to bury the battery pack; again, try and keep it separate from the recorder in order to cause less disturbance.

If you have to dig, lay down a ground sheet for the soil then carefully remove a layer of turf which will be replaced later. Make the hole large enough for the equipment and then line it with a waterproof bag or bin liner. Ensure all the camera settings are correct, that the camera is pointing in the right direction and give it a test if you are using the VMD facility. Cover over and camouflage the area, checking that all cables and lenses are concealed.

Ensure that you have not left any tools behind and sprinkle the area with animal repellent crystals (Methyl Nonyl Ketone) to prevent foxes and other animals from digging it up. It has also been suggested that if you sprinkle the area with human hair (from a hairdressers), it will deter foxes.

After moving clear, you may want your back up to carry out a walk past or drive past to check the concealment. Make a note of where the equipment is concealed, draw a sketch or take a photograph in the event of someone else having to recover it. When you depart, carry out some anti surveillance in case you have been seen and followed away.

Camera is concealed in this roadside marker post. You may have to deploy a number of posts as decoys in order for it to become inconspicuous

The Envirocam can record up to four cameras simultaneously onto a removable hard drive

## Bushnell Trail Cameras

Another ingenious camera system from the USA is the Bushnell Trail Camera. Originally designed to be left in a forest to photograph wildlife such as deer and badgers. It is fairly small and can be attached to a post or tree pointing towards the target. Inside, it has batteries that last a number of months, a slot for the SD card onto which it records, and the programming buttons.

On the exterior, it has the lens, a PIR movement sensor, a flash (which can be disabled) and an array of infra red LEDs for night photography. Once set, the camera can be left in situ until it detects movement. Depending on how the camera is programmed, it can take a 15 second video clip or take a series of still images which are stored onto the SD card as JPEG files. The latest unit (Bushnell Trophy Cam) is fairly small measuring 4" x 5.5" x 2.5". It is excellent for long term monitoring of remote sites, gates or access routes.

Typical Bushnell Trail camera

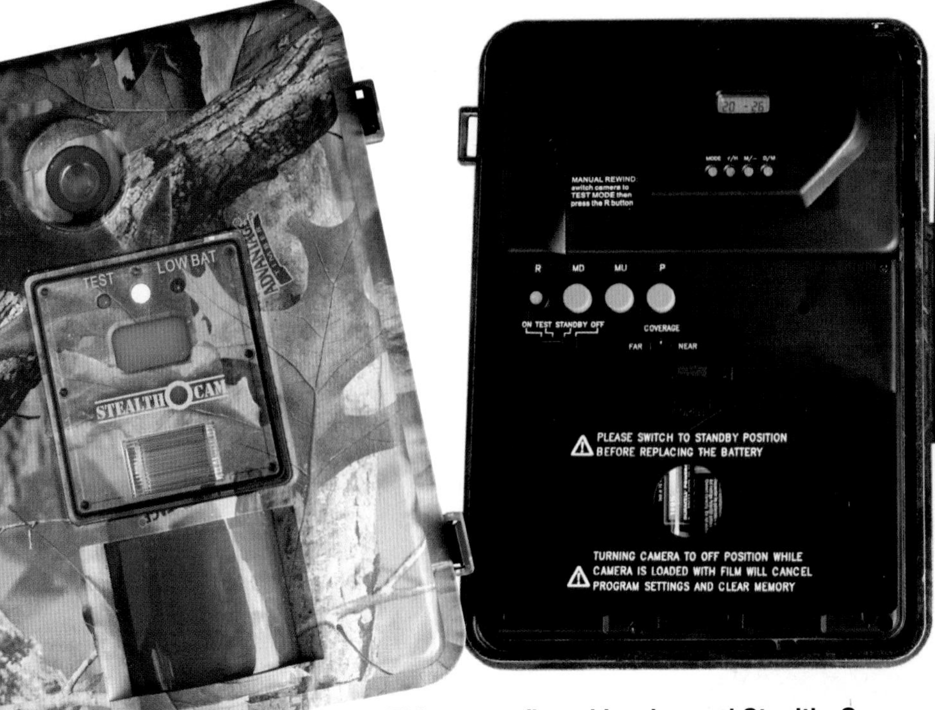


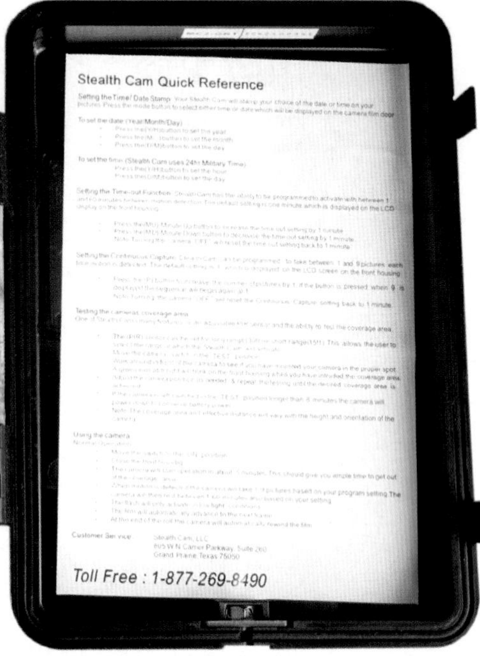


This camouflaged hard-cased StealthoCam records on a 35mm film as opposed to the Bushnell unit shown below which stores imagery on an SD card

## AUDIO MONITORING

Conversations taking place in a room or specific area can be listened to by using the following technology:

- Hard Wired Systems
- Transmitted Radio Signals
- Cellular Network

### HARD WIRED SYSTEMS

- **Hard Wired Devices**

A microphone placed in the target area can be concealed almost anywhere. A cable must run from the microphone to an amplifier (which gives the signal clarity, especially over long distances) or directly into a recorder. Headphones can then be connected in order to monitor the conversation.

Obviously, concealment of the cable is the most important factor when using this method. Redundant cables that are already in situ (such as unused telephone/computer cables or mains wiring, that are often found in offices) can be used to carry the signals from a microphone to the amplifier.

Hard wired microphones can be located in the target area, buried in wall cavities or even listened to through the wall

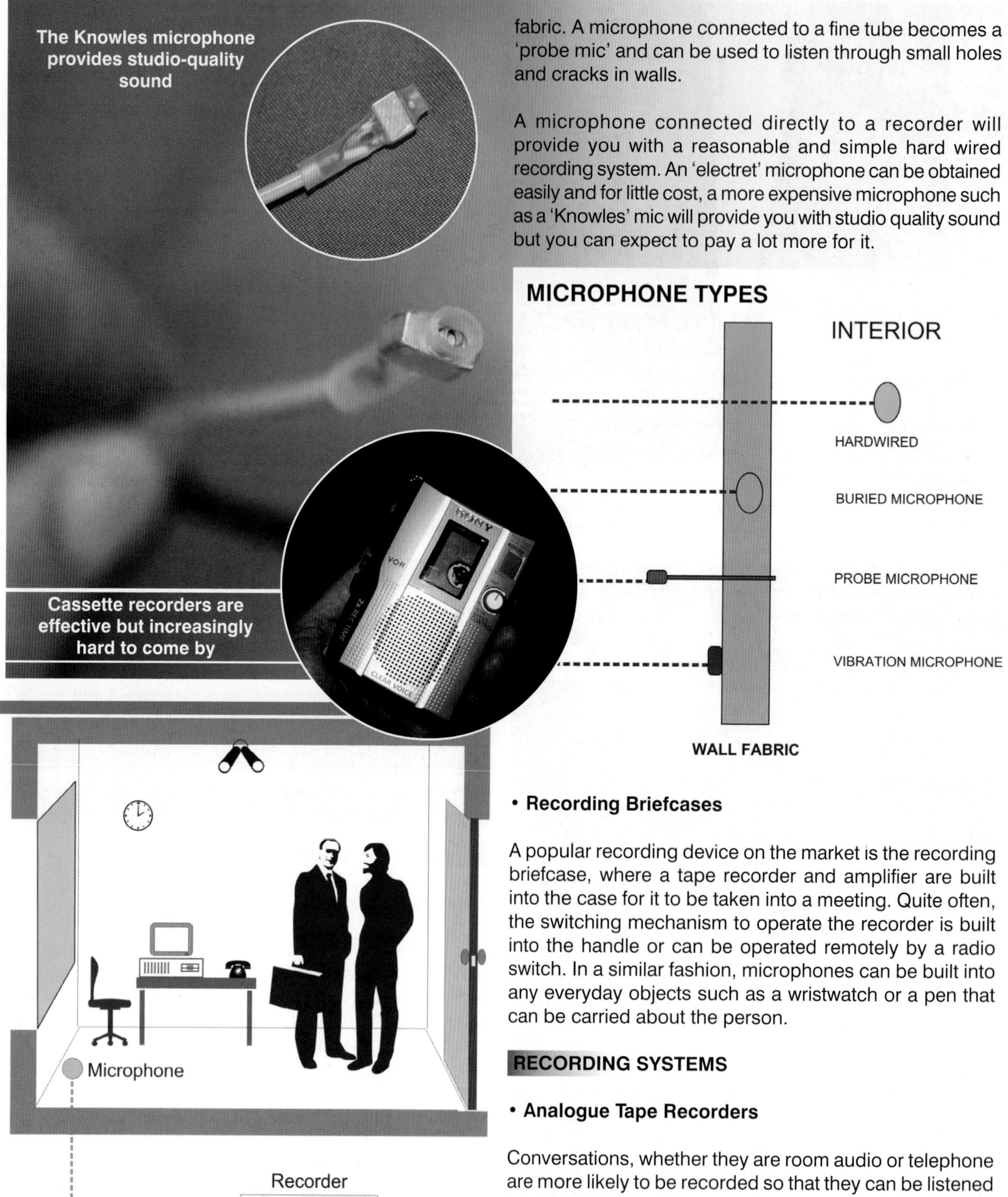


The Knowles microphone provides studio-quality sound

Cassette recorders are effective but increasingly hard to come by

A hard-wired microphone connected to a recorder via an amplifier

fabric. A microphone connected to a fine tube becomes a 'probe mic' and can be used to listen through small holes and cracks in walls.

A microphone connected directly to a recorder will provide you with a reasonable and simple hard wired recording system. An 'electret' microphone can be obtained easily and for little cost, a more expensive microphone such as a 'Knowles' mic will provide you with studio quality sound but you can expect to pay a lot more for it.

- **Recording Briefcases**

A popular recording device on the market is the recording briefcase, where a tape recorder and amplifier are built into the case for it to be taken into a meeting. Quite often, the switching mechanism to operate the recorder is built into the handle or can be operated remotely by a radio switch. In a similar fashion, microphones can be built into any everyday objects such as a wristwatch or a pen that can be carried about the person.

## RECORDING SYSTEMS

- **Analogue Tape Recorders**

Conversations, whether they are room audio or telephone are more likely to be recorded so that they can be listened to at a later time. There are many different types of tape recorders available and some that can record for six hours or more on a single side of a cassette. Cassette tapes are not very common these days and are of a poorer quality than digital, although they are still used.

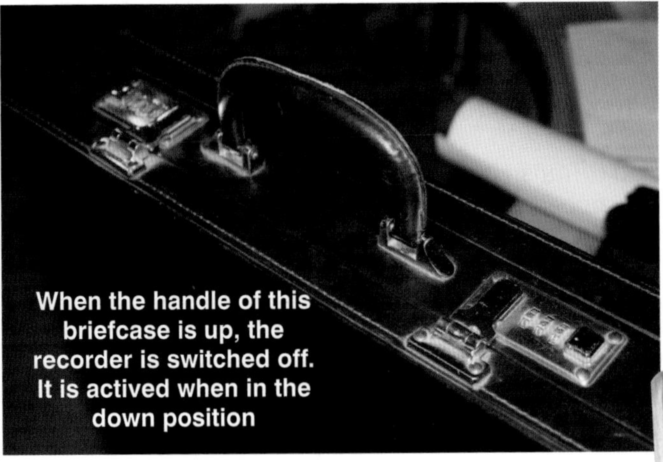

When the handle of this briefcase is up, the recorder is switched off. It is actived when in the down position

• **Voice Activation**

Many recorders have a voice activation facility or 'VOX' as it is often called. This enables you to set the level of noise to be recorded and therefore the recorder will remain dormant until a sound such as a voice is heard, then start recording. In surveillance this can be very unreliable (except for telephone tapping) as the VOX system will pick up every other external sound. If you wish to record conversation in an office for example, the VOX will also activate if it hears a telephone ring, a radio playing in the background or a door slam. This system will not work in vehicles as the engine noise, road noise and car stereo/ radio will also activate the recorder.

• **Digital Recorders**

Digital recorders are very common in the form of memo recorders or Dictaphones and produce very high quality reproduction.

Using these devices has its 'pros and cons' but the main advantages are:

- They are small, lightweight and easy to conceal
- Exceptional audio quality
- Very power efficient
- They can record for over 30 hours
- The date and time is stamped onto the recording
- You can connect to an external microphone
- They can be used for telephone monitoring
- Can be connected to conventional tape recorders
- Recording can be downloaded and sent by email

These devices are approximately 3 x1 x 9cm in size, weigh about 50g and can be concealed easily in a shirt pocket. When they were first introduced they were very expensive but they can now be obtained for as little as £35.00.

A covert miniature digital recorder manufactured under the 'EDIC' range are very small and store audio recordings on a flash memory. The devices can record up to 1,200 hours of conversation.

EDIC Mini shown in comparison to a regular matchbox

**Electronic Stethoscopes**

A surveillance device often referred to as a 'Through Wall Microphone' consists of a ceramic contact microphone that is placed onto the wall adjacent to the room you wish to monitor. The microphone picks up the audio vibrations that travel through the wall like a large eardrum. The microphone is connected to a high gain amplifier to which headphones or a recorder can be connected; it can also be used to listen to the floor above or below you.

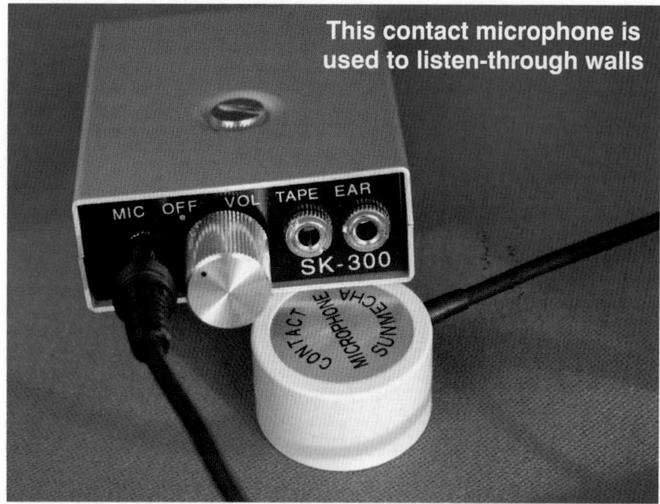

This contact microphone is used to listen-through walls

## Mains Carrier Systems

This system has a special microphone unit that draws its power and also transmits its signals through the electrical ring main in a building. It operates in very similar ways to a domestic 'Baby Monitor' whereby a listening unit is plugged into the mains socket of the baby's room. In another part of the house, a similar receiving unit is also plugged into the wall and can listen to the sounds of the baby crying.

The audio is not transmitted through the air by radio but the signal is 'carried' along the mains wiring system in the house. Purpose built eavesdropping devices can be covertly installed in the mains system to operate in this way or, the electronic components inside the baby monitor can be removed and adapted. Such units cost around £20.00 in a baby store.

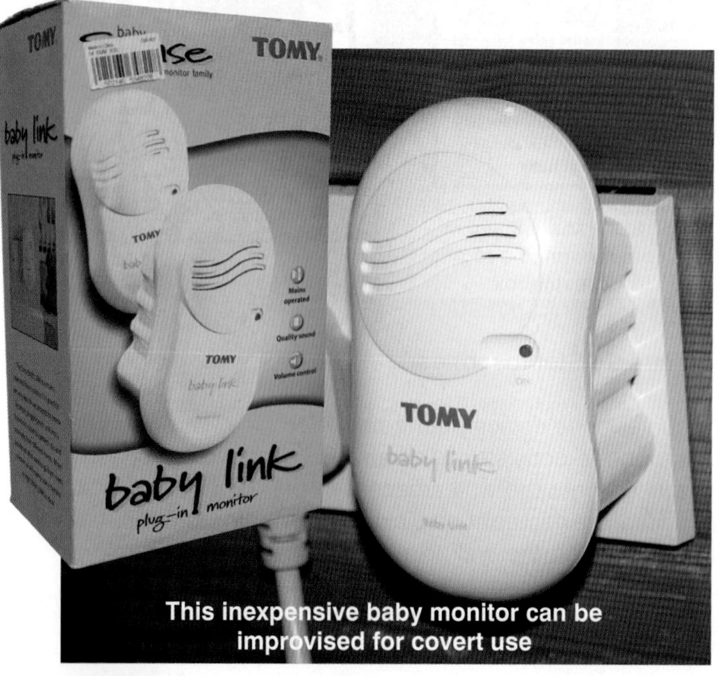

This inexpensive baby monitor can be improvised for covert use

## RADIO TRANSMITTING MICROPHONES (BUGS)

### • Transmitted Radio Signals

Radio Transmitters (Bugs) are small devices that can be left concealed in the target area. They will pick up conversations via a microphone and then transmit the signal to a receiving unit located nearby. This receiver can be monitored with headphones or be connected to a recorder.

Transmitters can be manufactured and supplied as 'stand alone' units or disguised in everyday objects such as calculators, pens, mains power sockets or built into briefcases.

Transmitters require an electrical supply in order for them to operate. They can be battery powered, mains powered, telephone line powered, solar powered, or a combination of all four.

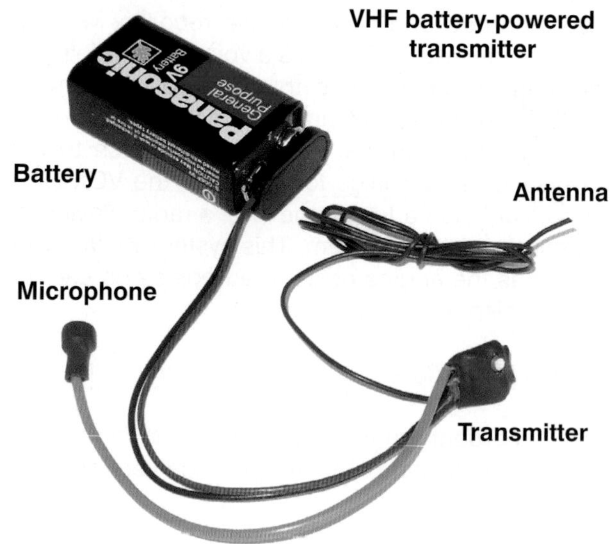

VHF battery-powered transmitter

### • Combined Room and Telephone Transmitters

This device is also powered from the voltage found in telephone cables (approximately 49 volts) and is able to transmit room audio via a microphone. However, when the telephone is used the microphone is cut off and the telephone conversation is transmitted. When the telephone handset is replaced, it switches back to monitor the room.

All of these transmitting devices can be easily located with counter measures using equipment such as Radio Frequency (RF) detectors, but only when they are transmitting. Be aware, when carrying out counter-surveillance sweeps using RF detectors such as the Scanlock, OSCAR or CPM700, that a transmitter that is switched off during an electronic search or sweep will not be located easily as it will not be emitting radio signals (RF).

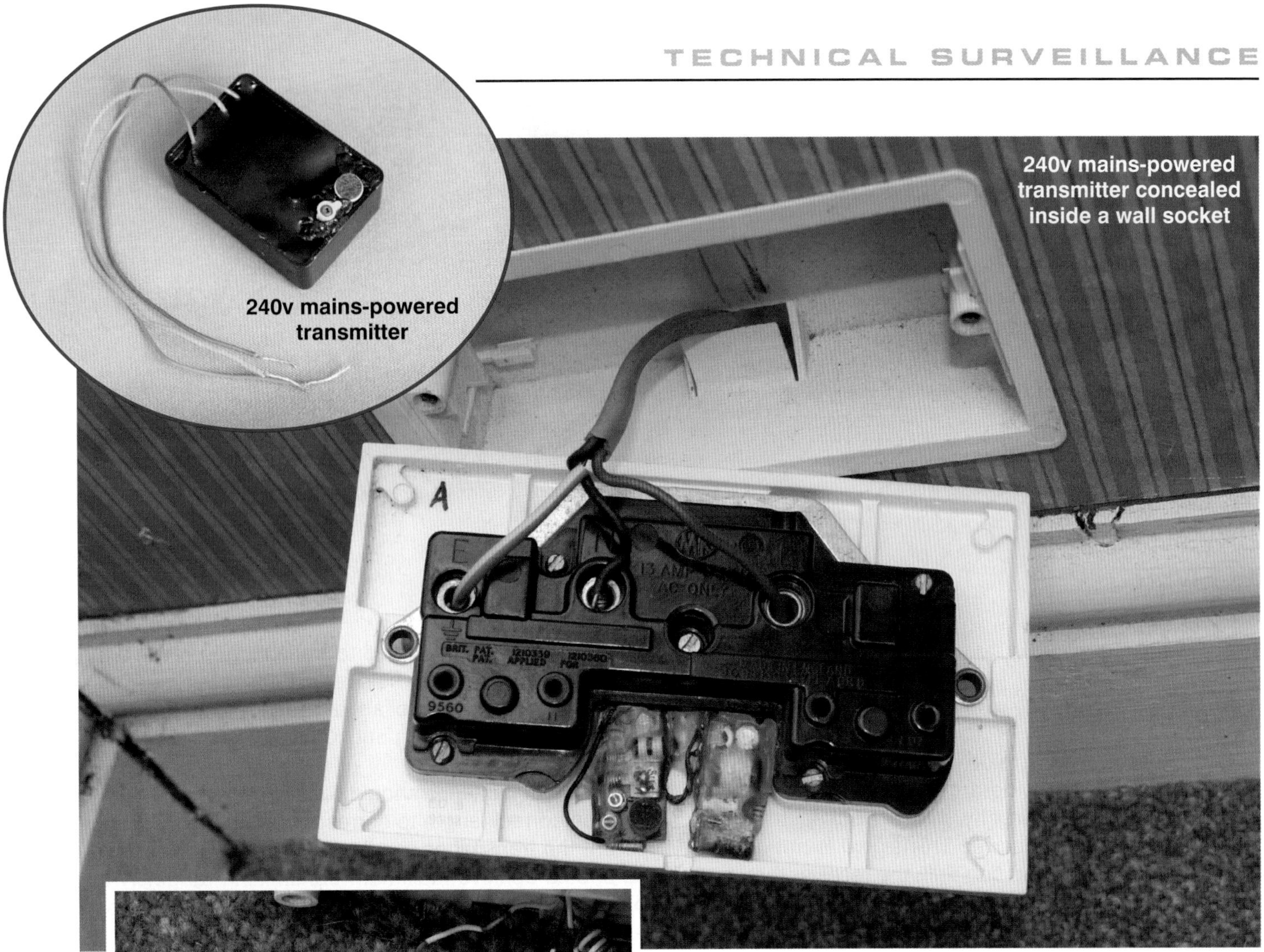

**240v mains-powered transmitter**

**240v mains-powered transmitter concealed inside a wall socket**

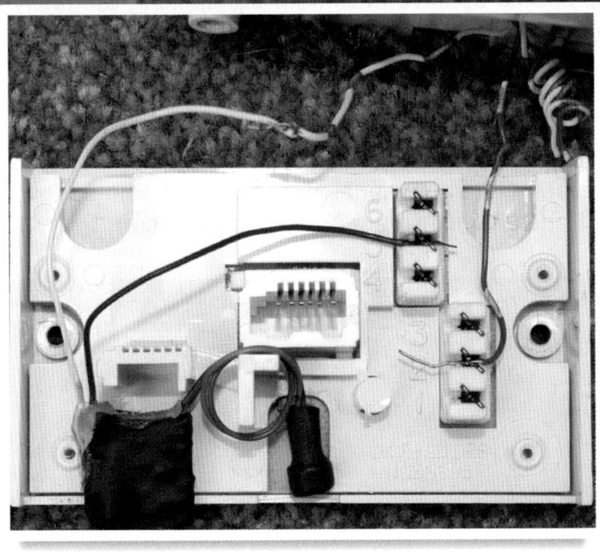

**• Voice Activated Transmitters**

Voice activated transmitters, although using up very little power whilst 'asleep', will power themselves up and start transmitting when a certain audio level is picked up such as voices and conversation.

These devices can be unreliable because any noise can trigger the transmitter such as ringing phones, passing traffic, radios or TV sets. If you are carrying out an electronic sweep it is advisable to play music from a CD player in the room that is being searched. This will activate any voice activated devices, that will otherwise will go undetected.

**Types of RF Transmitter**

There are two common ways in which these devices transmit signals, they are free oscillating or crystal controlled.

The free oscillating transmitter is normally a cheaper device to buy and should not be relied upon for professional purposes as the signals tend to 'drift'. They normally operate within the 'air band' frequencies of 108-138Mhz. The transmitted signal is propagated in a similar manner to water leaving a hose pipe that is being swayed from side

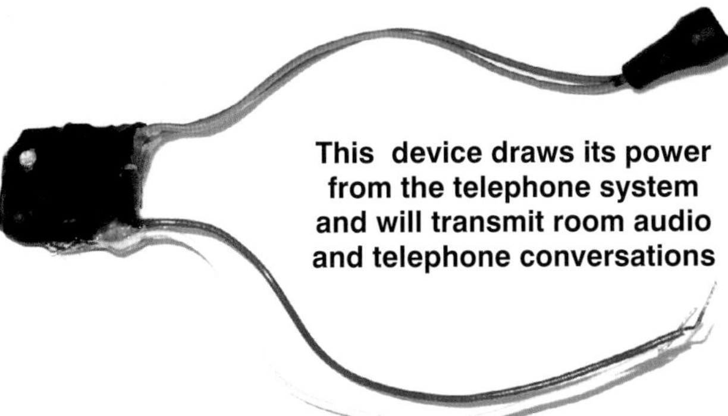

**This device draws its power from the telephone system and will transmit room audio and telephone conversations**

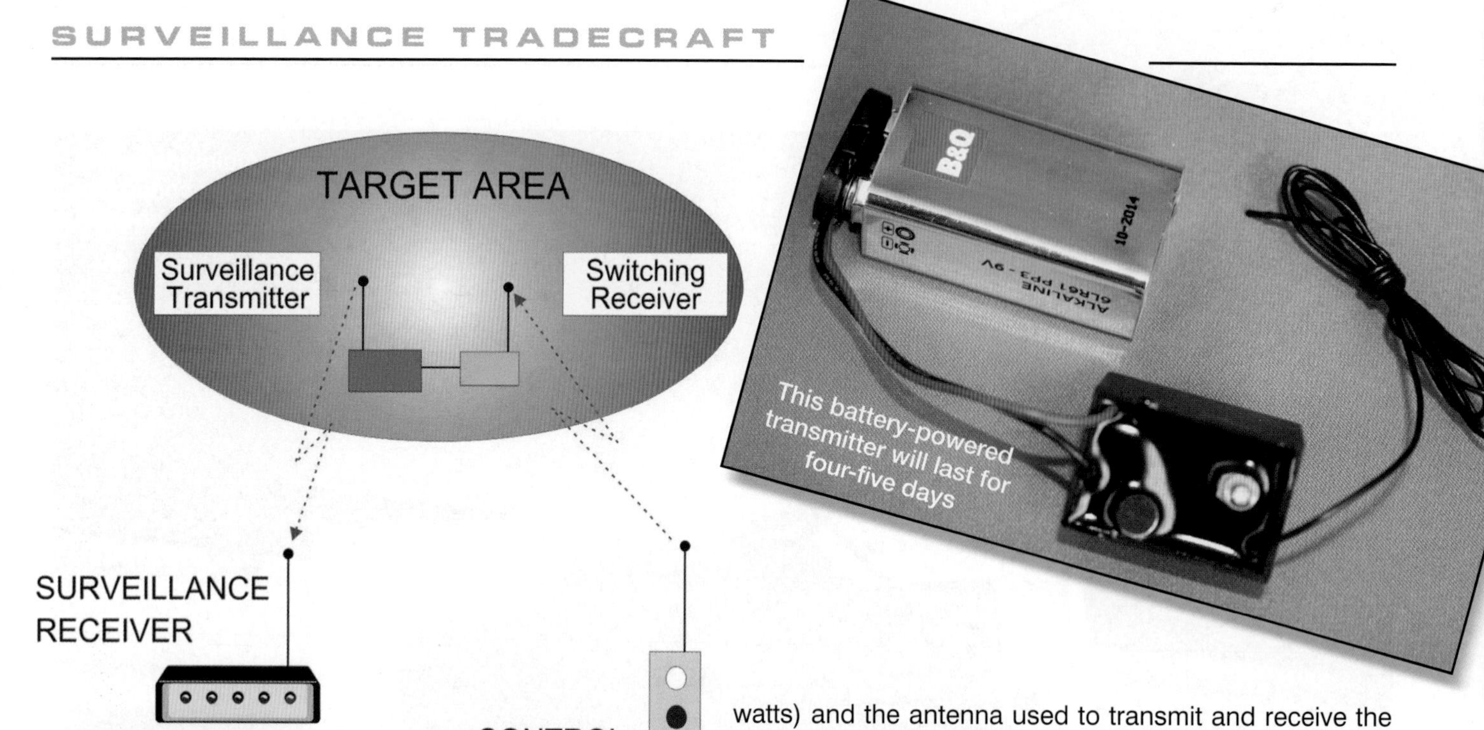


This battery-powered transmitter will last for four-five days

to side, the water spray will cover a wide arc and will not always land directly into a bucket, the radio receiver. This signal is not 'locked' and can drift; the receiver therefore, has to be continually tuned and would not be suitable for unmanned monitoring.

The crystal controlled signal is locked and is propagated in a similar manner to a fast steady jet of water, leaving a hose pipe and falling directly into a bucket. These signals are transmitted on a very narrow band to a dedicated receiver. They are very reliable because no tuning is required and the audio clarity is excellent. They are also more energy efficient than their free oscillating counterparts - but more expensive.

**Transmitting Frequencies**

The crystal controlled devices sold in the United Kingdom normally operate in the UHF band (318-490Mhz) or the VHF band (169-174Mhz).

Free oscillating devices often operate in the VHF band only and may use the frequency bands for commercial radio (88-108Mhz) or the Air Band (108-138Mhz).

**Transmission Range**

All devices have different transmission ranges; range is dependent on the power output of the battery, the power output of the antenna (normally stated in watts or milli-watts) and the antenna used to transmit and receive the signals. A standard hand held radio transceiver may push out 3-5 watts, whereas an average eavesdropping transmitter may only push out 10mw-50mw.

The transmitter antenna should, ideally, be vertical and has to be the correct length to correspond with the frequency used. If the transmitter has 'line of sight' to the receiver, you should achieve maximum transmitting range. When objects such as buildings, trees or hills come between them, the range will be drastically reduced.

The use of a high gain Yagi antenna will greatly increase your radio reception range. The Yagi antenna is similar in appearance to a TV aerial and should be pointed towards the transmitter to obtain maximum reception.

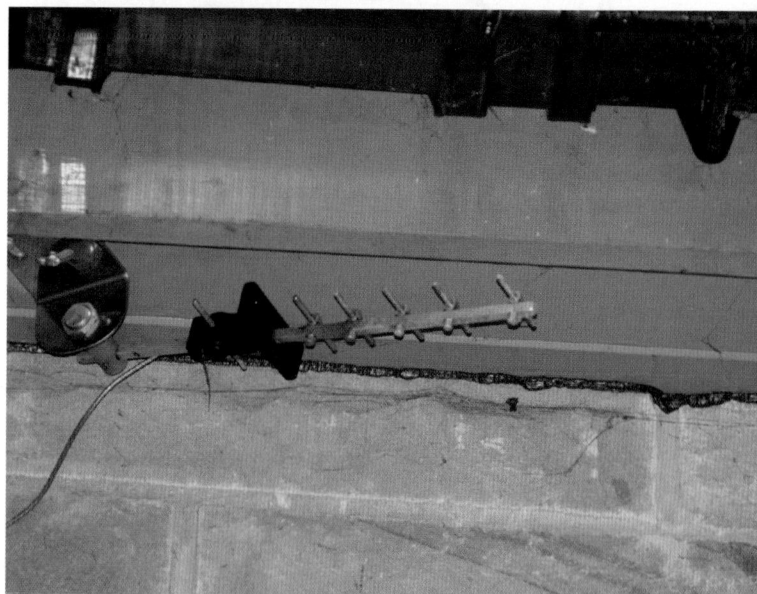

**This 20cm-long and discreet Yagi antenna is excellent for receiving transmissions over a long distance**

At times, we may have to monitor a transmitter from a considerable distance away. Transmitters bought from the run of the mill 'spy shops' will not be able to transmit for more than 300 metres for the reasons mentioned above. It would be difficult for these same devices to be installed in a vehicle to monitor conversations due to the shielding of the metal car body. If the engine is running, you will also encounter interference.

### Encrypted Transmitters

There are a number of suppliers that produce encrypted transmitters. The radio signal is 'scrambled', so it cannot be intercepted and listened into, like your standard device. However, RF locator/detectors can find signals transmitted from these devices, as easily as any other.

### Stage Microphones

One of the most effective audio transmitters available is a stage microphone used by performers on stage. The system comprises of a small transmitter (UHF or VHF), which is connected to a high gain microphone. This transmits to a dedicated nearby receiver with two antennas to ensure positive reception. The range is limited but the audio clarity is superb and far outclasses any surveillance device on the market today and in some cases, at a fraction of the cost.

### Radio Receivers

#### • Crystal Controlled Receivers

Crystal controlled transmitters normally come packaged with a dedicated receiver, the audio clarity received is excellent quality. Some receivers are the size of a cigarette packet and can be connected to a recorder.

#### • Tuneable Receivers

Tuneable receivers are normally used to receive 'free-oscillating' signals that operate in the 'Air Band' frequency range (108-140Mhz) and special receivers are available for this. These free oscillating devices tend to suffer from 'signal drift' and so constant fine-tuning is necessary to keep the signal clear; overall, they are not very reliable.

#### • Scanners

Radio scanners are receivers that are able to receive signals over a very wide frequency range. Individual frequencies can be stored into the scanner and then selected at random. If many devices are used on different frequencies, only one scanner will be needed rather than many dedicated receivers.

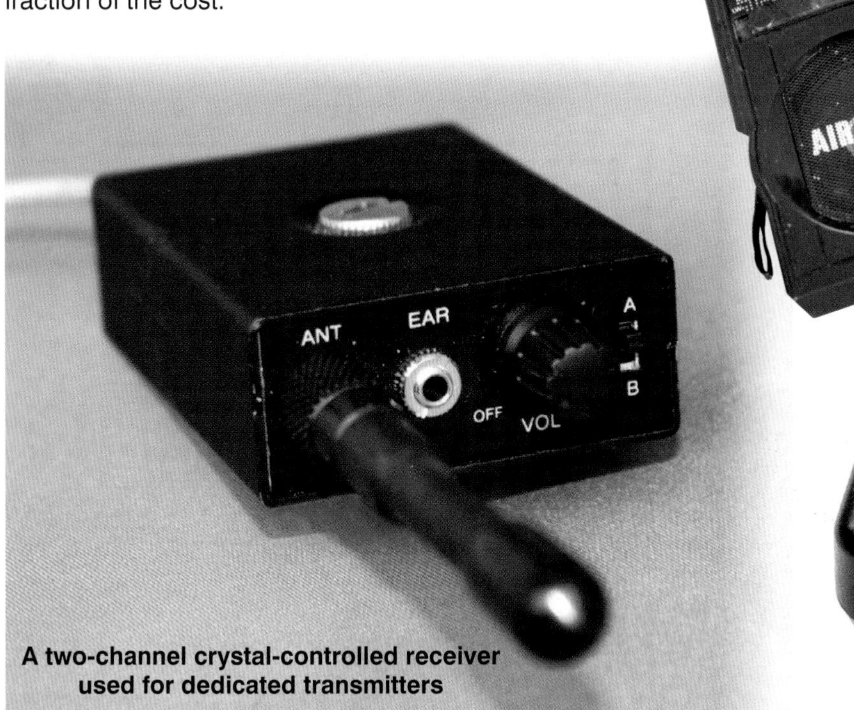


A two-channel crystal-controlled receiver used for dedicated transmitters

This device is used to jam cell phone signals in its vicinity. They can be bought on the open market but are illegal to use in the UK

Cellular Network Transmitters

In some respects, the radio microphones mentioned above are now outdated and have been replaced by their digital counterparts that transmit over the mobile phone network. This provides quality audio which can be sent over an infinite distance, as long as there is a phone signal in the area being monitored.

A basic device can cost you about £30.00, is the size of a match box and lasts for about 4 days on one battery charge. It has a SIM card inserted into it and therefore has its own telephone number. When dialled from a mobile phone or landline, the device 'opens up' and conversation in the vicinity can be heard. It can also be programmed to lay dormant but transmit to a pre-programmed telephone number on voice activation.

If you need to monitor conversations taking place in a vehicle, this is probably one of the most effective ways of doing so and the power supply can be obtained from the car's power system, if need be.

These devices can be purchased ready concealed in everyday objects such as a trailing power socket or a clock. They can also be improvised by using an old 'Pay-as-You-Go' mobile phone.

A low-cost popular GSM bug available from many spy stores

This high-grade GSM bug has two microphones for extra clarity

Make the following settings via the phones menu to adapt the telephone:

- *Turn the Ringer Tone OFF (to make it covert)*
- *Turn off the Display Light (to preserve power)*
- *Set the phone to Auto Answer (so it answers itself)*
- *Connect the hands free kit (to remote the microphone)*

When you dial into the phone it will not ring as you have turned the ringer off. After the second 'ring' the phone will 'auto answer' and open up the microphone in order for you to listen in (only with the hands free kit connected). Not all phones are able to do this but give it a try.

## TELEPHONE MONITORING

Intercepting telephone conversations is probably the most effective way of gathering information technically and can be acomplished in the following manner:

- Hard Wired Telephone Tap
- Transmitted Signals
- Induction Telephone Tap

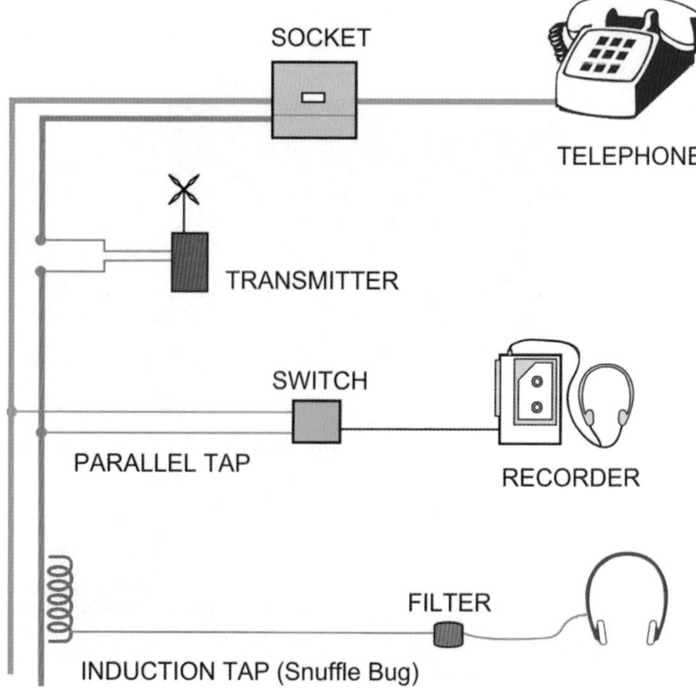

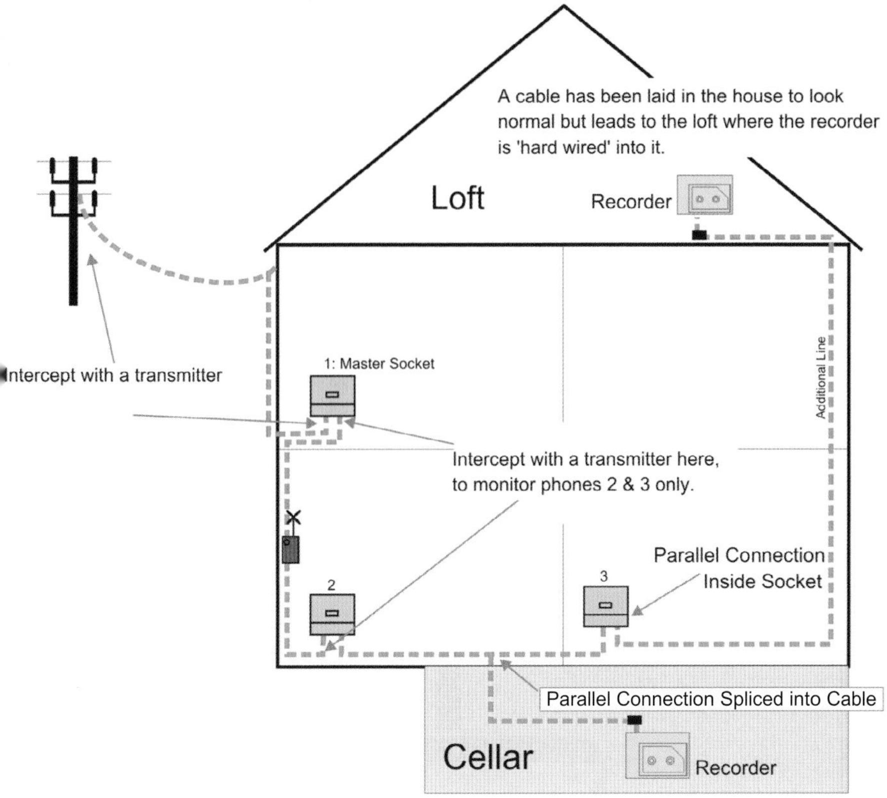

A cable has been laid in the house to look normal but leads to the loft where the recorder is 'hard wired' into it.

Loft

Recorder

Intercept with a transmitter

1: Master Socket

Additional Line

Intercept with a transmitter here, to monitor phones 2 & 3 only.

2

3

Parallel Connection Inside Socket

Parallel Connection Spliced into Cable

Cellar

Recorder

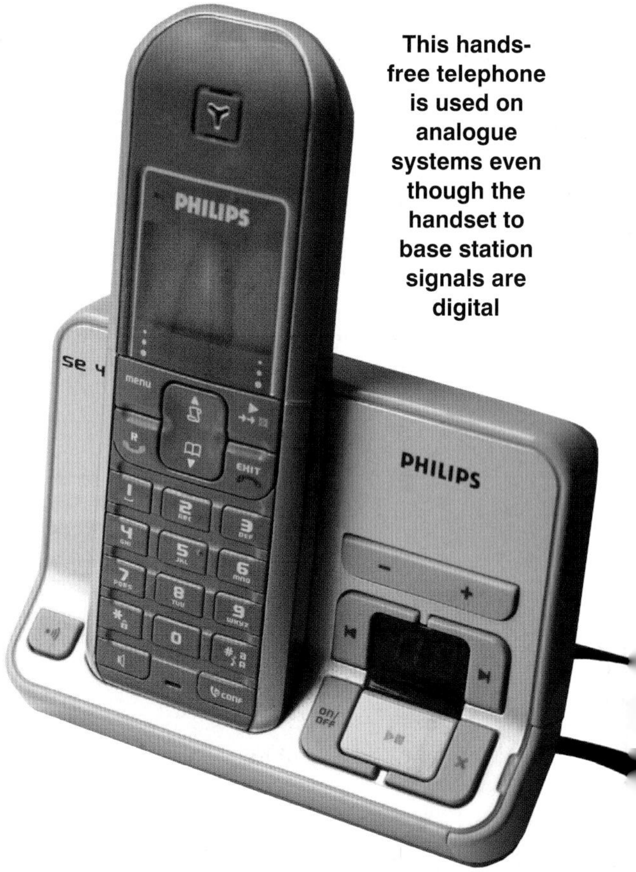

**This hands-free telephone is used on analogue systems even though the handset to base station signals are digital**

Telephone systems can be divided into two categories. Analogue or Digital. Analogue is the system normally used for domestic (home) systems and small businesses. The signals carried through the system cabling have not been processed and can be listened to effectively by attaching a pair of headphones.

Digital systems are more likely to be found in offices and businesses, these signals are converted into digital code before they are sent through the system. Due to this, the signals cannot be intercepted by conventional methods. We will later look at the methods of intercepting digital systems but first we will look at analogue telephone systems.

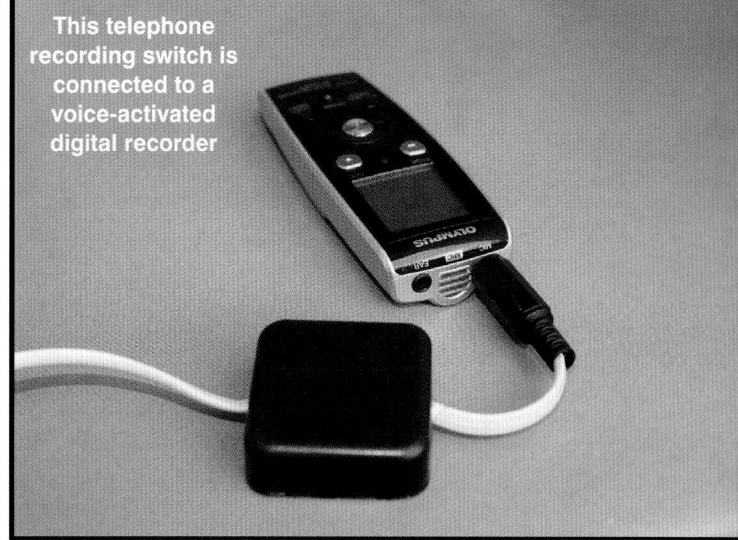

**This telephone recording switch is connected to a voice-activated digital recorder**

## ANALOGUE SYSTEMS

### • Hard Wired Telephone Tap

A tape recorder can be connected by various means to the telephone system and can intercept conversations taking place over one particular target telephone, or from any other telephone extension that is being used on the same circuit.

The recorder has to be physically connected to the telephone line and the signals pass through an interfacing switching device that stops and starts the recorder as the telephone handset is lifted. These switches can operate by voice activation (VOX) or by voltage 'relay' switches. This system is very effective and the recorder can be located in another part of the building some distance away from the target telephone. If you are unable to use the existing wiring, you may have to lay a separate cable that looks as if it is part of the system and run it to a safe, concealed area.

The switching device or tape recorder may be manufactured with a standard telecom plug fitted. If this is plugged into an unused socket it should record any of the telephones on the same circuit. If it is not feasible, or

PROHIBITED from direct or indirect connection to public telecommunication system. Action may be taken against anyone so connecting this apparatus.

This telephone transmitter is fitted in 'series' by splicing it into the wire that leads to terminal 5 in the telephone socket. Terminal 2 could also be used.

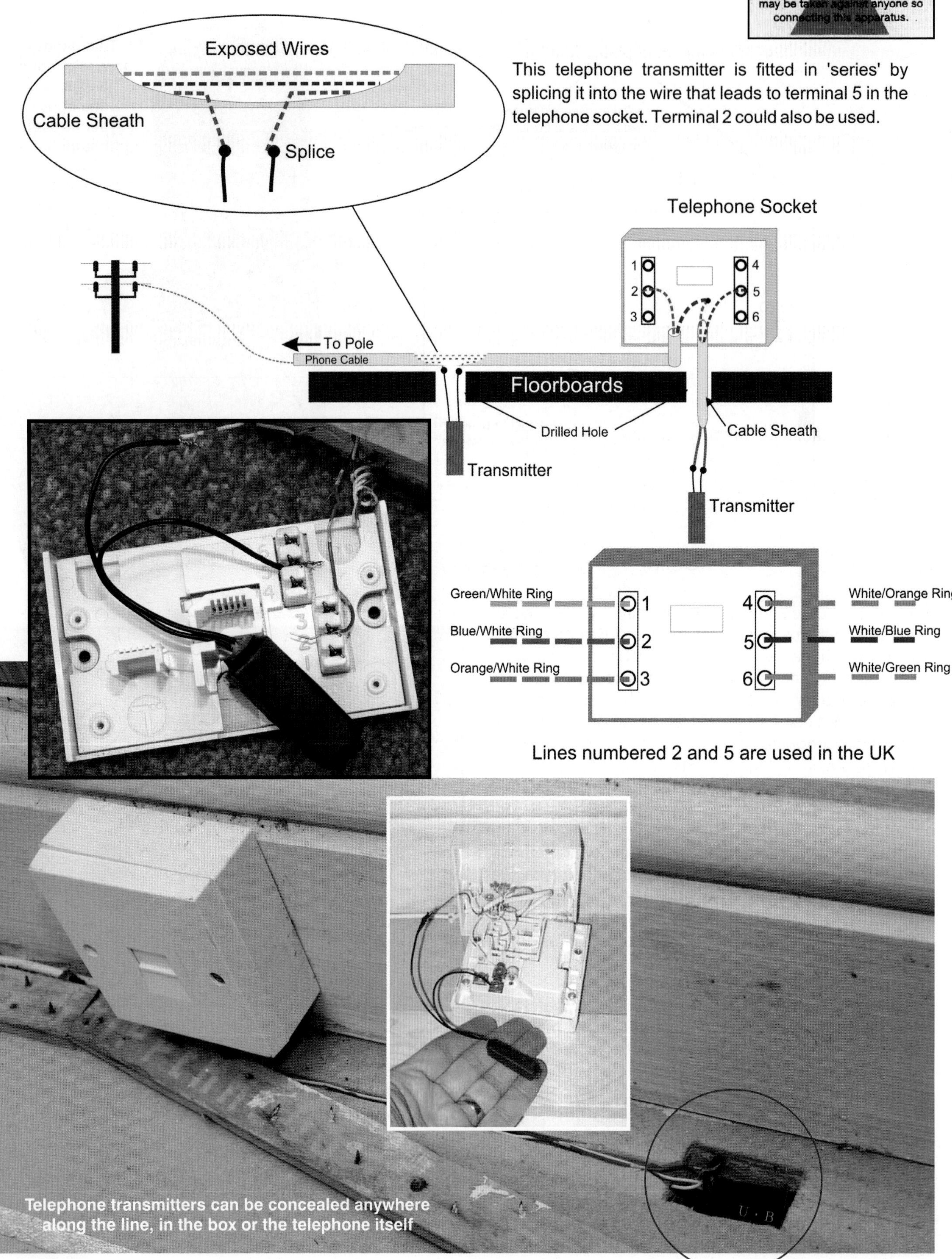


Lines numbered 2 and 5 are used in the UK

Telephone transmitters can be concealed anywhere along the line, in the box or the telephone itself

This telephone transmitter is spliced into one of the lines that leaves the telephone

covert to plug it into the wall socket, the plug can easily be removed, the two 'outside' wires made bare and then connected into the junction box or spliced into the two correct wires. These devices are normally to be connected in 'parallel' to the wires numbered '2' and '5' in a conventional socket in the UK. This will enable all the telephones on the same circuit to be recorded and the recorder can be located in a safe place.

A digital recorder can also be used to record the conversation if concealment and recording time is a major factor. The digital memo recorders can store many hours of recording time. A hard wired recording system will not be located by RF detectors.

**Telephone Transmitters**

In a manner similar to that of a room transmitter, telephone transmitting devices can send conversations over the air to a nearby receiver. The transmitters have to be connected to the line by splicing at a point between the telegraph pole and the target telephone or inside the telephone itself. Whether one telephone or many extensions will be intercepted will depend on how and where the device is actually installed.

There are various telephone devices available: the more common types rely on the telephone line voltage to operate them. Some have a rechargeable battery built into them to provide extra transmitting power. Telephone transmitters can be supplied as 'stand alone' units or come ready-made built into telephone sockets and adapters. In an analogue system, the wires connected to terminals 2 and 5 carry voice transmissions and it is one of these that the device is connected to.

When carrying out electronic searches ensure that the telephone handset is removed from its cradle and a dial

Recorder/receiver for monitoring telephone conversations

tone obtained, otherwise no signal will be transmitting for the RF detector to lock onto. In addition, do not assume that transmitters will be connected to the lines or junction boxes that you can see. Double check to see if any cables spur away to where transmitters may be 'remoted' to avoid detection.

The receiver / recorder will be located nearby and will lay dormant until the telephone handset is lifted and a transmission made. This is automatically picked up by the receiver, which then activates the recorder. The recorder then shuts down after the conversation has ended and the handset has been replaced.

• **Cellular Telephone Transmitters for Land Lines**

This device (sold as the 'Matrix') is a mobile phone which is used to transmit a land line telephone conversation. A single phone number is stored in the mobiles memory as it is this number that will automatically be dialled. It plugs into a spare phone socket or is spliced into the line that needs to be monitored. It has a switching system and a small battery pack for it to operate. When the target phone makes or receives a call, the switching system detects a drop in line voltage and activates the switch. The switch causes the mobile phone to dial the stored number and you can then listen to the conversation taking place. The mobile phone requires a SIM card on a pre-pay tariff and transmission range is not an issue as it uses the mobile phone network.

**THE 'MATRIX'**

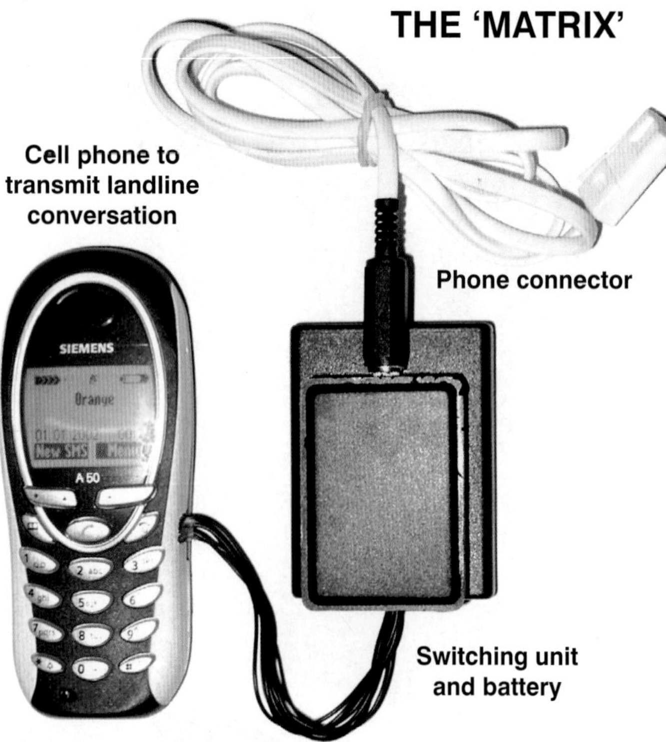


## DIGITAL TELEPHONE SYSTEMS

Telephone conversations on digital systems can be difficult to intercept as the signals are 'coded' or processed.

In order to monitor and transmit these signals, they have to be intercepted before they are digitalised. This means that a transmitter has to be installed to catch the signal as it leaves the 'curly' lead from the handset and before (or where) it enters the printed circuit board and becomes digital.

Once the correct pair of wires that lead to the handset ear-piece are identified you should be able to connect your transmitter. In digital systems, the power through the system is very low, therefore any transmitter will require its own power source and switch.

• **Fibre Optic Switch**

One switching system incorporates two light sensors which 'see' the ambient light from two short fibre optic cables. Two tiny holes are drilled into the telephone body (one in the handset cradle, the other on the top surface of the phone) and the fibre optics 'see' the light levels and activate a switch. The sensor that is set into the handset cradle will be in darkness when the handset is resting, the sensor on the surface of the phone will be in the light. This difference in light from each sensor sets the switch in the 'off' position.

When the handset is lifted from the cradle, the two sensors now pick up equal amounts of light that activates the switch and cause a transmission. This system is very clever but over-sophisticated when there are easier methods of carrying out the same task.

• **Hard Wired Recorders/Computers**

You do not necessarily require a tape recorder as there are interfaces available that allow telephone conversations to be recorded on a personal computer. In addition to the conversations, you will be able to tell the date, time and duration of any calls received or made. As with analogue systems, a device is available that can be attached directly to the digital telephone cabling but in this instance it converts digital signals to analogue, prior to being recorded. These digital devices are very expensive.

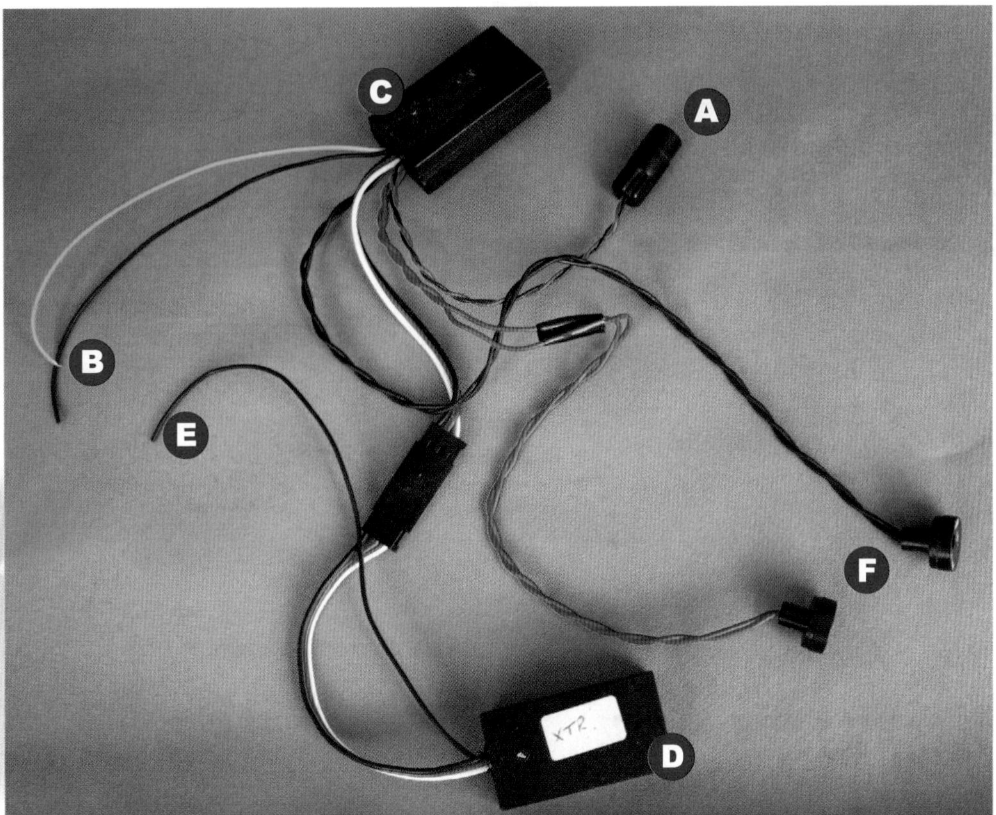


## DIGITAL TELEPHONE TRANSMITTER

| | |
|---|---|
| A | Battery connector |
| B | Wire connectors |
| C | Switching unit |
| D | Transmitting unit |
| E | Antenna |
| F | Fibre optic sensors |

Digital telephones can be monitored by computer

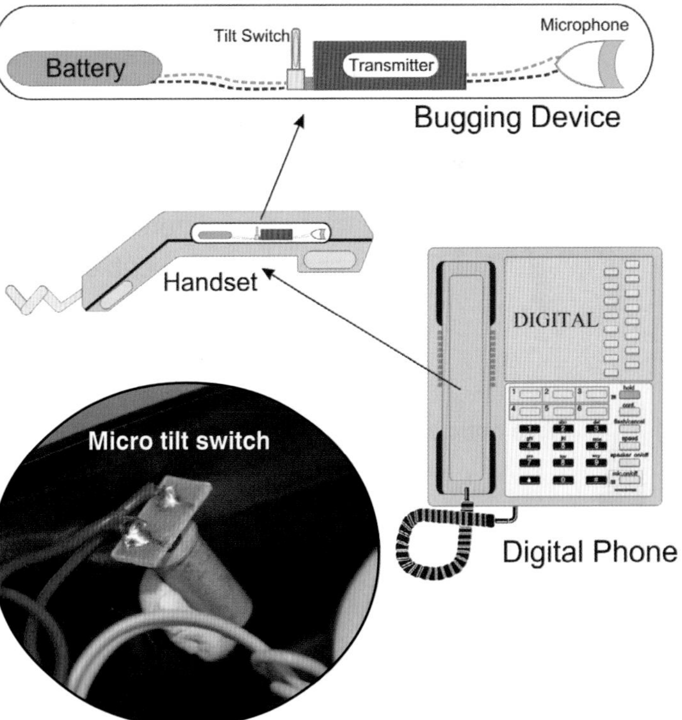


• **Handset Tilt Switch**

Another and much simpler system of monitoring digital systems is a normal room transmitter, but it is installed into the actual handset and has its own power supply which lasts for about one month. The microphone is able to pick up the voice of the person holding the receiver and also the person on the other end. In some devices, two wires are also connected to the telephone earpiece in order to hear the other side of the conversation. As it is battery operated, you would not want the batteries to go flat within a number of hours and so a small 'tilt' switch is used in order to power and activate the device. When the handset is resting in the cradle the device is dormant. When lifted up to the ear, the tilt switch activates the device and transmits. If you are carrying out TSCM sweeps with an RF detector, ensure that you pick up a telephone handset to activate any transmitters also shake the handset in order to activate any tilt switches.

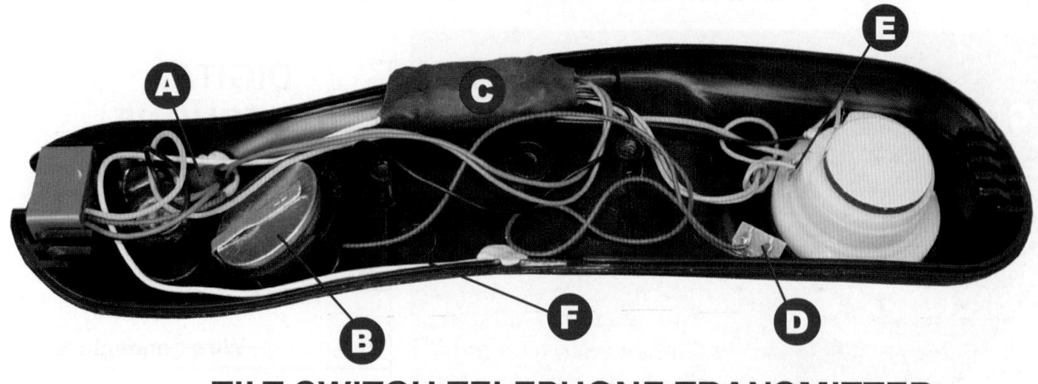


| | |
|---|---|
| **A** | **Microphone** |
| **B** | **Battery** |
| **C** | **Transmitting device** |
| **D** | **Micro tilt switch** |
| **E** | **Earpiece connections** |
| **F** | **Antenna wire** |

**TILT SWITCH TELEPHONE TRANSMITTER**

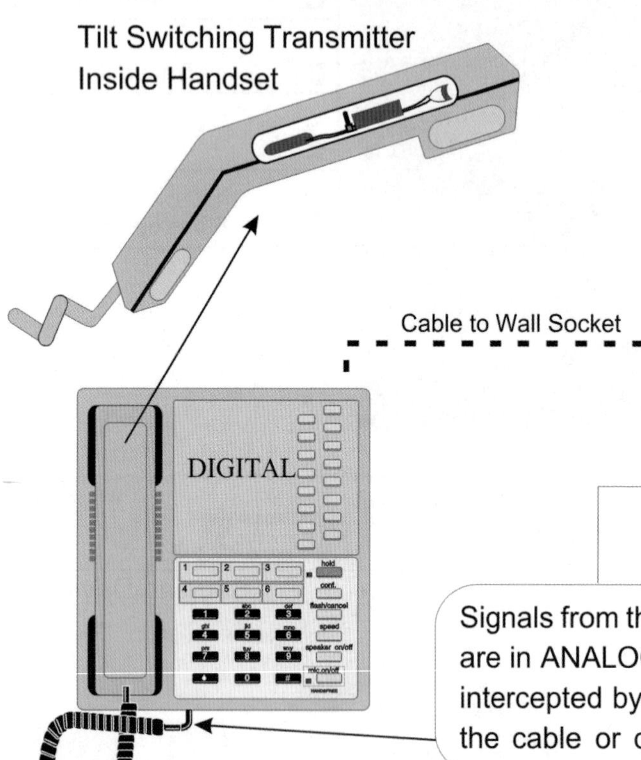


Digital to Analogue Converter

Wall Socket

Hardwired Recorder

Various methods of switching can be used such as Voice Activation or Fibre Optic Light Sensors which detect when the hand set is lifted from its cradle.

Signals from the handset to the base unit are in ANALOGUE form. Signals can be intercepted by splicing a transmitter into the cable or connector within the base

## ISS CASE

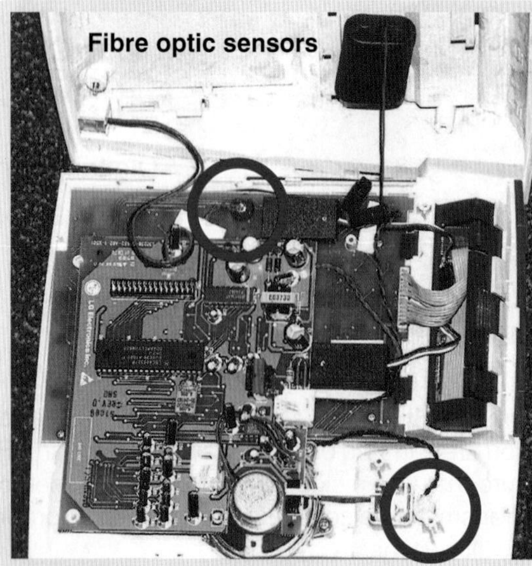


A number of years ago, we carried out a sweep of a company premises for listening devices. In the boardroom there was a 'Meridian' digital phone on a small table. Even before unpacking the TCSM kit, I picked up the phones handset, looked at the phone and instantly knew the phone was bugged! I could see a small dot where the handset sits in its cradle and knew straight away that it was a light sensor. I then set up the Scanlock and swept the phone, when I lifted the handset, it got a negative reading which meant that the battery was flat and not transmitting. The phone was internally inspected and my assumptions were correct.

Nothing else was found during the search but when the client was told of our findings he said, 'Oh, is that where it was, we bugged a member of staff about a year ago'. Personally, I think that they hired us solely to locate this 'rogue' telephone bug that they had installed and had gone astray.

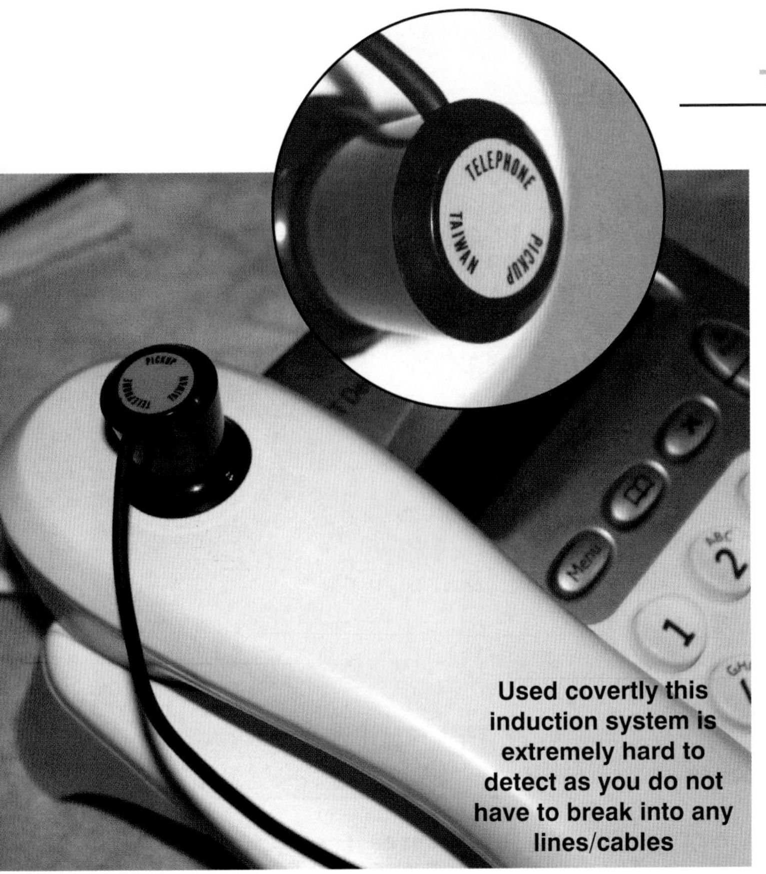


**Used covertly this induction system is extremely hard to detect as you do not have to break into any lines/cables**

- **Induction Telephone Tap**

This device often referred to as a 'Snuffle Bug', can be used in conjunction with a transmitter or hard wired into a recorder. The snuffle bug is placed on the outside of the telephone wiring and picks up signals by 'induction'. Every wire that has a current running through it such as a phone line - radiates a magnetic field. This device is able to read the signals carried along this magnetic field. The advantage of this device is the fact that the telephone line does not have to be 'broken into' which makes it very difficult to detect and leaves no trace of tampering.

A cheap common device that works by induction is called a 'telephone pick-up coil'. It is a small device that is connected to a recorder, at the other end is a small black device housing a coil with a rubber sucker on the outside. The sucker is connected to the telephone receiver (next to the earpiece) and picks up the signals. Although not covert, it is a suitable cheap device if you need to record telephone conversations. To some extent, it will also work if you place the sucker close to the telephone cabling.

**Monitoring Mobile Phones**

I have trialled and used some sophisticated software that you can download onto a mobile phone by Bluetooth. Once installed on the target phone it can carry out various actions.

If the target sends or receives a text message, you also get a copy sent to your mobile phone. If the target phone makes or receives a call, you also receive a text to say that the phone is in use and the number it has dialled (out or in). The latest software programmes also let you listen-in to the conversations taking place on the target phone.

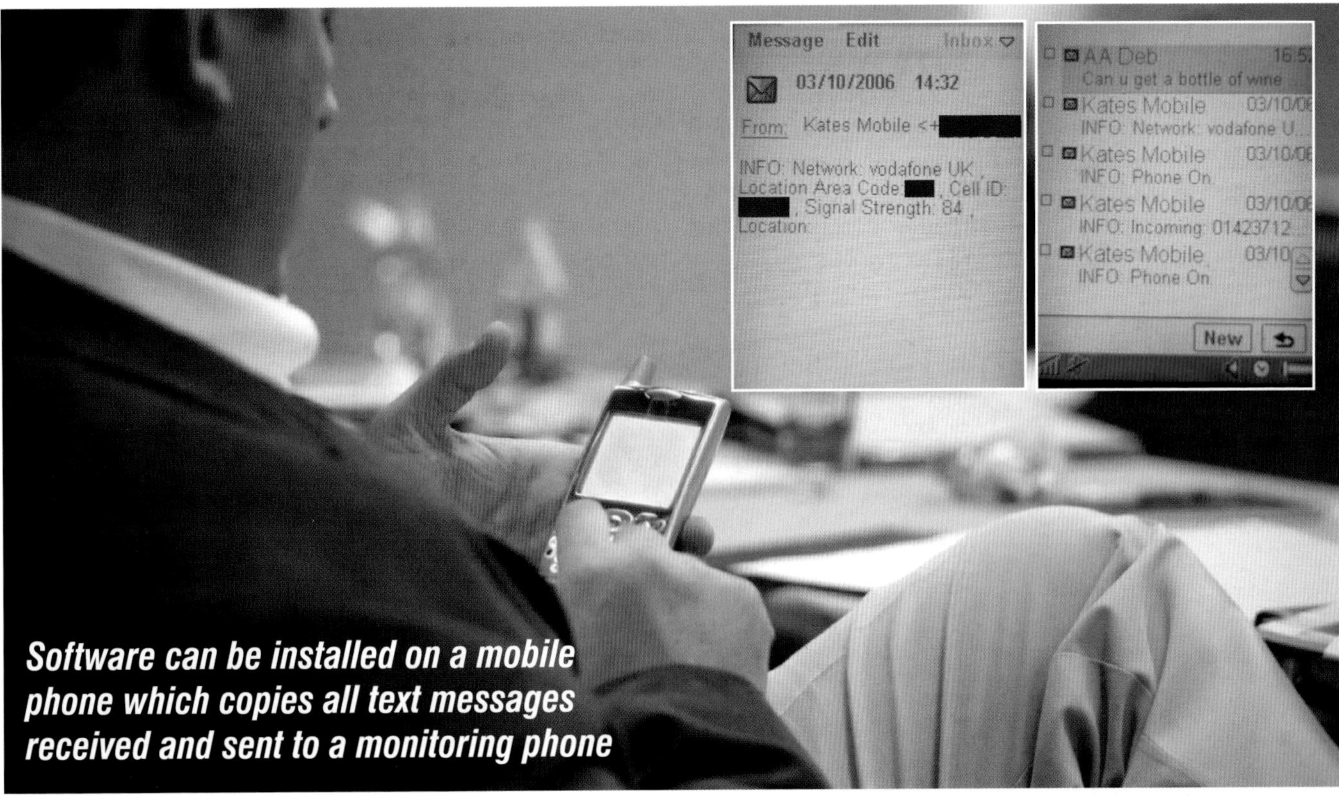


***Software can be installed on a mobile phone which copies all text messages received and sent to a monitoring phone***

## COMPUTER AND DATA MONITORING

### SIM Card reader

A cheap device can be used for retrieving text messages that have been received on a mobile phone and then deleted. The phone SIM card is inserted into the device which is then plugged into the USB port of a computer. The software then recovers the deleted messages and also deleted phone book entries. This device is fairly good but if the target's mobile phone saves its messages onto the phone rather than the SIM card, it will not work.

The SIM-card reader will recover deleted text messages

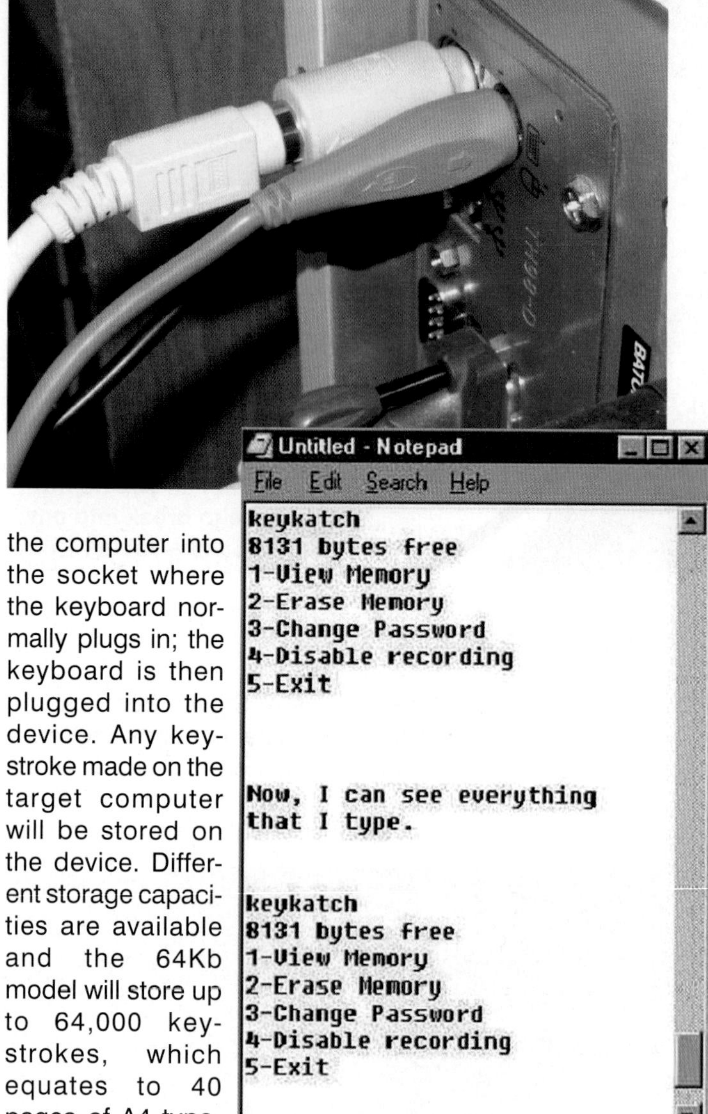


Key logger in situ is hidden amongst the 'spaghetti' (cables)

### Computer Monitoring

It is fairly simple to establish what an individual is doing on a computer, in particular what they are doing on the Internet. There are a number of ways of doing this and you don't need to be technically minded or computer savvy.

- **Keyboard Logger**

This device called the 'Keykatch' has been around for many years now and is still very effective for recording the keystrokes made on a computer keyboard. This identifies what a target is typing into a computer and is useful for establishing log in information and passwords.

It is about an inch long and it connects into the back of the computer into the socket where the keyboard normally plugs in; the keyboard is then plugged into the device. Any keystroke made on the target computer will be stored on the device. Different storage capacities are available and the 64Kb model will store up to 64,000 keystrokes, which equates to 40 pages of A4 typescript.

A USB and a PS2 key logger

The device can be interrogated whilst still connected to the target computer or be removed and interrogated elsewhere. All that you need to read the device is a word processing package such as Windows Notebook or Microsoft Word. After a password is entered into the keyboard, it is recognised by the device and a short menu appears on the screen giving you various options to view the data or erase it.

If you choose 'view', the stored data suddenly appears on the screen and can be read as a normal document full of information. The file can then be saved on a memory stick and the device 'emptied' of all data ready to start again.

## COMPUTER MONITORING SOFTWARE

**• Spector Software**

Another simple and very effective method of viewing activity on a computer is with a software programme called 'Spector', produced in the USA by Spectorsoft. If you can imagine a camera inside your computer which takes a snapshot of the screen every five seconds and then stores the pictures in a hidden file for you to look at later on, then this is what 'Spector' is capable of doing.

The software, downloaded or supplied on a CD, takes about 3 minutes to install and is immediately in use with no fuss. By accessing the hidden file with a password, the screen shots can then be reviewed using the on screen buttons similar to a video recorder which has play, rewind and fast forward which help you scan through the snapshots.

It is an amazing piece of software and anything that appears on the screen will be recorded.

- *All applications and programmes*
- *Typed letters*
- *All web sites visited*
- *Email activity*
- *All keystrokes typed*
- *Screen snapshots*
- *All chat net activity such as msn*

If you need to know what someone is doing on a computer, this programme is first class.

**• Remote Computer Monitoring**

There are numerous computer software packages on the market that enables a person to monitor the activity taking place on a target computer from a remote location. One common package similar to Spector is called 'eBlaster'.

This programme carries out the same monitoring activities as Spector but you do not need access to the machine in order to examine the information or screen shots. With eBlaster, whenever the target computer goes on-line it will secretly send an email to a designated email address with all the computer activity and screen shots. It will do this every 30 minutes or once a day depending on how you program the software.

A special feature of the programme is that every time the target receives or sends an email, you also receive a covert copy of it in your designated email post box. Going further into the depths of cyber spying, you can also tell eBlaster that you only wish to receive emails with a selected word in it. So, if you only want emails mentioning 'theft', you tell eBlaster so that it filters them out and sends them on. This is a very powerful monitoring tool indeed.

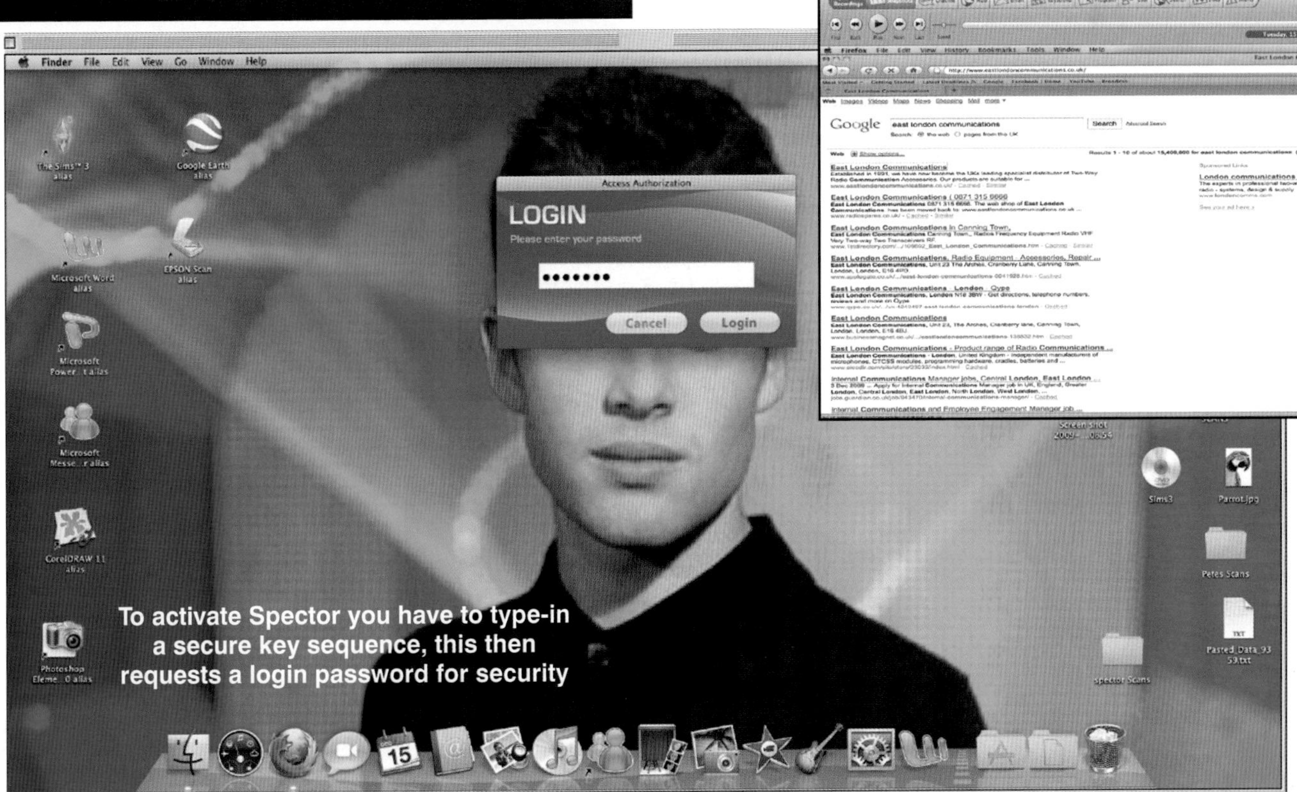


To activate Spector you have to type-in a secure key sequence, this then requests a login password for security

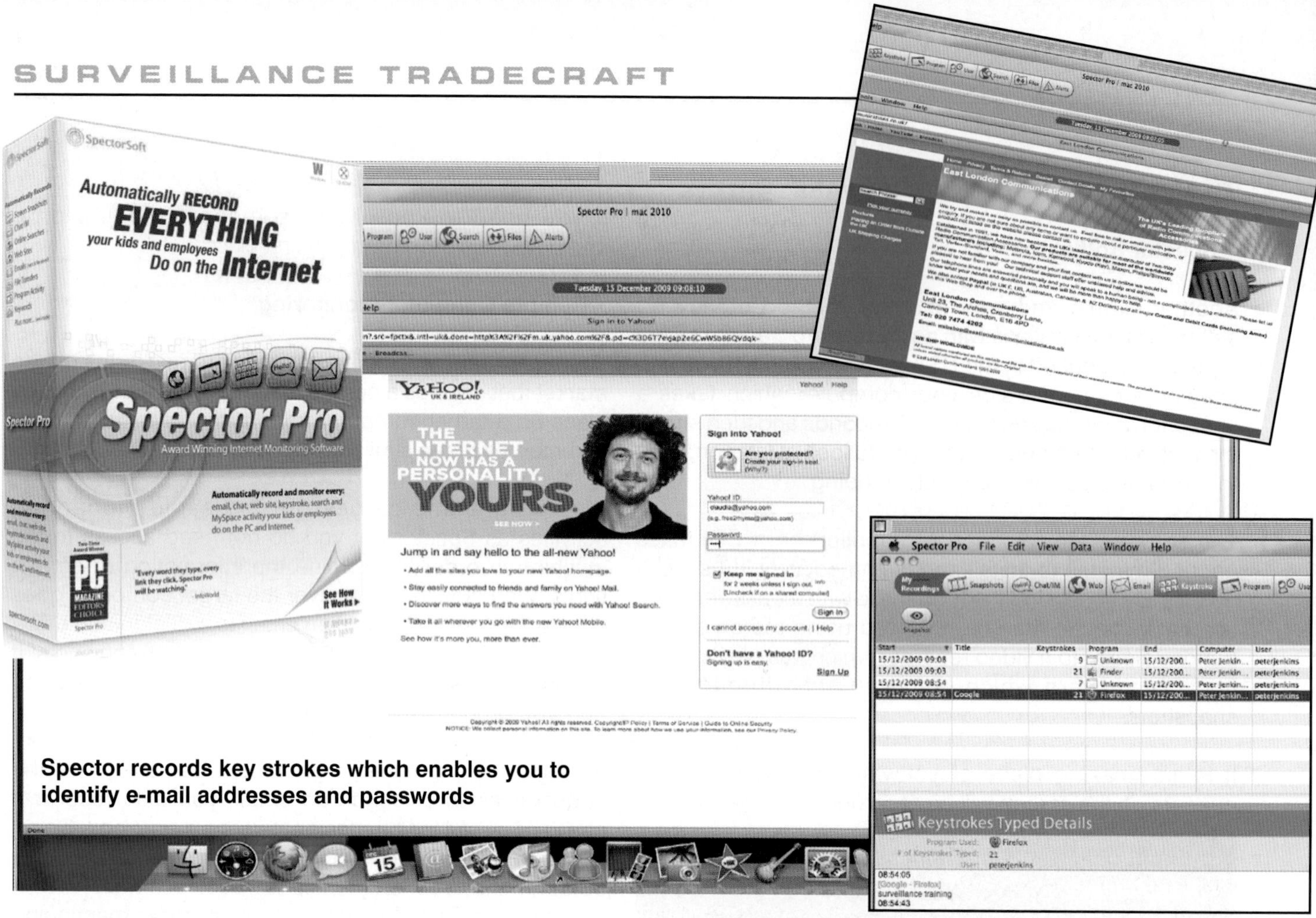

Spector records key strokes which enables you to identify e-mail addresses and passwords

### Snoopstick

The 'Snoopstick' looks just like a memory stick, in fact that's what it is but has a piece of spy software loaded onto it. It is used so that you can monitor a live computer from anywhere in the world.

When you plug the device into the target computer's USB port, it opens up an installation programme. It puts a programme onto the target computer and retrieves the target computers unique IP address, putting this information onto the Snoopstick which you then remove.

Get on a plane, fly to another country and go on the internet with your laptop. You place the same device into your USB port and the operating menu appears on screen. Click on 'View Remote Activity' and you will now be able to see 'live' what the target is actually doing on-line at that moment in time, wherever you are.

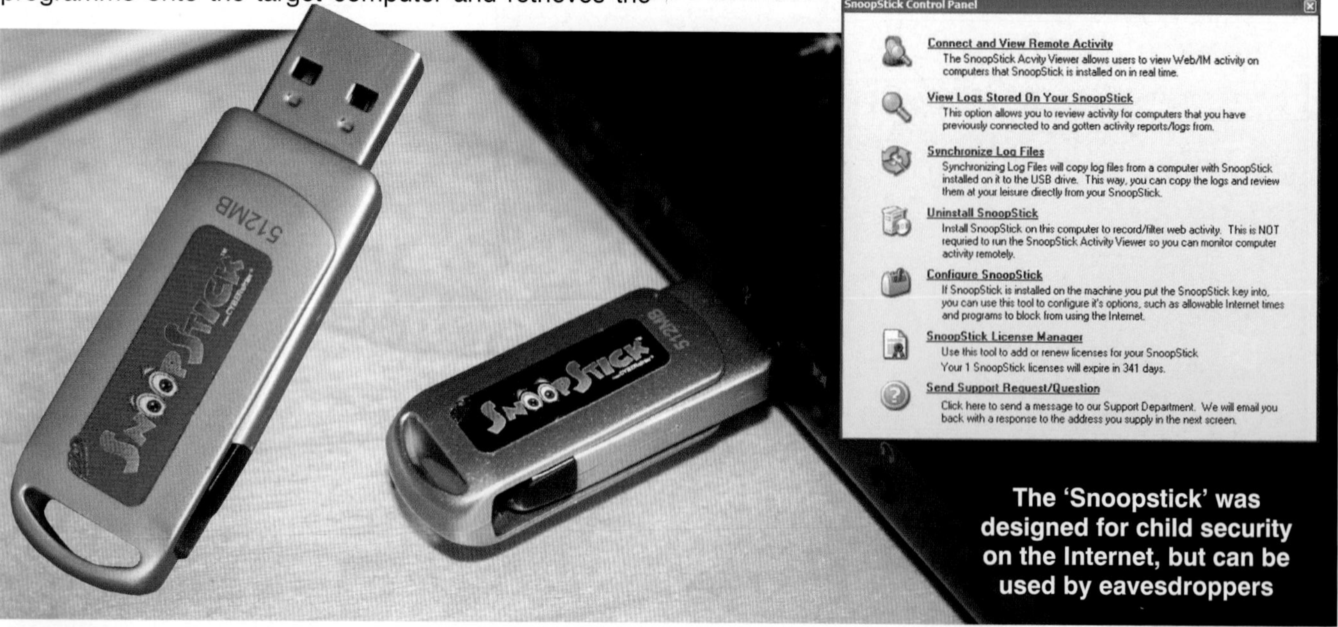


The 'Snoopstick' was designed for child security on the Internet, but can be used by eavesdroppers

## TECHNICAL SURVEILLANCE COUNTER MEASURES (TSCM)

Electronic surveillance counter measures is a very technical and complex subject which cannot be covered in half a chapter. There are many people who advertise a search and sweep service but, in my opinion, the majority are just going through the motions without really knowing what they are doing, what they are looking for and with insufficient equipment or training.

If you spend thousands of pounds on purchasing an RF detector such as Audiotel's 'Scanlock', without having the training to use it or understand its capabilities then it is of no use to you. The Scanlock is a first class RF detector/ locator (and mains carrier detector) but it will not locate a hard-wired recording device such as a buried microphone or a transmitter that has no power source. If you have to use or hire a counter measures team, do not be afraid to quiz them about their qualifications and do not be impressed by the cost of the equipment. Anyone can have a Rolls Royce if he has the money, but not everyone can drive it properly.

De-bugging equipment is very sophisticated but it is easy to operate and is user friendly. However, unless you know exactly what you are looking for and how devices are connected, concealed and operated, it is very easy to miss them in your search.

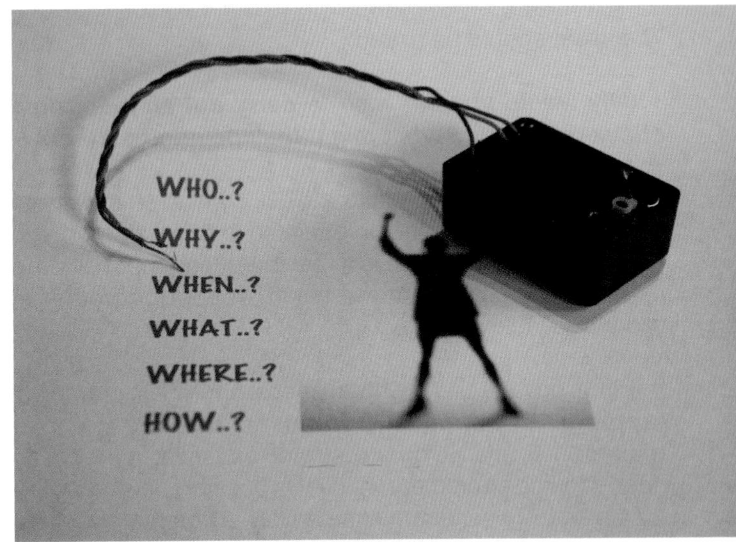


**Threat Assessment**

We have often received telephone calls from clients stating, 'I think that our office or telephones are being bugged'. 'Okay', I reply, 'Where are you telephoning me from? 'Why, the office of course!' is often the reply; and then the client suddenly realises how stupid he is as he has just informed the eavesdropper that he is on to them.

If you have a client that claims that he may be the victim of electronic surveillance it is very important to carry out an initial 'threat assessment' in order to establish the level of the threat and the likelihood of an electronic or technical attack.

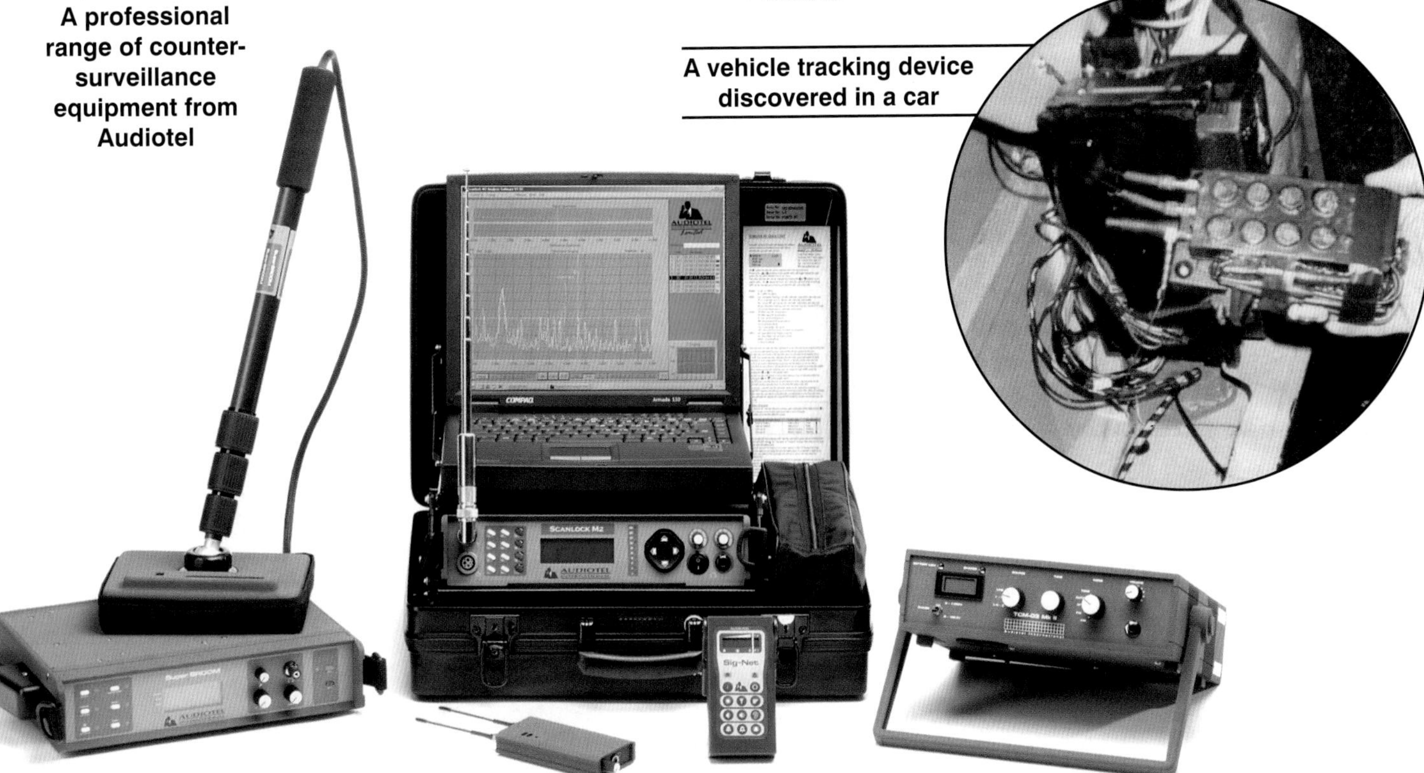

**A professional range of counter-surveillance equipment from Audiotel**

**A vehicle tracking device discovered in a car**

The client should be asked:

**• *Why would anyone wish to carry out an electronic attack on you and what might they be interested in?***

If your client is being monitored, ask by who? If they have a genuine reason for being attacked in this way then you can judge whether there is a real threat and, possibly, the expense and effort that the threat would go through in order to attack your client.

If it is a private client who suspects that their partner is tapping the phone due to suspicions regarding a matrimonial affair, you would not expect to see costly sophisticated equipment which has possibly been installed by a private investigator. Alternatively, a commercial client who has high value confidential information that would be of use to competitors, might be attacked with more expensive and sophisticated equipment.

If the client states, 'I don't really know why or who would want to monitor us', then you must get to the bottom of why you have been called in. Do not forget that there are people around who suffer from paranoia; on the other hand, do not become complacent, there may be a real threat.

***Extracts from the paranoia letter***

*I'm being hypnotised by a bugging device that is inside the body. It's a two way receiver and microphone.*

*I payed £400 to have my ears scanned but they said there was nothing there. I even had the filing in my teeth removed and teeth taken out...*

*I thought I could have swallowed it but why didn't it come up when I vomited...*

*I don't know why they are hypnotising and torturing me, I've been to the police...*

*There must be two receivers, I think now I've had two bugging devices pushed up into my nose. I have no recollection of when this happened though.* [SIC]

**• *Who do you suspect of attacking you in this way?***

There could be one potential threat, there could be many, for a variety of reasons. If they are under attack, how was the device planted? Was it by an employee, a visitor or by unauthorised access such as a mock break in?

**• *What are your reasons for suspecting that you are being monitored?***

If the client is convinced that information is being 'leaked' or confidential information has got back to them via a circuitous route, there is obviously a breach of security. Many clients automatically suspect that they are being 'bugged', but check to establish if the 'leaked' information could have got out by any other means and consider:

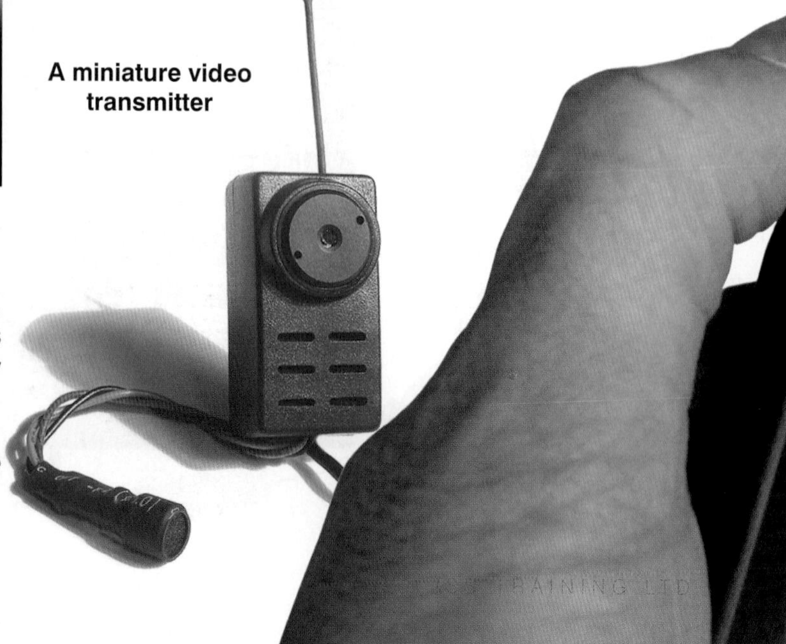

**A miniature video transmitter**

- *Loose talk by staff*
- *Disgruntled employee*
- *A confidence being broken*
- *Confidential waste and refuse being examined*
- *Documents left on desks*
- *Unauthorised access to computers and files*
- *Dictaphone tapes left out on desks*
- *A 'mole' in the company*

**• *Who has leaked the confidential information?***

If the details of a confidential conversation have got back to the client, he should recall the place and circumstances in which the conversation took place. If it was in an office or boardroom, you can suspect that these may be vulnerable target areas. If the conversation took place over the telephone, this is obviously a prime area to check and search.

**• *If a device is found, what are you to do?***

If a device is found there are a few options that are open to discussion with the client. Remember, if you locate one device do not pack you bags and go home. Continue your search for other devices, some may have been planted to act as decoys.

**• Remove the device?**

If we remove the device, there will no longer be a threat but the buggist will know that his operation has been compromised. This will either make him go to ground or attempt a further attack.

The 'SpyFinder' is a useful tool for locating concealed pinhole cameras. The camera lens is detected by the reflections of bright flashing lights seen through the device's viewer.

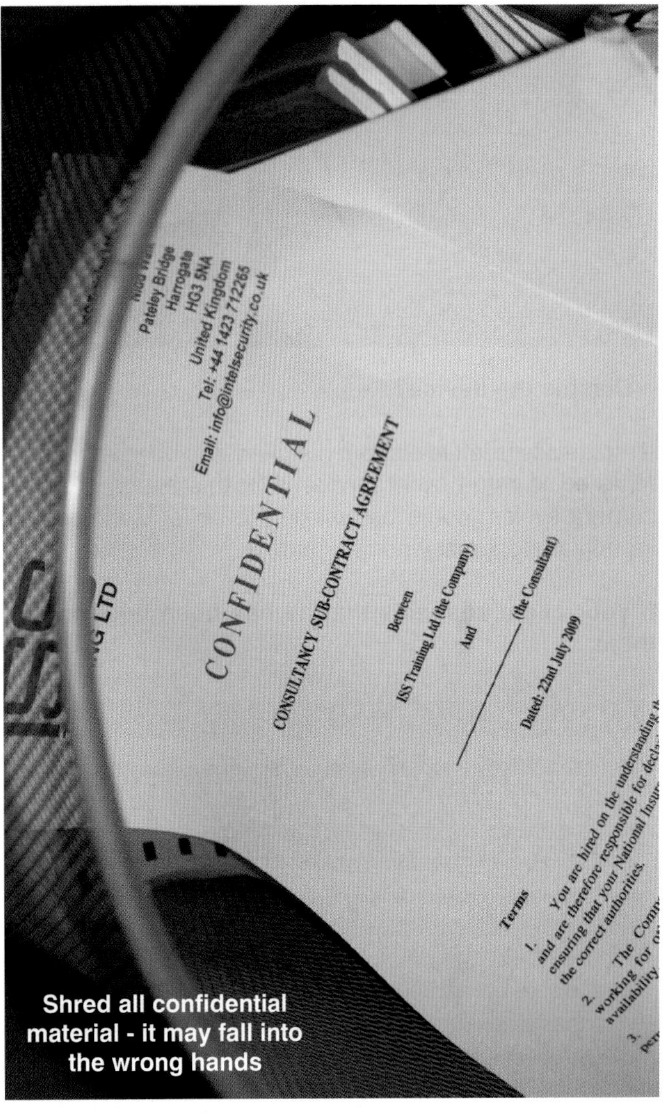


Shred all confidential material - it may fall into the wrong hands

**• Leave it in situ?**

You could leave the device in place and then provide false information (dis-information) to the buggist. If this is done, you should be careful as the buggist may have heard your attempts to locate the device.

During searches, everywhere has to be examined

**This telephone junction box found attached to most modern houses is extremely vulnerable to attack and easily accessed**

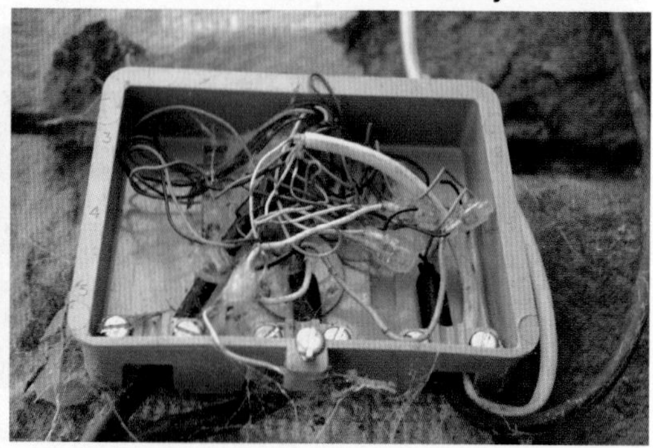

- **Disable the device?**

If the device is left in situ but disabled, the buggist may be tempted to return and service it. In this event, a covert camera system could be installed to cover it, in order to identify the buggist when he returns.

**If your client suspects that he has been bugged, tell them:**

- Not to panic.
- Continue to use the telephones in a normal manner but avoid discussing sensitive issues. To stop using the phones altogether may alert the buggist.
- To contact a search team as soon as possible using a 'secure means'. He should prepare for them a 'threat assessment'.
- Not to employ a local private investigator to carry out the search as he may have installed the device. Look for someone out of the area and check their qualifications.
- Do not use the 'suspect' phone for confidential matters.
- Use a mobile cell phone in a 'clean' area to discuss counter-measures or sensitive information.
- Do not try to locate any devices themselves. Do not telephone the police or the phone company as they will not be able to help them.
- Secure any suspected areas in the event the buggist attempts to retrieve any devices before a search team arrives.

After this has been discussed, you should arrange for a professional and qualified person to carry out the sweep/ search. It is strongly recommended to use only those practitioners that do this solely for a living. A private investigator may advertise a sweep service but he may also carry out accident enquiries, tracing missing persons, process serving and debt collection. The phrase, 'Jack of all trades but a master of none' comes to mind. There are qualified people out there who have many skills but would you expect your plumber to be able to fix your roof, tarmac your drive, re-point the walls and re-wire you house?

**During a search in this company boardroom, ISS discovered a fibre-optic telephone transmitter (below)**

## COUNTER ELECTRONIC SURVEILLANCE EQUIPMENT

Listed below are a number of types of equipment that a counter surveillance team would be expected to use in an electronic search. These devices all have limited use but should tell you that a device is present. An electronic search should be backed up by a physical inspection, as it is only the eyes that will find a device or any evidence of tampering.

- **Radio Frequency Detectors/Receivers**

Counter surveillance receivers such as Audiotel's Scanlock, the OSCOR or CPM700 are able to pick up signals from active transmitters and are then used to locate them to within a few inches. They are also able to detect 'mains carrier' transmitting systems and radio telephone taps.

**A multi-meter is a useful tool for detecting line voltage irregularities which may indicate listening devices are present. If detected a physical search has to be conducted**

- **Non-Linear Junction Detectors**

The 'NLJD' or Harmonic Radar is often referred to as 'The Broom' which is actually a trade name. They are used to identify and locate printed circuits, cables and microphones that may be buried in walls, cavities or furniture. The NLJD will locate any inactive transmitters or devices.

- **Hand Held RF Detectors**

Smaller portable, hand held RF detectors are cheaper alternatives and often used by close protection teams. I would not recommend using one for a major search and be aware of the 'cheap and nasty' ones that sell for about £150.00 as they are virtually useless. Audiotel's Delta V is a hand held device, that is portable and very effective in locating transmitters.

The Sig-Net is also a hand held receiver, which identifies and locates devices using the cellular network. This receiver can be left in an office whilst a meeting is taking place in order to protect 'real time' in the event of anyone activating a cellular device.

- **Spectrum Analysers**

These devices allow you to see a visual display of the radio signals in the locality via an oscilloscope. To a trained person, these signals can be interpreted and establish if a transmitting device is present. Modern counter measures receivers use PC based spectral analysis software for faster response and location.

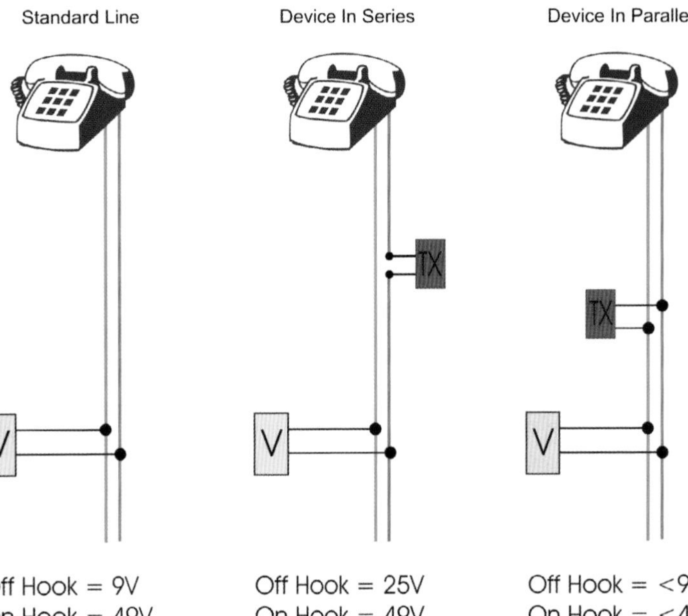

Audiotel 'Scanlock' shown being used to carry out a sweep for RF devices

It pays to use more expensive search equipment such as the Delta V (left). Cheap units are not as effective

• **Time Domain Reflectometer**

This device is used to detect breaks and splices in cables. Quite often it is not possible to follow a cable along its length and so a TDR will identify where a cable has been broken and repaired or a device attached. An experienced operator should be able to tell where the 'break' has occurred in order to examine it physically.

• **Multi-Meter**

This is used to measure line voltages and other current measurements especially within telephone wiring. A measurement taken across the line (at terminals 2 and 5) should give you a reading of 49 volts when the handset is in the cradle (on hook). When removed (off hook), the voltage drops to about 9 volts.

If a device is installed in series on the line, the voltage measurement when off hook should increase from 9 volts up to 25 volts due to extra resistance. If a device is installed in parallel on the line, both the on hook and off hook voltages would be less than normal (below 9 and 49 volts respectively). This amount will differ according to the type of device used.

A physical search has to be carried out in addition to an electronic sweep

Audiotel 'Superbroom' and 'Scanlock'

## LEGAL ISSUES

In the United Kingdom, there is a belief within the investigative industry and those that sell surveillance products that there is a 'grey' area regarding the use and legalities of electronic surveillance equipment. There is in fact no grey area but law, which clearly defines black from white when it comes to using this equipment.

There are various Acts, which govern electronic surveillance in the UK, these include:

- *Regulation of Investigatory Powers Act 2000*
- *Interception of Telecommunications Act 1985*
- *Intelligence Services Act 1994*
- *Security Service Act 1989*
- *Police Act 1997*
- *Wireless and Telegraphy Act 1949*
- *Human Rights Act 1998*
- *Data Protection Act 1998*

**Public Authorities**

For 'Public Authorities' such as the Police, Customs and Excise, the Security Service (MI5) to carry out a technical surveillance, they have to have a signed authority and warrant from the Secretary of State. This authority is given under the terms of the Interception of Communications Act 1985 where warrants will only be issued if the warrant is deemed necessary in the interests of national security, or for the purposes of safeguarding the economic well being of the UK. This is normally used against threats from overseas in order to prevent or detect serious crime. This type of surveillance is classed as 'intrusive' under the Regulation of Investigatory Powers Act 2000.

In order to install these devices, the authorities will require permission (again from the Home Secretary) to enter premises to do so. Authority will be granted on the grounds that the information is likely to be of substantial value to the authorities and that technical surveillance is being used as a last resort when all other avenues have failed.

**Radio Transmitters**

Using ANY radio transmitting equipment without a licence in the UK is an offence under the 1949 Wireless & Telegraphy Act. You could also be liable to confiscation of any other related equipment used at the unlicensed station or premises and/or a fine of up to £5,000 and up to six months imprisonment.

Therefore using any transmitting bugs (whether used on private property or not) is an offence. This includes the improper everyday use of transmitting equipment such as Public Mobile Radio (PMR) or walkie-talkies.

**Interception of Telecommunications (Telephones)**

It is an offence under the Telecommunications Act 1985 to attach a device or telephone instrument to a British Telecom line/system which has not been authorised by B.T. regardless of whether it is on private property or not. In addition, the recording of a person without their knowledge of the fact is also illegal under the Data Protection Act, hence why some recorders emit a bleep. In addition, you may have noticed that sometimes when dialling certain companies and call centres, they have a warning message at the start of the call informing you that all calls are being monitored for training purposes. This message is really a 'get out' clause in order for them to legally monitor and record offensive customers.

Some telephone recording machines have a 'green circle of approval' and therefore can be connected to your phone system. However, if it has been modified in anyway (by cutting off the connector plug) or is not used according to the instructions, this invalidates the approval.

**Audio Recordings Not Using Transmitters**

A recording made with tape recorders and hardwired microphones is perfectly legal in the United Kingdom and can be used in evidence so long as the integrity of the tapes (evidence) is preserved.

## CONCLUSION

Technical surveillance can be a very complex subject but due to the many devices available on the open market today, they are made very user friendly. The majority of the devices mentioned above are devices that had a genuine commercial use before being adapted for surveillance use.

Counter surveillance is very complex and should be left to a qualified expert. If you carry out searches, remember that you have to leave the premises with your hand on your heart and be able to say, 'Yes, that office is clean'. If a client later finds a device and can prove that it was present when you carried out your search, and has lost information as a result, he is likely to sue you. Be careful.

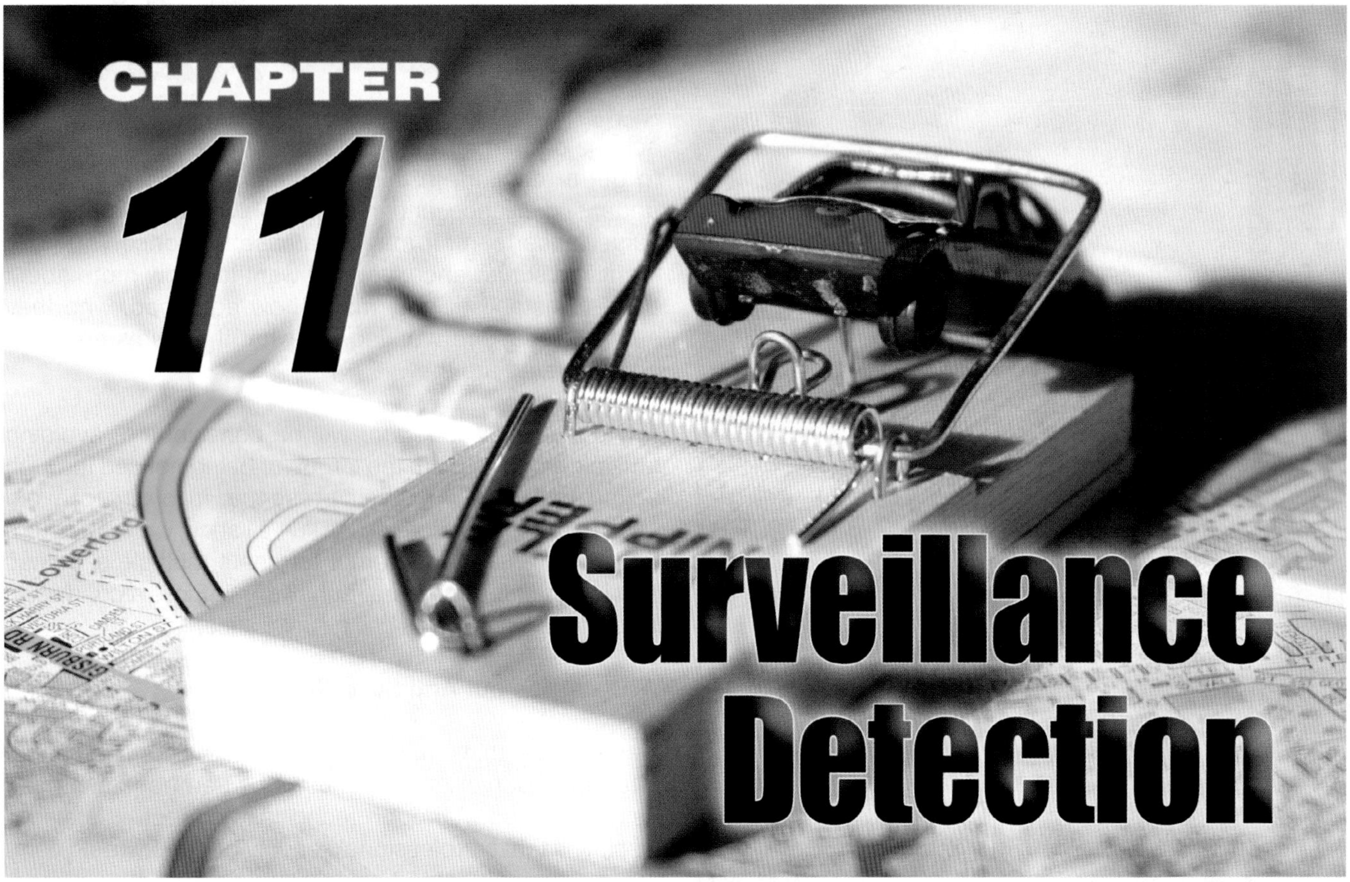

# CHAPTER 11

# Surveillance Detection

This chapter deals with surveillance detection by the use of anti and counter surveillance. There are measures that you or the target of a surveillance can carry out in order to detect and identify if surveillance is present. Anti surveillance (AS) is a misunderstood practice that is frequently confused with counter surveillance (CS). Anti surveillance and counter surveillance are two very different types of surveillance detection.

- **Anti-Surveillance**

Anti-surveillance are the actions or manoeuvres that a person carries out in order to confirm that he is under surveillance and by whom. Anti-surveillance manoeuvres (or 'drills' as we call them) are the actions that a person who suspects that he is being followed will carry out. These drills will, hopefully, draw the surveillance into a position where surveillance can be identified.

- **Counter Surveillance**

Counter Surveillance is defined as the methods or actions that a third party (person or team) carries out in order to identify the presence of a surveillance team and further identify the makeup of the surveillance team, to gather intelligence about them.

In a nutshell, anti surveillance is what we would do ourselves in order to detect if surveillance is present (we check our own back), and counter surveillance is when we bring in someone else to detect it for us (you get someone to check your back for you).

## ANTI SURVEILLANCE

As we have defined, anti-surveillance is described as the actions or manoeuvres that a person carries out in order to get a reaction. In this way he will confirm that he is under surveillance, and then, possibly evade and lose the surveillance team. It may be a case that once you have identified surveillance, you will want to know more about them to establish: how many, how equipped, who they are, who they are working for, what their aims are, how sophisticated are they.

Any surveillance operator will be conscious of avoiding multiple sightings with the target; or being noticed through acting unnaturally in their presence, in order to avoid compromise. Therefore in anti surveillance, we want to turn this on its head and attempt to create multiple sightings and look out for unnatural behaviour in those around us, in order to expose them as being surveillance.

**Who carries out Anti Surveillance?**

Many people think that anti-surveillance is something that a target of surveillance carries out when he thinks he is being followed. Although technically correct, it is also a discipline that a professional security operator would carry out in order to identify if he was subjected to surveillance.

If I am working abroad, after arrival at the hotel, I usually carry out some anti surveillance measures as I familiarise with the area. After an hour or so I may go for a walk around the town or city and carry out subtle anti surveillance drills, as described below.

I plan the route that I will walk the following morning to the training venue to include 'surveillance hazards' or choke points. Without becoming paranoid, a simple and effective anti surveillance routine can be built into your day to day activity without even thinking about it.

To keep things simple, I have listed certain 'drills' that a person would carry out themselves in order to detect surveillance.

Anti-surveillance measures can be carried out covertly or overtly, on foot, by vehicle, public transport and also in combination. Covertly, where you carry out very subtle drills in order to identify a surveillance presence without them realising the fact or, overtly, where you carry out obvious drills to let them know that you are looking.

***The concepts of anti and counter surveillance are often misunderstood***

**CHOKE POINT** **If used correctly narrow 'choke points' such as these can force a surveillance operator to follow you. However, an experienced surveillance team should recognise this a possible 'AS' trap**

## ANTI SURVEILLANCE WHILST ON FOOT

Being followed on foot will mean that any surveillance will be reasonably close to you also on foot; so the risk of them being noticed is much greater, this can be used to your advantage.

Therefore a number of drills have to be carried out to identify surveillance. Just looking behind you does not identify surveillance - it identifies those who are behind you. However, if you see those same people later on, especially in a different place and you have seen them at least three times, then alarm bells should start ringing.

If you are trying to identify surveillance, you need to draw any possible team (or individual) into an area where it makes it easier for you to spot them. In London, for example, if you are on Oxford Street where there are hundreds of people close together, it will be difficult to get multiple sightings of someone as they mix in with the crowd. Therefore, you will need to move off the street and into a quiet area where you have the advantage. Do not be too quick to venture into very quiet areas as an experienced team may pick up on this and not send anyone in as they do not want to be exposed.

Let us take a look at the various drills one can carry out yourself in order to detect surveillance. Firstly, we shall look at foot drills and then, mobile drills.

Remember, on foot, we are looking for a number of things: multiple sightings, unnatural behaviour and a person's demeanour and appearance. If you recall, surveillance operators will be the 'grey' person, upright bearing, not too young or too old, casual comfortable footwear, practical loose clothing (possibly branded) and they will have some means of communication, so look out for a clenched fist or a pressel switch.

## FOOT ANTI SURVEILLANCE DRILLS (DRILLING)

• Look directly behind you frequently. This can be overt or covert; overt if it is obvious that you are looking back which will spook the surveillance team. Covertly, you would cross the road (in order to look back) but listen and wait for a stream of traffic to pass first. This gives you the opportunity to look back several times without it being obvious that you are looking back.

To be even more covert, cross the road at a pelican crossing, do not press the button but pretend to. This now gives you a reason to stand at the side of the road and look back and forth several times (and for quite a while) because the green man isn't going to change.

**A pedestrian crossing gives you a reason for stopping and looking back covertly in the direction from whence you came**

**The use of the reflections in shop windows and doorways is also another method of being able to look back without being too obvious. It may also create a force past, described below**

• Enter a shop, large store or mall. Politely hold the door open for those behind you giving a chance to look back or use the doors reflections.

If no one follows you in, you can then look out of the store window at your surroundings and the reactions of those in the area. You may see someone going for a trigger such as quickly moving into a phone box, peeping around corners or they may even walk past to see where you are.

• Frequently turn about and change direction, though this is quite overt. If you change direction, have a reason for doing so such as looking in a shop window, hopefully this will create multiple sightings of the same person - if they are not carrying out regular 'handovers'.

• Drop a piece of paper and see whether it is picked up and examined. A surveillance team will be wary of this but if you provide some juicy bait such as an ATM receipt (a mock receipt), they will attempt to recover it.

• Enter a telephone box and use it to observe your surroundings. When you leave, keep a close eye on it in case a surveillance operator is 'clearing' the box for information. Be aware that many people now carry mobile phones and so using a public phone may alert watchers.

**Going into a shop gives you the opportunity to observe peoples actions on the street**

**A piece of paper dropped at an ATM may get retrieved by a surveillance operator**

• Walk into areas where there is little pedestrian activity such as a quiet neighbourhood or multi storey car park. If the team is poorly trained, they will be drawn in.

• Use large department stores with many exits and levels. Upon entering, suddenly stop to look at the information board. Look out for unnatural behaviour as someone follows you in and then suddenly realises that you are right there in front of them, they may be forced to walk past you. Use escalators to your advantage, take an escalator up or down, move away from the exit and observe those that follow you off. You should be looking for eye contact, use of pressel and an earpiece. If a suspect walks past, lookout for them looking back at you.

• Walk through narrow walkways or choke points. If the team are not familiar with the area they will probably send at least one person down there.

• Walk three sides of a square. Walk along a street, covertly noting those behind you as described. Change direction and take another covert look back, noting those that follow you around the same corner on either side of the street. Now, take a third change in direction, again looking back and noting if you have seen anyone take the same changes in direction.

A person seen once, is just a person on the street, the same person coming around the same corner is likely to be a coincidence but seen a third time should arouse suspicions. This, combined with a bit of un-natural behaviour should indicate whether that person is surveillance or not.

• An effective method to create a reaction is to create a loss such as turning a corner then suddenly entering into a shop to hide, whilst observing what is happening outside. An inexperienced team will soon be noticed by their mannerisms and apprehensive body language as they desperately try to re-locate you.

**If there is no way to go around at least one operator will be drawn down this narrow street**

# CLEARING A PHONE BOX

**Clearing a phone box is still taught by some enforcement agencies, however, if carried out, should be done with extreme caution**

• Turn a corner and suddenly stop, a term known as 'corner hanging'. This may force a watcher to go around the same corner and as they do so you observe their actions; do they walk past casually or are they startled like a rabbit caught in headlights? If they do casually walk past you, can they resist the temptation to look back at you?

• Using public transport can cause confusion and create anxiety in the team, especially if you are changing from one type of transport to another. At least one of the team is likely to be close in order to keep control. Some tactics are very overt:

- Wait at a bus stop and then don't get on but let the others in the queue.
- Stay on the bus to the terminal or final destination, notice who else gets on and remains on the bus with you.
- Get on a bus and get off at the next stop.
- Stand on a train platform and attempt to be the last person to board it, noticing if anyone else is hanging around on the platform.

**A surveillance operator may be drawn on to the railway platform or close by**

- Take a train but then get off prior to your stated destination.
- Get onto a train and then quickly get off before it moves away, see who does the same.

Some of these drills are quite overt and should only be used if you are really struggling to identify a team. Be aware that these drills are likely to make the surveillance team abort what they are doing.

• A new favourite is to scan the area for Bluetooth devices with your mobile phone, especially whilst in confined areas. A surveillance team may have their mobile phone's Bluetooths unintentionally switched on or they may be even using a Bluetooth earpiece headset to communicate with.

In addition to forcing multiple sightings of a surveillance team, we must look out for unnatural behaviour from suspects such as:

• People peeping around corners, peeping over stands, peeping through doors and windows

• Mirroring: someone copying your actions, e.g. you cross the road and they also cross the road. This will identify unsophisticated surveillance.

Look out for loitering. This operator is inadvertently paying too much attention to this women's clothing rack!

## ISS CASE

On a training exercise when I was the target, I boarded a train and scanned the area with my mobile phone's Bluetooth facility, noting who was in the vicinity as certain names/phones come up. Later on I did the same whilst in an art gallery and identified the same name as before. The same name was also present on the train on my return journey about an hour later thus creating 'multiple sightings'. Ensure that your Bluetooth is switched off.

Look out for any cross-contamination between operators

• A person being fixated on you or the target. They have a bad habit of staring at you and not noticing what is going on around them

• Being Isolated and standing out without any cover. Look out for the person with no reason for being there and just 'hanging around'. If you move towards them, they will feel very uncomfortable and either 'act' or attempt to move into some sort of cover. Are they fidgeting or acting in a dubious manner?

Be aware of people 'hanging around' for no reason

• Are they talking to themselves on the radio. Any serious surveillance team will have some form of covert communication, so you are looking for those talking to themselves whilst also noting their body language. Any possible surveillance using mobile phones may also be easy to spot as they all have a phone up to their ears at the same time or are wearing hands free Bluetooth earpieces.

• Try to get a look at the suspects hand or fist. If they are holding a pressel, this can often be seen if you know what to look for, is the persons hand relaxed or is it clenched tightly. It may be a sign of nervousness or they are trying to hide something.

Large open areas such as this can let you observe from a vantage point. However, a surveillance team will endeavour to do the same.

• Do they have a vacant expression on their face, this is quite a unique look! Whilst an operator is struggling to hear radio transmissions they may stop and appear to look into the distance, with mouth open and a gormless look on their face, especially from novices or amateurs.

• Look out for those who continually touch their earpiece. This is a sign of a lack of confidence, as the person is afraid that it may fall out. If you are able to get close enough an earpiece is something to be looking out for.

• If you carry out a U turn or hold a door open for the person behind you, do they deliberately avoid eye contact or are they reacting strangely when face to face.

• Look out for cross contamination. If you suspect an individual then keep a close eye on him. He may identify another watcher by hand signals, eye contact, a nod of the head or communicating by a mobile phone.

• Indirectly challenge anyone suspected of following you by asking them for directions or the time and note their reaction. If you notice a professional style watch (G Shock etc) this should also add to your suspicions.

• You may also want to make a direct challenge to someone you suspect as surveillance. 'Are you following me you bastard?' can really put off a surveillance. The operator will now have to pull off from the team and it is likely that as a consequence, the whole team would also have to lift off. If you really want to put them off, take a photograph!

If challenged indirectly, 'Excuse me, can you tell me the time'. This will spook the operator and get him concerned; he will want to get out of the way soon afterwards. His response and body language should tell you a lot and if you ask him the time, you may get a glance at his G Shock wristwatch, compass or a covert earpiece.

An unprofessional team is easily spotted and very easily caught out because they act unnaturally and they do not carry out the correct procedures which prevent multiple sightings. An experienced surveillance team is more likely to carry out tactics to ensure that they are not spotted, and if they suspect that they are being drawn into a compromise, they are more likely to 'lift off' from the surveillance and let the target run rather than confirm his suspicions.

## ANTI SURVEILLANCE WHILST MOBILE

We shall now look at the anti surveillance measures carried out when mobile in a vehicle or on public transport. We shall also look at the various times that a target or person will conduct anti surveillance drills in order to detect surveillance, which is quite important.

Remember that anti surveillance is defined as the actions that a person would take or do, in order to detect if surveillance is present. The person is aiming to draw the surveillance in, by generating two things; multiple sightings and unnatural behaviour.

A large team is difficult to detect whilst someone operating on their own should be fairly simple.

## MOBILE ANTI SURVEILLANCE DRILLS (DRILLING)

In a similar fashion to the drills carried out on foot, these drills can also be covert and subtle or overt, where it is obvious to the followers what you are doing. Again, a number of drills have to be carried out in order to identify surveillance. Just looking behind you does not identify surveillance - it identifies those who are behind you. Consider the following:

• Note any suspicious vehicles in the street or watchers that may be providing a trigger, especially if they are 'two up'.

• Whenever you first set off, note if anyone pulls out immediately behind you, this is amateurish and very unprofessional, which may tell you the level of sophistication of the surveillance team. Make a note of the vehicle behind you as you encounter the first or second turning after departure.

Watch out for operators sat in parked vehicles

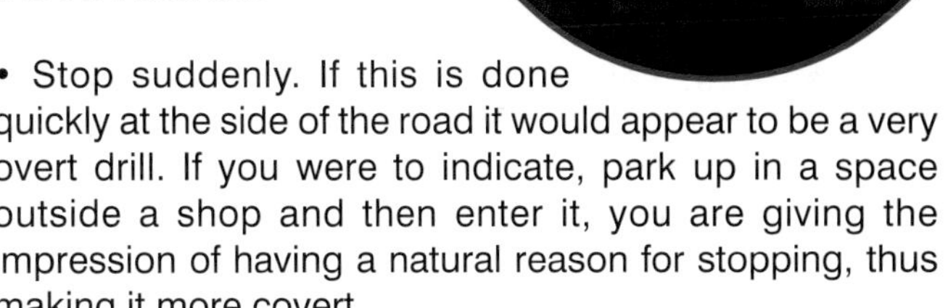

• As you depart, continue in your original direction for a short distance and then make a turn to see if that same car is still present. If it is, it may be a coincidence, so you now have to create a third drill in order to confirm or deny that it is surveillance.

• Stop suddenly. If this is done quickly at the side of the road it would appear to be a very overt drill. If you were to indicate, park up in a space outside a shop and then enter it, you are giving the impression of having a natural reason for stopping, thus making it more covert.

As you stop you should be noting the vehicle that overshoots and drives past - unless he suddenly pulls in somewhere behind you. You are looking for specific signs; the

This orange car is unlikely to be a surveillance vehicle

By pulling over suddenly you may force the surveillance team past

driver looking at you, the driver talking to himself, a small antenna on the back of the vehicle, the driver looking back as he passes you.

Once passed, he may turn off at the next side road and an amateur is likely to do this quite aggressively as he rushes to 're-plot'. Also, note the type of vehicles that pass you. A yellow Mustang convertible is unlikely to be surveillance. If a car passes you and parks up in front, take note if the driver actually gets out of his car or whether he sits there.

Also, don't forget to keep an eye on what is going on to your rear. You may note other vehicles peeling off the main road or manoeuvring to park up and get a trigger.

• As you depart, continue in your original direction for a distance and then do a 'U' turn, taking you back past the spot you have just left. You should look at the other vehicles as they pass you to observe the body language of the oncoming drivers. Ensure that you travel some distance first otherwise you will not 'break the box' and will not draw in the surveillance.

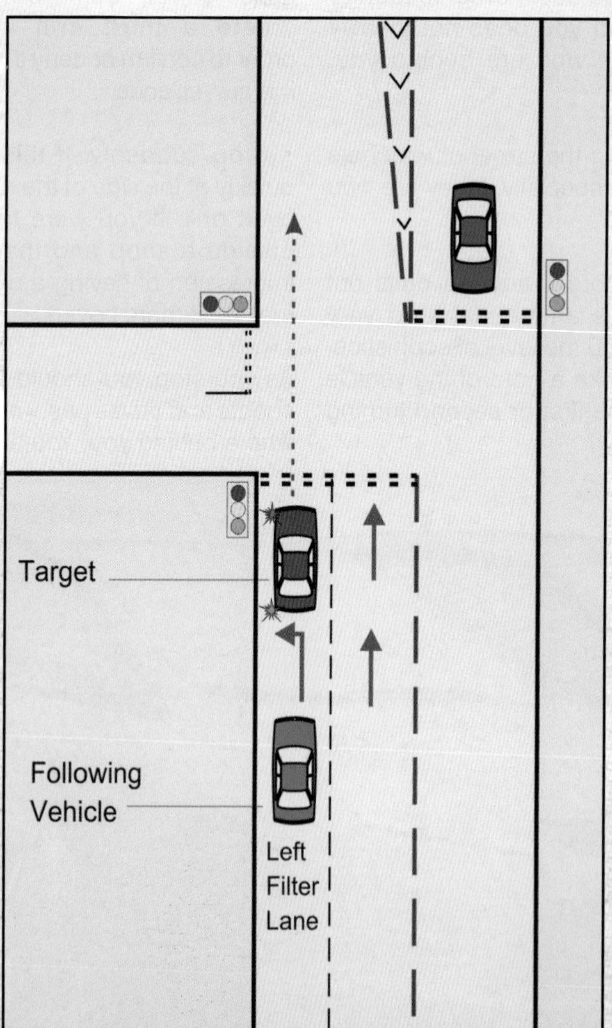


• Drive around a roundabout several times to throw watchers into chaos. This is a very aggressive drill and will immediately alert the team to your drilling.

• Jump a red light to see if you are followed across. Again this is a very unsophisticated and obvious drill; unless you time it right so that you arrive at the junction just as the lights change after a 'long green'.

• At a junction or crossroads, indicate to turn but then move off in a different direction. If the cars behind you also indicate, then cancel their indicators and follow, you suspect possible surveillance.

• On an approach to a junction with multiple lanes and a filter lane - such as a crossroads controlled by lights. Manoeuvre into the filter lane is if you were going to turn. When the lights go to green, continue straight (rather than turn) and this will force the watchers to either go

Use hill gradients to naturally slow you down - this can cause a surveillance team to 'bunch-up' behind you

Be aware of the target 'lane-hopping' in order to draw the surveillance team who may mirror his actions

with you (and thus identify themselves) or they will be forced to make the turn and consequently lose contact.

• Frequently alter your speed by slowing down then speeding up, note if the following cars overtake you or keep to the same speed and mirror your actions. This can be an obvious drill but if you use slow moving traffic on a dual carriageway to deliberately slow you down, you can be more subtle about it. Likewise, drive up a long hill and slow your speed down. The cars behind will be forced to close up on you and possibly overtake.

• Stopping immediately after taking a left turn may cause at least two of the cars to overshoot but again this is quite an overt drill. To give a reason for stopping, get out of the vehicle or pretend to look at a map or make a mobile phone call.

• If held in traffic, examine the car behind you closely and also its occupants. If it is 'two up', look for their body language or look for signs of talking into a radio. Watch out for the driver that 'creeps up' behind you when coming to a halt at traffic lights.

When obtaining fuel this gives you the opportunity to look around for potential surveillance triggers

Changing from major roads to minor roads in rural areas will draw in a surveillance

• Take the motorway, changing speed frequently from high to slow. Come off at an exit and then rejoin the carriageway to see the actions of the cars behind you.

• Pretend to break down on a motorway to see if anyone stops behind you, they shouldn't but an amateur would. A more professional team will continue to the next junction and wait there.

• Drive into more rural areas using narrow lanes whilst observing the vehicles behind you. Driving at a slow pace along very straight roads is really difficult for the surveillance team.

It is ideal for a surveillance team to dominate all of the lanes of traffic to avoid being drawn into 'mirroring' the target

**If the target suddenly stops and you are forced to overtake do not drive aggressively as you peel off**

• Lane hop. This is where you have multiple lanes and switch from one to the other. This is an overt drill but may force someone on their own (or an amateur) to mirror your actions.

• Driving into dead ends or a cul de sac can often be effective, especially if the road is not marked as being so. This may force one of the surveillance cars to follow you in and you will be able to note the reactions of the driver.

**Be Aware of the Lost Driver**

If a target drives around a roundabout twice, he may not be drilling - he missed his exit. If he then suddenly hops from one lane to another, he still might not be drilling - he is trying to find his way but, if he carried out a third manoeuvre, alarms bells should alert you to the fact that he has now carried out three drills, which is more than a coincidence. A sophisticated person will carry out the drills over a period of time or distance, making them much more difficult to detect. Whereas an amateur will do them one after another in close proximity to each other.

Think to yourself, what actions will a lost driver carry out? He will:

- *Suddenly stop at the side of the road*
- *Frequently change direction*
- *Go twice around a roundabout*
- *Enter a dead end or one way street*
- *Go twice around the block*
- *Indicate to go one way and then suddenly change his mind*
- *Switch from one lane to another*
- *Speed up then slow down*

All of these are classic signs of someone carrying out anti surveillance. Therefore we can establish at an early stage whether a target is lost or is carrying out anti surveillance. If a target starts to carry out these 'odd' drills in his home town there is a chance that he is drilling as he should know his way around. Whereas, if he were miles away in an unfamiliar area, these manoeuvres might indicate that he is lost; so, be careful.

**Long straight roads in rural areas make it easier to identify what vehicles are behind you**

**If the target suddenly carries out aggressive manoeuvring you will have to decide quickly whether he is 'drilling' or just lost**

## ANTI SURVEILLANCE ROUTES (SURVEILLANCE DETECTION)

Anti surveillance routes can be unplanned or planned. The former, if you are out and about and then suddenly suspect that you may be under surveillance; in this case you will want to carry out some subtle drills as described above. If, in advance, you suspect that you may be the subject of surveillance you may want to pre-plan an anti surveillance route on foot, by car or even using public transport.

Often, when working abroad, the team will go out for the evening of arrival to see the local area. During this, we will carry out some subtle anti-surveillance without really planning it or even thinking about it. Also, at this time, we might make note of various choke points where a surveillance team could be drawn into a trap.

A Close Protection Officer (CPO or Bodyguard) working on his own, may plan a simple anti surveillance route in order to chauffer his Principal from a hotel to a conference. The route should be simple and straight

## ISS CASE

On a trip to Finland, I devised a route to the training venue that ensured that I was not being followed. In the morning, I would leave the hotel, noting who was in or around the lobby. Leaving the hotel, I would note anyone hanging around on foot or in a nearby vehicle. I would walk to a nearby indoor shopping mall, carrying out a look-back as I crossed the street and also a second look-back using the reflections in a shop window after changing direction. Upon entering the mall, I'd do another subtle look-back as I held the door open for someone close behind me.

Upon entering, I'd go straight onto an escalator. Whilst travelling upwards, have another look-back at the mall entrance for anyone also entering.

Once at the top of the escalator, I would stop at a convenient coffee stand order a coffee and observe the top of the escalator and the nearby glass elevator for anyone coming up to the same level. I would then buy an English newspaper from a news stand and make my way back to the hotel, carrying out a few other subtle drills on the way.

forward, not deviating from the main route too much. It should be devised in order to create multiple sightings

This type of anti surveillance route is okay if used with caution. If I were to do this every day, a surveillance team will note that it is part of my daily routine (morning coffee and a paper) and they are most likely to let me 'run' when I leave the hotel because they know from previous surveillance 'serials' that I will be back at the hotel in 15 minutes with a daily paper and a Starbucks. Therefore, it may not always identify surveillance if you use the same routes, which is why CPO's use different routes for their principal.

### Let's Catch Them Out!

However, if you detected surveillance this way, you could now turn this routine habit into an advantage in order to lose the surveillance. Every morning, you leave the hotel and carry out the same boring visit to Starbucks and the news stand. You do it every day for five days and the surveillance team become bored, complacent, let you run when you enter the mall and head up the escalator.

Because they know you will be back down in a few minutes (and they do not want to risk being compromised) they will use this routine to their advantage (or so they think) to prevent exposure.

So what do you do to evade them? Confirm that you have not been followed into the mall or up a level and then carry on straight out of the other side. Enter into a large department store, down a level within the store and out at the other side of the mall into a cab waiting at the taxi stand!

This all sounds very 'TV' but it works! Treat everyone as suspicious and do not ignore:

- *People in suits*
- *Females*
- *Old people*
- *People walking dogs*
- *Taxi drivers*
- *Shop/Kiosk operators*
- *Delivery persons*
- *Street sweepers*
- *Beggars & tramps*
- *Street traders*

Make a conscious effort to remember what shoes any possible surveillance is wearing. Whilst it is easy to change appearance and clothing, shoes are rather bulky and therefore difficult to disguise. If the operator is changing clothes, it is unlikely that he will change his footwear.

**_Do not ignore tramps and beggars, take note whether their hair is clean or finger nails are dirty. Pay attention to detail_**

**A student from a foreign enforcement agency described how one of their operators dressed as a vagrant was shot dead by a drugs gang. The gang were initially happy with the tramp after questioning him, but a more inquisitive gang member made him strip off revealing a very clean pair of Calvin Klein underpants. This was his undoing.**

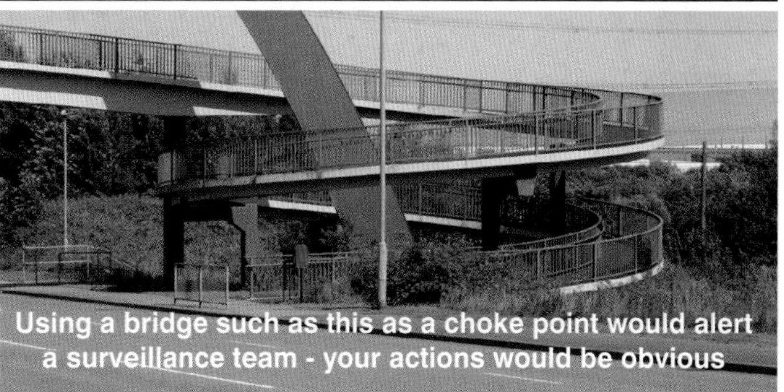

Using a bridge such as this as a choke point would alert a surveillance team - your actions would be obvious

# THREE SIDES OF A SQUARE

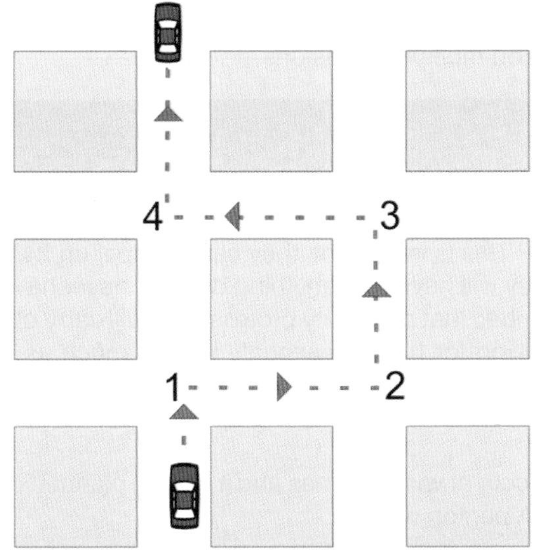


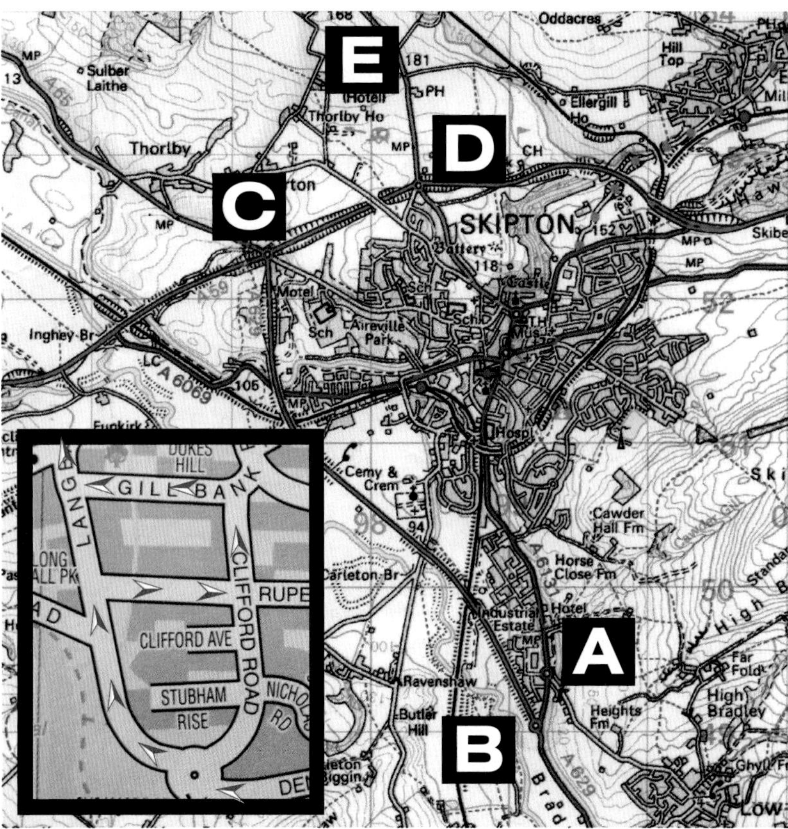


**Taking three sides of a square is a classic anti-surveillance drill by foot or vehicle. It can be carried out on a small scale such as a housing estate or city block, or on a larger scale such as in a town or county.**

**In the diagram, if we leave point A to get to the pub at point E we could either go straight through town or 'box round' the west side of town in order to create changes in direction**

**Mobile Anti Surveillance Route**

Should you want to drive from A to B, you need to choose a route that is straight forward, does not deviate from the main route and can harness a number of covert anti-surveillance drills.

As you drive off, check your mirror and note the first car and second car that appears behind you. Change direction, again keeping note of the few cars that are still behind you but do this a good distance away from your start point otherwise you may not have broken the surveillance 'box'. Carry out a number of the drills described above and if you want to create a stop, have a reason for doing so such as a petrol station or a shop. After this, drive off for a short while, carry out another stop - with a reason - and observe.

Use slow and heavy vehicles in front to make you slow down, this will force a surveillance team to 'bunch up'. Then overtake the slow mover to see the reaction in your mirrors; but remember, anyone else on the road is likely to do the same.

If it is covert, try not to be too aggressive, do not use the drills such as going around a roundabout, changing direction or stopping without a reason.

Remember from the chapter on mobile surveillance what a typical or ideal surveillance car would look like. The vehicles you need to look out for may have the following characteristics:

- *Safe & well built*
- *Roadworthy*
- *Common make & model saloon or small van*
- *Dark or neutral colour*
- *At least a 1.6+ sized engine*
- *No noticeable markings*
- *Possibly automatic transmission*
- *Air conditioning*
- *4 door*
- *May have an antenna*

This is not to suggest that you ignore every other vehicle that you see on multiple occasions.

## WHEN WILL A TARGET OF SURVEILLANCE CARRY OUT DRILLING?

So when will a target carry out anti-surveillance manoeuvres or drills? This is important, they can't keep it up 24/7 otherwise they will never get anything done or never have a life. Remember, that a security professional will carry out a form of drilling for his own security just as much as a target of surveillance would. A good example would be a close protection officer after picking up his principal.

Drilling will occur at various times and it can be planned or unplanned. A person will drill:-

1. WHEN THEY FIRST APPEAR
2. PRIOR TO ANY ACTIVITY
3. AFTER ILLEGAL ACTIVITY
4. ON RETURNING TO THEIR HAVEN
5. WHEN THEY SUSPECT SURVEILLANCE

• **When they first appear**

For instance, on leaving the house he will be looking up and down the street for anything suspicious. He gets into his car and drives away looking for anyone else moving off at the same time or pulling out behind him (unprofessional surveillance). After that, he may circle the block or carry out any of the drills mentioned above. A professional surveillance team should pick up on this drilling activity the first or second time it happened and would then widen their surveillance stake out 'box' on any subsequent surveillance. A professional security operator or close protection officer would continue to drill for some distance from the home address so that the surveillance team (if there is one) breaks the 'box' and are into the follow phase and are thus easier to identify.

• **Prior to any activity**

A criminal may carry out some form of drilling prior to carrying out any activity. A close protection officer may also carry out some subtle drilling prior to delivering his Principal at his destination.

• **After illegal activity**

Savvy criminals will do this drilling after an illegal activity just as much as prior to it. A criminal may be happy that he is not under surveillance before the criminal act but he may have picked up a surveillance at the activity site by a team watching the other party who then switch targets.

An intelligence officer, if he does not have counter surveillance deployed will also carry out anti surveillance prior to, and after a meeting for this same reason.

• **When returning to his haven**

Prior to returning to his home, office or wherever, a person may also carry out some form of drilling in the event they have picked up a surveillance. Drivers of security vehicles or those that work in banks or run the risk of kidnap, should do this as part of their daily routine on their way home, in case criminals are trying to identify where they live.

• **When the Target suspects surveillance**

It is likely that criminals will drill at the times mentioned above. However, depending on their awareness level, they will also start to drill when they have been 'spooked' or when they suspect surveillance is present. This will occur if they notice 'unnatural behaviour' or have 'multiple sightings' of the same person or car. Keep it in mind that there are other people in the world than just the surveillance team. It may be a case that the target is so alert because he has been spooked by someone totally unconnected with the surveillance.

## ISS CASE

On one particular surveillance we followed a delivery driver for a major builders merchants who was suspected of stealing materials. He would leave the yard in the morning but prior to an illegal delivery, he would park up for 5 minutes, wait and then circle the block to make sure that he was not being observed before he dropped off the goods at a building site.

The drilling was identified and we just hung back a little and didn't go in too hard because it told us he was about to do something. This primed the team who had their cameras ready and prepared for a walk past. In addition, we now expected the target to drill when he left the site and so we gave him a wide berth on his departure and loosely bounced him away from the site.

On a separate occasion we subcontracted a surveillance job to a private investigator who came back with a negative report and no evidence of the target's activities. I was told, 'he was starting to drill, so we let him run and so dropped the surveillance'. In this particular case it was the wrong answer to give. He was drilling in the area that he was suspected of visiting. The team let him run and did not check the target area.

**SWITCH ON!** **If the gentleman in this series of photographs had performed anti-surveillance and picked up on the fact they were being followed, they would not have met up**

**Don't lift off!**

As we have just mentioned, a target will drill just prior to an activity so therefore a surveillance team should detect the drilling at an early stage, this drilling is what we call a 'switch on'. Basically, you have to 'switch on' because something is about to happen. Inexperienced investigators do not realise this, they notice drilling, thinking that they will be spotted and so 'lift off ' when they should really be doing the opposite. Switch on, because things are about to happen and they need to keep control, but with caution.

## ISS CASE

On a recent foot course in London, two targets were under surveillance at the same time by two separate teams. The teams were briefed that if their target were to meet up with anyone else, then covert video was to be obtained of the meet and of any exchange of packages.

One of the girls on the course was designated to go in close with a covert camera in her handbag if the meeting took place. The target (Echo 1) was under surveillance for about an hour when she met up with an associate outside the National Gallery in Trafalgar Square. Just before the meet, she carried out some anti surveillance drills to clear her back.

Alpha 1 and Echo 1

Exchange takes place

At the post exercise debrief, it was established that the team member with the covert video bag wasn't able to obtain any video and was asked why. The reply was, 'Well, the target was drilling and on the lookout, so I decided not to go in too close with the camera'. If she had thought about it, there was no reason not to go in hard and close. Trafalgar Square is an extremely busy place, with people everywhere - especially with cameras.

Secondly, and more importantly, the fact that the meeting took place after the two targets had carried out some drilling, suggested that they were satisfied that they were not being followed. A perfect opportunity to get in close.

***Just because a target is conducting overt or covert anti-surveillance, it does not mean you will be detected!***

**What to do if you find yourself being followed**

You have carried out a number of drills and you have confirmed or strongly suspect that you are actually under surveillance, so what are you going to do, what are your options?

First of all, stay calm and do not panic. You have to decide, do you want to identify the followers and the make up of the surveillance team or do you want to evade them? A number of things can be done:

• You can try to out race them but this would immediately alert the team who are most likely to let you run. You will not achieve much and possibly cause an accident in the process.

• Inform someone: your team, the police or a friend who may be able to help you. If you are really concerned, inform the police that you are being followed and pass the details of the surveillance team to them with an excuse that you are carrying a large amount of cash and are in fear of being robbed!

• Keep driving until you are in a safe area such as a public place or a police station but do not go to your destination. That may have been the aim of the surveillance and you have just given it to them on a plate. Keep to the main roads if possible.

**Motorway service stations often have service roads which can be used as quick escape routes**

**If you feel threatened do not hesitate to head for safety. Do not be forced into a car chase**

• Make a written note of any vehicles or of the drivers. Use the mnemonic SCRIM to help you:

| |
|---|
| **Shape (hatch back)** |
| **Colour (dark blue)** |
| **Registration (05 D 35231)** |
| **Identifying Marks (Tow hook)** |
| **Make & Model (Opel Corsa)** |

• Think twice before you stop and confront them, directly or indirectly, they could be dangerous.

• Continue, but deviate from your route in order to identify more of the team - but this should be treated with caution.

• Continue and lead the followers into a trap by telephoning for help. This once happened to a colleague who ended up on his own and tried to continue with the surveillance when his back up was detached. He was spotted and the target entered a multi-story car park where two of his 'not so nice' friends were waiting with iron bars.

• Arrange for simple counter surveillance in order to identify the surveillance team and to learn how sophisticated they are.

A target, or person, may leave his home totally unaware but remember that the two most important things that will get a surveillance noticed: multiple sightings and unusual behaviour. The first time you notice someone, you are none the wiser. The second time could just be coincidence but the third time is a positive identification so any anti-surveillance has to be a combination of at least three drills.

**Conclusion**

An unprofessional team is very easily spotted and therefore caught out. An experienced surveillance team is more likely to carry out tactics to ensure that they are not spotted. If they suspect that they are being drawn into a series of drills, they are more likely to keep their distance and not be drawn in.

It is better to let the target run rather than suffer a compromise. A target left to run can be picked up another day. One that has noticed you, will be on his guard for a very long time afterwards.

## DON'T FORGET TRACKERS!

The use of tracking devices are imperative when conducting surveillance on very aware targets or targets who carry out drilling as a matter of routine. A target can go around a roundabout as many times as he wishes, or jump from one lane to another but it doesn't matter because the surveillance team can keep their distance, back off and let the tracking system do the work it was designed to do.

Conversely, you can drill as much as you want but will not notice any surveillance. If you are in the close protection industry, your daily IED checks should also extend to checking for trackers so learn where they are placed and how they are used.

## COUNTER SURVEILLANCE

As we defined earlier, counter surveillance is defined as the actions that a person or team carries out, in order to detect that a person is under surveillance and to identify the composition and makeup of a hostile surveillance team.

These actions can be planned or unplanned and can be carried out either covertly or overtly. Or, in other words, we let the watchers know you are aware of their presence, or by letting them appear to carry on undetected.

For ease of reference, I shall refer to the 'Principal' as the person potentially under threat of surveillance.

- **Unplanned**

Unplanned is when a principal realises he may be under surveillance and calls upon a team (or person) to either confirm or deny if surveillance is present - this may switch to a planned operation later.

- **Planned**

This is where a principal walks or drives (or is driven) a pre planned route through a series of choke points, monitored by a third party to either confirm or deny if surveillance is present by multiple sightings. These choke points have to be a tactical distance apart in order to rule out multiple sightings of third parties and minimise co-incidental sightings of them.

**Protection**

Close Protection Officers (CPO's) that are responsible for their principals safety, often carry out counter surveillance especially when there is a high threat level. Anyone who is a serious threat and intends to carry out an attack or kidnap will most probably do his homework and carry out some reconnaissance and surveillance beforehand.

The counter surveillance team (CST) will carry out various checks and observations in order to establish whether there is a surveillance presence in the area where the principal is housed and also when the principal is on the move. The CS team should be very alert, very observant and fully understand the principles of surveillance. You have to know surveillance and understand its methods in order to detect it.

## ISS CASE

A colleague once received a telephone call from his girlfriend who said that she was being followed. Carl told her to drive to a nearby retail park and enter the Ikea store where she could spend a lot of time. This gave Carl time to make his way to her. Upon arrival he identified where his girlfriend was parked and then took a look around, he soon identified the guy he suspected had the trigger on the car and took a number of photographs of him. Carl then rang his girlfriend and told her to go back to her car, drive a short distance to the other side of the retail park and enter another store, which she did. Carl then managed to identify a second operator who reacted when she moved off. When she parked up, Carl managed to photograph the second guy who was now taking video of his girlfriend.

It was established that Carl's girlfriend was being followed by private investigators on the instructions of her former husband. The private investigators he hired were soon identified and both former husband and the detective agency they were from received copies of the pictures that Carl had taken of them!

The funny thing about this story is that I was talking about it on a training seminar a few years later. One of the audience came up to me afterwards and said, 'We've wondered for ages who took and sent those pictures of our investigators, the client never paid our bill!'

A good example of unsophisticated and unplanned counter surveillance.

### The Hostile Planning Cycle

Many readers of this book will be Close Protection Officers (CPO's) or those involved in static or residential security teams. They are employed for one reason - to protect. To protect their Principal or premises from attack, kidnap, intrusion or theft.

There is no doubt that anyone (or place) that is targeted for attack will have surveillance conducted on them at some stage. Whether it is an attack by sophisticated terrorists, an assassination by a stalker or a burglary by low level criminals, all attacks would have gone through some prior planning in a process what is known as the 'hostile planning cycle'. As part of this cycle, surveillance is present and it is at these times when the attackers are vulnerable (if they can see you - you can see them) and therefore possibly be identified before an attack takes place. The cycle is made up of the following phases:

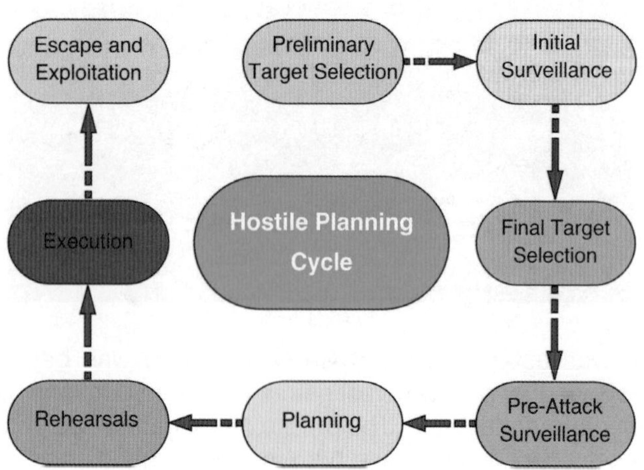


### Phase 1: Preliminary Target Selection

The attacker will initially decide who to attack and why. For example, to attack the base of an occupying military unit in order to disrupt and obtain publicity. It may be that the attackers have a list of potential targets, therefore they will now move into the next phase.

### Phase 2: Initial Surveillance

The attackers will now conduct their probing recces of a target in order to identify weaknesses and strengths. They will not necessarily be going in close but they will be looking for: overt and covert security patrols, perimeter protection, access control, CCTV, alarm systems, vulnerabilities, routines such a shift patterns and also escape routes. If they find that their target is too well protected and too risky to attack, they go back to Phase 1 and start again. During this initial surveillance phase, the attackers will be vulnerable to detection, mainly by multiple sightings or behaving un-naturally in the vicinity.

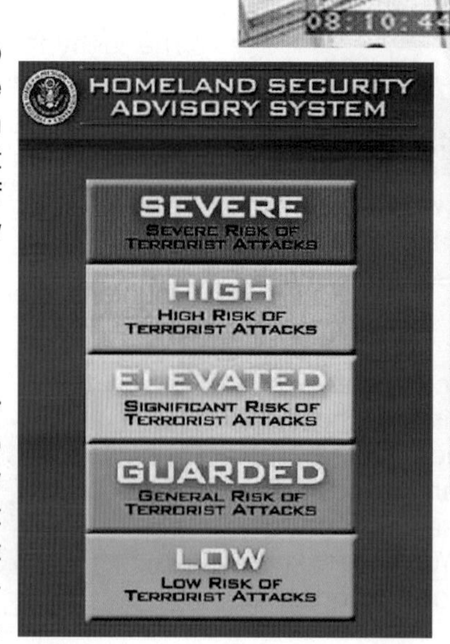


# WARNING!

**_Any surveillance detection team relies on observing unnatural behaviour in potential attackers or having multiple sightings of them whilst they carry out their recces._**

**_The sophisticated and 'switched-on' attacker is not necessarily presenting himself in this way anymore. Only one walk past and never seen again. Only one drivepast (by someone else) and never seen again, and they won't be seen sat in cars for hours on end nearby._**

### Phase 3: Final Target Selection

Once the attackers have carried out their basic intelligence gathering recces, they will select a vulnerable target to attack. They will now proceed to gather as much information as possible to make a successful plan, some of which will again be surveillance led (the next phase). They will obtain information on the target by obtaining: press cuttings, the Internet, brochures, maps and plans.

**Weeks prior to the 7 July 2005 London attacks, terrorists visited the city to conduct reconnaissance and carry out a dummy run as shown in this photo**

**Phase 4:** Pre-Attack Surveillance

The attackers will now probe deeper at their intended target to obtain detailed intelligence. Rather than just carrying out 'drive bys' they may conduct static observations of the site, follow individuals such as VIP's, staff or delivery vehicles. They may even infiltrate the site itself under the guise of carrying out deliveries or even obtain employment at the site. Again, during this phase the attackers will be vulnerable and open to detection.

**Phase 5:** Planning

All of the intelligence the attackers have obtained will be collated and used to form the basis of an attack plan; what weapons or explosives to use, how to get in, how to carry out the attack (normally by surprise) and how to escape.

**Phase 6:** Rehearsal

The attackers will conduct rehearsals. They may do this at a safe site with similar characteristics to the target or it may be done over a plan, map or a model. The plan will need to be fine tuned to rehearse; routes, timings, RV's, deceptions, the attack itself and also escape routes in the event things go wrong.

**Phase 7:** Execution

If the attackers get to this phase, there is a chance that they will succeed in their attack plan as it is now too late.

BBC NEWS

As it happened: Mumbai attacks 29 Nov

Profile: Mohammad Ajmal Amir Qasab

BBC NEWS

7 JULY BOMBINGS

LONDON ATTACKS

Russell Square

At 0850 BST a bomb exploded on Piccadilly line train number 311 travelling south from King's Cross station to Russell Square.

However, their mission can still be disrupted by vigilant security.

**Phase 8:** Escape & Exploitation

The attackers will want to escape capture (unless they are suicide bombers) and will have planned an escape route. It is also likely that they will have pre-planned a public statement or video in order to maximise publicity for their cause.

Having looked at the different phases of a surveillance; the Stake Out, the Pick Up the Follow and the Housing, there are procedures that we can use at each phase in order to identify and detect watchers. The counter surveillance team have to think 'surveillance' and if they were to carry out a surveillance on their principal, how would they do it.

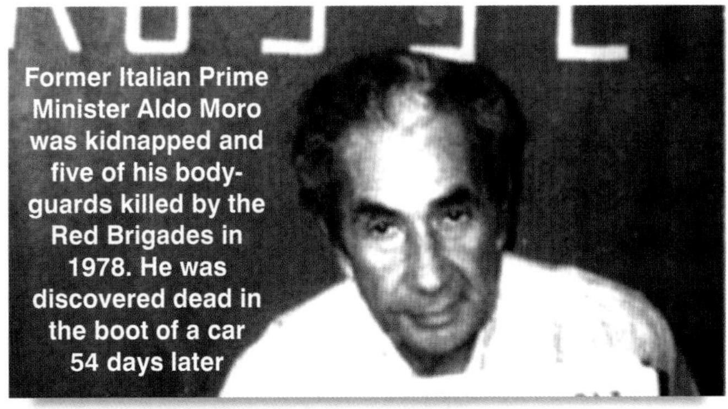

BBC Mobile

News | Sport | Weather | iPlayer | TV

NEWS EUROPE

Home | World | UK | England | N. Ireland | Scotland | Wales | Business | Politics | Health | Education | Sci/E

Africa | Asia-Pacific | Europe | Latin America | Middle East | South Asia | US & Canada

13 December 2010 Last updated at 20:28

Stockholm bomber 'aimed to kill many people'

**A man who blew himself up in Stockholm was carrying three explosive devices and intended to kill as many people as possible, prosecutors say.**

Chief prosecutor Tomas Lindstrand said police were "98% sure" that the man was Iraq-born Taimour Abdulwahab al-Abdaly.

Abdaly, 28, is believed to have died minutes after setting off a car bomb on Saturday. Two other people were hurt.

Seven US FBI bomb experts are heading to Stockholm to help the investigation, Sweden's intelligence agency said.

Although Abdaly was a Swedish citizen, he ha[...] been living in the UK.

British police have been searching a house in [...] where Abdaly lived.

Mr Lindstrand said Swedish police were now [...] bomber's target had been before he blew him[...]

"He had a bomb belt on him, he had a backpa[...] carrying an object that has been compared to [...] all blown up at the same time, it would have b[...]

A car containing gas canisters blew up first in [...] the area of Drottninggatan at 1700 local time [...] minutes later by a explosion in a street about [...] killed the bomber.

**Suicide bombers may be identified by unnatural behaviour or their demeanour, but by this stage it could be too late.**

**They do not necessarily plan for an escape...**

## THE NEED FOR COUNTER SURVEILLANCE

Why people and vehicles are subjected to counter surveillance are many:

- To identify if a principal is being targeted prior to attack/kidnap by a hostile element
- To identify if a person's back is clear before or after a meeting. It could be a company CEO involved in a buy out or merger
- To identify journalists and Paparazzi so that a celebrity can go about their normal life unhindered
- To clear (or clean) an intelligence agent prior to conducting clandestine operations
- To clear an undercover operator as he arrives or departs from a sensitive operation or meeting
- To check that an informant's back is clear before a meeting with his handler
- To identify any potential criminal activity such as robberies on 'cash in transit' vans

## THE START POINT

Some CS teams make the mistake of sitting up where they can see the principal's house or premises. This in some respects is wrong because they are probably sitting where a surveillance person would. The CS operator should take a look at the area and think to themselves, 'if this were under surveillance, where would someone sit and get a trigger from?' Where would someone sit if they were covering the right option out etc. You then need to remove yourself from these locations but in a position to observe them. This should be taken into account at all of the choke points and not just the start point. If a hostile surveillance is already in position before the CS team arrives, they may be difficult to identify, as they will not be moving around but settled in for the wait.

The 'Paparazzi' can be a threat and a nuisance

It is this principle that forms the basis of counter surveillance when trying to pre-empt where and what an operational team would do.

If you carry out a walking patrol in the area of the principal's home, you should be looking for:

**CONVOY** **Close Protection Officers from the Government's Diplomatic Protection Group escort the Prime Minister through London on his way to an official engagement**

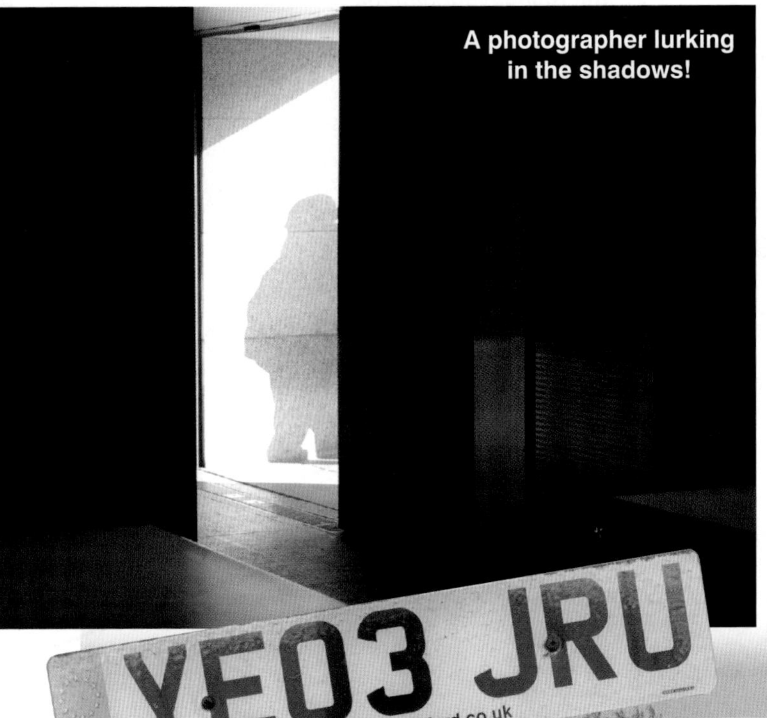


A photographer lurking in the shadows!

In addition the dealer's website their address may also be displayed

- The small detail on registration plates that may tell you what area it is from
- Paperwork on seats
- Radios or radio parts
- Maps
- Fast food wrappings
- Old newspapers
- Antennas on cars
- Cars that are reversed parked (combat parking)

Look for cars that appear to have 'doubled up'. Surveillance operators often get bored and co-locate with disregard to cross-contamination

- Likely trigger positions that a surveillance team may use. Remember: vans, cars, buildings or rural OP's

- People sat about in vehicles who try to avoid your gaze or people on motorbikes.

- Make a note of empty vehicles and their contents, things to look out for are:

The open rear window catches the eye. The passenger is pointing and evidently talking to somebody in the back - possibly a team biker as in this case a motorbike is parked at the rear

- Approach and confront anyone you find suspicious and note their reactions or any indicators to suggest that they could be surveillance.

- Widen your search area and check along the escape routes.

Whether it is a home address, hotel or even a petrol station, when the principal moves, so do the surveillance team and you should note any sudden movements from other vehicles or people in the area.

This lie-up position is covering the roundabout and the A65

This lie-up position is also covering the roundabout and the A65

A65

A59

LAYBY ON EITHE
SIDE OF ROAD

Courtesy: www.wtp2appspot.com/wheresthe path

A detailed sketch of the hotel area

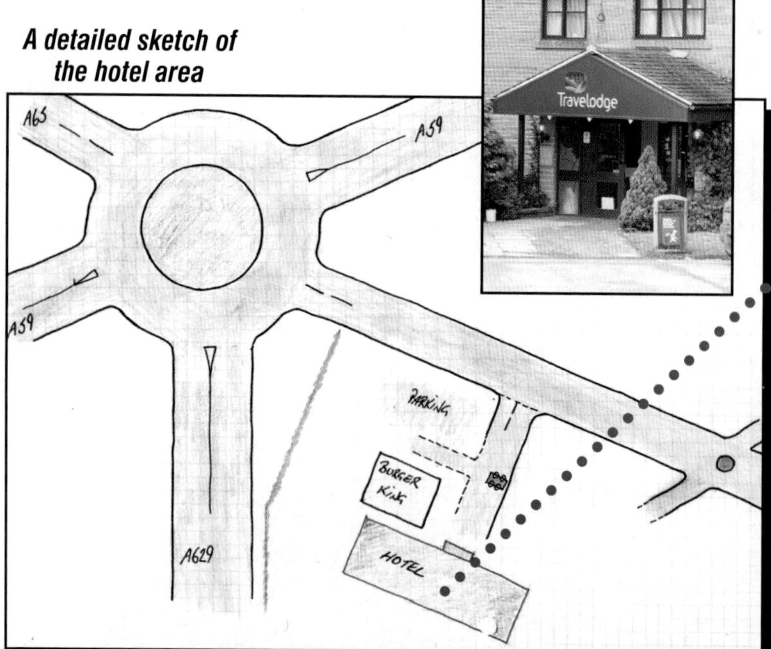

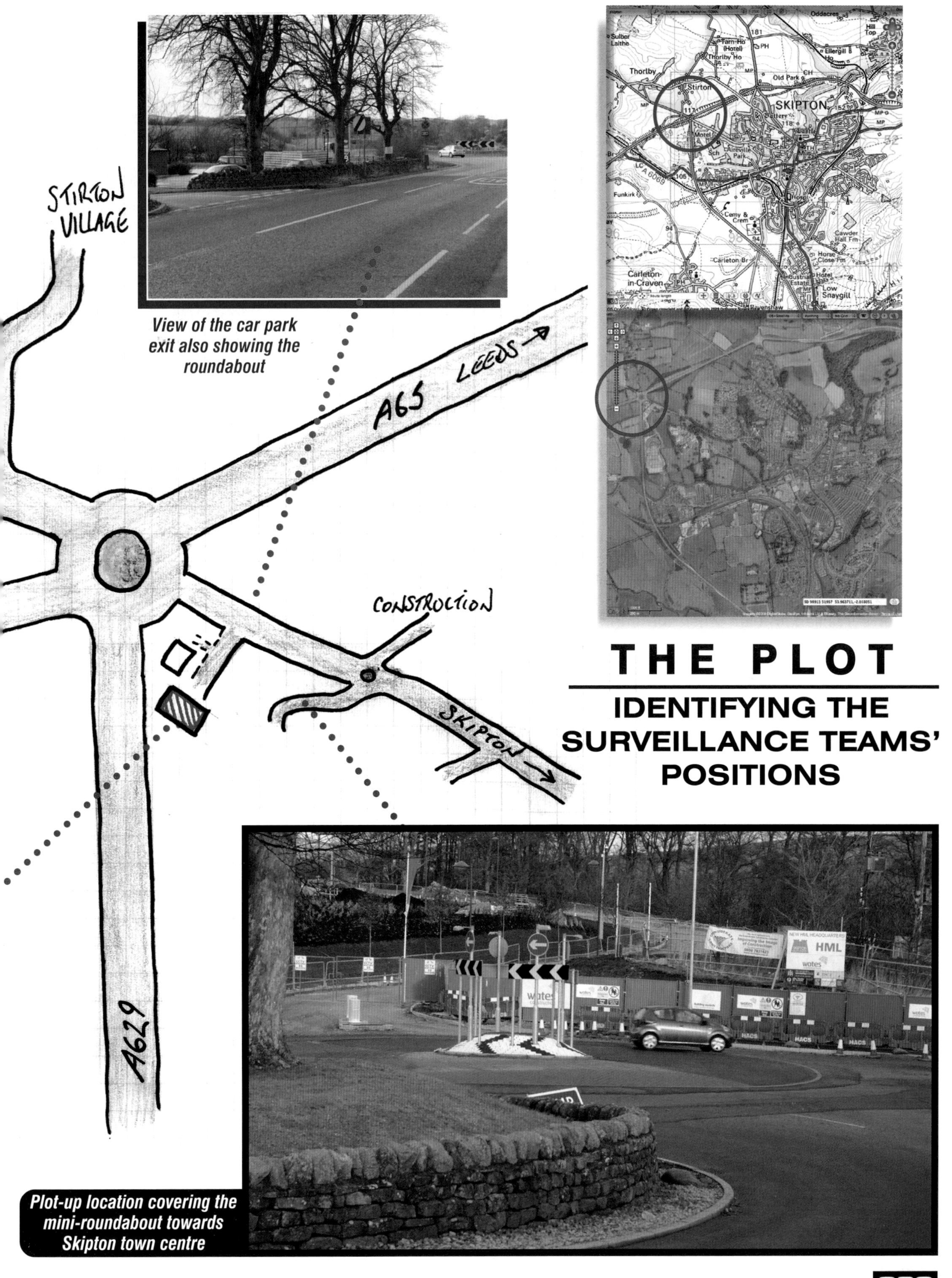


View of the car park exit also showing the roundabout

Plot-up location covering the mini-roundabout towards Skipton town centre

## THE PLOT

### IDENTIFYING THE SURVEILLANCE TEAMS' POSITIONS

Be aware of any cars reacting when the Principal moves off

## SURVEILLANCE DETECTION ROUTE (SDR)

Your principal wants to get from A to B. Before arriving at B, he wants to make sure that he is not under surveillance and his back is clear; therefore, he has to be run through a counter surveillance route, also known as a Surveillance Detection Route (or SDR).

This route should be as natural as possible without deviating from the most logical route otherwise it will be identified by the surveillance. It will require at least three separate choke points that can be monitored by the counter surveillance team when the principal passes through them. We say a minimum of three because we are trying to create and establish multiple sightings of people or their cars so that the sightings are more than just a coincidence. To be on the safe side you could also use four choke points.

The Principal travelling through East Harling will be forced over a bridge. There are no immediate parallel routes that the surveillance can take and therefore they must use the bridge

Counter surveillance can either be carried out by a full team or by a single person. Carried out single-handed can prove to be hard work and is likely to mean that the principal will have to stop on one or two occasions, which may not always be practical or safe to do so. The CS should be armed with a camera or video recorder to film activity and scrutinise it for un-natural behaviour. In addition, potential sightings can be recorded for cross referencing against further sightings.

Each choke point should be observed for routine activity and you should get a feel for the environment. Should a surveillance team arrive, you should be able to notice the difference in tempo and activity from certain individuals or vehicles.

### MOBILE CS ROUTE WITHOUT STOPPING

Let us say that we have a diamond courier who collects diamonds from a secure unit at an airport and delivers them to his company on a weekly basis, his company premises are unmarked and the location secret. He uses a plain vehicle so that he does not attract attention. The courier wants to go straight from the airport to the company without having to stop en-route.

The CS team (comprising of three operators) should look at the route and choose at least three 'choke points' that the Principal has to pass through that can be easily

At a junction where the Principal is required to turn right there is a chance he will be held due to oncoming traffic. This is good as it will not only stall the Principal, but force any surveillance to 'stack-up' behind him

monitored with one operator observing each choke point. This can be carried out by examining a map of the route prior to actually going out on the ground for a more detailed recce.

Ideally, the route should not be one continuous road over a long distance as there is a fair chance that other 'innocent' road users are using the same route. Therefore, keep the route as natural as possible; put in at least two changes of direction to minimise third parties and to draw in the surveillance team.

A choke point does not necessarily mean a narrow channel such as a bridge but needs to be somewhere that you can monitor securely which gives you the maximum possibility for identifying any surveillance vehicles. Mobile choke points can be:

- **Road junctions**
- **Roundabouts**
- **Bridges**
- **One way streets**
- **Long straight roads**
- **Retail Parks**
- **Quiet roads**
- **Entry to a motorway or service stations**

# MOBILE ROUTE WITHOUT STOPS

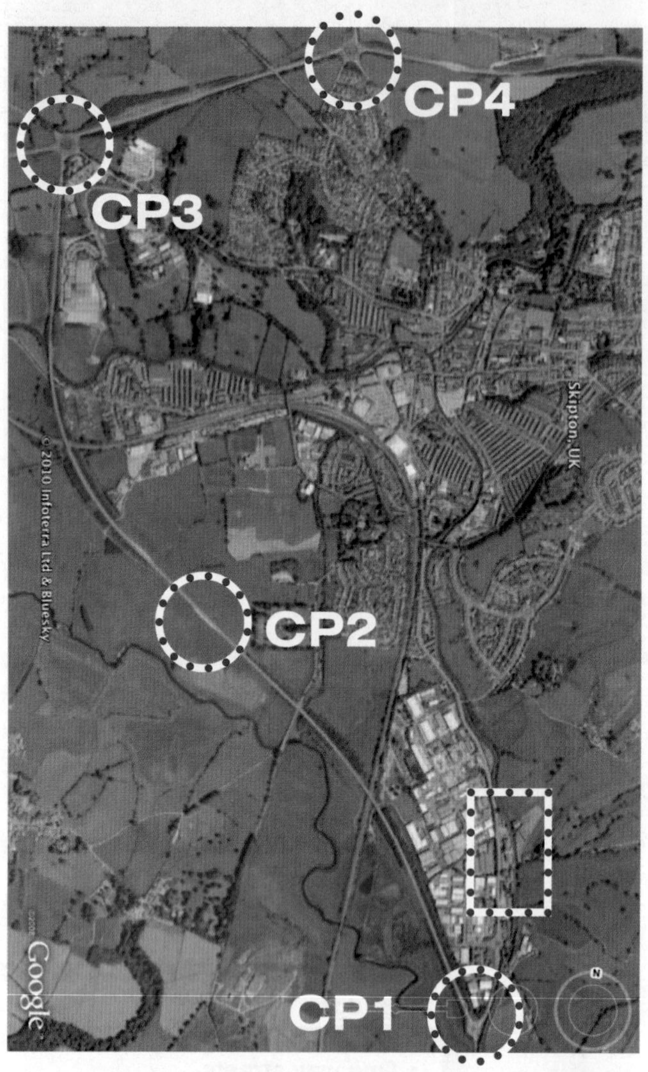

This short route demonstrates various types of choke points. The most direct route is through Skipton town centre. However, this route is not drastically out of the ordinary and incorporates several changes in direction.

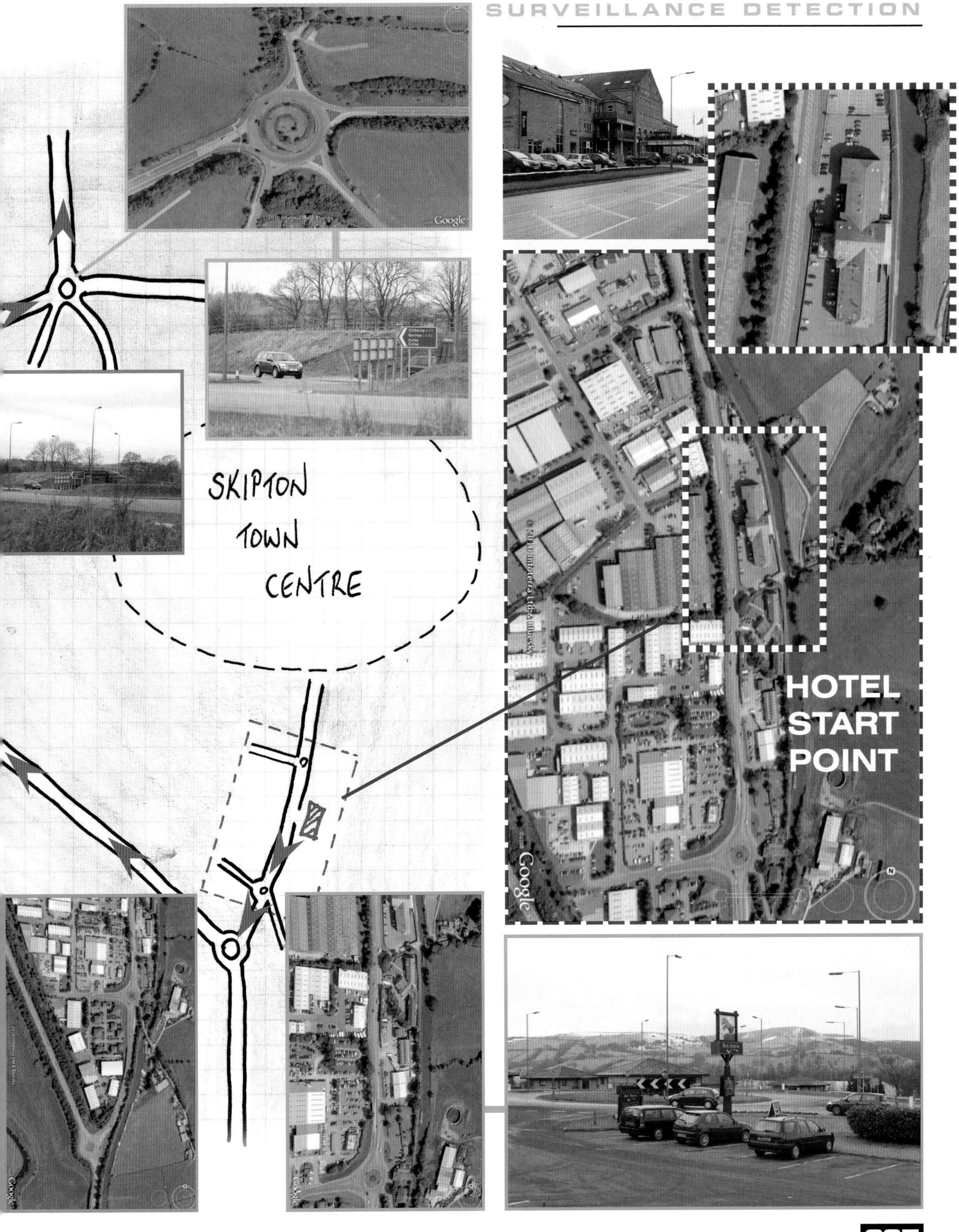

SKIPTON
TOWN
CENTRE

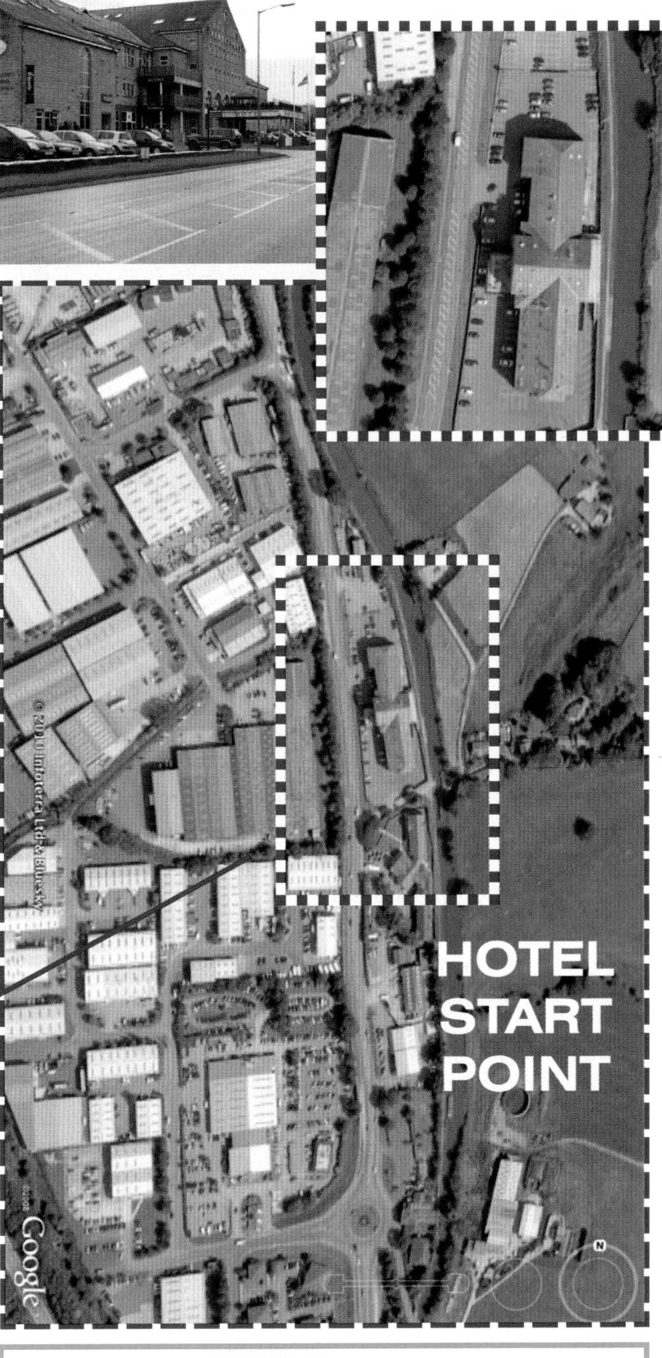

You can monitor the choke points from wherever you feel is a good position. You can be in your car, on foot, in a café or other building close enough to identify vehicle registration details. Try to avoid choke points at very busy roundabouts, busy junctions or on fast roads as it will be difficult to note vehicle details.

## CHOKE POINT 1

CP1 is a crossroads junction where the principal's route takes a right turn. A right turn is chosen on purpose. If he were to turn left, he may approach the junction and if traffic is light, he can pull straight out and turn. Whereas, if turning right, he has to wait for the traffic to clear from both sides which means that there is a chance he will be held at the junction. This is what you are trying to achieve so that the traffic behind stacks up in order for you to identify surveillance vehicles.

This junction should be monitored to:

- Identify the details of at least 8 to 10 cars that are behind the principal (colour, make, registration). Sometimes it is difficult to note all of them and so a memo recorder is useful to note the last three digits of the registration. We say at least 8 cars because if a three man surveillance team is used, they are likely to be spread out and the trail car could be some distance away.

- Identify the cars that make the right turn in the same direction of the principal.

- Observe the roads leading into the junction. A surveillance team may carry out a handover here, so watch for someone turning left or going straight on and then carrying out a U turn to get back into the follow.

- Log and record all sightings.

The CS team leader will decide how the information is to be collated so that a pattern of multiple sightings is identified. Normally each person at a choke point will report his findings to the team leader or a control point. This must be done as soon as possible.

Entry to a motorway or highway can make a good choke point as a surveillance team will be forced to join also. In addition, when exiting the motorway this will possibly identify the same vehicles as they exit also

Principal in white van held whilst waiting to turn right. Note the cars registration that overshoot and take note of any antennas

Note the vehicles that stack-up behind the Principal

Note any other vehicles that appear to be hanging back from the convoy. Note all registration numbers

Note any erratic driving and also look out for the car that originally overshot coming back towards the junction

Any potential surveillance is also likely to turn right after the Principal. Make a note of the 10 vehicles that are behind him

## CHOKE POINT 2

CP2 is a roundabout where the principals route goes straight across at the second exit. Again, you will have to position yourself so that you can monitor all of the vehicles approaching the roundabout and all those exiting at the same exit. You will need to look out for:

• Cars switching lanes at the last minute on approach to the roundabout in preparation for a handover.

• Cars closing up on the principal to avoid a loss at the roundabout.

• Cars going all the way around the roundabout whilst they carry out a handover or a car taking the first exit and then carrying out a quick U turn to get back into the follow.

All sightings and details of vehicles are now reported to the team leader. He will cross refer the sightings at CP1 with those at CP2 to identify if any of the cars sighted are the same.

If a number of cars have been sighted at CP1 and CP2 it does not necessarily mean that they are surveillance. It could be a coincidence which is why we have a third choke point, or even a fourth, to confirm.

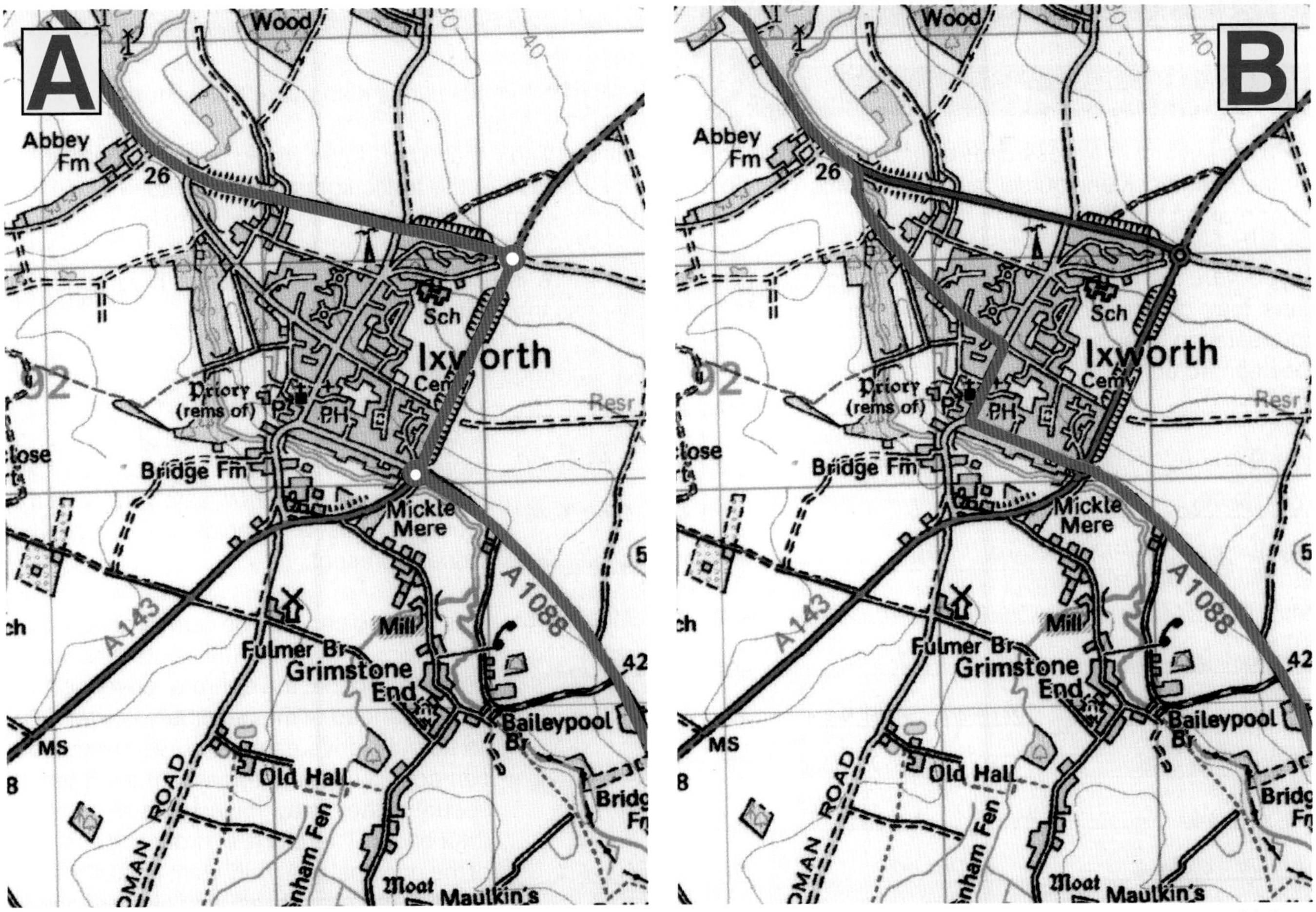

The most direct and quickest route through Ixworth is on the main road where you encounter two roundabouts which can be used as choke points [A]. However, if the Principal goes through the centre of the village, the various changes in direction can also be used as choke points. Map [B] is the preferred route as you are likely to encounter less traffic

**CHOKE POINT** A roundabout can make a good choke point as it is likely that you will see a surveillance team 'stacking-up' behind the Principal. Look out for cars going around the island as they carry out a handover

## CHOKE POINT

CP3 is a left turn at a crossroads controlled by traffic lights. Rather than position yourself before the lights, plot up just after making the left turn.

If you were to monitor before the lights, a good number of cars may go straight or right, which you are not really interested in, therefore the left turn catches all. From your position note:

- All of the vehicles that also make the left turn.

- It is unlikely that a handover would be carried out at the junction due to the traffic lights. One may take place just after the lights and you may see this happen.

- If there is a 'cut through', an operator may take it to by-pass the lights

| CP 1 GOLF | CP 2 HOTEL | CP 3 INDIA |
|---|---|---|
| X168 YUG White Fiesta | PH06 CDE Blue Toyota (taxi) | KL03 PBK White Pick Up. |
| YL04 DPH Green Golf. | FP05 HDC Blue Vectra | YL04 DPH Green GOLF |
| ?? CDE Blue Toyota (TAXI) | WF04 ?? Black Range Rover | DY 778B. Blue Renault 5 |
| Bus! | Y431 LAB Silver Focus | FP05 HDC Blue Vectra |
| FP05 HDC Blue Vectra | HD07 PIJ White Merc | WL07 GBL White Toyota (Taxi) |
| Y431 LAB Silver Focus | YL04 DPH GREEN GOLF | HD07 PIJ White Merc. |
| DS06 CMF Pale blue Audi | ?? DKJ Motorbike - White Helmet | 7.5 Ton Wagon |
| TM01 KAY Yellow Mini | BK04 DBA Maroon Fiat Punto | DLJ 041X Red Fiesta |
| WS48 BMJ Grey Honda | - POLICE CAR. | S174 HDL Silver Honda |

**This chart shows that the green VW Golf and the blue Vectra were sighted at all three choke points which indicates likely surveillance**

All sightings are again reported to the team leader to identify if any of those vehicles noted at CP1 and CP2 are also sighted at CP3. If one or more vehicles have been sighted on all three occasions, you can now safely say that it is more than just a coincidence and surveillance is present.

This method can also be carried out with two operators. However, the route has to be designed so that the operator covering CP1 can get ahead of the principal to cover CP3. To actually drive past the surveillance team can actually pose a threat to the CS teams security (they may have been seen more than once). Therefore, in order to get ahead of the principal, you may want to take a faster parallel route such as a dual carriageway whilst sending the principal along a slower minor road.

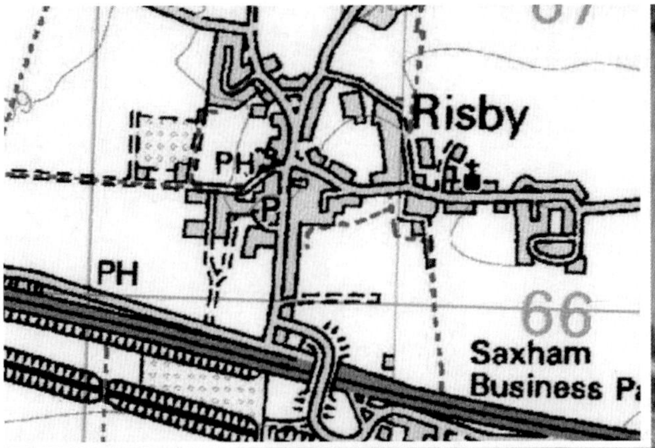

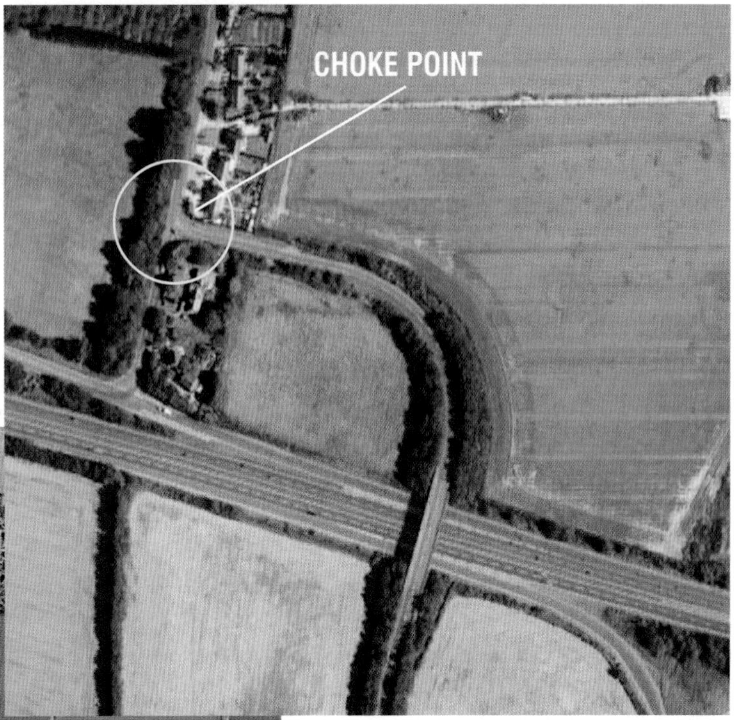

This T-junction follows the exit off a dual carriageway. Any surveillance will be forced to come off following the Principal and reach the T-junction. You will be able to monitor all of these vehicles and it is likely you will witness a handover

## MOBILE CS ROUTE WITH STOPS

Our principal is an undercover officer who is meeting with an aware and hostile criminal. When he leaves the meeting, the officer needs to ensure that he is not followed away in order to preserve his identity and his personal security.

Surveillance detection routes with stops can pose a risk to the principal because he has to stop, therefore any stop has to be logical, consistent and should have a purpose. By stopping, we can force a surveillance team to react in a certain way and so possibly identify them. The principal can also proceed on foot when he stops, which again will force the surveillance team to react as they deploy on foot. A mobile CS route with stops can also be covered with a minimum number of personnel, even just one person.

Prior to the operation, the principal is briefed on the time he is to depart and the exact route he is to take. If he has to make changes in direction, these turns are to be given in detail and at easily identifiable places i.e. opposite a large advertising board or a petrol station. He is told exactly what to do at each stop.

Changes in direction should be easily identifiable to avoid confusion

After briefing the principal, he should leave being confident of what he has to do. If his instructions are written down, care has to be taken that any surveillance does not see him constantly referring to notes, it will make them suspicious.

Choke Points do not necessarily have to be manned from your car. You can be within a building such as a cafe or out on foot

**When the Principal stops at a choke point you should monitor the area for potential surveillance. You should note the cars that come in behind the Principal and those that carry out erratic manouvering whilst they obtain a trigger and replot to cover their options**

The principal should be briefed to:

• Depart on schedule

• Drive normally, not faster or slower

• Fully understand the route being taken

• Make no attempt to try and spot surveillance himself. That is what the CS is for

• Do not react or start to carry out anti surveillance drills

• Do not speed in order to make ground if he gets held up in traffic, this may be considered as drilling

• Do not carry out U turns or make aggressive manoeuvres if he misses a turning. Again this may be considered as drilling. You do not want the team to 'lift off', you want to lure them in

• Follow the instructions to the letter

**Surveillance operators should not leave their 'working tools' on the seat**

Ideally, the principal should not know or be able to recognise any of the CS team. Should he get lost or confused it is possible that he may approach one of them to ask directions and thus compromise you by association.

Whoever plans the route has to consider changes in direction and also the reasons for stopping.

# LEAPFROGGING

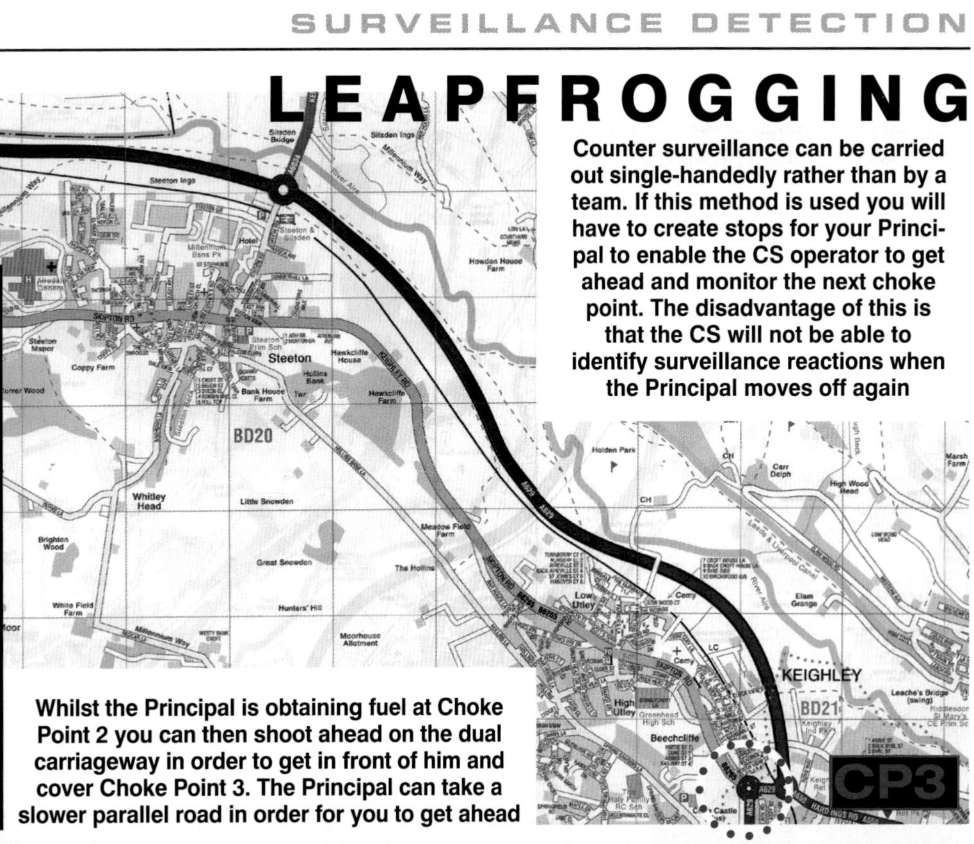

Counter surveillance can be carried out single-handedly rather than by a team. If this method is used you will have to create stops for your Principal to enable the CS operator to get ahead and monitor the next choke point. The disadvantage of this is that the CS will not be able to identify surveillance reactions when the Principal moves off again

CP2

CP3

Whilst the Principal is obtaining fuel at Choke Point 2 you can then shoot ahead on the dual carriageway in order to get in front of him and cover Choke Point 3. The Principal can take a slower parallel road in order for you to get ahead

**GOTCHA!** The practice of clearing a target's vehicle by surveillance operators is not always a good idea, especially if it is a sophisticated target that may employ counter surveillance. In this sequence the Principal's vehicle is being checked while he is away. The surveillance operator is identified along with his car.

Consider various choke points to stop at:

• If one is a café or shop, make sure that it will be open when the principal comes through. Ensure he has cash

• If you use a car wash or a petrol station, ensure that the car is dirty and not already full of fuel

• If you use a florist to stop and buy flowers don't let the principal leave them on the back seat to die or leave them in the car for three days

• If you visit a launderette, take something in to be cleaned

Your stops can have a theme to them but do not make it appear odd or unusual. For example, stopping at one electrical goods shop and then visiting another and then another would not seem out of place - you're comparing prices. Whereas, a coffee shop, followed by another and then another, may seem odd.

**Note those on foot in the vicinity of your Principal and observe their body language**

## CHOKE POINT 

CP1 is a busy coffee shop just off a main road with its own car park. The principal is instructed to park in a particular place, proceed on foot and enter the store. He is to remain in there for at least 15 minutes to have his drink before leaving.

The CS operator covers the coffee shop by plotting up and observing the approaches and general area; as the principal arrives, he will be looking out for and noting:

- The next 8 or so cars that are behind the principal

- Cars that quickly turn off after the location or just before it as the surveillance team plot up

**Look for cars that are 'two-up' and the occupants appearing attentive**

- Any cars that follow into the same car parking area or appear to be manoeuvring for a trigger from across the street or nearby
- Erratic manoeuvring from cars as they position themselves, reverse park, nose forward to get a view or carry out a drive past

- Unusual body language from drivers in cars, anxiousness, constant head turning, talking to themselves or visible radios

- Any persons getting out on foot and acting odd without any reason for being there

- Anyone going into the coffee shop (it may be that a surveillance team would not follow him into the coffee shop if they are considering 'loss/gain')

Once the CS operator is satisfied he has enough information, he uses the delay of the principal having coffee to get ahead and drive to the next choke point.

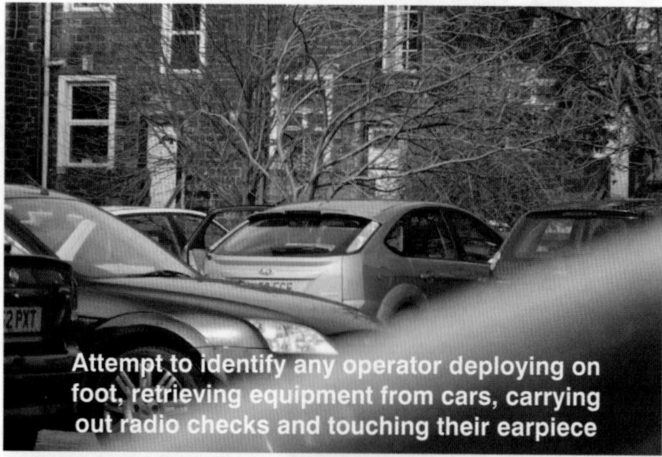

**Attempt to identify any operator deploying on foot, retrieving equipment from cars, carrying out radio checks and touching their earpiece**

## CHOKE POINT 2

CP2 is a petrol station where the principal is instructed to obtain fuel. The CS operator has arrived first and waits for the principal and the same procedure as above starts again, noting down as much as he can to cross reference any sightings with the first stop.

When the principal enters the kiosk to pay, he then moves on to the next choke point, CP3. If there are two operators carrying out the counter surveillance, one would remain in situ whilst the other moves on. The one remaining would be checking the area for activity and sudden movements when the principal departs. Any sightings should be cross referenced with your partner.

This car is located at the exit of a car park and appears as if it is on a 'mission' by the way it is parked (note the wheels)

## CHOKE POINT 

CP3 is a large retail park with an indoor shopping mall, the principal is instructed to enter the mall and obtain a balance from an ATM machine and then visit a travel agents (some distance from the ATM) where he is to ask about cheap flights to Zurich on a particular date.

Deploying on foot at the mall should present many indicators of a surveillance team. Firstly, any vehicles noted here should now be cross referred with the other two stops. If none are noted then you can presume that surveillance is not present. If one or two (or more) cars are identified then you can assume that surveillance is present. You now have the dilemma of what to do next.

If you decide to continue the CS plan, consider these options:

• Observe the principal's car whilst he is away from it. A surveillance operator may carry out a walk past to note anything of interest inside, check his parking ticket or even put a tracker under his car

A surveillance operator will consider loss versus gain. You may have to create a trap which will draw them in such as a travel or estate agent or a hotel reception

• Observe the whole area of the car park from above, look for anyone acting with urgency as he parks up or gets out of his car. His body language may give him away as he pats his pockets for his mobile phone and wallet or fiddles under clothes to adjust his body-worn radio

• Observe the entrance to the mall, which the principal went through. A surveillance team will close up here so that they do not lose their target and will be channelled. You should be noting: people talking to themselves, pressels in hands, diver's watches, earpieces and those acting with a sense of urgency

• Use height from upper floor balconies to assist you to overlook an area but remember a surveillance is also likely to do the same

• When the principal uses the ATM, note any reactions you get from other pedestrians such as; hovering in the mall, sudden stopping, people quickly getting out mobile phones or someone getting in very close to the principal as he uses the machine. When he walks off, look for sudden movement and if the principal drops a small piece of white paper, it may get picked up by the surveillance thinking it is a slip from the ATM

• The travel agency should be some distance from the ATM machine. If they were next to each other, the principal would not break the surveillance 'box' as he goes from one to the other so he has to move in order to make the surveillance move

• At the travel agents you are looking for reactions to a stop and note the pedestrian activity and cross reference any sightings. Hopefully, entering the travel agents will tempt an eager surveillance person to go in as well.

**Mobile CS Route at Night**

Consider all of the above points when selecting a detection route to be carried out at night time. Obviously, it will be more difficult for you to identify colours of vehicles and registrations and so you may have to be right on top of your chosen choke point. If at all possible, attempt to observe the choke point and vehicles from behind, otherwise the cars headlights will blind you making it difficult to obtain details.

***Your choke point at night has to be in a position where vehicles are forced to slow down, such as approaching a junction. This enables you to obtain the registration number***

A memo recorder is essential for noting vehicle details as they come through a choke point

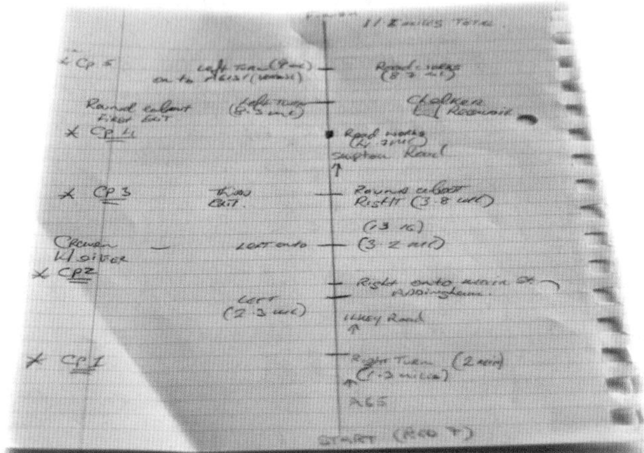
Your CS route should be simple and clear for the Principal to understand and follow

### Detected or Not Detected

If no surveillance is detected, you can call your principal by mobile phone and tell him that he is clear to run and that is the end of the job. In the days prior to mobile phones, a system would have been needed to indicate to the principal if he was clear or not. This may have been by briefing him; 'When you come out of the shopping mall and head back to your car, if you see a man standing in the entranceway wearing a high-vis vest with the words 'COMAG' on the back of it then you are clear to run. If you do not see him, you are to return to your car and wait for someone to approach you from the CS team and he will escort you'.

A CS team preparing a briefing

If surveillance is detected you now have several options open to you. The priority may be to go overt to protect and escort your principal to safety. The other option, (which could be risky) is to run the principal through a fourth choke point (that you have either planned or improvised) in order to further establish the make up of the surveillance team and take photographs or video - if you have not already done so. It may be that you want to run them into a trap to effect an arrest or just approach them to cause a compromise.

It may be that you now want to investigate the threat further and follow the surveillance. If this is your decision, do so with extreme caution and not single-handed. Ensure that you keep well back and use distance as much as you can at the back of the hostile team. Ensure that you do not get in between any of them and watch out for stragglers, especially after they have carried out a handover. If they have a biker, it is likely that he will be hanging at the rear of the convoy so be aware of any motorbikes that hang behind traffic.

If the hostile team is followed, you will either take them back to their base (hotel or office) or it is likely that they will lift off and RV at a suitable spot, quite often a café or fast food outlet where they will carry out a quick debrief over coffee. At this stage they will probably drop their guard as they switch off and therefore you can use this to your advantage to obtain closer identities of the team.

### AUTOMATIC NUMBER PLATE RECOGNITION (ANPR)

ANPR is widely used over Britain's roads in order monitor cars movements in the fight against crime. A portable system is available such as CitySnyc's 'JET Roadrunner' where a camera can be placed in a building or in a vehicle parked at the side of the road. The system records the number plate of each vehicle that passes and can read up to four lanes of fast moving traffic simultaneously. The intelligent software is able to store and log all sightings and alert you of any repeated sightings of the same plate.

A portable ANPR system can be located in a car and parked on the roadside to monitor all vehicle activity

ANPR is being used more and more in public car parks and is a very effective way of collecting parking fines

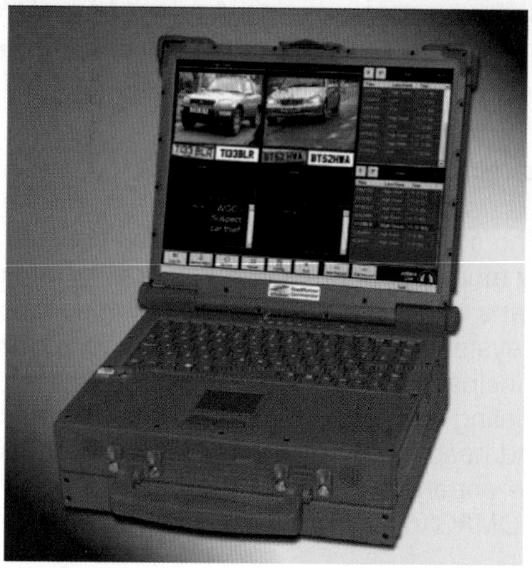

Courtesy: CitySync Ltd

ANPR is more likely to be used in long-term counter surveillance projects or very high risk perimeter monitoring.

**Don't forget trackers!**

Remember to carry out a thorough search of the principal's car for trackers. You may have planned and executed an excellent counter surveillance route and established that surveillance is not present but if there is a tracker fitted, you will never see them because they will not be there, letting the tracker do the work.

**Conclusion**

Having learnt most tactics relating to surveillance, you should be able to think to yourself, 'If I were to be put under surveillance, what would I do in order to identify the watchers and what would I do to draw them out into the open?'

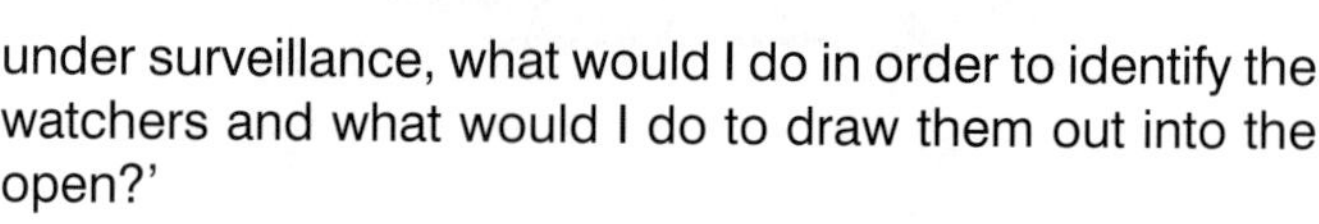

An unprofessional team is easily spotted and very easily caught out. An experienced surveillance team is more likely to carry out tactics to ensure that they are not spotted. If they suspect that they are being drawn into a compromise, they are more likely to 'lift off' from the surveillance and let the target run.

Ensure that you do not get seen by the surveillance, they only have to see you on two occasions to get concerned and realise that counter surveillance is in place.

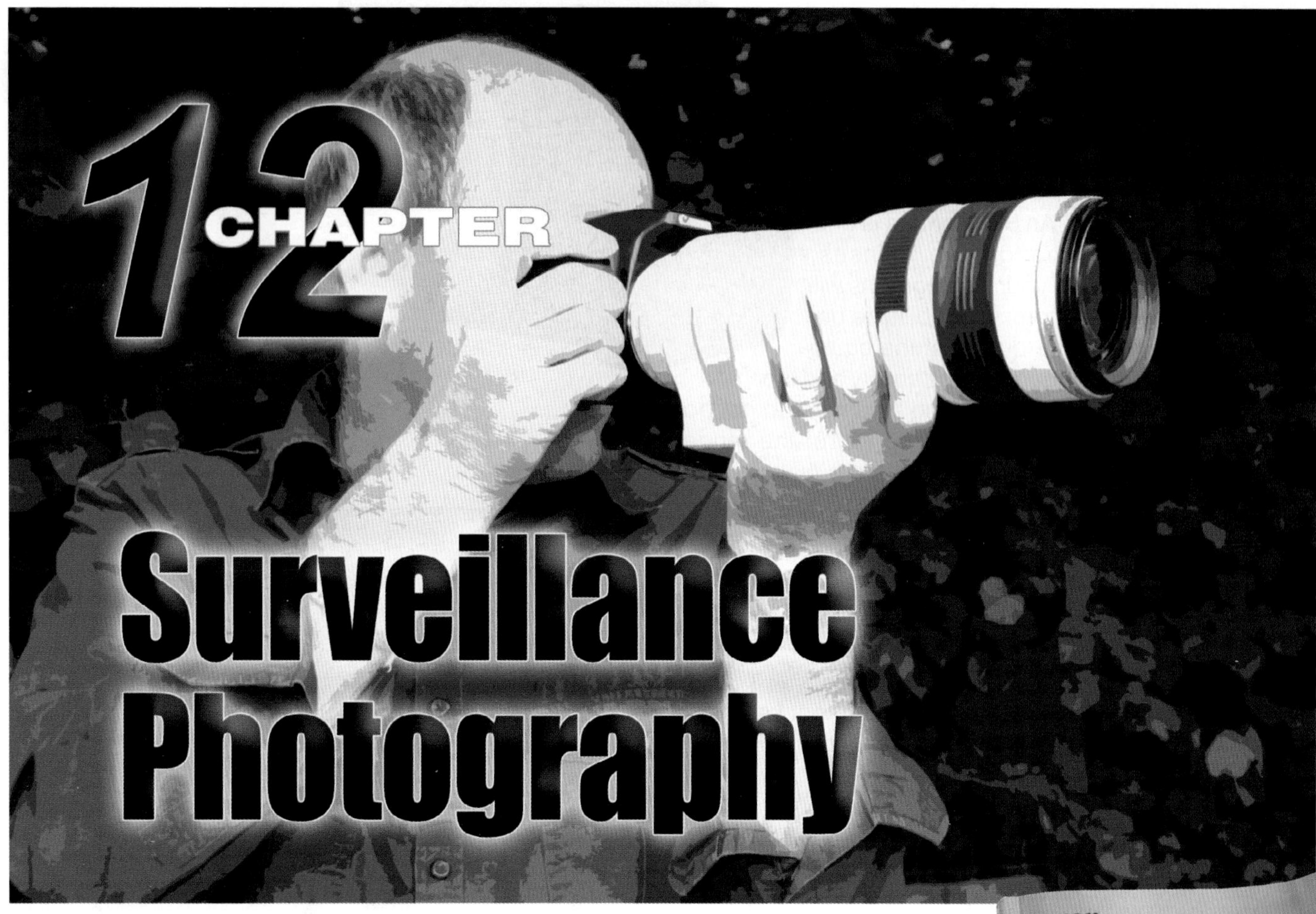


Many investigators and surveillance operators prefer to use video footage rather than stills, because still photography can be quite technical to the novice. However, it is just as easy to fail with video as it is with a stills camera. On the commercial surveillance circuit, many clients prefer video evidence, especially in relation to 'personal injury' investigations.

This chapter deals with aspects of digital photography, still and video in relation to surveillance. It is not intended for the reader to become a professional photographer but deals with the various aspects that will enable you to produce a quality photograph taken in poor conditions such as bad light and with the use of telephoto lenses.

If you are watching an individual or a premises for a long period of time to obtain photographic evidence it is imperative that you know your photographic equipment and its abilities. It can be embarrassing having to report back to a client after twenty hours of observations with a photograph which is either blurred, out of focus or under exposed. The photograph is often the product that the client is buying.

After you have read this chapter it would be wise to go out and experiment with your camera and practice some of the techniques that have been described. At the end of this chapter there is a short practical exercise for you to carry out for this purpose. Going straight out on a surveillance task with a new camera is asking for trouble. Read the instruction manual, play with the camera and then read the manual again to discover something new.

## DIGITAL STILLS PHOTOGRAPHY

There are many cameras available and choosing one can be difficult. A brand name Digital SLR (single lens reflex) camera such as Nikon, Canon or Sony is ideal. An SLR camera is one which has inter-changeable lenses. Ultimately, the quality of your photographs will be a combination of factors: your ability to use the camera correctly, the quality of the equipment, your personal judgement, the quality and type of lens that you use. When choosing a camera do not go for the most expensive; an expensive top of the range camera will give you hundreds of different features but you are likely to only use a fraction of them.

- Ask an experienced user for of their advice and recommendations. Do not rely on a camera shops advice, all they want to do is close a sale
- Choose a camera that will withstand knocks and rough handling, get a black one, not silver in colour
- Make sure the camera feels comfortable and balanced in your hands and the controls are simple and quick to use
- Operating the camera may appear complicated at first, after a few days handling, you will become accustomed to it
- Ensure that it has a Spot Metering facility
- Make sure it has automatic, shutter and aperture priority exposure modes
- Ensure the resolution is at least 10 Mega pixels
- Choose lenses with focal length and speed in mind. As a basic kit, I would choose an 18-55mm and a 55-250mm lens.

Two lenses suitable for general photography

### Digital SLR Cameras

Digital cameras operate in the same way as conventional wet film cameras however, instead of capturing the image on a film, the image is read by a series of light sensors which convert it into signals and that are stored on a memory card as an image.

This card can then be read on a computer and the image downloaded for printing or manipulation with suitable software. A photograph taken with a digital camera can be quickly and simply downloaded onto a lap top computer and sent by email to anywhere in the world within minutes.

### Image Size and Resolution

Image size and image resolution are two different processes and a detailed explanation can become very technical. In simple terms, the image size is the actual size of the picture if it were to be printed on paper. The image size can be altered in the cameras settings menu, the larger the size, the more memory it will take up. Personally, I set this to the largest size possible as you can always reduce the size afterwards. Setting it small and then enlarging the picture later can reduce its quality considerably.

An image is made up of 'pixel elements' or pixels. A pixel is a tiny dot of colour and a digital image is made up from millions of these dots. Normal viewing of a picture is crisp and sharp but if you enlarge the picture or view it with a

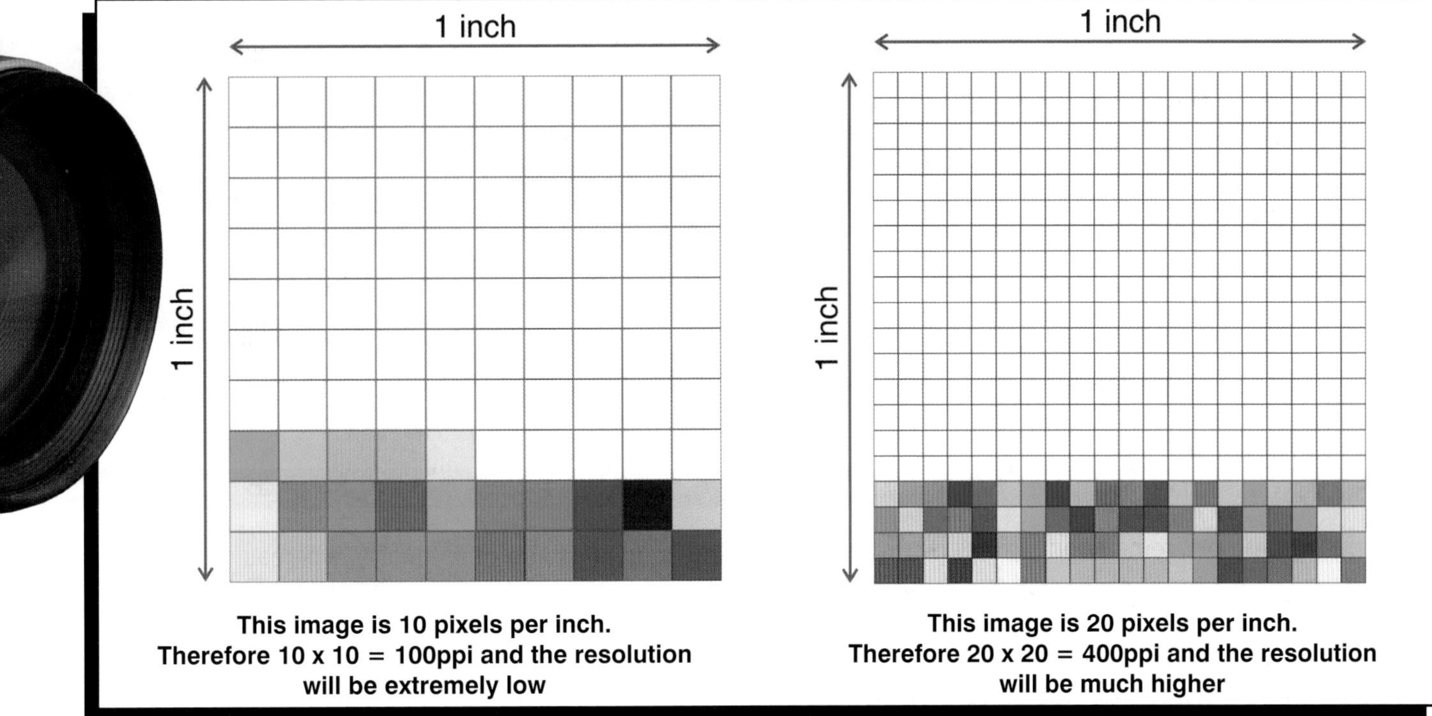


**This image is 10 pixels per inch. Therefore 10 x 10 = 100ppi and the resolution will be extremely low**

**This image is 20 pixels per inch. Therefore 20 x 20 = 400ppi and the resolution will be much higher**

magnifying glass you will notice the individual pixels and the image becomes blurred or 'pixelated'.

The more pixels that you have in an image, the sharper it will be. For instance, a picture with an image size of 3.99cm x 6cm with an image resolution of 72 pixels per inch (ppi) means that there are 72 pixels for every inch. It also means that the dimensions of the image in pixels is 113 x 170 which is not very sharp as each pixel will be 'stretched' and enlarged over this area and when printed could be quite blurred.

However, the same 3.99cm x 6cm image with a resolution of 300 ppi would give you pixel dimensions of 471 x 709 and will be printed at a very sharp resolution.

These settings are important and are dependent on what you are going to use the images for. When a picture is taken, most cameras store them on the memory card at 72ppi; the image size will be whatever you have set on the camera.

If you intend printing the pictures or want to include them in a document, I would suggest that you alter the image to 300ppi. If they are only going to be used for viewing on a computer or used on the internet as a webpage, then keep them at 72ppi. A computer screen can only display images at 72ppi, so it is pointless having an image of 300ppi used in a website as it will be no sharper but it will be a very large file to download. Note the file size in the images below.

The image size and resolution can be altered using software such as Adobe Photoshop Elements or Microsoft Office Picture Manager. Google's 'Picasa' is a free download and is simple to use for image processing and filing.

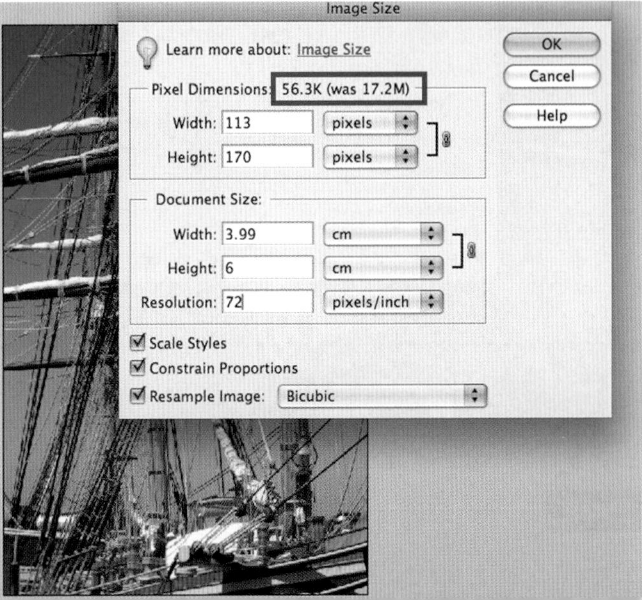

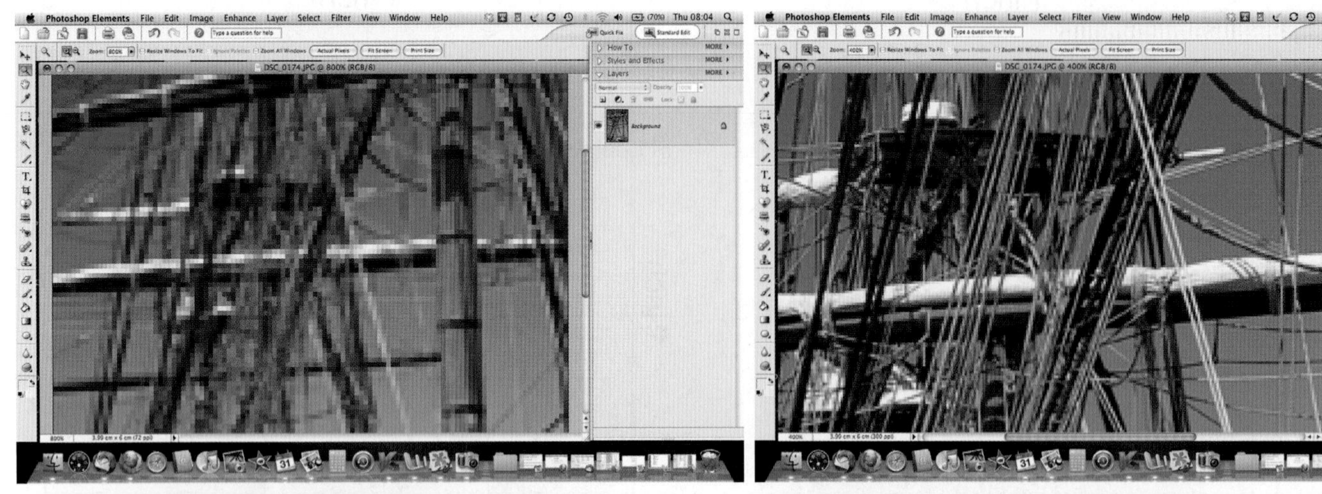

To keep things simple, remember:

- The more pixels in the image, the better the quality it will be when printed
- The more pixels, the larger the file size. So, if you intend emailing the picture, keep it small
- For images used on the internet, set the resolution to 72ppi
- For printing on paper, set the resolution to 300ppi

## IMAGE COMPRESSION

When a picture is taken, it is stored on a memory card and digitally compressed so that it does not take up too much memory space. However, a high compression setting means that the image is really squashed together and in doing so loses some of its quality, whereas, a low compression is a larger file but of better quality. The 'quality' or compression setting can be altered through your cameras menu settings. I always have my camera set to take the highest quality (lowest compression) although the draw back is that you cannot store as many pictures on a

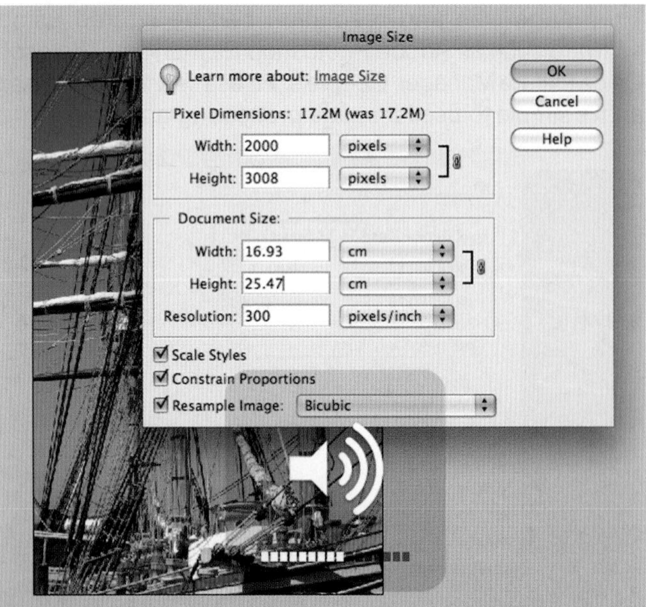


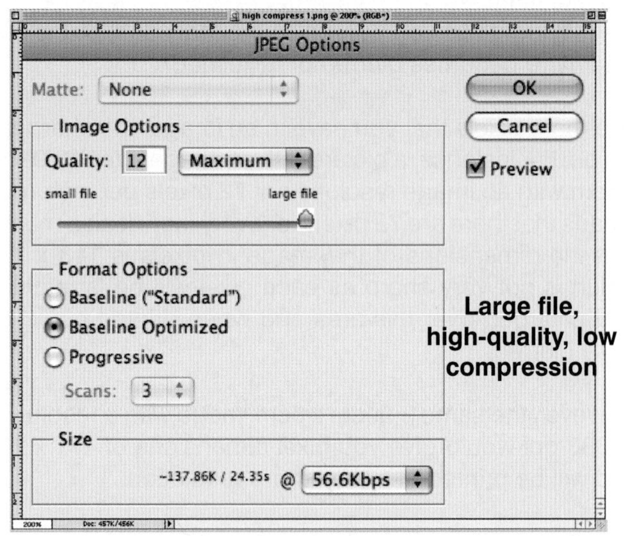


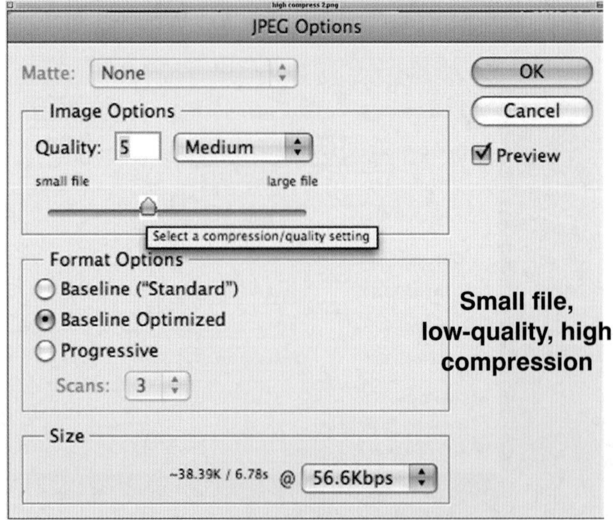

memory card. However, it is far better to save images at the highest quality and work down as you cannot store an image at low quality and then manipulate it to look better later.

Another disadvantage of having the camera set to the highest quality is 'shot time lag'. This is a delay that occurs when you cannot take shots in quick succession because the images are being processed by the cameras computer. However, a high-end professional camera should not have this problem.

If you have altered an image by computer and saved it, the programme may ask you if you want to save it at a high, medium or low quality. When you click save, the picture is compressed again. If you want to save it for use on the web, choose low quality but if it is for printing choose high quality.

**RAW Images**

Your digital camera will probably store the image as a JPG file onto the memory card. A JPG is a file that has been compressed by the camera in order to store as many as possible on the card. However, on most good cameras you can choose to save the images in RAW format. This means that the image is not altered or compressed and therefore the nearest it can possibly be to the original when it was taken. The drawback is that you will store less images on a card as they are very large files. Most professional photographers shoot in RAW as so much can be done with them in the digital darkroom. You will need a good software package such as Photoshop in order to open up RAW files.

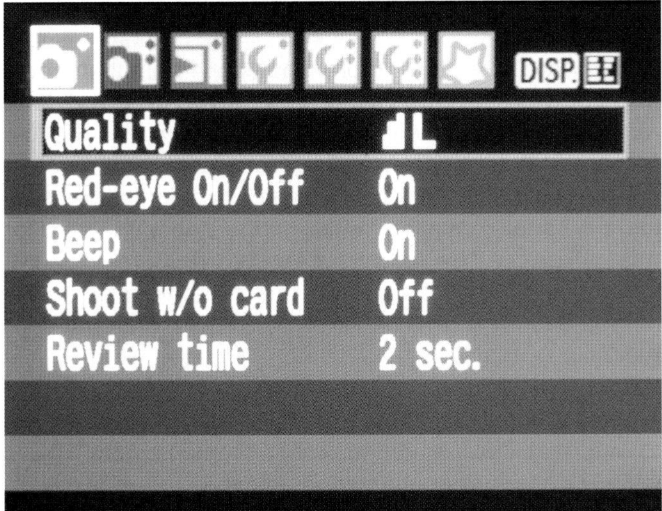

**Note that when RAW format is selected the number of images stored on the memory card is greatly reduced**

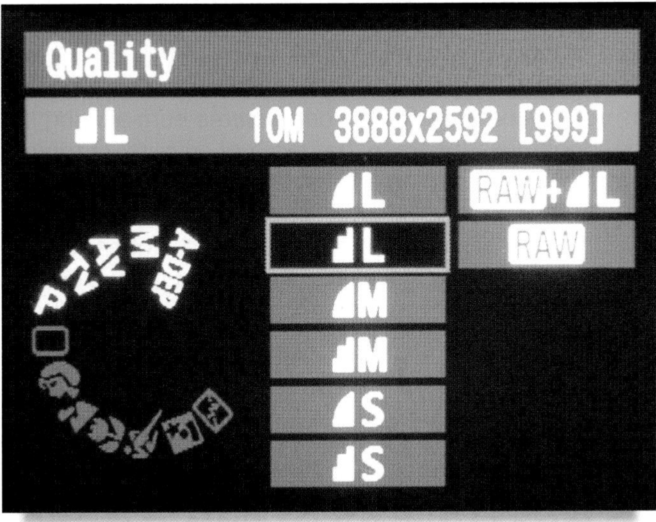


Raw files (stored as .CR2 files) can be processed and manipulated to reveal objects that the eye cannot see on a normal JPG file. We recently used an 800mm lens to photograph a van arriving at a target site from about 2km away. By tweaking and filtering the colours, we were able to reveal the colour and shape of the logo on the side of a van.

Police and other enforcement agencies tend to use RAW as standard because it is the nearest you will get to the original. As a JPG is a compressed file, it could be argued technically that it has been modified but more is mentioned on this subject in the chapter on evidence.

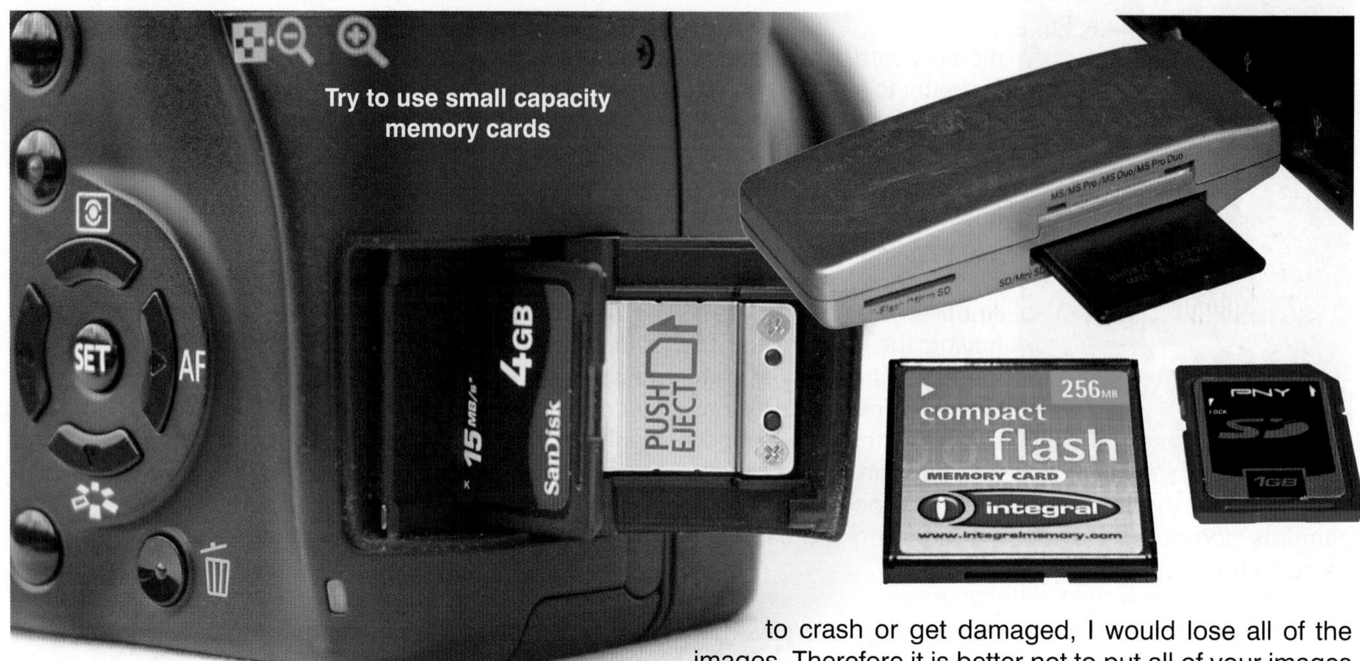


## Memory Cards

Every digital camera stores the images onto flash memory cards and there are various types: Secure Digital (SD), Compact Flash (CF), and Memory Stick (MS) to name a few. The cards can be removed from the camera and read by a computer. Always remember to switch off your camera before removing or inserting a card or you may damage it.

Each card will have a storage capacity normally measured in Gigabytes (Gb). At the time of writing, an 8Gb is the largest capacity card available and can store thousands of images. Personally I use 2Gb cards, any larger will encourage me to store more pictures and if the card were to crash or get damaged, I would lose all of the images. Therefore it is better not to put all of your images in one basket.

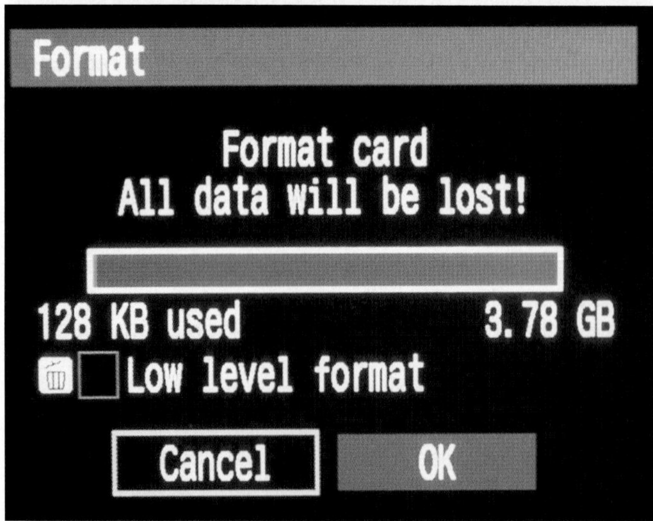


**Reformat the SD card regularly but be aware all images will be permanently erased**

A 1Gb card can store approximately 644 small images, 356 medium images and 204 large images. It is recommended to download the images from the card to a computer as soon as possible. If you want to write protect the card so that the images cannot be accidentally erased, there is usually a sliding switch on the side of the card for this purpose. The images can be transferred to the computer either by connecting the camera directly to the computer with a USB cable or by using a memory card reader.

After erasing all of the images on the card, it may be wise to re-format it so that you maximise storage space. This is usually done through the cameras menu.

## Manipulating Digital Photographs

Most of the digital photographs taken in this book were processed with Adobe Photoshop software. This package lets you do many things to your pictures from altering the size, brightness/contrast, the depth of colours, cropping, re-touching and adding special effects.

My camera's settings are always on the highest quality (maximum resolution) and also the largest picture size so when an image is brought across to the computer it can be as much as 3.8Mb in terms of file size. The actual image size is 137cm x 91cm which is very large to use in a document. Therefore, to make the image more manageable, I would firstly crop it to cut out any unwanted stuff around the edges; then I would re-size the image, making it 15cm x 11cm and set the resolution to 300ppi. As a consequence, the file size is then reduced to 448k.

Use the 'Crop Tool' in Photoshop to select the part of the image you wish to retain - do this before you resize the file

### Power

Digital cameras use up a lot of battery power. If your camera takes standard size batteries, it is recommended to use hi-power (2100mAh) rechargeable ones. Due to their lower cost and the fact that rechargeable batteries last longer.

Your camera is likely to have an LCD screen in order to make adjustments to the camera's settings

Images taken can be reviewed on most digital cameras

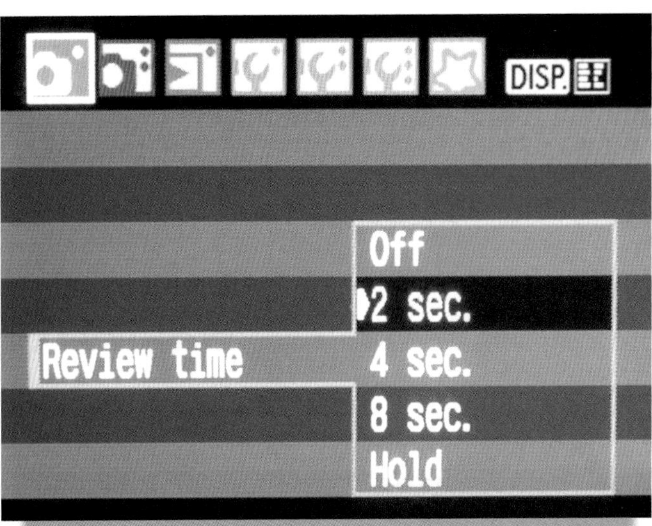


If you do not need to review each image as it is taken, switch the viewer off to preserve battery power

**If not using your camera for a while, remove the battery. Always ensure you have a fully charged spare.**

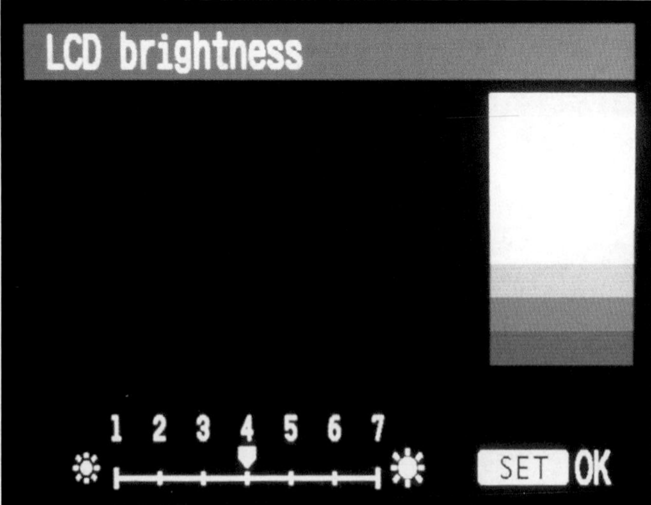


**Reducing the screen's brightness, will save battery power and prevent illuminating your face at night-time**

and also to review the images taken. If possible, manually turn this off, as the screen is a large drain on the batteries. If your camera has a conventional viewfinder use it to compose the shot rather than the LCD screen.

## DIGITAL SINGLE LENS REFLEX (D-SLR) CAMERAS

### HOW A DIGITAL CAMERA WORKS

A camera is a light proof box with a light sensor called a Charge Coupled Device (CCD) at one end (instead of film) and a lens at the other, which focuses light onto the sensor.

There are two things that control the amount of light that enters the camera and hits the sensor:

- *The diameter of the lens, which we call aperture*
- *The length of time the aperture is held open (shutter speed)*

Different combinations of these two factors give different effects to the image, which are very important and are described below.

A correct exposure is where the camera reads the amount of light available and sets what it calculates to be the ideal aperture and shutter speed. Some area of the picture maybe in shade and another in bright light and so the cameras meter calculates an average to obtain a correct exposure.

**Correct Exposure is a combination of aperture setting and shutter speed**

**Aperture**

As stated, the aperture is the size of the hole that allows light to reach the sensor and is controlled by a diaphragm inside the lens. The size of the aperture can be altered and is given a numerical value which represents the size. These values are called **'f'** numbers or **'f stops'** and follow in sequence:

**f1.4 2.8 4 5.6 8 11 16 22**

**f2** being the widest aperture, letting in a lot of light and **f22** the smallest, letting in less light.

The series as a whole is arranged so that each **f** number lets in twice as much light as the previous number.

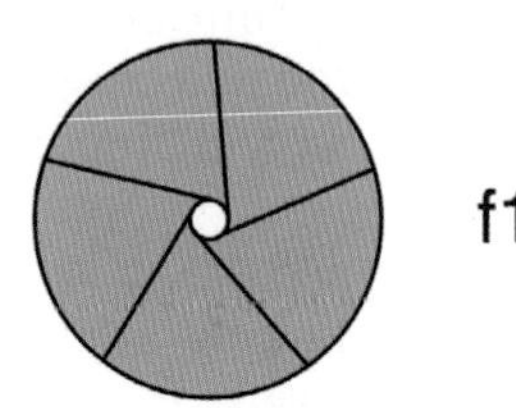

f16

***So why is aperture so important to the surveillance photographer?***

A wide aperture such as a f2.8 will allow in plenty of light and this is needed in a low light situation which is common in surveillance photography, especially in the early morning or in the evening. In addition, a

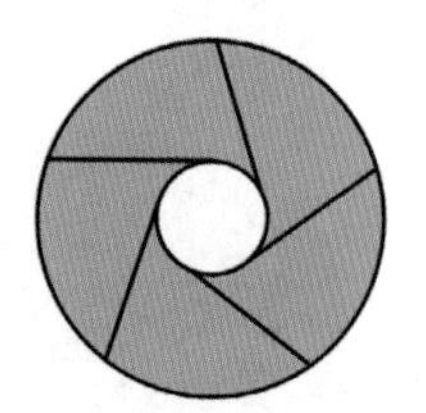

f8

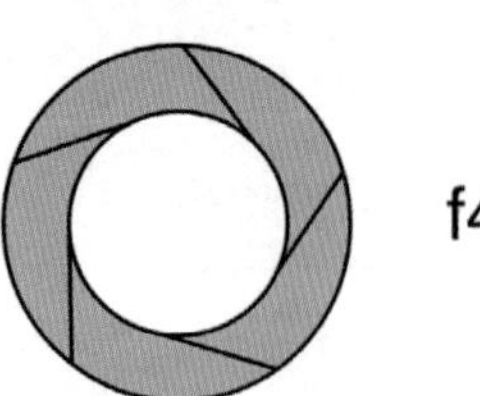

f4

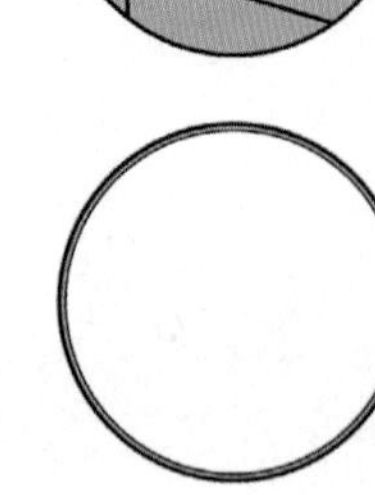

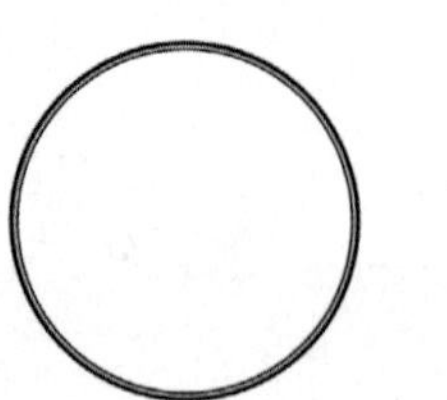

f2

larger aperture will allow you to use faster shutter speeds, which is important with a telephoto lens. Whether you use a small or large aperture also has a strange effect on the image which we call 'depth of field' and is described below.

**Shutter Speed**

Shutter speed is the amount of time the shutter is held open to allow sufficient light to fall on the sensor before closing again.

Shutter speed is measured in fractions of a second, such as:

**This photograph was taken with a slow shutter speed of 1/15th of a second which gives the "blurred" effect caused by the motion of the bus**

| 1/15 | 1/30 | 1/60 | 1/125 | 1/250 | 1/500 | 1/1000 |
|---|---|---|---|---|---|---|

They are similar to the aperture **'f'** numbers in that each shutter speed either doubles or halves the one next to it. Shutter speed is important especially when shooting in low light, moving subjects and with telephoto lenses.

When you take the first pressure on the shutter button, it focuses the lens and takes a reading; it calculates what it considers to be the best aperture and best shutter speed to use. Both are related by inverse ratio because as you alter the shutter speed, the aperture is also affected. The slower the shutter speed, the smaller the aperture. The wider the aperture, the faster the shutter speed.

**The first image the exposure was set on f8, the second f5.6 and the third f4. Note the difference in exposure as the aperture is opened wider**

Exposure control on a Nikon camera

**The aperture and shutter speed are inversely related (i.e. the faster the shutter speed the larger the aperture)**

## EXPOSURE MODES

Many cameras have different exposure modes and your camera's manual should explain what modes are available, such as:

- *Automatic*
- *Program*
- *Aperture Priority*
- *Shutter Priority*
- *Manual*

- **Automatic Exposure**

Most SLR cameras have an automatic mode and it is usually identified by a green symbol on the mode dial. In this mode, all that is needed to take a picture is to point the camera which takes a meter reading and automatically sets the camera's aperture setting and shutter speed to obtain a correct exposure - it will also pop up the flash if needed. This is a good setting for the novice but not always ideal in surveillance photography where more control over the camera is required.

Exposure control on a Canon camera

- **Program Mode**

In this mode, the camera takes an exposure reading and suggests the best settings to use. Turning the control dial can manually alter the shutter speed and the camera selects the correct aperture to match. This mode is used to give you more control over which shutter speed or aperture to use in order to obtain certain effects.

Let's imagine you've just taken a meter reading and your camera suggests an exposure of **1/125**sec at **f8.** To achieve the same exposure, you turn the control dial to use any of the following aperture and shutter speed combinations:

| 2.8 | 4 | 5.6 | 8 | 11 | 16 |
|---|---|---|---|---|---|
| 1/1000 | 1/500 | 1/250 | 1/125 | 1/60 | 1/30 |

The combination you choose depends on what type of effect you are trying to achieve.

- **Aperture Priority**

When in this mode, you manually set the aperture setting and the camera automatically sets the shutter speed.

**Highlighted in red you can read the camera's shutter speed and aperture setting in the display**

For example:

If aperture **f16** is selected, the camera may automatically set a shutter speed of **1/15** sec

If aperture is set to **f5.6** the camera may then choose **1/500** of a second

In surveillance photography, this mode should rarely be used except when depth of field is important such as taking pictures:

- *Through fences or foliage*
- *Close up objects or documents*
- *When you need to place a subject in its surroundings*
- *Filming in low light when you need the largest aperture*

Depth of field is explained shortly but we tend to use this mode in poor light so that the widest aperture can be set on the camera.

- **Shutter Priority**

When in this mode, you manually set the shutter speed and the camera automatically sets the aperture.

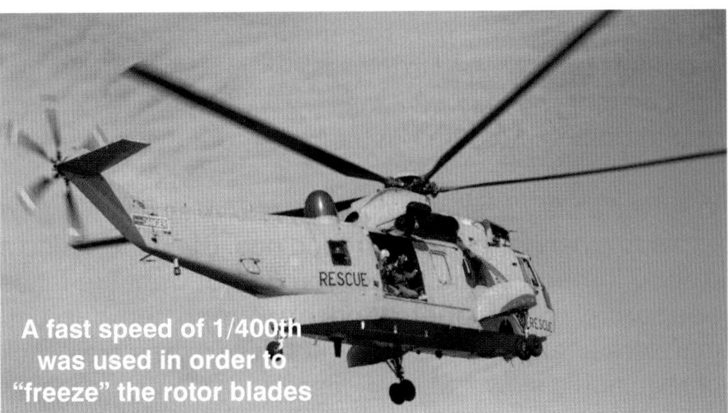


A fast speed of 1/400th was used in order to "freeze" the rotor blades

Your choice of shutter speed affects how moving subjects will appear in the picture. Slow shutter speeds such as 1/15 or 1/30 of a second, will blur moving subjects. Fast shutter speeds such as 1/250, 1/500 or 1/1000 of a second can be used to freeze the action of a moving subject. Fast shutter speeds are required when using telephoto lenses to prevent camera shake.

- **Manual Mode**

This mode is used when you require full control over exposure. Photography in this mode would only be recommended for the experienced photographer as the aperture and shutter setting are controlled separately and independently.

## DEPTH OF FIELD

Depth of field is the extent of the picture that will be in focus when set at a given f number.

For example, if we focus the camera on a tree in a field some 50 metres away, the tree will be sharp and in focus. An area in front of the tree and behind it will also be in focus but only for a certain distance. This area in focus is called the depth of field.

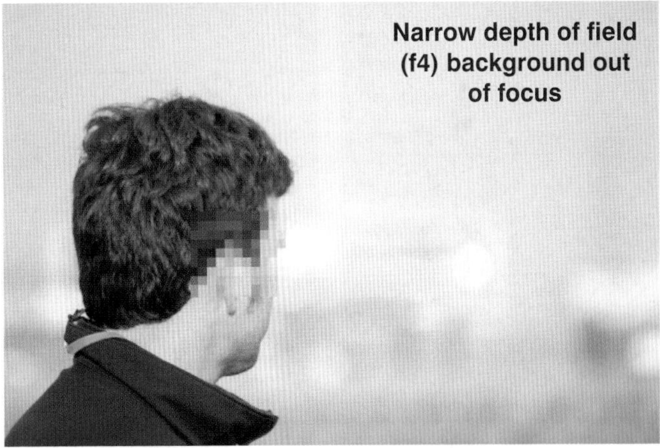

**Narrow depth of field (f4) background out of focus**

**Wider depth of field (f11) background more in focus**

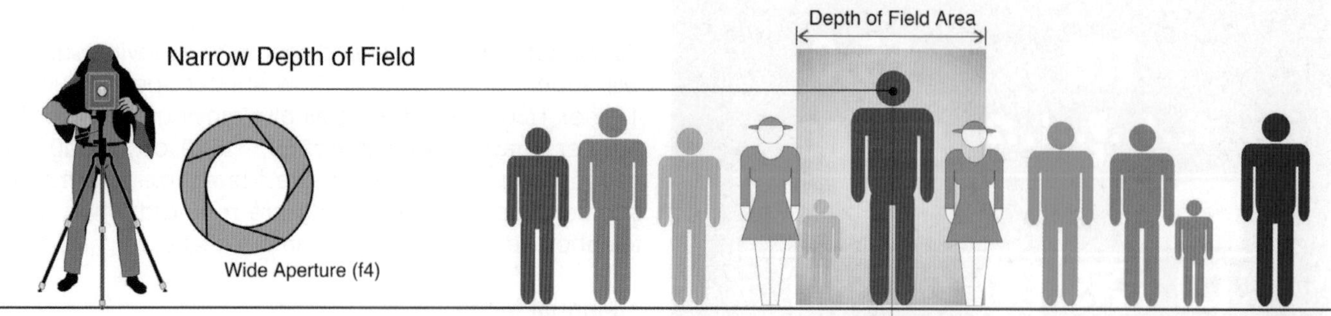


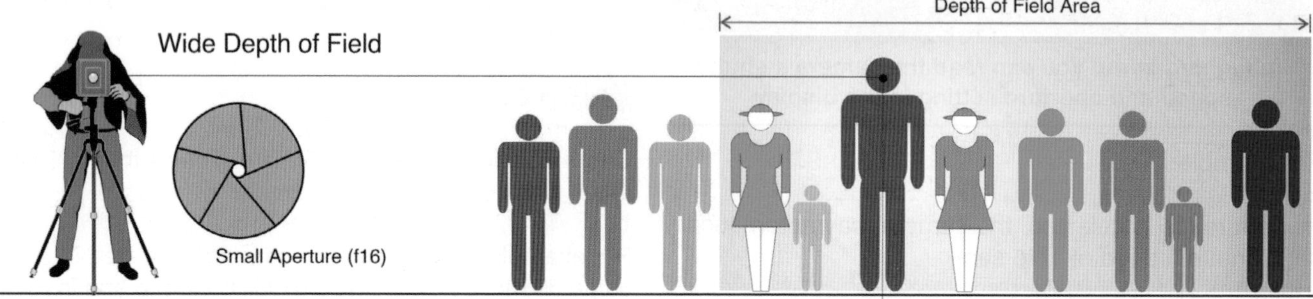


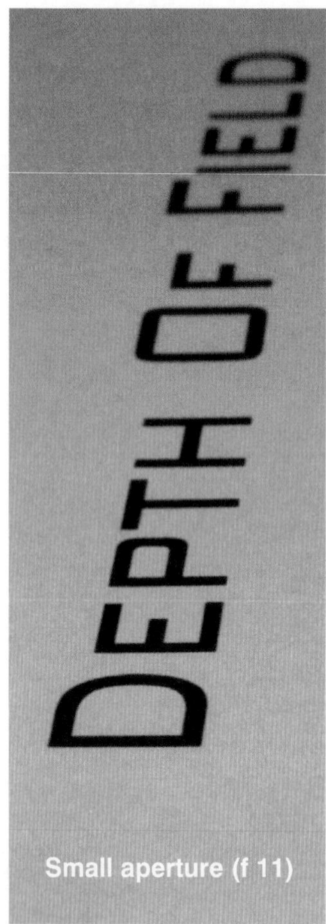

Small aperture (f 11)

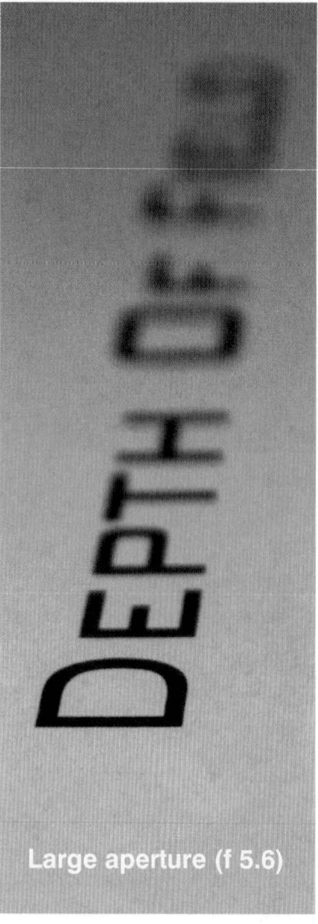
Large aperture (f 5.6)

As the size of the aperture decreases (small hole, f22), the depth of field lengthens bringing more of the picture in front and behind the subject into focus. Conversely, increasing the aperture (large hole f4.5), the depth of field is shorter and only the tree will be in focus.

The size of this depth of field area varies and depends upon three factors.

- *The aperture the lens is set to*
- *The focal length of the lens*
- *The camera to subject distance*

If you were to take a portrait picture of a person on holiday with a mountain in the background, you would need to set a small aperture (f11), this will alter the depth of field so that the person and the mountain are all in focus together. If you wanted to take a portrait picture of a model on a beach, you may want to use a wide aperture (f4.5) so that the model is sharp but the background is a blur.

In surveillance you should normally maximise depth of field to place a person in their surroundings. If you are taking a picture through a wire fence, you do not want the fence appearing in the photo and obscuring the subject, therefore use a small aperture but this has the drawback of requiring a slower shutter speed.

## OTHER EXPOSURE MODES

We have discussed the main camera modes; Automatic, Program, Aperture Priority and Shutter priority. There are also a number of other exposure or 'scene' modes available on a D-SLR camera. You will note on the selector dial a few images such as a face, mountain, flower, sportsman and the moon. These modes help you quickly select the best priority settings for different circumstances.

### Portrait

This mode automatically makes aperture priority with a large aperture (fast **f** stop). This is used to take portrait photographs so that the background is always blurred (minimum depth of field) and makes the subject stand out.

### Landscape

This mode gives the opposite effect and selects aperture priority but the aperture set is as small as possible (slow f stop) so that a maximum depth of field is always obtained.

This night-time photograph was taken using a large aperture and a slow shutter speed (f 3.5 - 1 second)

### Close-up

Close-up mode is similar to portrait mode where depth of field is important. The camera will take a maximum and minimum focus reading of the subject and calculate the ideal aperture to be used to obtain most out of the picture in focus

### Sport

This is a quick fix for surveillance photography as the camera will automatically set the fastest shutter speed possible for a correct exposure. The camera will also shoot on continuous rather than one shot at a time.

### Night

This mode sets a high ISO rating and selects the best aperture to shutter settings. The flash is also likely to come on automatically.

## CAMERA LENSES

The lens is the device which focuses the light onto the sensor to form an image; that image must be sharp in order to produce clear pictures.

- **Focal Length**

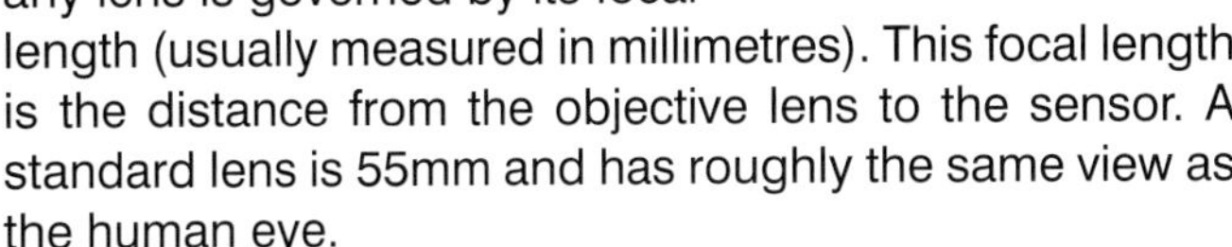

The amount of view seen through any lens is governed by its focal length (usually measured in millimetres). This focal length is the distance from the objective lens to the sensor. A standard lens is 55mm and has roughly the same view as the human eye.

There are a wide range of lenses available and for the surveillance photographer lenses of 300mm are normally adequate to bring your subject in close enough. Zoom lenses (lenses with varying focal length such as 28-70mm, 70-210mm or 100-300m) are ideal and enable you to frame the picture. A lens of 28mm or less would be considered a wide angle lens.

In digital photography, the focal length of a lens is different to that of a 35mm wet film camera. A digital lens is 1.5 times better than its old counter part in terms of focal length. In simple terms, a digital 300mm lens is the equivalent to a 450mm in old money and a 100mm digital lens is equal to an old 150mm lens. As the system is digital, you now have the advantage of being able to zoom into the picture electronically to bring it even closer after the picture is taken.

Sports photographers and the paparazzi are often seen with long lenses of 300mm and above but you will note that they are also very wide in diameter. This is because they have been designed to let in as much light as possible and their speed can be as fast as f1.8. This enables the photographer to use faster shutter speeds in order to freeze action.

Depth of field is normally very narrow with these lenses, especially when using wider apertures, therefore focusing on the subject has to be precise. You will also note that many of these lenses are coloured white, this is so that they reflect heat rather than absorb it, which can distort the lens.

Keep all fittings clean of dust and dirt and replace caps when necessay

• **Lens Speed**

As previously mentioned, a large aperture will let in more light than a smaller aperture. Each lens has a 'speed' and is marked on the lens barrel as an f stop and is the widest possible setting.

For example an average 50mm lens will have an aperture range of f3.4 to f16, the speed of this lens is f3.4. An average 300mm lens will have an aperture range of f4.5 to f22 so its speed will be f4.5.

• **Tele-Converters**

Tele-converters offer a cheap way of extending your lens' focal length. It is a small cylindrical tube that is fitted between the camera and the lens; a 2x converter doubles the focal length so that a 200mm telephoto now becomes a powerful 400mm. However, there is a disadvantage as your aperture settings will also be reduced by 2 f stops. If your 200mm lens is an f4 it now becomes f8 and so shooting in low light may be difficult.

**The speed of the lens is normally marked on the lens barrel as a ratio. In this case 1:3.5-4.5**

## Lens Filters

Special effect filters have no real purpose in surveillance photography. However, it is recommended to fit a skylight filter to each of your lenses. This will give a slightly better colour rendition to your photographs but more importantly it will protect the front of your lens from scratches. It is far cheaper to replace a scratched or cracked filter than it is to replace a lens.

A circular 'polarising' filter can give you two different effects. You can turn it to see straight through glass where there is an abundance of reflections. For instance; if you are photographing someone sitting in a car but cannot see through the window due to reflections. Alternatively, you can use the reflections in a shop window to your advantage; point the camera at the window, adjust the filter and you can now photograph what is behind you or oblique to you in the reflection. Be aware that the filter is slightly dark and so you will lose 1 or 2 stops, which may have to be compensated for by over exposing.

**Image taken shooting directly into a window at 45 degrees. The image captured is a reflection using a polarising filter**

**A circular polarising filter can be used to photograph through reflective windows, or conversely, use the reflections to take a photograph of the scene behind you**

**These images were taken from a distance of 50 metres, hand-held with a 400mm lens. The sharper photo was taken at a shutter speed of 1/320th, whilst the other was taken at 1/90th of a second**

### Shutter Speed and Telephoto Lenses

In surveillance, fast shutter speeds are normally required because we are using long lenses and we have to overcome image blur caused by camera shake.

With telephoto lenses, in addition to the picture being magnified, camera shake is also exaggerated. Therefore, try to use a support or tripod whenever possible. If the camera has to be hand held, use the following table as a guide to selecting a shutter speed that will help you prevent blur.

For every mm of focal length lens used, use a reciprocal shutter speed; for example:

| Lens | Shutter Speed |
|---|---|
| 50mm | 1/50th |
| 100mm | 1/125th |
| 250mm | 1/250th |
| 500mm | 1/500th |

In poor lighting conditions, you will not always be able to obtain an ideal shutter speed. For example, if the weather is very dull and you have a 300mm lens fitted to the camera, the camera's exposure meter may tell you that a speed of 1/125 sec is required. If this is so, either use a support or try to hold the camera as steady as you can to prevent blur. There is also another technique that you can use to obtain faster shutter speeds called 'pushing' which is described below.

**Lenses should only be cleaned with the correct cloth or brush and not dirty tissues!**

### Film Speed and ISO

The term 'film speed' is used to describe how light sensitive a wet film is and it is measured as an ISO rating. A 'fast' film of 400 ISO reacts very quickly to light, whereas a 'slow' film of 100 ISO is less sensitive and reacts slower, requiring brighter light or a longer exposure.

A 400 to 800 film is good for surveillance as it enables the camera to take pictures at faster shutter speeds but the disadvantage is that the pictures often turn out grainy (hence the poor quality of long range photographs of famous people in some celebrity lifestyle magazines).

In digital cameras, there is no film but the sensor reacts in a similar manner and they still have speed ratings. The ISO is normally set automatically by the cameras meter to either 100 or 200 ISO. However, the ISO rating can be altered manually, or 'pushed' as it is called, which alters the sensitivity of the meter.

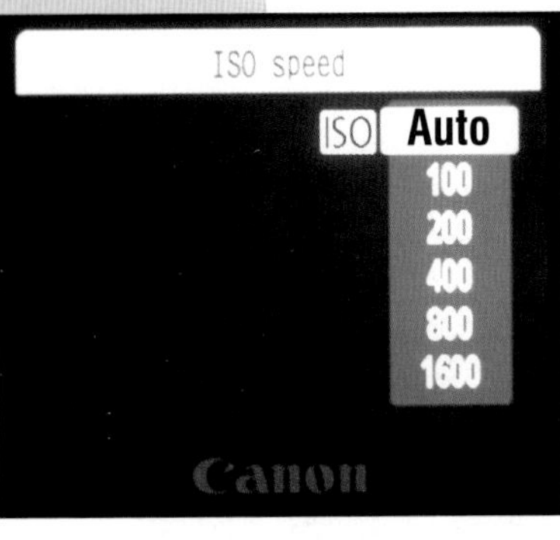


For example, you are using a f4.5, 300mm lens in low light and take a reading in program mode. The camera gives you the maximum aperture of f4.5 but the shutter speed it selects is 1/90th of a second. This shutter speed is far too slow for the long lens as camera shake is inevitable. Remember, we need a shutter speed of at least 1/300th to match the focal length.

Therefore, if we now manually alter or push the ISO setting up to 1600 (see your manual on how to do this) and take the same reading, you will note that the aperture is still 4.5 (because it can't open any larger) but the shutter speed is now 1/500th of a second and much faster. This is what we are trying to achieve to get a steady shot in low light. So, if you are in an OP and shooting in twilight, you may want to consider pushing the speed.

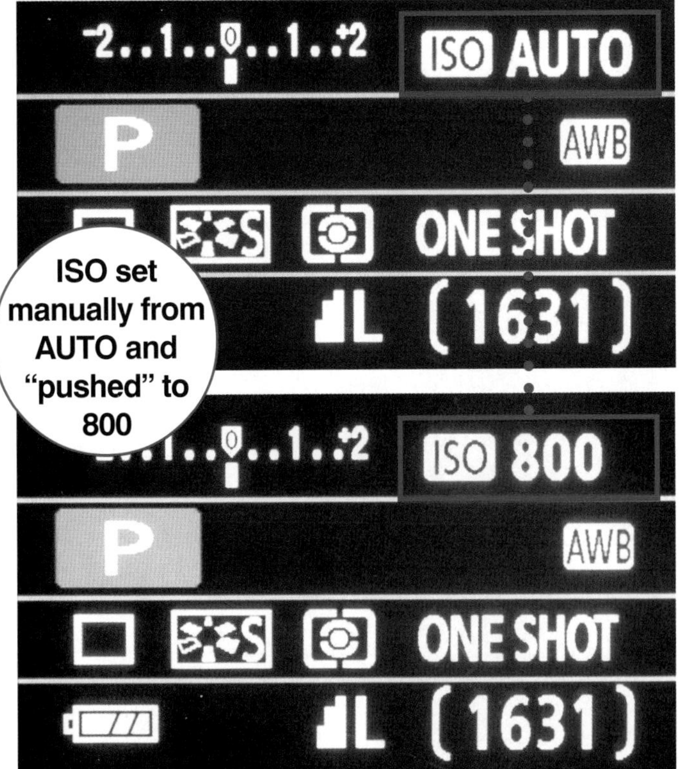


**IMAGE 1**

**IMAGE 2**

**These two images were taken at the same time with a focal length of 117mm looking across a valley. The dark image is the nearest to what the naked eye can see, the second image was taken by adjusting the cameras' ISO and shutter speed setting.**

**Image 1: At night, what the naked eye can see. Settings: ISO 800, 4 seconds at f5.6**

**Image 2: After pushing the camera's settings. Settings: ISO 12,500 15 seconds at f5.6**

As with wet films, the higher the ISO, the more grain in the picture; the higher you push the speed, the more 'noise' will appear in the images, normally as red and blue specks. The top of the range cameras will have a built in noise reduction facility but you can normally get rid of it in Photoshop using the 'noise reduction filter'.

If you push the ISO, **Don't forget** to reset the ISO back to automatic afterwards. In surveillance photography, I would consider this as one of the most used functions on the camera.

A controlled breathing pattern is essential

# KEEPING YOUR CAMERA STEADY

Your feet should be shoulder-width apart one foot slightly in front of the other

Support the weight of the lens barrel with your left hand

Your left hand is also used to control the zoom and focus controls

A quick release catch enables you rapidly attach your camera to a support such as a monopod

When holding the camera (portrait) try and support the weight of the camera from below (left) rather than above (right)

**Use a post, for example, to help steady the camera when using telephoto lenses**

## Keeping Your Camera Steady

The way you hold your camera will greatly affect your picture taking and make the difference between a pin sharp picture and a blurred image. You may have spent a lot of money on a camera but it will not give you a faster shutter speed, therefore the picture quality starts with you, by holding it correctly.

The following will you help take sharp pictures:

• Use a monopod or a tripod whenever possible, if this is not possible, turn your body into one

• Grip the camera firmly with the right hand, with your forefinger resting gently on the button and the remaining fingers griping the side of the camera body. Your thumb should be pressed against the back of the camera

• Do not hold it too tight otherwise your hand will shake

• The left hand should be placed under the lens barrel to take the weight and also used to focus and control the zoom. Held like this you should be able to remove either hand and still have a tight grip of the camera

• Keep your elbows tucked into your body for support - important

• Stand in a position where you will not sway about, your feet should be shoulder width apart and one foot slightly in front of the other for maximum stability

• If kneeling or sitting, tuck your elbows into the insides of your knees

• Breathe out a little, hold your breath, squeeze the shutter gently. Do not snatch it or the camera will tilt

• Use a support to lean against especially when using slow shutter speeds. Do not rest the lens barrel on anything solid, rest your hand on the surface with the lens on top.

• If you have to turn the camera in order to shoot vertically, your right hand should be below the camera in order to support the weight.

• Use a fast shutter speed when possible, push the ISO setting

• If you are in a vehicle, switch off the engine and rest against something

• If your lens has stabilisation, switch it on

This foam pipe lagging is useful for resting a lens on a lowered car window

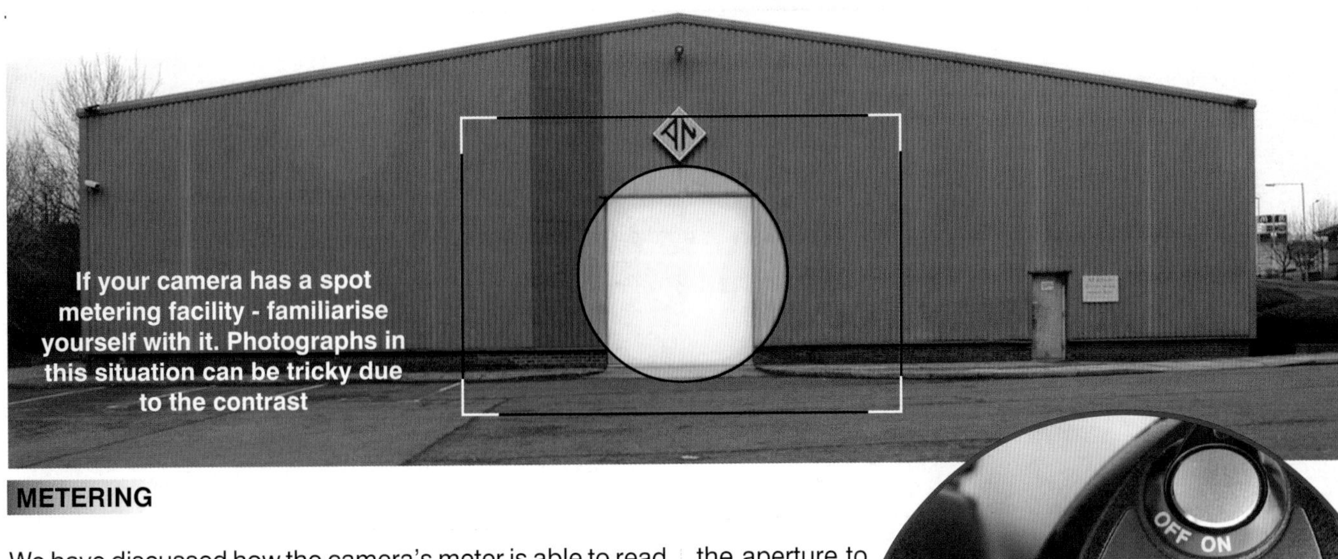

If your camera has a spot metering facility - familiarise yourself with it. Photographs in this situation can be tricky due to the contrast

## METERING

We have discussed how the camera's meter is able to read the amount of light and adjust the settings accordingly to obtain the correct exposure. Metering systems vary from camera to camera but most modern cameras work on 'multi-pattern' metering. The camera's 'eye' is split into separate individual 'cells', it then averages the amount of light read in each of these cells to give a correct reading.

### Spot Metering

If your camera has a spot metering facility you will find this may be one of the most important features when taking covert photographs in tricky lighting situations.

When the 'spot' button is pressed, the metering system restricts its reading to a circular area marked in the centre of the viewfinder. Therefore any light outside this area is ignored. This is useful when your subject is surrounded by bright features or your subject is surrounded by dark features.

- **Surroundings too Bright**

If we have to take a photograph of a man who is standing in front of a white garage door loading a white van, the camera's meter would normally read all this 'whiteness' and close down the aperture to obtain an average exposure.

In doing so, the man will turn out very dark and under exposed. With spot metering, the spot is placed over the image of the man and the photo taken. The meter reads only the light from the man, ensuring a correct exposure. A similar situation would occur when your subject is standing in front of a bright window, in a snowy location or when the sun is behind him causing him to silhouette.

- **Surroundings too Dark**

If you are shooting into a lighted garage in poor light, a normal exposure would read all the dark areas and open the aperture to obtain an average exposure; the man would appear bright and over exposed. The 'spot' should be placed over the subject to ensure that the subject is correctly exposed.

### Exposure Compensation

If your camera does not have a spot metering facility and you find yourself taking photographs in similar conditions, you may be able to adjust your camera manually by over-exposing or under-exposing the picture by 1 or 2 stops (f numbers). Care should be used when using the exposure over ride control so that you do not compensate the wrong way. If the surroundings are too bright, over expose; if they are too dark, under expose.

Over-exposed photo to lighten-up the inside of the building

-2 • • 1 • • ↓ • • 1 • • (2+)

-2 • • 1 • • ↓ • • (1) • • 2+

-2 • • 1 • • (↓) • • 1 • • 2

The EV setting can be easily changed by holding down the correct button on the camera (note: AV on a Canon)

Many photographs taken of snowy scenes on automatic mode often appear too dark or grey. This is because the camera's meter has read a lot of light from the snow and as a consequence, closed the aperture down to compensate. To override this, the camera's EV (Exposure Value) settings can easily be changed - check the instruction manual. If you want to brighten the image increase the exposure; if you want to darken the image, decrease the exposure.

If you alter this setting remember to reset it to zero afterwards, otherwise all of your other pictures will be incorrectly exposed.

## FOCUSING

There is nothing worse than having a photograph that is out of focus. Auto-focus lenses have the facility to be operated manually and this is often used in surveillance. They also offer continuous auto-focusing which will 'track' an approaching car.

The eyepiece has to be adjusted using the dioptric knob which focuses the eye to the camera

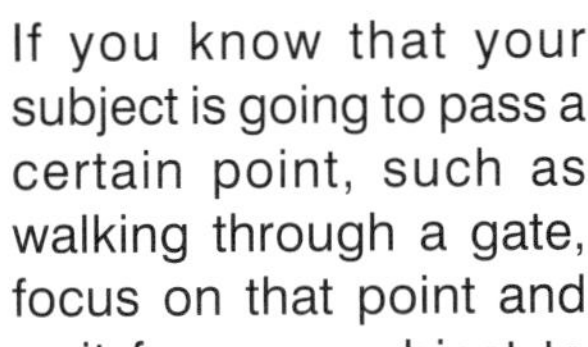

Don't forget to reset the EV meter back to 'zero' after making adjustments, or all of your subsequent pictures will be exposed incorrectly

Various techniques can be used when manual focusing is required:

- **Predictive Focusing**

If you know that your subject is going to pass a certain point, such as walking through a gate, focus on that point and wait for your subject to appear.

- **Follow Focusing**

If your subject is moving then you will have to continually adjust the focus with your free hand as the subject moves. This technique can be tricky and requires practice. Maximum depth of field should be used if possible.

**The manual focus switch is normally found on the lens barrel. Remember its status, otherwise you will take pictures that are out of focus**

**The photographer is some 300 metres from the crane. These pictures show the difference in focus, this is after only a tiny manual adjustment has been made**

Manual focusing is required in this situation in order to prevent the camera automatically focusing on the branches rather than the target. Similarly, if you are indoors shooting through blinds, for example, you want to focus manually beyond the blinds

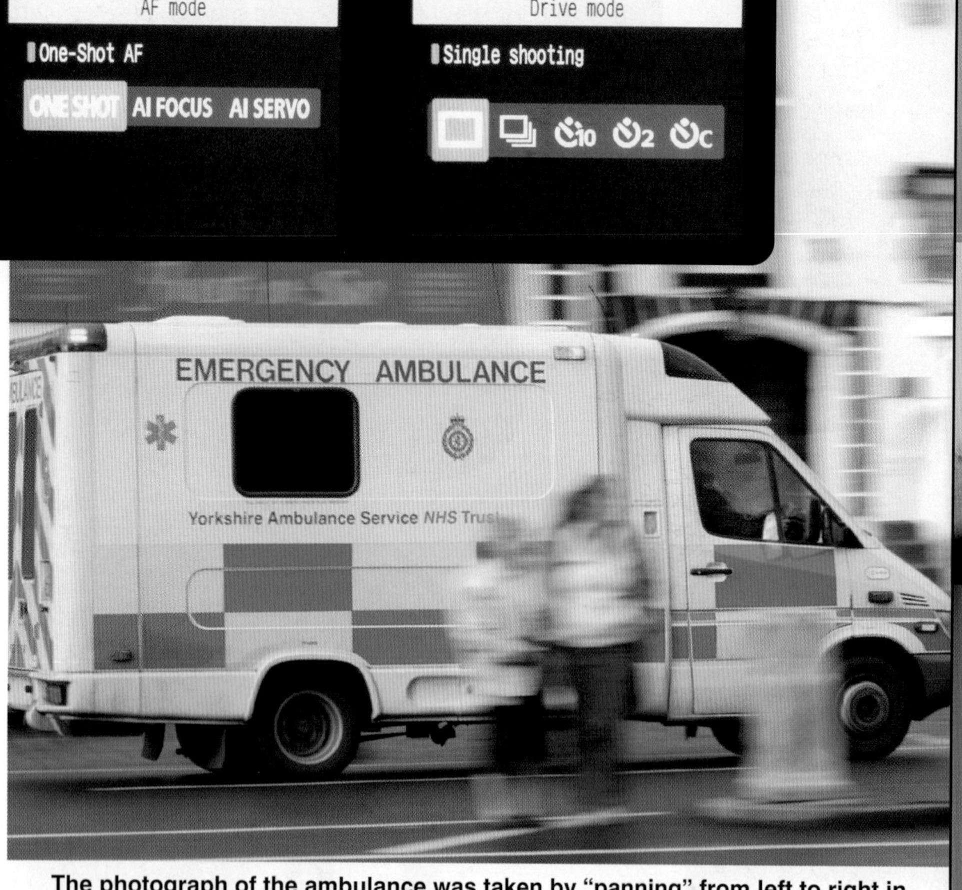


The photograph of the ambulance was taken by "panning" from left to right in order to "overtake" the ambulance. The camera was set to Servo focus which continually tracks and refocuses on the moving target. It is also wise to set the drive mode into rapid fire (multiple shooting)

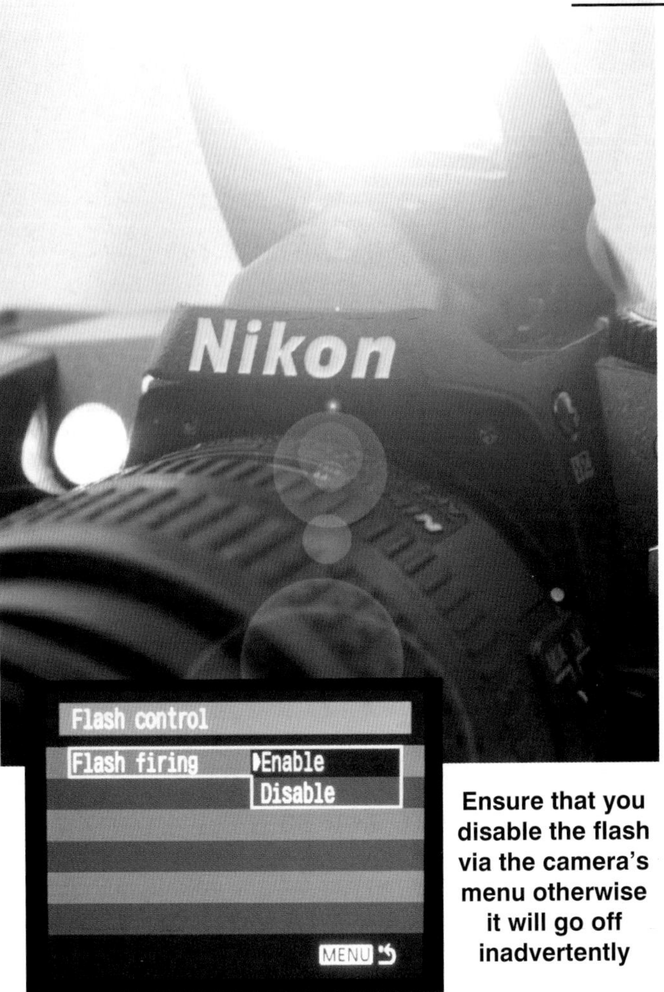


Ensure that you disable the flash via the camera's menu otherwise it will go off inadvertently

**Camera's Clock**

Most digital cameras have a time and date facility that is stored when the picture was taken within the image. Ensure that the clock is synchronised correctly to your watch and any other cameras. A photograph with an incorrect time on it could be disadvantageous if it is to be used in legal proceedings. This function also assists when matching up photographs with your surveillance logs, making reading and collation of reports simpler.

**NIGHT PHOTOGRAPHY WITH IMAGE INTENSIFIERS**

Good quality intensifiers are not cheap and can cost a few thousand pounds but when combined with a Digital SLR camera, they can help you obtain excellent still photographs in dark situations. The device is fitted between the camera body and the lens and intensifies the minutest amount of light in the sky. It is imperative that you use a tripod or support for the camera and if you have image stabilisation ensure that it is switched on and set the focus to manual. If you are totally covert and close to your target remember to disable any lights, red eye reduction flash or LCD displays.

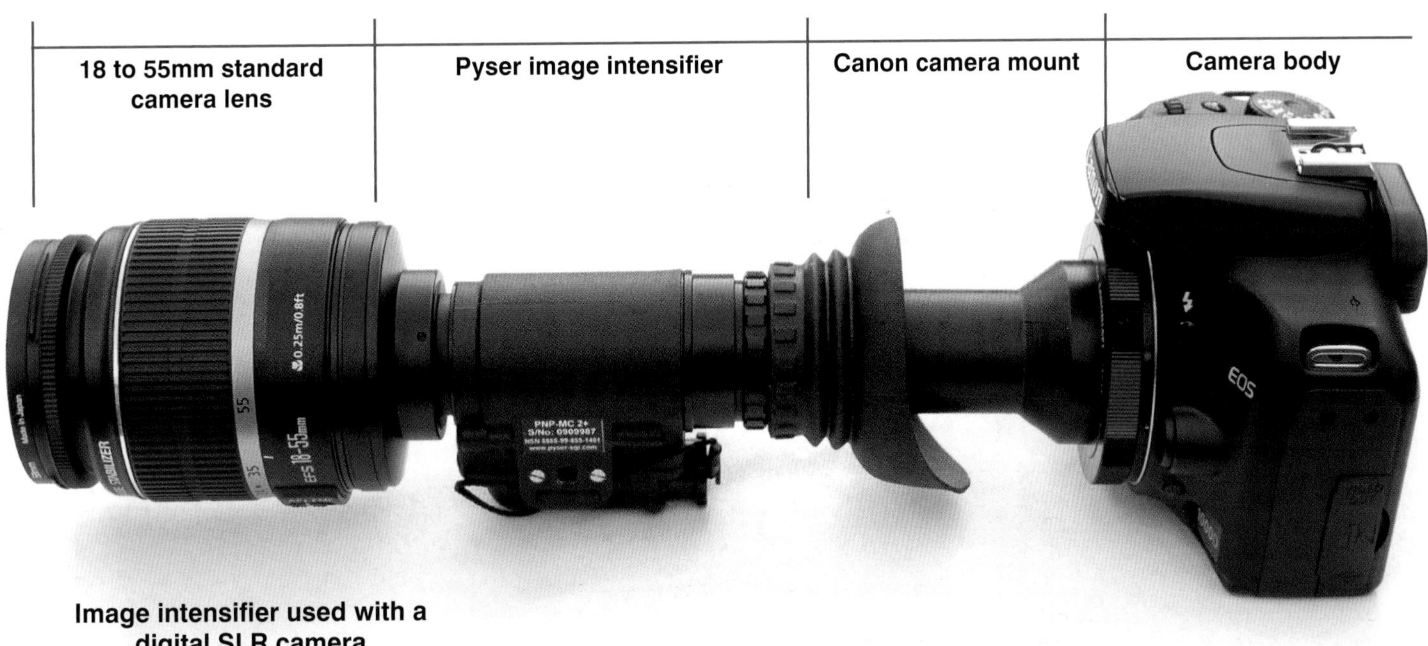


**Image intensifier used with a digital SLR camera**

# PANORAMIC PHOTOGRAPHY

Manually set the ISO rating to at least 1600, be careful not to push it any higher as you will experience 'noise' and lose quality on the image.

You will need to shoot on the fastest shutter speed possible to prevent blur. In order to do this, set your camera onto manual exposure mode as you want to use the largest aperture to allow as much light as possible through the lens. The shutter speed needs to be fast enough to prevent blur but slow enough to capture the dark green image which is produced. The beauty about digital photography is that you can review the images immediately so take a few pictures on different shutter speeds to obtain a good exposure. Try it set between 1/20th and 100th of a second. If you have an independent IR illuminator such as a torch or beacon, this will assist in very dark and shadowed areas.

## PANORAMIC PHOTOGRAPHS

Quite often you may be required to take a panoramic photograph (if the subject covers a wide area or you need to record detail over a large area) using a telephoto lens. This is done by taking a series of photographs and then panning the camera slightly to one side after each shot is taken. The resulting photographs are then joined together to form an overall picture.

It is important to hold the camera so that it pans horizontally and a tripod is useful. Take the series of pictures from left to right, each one just overlapping the last. This overlap assists in lining them up and joining them together which can be done on Photoshop by manually joining the images together or using the 'stitch' facility where the computer intelligently joins them up.

Photographs taken through an image intensifier

*There are many downloads of the Internet used to "photostitch" panoramic photographs automatically*

# PHOTOGRAPHIC ACCESSORIES

*The following are photographic accessories that I have found to be useful whilst carrying out surveillance work.*

Bean bags are ideal for supporting cameras and lenses on uneven surfaces

'Cammo' camera 'Armor'

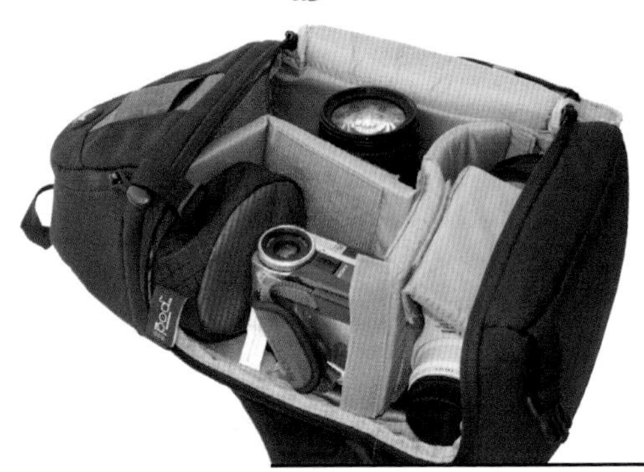

Typical camera rucksack will hold your camera, lenses, accessories and your copy of 'Surveillance Tradecraft'

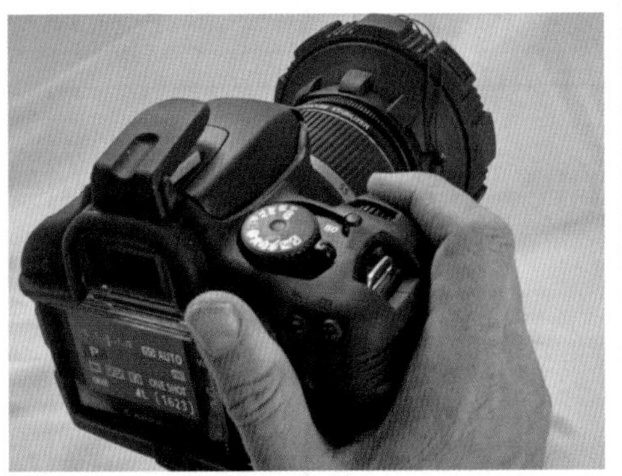

Camera 'Armor' is a useful way of protecting the camera whilst still enabling you to use the controls. The strong rubber shield is available in different colours, including camouflage

PHOTOGRAPHS COURTESY: Shai Gear LLC, www.spiderholster.com

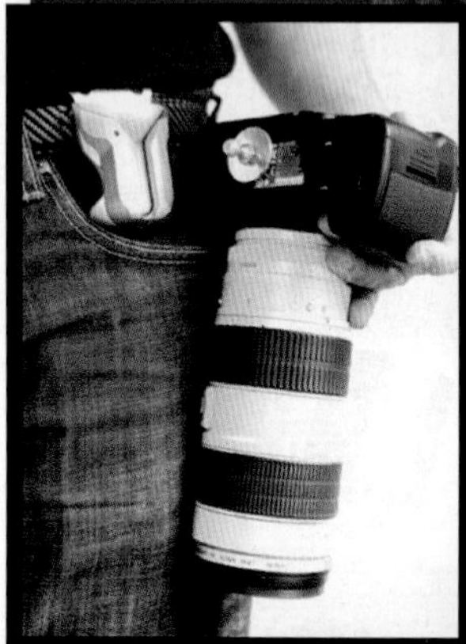

The 'SpiderPro' holster comes as part of a belt system, or a device which can be clipped on to an everyday belt

The 'SpiderPro' holster system is an excellent method of carrying your camera and keeping your hands free to perform other tasks and is easily concealed under a coat

LensCoat.com provide tailored protective camouflaged neoprene covers for camera bodies and lenses

Urban OPs require large, tall tripods in order to take the weight of cameras and telephoto lenses.

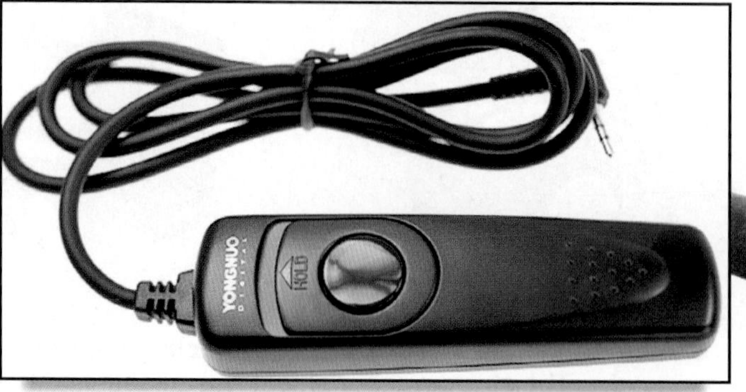

Right: A shutter release is essensial when using telephoto lenses otherwise the camera will shake as soon as you touch it

Cover supplied by www.wildlifewatchingsupplies.co.uk

This camouflaged cover is lined with fleece material to keep the camera warm and also incorporates a pouch which holds a chemical hand-warmer.

1.4x lens extender transforms a 300mm into a powerful 420mm lens

The Sony Cybershot is a compact digital camera and has as many functions as a DSLR camera

A gorillapod tripod can be fixed to virtually any object

A small sturdy tripod is a must addition to your camera kit

A cheap skylight filter is a low-cost way of protecting a lens from scratches (it is cheaper to replace a filter rather than a lens)

# COVERT INFRARED PHOTOGRAPHY

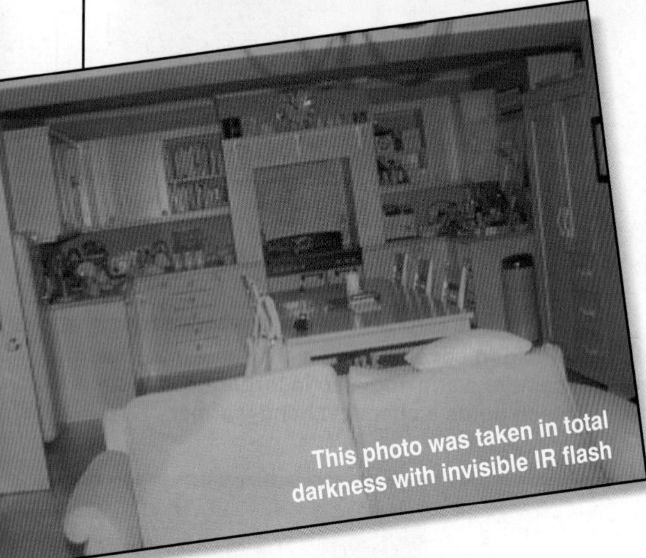

This photo was taken in total darkness with invisible IR flash

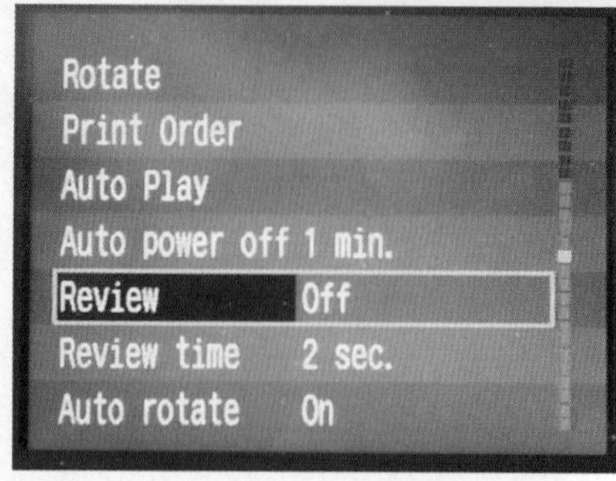


Covert imagery can be taken in complete darkness with the use of infrared flash and a suitable camera. The majority of SLR cameras have an internal IR filter, which is built into the body of the camera. This is used to filter out any natural IR light from reaching the sensor as it will have an adverse effect on the final image. Therefore, your SLR camera has to be specially modified to remove the IR filter.

The flashgun is screened with a piece of IR filter glass which is dark red in colour. The filter has to be fitted so that any stray white light does not escape from the flash in order to remain covert.

## THE CAMERA SETTINGS

Go through the camera's menu and adjust:

**Review:** Off, this prevents the rear screen from automatically lighting up.

**LCD Brightness:** Low, this keeps the viewing screen brightness down when you review the images.

**ISO:** Set the camera's ISO to 800 for optimum shutter speed.

**Red Eye:** Off, this prevents a beam of light firing out of some cameras.

**Manual Focus:** This prevents the camera shooting out a beam of 'focusing' red light. The disadvantage being that it can be tricky to focus on your subject in total darkness. IR light also focuses at a different point to natural white light. If you are focusing on an object 50cm away, the actual IR point of focus will be approximately 5cm behind the object.

**Auto Focus:** When the camera's lens is set to auto focus, a beam of light is emitted from the camera. If the situation is secure and permits you to get away with it (such as being close up or indoors) then us it.

The camera's mode should be set to manual (M). You will now have to manually adjust the shutter speed and aperture to the desired settings. A bit of experimentation is now required by bracketing the shutter speed. Always try to use the largest aperture possible (f3.5 or f4.5). However, if shooting very close up, set this to f8 in order to maximise depth of field.

With your camera's aperture set to f3.5, set the shutter speed to 1/125th and take a picture. Review the image; if it is too dark, then slow the shutter speed down to 1/90th. If it is too bright, then use a faster shutter speed of 1/350th. Experiment!

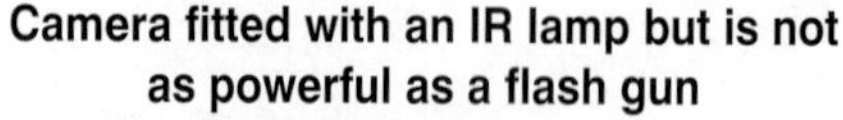

**Camera fitted with an IR lamp but is not as powerful as a flash gun**

**Both of these photographs taken in total darkness with IR flash at different camera settings**

**1/125th sec at f5.6**

**1/350th sec at f5.6**

This circular 'grabmat' is used at the front of an OP to place your camera and other equipment on

If you have to 'bug out' grabbing the draw chords pulls the mat over the equipment quickly for an escape

# PRACTICAL EXERCISE

## Carry out this exercise, it will help you find your way around your camera

- Synchronise the date & time with the speaking clock.

- Take a photograph of a person at least 100m away with a 250mm lens. Your minimum shutter speed should be 1/250th.

- Take the same photograph but push the ISO to 1600 to give you a faster shutter speed (make a note of what it is). Examine the difference in 'noise' when you compare both images. **Remember to reset the ISO back to automatic afterwards.**

- Take two pictures of a flag blowing in the wind. One with the flag frozen, the other with the flag blurred. The pole should be sharp in both images. This should be done in shutter priority mode.

- Take two photographs close up displaying 'depth of field' using a short focal length lens (approx 50mm). Take one image with an aperture of f4.5, the other at f19. Now carry out the same exercise with a 120mm lens.

- Take a photograph of a person 3 metres away but have the background out of focus.

- Take a photo of yourself with the self timer.

- Take the same photograph but have the person and background in focus.

- Take a photograph in low light without the flash popping up.

- Take a photograph of a vehicle moving from left to right to capture the driver. Set the shutter release to 'rapid' or multiple rather than single shot.

- Take a photograph of a vehicle moving away from you to identify the registration plate. You may need to set the camera to continuous focus or 'servo' focus.

- Take three photographs of a building: one at normal exposure, the other over exposed by 2 stops, the other under exposed by 2 stops. **Remember to reset your EV meter back to zero.**

- Create a folder on your computers desktop called 'tradecraft'

- Download the images from the camera to the folder.

- Resize a picture to 15cm by 10cm at a resolution of 300ppi and then save it as a file called 'test.jpg'.

- Open the same image and again resave it with a different file name at a smaller file size (approx 250KB) by reducing the ppi to 72 and then email it to yourself.

- Re-format the SD card to remove all of the images.

**SUMMARY**

- *Hold the camera steady, use a support if necessary*
- *Use a fast shutter speed to prevent camera shake*
- *Adjust the ISO if shooting in low light*
- *Use spot metering or adjust exposure if necessary in contrasting light*
- *Maximise depth of field whenever possible*

These digital video tape cameras are fairly robust and good for surveillance

## VIDEO PHOTOGRAPHY

Video cameras (camcorders) are now used more often in investigative work than DSLR cameras. Personally, as a medium I prefer still photography to video but clients often prefer video. If you are investigating 'personal injury' type claims, then video is essential in order to record physical activity and movement.

To this end, if you are watching an individual or premises for a long period of time to obtain video evidence, it is imperative that you know your photographic equipment's abilities and limitations inside out. The best way to improve your technique is to actually watch the tapes after you have shot them and learn by your mistakes. The video is your 'product' and is what you are selling to your client - it has to be first class.

### Video Cameras

The majority of camcorders today store their data digitally and this can be in various formats. Video tapes are still used but the footage can also be stored on a CD, DVD or SD Card. They can also be stored on the cameras own internal flash hard drive. It is all down to personal choice but personally I prefer a medium that I can take away such as a tape or a CD. Otherwise the camera has to be connected to a computer, the data transferred across and then burned onto a DVD. Sony equipment is a reliable brand and their cameras have the majority of features that I require for surveillance, such as:

- **Minimum of a x 20 Zoom Lens (Optical)**

All cameras have a zoom facility that allows for you to obtain a wide angle picture or to zoom in for a close up. If you can, obtain the highest number of optical zoom possible as this enables you to film from a distance without losing any picture quality. At the time of writing, the highest optical zoom available is x48.

During 'optical' zoom, the zoom control is adjusted and the actual glass lens inside the camera moves, thus bringing the picture closer or further away. During digital zoom, the image is electronically processed to appear closer, however, this has an adverse effect as you lose picture quality the closer you zoom in and the image will become pixelated.

Technology is improving all the time and cameras are currently available with x1000 digital zoom. Not only will the quality be poor at the top end of the zoom but it will be extremely difficult to hold the camera steady. I would recommend that you set the zoom facility on your camera to 'optical' only via the settings menu, this prevents you from being tempted to go into the digital zone.

The latest digital cameras do not have an eye-piece to look through - the screen must be flipped out which is a disadvantage in low light

Famaliarise yourself with every control on the camera

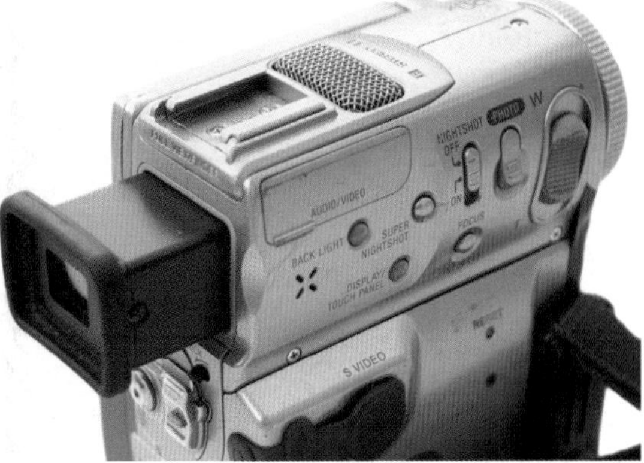

Insert a blank plug in the microphone socket

## Focal Length Conversion

If you are familiar with still photography, you will be used to focal length given in millimetres: a wide angle lens would be 28mm, a standard lens 50mm and a telephoto lens of 210mm and upwards. In video photography (and some digital still cameras) a 'times' ratio is used (e.g. x6) rather than a measurement. The table below describes the corresponding times (x) scale with the focal length of a stills camera.

The formula used is: **times (x) divided by 0.03125 = focal length in millimetres**

For example: **x 6 on a video divided by 0.03125 = 192 which equals a 192mm lens**

| TIMES | FOCAL LENGTH |
|---|---|
| x2 | 32mm |
| x4 | 128mm |
| x6 | 192mm |
| x12 | 384mm |
| x24 | 768mm |
| x40 | 1280mm |

- **Anti-Shake Feature**

The majority of camcorders have an 'anti-shake' feature built-in. Camera shake is more apparent when using video, especially when filming at the top end of your zoom so ensure that this is switched on.

- **Ability to playback through the viewfinder or screen**

Some view finders are monochrome (black and white) only. You will pay more for a colour viewfinder but they are better if you are having to record and give descriptions at the same time. Be aware that some of the latest camcorders do not have an eyepiece viewfinder, they only have a screen which pops out at the side. This can be a disadvantage if you are filming in low light or at night as the light from the screen will light up your face.

- **Manual Focus as well as Auto Focus**

Not all cameras can be focused manually but I consider this an essential feature in surveillance photography. One of the main problems seen with video evidence is the fact that the picture is often out of focus. Most camcorders utilise an 'auto-focus' lens but they also have the facility for this to be disabled manually.

Quite often you will be in your car filming your target who is walking down a street or getting in and out of a vehicle.

## CAMERA CONTROLS

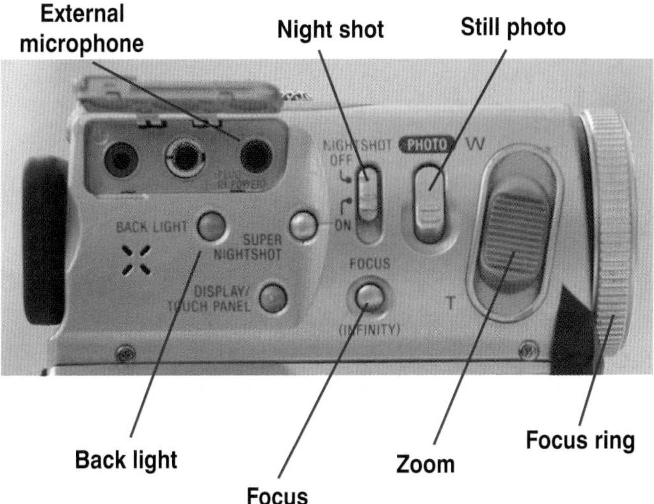

Imagine you lift your camera up and start recording; vehicle passes between you and the target, the lens now auto focuses on the passing vehicle whilst turning your subject into a fuzzy blob; once the obstruction has passed, the camera starts to refocus on the target but then locks onto the dead fly on your windscreen and remains focused there until the subject has disappeared out of shot. Not good.

Similarly, if you are in a rural OP filming through undergrowth or through a chain link fence, a camera set to auto focus is likely to focus onto the fence rather than on your target in the distance.

- **Standard and Slow recording speeds**

Cameras have the facility to record at Standard Play (SP) or Long Play (LP). This is a good feature but try to use SP whenever possible to obtain a better picture quality. You may consider using LP if you are going to place a camera on constant record. In this mode, you will achieve up to three hours continuous recording on one tape.

- **Back Light Compensator**

If your target is standing in front of a white or bright background, the camera's aperture will close down and make your picture appear very dark. By altering the exposure you can override this and brighten up the whole picture; this is also useful when shooting towards the sun.

- **Memory Stick**

Many camcorders have a 'Memory stick' which slides into the camera to store still photographs. In addition, you can also take still frames (snapshots) from the videotape as you watch it and store them on the memory stick as JPEG files.

- **Night Shot Capability**

Many of today's camcorders incorporate a 'Night Shot' facility, enabling you to record pictures in total darkness or zero lux. The camera can be switched from daylight mode to night mode quite simply. The camera will have its own small infra red (IR) lamp, which provides IR illumination for about two to three metres. Alternatively, an external lamp such as the SONY HVL-IRM can be used to flood the area with strong IR light.

Video camera fitted with an infrared lamp

It doesn't have to be complicated to covertly video from your car

Camouflage tape protects the camera when used outdoors

*Use of the NightShot system is useful for close target reconnaissance*

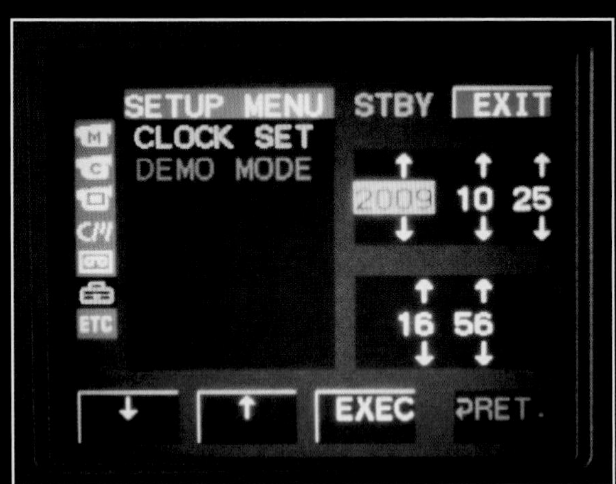


***• Don't Forget to Synchronise...***

***If you are using two or more cameras on the same investigation, ensure that all the timers are synchronised. This should be a professional habit carried out on every morning of the surveillance by all operators.***

**Poor Video**

When filming, be aware that the following could reduce the quality of your footage:

**• Over use of Zoom**

It is irritating to watch videos where there is an overuse of the zoom control. Because it is there, we feel that we have to use it but it can be very frustrating to watch footage that continually zooms in and out of shot. Don't touch it.

**• Camera Shake**

Camera shake is very noticeable when using video, especially when filming at the top end of your zoom. The way you hold your camera will greatly affect your picture taking and make all the difference. The following should assist in taking a steady shot:

• Grip the camera firmly with both hands and support the lens.

• Stand or sit in a position where you will not sway about, use a support to lean against, keep your elbows tucked into your body for support

- *Hold your breath or use shallow breathing*
- *If filming from a vehicle, turn the engine off*
- *Ensure your camera has an 'Anti-Shake' feature*
- *Use a support such as a mono-pod or tripod*
- *Radios and Mobile Phones*

If you are filming, ensure that your mobile phone or radio is away from the camera whilst you transmit/talk, otherwise the radio waves disturb the cameras electronics and cause interference on the film.

**• Sound/Audio**

Video evidence rarely requires sound on the tape unless voices or certain sounds need to be heard as part of the evidence. A dummy plug (2.5mm jack plug) pushed into the external microphone socket disables the built in microphone and prevents recording any unwanted sounds. Radio voice procedure, background noises/voices and even the odd piece of bad language do not need to be recorded. Remember, your original tape may be played back in open court.

**A camcorder fitted with a Pyser image intensifier used for filming at night-time**

## COVERT VIDEO CAMERAS

Quite often, you will have to get out on foot and take your camera with you. Obviously you will not want to walk around the streets with a camera overtly in your hand (unless the situation permits it) and so there are various methods in which it can be concealed. The crudest way is to put your camcorder in a bag with a hole cut in it for the lens to see through, commonly known as a 'Bag Fit'.

This is a good photographic aid as you do not always have to be 'face on' to the target. You can be to the side, in front or behind him to get your film. If you had to follow someone around a supermarket the bag can be put into a shopping trolley.

**The Bag Fit**

This sports bag has been fitted with a wooden cradle inside in order to hold and steady the camera without it rattling around. The camera can be pushed into it so that a clear picture will be obtained.

The hole is cut in the correct place and then camouflaged by gluing a piece of wire mesh over the hole on the inside of the bag. Other ways of camouflaging it are with a baggage tag or a pair of sunglasses for the camera to see though. If you are going to use a bag fit, ensure that you:

- Set the focus to infinity. Do not use auto-focus as the lens will constantly be re-focusing as people move between you and the target.

- Set to Wide angle. Pull the zoom right back so that you are at the widest possible angle, this ensures that your target is captured in the frame.

**Technique**

Using a bag fit takes practice, it has to be held steady and pointed in the right direction, not at the sky or the floor. It also has to be carried naturally down by your side and not out to one side as if there is a bomb in the bag - you have to be relaxed with it.

**This Sony camcorder can be connected to a pinhole lens camera for covert use**

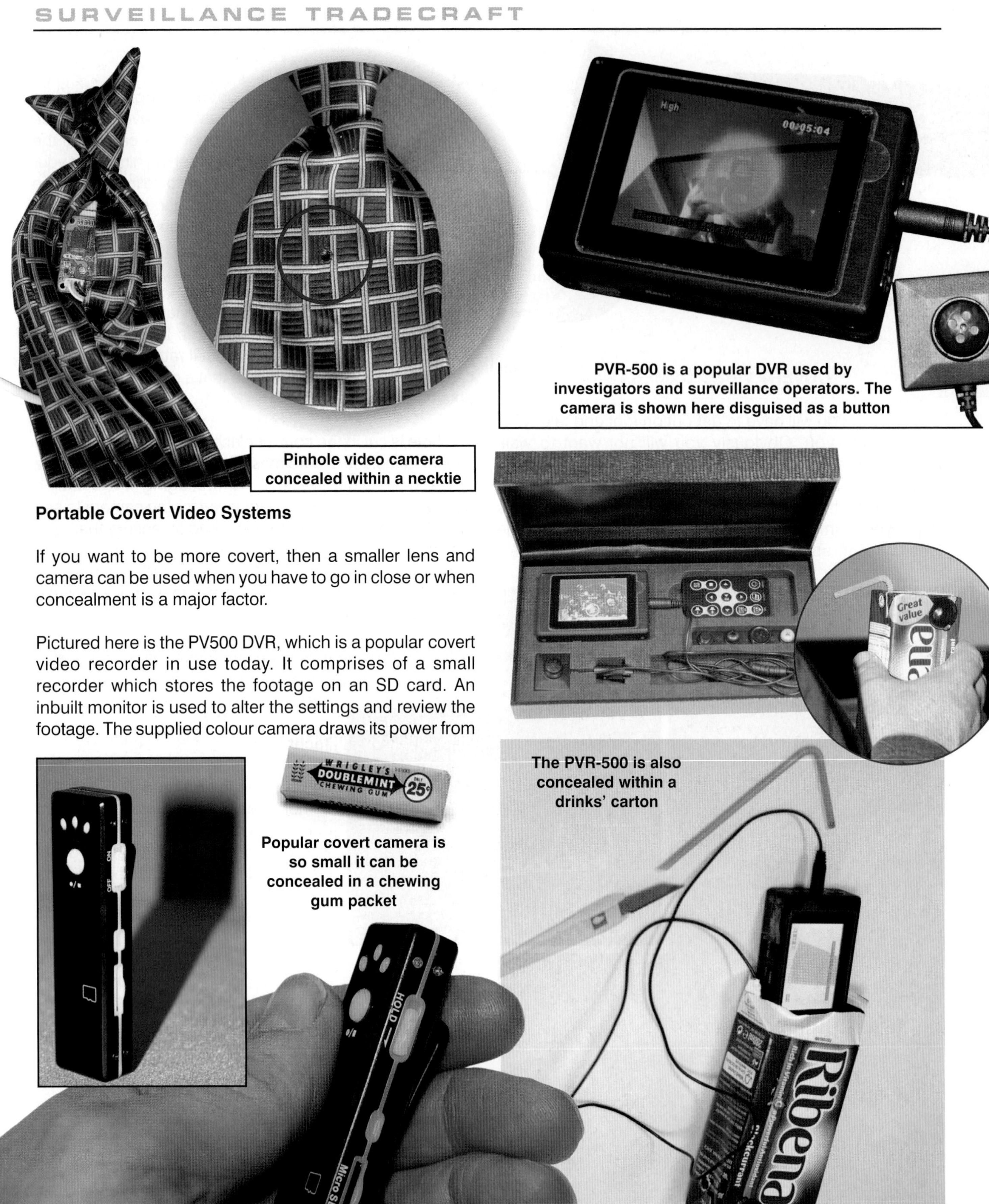


PVR-500 is a popular DVR used by investigators and surveillance operators. The camera is shown here disguised as a button

Pinhole video camera concealed within a necktie

**Portable Covert Video Systems**

If you want to be more covert, then a smaller lens and camera can be used when you have to go in close or when concealment is a major factor.

Pictured here is the PV500 DVR, which is a popular covert video recorder in use today. It comprises of a small recorder which stores the footage on an SD card. An inbuilt monitor is used to alter the settings and review the footage. The supplied colour camera draws its power from

The PVR-500 is also concealed within a drinks' carton

Popular covert camera is so small it can be concealed in a chewing gum packet

Pinhole lens within zipper pull

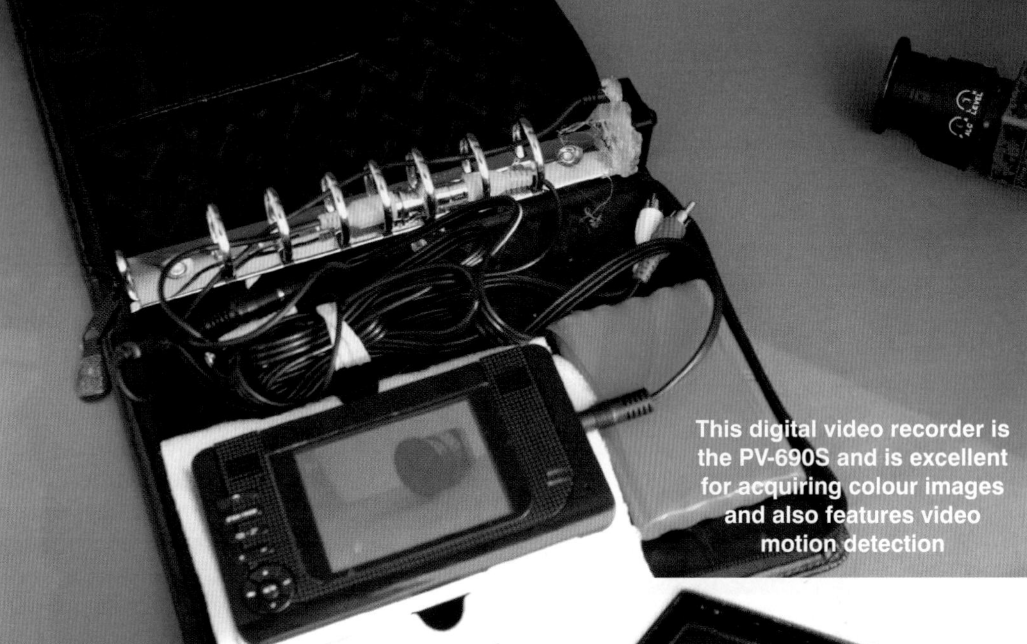

This digital video recorder is the PV-690S and is excellent for acquiring colour images and also features video motion detection

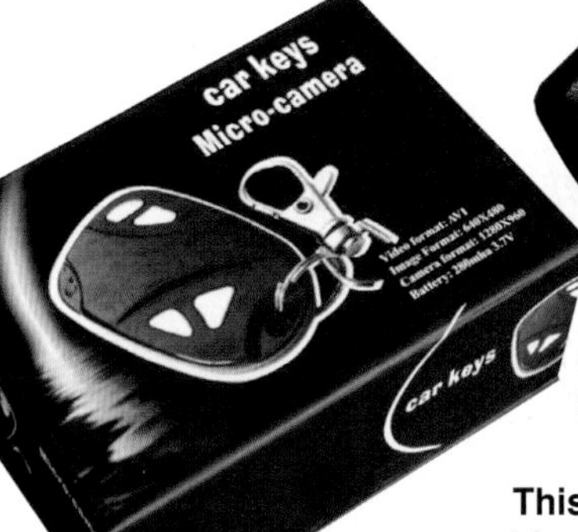


This innocuous key ring can record video and audio for 90 minutes before its battery fails

One of the latest miniature audio-video recorders which records directly onto an SD card

the DVR and comes with a selection of buttons and screws in order to aid concealment. There are many variations of this type of camera available and each have varying capabilities such as time and date stamp and motion detection recording. This particular recorder will run for about 2 hours on one battery charge and will continuously record for over an hour on a 1Gb card.

Test purchase: Images taken using a covert video camera

This miniature video camera is attached to an image intensifier for videoing at night

## Flash Recorders

These miniature recorders come in various disguises such as pens and key fobs. The key fob is a current favourite as it is simple to use, very portable and has a very good image quality, especially in poor lighting conditions. It can take either JPEG still images or video which it stores on its internal 4Gb memory. The re-chargeable batteries last for approximately an hour and a half so it can be left for short term, continuous recordings.

It is simple to use by connecting it to a computer with a USB lead; it acts like a memory stick and the images and video are easily viewed. The latest key ring cameras also have voice activation and motion detection. The fire alarm in the picture conceals a flash camera with motion detection and is ideal for videoing covertly in lobbies and hotel corridors.

## Conclusion

Photography can be complicated but does not necessarily need to be. I have seen many operators spend hundreds of pounds on photographic equipment without learning how to use it properly, a great waste and a shame. If you learn a few basic rules such as choosing fast shutter speeds and keeping the camera steady, you should be able to produce clear pictures for your client.

If you buy a new camera, read the instruction book and experiment with it. After a few days, read the book again and I am sure that you will learn twice as much. Why spend many hours on surveillance when at the crucial time your evidence is lost because you did not understand how to use your equipment?

This motion detection video camera is concealed in a fire alarm and is quick to deploy in offices and hotels

# 13 CHAPTER

# Evidence & Law

If we are going to carry out a surveillance, we obviously have a reason for doing so; the ultimate aim may be to gather information that will be used in a court of law as evidence.That evidence has to be accurate, fair, credible and accounted for. We must record our observations in a manner that is accepted by the courts and in particular the Criminal Procedures Investigations Act 1996 (CPIA) especially as our evidence will most likely be disclosed to the 'other side'.

The Hague (European Court), Netherlands

We may have carried out a surveillance which required detailed planning, had taken place over a number of days and achieved a positive result. But, if we have not recorded our evidence correctly (especially if it is a criminal matter) then the whole case could be thrown out of court on a procedural matter.

These subjects are often very boring but are essential knowledge for the professional surveillance operator whether working privately or for a Public Body or Enforcement Agency.

## EUROPEAN CONVENTION ON HUMAN RIGHTS

In 2002 in the United Kingdom, we saw the introduction of the Human Rights Act 1998 (HRA). Stemming from this, in relation to surveillance, the Regulation of Investigatory Powers Act 2000 (RIPA) was born. In simplified terms, this

Headquarters of MI5 - the Security Service - technically a public body

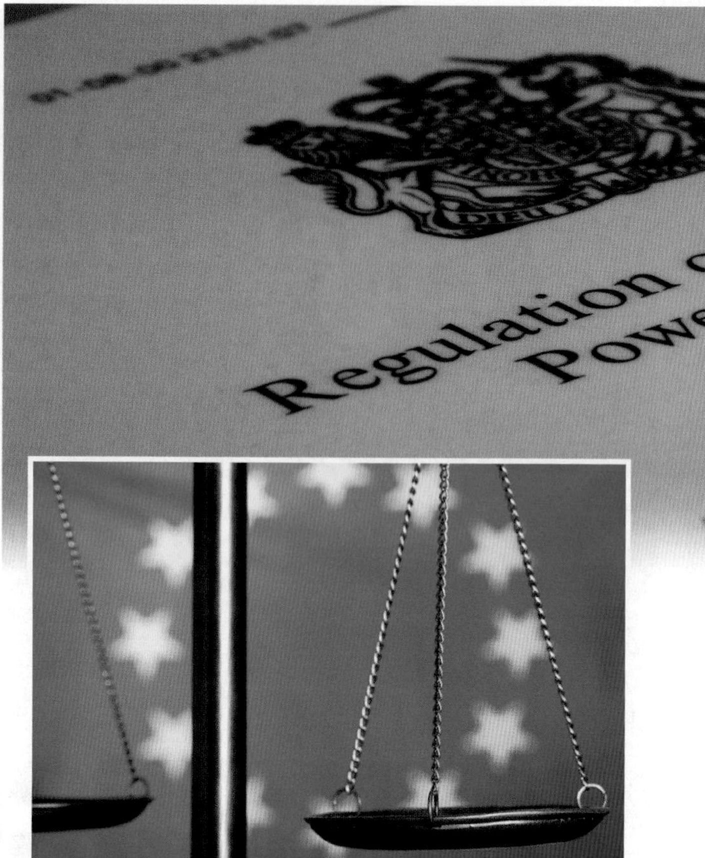


means that any 'Public Body' has to be accountable for carrying out surveillance in order to prevent a persons human rights being violated, especially when personal and private information is being collated.

By Public Body we mean any organisation that comes under the 'Public' umbrella such as:

- Police
- Customs & Excise
- Security Service
- Inland Revenue
- Department for Work & Pensions (Social Security)
- Trading Standards
- Environment Agency
- Local Authority
- Social Services
- National Health

Private Investigators, Surveillance Operators or Security Consultants are not public bodied and so technically they do not have to seek any approval or authorisation in order to mount a surveillance. However, if a private investigator is carrying surveillance work on behalf of a public body, that body should still obtain authorisation in accordance with RIPA.

Prior to RIPA, any public body could put someone under surveillance for whatever reason, without authority and not be accountable to anyone. Since 2002, someone in public authority has to be made accountable in the event of things going wrong, procedures not being adhered to correctly or in the event of miscarriages of injustice.

**RECENT EVENT**

***In February 2008, it was reported that Sadiq Khan, a Labour minister was bugged whilst talking to prisoner Babar Ahmad in jail whilst he was facing extradition to America on terrorism charges.***

***Whilst the bugging of a cell, member of parliament or prisoner has other legal issues and implications, the actual bugging would have had to have been authorised by someone at the very top of the Intelligence Services, Police or Government. The person placing the device would not necessarily be responsible if he had authorisation from above.***

To be accountable, public bodies need to:

- Apply for authorisation
- Have tried all other investigative means
- Authorisation has to be granted by a person of rank, grade or a qualified authorising officer
- Receive authorisation and carry out surveillance in accordance with RIPA 2000

When a Public Body seeks authorisation, the Act requires them to follow human rights principles. In particular, they will be required to justify why they propose to use the powers in terms of **legality, necessity** and **proportionality.** The case officer or authorising officer in relation to the application must ask the following questions:

- *Is my proposed action lawful?*
- *Is it necessary?*
- *Is it proportionate? (or is it using a sledgehammer to crack a nut)*
- *Is my action non-discriminatory?*

An authorisation for directed surveillance may be granted:

- *When needed for a particular case (no other means)*
- *In the interests of national security*
- *To prevent and detect crime or prevent disorder*
- *In the interests of the economic well-being of the UK*
- *In the interests of public safety*
- *To protect public health*
- *To Assess, collect any tax, duty, levy or other charge payable to a government department*

**Authority is not immediately required when responding to an event**

Authorisation is not required when immediately 'responding to an event'. For example, an Environmental Crime Officer is on his way home from work and sees someone fly tipping from their car into a lay-by; so he follows them in order to confirm the vehicles registration and establish the address of the offender. This would not need authorisation as he is responding to an event. However, if the officer needed to protract the surveillance for a few more hours he would be able to obtain verbal authority over the phone from his superior. He would not be allowed to return and continue the surveillance the following day as that would then be 'directed' and would warrant full authorisation.

Many corporate security teams for large organisations that we have trained in the past do not have to comply with RIPA as they are not a public body. However, they do carry out their own internal authorisation procedures based on RIPA in order to ensure 'best practice' if ever challenged in Court.

Quite often, I have seen on the websites of private investigators the phrase:

> ***'We conduct surveillance in accordance with the Human Rights Act and the Regulation of Investigatory Powers Act in order to protect you, the client'***

'Why? You don't need to and who do you go to for authorisation? It's a bit of a gimmick to lure unsuspecting clients to part with their money as the investigator tries to show off his supposed legal prowess and knowledge when he should really be reading another John Grisham novel!

> Investigations are conducted and managed within the guidelines of RIPA - The Regulation of Investigatory Powers Act 2000, following on from The Human Rights Act 1998.

In 2006 MI5, the Security Service had a height restriction of 5ft 11" but this should not deter tall people from working in the industry

## KEY DEFINITIONS

**Surveillance (under RIPA 2000 (Section 48 (2))**

• Monitoring, observing or listening to persons, their movements, their conversations, activities or communications

• Recording anything monitored, observed or listened to in the course of surveillance and

• Surveillance by or with the aid of a surveillance device

• Covert

• If it is carried out in a manner that is calculated to ensure that the persons who are subject to surveillance are unaware that it is or may be taking place

### DIRECTED SURVEILLANCE

Surveillance is **directed** if it is covert but not intrusive and is undertaken:

• For the purposes of a specific investigation or specific operation

• In such a manner as is likely to result in the obtaining of private information about a person and

• Otherwise than by way of an immediate response to events or circumstances, the nature of which is such that it would not be reasonably practicable for an authorisation under this part to be sought for carrying out the surveillance

### INTRUSIVE SURVEILLANCE

Surveillance is **intrusive** if, and only if, it is covert surveillance that:

• Is carried out in relation to anything taking place **on** any residential premises or **in** any private vehicle and

• Involves the presence of an individual **on** the premises or **in** the vehicle or is carried out by means of a surveillance device.

• **Residential Premises**

• Any premises occupied or used by a person however temporarily, for residential purposes or otherwise as living accommodation including hotel or prison accommodation that is so occupied or used. Such accommodation might be in the form of a house, yacht, a railway arch or other makeshift shelter. It includes hotel rooms, bedrooms, barracks and prison cells but not any common area to which a person is allowed access in connection with his or her occupation.

• **Private Vehicle**

• Any vehicle which is used primarily for the private purpose (family, domestic & leisure use) of the person who owns it or of a person otherwise having the right of use to it. This does not include a person whose right to use the vehicle derives only from having paid, or undertaken to pay, for the use of the vehicle and its driver for a particular journey. A vehicle includes any vessel, aircraft or hovercraft.

Intrusive surveillance must only be used in cases of serious crime where there are reasonable grounds for believing it is necessary for the specified action to be taken. The evidence obtained is likely to be of substantial value in the prevention or detection of serious crime and where the action it seeks to achieve cannot reasonably be achieved by any other means.

**CODE OF PRACTICE**

***Pursuant to Section 71 of the Regulation of Investigatory Powers Act 2000***

***This code applies to every authorisation of covert surveillance or of entry, on or interference with property or with wireless telegraphy carried out under section 5 of the Intelligence Services Act 1994, Part III of the Police Act 1997 or Part II of the Regulation of Investigatory Powers Act 2000 by public authorities which begins on or after the day on which this code came into effect.***

Although Article 8.2 of the HRA uses the phrase 'Public Authority', private individuals should be aware of the Article which deals with the **Right to Respect For Private and Family Life** (Article 8.1).

**8.1** Everyone has the right to respect for his private and family life, his home and his correspondence.

**8.2** There shall be no interference by a public authority with the exercise of his right except such as in accordance with the law and is necessary in a democratic society in the interests of national security, public safety or the economic well being of the country, for the prevention of disorder or crime, for the protection of health or morals, or for the protection of the rights and freedoms of others.

We mention these Acts as the private surveillance operator should be aware of them in the event that he is asked to carry out surveillance on behalf of a public body. Any public body or enforcement agency involved in investigation or surveillance work should already be familiar with procedures involved with obtaining authorisation, the HRA and RIPA 2000.

## PRIVACY

The Human Rights Act 1998 together with the Regulation of Investigatory Powers Act 2000 can be a minefield and very confusing to the lay person. In summary, I would suggest that you continue with your surveillance as you have been in the past but keep in mind what you would consider as morally acceptable, fair and how **you** would expect to be treated in the same circumstances.

**It is important to minimise collateral intrusion when filming the target. In other words, don't take video of members of the public unnecessarily**

# LEGAL CASE FILE

A court case relating to a 'personal injury' surveillance (Joyce Elliot v Rhondda Cynon Taff Council) private investigators had obtained video film of their target carrying out physical activities which contradicted her claims. The conclusion made by the district judge at the court hearing, was to the effect that (in view of the video evidence), the claimant (target) was exaggerating her claim for injuries.

The video film was taken from a public place but provided detail of activity filmed through her front door and windows. The claimant and her legal team used this as a basis to apply for an appeal against the judge's decision on the grounds that the video film was inadmissible as it infringed the claimants human rights under Article 8.1 (as it was a contravention to her right to privacy).

The judge added that the evidence (video tape) was justified because the surveillance operative did not trespass onto private property to obtain the film nor was the claimant filmed in an embarrassing situation. The judge did accept that there was a breach of privacy but it was minimal. Thus the application for appeal was not granted.

**RIPA Misconceptions by the Media**

The media are often found using the headlines, ***'Local Council using Anti Terror Laws to catch Fly Tippers and Dog Fouling'*** where they ramble on about local authorities who have put fly tipping hot spots under surveillance with a CCTV camera. The reporters and their newspapers are just sensationalising a story without really understanding the process and what RIPA is all about.

**Snoopers want to use 007 bugs to catch the fly-tippers**

HOW IT WORKS

VEHICLE tracking systems ca used to find the location monitor the movements of trucks, motorcycles or ships
The magnetic devices ar size of a matchbox and have roots in the maritime indu
They were then adopt companies to monitor fl vehicles and by the police an eye on suspects.
The Environment Agen radio frequency track tems, instead of the mo ventional GPS satellite d
Radio devices can through walls, covered a places with many high s – a flaw for GPS.
Once engaged, the tra emit a continuous signa picked up by a radio operated by Agency waiting nearby.
The devices give a information about exa a vehicle is, how fas driven, where it's be long it stayed.

**Council used Terror Act to spy on us over school places**

By **Jo Willey**

A MOTHER has branded a snooping council "ludicrous and completely outrageous" for spying on her family to ensure her children were in the correct school catchment area.

Jenny Paton, 40, says a council worker used controversial powers to monitor the comings and goings of herself, her partner Tim Joyce and her three children for nearly three weeks.

A log reveals they were spied on 21 times to check they lived at an address within the catchment area for Lilliput First School in Dorset.

Officials were allowed to spy on the family using the Regulation of Investigatory Powers Act (Ripa).

The act was primarily brought in to fight terrorism – but some councils are using it to monitor trivial offences, leading to it being dubbed a 'snooper's charter'.

**Futile**

Yesterday, at the start of a landmark Investigatory Powers Tribunal hearing in central London at which she hopes to prove the spying was unlawful, Ms Paton hit out at the surveillance in February and March last year.

She told the hearing: "Some of the operational aspects are ludicrous and completely outrageous and I think we all need protecting from the way local authorities are using Ripa.

"This is about saying 'No more'

Picture: SEAN DEMPSEY

Jenny Paton at the hearing yesterday

Under the Freedom of Information Act (FOIA), a journalist will establish that a local authority will have applied for so many RIPA authorisations for surveillance over the past year and this forms the basis of their headline.

**Phones tapped at the rate of 1,000 a day**

Councils are intercepting calls, emails and letters

Put into perspective, local authorities were conducting surveillance well before RIPA came into effect. RIPA just makes it more accountable and quantifiable.

Whether you are a terrorist, a fly tipper or you let your dog foul the street, the same legislation applies **equally** to both to conduct surveillance. Fly tippers were around well before Al Qaeda but we do not see the headlines ***'Al-Qaida Terrorists Apprehended Using Anti Dog Fouling laws'!***

## PROTECTION FROM HARASSMENT ACT 1997

This Act is briefly mentioned as a number of investigators have been threatened with being taken to court for harassment by a target who had compromised them.

This act has often been referred to as the 'Stalker's Act' and is designed to catch all types of harassment, not just offences such as stalking. It can also include neighbourhood disputes, anti-social behaviour, racial hatred, bullying and domestic violence. Extracts here are taken from the Protection from Harassment Act 1997, Chapter 40.

The Act states that a person must not pursue a course of conduct which he/she knows (or ought to know) amounts to the harassment of another. It is not necessary to prove that the person intended that his/her conduct amounted to harassment. The test is whether a reasonable

If you have been compromised, it is better to 'lift off' rather than risk accusations of harassment

person, who had the same information would think that it amounted to harassment. It does not apply to a course of conduct if the person who pursued it shows:

• That it was pursued for the purpose of preventing or detecting crime

• That it was pursued under any enactment or rule of law or to comply with any condition or requirement imposed by any person under any enactment or

• That in the particular circumstances the pursuit of the course of conduct was reasonable

**Definition**

Harassment is not defined by the Act, the courts will probably have to rely upon the dictionary definition (to worry, pester, annoy, distress). Factors which may be taken into account:

- *Where and when the conduct (harassment) occurred*
- *The relationship between the harasser and victim, and*
- *The previous dealings between the parties*

In criminal proceedings, harassment must have occurred on at least two occasions, although a civil claim may succeed where there has only been one incident, especially if there are reasonable grounds to believe that the harassment may occur again.

**Criminal Offence of Harassment**

**The Act creates two criminal offences:**

• **Harassment**

It is an offence to pursue a course of conduct which amounts to the harassment of another when the harasser knows (or ought to know) his conduct amounts to harassment. The offence is arrestable and is dealt with in the Magistrates Court. If convicted a person can be sentenced to up to six months imprisonment or fined up to £5,000, or both.

• **Causing Fear of Violence**

This is a more serious offence. The offence is committed if a person's course of conduct causes another person to fear, on at least two occasions, that violence will be used against him/her.

This offence can be tried at the Crown Court. The maximum sentence is five years imprisonment, unlimited fine or both.

## CIVIL OFFENCE OF HARASSMENT

A person who is or may be the victim of a course of conduct amounting to harassment can bring a civil action. This claim will be heard in the County Court or in the High Court. The Court can award damages including damages for anxiety and any resulting financial loss.

The victim or potential victim can also ask the Court to grant an injunction restraining the person from any conduct which amounts to harassment. If the person does anything which is prohibited by that injunction, he or she can be sentenced to imprisonment for contempt of Court.

### In Your Defence

It is a defence to show that the person's course of conduct was instigated for the prevention or detection of crime, or was authorised by statute (bailiff), or it was reasonable for purposes of protecting him/herself or another person or property.

If the Secretary of State certifies that in his opinion anything done by a specified person on a specified occasion related to:

- *National security*
- *The economic well-being of the United Kingdom, or*
- *The prevention or detection of serious crime*

was done on behalf of the Crown, the certificate is conclusive evidence that this Act does not apply to any conduct of that person on that occasion. The Act, like any other, is hard to understand but nevertheless, important.

### Criminal Procedure and Investigations Act (CPIA) 1996

Surveillance may be carried out in any public place so long as trespass is not committed (see below). A public place can be defined as a place or premises to which the public has access or has access subject to conditions, and where a reasonable person would have no general expectation of privacy, or would expect privacy to be significantly reduced.

This extends to private land which is capable of being overseen by the general public such as driveways and gardens. A public place also includes private areas that are open to the public such as parks, zoos and fairgrounds, whether by free admission or by payment.

Not so much for the private individual, but a public body when carrying out surveillance should be familiar with the R-v-Johnson 1988 rules where there are set guidelines for carrying out surveillance in public places. This is essential when carrying out surveillance from an observation post on someone's private property such as a house, and with special regards to the disclosure of the evidence obtained. All evidence obtained must be revealed, as it will be required to be disclosed to the 'other side'. However, surveillance methods, tactics and in particular the location of observation posts do not have to be disclosed for fear of reprisals against the owner of the property.

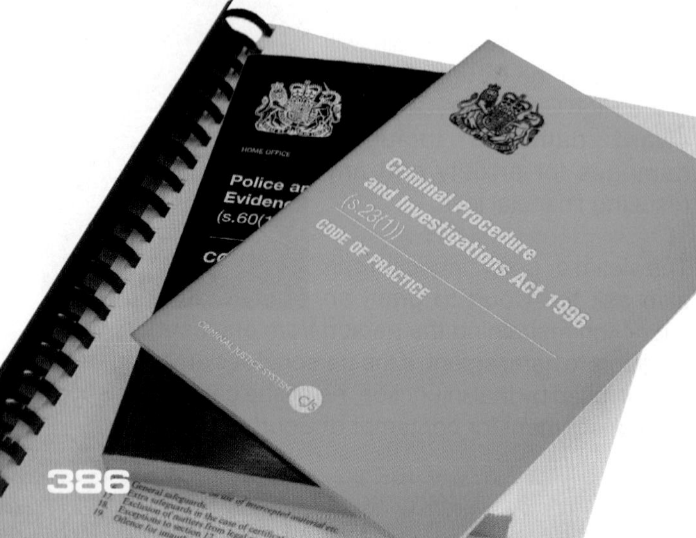


### Trespass

We can take photographs or carry out our enquiries in a public place. We can also be in a public place and take photographs looking into a private place if it would be deemed reasonable that we did not have to make an effort to do so, such as climb up a ladder to look over a wall.

The distinguishing feature of trespass in modern law is that it is a direct and immediate interference with person or property, such as striking a person, entering his land or taking away his goods without his consent. The act of trespass is a 'tort' (a civil wrong) not a crime and therefore it is not necessary to prove that it has caused damage. The sign '*Trespassers will be Prosecuted'* is therefore usually misleading and should actually read, *'Trespassers will be Sued'.*

The placement of a tracking device on a vehicle parked on private land such as a driveway would be deemed as trespass to land, as opposed to being attached in a public place such as a supermarket car park. However, by attaching the device to a car you would also be considered to be interfering with property and so causing a trespass.

There are three types of trespass: to the **Person,** to **Goods** and to **Land.** Trespass to land, usually takes the form of entering it without permission; remaining on land after the owner has withdrawn his permission for you to be there is also a trespass.

### Use Of Trackers

The use of trackers by the public in the UK is open to examination for the reasons stated above in relation to trespass. The use of a tracking device only provides information regarding its location or a vehicles. It does not provide any personal or private information about an individual and therefore cannot infringe a persons human rights.

Some would argue that a tracking device is considered 'intrusive' rather than 'directed' surveillance as far as RIPA is concerned but the Surveillance Commissioner in the

*The use of a tracking device is considered as directed surveillance, rather than intrusive as it only gives you the vehicle's location*

use of a Tracker (not manufactured or adapted to capture & send an audio or video signal) is not intrusive, provided that the surveillance itself is lawful, and no offences are committed in attaching or removing the tracker (Trespass)'.

He views the use of a tracking device as a surveillance tool, and therefore no different than a camera.

However, Part 3 of The Police Act 1997 states that property interference, entry onto or into any private property (including deploying surveillance devices (trackers)), on vehicles trespassing on private land is considered intrusive.

The Act recognises that surveillance will encroach on the privacy of an individual and therefore imposes strict controls over the authorisations of those operations which involve interference with private property.

Some would argue that deploying a tracker on a vehicle is classed as 'Vehicle Interference'. However, vehicle interference comes under the Criminal Attempts Act 1981 which is where an offence is committed by a person interfering with a motor vehicle or a trailer (or with anything carried in it or on it), which is more than merely preparatory to the commission of a theft. Therefore, if you are deploying a tracking device, you are not intending to commit theft.

## DATA PROTECTION ACT 1998

The Data Protection Act 1998 came into force on 1st March 2000. It sets rules for processing personal information and applies to some written paper records as well as those held on computers. The Act applies to 'personal data' that is about identifiable living individuals.

The Data Protection Act is extremely complicated and therefore only the fundamentals that would effect the surveillance operator are covered here.

declares that the in the United Kingdom, any person who compiles or holds private information, whether you are a private investigator, security consultant or even the owner of a video rental shop (who may store names and addresses) you are required by law to be registered with the Data Protection Registrar. Failure to do so can result in heavy fines and/or imprisonment.

Anyone processing information or personal data (be it on computer, video, photographic or written on paper) must comply with the eight enforceable principles of good practice, which states that information is:

1. Fairly and lawfully processed
2. Processed for one specific and limited purpose
3. Adequate, relevant and not excessive
4. Kept accurate and up to date
5. Not kept for longer than necessary
6. Processed in accordance with the data subject's rights
7. Acceptable security measures are used to prevent unauthorised use or misuse of data
8. Not transferred to foreign countries without adequate protection

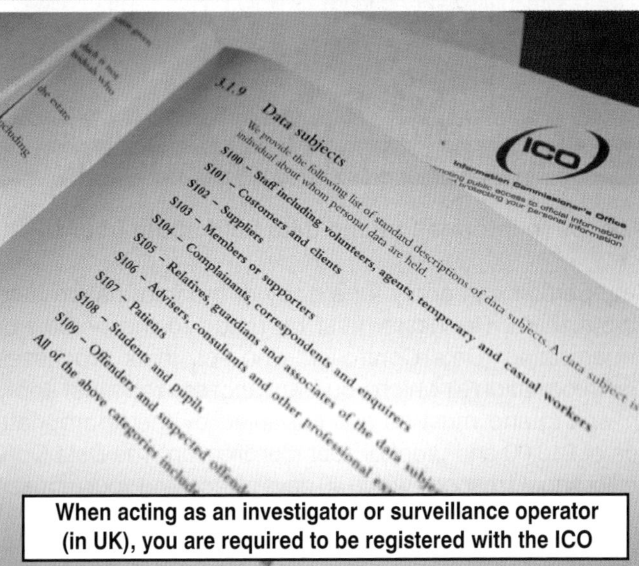


**When acting as an investigator or surveillance operator (in UK), you are required to be registered with the ICO**

The person holding the information is referred to as the 'Data Controller', the person which has information stored about them is referred to as the 'Data Subject'.

Personal data covers both facts and opinions about the individual and also includes information regarding the intentions of the Data Controller towards the individual.

### The Data Subject's Rights

The reason and concept of the Data Protection Act was to partially provide some sort of fairness and security for the 'Data Subjects' or 'us', the general public. As so much information is being stored and processed by many organisations, it was deemed that this information should be kept accurate, truthful and fair. The Act also makes provision for the 'Data Subject' so that he or she is able to find out what information is held about themselves on computer and/or on paper files. This is known as the 'right of subject access'.

The Act also allows individuals to apply to the Court to order a Data Controller to rectify, block, erase or destroy personal details if they are inaccurate or contain expressions of opinion which are based on inaccurate data.

*PETE'S LINK:* www.ico.gov.uk

**Any information relating to your targets should be destroyed as soon as it is no longer required**

### Access to information and data held about you

Any person can apply for a copy of the information held about them. Requests must be made to the person or organisation (Data Controller) who you think processes the information to which you want access. You must apply in writing and must be accompanied by the appropriate fee of £10.00 and proof of your identification. The Data Controller should respond within 40 days of receiving your request.

Individuals are entitled to be told if any personal data is held about them and if so:

- To be given a description of the data
- To be told for what purposes the data is used
- To be told the recipients to whom the data may have been disclosed

**WARNING: Some investigation agencies are using financial and credit databases such as Experian and Equifax when carrying out research into their targets, especially to establish whether they are still living at the address. This is in fact a breach of conditions set down by these companies (and a breach of the DPA) as the information is supplied for obtaining credit scores for lending only.**

You are also entitled:

- To be given a copy of the information with any unintelligible terms explained
- To be given any information available to the controller about the source of the data

Theoretically speaking, if a target of surveillance were to find out which investigation agency or person has them under surveillance, they would be legally entitled to view any information or data (surveillance logs, video tapes) that has been obtained about them. There are various exceptions to this rule which includes surveillance by a public body. So if you get compromised, ensure that the target does not identify you and keep your fingers crossed that he is unaware of the DPA!

This subject can be a minefield, the Data Protection website is very clear and helpful. To register you have to notify that you are a Data Controller by submitting the relevant forms with a fee of £35.00 per year. Failure to do so is a criminal offence and can result in a fine and/or imprisonment.

### Data Protection Act in Relation to Covert CCTV

The DPA takes into account the use of domestic CCTV systems for your own private security and does not expect every householder to register with them. However, the Act gives certain exemptions to the above eight enforceable principles for a CCTV camera mounted on private and domestic property.

Section 36 of the DPA states that:- Personal data processed by an individual only for the purposes of that individual's personal, family or household affairs (including recreational purposes) are exempt from the Data Protection Principles.

Overt CCTV has to be advertised, displaying information about the data controller, unlike this sign

If a person **enters** the property covered by CCTV the owner does not need to put up notices stating that the person is entering a CCTV covered area. Nor is he required to provide a copy of the film he has taken to the Data Subject if they make a formal request.

However, if that CCTV camera picks up images outside the premises, such as a pedestrian walking past, or a camera overlooks his neighbours garden then the above eight principles have to be considered and a sign put up.

However, if your camera is **covert,** Part 1 of the DPA CCTV Code of Practice states:

***In exceptional and limited cases, if it is assessed that the use of signs would not be appropriate, the user of the scheme must ensure that they have:***

***a) Identified specific criminal activity.***

***b) Identified the need to use surveillance to obtain evidence of that criminal activity.***

***c) Assessed whether the use of signs would prejudice success in obtaining such evidence.***

***d) Assessed how long the covert monitoring should take place to ensure that it is not carried out for longer than is necessary.***

***e) Documented (a) to (d) above.***

***Information so obtained must only be obtained for prevention or detection of criminal activity, or the apprehension and prosecution of offenders. It should not be retained and used for any other purpose. If the equipment used has a sound recording facility, this should not be used to record conversations between members of the public.***

Therefore you are able to install covert CCTV so long as you comply with the above codes of practice and the enforceable principles of the DPA.

## EVIDENCE GATHERING

Let us now examine various aspects, which help us to notice events, recognise and describe people.

### Target Detail

On arrival at the target address, make a note of the surrounding details. Should you be keeping a house under surveillance, it is possible that you may not see any sign of life for many hours. This can be disheartening for the investigator and makes him doubt that there is anyone at home but the target could be a late riser or might have left home prior to you arriving.

Rather than make a pretext visit or phone call to the house, your powers of observation will tell you if anyone is present. Things to look out for are:

## QUICK CHECK LIST

- The state of the curtains and windows
- Are there any lights on?
- Chimney smoke
- Milk on the doorstep
- Dry patch on the driveway after rain
- Cats waiting to be let in or dogs barking
- Steam from bathroom window or vents
- Birds flying off when disturbed
- Noise from machinery such as tools or lawnmowers

You may not always be in a position to observe any of the doors and so any of the above indicators will tell you that someone is present and may give you prior warning of them leaving.

Should there be two exits from the property you may have to put a 'trigger' on each. Alternatively, consider putting some sort of 'tell tale' marker on the rear gate/door such as a stone or stick against the gate. If the gate is used it will be disturbed.

On or off? Remember the status of the lights

In addition to being visually aware, you should also rely on your hearing. You may hear the sound of doors and gates opening or car alarms being unset. This will provide those extra seconds of warning to have your camera up and ready or to put the surveillance team on standby.

A 'tell-tale' such as this twig will reveal if anyone has opened the gate

A lack of snow in this area indicates a car has recently driven away

An extractor fan such as this may release steam indicating someone is up and about

Look for 'tell-tale' signs of occupancy such as smoke from the chimney

Heat from an exhaust pipe can reveal if the vehicle has been recently driven

## DESCRIBING PEOPLE

It is not always possible to obtain a photograph of your target and so a full description of him should be taken from those instructing you, so that he is immediately recognisable. In addition, you may need to describe the target in your written reports and so the list below should help you memorise the identifying characteristics.

The well known actors David Haig and Kevin Spacey, have sometimes been mistaken for the author!

### Photographs of Targets

Whenever possible obtain photographs or video of your target, obviously the more recent the picture the better and establish whether your target has changed since it was taken, for example, has grown a moustache, now wears glasses or has altered their hair style. Do not pay lip service to identification photographs, study them and examine facial detail and bodily details so that the target is instantly recognisable when being seen for the first time.

Sometimes comparisons can be difficult, so carry the photograph with you on the task and use it. There is no point in having a photograph if it is going to be left at the office or the car, especially when identification is not easy. The military use a mnemonic 'A to J' in order to describe people:

# IDENTIFYING THE TARGET

"...That's Alpha 2 out and Foxtrot left"

Alpha 2 - Julian Winton

JOHN RHOSTT - ALPHA 1
A. 45-50 YRS
B. MED- FIT
C. CAMMO TROUSERS
D. WINGED DAGGER TATTOO ON WRIST
E. 5'9"- 5'10"
F. SQUARISH- TASH
G. CONFIDENT SWAGGER
H. DARK, CURLY, RECEEDING
I. I.C.1.
J. BOBBY BALL COMEDIAN

| | |
|---|---|
| A | Age |
| B | Build |
| C | Clothing |
| D | Distinguishing Marks |
| E | Elevation (Height) |
| F | Face |
| G | Gait |
| H | Hair |
| I | I.C. Code |
| J | Just Like (resemblances) |

Quite often you will have to describe certain persons in your reports. Even if you recognise your target from a photograph, it is always wise to add a description of that person to your log or report. The descriptive list shown above should be sufficient for most purposes.

**Characteristics and features vary and could be described in the following ways:**

### • AGE

To estimate age, compare the target's age with your own or someone that you know. If you find this difficult, try to 'bracket' their age. If you feel that they can not be older than 50 but are not as young as 40, we can estimate that the target is approximately 45 years old. When making notes such as your surveillance log, do not be too precise when estimating ages and put them down in brackets (35-40 years). Be aware that beards and baldness can make men appear much older than they really are. ☹

### • BUILD

Build could be considered as: Slim, Medium, Heavy, Well Built, Proportionate, Stout, Stooped, Small, Athletic, Muscular and Wiry. Be aware that peoples clothes can often alter your perception of build, especially heavy coats.

### • CLOTHING

Smart, Scruffy, Casual, Business-like, Sporty, Industrial, Designer.

### • DISTINGUISHING MARKS

Tattoos or Skin Marks. Obtain the design of the tattoo and their locations. Tattoos are designed for showing off and are often found on the forearms. Some people have very distinguishing marks such as birthmarks, blemishes and scars.

LONDON SHOOTFIGHTER fighter
WWW.LONDONSHOOTFIGHTER

### Spectacles and Jewellery

• Spectacles: Round, Square, Horn Rimmed, Metallic, Bi-Focal, Tinted

• Jewellery: Rings, Necklaces, Medallions, Broaches, Earrings, Hair slides, piercings

COURTESY: ITV

### Speech

Regional accents are not always distinct but attempt to put the accent to an area, even if it is only North, South, Midland or West Country. Consider the tone and volume such as quiet, soft, loud, slurred, educated, clipped

## • ELEVATION (HEIGHT)

Height can be estimated in a similar manner as we would for age. Compare the target's height to yourself or someone you know and bracket accordingly. In addition, you can compare the target against his surroundings such as a door frame (6 feet 6 inches) or a car roof. Height can sometimes be difficult to estimate as the persons build can often alter our perception especially if they are higher up than you, such as on a doorstep.

## • FACIAL FEATURES AND COMPLEXION

Pale, Fair, Tanned, Olive, Rashy, Weathered, Dark, Freckly

### • Shape of Face

When looking at faces there are many features that make up the face apart from the overall shape

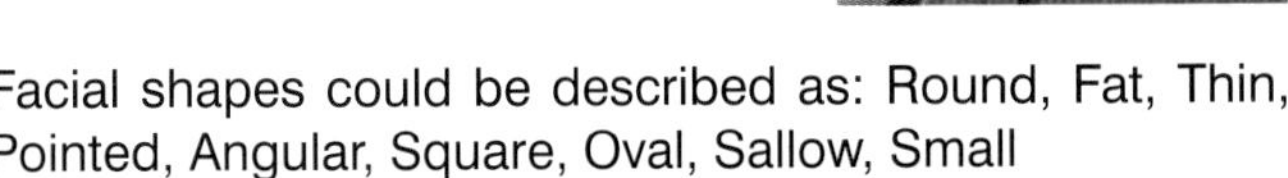

Facial shapes could be described as: Round, Fat, Thin, Pointed, Angular, Square, Oval, Sallow, Small

### • Eyes

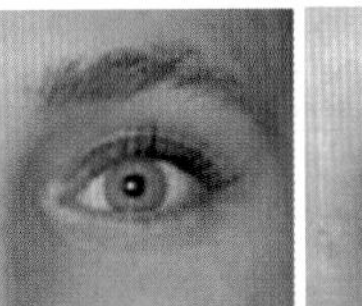

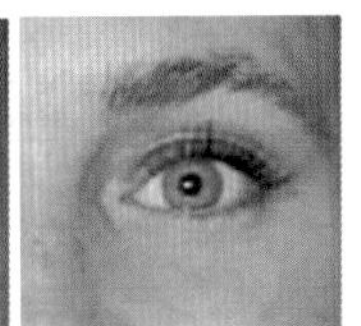

Large, Small, Squint, Slanted, Bloodshot, Piggy, Piercing, Hooded Lids, Wide, Colour

### • Eyebrows

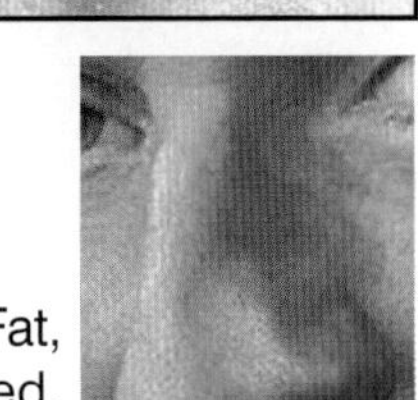

Thick, Thin, Bushy, Arched, Plucked, Narrow, Joined, Slanted, Straight

### • Noses

Small, Large, Button, Hooked, Roman, Fat, Bumpy, Snub, Bulbous, Wide, Pointed, Squashed

### • Teeth

White, Discoloured, False, Capped, Chipped, Crowned

### • Lips

Fat, Thin, Colour, Pale, Pouting

### • Chins

Square, Round, Pointed, Long, Double, Angular

### • Facial Hair

Moustaches: Military, Droopy, Handlebar, Bushy/Thick, Tooth-brush, Mexican, Thin, Walrus, Clipped, Waxed Beards: Stubbly, Unshaven, Pointed, Long, Straggly, Short, Designer

## • GAIT

Most people have a unique and identifiable gait in the way they carry themselves and move whilst walking

• Posture and Bearing: Upright, Slouched, Stooped, Round Shouldered, Head Drooped, Lethargic

• Gait and Pace: Fast, Slow, Bouncy, Marching, Skipping, Plodding, Springy, Dainty, Lethargic, Limping, Shuffling

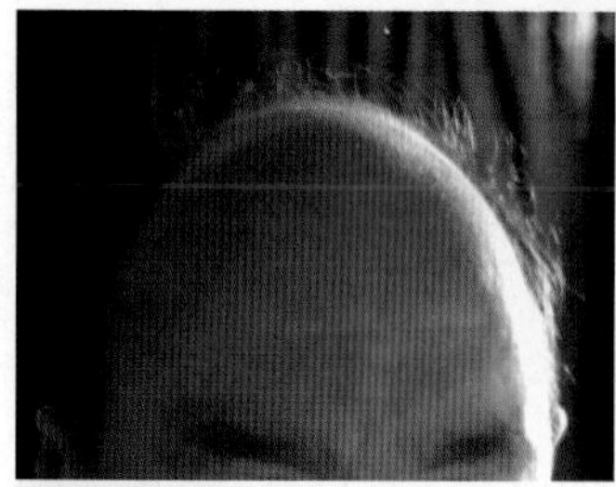

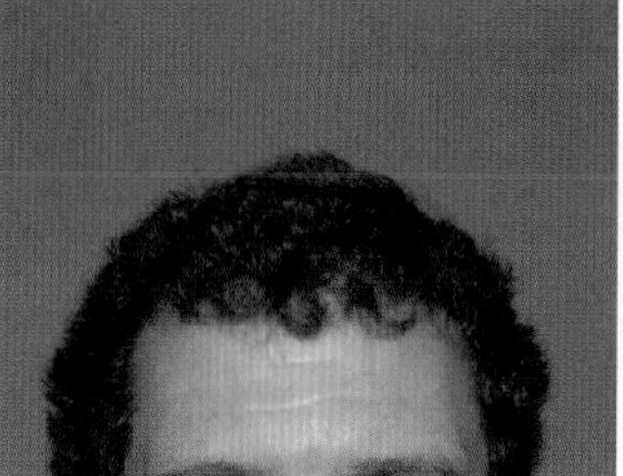

## • HAIR

Hair can be described in many ways but we divide hair styles into three sub-categories:

• **Colour:** Light, Dark, Fair, Streaked, Bleached, Tinted, Coloured, Black, Brown, Grey

• **Length:** Cropped, Short, Balding, Collar/Shoulder Length, Long

• **Style:** Tidy, Scruffy, Wavy, Permed, Straight, Thick, Thin, Curly, Receding, Greasy, Fringed, Styled, Spiky, Bobbed

Some people have unique hairstyles



## • ETHNIC ORIGIN

Your description of origin should be treated as being descriptive rather than a guess. Terms to be used could be: White, Black, Asian, Arabic, Hispanic, Oriental, Latin, Scandinavian, East European.

## • RESEMBLANCES

Does the target resemble anyone famous? A television personality or a politician, for example. If you use this method to describe a person, ensure that it's someone that most people will recognise!

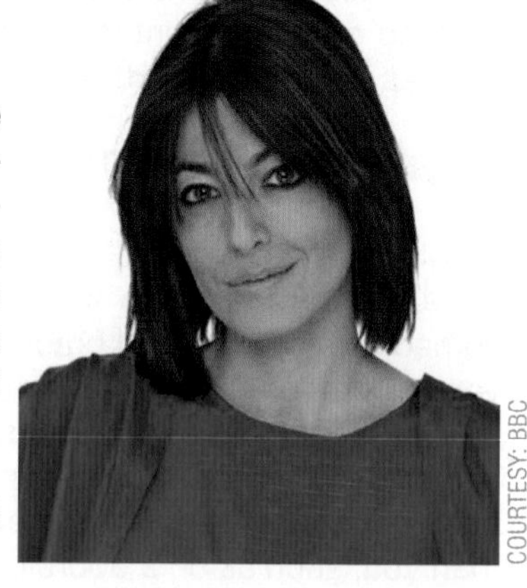

## • DETAILS OF VEHICLE

Any vehicle detail that you can obtain regarding the target will be extremely useful. When vehicles arrive on the scene of an observation, or you arrive there to find a vehicle, it is important that you record as much detail as possible about them. Today, many vehicles are designed by computer and consequently appear to be a similar shape such as the Laguna, Mondeo or Corolla. Therefore it is also important to recognise the car's logos and badges.

| Major Categories Description & Code | Sub Group Description | Code |
|---|---|---|
| | | |
| Asian or Asian British (A) | Indian<br>Pakistani<br>Bangladeshi<br>Any other Asian background | A1<br>A2<br>A3<br>A9 |
| Black or Black British (B) | Caribbean<br>African<br>Any other Black background | B1<br>B2<br>B9 |
| Chinese (C) | Chinese | C1 |
| Mixed (M) | White & Black Caribbean<br>White & Black African<br>White & Asian<br>Any other Mixed background | M1<br>M2<br>M3<br>M9 |
| White (W) | British<br>Irish<br>Any other White background | W1<br>W2<br>W9 |
| Or any other ethnic group (O) | | O1 |
| Not Stated (N) | | NS |

# VEHICLE SHAPES

- **Make and Model**

The make could be either a Ford or a Vauxhall, the models possibly being a Focus or Vectra respectively.

- **Shape**

In addition, there are variants such as estates, saloons, hatchbacks and convertibles. If you do not know what make it is, provide a detailed description.

- **Colour**

Colours are fairly straight forward with variants in shades and metallic finishes. Make a note of the state of repair and body work, does it have any modifications?

- **Registration Marks and Numbers**

Registration numbers are unique to every vehicle and are the best means to recognition.

**Identifying Features**

Note any unusual marking or ornaments such as stickers, furry dice, nodding dogs and tow hooks. In busy traffic you may only get a brief sighting of a sticker in a rear window when the car is way ahead of you, this may be the only indicator to provide its location in a long queue of traffic.

Remember, if the target drives a powerful car, it will be necessary for the surveillance team to use powerful vehicles also.

## MISTAKEN IDENTITY

**Charles De Menezes (left section) was mistaken for 21/7 London bomber Hussain Osman (right section). De Menezes was shot dead by the security forces on a Tube train**

## NIGHT VISION

After being in a well lit area and then moving into the dark, it takes approximately 20 minutes for your eyes to get accustomed and about 40 minutes to become fully adjusted. This adjustment is what we call 'night vision' or getting used to the dark.

At the back of the eye is the retina which is made up of cells, these cells (of which there are two types) are formed in the shape of rods and cones. The cones (in the centre) are sensitive to coloured light but not shades of grey. Alternately, the rods (surrounding the cones) are not sensitive to colours but are sensitive to shades of grey. During the daytime, the cones cells are used to transmit light to the brain, as darkness takes over, the rods take over.

If you are observing at night, do not stare directly at the object, but look slightly to one side so that you are using the area of the rods. If you look directly at the target, it will be covered by the cones and in effect causing a blind spot.

When we go from one extreme to another such as a well lit area into darkness, it takes some time for the cells to change role and so we have this 20-40 minute period of 'getting used to the dark'. The suggestion that carrots help you to 'see in the dark' is true to some extent. Carrots are rich in Vitamin 'A' and it is known that Vitamin 'A' stimulates the cells that we have mentioned.

Once night vision is obtained, it is easy to lose it again by looking at bright lights or through night vision scopes. It also takes much longer to regain your night vision after losing it, therefore when observing at night consider the following:

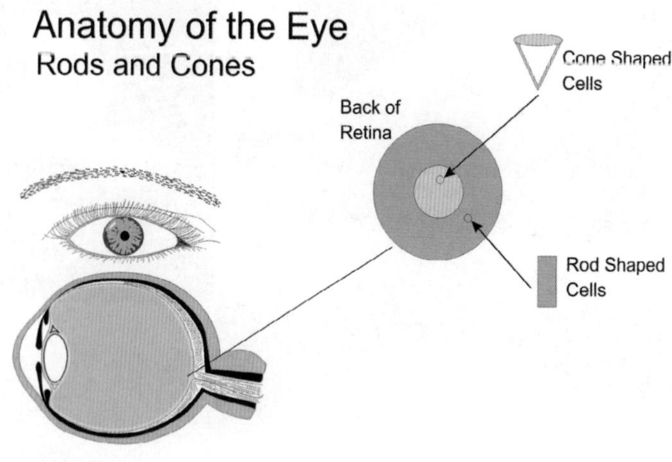


- Scan areas of observation slowly
- Do not look directly at the object, the eye has a 'blind spot' so look slightly to one side
- Do not stare at an object, your eyes will play tricks on you
- Avoid looking at bright lights, this will ruin your night vision
- Keep your eyes closed when exposed to light such as car headlights. If necessary, just keep one eye open
- Rest your eyes frequently
- Looking through a night vision scope can ruin your night vision

*Troops on night operations sit in the dark for at least 40 minutes before deploying*

COURTESY: DOD

## SPECIAL CASE FILE

### RECCE PATROL - FALKLAND ISLANDS WAR 1982

*During the Falklands Campaign I served in a small reconnaissance unit tasked with carrying out forward recce patrols and OPs ahead of the main fighting units. When the patrol moved at night, I was one of two scouts whose responsibility up ahead, was to stop, listen and look to our front for enemy positions or patrols using image intensifying scopes.*

*This was extremely hard work. Once I had 'cleared' to my front, my partner Jan would move forward to clear his front and then I would come through and so on, with the patrol following not far behind us. What made the job even more difficult for us was the fact that we would stop every 50 paces or so and scan through the night sight, in doing so we would lose our night vision in that eye. When we patrolled forward, visibility was difficult as we were now effectively blind in one eye.*

Soldiers preparing to carry out night time operations (such as going into a night assault by helicopter) will often sit for 40 minutes in darkness to enable their eyes to become accustomed to the dark. The troops may wait in a special area illuminated by red light (which does not effect night vision) or all of the lights inside the aircraft may be switched off.

## MEMORY AND PERCEPTION

### Perception

Noticing detail is very important but our minds can often play tricks on us without us being aware of it. For example, read the following sentence and then write down how many times the letter F is used:

FINISHED FILES ARE THE
RESULTS OF YEARS OF
SCIENTIFIC RESEARCH
COMBINED WITH THE
EXPERIENCE OF YEARS

The first time I read this I counted three, when there are actually six! If you think I am mistaken, then count again....

**F**INISHED **F**ILES ARE THE
RESULTS O**F** YEARS O**F**
SCIENTI**F**IC RESEARCH
COMBINED WITH THE
EXPERIENCE O**F** YEARS

This is a common mistake as your brain plays tricks on you all the time. We discard the word 'of' because it does not require much thought and is not one of the main words we are looking at.

Here's another one...,

**DO not read the words, say aloud the colour of each word**

YELLOW BLUE ORANGE
BLACK RED GREEN
PURPLE YELLOW RED
ORANGE GREEN BLACK

Try to educate your memory. There are three different ways in which we memorise detail. On surveillance courses we show a number of items to the students; they have one minute to look at them and remember them, after which they have to write down and describe what they can remember. A number of tests carried out over a few days certainly improves their memory and their attention to detail.

***Study the image overleaf for one minute, then close the book and attempt to write down the list of objects. Pay attention to detail and count how many there are as this helps***

People have different ways of remembering the objects, some use 'association' where the set of cars keys would be linked to a petrol receipt or the packet of sweets would be linked to a toothbrush. Others think to themselves a bizarre story in which they link the objects together such as: *I left the house with my CAR KEYS in my hand, I looked at my WATCH because I was late, I had to fill up with PETROL and I bought some headache TABLETS at the same time.*

Others may group the objects into rows or clusters, such as the top row, the middle row and the bottom row. Everyone has their own personal way of remembering details, so use whatever system suits you.

# TEST YOUR OSBERVATION SKILLS

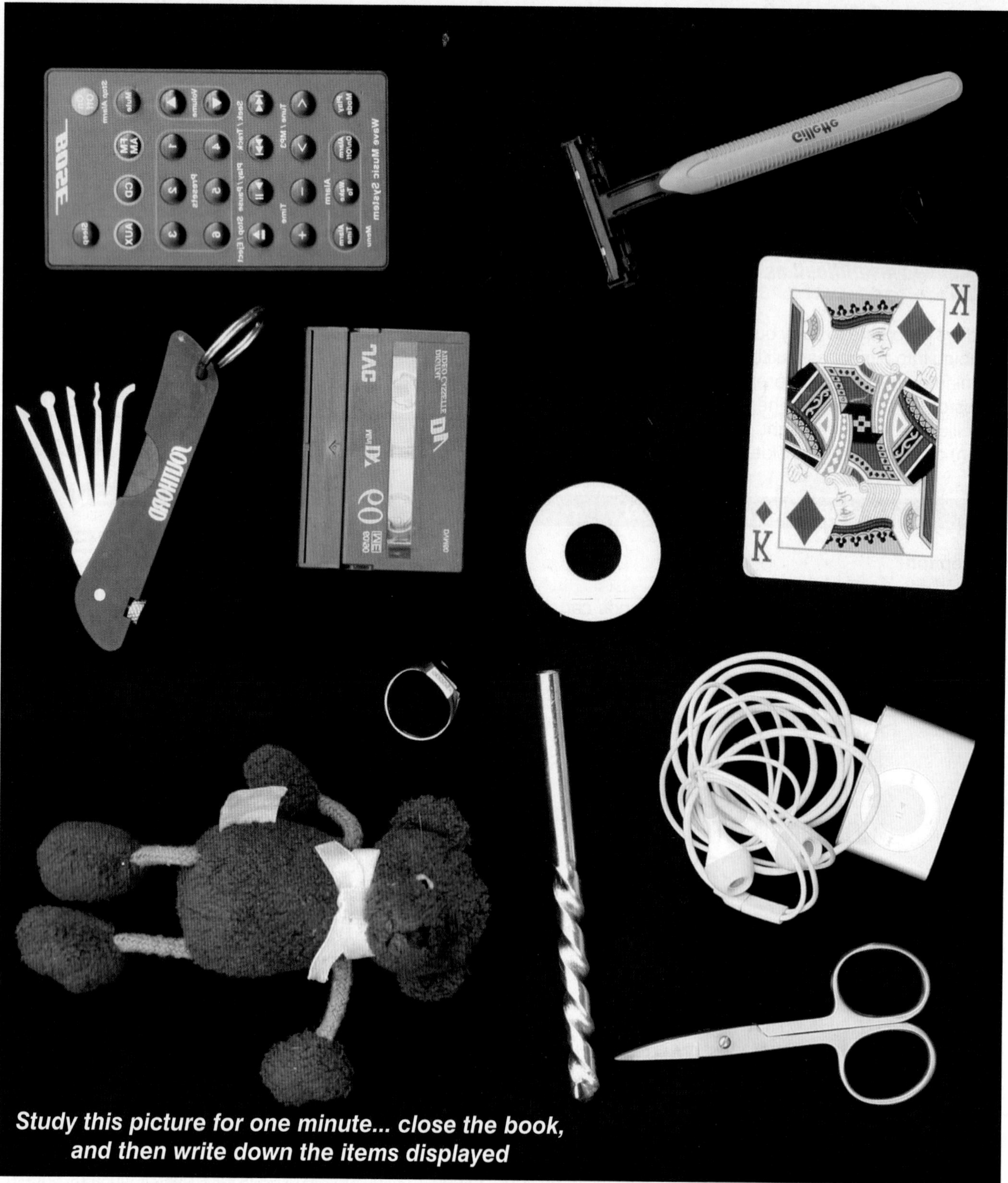

*Study this picture for one minute... close the book, and then write down the items displayed*

**Answers on last page of chapter**

## SURVEILLANCE LOGS AND REPORTS

As a member of a surveillance team, you should keep an accurate log of exactly what occurs and what action is taken. The team leader may keep a more detailed log of team events (Master Log). It is important that all team members synchronise their watches and timers on photographic equipment so that the surveillance logs coincide with each other and there are no discrepancies. Remember all oddities may be brought to the attention of a court and could discredit your evidence.

Should you be in a static OP, you may be able to write down a fair amount of detail about the target area and the events taking place. Should there be two operators on the same task, there is no reason why one keeps the log, so long as the other signs and witnesses it on completion.

Depending on the nature of the enquiry, it will effect how you log and produce your written reports. It is recommended to have the surveillance logs typed up and submitted with accompanying photographs or video tape. Reports in this format include all details and log events in a chronological order.

**Official government surveillance log has its pages glued, stapled and tape-bound. All pages are numbered**

### Surveillance Logs

All timings, incidents and information should be recorded in a chronological order and preferably written down in note form. The notes that you make will be regarded as contemporaneous and will possibly be used as evidence and would have to be produced in court. Your notes may be written on anything at the time of the incident; pocket book, log sheets or even the back of a cigarette packet, but once written they should be preserved as evidence, more importantly so if you are investigating a criminal activity.

All entries into the log should be made as soon as practically possible after the event which took place. If there is a large time span between an event taking place and the entry being made, it may be worth mentioning this in your log. Try and use block capitals when recording names, addresses and place names. It makes them clearer to read and it is important information that easily jumps out from the page.

It is not always necessary to use prepared log sheets but they are simple, easy to read and make life easier when they have to be typed.

It is not always practical to handwrite a log, and so a running commentary, or details of an event may have to be kept on a dictaphone or a memo recorder The details on the recording should be written up as soon as possible. On occasions (such as Criminal Investigations) the dictaphone tape will also have to be retained and preserved as evidence.

### No ELBOWS!

When compiling our surveillance log sheets, there are certain guidelines that can help preserve the integrity of the log and its content and we use the mnemonic **'No ELBOWS'** to remind us. There should be no:

#### ERASURES

If you make a mistake, you should not obliterate the mistake with pen, rub it out or use correction fluids. If you make an error, draw a single line through it (so that the error can be read) and write the correction immediately afterwards. The loggist should initial any mistakes and all entries should be made in ink.

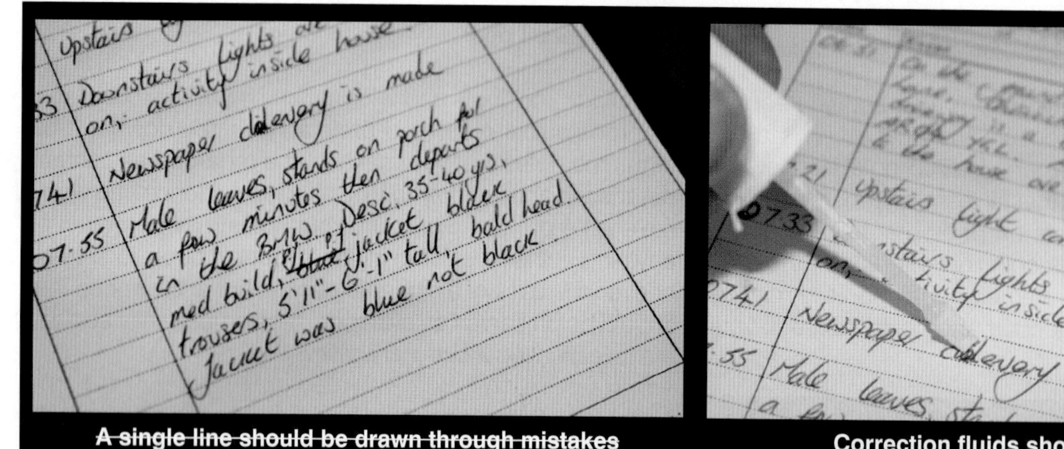


~~A single line should be drawn through mistakes~~

Correction fluids should not be used

## LOOSE LEAFS

Ideally the sheets of a logbook should be bound with glue and each page serial numbered (as are the Police and Enforcement Agency Logs). In this way entries are made in a chronological order and it cannot be open to suggestion that extra pages were added at a later time and also any removed pages will be identified.

## BLANK SPACES

Some people leave a blank line in between log entries in order to make it clearer that it is a separate event. This is in fact bad practice as it could be suggested that you have left the line clear in order to add an entry at a later time. Should an entry leave a large gap, this should be struck out to prevent any further additions. A line drawn straight across the page normally indicates the end of the surveillance or day's entries.

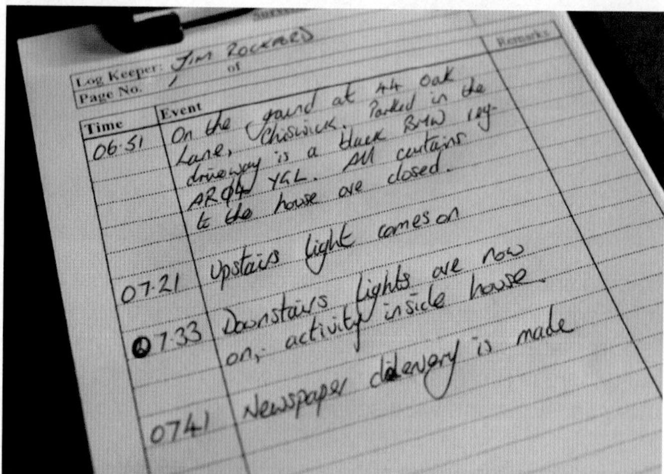

## OVERWRITING

As mentioned above, if you make a mistake, do not write over the top of the error or cram the correction into the text, use a fresh line.

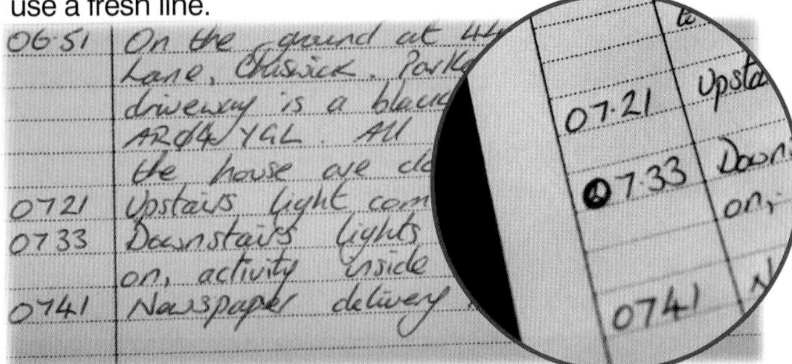


**In this log you will note each entry is continuous without leaving blank lines**

## WRITING BETWEEN THE LINES

Do not cram words in between the lines of text if you realise that there is an addition you need to make to your log. If you realise that you have made an error or there is something that you wish to include in the log, then add it to the end of the log commencing with the phrase 'Belated Entry' and timed at the time the event took place and also noting when the belated entry was made.

## SEPERATE PIECES OF PAPER

If at all possible, use bound surveillance logs. Separate log sheets are acceptable but can be left open to abuse and the suggestion that they were not the originals. If you use separate log sheets, ensure that you number the pages 2 of 2, for example. If for some reason you record your

observations on a scrap piece of paper as it was the only thing to hand, then this must be preserved and retained with the log sheets. An entry should also be made in the log referring to it as an exhibit.

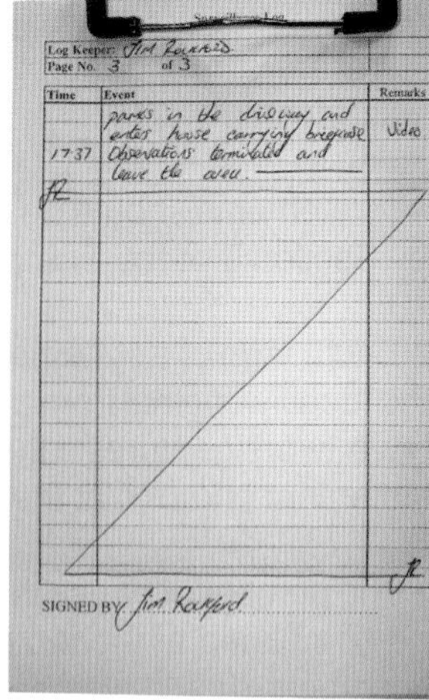


If your surveillance logs are maintained keeping all of the above in mind, it will be more easily accepted as reputable evidence. Remember, if you are using a dedicated loggist, the accuracy of your reporting over the radio net has to be precise. If there is a stop, say exactly where it is as the loggist will be relying on you to pass this information back to them.

### Witness Statements

If you are providing a surveillance service for a solicitor or insurance company, it is most likely that they will require a statement to accompany your report and surveillance logs. It is highly likely that the statement will be served upon the other parties to the proceedings.

A surveillance log or report cannot be just put into a legal file to be used in Court proceedings as evidence. Therefore a system is in place under the Criminal Justice Act 1967, Section 9, whereby a 'Statement of Truth' launches your evidence into the legal system. In the police world, this statement form is often referred to as 'Form MG11'.

Statements in this instance can be made in one of two ways; your surveillance log of events can be contained within the body text of a statement, or a brief statement can be written and used with your surveillance log attached as an Exhibit. For example, if your log is attached as an exhibit, it would look something like this (see documents over):

Here are a few general rules to consider when making statements:

All statements should be prepared in the format prescribed by Section 9 of the Criminal Justice Act 1967:

• Each page of a statement should be signed in blue ink (to the identify original from a photocopy). The first page should have two signatures: one at the caption at the top of the statement and one at the base of the page.

• The number of pages that comprise that statement should be completed at the top of the statement. Each continuation sheet should also be numbered in sequence.

• The first paragraph should be used to introduce the witness and should include a brief background, experience and qualifications.

• Statements should not contain hearsay, opinion or conjecture. They should be factual and written in the first person (I did this, I saw that etc) and in a chronological order.

• If you need to produce some real evidence such as a photograph or videotape, you should make reference to it in the statement e.g. "I produce a video tape reference PIJ1"

• The reference will be the initials of the person producing it followed by a sequential number.

• If the statement is typed it is recommended that it is in the following font and format:

- Font - Times New Roman
- Font size - Twelve pitch
- Line Spacing - Double
- Justification - Fully justified
- Paragraphs (unnumbered)

## WITNESS STATEMENT

**(CJ Act 1967, s.9; MC Act 1980, ss.5A(3) (a) and 5B; C.P.R 27.1.2005)**

**Statement of:** Darren Paul Finch

**Age if under 18:** Over 18

**Occupation:** Commercial Investigator

**This statement (consisting of one page, each signed by me) is true to the best of my knowledge and belief and I make it knowing that, if it is tendered in evidence, I shall be liable to prosecution if I have willfully stated anything in it, which I know to be false, or do not believe to be true.**

**Signature:** D. Finch

**Date:** 14th February 2010

**STATES:**

I am Darren Paul Finch of DPF Associates, 84 Thames Road, London, W1 5DL. I am a commercial investigator and have been carrying out investigative work for the past 11 years. Prior to this I was a member of the HM Forces carrying out surveillance and intelligence work within the Royal Military Police.

On 28th January 2009 I carried out surveillance at the premises of 'Kwikly Exhausted Ltd', located at 113 Jeremy Street, Keighley, BD21 3DF to monitor all deliveries made at the premises. I commenced my observations at 08.30 hours and completed at 16.30 hours when I left the area.

During my observations, I noted various vehicles making deliveries to the premises and these are recorded in my handwritten surveillance log which was maintained at the time.

The surveillance log is exhibited hereto and is marked as Exhibit 'DPF 1'.

**Signature:** D. Finch D. Finch

**Signature witnessed by:** C. Fillers

**Page 1 of 1**

*Or if contained within the body of a statement like this:*

## WITNESS STATEMENT

**(CJ Act 1967, s.9; MC Act 1980, ss.5A(3) (a) and 5B; C.P.R 27.1.2005)**

**Statement of:** Darren Paul Finch

**Age if under 18:** Over 18

**Occupation:** Commercial Investigator

**This statement (consisting of one page, each signed by me) is true t that, if it is tendered in evidence, I shall be liable to prosecution if I or do not believe to be true.**

**Signature:**

**Date:** 14th February 2010

**STATES:**

I am Darren Paul Finch of DPF Associates, 84 Thames Road, London, W1 5DL. I am a commercial investigator and have been carrying out investigative work for the past 11 years. Prior to this I was a member of the HM Forces carrying out surveillance and intelligence work within the Royal Military Police.

On 28th January 2009 I carried out surveillance at the premises of 'Kwikly Exhausted Ltd, located at 113 Jeremy Street, Keighley, BD21 3DF to monitor any collections of tyres made at the premises. I commenced my observations at 08.30 hours and completed at 16.30 hours when I left the area.

During my observations, I noted various vehicles making deliveries to the premises and these are as follows:-

08.30 Observations commenced.

10.47 Arrival of a blue Toyota tipper truck vehicle registration YG05 SHD, a delivery of exhaust pipes were delivered.

11.04 The above vehicle departs.

11.57 Royal Mail Postal Delivery

13.16 A grey Ford Transit van arrives, approximately 30 used tyres are loaded into the van. The driver would be described as: male, 35-40 yrs, heavy build, wearing dark green overalls and a 'Ford' baseball cap, 5'8"-5'9" tall, goatee beard, greying collar length hair. Video is obtained.

**Continuation Statement of: Darren Paul Finch** **Page 2 of 2**

13.36 The above vehicle departs

15.53 A yellow DAF 7.5 ton lorry vehicle registration YS06 ODH arrives and makes a delivery of 8 tyres.

16.00 The above vehicle departs.

16.30 Observations are terminated and depart the area.

A copy of the video tape is exhibited hereto and is marked as Exhibit 'DPF 1'.

**Signature:** D. Finch **Signature witnessed by:** C. Fillers

## EYE WITNESS TESTIMONY AS EVIDENCE

If you find yourself in court giving evidence, it is possible that the Defence barrister will attempt to discredit your evidence or put your 'witness testimony' in some doubt in order to confuse a jury, especially when there is a doubt about a person's identity.

In a famous case (Regina -v- Turnbull and Others 1976), certain witnesses to an armed robbery were called to give evidence at the robbers' trial, Turnbull was the getaway driver in the robbery. These witnesses saw the robbery take place but their testimony was put to question by the Defence. Many questions were asked:

- *How far away from the Defendant were you?*
- *If across the street was the road busy at that time of the day?*
- *Could passing buses obscure your view?*
- *How long did you have him in sight for?*
- *Are your sure it was him?*
- *How can you be certain?*

## CASE SUMMARY

In summing up, the Judge Lord Widgery, informed the jury that there should be a special need for caution when considering eye witness evidence and said that a single witness can make mistakes, several witnesses are likely to paint a more realistic picture of events but they can also still be mistaken. This case set a precedent and barristers now use this case as a guide when cross examining eye witnesses when identification is in doubt. Lord Widgery speaking for the English Court of Appeal in R-v-Turnbull referred to four guideline matters which a trial judge, when instructing a jury or himself, if sitting alone, must consider.

**1.** ...whenever the case against an accused depends wholly or substantially on the correctness of one or more identifications of an accused which the defence alleges to be mistaken, the judge must warn the jury of the special needs for caution before convicting the accused in reliance on the correctness of the identification or identifications...

**2.** ...he should instruct them as to the reason for the need for such a warning and should make some reference to the possibility that a mistaken witness can be a convincing one and that a number of such witnesses can all be mistaken...

**3.** ...direct the jury to examine closely the circumstances in which the identification by each witness came to be made...

His Lordship then set out a number of factors one might consider when deciding whether or not there is evidence before the Court which would impact positively or negatively upon the correctness of the testimony, and continued:

**4.** ...remind the jury of any specific weaknesses which had appeared in the identification evidence. Recognition may be more reliable than identification of a stranger; but, even when the witness is purporting to recognise someone whom he knows, the jury should be reminded that mistakes in recognition of close relatives and friends are sometimes made...

His Lordship went on to state:

...If the quality is good and remains good at the close of the accused's case, the danger of a mistaken identification is lessened; but the poorer the quality, the greater the danger. In our judgment, when the quality is good, as for example

## LEGAL CASE FILE

***In the case of the murder of Jill Dando (a British newscaster shot dead in 1999 on her doorstep ), a man called Barry George was tried for her murder. He was convicted on the grounds that forensic evidence from a firearm was found on his clothing. The prosecution had several witnesses who stated that they saw a man acting suspiciously in the area before, at the time and after the murder. However, each description given by the witness was different from each other and thus not accurate enough to convince the jury that George was at the scene of the crime.***

***Barry George was finally acquitted after he appealed against his conviction and he was set free.***

when the identification is made after a long period of observation, or in satisfactory conditions by a relative, a neighbour, a close friend, a work mate or the like, the jury can safely be left to assess the value of the identifying evidence even though there is no other evidence to support it; provided always, however, that an adequate warning has been given about the special need for caution....

If we take the case of **R-v-Turnbull and Others,** and can give answers to the points raised, we can be confident in our evidence. Using the mnemonic ADVOKATE we remember the points which need to be made in detail which you may be cross examined about.

# ADVOKATE

## A AMOUNT OF TIME

How long was the target in view for?

## D DISTANCE

How far away was the target from you?
Were you using optics such as binoculars or telephoto lenses?
Was the target so close that you had to avert you eyes?

## V VISIBILITY

What was the weather like? Was it foggy? Was the sun in your eyes?
Were you having to look in your rear view mirror, was it a back to front image?
Do you wear glasses? Were you wearing them at the time?

## O OBSTRUCTIONS

Were you looking across a busy street, heavy with passing traffic?
Were you having to peer through heavy foliage?
Was there a lot of pedestrian activity?
Did the target go out of sight at any time?

## K KNOWN OR SEEN BEFORE

Had you seen the target before?
Was he known to you?
Did you have a photograph to recognise him from?
Had you carried out surveillance on him before?

## A ANY REASON TO REMEMBER

I had reason to remember because that day in question was my birthday.
I remember the jumper he wore because I have one exactly like it.
I remember him because he had a likeness to.....

## T TIME LAPSE

Could your memory fail you?
What was the time span between seeing the incident and making your notes and statement?
What was the time span between seeing the incident and the identity parade?

## E ERRORS OR DISCREPANCIES

Is it possible.........?
Is it possible that you are mistaken?
You have stated this, another witness has stated that, could you be wrong?

*Under cross-examination you will be asked how far away you were from the target... were there any obstructions or distractions?*

*I have given evidence in Court when the Defence barrister went systematically through the list above. At the time I was still a 'young investigator' and had no knowledge of R-v-Turnbull or ADVOKATE but I was able to provide the correct answers to his cross examination. This was only due to correct log keeping at the time, quick thinking and having the confidence in my own evidence.*

Remember a defence barrister will want to:

- Shorten the time span that the target was in your sight
- Extend the distance between you and the target
- Cloud your view
- Prove that the view was fully or partially obstructed for a short period of time
- Intimate a wrong identity
- Question your judgement and memory
- Put to you any discrepancies, such as errors in your log keeping
- Put doubt in the minds of a jury

## PRESERVATION OF PHOTOGRAPHIC EVIDENCE

The aim of the majority of surveillance tasks is to obtain photographic evidence of an event taking place or to prove that a person was in a particular location at a certain date and time.

Should these photographs or video tape be used in legal proceedings (especially criminal) then they should be handled, preserved and exhibited as any other evidence would be. There should be a documented record of the evidence when it is transferred from one person to another for reasons of continuity. This is essential when handling evidence to be used in criminal proceedings.

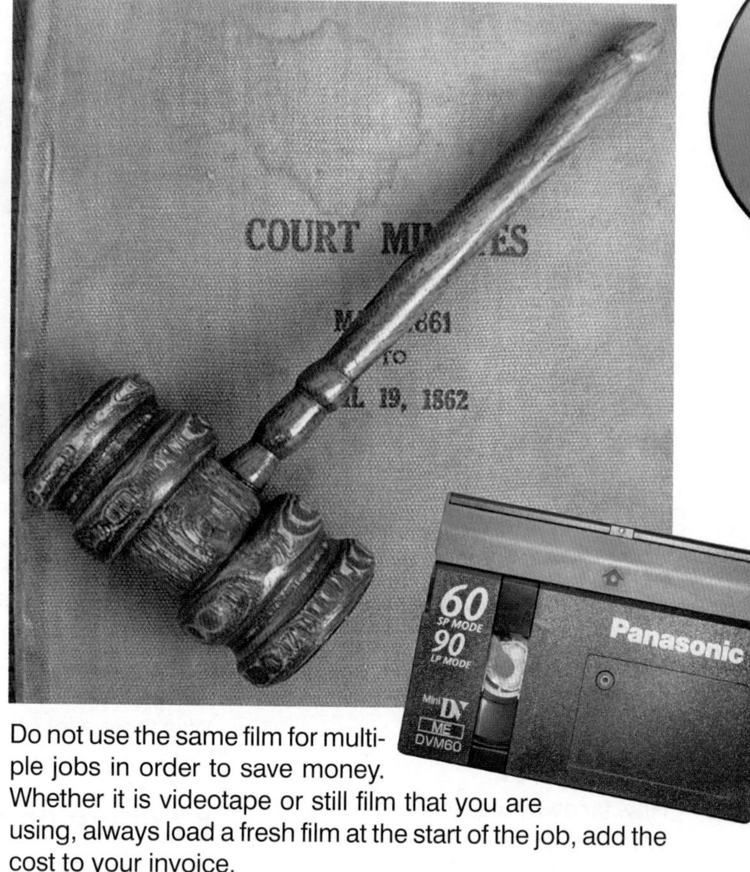


Do not use the same film for multiple jobs in order to save money. Whether it is videotape or still film that you are using, always load a fresh film at the start of the job, add the cost to your invoice.

Having taken the photographs on a digital camera, you can do one of a number of things: retain the medium that it was recorded on such as an SD card and preserve this as your 'original' and then print off the pictures, however, this can be quite costly if you carry out a lot of surveillance and because they are so small they are easy to lose. Or, you could use the most common way and transfer the images to a CD or DVD and retain this as your original. Then make a second copy from which you can work from. It is then likely that you will need to make a statement to this effect.

A handy device called an 'EZ DigiMagic' is designed for this purpose. You insert a blank CD or DVD into it and then insert your SD card into the appropriate slot.

EZ DigiMagic machine

At the touch of a button, everything stored on the SD card is automatically transferred and burned onto the CD.

In the matter of video taped evidence, your original recording should be retained (Gold Copy) and kept safe. A copy of the Gold material should be made (Silver Copy) in its entirety and this used as a 'working' copy to make further copies or make edited versions (known as your Bronze Copies). The original tape should be labelled, secured and retained as evidence.

Many video recorders store their data on hard drives, especially long term recorders which are very expensive. It is accepted by the Courts and is the procedure for Enforcement Agencies to copy the data on these disk drives 'Gold Copy' in its entirety onto two DVDs. One of which is retained and kept safe whist the other is used to make edited versions and take stills from.

### Camera Data Backs

Most digital still and video cameras record the date and time onto the image, therefore ensure that you synchronise the cameras clock to the correct time each time you use it. Digital SLR cameras store the date and time together with other details such as exposure settings within the data of the photograph.

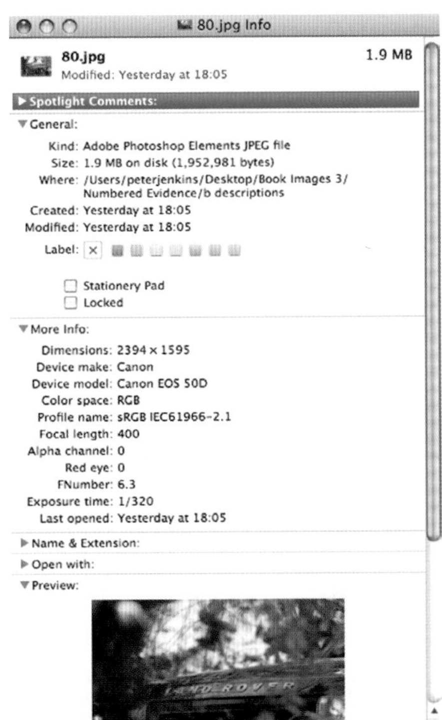


## SURVEILLANCE BRIEFINGS & DEBRIEFINGS

A surveillance briefing should last no more than 30 minutes if it is not too complex. You can only brief up to the 'stakeout' phase because after that, it is the target that dictates what happens, unless you have various SOP's or 'standard operating procedures' you may want to effect if the target visits certain areas or meets up with someone.

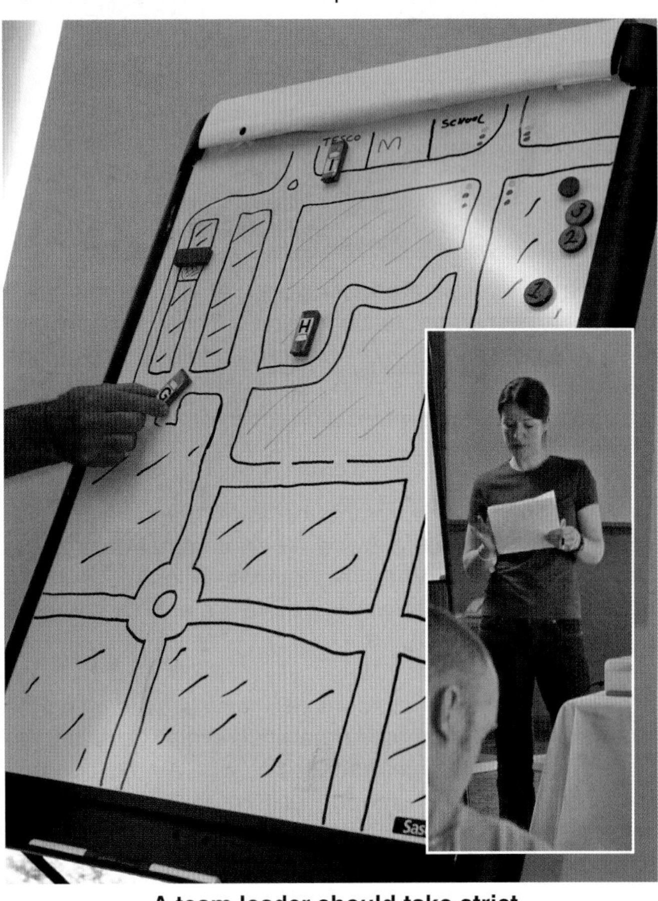


A team leader should take strict control during a debrief

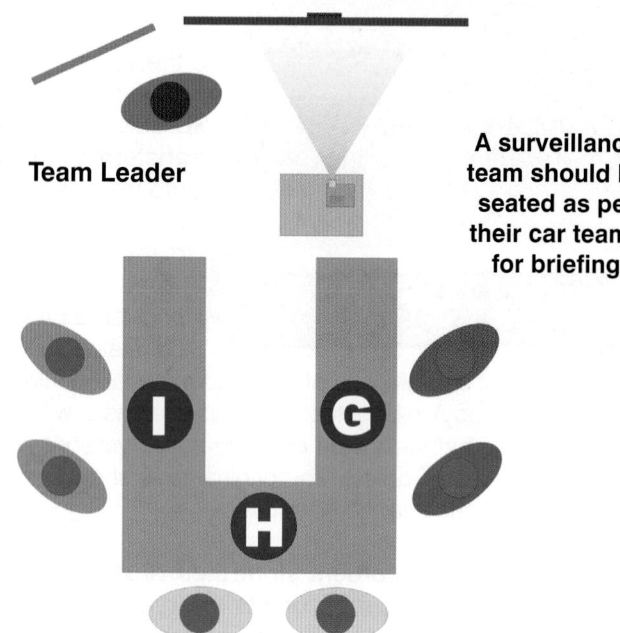


A surveillance team should be seated as per their car teams for briefing

The briefing is separated into particular phases and each phase is explained below. Something will normally go wrong in surveillance, especially with large teams because no one knows what the other is doing or what their tasks are. This is down to lack of communication and information from poor briefings.

Most briefings in the commercial surveillance world are carried out by email followed by an informal chat at the rendezvous point (RV) the night before or on the morning of the surveillance. Especially if there are only two or three of you on the team.

If the surveillance is more complex, has a large team or has a number of tasks, a more formal briefing may be given. We train a number of surveillance teams who always conduct formal briefings which is good, it ensures that all of the bases are covered. In addition, many teams at government or enforcement level carry out surveillance 'two up' or in other words, the vehicle is crewed by two persons rather than single crewed (one up). We use a simple system to conduct a briefing and it can be used for both quick briefings as well as long complicated scenarios.

If you are responsible for the briefing, take charge of the team, instil order as it will reflect on you if the plan goes wrong. Conduct the brief to all as if they have no idea of the plan, assume no knowledge. It may be that some of those who you are briefing carried out a recce or drew up plans. It is too easy to fall into the trap of missing out an important part of a brief such as describing the target house by saying, '..Okay you all know where and what the target looks like...' rather than describing it in full. Make sure you do, because there will be someone on the team who doesn't have this knowledge and the task will fail because of it.

## THE SURVEILLANCE BRIEF

### Prelims

Prior to the actual brief, the team needs to be seated in a particular order in the briefing room, they should be seated in car teams so that you can refer to one call sign collectively rather than having to keep asking, 'who's in call sign Golf?' and so that they can map share if necessary. It is worth putting up the crew list on a wall or flip chart so that everyone knows at the outset who is crewed with who and in what vehicle.

| CALL SIGN | VEHICLE | CREW | RESPONSIBLE |
|---|---|---|---|
| Golf | Blue Vectra YG03 TAH | Darren (11) & Chris (14) | Darren I/c |
| Hotel | Green Golf TL07 CDE | Claire (21) & Ryan (16) | 2i/c Claire |
| Victor | White Van FL05 CMF | Paul (15) | Loggist |

Tell the team they need to take notes and hand out any relevant documents or photographs. When you have everyone's attention the following format can be given.

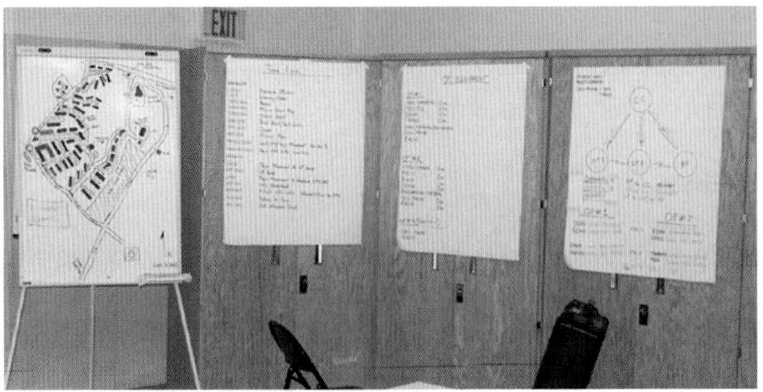


- Area
- Situation
- Tasks
- Execution
- Administration
- Command & Communications

For those with a military background, you will note that this format is similar to a NATO set of briefing orders.

• **Area**

In **General,** the target area is described so that the team get an initial feel of what the area is like and the extent of the area if it is known. This may also include briefing of any areas that are hostile, or areas to avoid.

A drive-by of the target's address may be required to finalise plans

Photographs of the target's start point are essential when conducting a briefing

In **Detail,** the actual start point, such as the target house is described detailing the property, garages, out buildings, parking spaces, any escape routes from the building.

To assist with the descriptions of the area, photographs maps and sketches are always worth a thousand words and so an aerial photograph or map image together with any photos taken on the recce is always useful. Using a projector to project aerial images and maps onto a magnetic dry wipe board is useful for briefings.

• **Situation**

This is where you provide background information about the target (and associates) which includes a description and his history. Provide the scenario behind the surveillance and what the overall general aims are.

• **Tasks**

Described here are the aims or tasks of the surveillance, what you actually want the team to achieve. It may be to establish whether the target is visiting a certain address or to establish whether the target is meeting with another person and to obtain video footage of the meeting.

**Execution Of Task (The Plan)**

In this phase we describe how we are actually going to conduct the surveillance, especially at the stake out or trigger phase. This is the big plan! The execution phase is given firstly as a general outline and then in more detail and is likely to be split into a number of separate phases.

• **Execution General Outline**

This operation is to be carried out in 7 phases to put the target under surveillance. We will move from here to the RV, once all set we will move to the target area, insert the van as the trigger and take up our plot up positions. Put the target under surveillance and lift off on completion and head back to the office for a debrief.

• **Execution In Detail**

Briefed here are the details of how we actually carry out the plan in detail together with timings. The example below shows this in detail.

| | |
|---|---|
| **Phase One:** | **Preparation for moving out** |
| **Phase Two:** | **Move to the target area** |
| **Phase Three:** | **Insertion of the trigger vehicle** |
| **Phase Four:** | **Stake out, where call signs will cover** |
| **Phase Five:** | **The surveillance** |
| **Phase Six:** | **'Lift off' and return to base** |
| **Phase Seven:** | **Debrief** |

**Timings:** Timings for briefings, rehearsals, moving out, being set, finish time, no movement

**Routes:** To the RV, to the target area

**ERV:** Where the Emergency RV is to be located or designated whilst on the ground, if moving.

**Actions On:**

Actions to be carried out in the event of certain outcomes and brief what to do in each circumstance.

*Compromises - hard & soft*
*Breakdowns*
*Accidents*
*Target doesn't show*
*Secondary targets*

• **Administration**

Special Equipment: such as tracking device or night vision scopes Special Vehicles: such as the observation van Safe Haven/Hospital: Identify where the nearest accident and emergency hospital is located and point it out on the map during the brief

• **Command & Communications**

Commander: who is in overall command of the team and his or her second in command (or 2i/c). The 2i/c should be in a different vehicle from the team leader.

Comms Channel: Brief which is the primary radio channel and which is the secondary in the event of someone else being on the same frequency. All mobile phone numbers should be exchanged and stored on speed dial.

Visual aids are important for explaining area locations

• **Questions**

On completion, you should then ask for any questions. This ensures that anyone not fully understanding the brief has their time to clarify matters. Once done, do not be afraid to ask questions to the team regarding where they are meant to be, what their task is and so on.

• **Rehearsals**

At the end of the brief, talk through on the magboard (using model cars if necessary), all the scenarios that can happen when the target goes mobile in order to put the plan into perspective.

# SURVEILLANCE OPERATION BRIEFING SHEET (SAMPLE)

## PRELIMS

| CALL SIGN | VEHICLE | CREW | RESPONSIBLE |
|---|---|---|---|
| Golf | Blue Vectra YG03 TAH | Darren (11) & Chris (14) | Darren I/c |
| Hotel | Green Golf TL07 CDE | Claire (21) & Ryan (16) | 2i/c Claire |
| Victor | White Van FL05 CMF | Paul (15) | Loggist |

Take Notes, issue A-Z maps, page 47

**GROUND (AREA)** (use sketch maps or projected maps for briefing)

In General: We will be operating in the area of the Worth Valley area between the towns of Keighley and Skipton. These two towns are linked by the A629 main road, a rail link with stops at Steeton and Connonly. There is also a link via the Leeds/Liverpool canal. The two towns are small market towns in rural areas.

**In Detail:** Charlie 1 is called '3 The Bank' 'The Bank' is a short cul-de-sac comprising of 3 newly built properties located on a slope and set back from Haworth Road (map page 47, D/4) in an older part of the town. Haworth Road runs east to west along the bottom of a small valley and is a fairly busy street with local shops either side and a number of rows of Victorian style terrace houses. It is a neighbourhood watch area.

C1 is a detached property in the top right corner as you enter the cul de sac. There is no access to the rear. To the left of the house is a garage with a white painted door and there are hanging baskets on the front door.

There is only one way out onto the main Haworth Road by car or foot. Where the target can turn either left or right. Here are no exits at the rear.

**SITUATION**

**Background:** Alpha 1 has been employed by 'Tyred 'n' Exhausted' car repair garage for the past 9 years. He has been on long term sick for the past 18 months due to a back injury sustained at work. Our clients have good reason to believe that he is working part time for a friend of his (George Royston) who owns GR Motors located on 22 Great Horton Road, Skipton.

**Target: A1** is Colin Traynor, 34yrs, thin build, 6'1" tall, brown short spiky hair.

**Address: C1** is 3 The Bank, Haworth Road, Keighley, BD22 7GK. (Tel: 01535 644155)

**Likely Associates: A2** is George Ryston, no full description

**C2** is GR Motors, 222 Great Horton Rd, Skipton, BD23 1DU

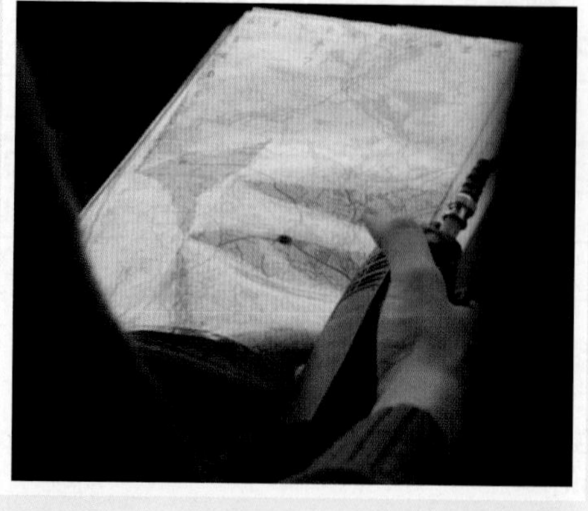

**Attachments & Support Elements:** The client is on standby to come out to join the team if the surveillance is successful as he wants to confront Alpha 1.

**OPERATIONAL TASKS**

1. To observe C1 in the event of A1 leaving and follow if necessary
2. If he visits C2, to obtain video evidence of him working there
3. To obtain any video of him whilst out and about

**EXECUTION OF TASK**

**General Outline**

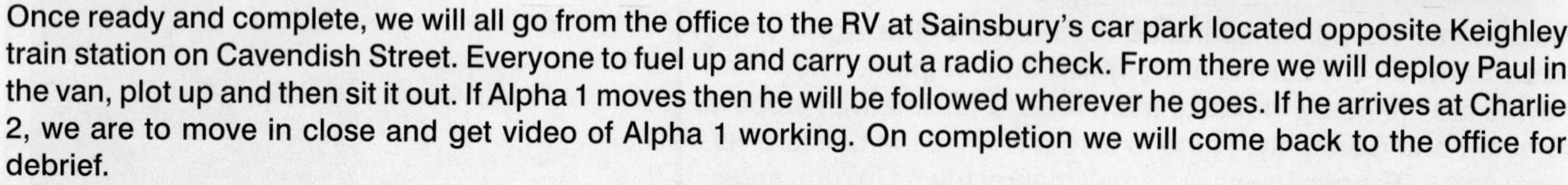

Once ready and complete, we will all go from the office to the RV at Sainsbury's car park located opposite Keighley train station on Cavendish Street. Everyone to fuel up and carry out a radio check. From there we will deploy Paul in the van, plot up and then sit it out. If Alpha 1 moves then he will be followed wherever he goes. If he arrives at Charlie 2, we are to move in close and get video of Alpha 1 working. On completion we will come back to the office for debrief.

**Execution in Detail**

**Phase One:** Final checks in the office tomorrow morning at 06.00hrs, ensure all cameras and radios are charged. Be ready to move at 06.20.

**Phase Two:** Deploy. We will drive from here to Sainsbury's car park taking the B2213 into town and left on Cavendish Street. Everyone to fuel up and carry out a radio check at the RV.

**Phase Three:** Insertion of the trigger vehicle. Chris from C/S Golf to join Paul in the van at the RV and drive him into position to get the trigger on Haworth Road. C/S Golf will then pick Chris up at the roundabout to the east side of Haworth Road.

**Phase Four:** Stake out, call signs will cover their options;

C/S Victor, to get the trigger on C1.
C/S Golf, to cover the left option, to cover the area of the mini roundabout.
C/S Hotel, to cover the right option, to cover the T junction by the post office.

**Phase Five:** The surveillance. On a standby, C/S Golf & Hotel to follow Alpha 1. If he gets some distance away from C1 C/S Victor to self extract the van and make ground to join the team. If Alpha 1 arrives at Charlie 2, we will insert the van in order to get a close video platform. Claire will also deploy on foot with the covert camera to obtain video footage of Alpha 1 inside the premises.

**Phase Six:** The 'lift off' and return to base. When it is decided, we shall extract the van, and move to the RV. Once everyone is happy we will move back to the office.

**Phase Seven:** The debrief. Once back at the office we will conduct a full debrief so that the logs and reports can be typed up. Any video obtained will need to be transferred to a DVD for the client.

**TIMINGS:** 06.00 RV at the office
06.20 Depart office
06.50 Arrive at RV
07.10 Van in Position at Charlie 1 and surveillance set.
15.30 Stand down if not finished earlier

**ROUTES:** Take the B2213 into Keighley and left on Cavendish Street by the college, Sainsbury's is 200m on the nearside.

**ERV:** ERV is Sainsbury's car park or dictated as we go along.

**ACTIONS ON:**

**1.** No Movement by 11am. Make a pretext telephone call it, if no one in, stand down

**2.** If A1 arrives at C2, we will move the van in to get a video position and Claire will go in and make a test purchase with the covert camera.

**3.** Compromise: A decision will be made on the ground.

**4.** Emergencies or breakdowns, we will tend to them at the time.

**5.** Loss of contact. Call sign Victor will cover C1, Call sign Golf to cover C2 and Call sign Hotel to search the area.

**ADMINISTRATION**

**Special Equipment:** All should have Sat-navs with the RV, C1 & C2 programmed in. One camcorder per vehicle, Claire in C/S Hotel has the covert camera bag.

Special Vehicles: The Van, C/S Victor

**Safe Haven/Hospital:** The RV or Airedale Hospital on the A629 north of Steeton

**COMMUNICATIONS & COMMAND**

**Commander:** Darren,
2i/c: Claire
Loggist: Paul

**Comms Channel:** Primary Channel Five
Secondary Channel One

Cell Phone numbers distributed

**Time Check:** Sync watches and camera timers

**Questions:** to and from team

## Team Debriefings

The team debrief is a very important part of the surveillance. It can be an informal affair over a drink in a café before the team disperses, or more formal back at the office, especially when large teams, complex surveillance or long term surveillance is being conducted.

The debrief is divided into three logical phases, which we will examine in turn.

- **Intelligence Debrief**
- **Operational Debrief**
- **Exposure Levels**

***Don't let debriefs get personal***

### • Intelligence Debrief

This first phase deals with the information or intelligence that was obtained about the target. This is where the surveillance logs are compiled to provide a master log of events which will be reported to the client.

The debrief should be chaired by the team leader or loggist. This part of the debrief should concentrate on:

- *Timings*
- *Places*
- *Routes*
- *Stops*
- *Activity*
- *Meetings*
- *Descriptions*

Remember, only what **the target did** should be discussed at this stage, this is very important as the client may be present. You have to be very careful of team members chipping in and adding what they did e.g. 'Well I could see the target but a woman approached me and started asking what I was doing so I had to move to another position and then my radio went down....etc'. It is not important at this stage, intelligence only!

You may have been working a long day and your aim is to get the debrief over and done with quickly and to get the report to the client. If you allow members to side track the debrief you will never finish.

Once the intelligence debrief is complete and logs, videos and photographs are done with, you can then move onto the next phase.

### • Operational Debrief

This is the time for the team to discuss what went wrong, what went right or was good and how you can improve or make any changes to the surveillance plan. It is also the time to be self critical and admit to any mistakes made so they are not repeated by you or anyone else, it makes a good learning place for all.

If a team member identifies certain areas to avoid, (maybe due to a third party), or finds a good position to 'lay up', or experiences a really bad road junction which is hard to get out of, then this should be discussed for all to benefit.

This part of the debrief should not get personal but constructive. We all make mistakes from time to time and the person pointing the finger at one member of the team should keep it in mind that it may be them that makes the next mistake. Don't let it get personal.

What we teach and practice is that any comments made at this stage are always confined to the debrief and that once proceedings are complete, we do not carry it on afterwards.

Be aware of this debrief getting out of control and going on for hours on end. In training, the easiest way to control this is to ask for each member of the team to provide one

SURVEILLANCE LOG BOOK REGISTER

01

| SERIAL NUMBER | ISSUE | | | | RETURN | |
|---|---|---|---|---|---|---|
| | SIGNATURE OF RECEIVING OFFICER | ISSUING OFFICER | DATE OF ISSUE | OPERATION NO NAME | OFFICER RECEIVING | DATE |
| | | | | | | |
| | | | | | | |
| | | | | | | |

good point and one bad point about the surveillance. Operationally, each person is set a five minute time limit to say what he has to and then finish.

**Remember: Intelligence is what the target did, Operational is what the team did.**

Once the operational debrief is out of the way, we can get on with the next which is equally important.

- **Exposure Levels**

Every time you go out on a surveillance give yourself 10 'lives' (or 'heat states' as they are often referred to). Now every time that you have any exposure to the target, knock off a life (or two). For instance, if the target goes into a hotel and you decide to go close in order to overhear what is being said at the reception, you may want to knock off one or two lives, as you have been in close and had some exposure to the target. You may now be down to a score of 9 or 8 but only if they have seen you.

Next, the target gets on a bus and you are the only person who is close enough to get on with him, and you make the decision to do so in order to keep control. Hopefully you can sit behind the target so you are not too exposed. The target gets off and another operator takes over and your own personal 'heat states' have now dropped down to a 6 or 7.

At the debrief, each member of the team is asked for their heat states and this is recorded by the team leader. It may also be wise at this stage to explain how you have reached your number.

Only you can tell how much exposure that you have had and if you are down to a 4 or 5, you should be asking yourself whether you would be safe working on the same target again the following day.

Be careful of being over paranoid or too cautious as we often tend to over-estimate our heat states (especially when new to surveillance). Personally, I always calculate a figure and then add 1 back on.

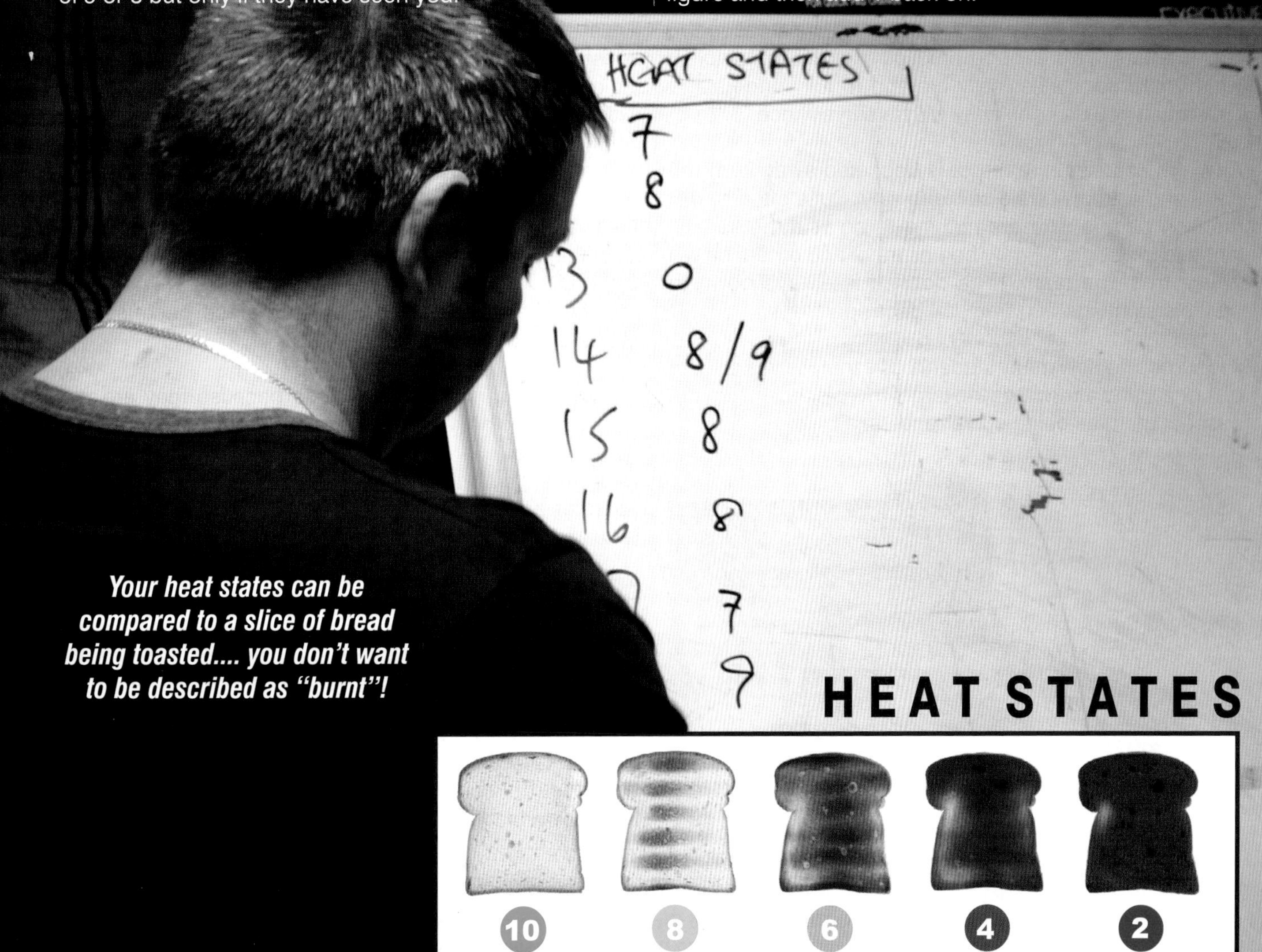


***Your heat states can be compared to a slice of bread being toasted.... you don't want to be described as "burnt"!***

As well as giving yourself a personal score, also do the same with the vehicles. If for some reason, call sign Golf has had a lot of exposure (it may have had a few long follows without any cover), then also give it a score out of 10. As above, if it is 4 or 5, you should consider changing vehicles for the next day or let some time lapse before you continue the surveillance with the same vehicle.

If you are a team leader or manager and working a number of the same operators on a regular basis, it may be worth considering keeping a 'Heat States Book'. If you are working in law enforcement or the military on long term operations against regular targets, it may be a consideration.

During training courses, the class often puts an unknown target under surveillance for a day. The target does not know any of the class and the class have never seen the target before. This is good practice in order to establish what your heat states really are and to fully understand how much you can get away with in surveillance.

After the exercise, the target is debriefed away from the class and asked who he saw and why. Quite often he will mention people who are nothing to do with the surveillance team, some he may be unsure of and others he will notice from the team. If he does, it is always down to multiple sightings or un-natural behaviour.

It is surprising how many students give themselves a score of 4 or a 5 and afterwards the target reveals that he did not suspect them as being surveillance at all.

Every time a surveillance operation is completed, list the operators and their scores in a book. Over a period of time it will tell you a number of things; if an operator is constantly coming back with scores of 9 or 10, it may indicate that he or she is hanging back all of the time without risking much and letting the others do all of the work, conversely, if someone is constantly coming back with a low score of say 3 or 5, you have to ask:

Are they too keen and being over zealous by going in hard all of the time?

Are they having to go in hard and close because the others are hanging back?

Are they going in hard and close because they are too stupid and do not really appreciate the risks?

Over time, you will build up a picture of how your team operates and performs, this is why our term 'Loss v Gain' is so important.

**Golden Rule**

Once the debrief is finished, it is finished. Sometimes people make mistakes and they can make big ones, which result in a compromise or an accident. At a debrief this 'finger pointing' and blaming can get very personal but we never let it carry on when we leave the debrief as it generates animosity. If you are blaming someone today, it will be you that screws up the next...

**List of Objects (answers to memory test on page 398)** Did you notice that the picture had been reversed?
**Gillette Razor, Set of Lock Picks, JVC Video Cassette, White Circular Disc, Pair of Nail Scissors, BOSE Remote Control, Drill Bit, Playing Card, Teddy Bear, iPod MP3, Gold Ring. Did you also note the purposely mis-spelt word 'Osbervation' (Observation)!**

Just like any other trade, everyone is always on the lookout for work. Many people in the surveillance industry operate as a 'one man band' and freelance to a number of other operators on the 'Circuit' or work part time for larger companies. There are also a few companies in the UK that employ operators on a full time basis.

Working for a company full time will help you gain a lot of experience in a short space of time but you will probably be required to travel the length and breadth of the country for a lot less pay but at least you will have some form of job security. Whereas, being self employed can often be a hit or miss affair with infrequent bursts of work, but once you get known and more importantly known to produce results, you should not have a problem getting work anywhere.

I often get asked, 'What kit should I obtain if I am starting up?' You do not need to spend a lot of money and do not buy the most expensive equipment you can find as it does not impress anyone, especially if you do not know how to use it properly. I would suggest the following: digital memo recorder, video camera, digital SLR camera, covert camera (such as the key fob), a laptop computer, handheld radio (with changeable frequencies) and a pair of binoculars. I would also suggest a small van but not necessary as you then have an asset to be employed (teams need a van) and you may also be able to carry out some static work single-handed.

**Have a current CV**

Summary

Peter Jenkins has been a corporate security consultant for the past 20 years specialising in surveillance work. He is the Director of ISS Training Limited and instructs on surveillance training courses for various private companies, government agencies, foreign military and federal enforcement units.

Prior to this Peter spent 12 years in the Royal Marines. He underwent recruit and command training for promotion acquiring a wide range of experience in soldiering, management and instructing. Broad spectrum of activities with varying degrees of responsibility includes Reconnaissance/Close Observation, Counter Terrorism, Administration and Instructing. He has operated and exercised all over the world.

Experience

**1989-Present** Manager of 'Intel Security Services' and then Director of ISS Training Limited, a supplier of surveillance training courses to:

- Allied foreign Special Forces units in Europe and the USA.
- U.K government enforcement agencies and authorities
- Close protection teams
- Corporate security teams

Personally responsible for the organisation, implementation and provision of surveillance training courses and programmes which have been accredited by Edexcel and the Northern College of Further Education.

Carrying out surveillance related investigations to the corporate and private sector investigating theft, fraud, copyright infringement, anti social behaviour, environmental crime and personal injury insurance fraud.

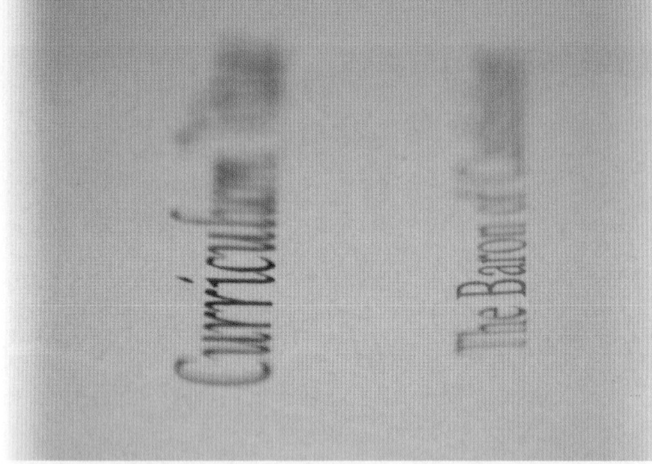

## CURRICULUM VITAE

Your CV is a very important document when looking for work and should be treated as such. Remember a CV will not get you a job, it is the key to getting you through the employers door.

Employing a professional CV writer can be a good idea but the results can become very samey and not be individualistic. I recently had five CV's arrive on my desk in the same week which was unusual. All of the CV's were in the same format and looked more or less identical except for the persons contact details. After a bit of research it became apparent that each person had been on the same close protection course where the students are also taught how to compile a CV. They had all used the same template that was provided rather than construct their own.

Keep your CV 'yours' and make it individualistic, I was once advised to print it on pale blue paper as it will stand out amongst everyone else's and it worked - I got the first job I applied for! Now that I have let that little tip out of the bag everyone else's CV will be blue from now on so choose a different colour!

Before you send an electronic copy by email, make sure you check the 'Properties' box to ensure that it does not have someone else's name or company details hiding in there. This is the first thing I check before I even read a CV. In the case mentioned above with the five CV's sent to me, each one listed the name of the CP course instructor and the company name! If you are using MS Word, from the top drop down menu, click File then Properties, then Summary and enter your own details or just leave it blank before saving.

Ensure that you put your full address on the CV. It is surprising how many leave this off, it is useful for an employer to know what part of the country you are based in. When including your date of birth also put in your age in brackets, yes it is simple maths but you want to make life easy for the employer.

If you are former military or police, try to keep it in a civilian context. Sure, list your experience and where you have worked but an employer does not want to know that you were trained using a TOBIAS ZX234 Blanket Stacking machine for Operation Safecracker in Pontystan, as he will not have a clue what you are talking about.

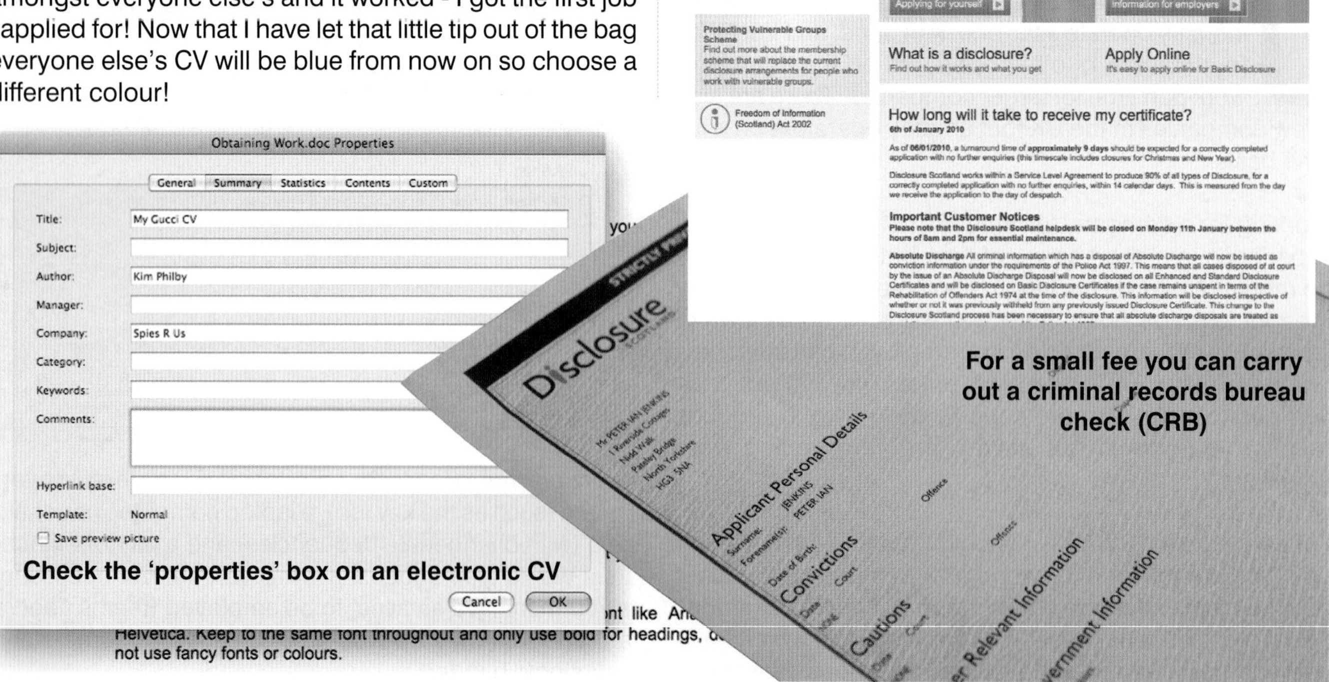


Check the 'properties' box on an electronic CV

For a small fee you can carry out a criminal records bureau check (CRB)

...nt like Ar... Helvetica. Keep to the same font throughout and only use bold for headings, d... not use fancy fonts or colours.

Occasionally it is best to keep the specifics of your past work record confidential until being interviewed

Keep the CV to about two pages in length and use a comfortable font such as Arial or Helvetica. Keep to the same font throughout and only use bold for headings, do not use fancy fonts or colours.

**EXAMPLE FONTS**

ARIAL
HELVETICA
TIMES
GARAMOND

Do not put in too many specifics but tailor it to suit the job offered, remember the CV is to get you an interview. Also think operational security, I received a CV from a close protection officer who had been working in Iraq who stated:

*I have carried out security survey and consultation at the offices and residences of:*

Sheikh Ghazi Al-Yarwar - President of Iraq.
Dr. Ayad Alawi - Prime Minister of Iraq.
Dr. Mowaffak Al-Rubaie - Iraqi National Security Advisor.

This tells me that this guy has no respect for operational security, he is trying to impress me, which he is not. If I give him a job, he is going to add to his CV the names of all my clients - so his CV went into the shredder.

If you have undergone surveillance training or had previous experience, name the training provider, the details of the course or what type of work you have been involved with, this is what he wants to know. Rightly or wrongly, some employers reject those that have been trained by a provider with a poor reputation, so it pays to do your research before embarking on a course.

The biggest 'must' is to get someone to check your CV for for spellllling and gramma. The second biggest 'must', is to ensure that the person checking it can read and spell! I have seen some appalling CV's in the past - if only they had had them checked. For those clever readers that noticed the two spelling mistakes in this paragraph, did you notice the word 'for' used twice in succession?

Post the CV with a brief covering letter stating what you are doing now and why you would like to work for their company. Finish it off by stating, 'I may contact you again in the near future in the event that you have a vacancy'. Give it a week or two and then telephone the company. If you have to get past a secretary, tell her that Mr. X is expecting your call (he is - you told him that you were going to get in touch). When you get through, ask him (or her) if your CV was received and whether there are any job opportunities. This telephone contact is probably the most important when looking for work and it is amazing how many people send off CV's but do not follow it through with a phone call, you literally double your chances of obtaining work, so get on the phone.

**For a small fee you can obtain entry in these specialist directories**

If you get a written response stating that nothing is currently available, ring the company up and thank them for their time getting back to you. Then call them back again in a couple of months because you never know what might turn up.

If you are told again that there is nothing available at that time, call again after about six weeks as circumstances may have changed, do not be afraid to pester. Remember - if you don't, someone else will get the job.

### Trade Bodies and Associations

It is worth joining a trade association such as the Association of British Investigators (ABI) or the World Association of Private Investigators (WAPI). Some of these associations have regular magazines which provides information on current equipment, legislation and good advice from other members. The ABI has a directory of members, they hold regular regional meetings - which is an excellent place to network and also an internet discussion forum which also advertises jobs. By being a member, it gives you some credibility as the Association has a selection procedure to show probity and credibility of its members.

There is also a publication called the 'Varsity Directory of Investigators' published by Shaw & Sons (www.varsityinvestigators.co.uk). For a small fee you can list yourself in a regional area and is widely used for passing work and networking.

### The Internet

#### Websites and Email

Even if you are a 'one man band' I would advise having a website, even if it is only one or two pages. People these days rarely use the Yellow Pages and are more likely to 'Google' for an investigator in their area. Once it is up and running, submit it to as many search engines as you can, this is the 21st century and this is how people out there will find you.

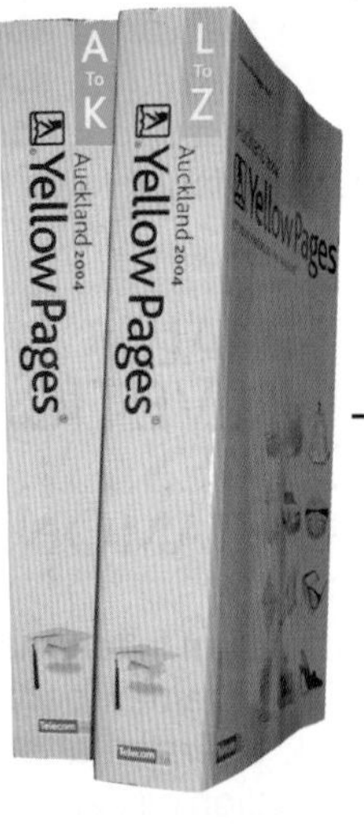


**Yellow Pages is still a good source to advertise in, but somewhat outdated due to the Internet**

# THE INTERVIEW

*A whole book can be written attending job interviews but whether it is a formal interview at the companies premises or a first meeting over a pub lunch, the following should be considered;*

Check yourself in the mirror - it only takes a few seconds

- Turn up early. If you are too early, go and hang out in a coffee bar until time. If you turn up late, you may as well not bother at all.
- Be smart, check your appearance in a mirror. You do not want to go in to an interview with egg yolk down your tie from the breakfast you have just had whilst waiting because you got to the venue too early.
- Don't smoke or chew gum, it's very un-professional.
- Relax.
- Do not ask what the rates of pay are straight away as it smacks of desperation - you should be told.
- Be polite and smile during introductions, make an effort to remember names of those you meet.
- Take a spare copy of your CV in the event it has been mislaid.
- Do not be afraid to ask questions, be prepared and have some ready, even write them down - it shows that you are inquisitive.

- Have a basic understanding of current legislation in respect of surveillance; Trespass, RIPA and Harassment.
- Answer any questions with a 'yes' or 'no' but add a short explanation and don't waffle on. If you are not sure, remain confident and say so.
- Do not negatively criticise any individual, company or previous employer - this industry is very small. Do not try to impress the interviewer with your powers of observation by stating that you spotted five spelling mistakes on their website.
- Do not name drop, 'I know Snoopy from B Squadron 22...'. The interviewer might also know Snoopy and ask you what you think of him.
- On leaving, thank them for their time and ask how will you get to know if you are successful. Don't be seen crossing your fingers as you go out of the door.

***Remember: you do not get a second chance to make a first impression.***

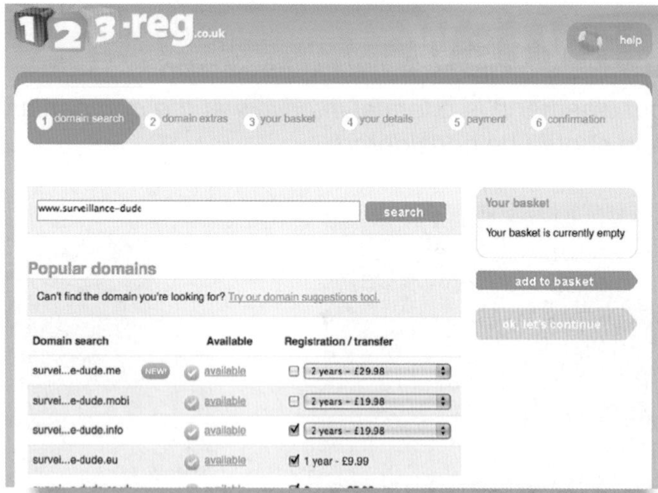


**It is not difficult or expensive to obtain your own domain name. Be wary of cheap or free web site building programmes - use a professional web designer such as www.castus.co.uk**

Try to avoid the free websites (they look cheap) and try to avoid making your own unless it is something you are very skilled at. There is nothing worse than a home made website displaying various bright colours and different types of font on a black background. It is not that expensive to have one made for you and buy a unique URL such as:

**www.intelsecurity.co.uk.**

Remember, your website is your shop window, you want people to come in and not walk past.

If you use a web based email provider such as Yahoo, Gmail or Hotmail, use a professional sounding email address such as investigator@hotmail... rather than bingedrinker@yahoo or Kevin007@hotmail.com. If you own a URL, this can also be used as your email address such as info@surveillance-tradecraft.co.uk

### Business Cards

Ensure that you have a professional looking business card printed and always carry them with you. There are a number of websites that produce quality cards such as www.vistaprint.co.uk, they are not expensive and have hundreds of design templates. Keep the design simple and classy and avoid using images such as 'eyes', 'gum shoe detectives' and people looking through binoculars, they can look tacky and everyone else is probably using the same design - try and be unique.

We had a close protection officer on a surveillance course who was always giving it the big 'I am'. He handed out his cards and the class were dumbfounded. There was a picture of a typical private eye wearing a trilby hat and a long coat leaning against a lamppost. Surveillance was spelt wrong, the phrase 'Pursuing Excellence' was also spelt incorrectly and his email address was missing a .co.uk!

Some operators working the security circuit use a PO Box as an address as they do not want to reveal their address, especially if they work from home. They are not

Whilst teaching surveillance in the USA to a specialist organisation, in addition to the class, a person turned up in order to 'Observe' the training. No one would tell us who he was or much about him, he was a bit secretive. I remembered from a previous visit to the USA when someone told me if someone gives you a plain white business card with just their name and mobile number on it, there is a chance that he is from the "CIA" or a government agency.

CHUCK MCREDFORD
EL: 202-385-

When we left the States, the mystery man gave me his card... yes it was plain white with just a mobile number on it.

expensive and you can have all of the mail forwarded to your address rather than having to collect it from the post office. However, they are not 100% secure as anyone can apply to the post office to ask who owns the PO Box number and they are obliged to give the information.

### Carding

**Information**

Category:
Entertainment & Arts - Radio

Description:
Here's a group for all Sam Spade fans on facebook. After you join please post the name or your favorite Caper.

Privacy type:
Open: All content is public.

There is a term on the security circuit called 'carding' and the practise is highly frowned upon. Simply, if one of my instructors were teaching on a course for one of my regular clients and he handed his card out to the team leader (or one of the class) it is very frowned upon and deemed as an attempt to 'steal' the client. On the close protection circuit, if you are on a team looking after a principal, it would not be correct to hand over your card to the principal when it is not your contract.

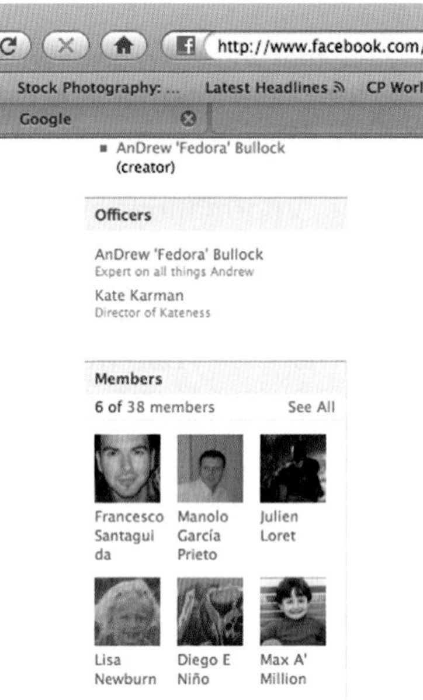


I am all for networking but normally anyone caught carding finds that it is their last job with that team. A good client will also tell you when he has been approached by someone else.

Also be aware of 'Facebooking' the client or other sites such as 'Linkedin'. It is not difficult for someone to look at your Facebook page to find out who your friends and connections are.

### Forums

Join an internet forum or two. Google 'surveillance forum' or 'investigator forum' and you will find plenty of them. They are a good place to obtain advice, offer advice, exchange ideas and hopefully obtain work. 'Close Protection World' is a good, well run and moderated Internet forum for surveillance operators and close protection officers.

### Administration

At the time of writing, surveillance operators and investigators do not have to be licensed to operate in the United Kingdom but there are moves to introduce licensing. The Security Industry Authority (SIA) in the UK is responsible for introducing licensing and their website is regularly updated.

Ensure that you are registered with the Data Protection Act. If you are carrying out investigations where you are obtaining private information about individuals you are required by law to be registered. The cost is in the region of £35.00.

It is not necessary but I would recommend that you obtain some insurance, especially professional indemnity insurance. Should you carry out a surveillance or investigation and the information you provide your client with was found later to be incorrect, they could sue you, especially if the information has had an adverse effect on them. It would be for them to prove that you were negligent but professional indemnity insurance covers you for this eventuality.

**Conclusion**

Some say that you are only as good as your last job in this industry but not necessarily so. What I will say is that you can work hard for 10 years in this industry and get good results but no one will ever tell you. However, as soon as you make one mistake - everyone gets to hear about it. But that's life!

Finding work can be a case of being in the right place at the right time and also down to luck - but you make your own luck.

## A FINAL WORD ABOUT SURVEILLANCE TRAINING

If you are new to surveillance and wish to enter the investigative sector to carry out surveillance work, it is imperative that you undergo some form of training. Not only will it teach you to do the job properly but prove to any potential employer that you are qualified and able.

There are many companies that advertise surveillance training and choosing one can be difficult. The author is director of the surveillance training company, ISS Training Limited; it is probably the longest established surveillance training company in the United Kingdom. Since 1998, ISS has trained over 2,000 surveillance operators from various backgrounds:

Working in a team environment can be rewarding

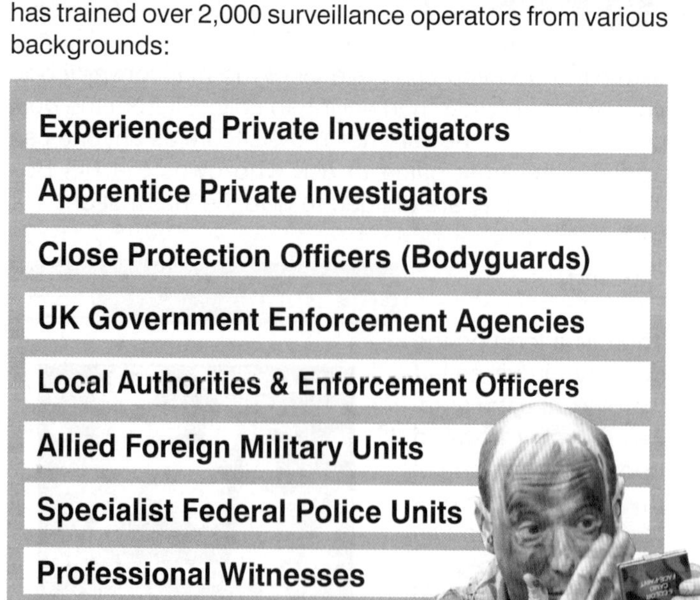

- **Experienced Private Investigators**
- **Apprentice Private Investigators**
- **Close Protection Officers (Bodyguards)**
- **UK Government Enforcement Agencies**
- **Local Authorities & Enforcement Officers**
- **Allied Foreign Military Units**
- **Specialist Federal Police Units**
- **Professional Witnesses**
- **Investigative Journalists**
- **Police Officers**
- **Security Consultants**
- **Researchers**
- **Security Guards**
- **CCTV Controllers**
- **Store Detectives**

**Investigative journalists have undergone training in order to get their covert "money shot"**

Many have travelled from all over the world to the UK for this training, including: Hong Kong, Brazil, Nigeria, Lebanon, Canada and the United States. In addition, an ISS mobile training team has conducted training in: Norway, Finland, Sweden, Denmark, Croatia, Northern Ireland, Germany, USA, Switzerland, Czech Republic, Eire, Canada, Singapore and Romania.

Essentially, there are two types of courses that are run. Those that are 'open' where any paying member of the public can attend and those that are 'closed' which are normally arranged for enforcement agencies, the military and specialist security teams, where the training is carried out in-house.

ISS was the first training company to develop the BTEC Level 3 Award and Certificates in surveillance training and this is something that we are very proud of. The awards provide surveillance operators with a recognised qualification in surveillance. Prior to this, there were no accepted BTEC qualifications in existence unless you had carried out official surveillance training with the Police or Ministry of Defence.

Since then, many other training companies have evolved and followed suit in order to provide a similar training product. ISS has been carrying out surveillance training for a long time and experience shows that we have learnt from our mistakes and like to think that we have got it right in all respects; we understand the clients needs, time frames and costs. We continually strive to improve and our quality assurance procedures ensure that we do this.

The success of ISS is mainly due to the expertise of the training team that instruct on the courses. They are drawn from various backgrounds such as Military Intelligence, Special Forces, Police and other enforcement agencies.

The equipment we use is updated regularly, is current, reliable and is what is used in the real world, especially the covert digital radio equipment. To ensure safety, cars are rented from a national company to keep the costs to the student down and to guarantee safe and reliable vehicles.

**The training is realistic but also safe. All our training vehicles are rented from a reputable hire company to ensure road worthiness and safety**

If, after reading this book, you decide that you wish to learn more and put your skills into practice, then get in touch with ISS. Our courses are normally held at a training facility in North Yorkshire for both men and women but we also often travel to a client's venue.

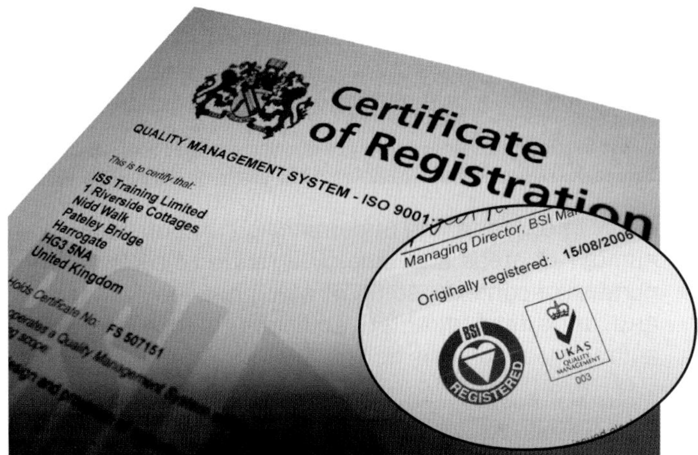


**ISS Training Ltd have Quality Management System approved by the British Standards Institute (BSI)**

edexcel
advancing learning, changing lives

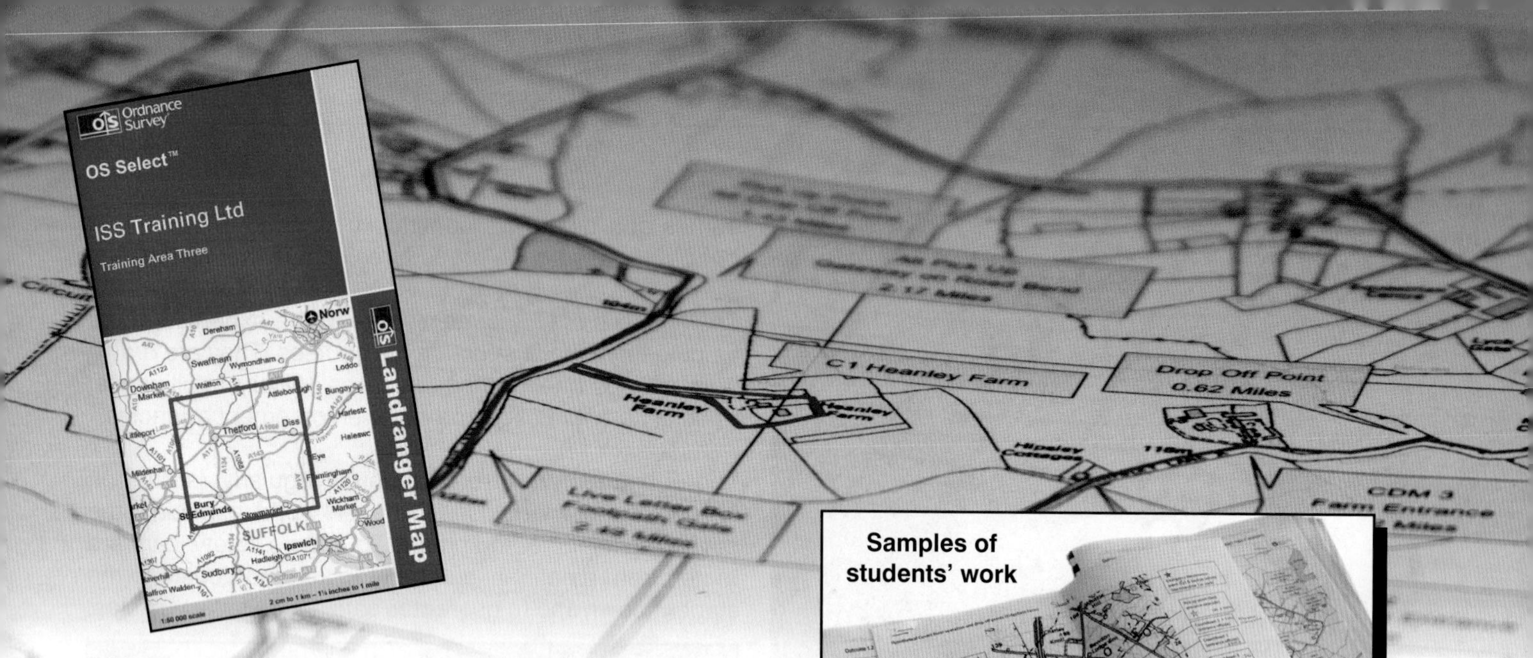

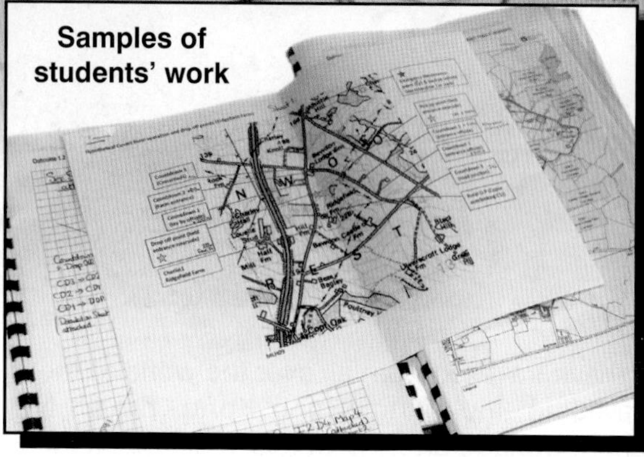

Samples of students' work

## What is a BTEC Level 3 Award or Certificate?

ISS surveillance training is set at Level 3. A Level 3 qualification is not based on the time that it takes to carry out the training or the length of the course but what the learner is actually required to do at the end of it. In the UK, this does not equate with a Police Level 1, 2 or 3 qualification as this is an entirely different structure and the two should not be confused.

Below is an explanation of how to distinguish between the qualification levels and is taken from what is known as 'Blooms Taxonomy'.

### ENTRY LEVEL

Employ, recall and demonstrate elementary comprehension in a narrow range of areas; exercise basic skills within highly structured contexts; and carry out directed activity under close supervision.

### LEVEL 1

Employ a narrow range of applied knowledge, skills and basic comprehension within a limited range of predictable and structured contexts, including working with others under direct supervision, but with a very limited degree of discretion and judgement about possible action.

### LEVEL 2

Apply knowledge with underpinning comprehension in a number of areas and employ a range of skills within a number of contexts, some of which may be non-routine; and undertake directed activities, with a degree of autonomy, within time constraints.

### LEVEL 3

Apply knowledge and skills in a range of complex activities demonstrating comprehension of relevant theories; access and analyse information independently and make reasoned judgements, selecting from a considerable choice of procedures in a familiar context; and direct own activities with some responsibility for the output of others.

### LEVEL 4

Develop a rigorous approach to the acquisition of a broad knowledge base; employ a range of specialised skills; evaluate information, using it to plan and develop investigative strategies and determine solutions to a variety of unpredictable problems; and operate in a range of varied and specific contexts, taking responsibility for the nature and quality of outputs.

**Or, in other words..**

As an easy example, a level 1 assessment question may be to 'list' the equipment you may take on a surveillance. Answer: camera, radio, Dictaphone etc... Whereas a Level 3 question in the same vein would be to 'identify and explain' the equipment you may take on a surveillance. Answer: A camera in order to photograph and record the witnessed activity...

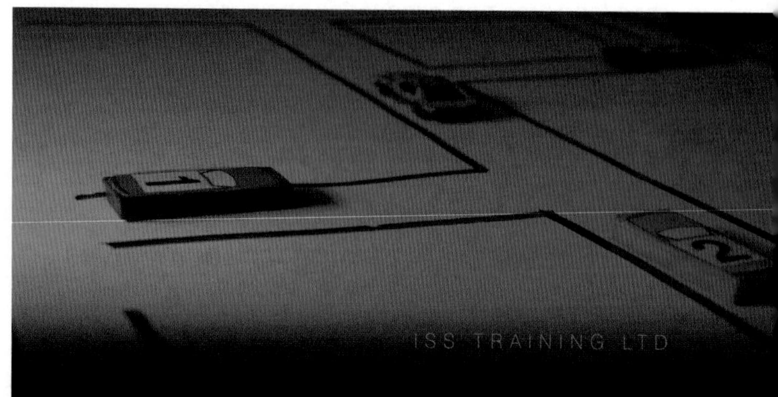

**Students assessment workbook**

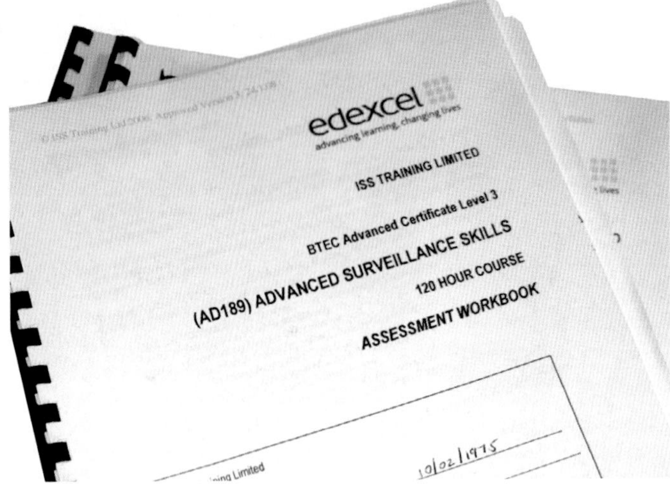


Together with the awarding body it was decided that surveillance skills should be set at Level 3 due to the type of work it involves and the fact that an operator is required to work on his own initiative most of the time.

The qualifications are also described as being an Award, Certificate or a Diploma, the difference being:

**50 hours - Award**

**50 - 150 hours - Certificate**

**150 - 250 hours - Diploma**

The Level 3 Award and Certificate in surveillance is assessed by both observation - which means that the instructors observe you conducting surveillance and note your ability - and also by the completion of a written workbook to demonstrate your theoretical knowledge. When designing the course ISS kept away from written tests, especially multiple choice as this does not reflect the learner's knowledge at Level 3 (a monkey could pass a multiple choice test on a balance of probability). We also kept away from a written answer test as we found that although some students have the aptitude for surveillance, they often find it difficult to put pen to paper when under a strict time limit.

Hence, a workbook was designed which the learner has to complete in his or her own time in the evenings throughout the training course. The design was also intentional so that students on residential courses carry on learning in their own time. Rather than going down town and hitting the pubs, they often sit quietly in the hotel bar as a group and go through the workbooks. This reinforces what they have been taught throughout the day so they are still learning in their down time.

## BASIC FOOT AND MOBILE SURVEILLANCE TRAINING

**BTEC Level 3 Award**

This basic five day course is very practical in content and over the years we have trained students from various backgrounds, many of whom have had no experience in the security industry but have used the course as a footing to enter into it.

Surveillance training courses in the Police or Military, are run over a period of weeks and months not days. ISS, or any other civilian training company could not be expected to provide this type of training on a budget that your average person can afford and so a fine line has to be drawn when calculating costs and training time.

Training is normally held with up to eight students per course. Five days is sufficient to teach and practice the basics (and some advanced techniques) for the student to then be able to go away and put into practice what he/she has been taught.

The students are not put under any undue pressure by the instruction team. They don't have to because what is being taught and what the students are expected to do, is quite demanding, especially for those who are not used to multi-tasking or using a radio. The instruction team are always there to help.

The course content is quite demanding and some periods are spent in the classroom. This is essential for teaching

**The basics are taught in the classroom before putting them in to practice on foot and in vehicles**

## ISS class photograph

the basic tactics and procedures that will later be practised on the street. As much time as possible is spent on the ground, be it on foot, in the cars or carrying out exercises. Surveillance is a practical subject and so you would not be expected to spend five days in a classroom.

All equipment is provided which includes covert radios, cameras, vehicles and fuel, so all the student has to do is turn up on the day with plenty of enthusiasm. By the end of the final exercise there is a good team spirit and the group is actually working as an effective surveillance team. It is surprising how steeply the learning curve rises during the week.

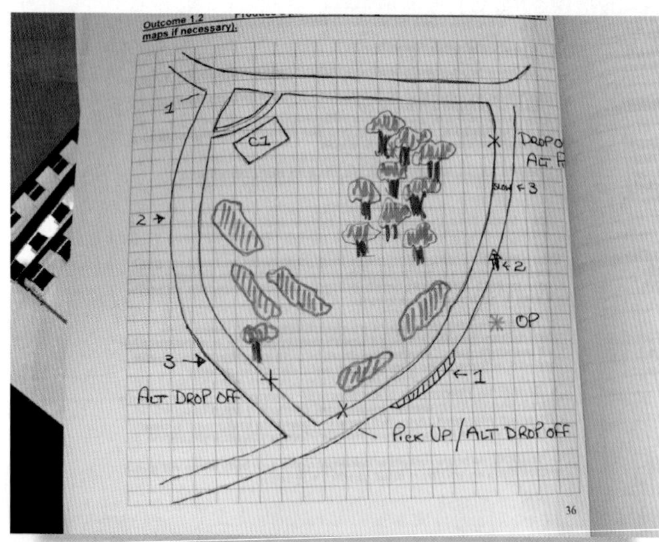


**Student recce sketch plan**

### TWO WEEK ADVANCED FOOT AND MOBILE SURVEILLANCE TRAINING

**BTEC Level 3 Certificate**

The first week of this course is the same as the 5 day course. In the second week the procedures and skills are taken to the next level in terms of more complex and technically difficult scenarios. The tempo is also raised in order to adapt to ever changing situations. New subjects are also introduced such as the deployment of a Close Target Recce team in rural areas, vehicle tracking, night surveillance, counter surveillance, covert video and public transport surveillance on rail networks.

**Level 3 surveillance training in Europe**

## TECHNICAL SURVEILLANCE TRAINING

This is a popular course of instruction covering technical surveillance. For anyone intending to carry out Technical Surveillance Counter Measures (TSCM) or 'sweeps' for bugging devices, you should attend this course as your first step up the ladder before paying out for any TSCM equipment. It will also give you an insight into what to expect in technical terms, as TSCM work can be very complex and costly. The aims of the course are to give an insight to the techniques used by the buggist such as:

- **Demonstrate how the devices operate and their limitations**
- **Demonstrate the reality from the hype**
- **Provide knowledge of concealment methods and how to avoid detection**
- **Provide knowledge of counter measures equipment**
- **Improvised bugging methods**
- **How to set up covert video systems**
- **Provide knowledge of the respective law**

Devices demonstrated on the course are:

- **RF Audio Surveillance**
- **Cellular Audio Surveillance**
- **Covert Video Surveillance**
- **Telephone Monitoring**
- **Vehicle/Asset Tracking**
- **Computer Surveillance**

This is not a course in technical counter measures but quite the opposite, which compliments training for the TSCM specialist. ISS teach the methods of how audio, video, telephone and computer eavesdropping takes place. If you are considering offering a TSCM service to your clients, then this training is a must.

**ISS ELECTRONICS' COURSE:** ***Students are taught a variety of telephone-tapping methods***

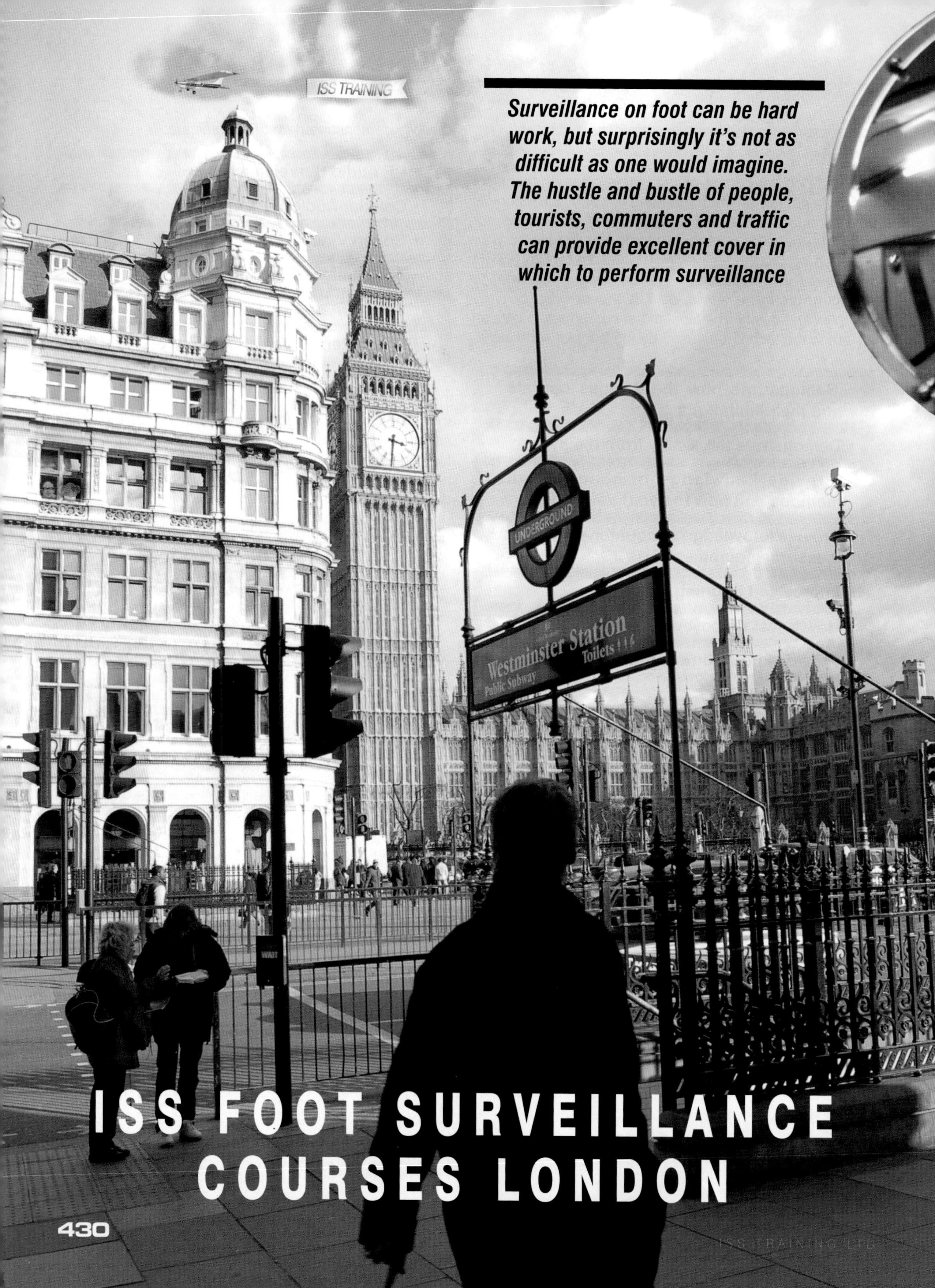


***Surveillance on foot can be hard work, but surprisingly it's not as difficult as one would imagine. The hustle and bustle of people, tourists, commuters and traffic can provide excellent cover in which to perform surveillance***

# ISS FOOT SURVEILLANCE COURSES LONDON

The Underground network is used extensively in this training

## FOOT SURVEILLANCE TRAINING IN LONDON

**BTEC Level 3 Award**

This three day course is for those who will be conducting surveillance and intelligence gathering in major cities where the target of surveillance is likely to use public transport networks and travel on foot rather than by car.

This training is also given to static security staff responsible for the security of major complex sites, stadiums, public buildings, indoor shopping malls and event venues, where covert security is necessary.

Based in Central London the course tests the students ability to conduct surveillance on foot in challenging and realistic situations whilst operating in residential, commercial and tourist areas. Much of the work involves travelling by foot on the underground rail network and by bus. Surveillance is also practised in large public buildings and stores with multiple levels and exits.

This course is quite intense and is suited for security professionals working in London or large cities.

## SURVEILLANCE DETECTION TRAINING

This three day course is designed primarily to teach students with a close protection background how to protect their principal against sophisticated threats through anti and counter surveillance.

If a surveillance team is observing your principal they are possibly gathering intelligence prior to carrying out an attack, kidnap or robbery. Either way, any surveillance team identified shadowing your principal poses a very significant and immediate threat.

**THE COURSE COVERS:**

- **The surveillance threat**
- **Planning and briefing**
- **Foot and mobile surveillance methods**
- **Recognising surveillance teams**
- **Covert and overt anti surveillance**
- **Counter surveillance routes**
- **Satellite vehicle tracking**
- **Realistic practical exercises**

**Skills are taught by experienced surveillance trainers**

On this course you are taught how to detect if your principal has been placed under surveillance. You will learn what to look out for and how to lay traps to confirm your suspicions by designing and implementing counter surveillance routes. By the end of the course you will be able to carry out advanced covert methods to identify the most sophisticated of surveillance teams.

**ISS PHOTOGRAPHIC COURSE:**
*Mastering the use of telephoto lenses in low light*

## DIGITAL PHOTOGRAPHY TRAINING

This two day course is for enforcement officers and investigators who use digital SLR cameras and video cameras in order to obtain photographic evidence.

Many investigators own and use their cameras on the 'auto' setting but this has little use in surveillance photography, especially when shooting in low light with telephoto lenses where fast shutter speeds are required.

The course is very practical in content and is suitable for the non technical person who wishes to learn and improve their photographic technique. This photographic training will give the operator the confidence to operate a digital SLR camera under surveillance conditions.

**THE TRAINING COVERS:**

- **Understanding digital cameras and images**
- **Basic principles of still photography**
- **Importance of exposure**
- **Shutter speed and aperture setting**
- **Advanced photographic skills in relation to surveillance**
- **Low light photography**
- **Telephoto lenses**
- **Transfer of digital images to computer or CD**
- **Processing of digital images for printing and emailing**
- **Continuity of photographic evidence**

## RURAL SURVEILLANCE TRAINING

**BTEC Level 3 Award**

This specialised course concentrates on all aspects of planning and carrying out surveillance in a rural theatre. It has been attended by civilians and enforcement agencies who operate in predominantly rural areas.

Students are taught how to plan, insert, occupy and work in an OP whilst being in uncomfortable conditions. The course also teaches methods of deploying and recovering video cameras in rural areas.

Students attending this course should be prepared for working outdoors whatever the weather, getting filthy and working long hours. **THE TRAINING COVERS:**

- **Planning, preparation and reconnaissance**
- **Camouflage, concealment and movement**
- **Construction of a rural hide**
- **Map reading and navigational skills**
- **Insertion, occupation and extraction from rural OPs**
- **Deployment of rural CCTV systems**
- **Risk Assessments**
- **Realistic Practical Exercises**

*Practical map reading exercise*

Students constructing camouflaged nets for later use in building rural OPs

Map reading and land navigation is taught in the classroom and on the ground

*Students undergoing specialist training in personal camouflage and concealment techniques*

## PROFESSIONAL WITNESS TRAINING

This two day course is for investigators and local authority officials that carry out evidence gathering in relation to anti-social behaviour.

Not only does the course teach urban static surveillance techniques but also involves legislation relating to the recording of evidence that will be accepted by the Courts. References are made to the Regulation of Investigatory Powers Act 2000, Criminal Procedure and Investigations Act 1996 and the Police and Criminal Evidence Act 1984.

**THE COURSE COVERS:**

- **Planning, preparation and reconnaissance**
- **Static surveillance methods**
- **Report and log writing**
- **Covert CCTV**
- **Preservation and continuation of evidence**
- **Eye witness testimony**
- **Legal procedure**

**Unmanned video equipment**

## NEWS OF THE WORLD

In the wake of the Leveson Enquiry into the role of the press and the police, (in particular the *News of the World's* 'Phone Hacking' scandal) undertaken by a 'Private Investigator', licensing has come to the forefront once again. The SIA are more determined than ever to regulate the private investigation industry.

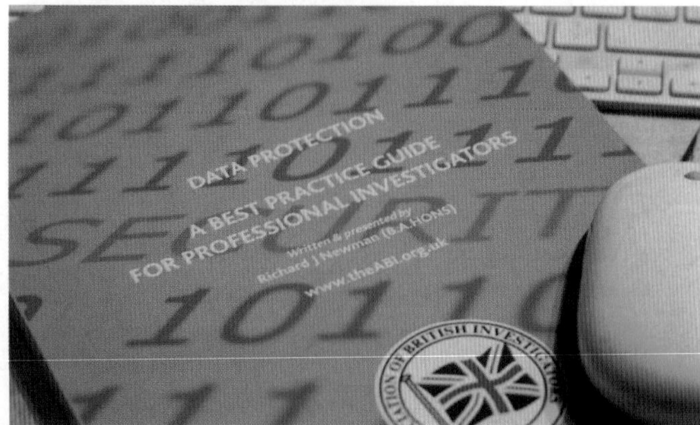

## PRIVATE INVESTIGATOR TRAINING

The Government recently stated that all Private Investigators will be required to be SIA licenced by the Autumn of 2014. The SIA requirements to obtain a licence are:-

***Prove identity***
***Have no criminal record***
***Have a Level 3 Award in Professional Investigation***

Licencing for Private Investigators is still 'work in progress' but the SIA's specification for core competency training is the Level 3 Award. At time of writing, the SIA have endorsed the Level 3 Awards presented by accrediting bodies EDI and iQ.

Any previous qualifications that are security or investigative related (including Police qualifications and experience), will not be accepted by the SIA: you still require the Level 3 Award. However, if you feel competent or experienced, you will be permitted to sit only the assessment test, rather than undergo a full course.

**Who Needs A Licence?**

This is an excerpt from the SIA's website: *'According to the Private Security Industry Act 2001, you will need an SIA licence if you are involved in any surveillance, inquiries or investigations that are carried out for the purposes of:*

*'Obtaining information about a particular person or about the activities or whereabouts of a particular person; or obtaining information about the circumstances in which, or means by which, property has been lost or damaged'.*

Anyone involved in providing contracted private investigation services will require a licence. If you are not offering a contracted PI service, you will not need a licence (such as a CPO conducting protective surveillance or a store guard following a suspected shoplifter), for which they should be licensed anyway in their own sector.

## ISS PRIVATE INVESTIGATOR TRAINING COURSES

This course is based on the SIA specifications for core competency training for Private Investigators. The requirements set out by the SIA is currently a minimum of 39 guided learning hours. The ISS course is 60 hours and is based upon teaching the basics of how to operate as a competent Private Investigator. The following topics are covered in some depth:

- **Digital Photography**
- **Open Source Intelligence**
- **Surveillance**
- **Running an Investigation Business**
- **Private Investigation**
- **Process Serving**
- **General Enquiries**
- **Statement Taking**
- **Legislation and Data Protection**
- **Tracing**
- **Report Writing**
- **Interviewing Witnesses**
- **Accident Investigation**

***All commercial surveillance operators will by 2015 require a licence***

ISS has taught a variety of military, federal and enforcement agencies from all over the world

## SPECIALIST MILITARY SURVEILLANCE TRAINING FOR HOSTILE AREAS

These specialist courses are designed for special military and government enforcement units who need to carry out surveillance as a means of intelligence gathering in hostile areas.

Since 2002, ISS Mobile Training Team has trained Special Operations Forces from Europe, Asia, Africa and the Americas. The training courses vary in content and duration from one week to six weeks duration. These courses are not available to individuals but to units and organisations by special arrangement only.

Firearms training is sometimes incorporated into the course

## OBTAINING WORK

After the course, many students often keep in touch and network between each other. Regrettably, ISS cannot offer employment after the course but we do recommend particular investigation companies who we talent scout for. Some training companies promise students work after completing their training but this is often a sales gimmick and should be carefully looked into before you part with any money.

If you feel that you want to learn more about ISS Training Ltd and the courses we provide, we can be contacted via our website **www.intelsecurity.co.uk**

In the meantime, ensure that you do not fall into the trap of making foolish mistakes. Surveillance is all about being patient, using your initiative and taking minimal risks.

**BTEC Level Three Assessment Questions**

Below is a list of questions taken from the BTEC Level Three Award workbook which is completed by each student in their own time during the course. After reading this book you should be able to answer them all.

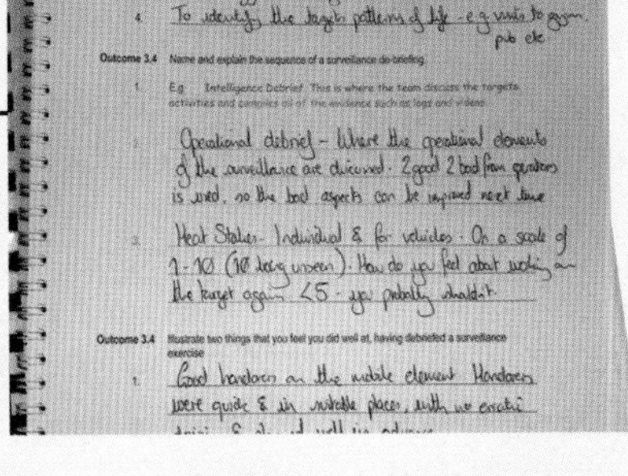

# SURVEILLANCE AWARENESS

**1.** Define the term surveillance

**2.** Identify four different types of surveillance and explain each.

**3.** Provide four examples of why surveillance is carried out.

**4.** Explain the importance of personal appearance and dress during surveillance operations

**5.** Explain at least three personal qualities of the 'ideal' surveillance operative

**6.** Describe three different types of surveillance teams

**7.** Identify and describe the certain main job roles within the surveillance team

**8.** Explain and list what basic equipment is required to carry out a surveillance task

**9.** Explain what the terms '7 x 50' means on a pair of binoculars

**10.** Explain why you should carry some form of identification whilst on surveillance and suggest what type of identification would be suitable

**11.** Explain what is meant by the terms: Eyeball, Nearside, Standby, Touch Red, Possible

# SURVEILLANCE COMMUNICATIONS

**12.** Define the following security code words: Alpha 2, Pluto/Ludo, Echo 1 & Bravo 2

**13.** Give the phonetic alphabet

**14.** Identify the alternative methods of communication and provide examples of when they would be used

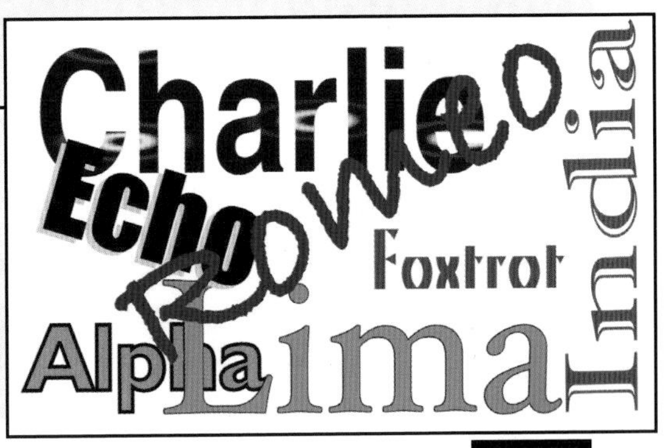

# PLAN, BRIEF & DEBRIEF A SURVEILLANCE OPERATION

**15.** Specify what information is required about the subject of a surveillance (apart from a description)

**16.** What considerations would you give to triggering a target that is very surveillance aware

**17.** Why is having knowledge of the targets 'awareness level' so important

**18.** Determine the various methods of 'triggering' a surveillance.

**19.** Carry out a physical reconnaissance of a target area and complete a recce report and sketch plan

**20.** Identify the logistical and resource requirements to conduct a surveillance operation.

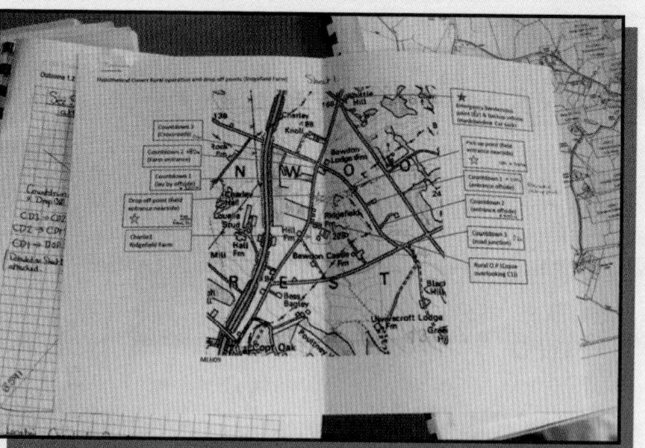

**21.** Explain how the sequence of a surveillance briefing is carried out providing information of each phase

**22.** Take active part in surveillance briefings and de-briefings.

**23.** Give three examples of the type of 'Operational Tasks' that may be given in a surveillance briefing

**24.** Name and explain the sequence of a surveillance de-briefing.

# MINIMISE PERSONAL RISK DURING SURVEILLANCE OPERATIONS

**25.** To minimise risks when coming to a halt on a mobile surveillance (or static whilst on plot), what should you consider in relation to your security and the security of the surveillance.

*'5' on the heat states!*

**26.** Explain what three things get a surveillance operator noticed which may lead to a compromise.

**27.** Explain how you interpret the principle of 'Loss v Gain'

# CONDUCTING FOOT SURVEILLANCE

**28.** Identify the four phases of a surveillance cycle

**29.** Explain when you would carry out a hand over whilst on foot and the reasons for doing so

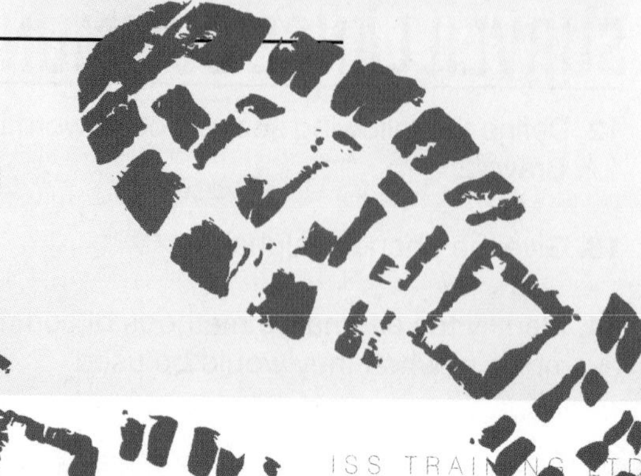

## IDENTIFY FOOT ANTI SURVEILLANCE MEASURES

**30.** Identify at what times a target is more likely to be surveillance aware

**31.** Give examples of the various foot anti surveillance measures (drills) a target may carry out

**32.** Examine the options that are open to a target who has carried out subtle covert anti surveillance drills and realises that he is being followed

## PARTICIPATE IN MOBILE SURVEILLANCE

**33.** Identify the requirements of an 'ideal' surveillance vehicle and state your reasons

**34.** Where would you consider a good location for a mobile handover

**35.** When would you consider carrying out mobile handover

**36.** If you are following an 'unsophisticated' target and you are dropped off from a vehicle, where should you normally get picked up and why

**37.** When alighting from your vehicle, what actions should you carry out

## IDENTIFY MOBILE ANTI SURVEILLANCE MEASURES

**38.** Explain the various mobile anti surveillance measures (drills) a target may carry out

**39.** Explain the difference between Anti Surveillance and Counter Surveillance.

## OBTAINING & COLLATING INFORMATION BY SURVEILLANCE

**40.** Specify under which legislation a Public Body has to obtain authority to conduct covert surveillance

**41.** Identify under the code of practice drawn from the above Act, what are the two types of surveillance and explain the difference between the two

**42.** State where can you obtain a copies of RIPA authorisation forms

**43.** When should we write or record a note of our observations?

**44.** Identify when recording your observations in a log book, what general rules should you follow in order to preserve the integrity of what is written (eg. No ELBOWS)

**45.** Produce an accurate surveillance log from one of the exercises.

**46.** Explain why there should be a special need for caution when obtaining or giving eye witness testimony (Judges statement in R v Turnbull 1976)

**47.** How would you describe a person (using the A to I method)

**48.** How would you determine a persons age, what could deceive you into thinking that they are younger or older

**49.** How would you determine a persons height, what could deceive you into thinking they are taller or shorter

**The written assessment is carried out in a student's own time by means of a workbook, rather than a formal test**

# EXPLAIN THE TECHNICAL AIDS TO SURVEILLANCE

**50.** Explain how GPS/GSM tracking equipment operates. State where it would normally be placed on a vehicle, and what factors need to be considered in order for it to work properly

**51.** Give examples of why tracking systems are used in support of conventional surveillance

**52.** Identify the different types of video recorders

**53.** Identify the basic controls of video cameras

**54.** Identify the common errors which cause poor video recordings

**Students are encouraged to obtain video evidence of the targets during exercises**

## SURVEILLANCE RESULTS?

I often get asked, 'What is your result rate doing surveillance?'. In some ways this is a tricky question to answer but I always give the same reply.

'A result is being able to put the target under surveillance for a period of time undetected. If he comes out, we will get the video but what we can never do is make them come out of the house. Therefore if we sit on a target for five days and he does not come out into the open, then it is not our fault, the client still gets billed for our time'. This is still a result.

## TOP 10 MISTAKES

### OF THE SURVEILLANCE OPERATOR

1. Carrying out single handed surveillance
2. Over exposure by not appreciating loss and gain
3. Not being aware of the 3rd party
4. Acting un-naturally
5. Having multiple sightings with the target
6. Wrongly assuming what the target will do
7. Not knowing your equipment
8. Lack of preparation, not carrying out a recce
9. Lack of concentration whilst on the job
10. Not getting on the ground early enough

PLEASE DON'T MAKE THEM

***Surveillance can be very boring and dull. It can also have moments of excitement, at times things get very serious and at other times you can also have a laugh in the process. I leave you with this final true story, the names have been changed...***

## MALCOLM'S STORY

I had the trigger from a bus shelter from across the street, it was February and bloody freezing. I had been there for two hours now without a change. We could only cover it and get a trigger on the exit of the underground car park in the event that he left. There were no slots to park up in and so muggings here was sat at the bus stop trying to keep warm.

We had a wealthy target under surveillance who lived on the seventh floor of a luxury apartment block which overlooked the Thames, the main foyer door to the block was controlled by an intercom security system so we could not get in any closer to trigger it.

There had been no movement on the first day and half way through the second day my boss (Dave) turned up to see what was happening - nothing but an icicle slowly forming on the end of my nose. He decided that we should enter the block and listen at the target's door for any noises such as a television or movement, that way we knew whether to come back in a few days time if no one was there. What we didn't want to do was use the intercom as he was very aware and this job was for a high profile client.

Dave was wearing a Barbour jacket and jeans and I had a North Face 'puffa' jacket on, not the type that you zip up but one that pulls over your head. We managed to gain entry to the block by 'tailgating' a visitor and decided to take the elevator up to the 6th floor and then walk up to the 7th floor by the fire escape. We crept long the plush carpeted corridor hoping we would not be disturbed or challenged, I kept a look out whilst Dave moved forward to listen at the door. I had moved past him to make sure it was clear and then moved back to cover the elevator and fire escape. As I squeezed past him in the narrow hallway he stood upright and pushed me against the wall.

As I moved, I heard a quick tearing noise. As I turned around to see what it was, I heard an even longer tear as the nylon shell on my puffa jacket had become snagged,

COURTESY UNIVERSAL PICTURES

I should have turned the other way. The little screw protruding from a dado rail tore the jacket wide open.

Oh my F***ing God! The whole content of goose down flowed from my jacket, landed around my feet onto the shag-pile. It then wafted in the air like a snow storm as I took a pace away from it. I didn't know whether to laugh or cry. I couldn't believe it - anywhere else but not this place, please.

Dave turned and looked on in disbelief as I stood there, like a fairy out of a Peter Pan surrounded by fluff. 'Let's go..' He said and we darted for the fire escape leaving a trail of fluff in the air as we went like a smoke screen. We got down to the 6th floor and I decided to empty my jacket pockets (or what was left of it - a limp bit of nylon with two fat sleeves), I took it off, having to pull it over my head and stuffed it behind a fire hose reel hoping that it wouldn't be found.....

We both got into the lift to go down and I saw my reflection in the wall mirror. We both burst out laughing as I now had fluff in my hair, ears, eyelashes, stuck to my lips and up my nose. I looked like Orville the f***ing duck!

Luckily we were not challenged on the way out and it took a lot of baby wipes to get rid of the fluff.

It has been a standing joke since - Johhny English and his assistant Boff. At least the target will be easy to spot when he goes mobile as all we have to do is follow the trail.....

Peter Jenkins
January 2010

# SURVEILLANCE TRADECRAFT

## SUMMARY

Compiling this book has been very hard work indeed and I certainly hope that it will be useful in your work as a surveillance operator.

Learning the fundamental and basic surveillance tactics are so important. They are the same in surveillance wherever you are in the world and in any theatre. The only difference is how you communicate over the radio to each other, as there are many different styles of commentary. Hopefully this book has covered all of the bases for you operate efficiently on your own or as part of a team.

A career in surveillance can be very rewarding. If you are in enforcement or intelligence sector, the results you are after can be very worthwhile and can bring a lot to the table. In the commercial sector a job well done is not only personally satisfying but also profitable. Working in a close knit team carrying out such a dynamic activity is one of the best jobs you can have. There are periods of boredom but there are also periods of excitement and humour and you will also benefit from the camaraderie.

If you are new to the profession, obtain proper training, plug at it steadily and learn from other peoples mistakes and not your own. In addition to being skilled in surveillance, integrity, honesty and trust also go a long way in to securing a rewardable career.

Remember to keep abreast of technology. Surveillance equipment is progressing very fast in terms of performance, size and cost. The same applies to legislation - it constantly changes and it is something that has to be monitored regularly. Being a member of a local or national association such as the Association of British Investigators certainly helps.

Ensure that you put 100% into your surveillance work and add plenty of enthusiasm. Treat your clients, your competitors and those that you work with respect and you will go a long way.

# GLOSSARY OF TERMS USED IN SURVEILLANCE VOICE PROCEDURE

To illustrate how effective this voice procedure is, we recently taught a Federal Enforcement Agency who's first language was Portuguese. Some of the class spoke very good English and one or two were not so good.

All the team had to do was to learn the 30 or so phrases used in the Glossary. The team were able to effectively communicate to each other and carry out surveillance even though English was not their first language. They performed excellently and soon became very fluent.

On the funny side, some of them finished the training thinking that they could now speak fluent English. By saying, 'Standby Standby, that's Alpha 1, out and foxtrot left towards blue six' doesn't really go that far when you are trying to chat up some English girl in a bar in Copacabana!

Rightly or wrongly a surveillance operators skill is often judged by the way he communicates on the radio. You can join a team that you have never worked with before but if you sound bad on the radio net, eyebrows will be raised and your ability will be questioned. Whereas, if you sound slick and confident on the radio, it displays that you know what you are doing and the team will feel comfortable working with you.

## EXPRESSION TO BE USED

| | |
|---|---|
| ADVANCE WARNING | Given prior to a hazard such as traffic lights or a roundabout |
| BACK UP | Second vehicle in the team supporting (backing) the Eyeball |
| BUS REQUEST | To be used instead of the term 'Bus Stop' |
| CANCEL MY LAST | Ignore my last message |
| COME THROUGH | Given after 'Hang Back' to bring callsigns through |
| COMMITTED, COMMITTED | The target is still travelling on a motorway |
| COMPLETE | Returned or Inside. E.g. 'India Complete' indicates that call sign India has returned to his vehicle after he has been on foot. Also used to indicate when a person has entered a building etc. |

| | |
|---|---|
| CAN YOU? | A call to the Back-up asking if they can take the eyeball. Often used with, 'Can you at...' followed by a location |
| CONTINUING STRAIGHT | Used when the subject is committed to the same road without any deviation |
| CONVOY | All vehicles comprising the surveillance team |
| C.T.R (Close Target Recce) | Close Target Recce'. Where operators conduct a close examination of a target premises |
| EYEBALL | Vehicle or Operative having primary visual contact with the target and who is directing the operation for the time being |
| EYEBALL REGAINED | Indicates target again in view, following temporary loss |
| FOXTROT | When someone is walking they are referred to as going 'Foxtrot' |
| FRESH GREEN / FRESH RED | Fresh means that a traffic light has just changed. A fresh green will indicate that the lights are likely to be green for a while and all of the team can get through |
| GOING ROUND AGAIN | Indicates that target vehicle is commencing a second, or subsequent, circuit of a roundabout |
| GONE | Indicating movement, i.e. 'Gone Left Left' |
| HANDLING | The person driving a vehicle is said to be 'Handling' |
| HANG BACK | Transmission from Eyeball, indicating to convoy that they should 'hang back' as the target vehicle is slowing and may stop |
| HELD | Indicates temporary stop by the i.e. held at traffic lights |

**INTENDING**
Indicates in which direction the subject is pointing or intending to move or likely to travel

**LEFT, LEFT at**
Indicates that the target vehicle has turned left, normally followed by 'at' or 'towards'

**LIGHTS AWAY**
At night, if you are unsure that it is the Target's vehicle which has moved, 'Lights Away' is called in order for another operator to check and confirm

**MANOEUVRING**
Indicating that the target vehicle is manoeuvring in a par park or the road

**MAKE GROUND**
Instruction from eyeball to another vehicle to close up

**NEARSIDE, OFFSIDE INDICATION**
States nearside/offside indicator is operating on the subject vehicle

**NO DEVIATION**
Indicates target vehicle is continuing straight ahead

**NO LONGER BACKING**
Used if you are backing and become blocked so that you are not actually in a position to 'back' and take over if needed

**NOT ONE, NOT TWO ETC.**
Indicates that the target vehicle negotiating a roundabout has passed first, second etc., exit. 'No Entry' roads are not counted as exits

**OFF, OFF**
Transmission by Eyeball, indicating that the target is now on the move. MOBILE is also used as a substitute

**ONE UP, TWO UP, ETC**
Indicates the amount of people in a vehicle

**ORIGINAL**
The term used when the target has resumed moving after a stop and is continuing in the Original (same) direction prior to the stop.

**OPTION**
Indicates a possible turning or route that that subject can go. i.e. '2nd option on the nearside'.

|  |  |
|---|---|
| OUT, OUT | Indicates that the target is alighting from a vehicle or is leaving premises |
| PERMISSION | Where an operator asks Eyeball for 'Permission' to interrupt the commentary to pass on a message. Commentary should not be interrupted without Permission on some teams |
| RADIO CHECK | Request from Eyeball to test comms' with the remainder of the team |
| RECEIVED | Used to acknowledge a message. ROGER also has the same meaning |
| RECIPROCAL | Indicates that target had done a 'U' turn and is returning along the same route. May be abbreviated to 'RECIP' or 'one eighty' |
| RELAY | The vehicle with the responsibility of relaying OR repeating the eyeball footman's messages |
| RIGHT, RIGHT | Indicates that target vehicle has turned right |
| SHADOW CAR | The vehicle being used to back up a footman |
| SHOWN OUT | If an operator is compromised they have 'shown out' |
| SO FAR? | When transmitting long messages, the term 'So Far?' is used to break up a message |
| STALE GREEN / STALE RED | Stale means that a traffic light has been that colour for quite a while. A stale green will indicate that the lights are likely to change to red at any time which will indicate that the team has to close up to get though |
| STAND DOWN | Indicates cancellation of whole operation |
| STOP, STOP | Indicates that target vehicle has stopped but not temporarily 'held' |

|  |  |
|---|---|
| STRIKE, STRIKE, STRIKE | Indicates designated operators will move in and effect arrest or searches etc. |
| STANDBY, STANDBY | Instruction issued by eyeball or Trigger, alerting the team to possible movement of the Subject |
| SUBJECT | Person subject of the surveillance, Target may also be used |
| TAIL END CHARLIE | Rearmost vehicle in convoy. Trail is also used |
| TAKEN FIRST, TAKEN SECOND ETC | Indicates that target vehicle has taken first, second, exit off a roundabout |
| TEMPORARY UNSIGHTED | Indicates a temporary loss of eyeball, due to terrain, traffic or other condition. |
| TOTAL LOSS | Indicates eyeball not regained following temporary loss. A total loss will normally be followed by a pre-planned search procedure |
| TOUCH RED | A call asking a team member to Touch Red is asking him to 'double tap' his brake pedal so that operators behind can see his position at night |
| TRIGGER | Term used for eyeball when they have to trigger or initiate the surveillance |
| UNSIGHTED | Indicates that the subject is out of your view |
| VISUAL | Used to indicate that an operator has a view of the target |
| WAIT | Used to indicate that operators should not transmit for the time being and to wait for further transmissions |

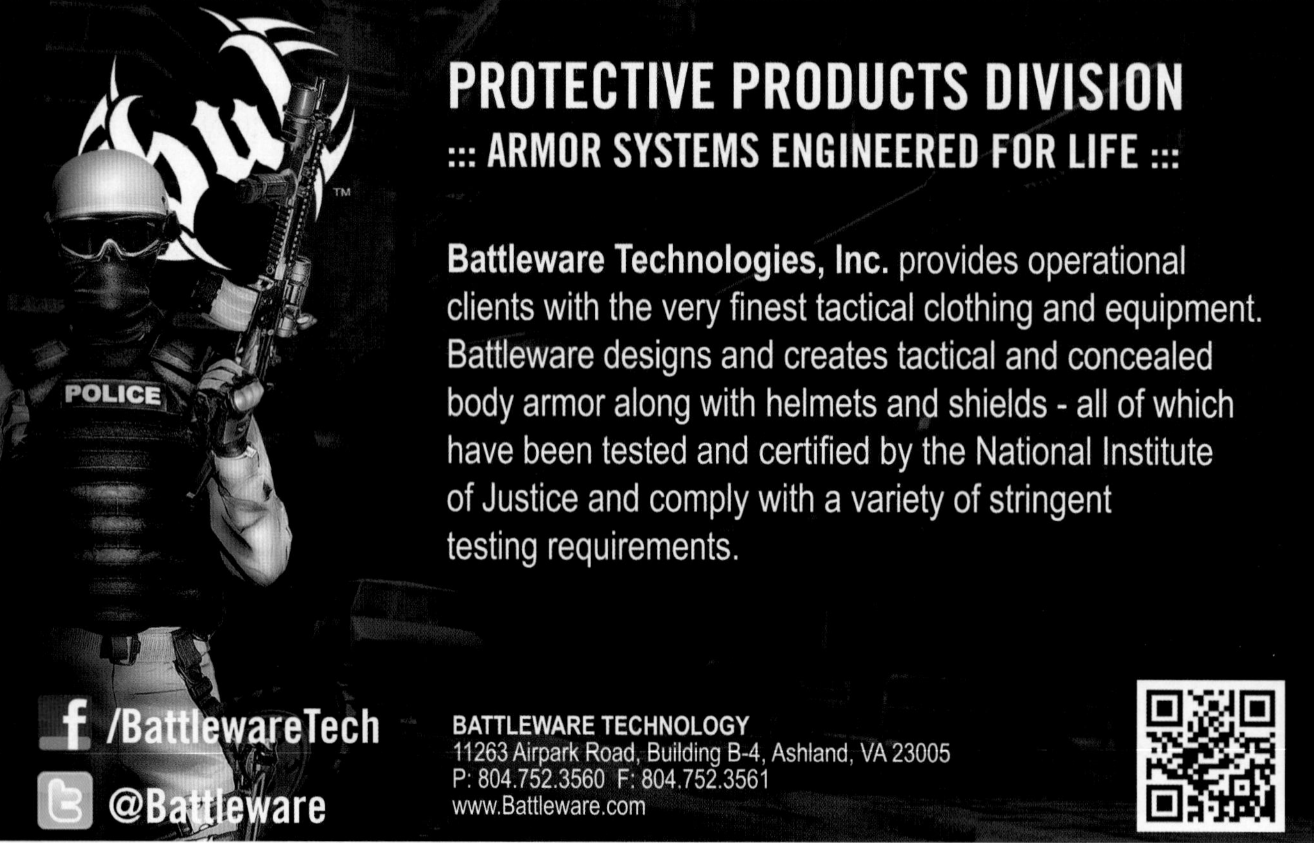

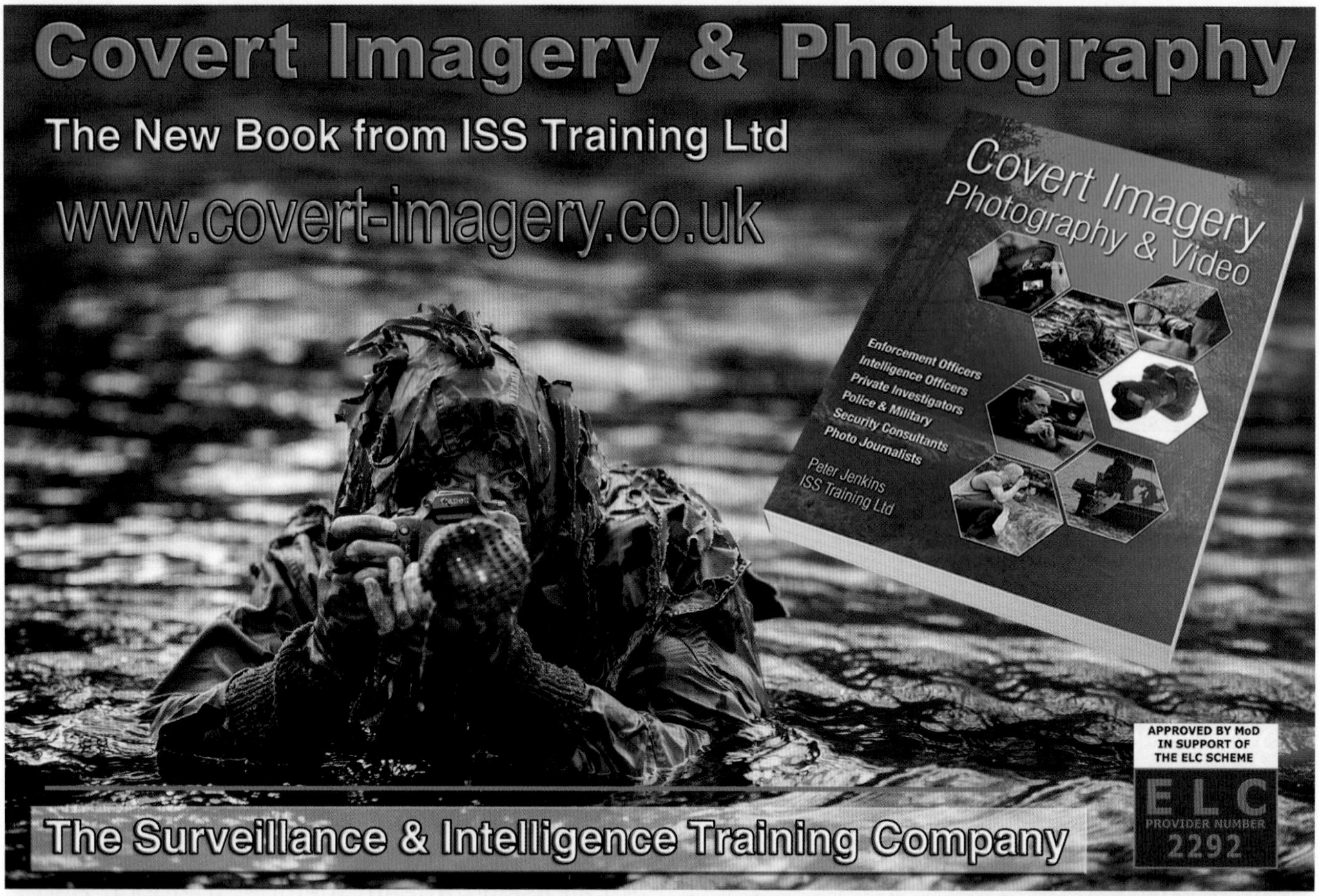
Covert Imagery & Photography
The New Book from ISS Training Ltd
www.covert-imagery.co.uk
Covert Imagery
Photography & Video
Enforcement Officers
Intelligence Officers
Private Investigators
Police & Military
Security Consultants
Photo Journalists
Peter Jenkins
ISS Training Ltd
APPROVED BY MoD IN SUPPORT OF THE ELC SCHEME
ELC
PROVIDER NUMBER
2292
The Surveillance & Intelligence Training Company

PROTECTIVE PRODUCTS DIVISION
::: ARMOR SYSTEMS ENGINEERED FOR LIFE :::
Battleware Technologies, Inc. provides operational clients with the very finest tactical clothing and equipment. Battleware designs and creates tactical and concealed body armor along with helmets and shields - all of which have been tested and certified by the National Institute of Justice and comply with a variety of stringent testing requirements.
POLICE
/BattlewareTech
@Battleware
BATTLEWARE TECHNOLOGY
11263 Airpark Road, Building B-4, Ashland, VA 23005
P: 804.752.3560 F: 804.752.3561
www.Battleware.com

NSI
GUARDING GOLD
UKAS
PRODUCT CERTIFICATION
0142
UKAS
QUALITY MANAGEMENT
0142
ASSOCIATION OF BRITISH INVESTIGATORS LTD

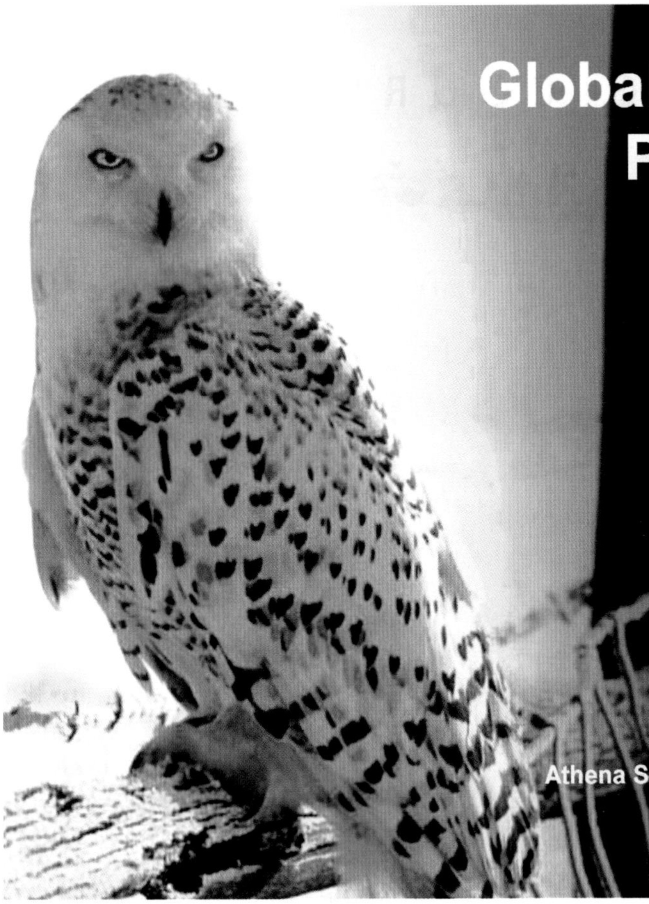

## SPECIALIST DRIVING COURSES

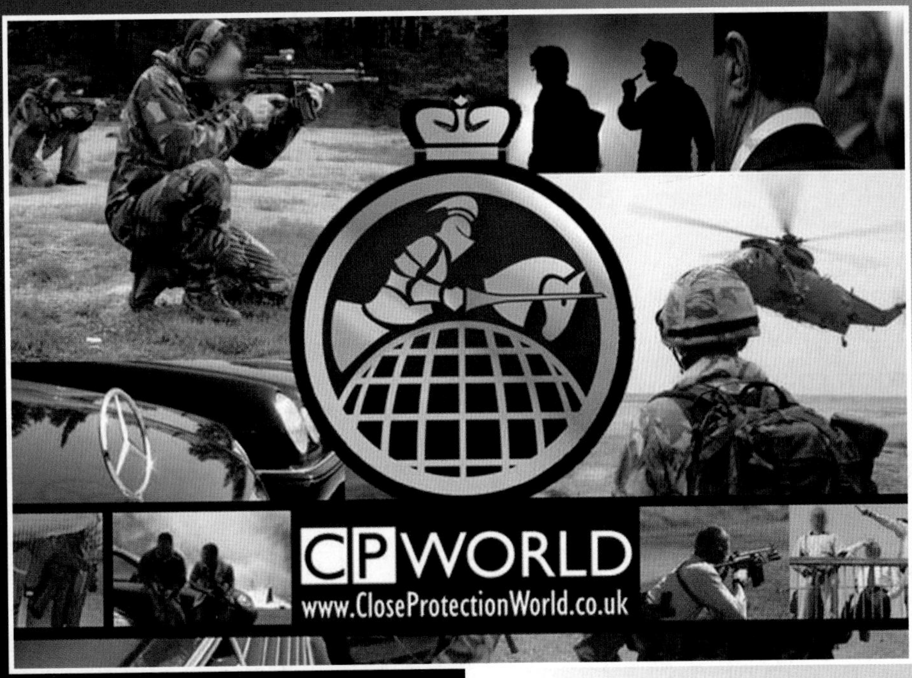

CP WORLD

www.CloseProtectionWorld.co.uk

British Bodyguard Association

Pursuing excellence through intelligence

Whether you are a seasoned security professional, or just setting out on a new exciting career path, the BBA will provide you with the most up to date information on current training providers, equipment suppliers, employment vacancies, a message forum and the great networking facility, BBA Chat.

**No other close protection organisation offers so much for so little.**

Since its initial formation in early 2007, the BBA has grown rapidly - in fact we are probably the fastest growing association of its kind.

We are now attracting membership not just from the UK but worldwide.

**Individual, Business and Corporate Packages Available**

www.the-bba.org.uk

We aim to unite and support both trained and aspiring bodyguards worldwide via our membership information programme and our magazine The Circuit

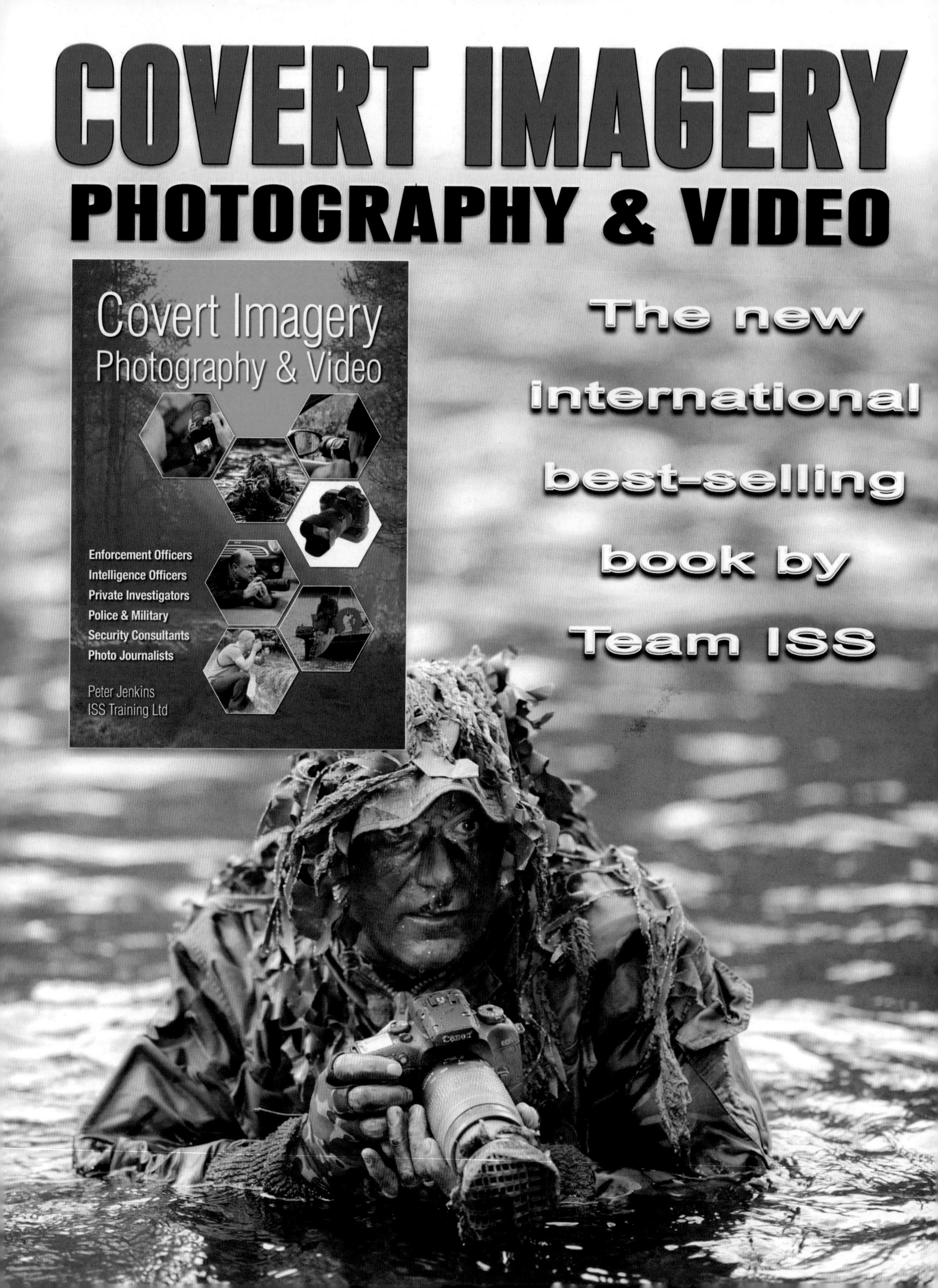

# INDEX

## I: INDIA



## J: JULIET



## K: KILO

## L: LIMA



## M: MIKE



## N: NOVEMBER



## O: OSCAR



## P: PAPA



## Q: QUEBEC

## R: ROMEO

S: SIERRA



T: TANGO



U: UNIFORM



V: VICTOR



W: WHISKY



X: X-RAY

Y: YANKEE

Z: ZULU